ALSO BY DAVID WILCOCK

The Source Field Investigations
The Synchronicity Key
The Ascension Mysteries

Praise for the Work of David Wilcock

"Alien enthusiasts who love corroborating proofs will find the large amount of new detail satisfying, and those who find Wilcock personally compelling will love the juicy details of his youth."

—Publishers Weekly on *The Ascension Mysteries*

"Wilcock also makes an intriguing case for the energetic influences of the celestial bodies on the recurring currents of history, and the mechanisms through which they may be directing them. At the very least, this book provides much food for thought. At its best, it is fuel for wonder and awe."

—New Consciousness Review on *The Synchronicity Key*

"Anyone interested in finding out how the universe works, not only mechanically but also spiritually, should definitely give this book a read."

—Quick Book Review on *The Synchronicity Key*

"David Wilcock is a leading thinker who makes a magnificent case . . . that a Golden Age is indeed within our grasp and can be brought into manifestation if only we choose to make it so."

—Graham Hancock, author of *Fingerprints of the Gods,*
on *The Source Field Investigations*

"We are *not* alone in this universe. And we have David Wilcock to prove it—and to guide us to this golden prophecy."

—James V. Hart on *The Source Field Investigations*

"A narrative as fast-paced and scintillating as a sci-fi novel."

—Kirkus Reviews on *The Source Field Investigations*

"David Wilcock is a dedicated and passionate investigator determined to understand this chapter in our collective history."

—New Dawn Magazine on *The Source Field Investigations*

AWAKENING

IN THE

DREAM

Contact with the Divine

DAVID WILCOCK

DUTTON

DUTTON

An imprint of Penguin Random House LLC
penguinrandomhouse.com

Previously published as a Dutton hardcover in June 2020

First Dutton trade paperback edition: August 2021

DUTTON and the D colophon are registered trademarks of
Penguin Random House LLC.
Permissions appear on page xi and constitute an extension
of the copyright page.

LIBRARY OF CONGRESS CATALOGING-IN-PUBLICATION DATA
has been applied for.

ISBN: 9781524742041 (trade paperback)
ISBN 9781524742034 (ebook)

Printed in the United States of America
1st Printing

*I would like to dedicate this book
to my wife, Elizabeth Wilcock,
as well as to you, the One Infinite Creator,
now reading this in your temporary
holographic projection as a seemingly
separate human being.*

Contents

List of Figures

PART ONE

CHAPTER ONE

Introduction

The light bulb was burning brightly—despite all the glass being shattered. Shards of broken glass jutted out from the metallic base of the bulb like angry teeth, catching the starry glint of the filament as it continued glowing. And there he was. A mysterious black man sat crying on the staircase of our family home. His filthy clothes were drenched in sweat and tears. He was shielding his face with both hands as he sobbed, resting his elbows on his knees. He was not invited. I had no idea who he was, what he was doing in our house, or why he was crying. Looking again to the fragile tungsten filament, lit up perfectly without the protective shroud of the glass bulb, it happened. *"Light bulbs cannot burn when the glass is broken. What I am seeing right now is impossible. My God, I must be dreaming! None of this is real! And yet here I am, right now! Awake in the dream!"*

At that moment, I was overwhelmed with emotions. My body, or whatever my mind decided that my body was at that moment, surged with an almost unspeakable power of ecstasy. I didn't know who the man was and now it didn't even matter. I had finally done it. After weeks' worth of practice and multiple failed attempts, I had awakened within a dream for the first time—becoming fully conscious and lucid. And now I had an agenda. The books had promised godlike abilities in a lucid dream, and I wanted to test them out. I willed myself to fly right through the thick brown wood of the front door—and it presented no resistance whatsoever. I glided above the white birch tree in our front yard—a much better experience than any climbing I had done in it as a boy. I quickly rose up and looked down at our house from a bird's-eye view, fully free.

I knew my body was safely asleep in my room, waiting for me to drift back to it as soon as I finished my epic adventure. In this form, I could go anywhere, be anyone, and do anything. I was a superhero. The only limit was my imagination. And as any practitioner of lucid dreaming will tell you, this phenomenon feels every bit as real as any waking experience you could ever have—if not more so. You transcend into a reality that words do not adequately describe, but might best be thought of as hyper-real. Your awareness becomes vastly more effective and all-encompassing than in any conventional state. Thoughts come rushing into your mind at an impressive speed, manifesting themselves into beautifully intricate structures before you even have a chance to ask the questions they answer. Limitless knowledge is there for the taking, with no effort whatsoever. And despite the awesome power of that experience, none of it seems to matter because you are so emboldened by the present moment. It is not at all uncommon for a lucid dreamer to conclude, "I have never truly been awake before."

Little did I know that within a few years, my lucid-dreaming research would plunge me into a world that seems completely supernatural by most people's standards. I would eventually come into direct contact with angelic, human-looking extraterrestrial beings who helped me completely reenvision science and spirit into a new and greater unified whole. The beings also helped me to identify a huge wealth of new evidence and proof that would help make the case. I would learn that these people initially reach out to you through dreams, synchronicities, and visionary experiences. They proved over and over again that they could predict the future as easily as if they were reading a book. And they would soon pass along the greatest message of all: namely that we are right on the threshold of a spectacular mass evolutionary event many have called Ascension. I have uncovered far more than enough scientific evidence to make a very compelling case for this, as I have presented in my previous books. For those of us who "do the homework" and prepare ourselves for this fascinating global transformation, our everyday lives will become indistinguishable from a lucid dream. The awesome popularity of superhero films may be another way in which our mass, collective subconscious mind is preparing us for what may be coming—far sooner than we would have ever believed possible. We may well find ourselves awakening within the dream we once were so convinced was reality.

These angelic beings also reveal that the only way to prepare ourselves for this mass awakening is to be genuinely dedicated to following a path of service to others—practicing forgiveness, compassion, patience, love, and understanding in our daily lives as our primary motivation. This is the core message of all great spiritual traditions. If we apply these principles as a regular practice, we have the potential to experience a quantum leap in human evolution that is almost unthinkable in its scope and power. The lucid-dreaming experience can give us a marvelous "sneak preview" of what our new lives as Ascended beings will be like. The study and analysis of dreams has always been a very essential part of my work that made everything else possible, and this book is the first time I have ever presented a deep examination of what I was doing and how I did it.

Protocols of Lucid Dreaming

The year was 1989. I was a sixteen-year-old student of the mystic scientist Dr. Stephen LaBerge through reading his groundbreaking book *Lucid Dreaming*. I was delighted to discover that lucidity was not that hard to achieve if you could already remember your dreams in the morning, as I often did. The key difference between waking and dreaming states is that in a dream, you can look at a particular area, look away and look back, and something will have changed. It may be subtle, such as a color or the position of an object, but it may also be quite dramatic—as in a completely different scene from the one you saw before. A wall in a house may turn into a lovely ocean beach just by turning your head, looking away, and then looking back at the same spot.

Dr. LaBerge encourages you to practice this exercise in your waking life. Look at a particular area, ask yourself if you are dreaming, look away from it and then look back. Check the area to make sure it still looks the same. Always be ready to be completely fascinated by the fact that something has changed—and think about how you might discover that you are actually dreaming, right now. That sense of childlike anticipation and wonder is a very important part of the practice. I had consistently practiced this meditation in 1989, and I had finally remembered to check my environment for unusual things while I was actually dreaming. The shattered light bulb and strange, uninvited man were what tipped me off that I had finally awakened in a dream.

The real "crown jewel" of Dr. LaBerge's method, however, is called MILD—which stands for Mnemonic Induction of Lucid Dreaming. The word *mnemonic* refers to something that helps assist your memory. To practice this technique, you first pick a day where you can sleep in and not wake up to an alarm. Right after you wake up, remain completely motionless and ask yourself, "What was just happening to me? Where was I? Who was I talking to? What was going on?" This is the key to remembering any dream. If you ask yourself, "What was I just dreaming?" you are not likely to get anywhere, because your dream will have seemed completely real as you went through it. Then, as you remember your dream, start noticing the things in it that would be impossible from a waking perspective. Perhaps you are talking to one person and then, in the middle of your conversation, they change into someone else. The objects and locations around you might spontaneously transform. You might be driving in a car and then find yourself walking indoors, quite seamlessly. In the dream, you usually ignore all these sudden changes and just follow along with whatever is happening to you in the moment. I will present a variety of examples of lucid dreams in this book where you can see for yourself how I spotted inconsistencies in the dream, in real time, which led to my realizing I was dreaming—and being able to consciously awaken within the dream experience.

Most important, after you have identified something strange, you then imagine yourself still being inside that same dream. Visualize yourself noticing whatever is out of place. Then allow your imagination to fully experience the joy and wonder of awakening in the dream. Let yourself feel that rush of excitement as you levitate objects with your mind, transform objects from one form into another, manifest anything you desire out of seemingly nothing, walk through solid walls, or levitate and soar like a bird through the air. These feats may be far easier than you think they will be, since in most cases you can do whatever you want quite easily.

Last, as you continue to visualize all of this happening and are feeling excited about it, you keep repeating a particular sentence in your mind, over and over again: "Next time I'm dreaming, I want to remember to recognize I'm dreaming." You might say it fifty times, a hundred times, it doesn't matter . . . and don't count them. The most important thing is to keep repeating the sentence. Eventually, as you repeat the sentence, everything around you will have changed and you are in a new situation, having new experiences. It is easy to be distracted and get pulled into another dream, but now you may notice that you are still repeating the same sentence. You then listen to what you are saying: "Next time I'm dreaming, I want to remember to recognize that I'm dreaming." Then you take a look around and recognize that you are indeed dreaming—right now! I have had dozens of successes with the use of this exact technique.

From there, your main job is to stay lucid and avoid snapping back into your body until you are ready to. Your single biggest danger is to have any thought of your body whatsoever as your dream goes on. You might think about the position of your head, your arms, your legs, whether you are hungry or need to go to the bathroom, any physical pains, or anything else that might be going on in the room. If this happens, you will find yourself right back in your body, awake, and you have to try again. As you practice more, you will notice that if you start thinking about your body, you don't lose the dream immediately. You will start seeing everything around you fading out into a gray mist. You now have only a few seconds left to try to stay awake in the dream.

In his book *Adventures Out of the Body*, William Buhlman recommends shouting out the words *Clarity Now* if everything starts fading away like this. You focus on keeping a small area visible, even if it's just a foot-wide circle at the center of your vision, and then widening the area as you keep shouting. Buhlman also recommends using both of your hands as if power is shooting out of them—the power to stabilize your dream reality. In the Carlos Castenada books, which I read during this period of my life, the alleged Yaqui shaman Don Juan recommends that you look at your dream hands. They will very likely look weird and scary, with fingers missing or distorted shapes, but it is a quick move you can make that will get you thinking about your dream reality rather than your physical one. Oddly, there is a difference between looking at your hands in the dream and thinking about your physical body in the bed. Once you become lucid, you will be able to tell the difference. If you keep your awareness fixed in the lucid experience and focus on whatever you see around you, everything is fine. If you start thinking about the fact that you also have a body that is somewhere else, and especially if you try to move your sleeping body or worry about it, you will snap right back.

Dr. LaBerge recommends a fairly similar technique to avoid losing your dream, which he calls "spinning." In this case, you lace your fingers together with both of your thumbs sticking up. Hold your thumbs high above your head. Look at your thumbs and then spin yourself around in circles. For some reason, if you do this, once you decide to stop spinning, you will usually find yourself walking around in a new reality, where you are still dreaming. I have used this trick on multiple occasions and it really does work.

The main books that helped me achieve this fascinating state over the years are *Lucid Dreaming* and *Exploring the World of Lucid Dreaming* by Dr. Stephen LaBerge,[1,2] *Conscious Dreaming* by Robert Moss, and *Adventures Out of the Body* by William Buhlman, who focuses on consciously inducing out-of-body states. In that case, Buhlman recommends some additional exercises while you are in deep meditation, such as visualizing yourself standing at the opposite end of the room you are in, and looking at yourself as you lie in bed. This was much harder for me than using Dr. LaBerge's techniques, but I did get it to work on more than one occasion. I found myself "snapping into" the vision of myself on the other side of the room, and from there I could float around, fly through a window, and see what my house looked like from the overhead view.

Other methods outside of techniques in books are available to aid you in lucid dreaming. For example, Dr. LaBerge invented the NovaDreamer, a sleep mask that can help signal when you are having a dream. The mask senses when you have achieved the rapid eye movement or REM state, and then flashes lights in your eyes. You will see these same flashes in your dream, since Dr. LaBerge discovered that whatever happens to your physical body will appear in your dream in some way. You may have noticed this happen when some kind of loud noise in the room appears in your dream in a very different form. The beeping sound of a truck backing up could start in your dream as a person screaming, for example. With practice, you can train yourself to look for flashing lights in your ordinary waking reality, and be ready to capture a dream in process whenever you see them. Certain modern versions of these lucid-dreaming sleep masks are still available for you to purchase online at reasonable prices, and many people have had great success using them.

Meetings with the Old Man

If the dream space and even your dreaming body is strictly a product of your awareness, as Dr. LaBerge and others have concluded, how can that world become so vividly realistic, solid, and three-dimensional once you are lucid and walking or flying around in it? I have spent plenty of time walking around, touching things, talking to people, and experiencing what seems to be a perfectly real world—even though it does keep changing as you move through it. At this point you are forced to start asking new philosophical questions. You can no longer take "basic reality" for granted. You may find yourself wondering if our normal, everyday life may also be an elaborate illusion—another dream within a dream. And who is the dreamer? Is there some cosmic intelligence, some awareness that is within each of us, who dreamed this entire universe into being? And if so, then what is reality? Perhaps even more important, *who* is reality?

Very soon after I achieved lucidity for the first time, I wrote a simple poem on October 6, 1989, entitled "A New Thought." At sixteen years of age, being constantly bullied and feeling extremely out of place in the world, I was starting to ask questions that demanded answers. I had been meeting with an intriguing, fatherly, and very spiritually powerful old man in my dreams ever since I was two years old. I often felt the presence of this man as if he was around me, just out of view, giving me gentle and peaceful suggestions on various problems I faced. Who was this old man? What was this old man? Did he have something to do with what we normally would think of as God? In an inspirational state, this was the poem I wrote as I explored those questions. I transcribe these words now off of a printout I made from my original computer, an Apple IIc that my parents had purchased for me two years earlier in the fall of 1984, along with its very noisy old dot-matrix printer:

> Within me there exists a presence, old as time yet fresh with ideas. I feel him there like I feel the gentle beating of my heart. He comforts me in my times of need, and watches over me in times of danger. I know not who he is, yet I sense where he has been. He has seen a simpler earth, where the skies were filled with wonder and the crops were generous in times of hunger. He has been there at every battlefield, every site of human emotions being put to the test. With him comes wisdom, feeling, and care. I feel that he is a guide to help me through the torment of living. He has been there since the beginning, when the state of existence and all of space in itself was merely a thought that pierced through the white nothingness. This thought became matter, and he began to shape it with his loving hands. He is more than an entity. He is more than my lord. He is more than a man. Do you know who he is?

This poem was partly a celebration of my first lucid dream. One interesting line in this poem is "He has seen a simpler earth, where the skies were filled with wonder," because I remember having a very clear visual image of UFOs as I wrote those words. As I documented in *The Ascension Mysteries,* I have had powerful UFO dreams ever since I was two years old. I would see cigar-shaped craft with no wings, floating and fluttering silently in my backyard. Sometimes I was alone and sometimes

I was with my mother. The feeling was always one of immense fascination. On many occasions I boarded these craft and found the old man waiting for me inside. He had gray hair, a gray beard, a slightly off-white robe, and sandals. He spoke very peacefully and lovingly. He was always patient and kind, never in the least bit rude or disrespectful. I actually felt more connected to him than I did to my own parents, and I would often cry when I woke up and realized that our latest conversation was "only a dream." I told my mother about many of these dreams, often in great detail, but left out the part about how I felt even closer to him than to her or Dad. At this point, she was keeping a written journal of her own dreams every morning in spiral-bound notebooks, and she was surprised by the level of detail that I would remember.

From as early as I can recall, going back to age two, the old man told me that I was going to be a very famous person. He knew I was meeting rock stars with my father, who had been a music journalist since Vietnam, where he was stationed during Woodstock in 1969, and who took me to rock concerts where we usually got backstage passes. The old man wanted me to observe these celebrities and learn what their strengths and weaknesses were, identifying the mistakes that I would want to avoid later in life. As a result, once I did have a public career, I ended up doing only a few conferences a year despite massive demand, as I could see how quickly these stars were burning out from constant touring. Most of them lasted just a few years before deliberately ending their careers in order to find relief. The old man also strongly emphasized the importance of my studying science, and wanted me to learn as much about it as I possibly could. He told me that something wonderful was going to happen on Earth, within my own lifetime. Some of us would have the opportunity to transform into something far more than a "normal" human being and become like superheroes. After I saw *Star Wars* in 1977, the old man began appearing as Obi-Wan Kenobi, the Jedi master who could levitate objects with his mind just like I often did in my dreams. I did think about the fact that in *Star Wars*, Darth Vader killed Obi-Wan and then Obi-Wan reappeared as a ghostly "light being." Similarly, in my dreams the old man had the same shimmering aura of light around him, and he didn't always seem completely solid and real.

My poem also featured the idea that "existence and all of space in itself was merely a thought that pierced through the white nothingness." Once I started college, I realized that there was a whole branch of philosophy built around this concept, known as existentialism, and I took some classes in it. The basic idea of this philosophy is that the only thing we can absolutely prove to be true is our own awareness. A lucid dream will definitely get you thinking like this. Everything else around you, including the entire visible universe, could be some form of an illusion that is created by your awareness.

My Greatest Wish: To Get Another Chance

Another important aspect of my first lucid dream in 1989 was that it finally granted my greatest wish. I had held on to this wish for eleven years—ever since I was five years old. By then, I already had been meeting the old man in UFO dreams for three years. When I first learned about UFOs from television, books, and movies like *Close Encounters of the Third Kind,* I got very excited because before then, I had no idea that there was a name for these unusual craft I had been seeing so often in dreams. In 1978, at age five, I was a kindergarten student, and I woke up one night to find that I was floating about three feet over my body in bed. I was watching my body breathe gently under the covers. I was clearly alive. In fact, I felt more alive than ever before. My floating body had the same yellow pajamas on with the red cuffs. My bedroom door was open and the hall light was on, as usual. I began floating down the hall feetfirst, though I had no control over it. I then stopped at the stairs. Some force suddenly turned my body 90 degrees and tilted my feet down. Now I started gliding down the stairs, again only about a foot below the ceiling. Unlike a dream, everything stayed vividly real. Nothing around me was changing. At this point, I became terrified that I was dying, and snapped back into my body.

I immediately started thinking I was a failure for getting scared. I felt that if I had been brave enough to understand that I was not dying, the next step would have been for me to fly outside. Night after night, I wondered if one of those tube-shaped silver craft would have been wait-ing for me outside the house. Even more so, I wondered if the old man would be in the craft, and I would finally get to meet him for real—and not just in another dream. The strong sense of fatherly connection that I had with the old man was a very powerful incentive. Every night, I apologized for being scared and prayed for another chance. I saved the "sacred pajamas" and never wore them again, and I still have them to this day. My prayers went on for two long years before I finally told my mother what had happened to me, and my dream of a second chance. She said that I had experienced something called extrasensory percep-tion, or ESP. She took me to a bookshelf under the cellar stairs with nice-smelling paperbacks she had been buying since the 1960s. My eyes immediately were attracted to a book that had ESP on the spine in big letters. It was *How to Make ESP Work for You* by Harold Sherman. The edition I read was released on January 1, 1968.[3]

I read the book and practiced the exercises, though I didn't get an-other out-of-body experience until I had my success with lucid dreaming as a teenager. However, I did have great success with other techniques. One of the ESP tools Sherman gave in the book was a how-to map for telepathic communication. I decided to test this out on my best friend at the time. As I lay there in bed one night, I kept visualizing Eric's face. I thought of his school picture, images of him smiling, images of him not smiling, just as many ways of visualizing his face as I could think of. At the same time, I was continuously telling him in my mind, "Eric, you will wake up in the middle of the night." As I kept doing this, I realized I needed to add something else to be able to validate that this had really worked. I then changed the phrase to "Eric, you will wake up in the middle of the night and think of gold." The next morning in the cafete-ria, I asked Eric how he had slept, without giving away anything about what I had done. Eric looked truly shocked. He told me he had bolted awake in the middle of the night and felt a ghostly presence in the room. I then asked him what his first thought was. He said he wanted to look at his watch. "What color is your watch?" I asked. "Gold," he replied. We were both awestruck as I told him about the telepathic experiment I had conducted the night before. Eric had already seen me bringing my ESP book to class every day, which I had covered over with a white piece of paper where I had written the words *Free Reading* on the cover. We were allowed to do "Free Reading" of books in school if we had finished our other work, and I was always one of the first kids to finish an assignment.

This surprising success led to my creating a "psychic club" with a few of my friends, including Eric. They would go around the corner of the kindergarten building, far out of my sight or earshot, and pick a number between one and ten. By following Sherman's protocols of going into a deep meditation and then taking the first piece of data that popped into my mind, however quiet or subtle it may have been, I was able to guess the correct number every single time. Now that I am an adult and my thoughts tend to be significantly more cluttered, this performance would probably be very difficult to repeat. At the time, I simply picked the first number I thought of in each case, once I knew I was in the proper meditative state, and I never second-guessed that original thought. I even knew when they had decided to try to trick me, and I stopped them and told them what their trick was going to be. They were about to choose a "fake number" for me to guess that would be different from the "real number" they had already picked. I saw a huge number seven fly toward me with brilliant rock and roll stage lights in my mind's eye as they walked away. I then saw them leaning in, laughing and whispering with each other, and I suddenly realized what was happening. I yelled out to them, "Come on back, you've already chosen the next number. It's seven." I thought they would be very excited about this, but it turned out they were so frightened that our "club" immediately broke up.

Years later, I would discover that Harold Sherman, the author of the ESP book, was one of a few key personnel involved in creating a formalized intuitive program for the government and military. Ordinary people can be trained to have ESP results that are every bit as good as these stories I just shared with you. Other key people who worked on this initial team were Ingo Swann, Dr. Russell Targ, and Dr. Hal Puthoff. The program came to be known as "remote viewing," where ordinary people could be trained to psychically travel to remote locations and view them. In most cases, neither the remote viewer nor the guide had any idea what the target would be. This is what the scientists called a "double-blind" study. Nonetheless, the best remote viewers could achieve up to 99 percent accuracy in describing a double-blind target. Remote viewing will become a central aspect of our narrative as we move on. I was fortunate enough to get some initial information on how to do it from Sherman's ESP book, and then I got the rest of the basic training from reading Dr. Courtney Brown's book *Cosmic Voyage* in 1996—with stunning results. In my case, I was able to use these protocols to pull in pages and pages of written text from a higher level of my own soul—the same part of me that was designing my dreams to help teach me various lessons. These words proved to have remarkable spiritual guidance and a Nostradamus-like ability to peer into the future with stunning accuracy.

Strange Childhood Experiences

Much of my early adventures are revealed in *The Ascension Mysteries*, but the spiritual aspects of the story admittedly drop off after 1992. What comes after 1992 in the personal sense is actually far more interesting, but it required a new book—which you are now reading—to cover it in proper detail, along with all the scientific data and documentation to back it up. The second half of *The Ascension Mysteries* discusses what I learned from a wide variety of insiders who have security clearances that in some cases are thirty-five levels of "need to know" above the president of the United States. I eventually found out that the UFO subject is no laughing matter. This was very different from how I felt in some of my earliest lucid dreams from 1989 and 1990, where I would fly up into the upper atmosphere, only to find myself aboard a spacecraft. I wasn't asking for this to happen—I just found myself suddenly getting pulled on board a super-advanced spacecraft with friendly people who were dressed like the old man. In some of my lucid dreams, I also visited a world where these people were walking around, but everything was made out of giant blocks of pure white stone that were perfectly polished and beautiful. There were pyramids, rings of stone like Stonehenge, domed buildings, and so forth. Anyone who saw me there was very friendly to me, and many of them seemed surprised to see me walking around.

At this point, I was still very much a skeptic. Dr. LaBerge believed the dreamworld was strictly a construct of your own mind. I confidently told the people I met on these ships that they were all figments of my imagination. They would just politely laugh and talk to me about things like my spirituality and future destiny. Since they kept sticking around and did not disappear after I looked away, I stayed in the conversation and decided to enjoy talking to my "subconscious mind." The "old ones" asked me a lot of questions. They listened to what I had to say, repeated it back to me, and gently pointed out contradictions in my thinking. In short, they were acting like loving, patient, and forgiving therapists. In a very nonconfrontational way, they asked me about my use of marijuana and helped me to see that I probably did need to quit at some point. I was definitely suffering from PTSD due to the almost unending abuse I had endured, such as from my fellow students who relentlessly attacked me for my abnormally high test scores and extra weight, prior to when I lost eighty-five pounds on a disciplined diet. In twelve-step recovery support-group terms, I was "self-medicating" with cannabis for a problem that was quite severe but otherwise undiagnosed. These unique conversations with the "old ones" strongly influenced my decision to major in psychology when I went to college.

Time to Start Asking Questions

In some of my more recent insider briefings that were not revealed in *The Ascension Mysteries,* I realized that there was a golden thread unifying many of these seemingly mysterious stories from my childhood. Why, for example, was I consistently sleepwalking and saying strange things as I walked around the house as a young kid? Why did I write a short story as a child in which I was picked up and taken in a spaceship to "Planet Z" and then became a very famous person? Why did I draw an "Intelligent Being" from Planet Z whose face looked almost exactly like a modern depiction of a Gray ET? Why did I draw a life-size image of a three-foot-tall being with unusually large eyes in my closet, and feel that he was my friend? Why did my mother once wake up to see a short human-looking being with a normal-size head walking out of her room in the middle of the night, while having an immense feeling of fear? Why did she have dreams of craft exactly like the ones I saw in my own dreams, again hovering in the backyard, while she was pregnant with my brother Michael?

Why did I wake up so many times in the middle of the night with extreme, life-and-death fevers throughout my childhood? Why would I feel like I had to scream louder than the enormous sound that was reverberating in my ears as this happened? Why would I get so many powerful hallucinations in these fevers, including many instances where the world around me was composed of geometric patterns? Why would I repeatedly wake up in the middle of the night, take a shower, pack my book bag, eat a bowl of cereal with milk, and walk out the side door, thinking I was going to school, only to then realize that it was still pitch-black outside? Why did this strange routine happen not once, not twice, but dozens of times, to the point where it became quite ridiculous? Why didn't I ever notice what time it was on the clock, or how dark it was outside, but instead went through the entire process as if I was in some sort of trance?

Why did I continue to feel closer and closer to the old man as I got older? Why did I feel like an intelligent, loving presence was always around me, guiding me and steering my life, causing me to write poems and stories like "A New Thought" from October 6, 1989, which I wrote when I was only sixteen years old? Why did I continue to have so many spectacular UFO dreams? Why was I constantly guided to read books about science, astronomy, DNA, body language, ESP, palm reading, Tarot cards, shamanism, ancient civilizations, and other strange mysteries? Why did I keep getting picked up by UFOs in my lucid dreams and meet with very friendly people dressed like the old man, who talked to me about my spirituality and the destiny of humanity? Why had I already written three short stories about being an extraterrestrial soul in a human body by the time I was a freshman in college, as I discussed in *The Ascension Mysteries*?

Skipping Ahead to the Good Stuff

If you read *The Ascension Mysteries,* you probably don't need to hear me tell you again about how my soul was shattered by the people around me, including my friend with whom I had started the ESP club. We don't need to review, again, how I started using cannabis when I was fifteen years old to self-medicate from the nearly suicidal depression I was feeling, and how it completely changed my circle of friends. We already discussed how I was inspired to lose eighty-five pounds of body weight starting a few months after I began using cannabis, as I found a new replacement for food as my escape mechanism. Nor do we need to cover how I finally conquered my addiction in my sophomore year of college, giving up the use of all drugs and alcohol as of September 21, 1992, by going to twelve-step support-group meetings. I felt as if I had no other choice if I wanted to stay alive.

What I did not say in the previous volume was that my mother quit first, in the hopes of inspiring me to do the same—and it worked. Although I described a variety of difficulties that my mother and I had with each other in *The Ascension Mysteries,* we were able to heal our differences and move into a truly wonderful relationship with trust, compassion, and mutual support. She was able to fully embrace the unusual events and conclusions I had come to. My mother also ran monthly conferences with me from 2009 to 2013, both in America and abroad, where she worked as a musician as well as a guest speaker.

Soon after I got sober, I started remembering my dreams again and writing them down every morning in notebooks—I still have all of them. It took a few months of drug-free living for me to start feeling happy again. I felt strongly compelled to keep documenting my dreams, whether I understood their deeper, hidden meanings or not. In those early months, I had recurring nightmares that I had relapsed and started using drugs again. I would be very relieved when I woke up and realized they were only dreams. We will review a few of these dreams in the next chapter.

About five months after I got clean, in February 1993, a close friend of mine gave me information that changed my life forever. His professor, who was the head of the physics department, openly told his class that UFOs were real. How did he know? He had worked in the higher echelons of NASA throughout the 1970s. At that level, everyone knew that Roswell was real, that other crashes had occurred as well, and that we had "reverse-engineered" much of our modern technological revolution since 1947 out of these ships—including computer chips.

That insider disclosure was the pivotal event that made me realize that my dreams of the old man, including the lucid dreams where I got picked up by wandering UFOs, as well as the mystical visions I was turning into short stories, may have been far more than fiction. There was some kind of strange connection between consciousness, dreams, lucidity, spirituality, ancient civilizations, ancient stone structures like the pyramids, and UFOs.

Perhaps my single most influential teenage dream featured me getting lured into and trapped in an underground facility where extraterrestrials were living and working on Earth. Some of them were using a strange technology to keep teenagers in a type of mind control. I had befriended one woman in the facility, but she couldn't break away like I was able to. I fought an incredible battle to make it to the control room, using a technology with which I could manifest an entire spaceship out of thin air or transform it into a battle suit that protected my body. This dream was so powerful that my friend Jude wanted to make it into a movie, and created an initial storyboard for it. I then wrote out the script as a short story, but after it was finished, it just sat in my archives. It was a total of 102 notebook pages: 60 in one book and 42 in a second, smaller one.

Notes from the Original Script

Here is an exact, unaltered transcript of my original writing from the pivotal scene where my character breaks into the control room and faces off against the military villain at the end. Remember that at this time, I was still just a seventeen-year-old high school student, so it is replete with some profane language and adolescent-dork angst. I feel it is very relevant to include this excerpt, as I had no idea that I would spend the rest of my life learning about underground bases, extraterrestrials, government cover-ups, and Ascension at the time this came in. I have now come to believe that this dream wasn't just a dream but was an insight into some very real information that I would later learn much more about. I speak about my character, Colin, in third person, referring to him as "he" and "his."

His drill cut through the doors like a spoon being pushed through Jell-O. He was amazed to see that the doors had been about 15 feet thick! He emerged into a bright room. The only words his stunned mind could come up with for him to say was "What the f—!" He was in what looked like a business conference room of the gods. Round, iridescent lights were attached to the side walls, making the room startlingly luminous. Bizarre, exotic sculptures of very alien creatures and machines adorned the room. The walls were white, apparently metallic. The floor was covered with a green carpet. Leafy, tall green plants stood up inside bizarre-shaped clay pots. In the center of the room, there was a desk and a chair in front of the desk. The chair was unlike anything he had ever seen before, but its soft cushions looked very comfortable. A layer of flat glass covered the desk, preserving the blotter and certificates underneath. At the desk, an older-looking human man with sandy gray hair was sitting. His eyes radiated a majestic evil force.

He looked grim and imposing, and quite powerful for his age. "Please sit down," he said to Colin, and motioned towards the chair with a wave of his hand. Nervously, Colin sat down, the bulk of his spacesuit-like robotic armor barely squeezing into the chair. He had changed his ship back into the suit for easier access, for he no longer needed the drill. His eyes never left the man's penetrating glance as he sat into the chair. The old man began to speak. "So. You really think you're something, huh? You come in here, kill my people and destroy my ship." He inclined his head towards Colin, tipping it to one side, and squinting his eyes. "Well, just tell me this," he implied, staring thoughtfully at Colin. "What didn't we do for you to make you happy? We provided you with what you needed. A place to stay, food when you were hungry, plenty of women your age to go after, and the parties you enjoyed so much in your life. A chance to live in a place where your only responsibility is to build things for us with your mind.

"We offered you a second chance. You could have played games every day that far exceeded anything you ever used to be able to get your hands on. You could have anything you want. Now you tell me, son, what's so damn bad about that!" He looked away. "You destroyed my ship. I think I'd like to know why." Colin stood up, aiming the anti-matter machine gun at his forehead. "Understand this, mother f___er," Colin said, his eyes glaring wildly. "No one—and I mean NO ONE—can ever tell me what to do with my life. How dare you attempt to force me to be your f___ing slave? You think I want to be a mindless drone of yours, working all day with glazed eyes, staring at nothing? F___ you! I can do a hell of a lot better than this . . . I can make anything I want. Don't try to stop me, you son of a bitch! No one can hold me down. I don't care who you are, or what you represent. If you try to keep me in your prison, I'm going to use all the force in the universe to smash you down."

Colin was unwavering throughout his whole speech. He realized how childish he had been, swearing to that extent, but it had felt really, really good. He got it all out. He was ready to pull the trigger and fire on this man. He just waited for his signal. "So, you want to be an individual," the man said to him. "You want to stand alone. That's fine. Plenty of our humans here work in the special areas of the hotel section, doing whatever they want. Some of them become teachers, others just build wonderful things. Why don't you just stay with us? We can provide you with anything you could ask for."

"Wrong," Colin said. "I want my freedom." He opened fire on the man. Antimatter explosions disintegrated his desk. The image of the man still sat, as though supported by some invisible chair. It looked very odd. His arms were still held with the elbows out as though he was resting them on his desk. The man's face was grinning and cackling insanely. "Nice try, Col," he said, "but I'm only a hologram. Tsk-tsk-tsk—it's too bad for you. You thought you could just kill me and end all of your problems. Well, it isn't that easy, bud. You're in my final chamber room. How are you going to get out? I can recreate every level. You're going to have to work your way back down. Hah—you're so tired now, I don't think you have it in you to fight through. Why don't you just stay with us? Your creativity is so extraordinary—there's so much we can do with you. We could promise you a very big role of leadership here, Mr. James. You could have a very exciting job. You can do anything you want here. Won't you let us take care of you? If you leave, you'll just go back to a life of schoolbooks and pimple-popping. Don't you want to use the extraordinary gifts we can give you?"

Colin felt unruffled. He knew exactly what he had to do. It flashed into his mind all at once. [Since he could create anything he wanted, just like in a lucid dream,] he crouched into a ball and, with his mind, he began to create himself. He knew that the image of the man and his ornate office no longer mattered. Everything went dark, and completely silent. Colin created a spiritual body for himself, enhancing his abilities by making himself like a demigod or a deity, with the ability to control the lives and destinies of the civilizations on a planet. He could drain oceans and move mountains.

His body got larger and larger, appearing to be a weblike network of twinkling, starry points of light; as he grew, the web changed colors from pink to blue to green to orange, always returning to white. He arrived at a shape that he thought to be quite colossal. He floated in space, staring into darkness. It became clear, then, what he had to do. In his mind he pictured a large, upright computer with two huge screens and a massive control panel. He decided to make it a universe-shaping computer, which would be used to make "corrections" in the universe, or to create new worlds.

The computer appeared before him. He appreciated the touch-sensitive keyboard and began to program his solution to the whole mess. ">SET UP EARTH IMAGE SCREEN LEFT," he typed. A beautiful, 3D hologram of Earth with its blue seas and swirling clouds appeared in the screen on the left, slowly revolving. ">ISOLATE ALIEN COMPLEX AND PLACE INTO INTERSTELLAR ORBIT," he typed. An image of the bullet-shaped alien craft appeared, rotating while spinning around the Earth in orbit. ">REMOVE HUMAN INHABITANTS, SHIELD THEM FROM SPACE. RETURN SPACESHIP TO ORIGINAL LOCATION." A cluster of people floated above the Earth, surrounded by a yellow field of energy. The ship suddenly shot like a blazing meteor out of the Solar System. It plunged headlong into the brightest star in the canopy of space. Colin identified the huge star as Virgo, a huge supercluster containing billions of galaxies.

"Interesting," he thought to himself. He began to type again. ">NEW PROGRAM SCREEN LEFT. CREATE NEW SOLAR SYSTEM, EARTH CONFIGURATION. EARTH PLANET WILL NOT BE POPULATED. CREATE FERTILE LANDS WHERE NEW CRADLES OF CIVILIZATION CAN BE ESTABLISHED, AND NEW CIVILIZATIONS CAN DEVELOP. TRANSFER HUMANS FROM SPACESHIP TO NEW PLANET, WESTERN HEMISPHERE." Ideas struck him. He decided to make it a "pleasure planet" with no wars, no money, and no laws. He returned the people to the mountainous area of New

York State that they had been in, and created a moderate shelter that looked like an ancient hotel. He created many pleasures of every kind on the planet's surface. There was no end to the fun that could be had there. He prepared to transfer himself to the planet. ">TRANSFER COLIN JAMES ENTITY TO ORIGINAL FORM. PLACE IN NEW YORK CRADLE OF CIVILIZATION." He held his finger over the "RETURN" button, ready to enter the command. . . .

Once I finished writing this story, I felt satisfied and never read it again. A few of my buddies read it and thought it was very good. Now I was in my sophomore year of college, and I was thinking about what the ex-NASA professor said. I realized that this dream might also have been more than just a dream. The government, in this case NASA, really did seem to be hiding major secrets from us. The disclosure soon ignited a passion for UFO research that has continued to this very day, and led to a successful and highly public career. Millions of people have been influenced by my work. It is not uncommon for someone to come up to me and tell me that my work helped them through very dark places in their life. However, up until now, I have been too afraid of public ridicule to tell the full story—but now is the time. I want you to know the truth. You may start finding a lot of personal connections in this story, and begin asking fascinating new questions. The reality you once took for granted may be a dream that you can awaken within.

CHAPTER TWO

Synchronicities, Dreams, and Archetypes

The lucid-dreaming practice I outlined in chapter 1 ended up being the "bait" that lured me into the world of dreams in general. Although a lucid dream is quite a marvelous experience, after you've had a number of them, you don't necessarily need to keep trying anymore. It's a lot of work, and adult responsibilities can easily distract you. On the other hand, if you can remember your dreams in the morning and write them down, they can become a truly remarkable, if not priceless, source of spiritual guidance and insight. Dreams are by far my most consistent and valuable source of spiritual guidance, and anyone can learn the language and tap into this resource for themselves. I have been writing down my dreams now for twenty-seven years, and I do my very best to never miss a single day. Up until now, I have never written in any depth about how I deciphered the language of dreams and used it for spiritual guidance. There is ample evidence that the language is universal, and that you can identify how your own personal experiences appear as symbolic messages in your dreams. Once you develop the practice and learn the language, you may be surprised at how radically your life will be transformed by dream data.

In writing this book, I went back and reread my dream notebooks from 1992 through 1996. This was the first time I had read them since I had written them down in many cases. I ended up being so obsessed with other aspects of my career that I never went back and looked at these early dreams again. I was stunned to discover a variety of fascinating "time loops," where events that were happening in my life as I was writing this book in 2019 were precisely predicted in 1992 through 1996.

The remote-viewing community has concluded that our own human consciousness exists outside of time. Right now, this type of phenomenon seems fantastic and hard to believe. However, I do feel that in our not-too-distant future, we will have a far more general understanding that everyone has prophetic dreams. If you start writing down your own dreams, it shouldn't take very long before some very interesting things start happening to you, including accurate future prophecies. I will give several very compelling examples of this as we go on.

Stunning Synchronicities

When I first started seriously researching UFOs in 1993, and even before, strange things kept happening to me. There were countless occasions when I would have my head buried in a book for what seemed like hours, only to suddenly wonder what time it was, look at the clock, and see a pattern of repeating digits. The two most common patterns were 11:11 and 3:33, but I also saw every other repeating combination—like 1:11, 2:22, 4:44, 5:55, and 12:12—as well as patterns of numbers counting up, like 1:23 and 12:34. In fact, I could actually measure how well I was doing by how often these number patterns appeared. If I was really focused on doing my research, I might see as many as five synchronicities a day. The numbers could appear just about anywhere, including scoreboards, cash registers, license plates, outdoor clocks, billboards, and the like. It is also very important to note that in almost every case, I would feel influenced to look at a particular spot before I had any conscious idea of what I would see there. My eyes were just drawn to a certain area, and there it was.

Once I became a driver, I had a ridiculous number of odometer synchronicities as well. This was before the days of GPS navigation. I might be driving to a particular location, make a few wrong turns, stop off at a store, think of another place to visit, and have a seemingly random trip. Then I'd drive home, and at the exact moment that I parked the car in the driveway and turned off the ignition, the odometer might have a pattern of three, four, or even five repeating digits in it. If this only happens to you once or twice, it might not seem to be significant, but if it starts happening as often as two or three times a month, it definitely gets your attention. There were many other occasions where I would be driving along and suddenly get the urge to look at my odometer, which I never normally did while driving, and I would see repeating digits.

As I have said in previous books, I had one exceptionally bizarre "event sequence" of synchronicities in what would otherwise have been a typical trip to the health food store for groceries. In this case the store was Robin's Food Warehouse in New Paltz, New York, which is no longer in business. By looking back in my notes, I tracked the first of these events to April 21, 1996. At the time, I was vegan and mostly lived on rice and beans, for that was all I could afford, working at two cents above minimum wage. I scooped my dry goods into plastic bags and at least two of them were precisely 0.99 pounds when I weighed them, though I made no apparent effort to be that precise. Other items came out to a triple-digit synchronicity number in their price. I only had $20 to spend, and the price tag came out to exactly $19.99. Then, on the way home, I reached a certain intersection in the middle of the country, on North Ohioville Road. I saw repeating digits on my odometer and repeating digits on my clock—5:55—at the exact same time. Even more bizarre was that on a subsequent trip to Robin's on September 19, 1996, I had the exact same type of synchronicity sequence take place. This time I again had a random scoop of rice weigh out at exactly 0.99 pounds. My grocery bill came out to $19.19, and the date I wrote on the check was the nineteenth. Then, as I drove back to the exact same intersection as before, my odometer hit 130444, and the three-digit gas odometer was at 333. I had wondered if I should travel back to that intersection at night and wait for some kind of UFO contact, but I was never brave enough to try it out. That same weekend, I booked a bus ride for my first trip to New York City. It turned out that the bus I needed to take would be leaving at exactly 5:55 P.M. This event took place less than two months before I started developing conscious telepathic communication with angelic extraterrestrial humans, as we will discuss later. This contact only developed after years of slow and deliberate buildup of trust with my so-called Higher Self that was clearly speaking to me in dreams each morning.

Better yet, the day after this happened, I recorded a CD with a friend of mine. Once we had finished it, he noticed that the CD's run time came out to exactly 55 minutes and 50 seconds—55:50. He then told me that perhaps that meant we should air it on his radio show. Right then I looked at the clock and it said 5:55. He was completely stunned, and I responded by telling him, in all honesty, that I didn't need synchronicities anymore to realize that I was a part of God. Immediately after I said that, a large hawk flew over our heads. This only caused my friend to be even more amazed. He called me the "Walking Synchronicity Machine."

In another case, I was driving to a job where I was playing drums in the pit band for a play at Dutchess Community College. I was running late, and thinking in the car about how I always seemed to have tension in my mind. I never seemed to have enough time to do the things I wanted to do, and I was frequently getting frustrated. Very clearly, I had the thought that I needed to meditate more often, calm down, not feel so stressed out, and not take life so seriously. At this moment, I looked at the clock and saw repeating digits. Simultaneously, rain began pouring down, where it hadn't even been a trickle before. This was a pivotal event that helped teach me to "read" a synchronicity. Whatever I was thinking about right before the synchronicity happened was important. The synchronicity was encouraging me to keep thinking along those same lines, or doing those same things. Again, synchronicity happened so often that I would become concerned if more than a day or two went by without any of these types of events happening. If the synchronicity stopped, then I knew I was "off" and needed to be more meditative and positive in my overall state of mind.

Dream Guidance

Ever since I got sober on September 21, 1992, at age nineteen, I clearly appeared to be getting direct messages from a higher aspect of myself on a daily basis through dreams. I finally started writing them down in the mornings in college-ruled spiral-bound notebooks as of October 23, 1992. It took quite a while to be able to decipher the language that the dreams were using, but with the help of various books and the repetition of a daily practice, their meanings started to become clear. I was eventually able to understand what the dreams were telling me in 95 to 98 percent of all instances. As the years went on and my research deepened, there were countless occasions when a dream would offer me some new insight into something I was reading about and studying. I was tipped off about threats and unforeseen situations on countless occasions, and was guided through a variety of different jobs and relationships that helped me to accomplish various goals. Anytime someone was attempting to deceive me, I would quickly be able to identify their true intentions thanks to my dreams.

I would often go back and review my dreams, such as a month later, only to find out that they had predicted the future in ways that I could not have seen beforehand. This system provided me with very consistent prophetic guidance on how to navigate innumerable life challenges successfully. Anyone who tried to get into my life and control me, including how I thought or what decisions I would make, quickly discovered that I would always defer to the "higher guidance." I will explore the great significance of the Law of One series later in the book, but one of my Law of One–inspired quotes, paraphrased by Dr. Scott Mandelker, is "Most of your peoples cannot differentiate between love and control," and I certainly have had extensive experience with that same phenomenon.

As I ventured into full-time work as a UFO researcher, author, and radio personality in 1998, I lived my adult life with military precision. I was constantly strategizing each minute of time during the day to try to optimize my effectiveness for the greatest good of humanity. If someone started talking to me for very long, it was easy to feel this was not the best use of my time, though I was invariably polite and respectful. The main friendships I developed after college were usually with insiders who were conveying highly classified and fascinating information. I rarely ever watched television or movies. I never wanted to leave the house for any reason except to buy groceries and run necessary errands.

I experienced karma—the negative and painful side of synchronicity—as almost instantaneous and utterly inevitable. I would marvel at people who would crash through life thinking they could "get away" with anger, jealousy, control, dominance, manipulation, lying, stealing, and other negative behaviors. It was also painful to note their own inability to see the consequences of their actions in their daily lives, regardless of how seemingly obvious the connection was to me. Any significantly upsetting attack against my basic happiness and peace of mind was usually followed by a distressing personal upheaval for that person, such as an unexpected accident or severe illness. In multiple cases, friends and associates attacked me heavily enough that they went through greatly debilitating and even life-threatening karma. It was surprising to see how often the karma would appear in such an obvious, undeniable fashion. I was always doing my very best to run a clean karmic game, with the precision and focus of an Olympic athlete. For many years, I was afraid to set effective boundaries, as I knew it would upset the other person, and I was afraid this might cause me additional damaging karma. This proved to be a gross error in judgment that I have since had to work very hard to process and integrate.

Dreams and Rapid Eye Movement

The first book I read on dream analysis was *Lucid Dreaming* by Dr. Stephen LaBerge.[1] This was later followed by his sequel, *Exploring the World of Lucid Dreaming.*[2] In addition to discussing lucid-dreaming exercises, Dr. LaBerge's books also gave a very valuable overview perspective on what dreams really are, as seen by conventional and Jungian psychotherapists alike. This view is notably different from the theories of typical cognitive scientists. I gained additional insights into this information through some of my college psychology classes, as well as books I read independently, such as those by Carl Jung.

First of all, a surprising number of people think they never dream. It is now fairly common knowledge that everyone dreams an average of two to three times per night. Scientists can detect this in the lab by looking at your eyes. While you are dreaming, your eyes dart around with the lids shut, in the phenomenon called REM, or rapid eye movement. Most people rarely bring any quality dream data back because of the violence of a morning alarm, and their overall lack of sufficient sleeping hours on any regular basis. It is far better to let your body wake up on its own time, and to set your alarm only as a last-minute protective measure. I often found myself waking up right before my alarm went off and turning it off ahead of time anyway, so it was easy to adopt this practice.

Most of these cognitive scientists believe that dreams are simply the brain's way of deciding which memories to store and which memories to throw away. The researchers realized that people would typically dream about things that had happened to them earlier that day, but in oddly symbolic ways that were different from what actually happened. They believe that our dreams are taking our thoughts and experiences from the previous day and transferring them from short-term into long-term memory. Other than that, the strange symbolic nature of the things that would happen in dreams was basically overlooked. Dreams are still often dismissed as the mostly useless chatter of a brain doing its best to stretch out and take a hot shower before the new day begins, filing away certain events and understandings for their long-term survival value.

Hypnotic Suggestion

By comparison, once you get into the opinion of psychology, and particularly Jungian psychology, things get more interesting. Psychologists were fascinated by the powers of hypnosis, where people could be given commands, or "suggestions," while in a hypnotic trance state. When I was only seven years old, I started reading books on hypnosis while also reading books on ESP. That same year, my brother and I had proven that hypnosis worked by convincing our father, while he was fast asleep, to buy us a sausage and mushroom pizza. We used a walkie-talkie at a very low volume next to his ear while he slept on the couch. Very quietly, we planted the "suggestion" of how delicious it would be to order a sausage and mushroom pizza. As soon as Dad awoke, he clapped his hands together and said, "Hey, boys, what do you say we go get a sausage and mushroom pizza?" This was the last time I ever hypnotized someone, as I feel it is an unethical practice that interferes with free will. A person given posthypnotic suggestions can be awakened, have no memory of what they were told to do, but then carry out the instructions they were given by some invisible but irresistible compulsion. Once put under hypnosis again, a person will remember everything they had been told before, and their instructions can be further modified. The best hypnotic subjects are "somnambulists," literally translated as "sleepwalkers." These are people who can talk, walk around, and perform specific actions while completely asleep. They can complete complex tasks requiring thinking and interacting with others, all while seemingly wide awake, and have no memory of what they did after they are brought out of hypnosis.

The original term for this hidden but accessible part of the mind that the hypnotist would speak to was the *unconscious*. Some of the books I read on hypnosis, dating back to when I was seven years old, had still used that term. The hypnosis books invariably warned you not to let anyone hypnotize you, because that person could get you to do just about anything—and it is far too dangerous to give anyone that level of trust. I remembered being very disappointed by that, as I felt like amazing things could happen if I were hypnotized. More recent psychologists had deduced that this hidden, obedient part of our minds did indeed have an active presence in our conscious thoughts and behavior—though we were not fully aware of it. As a result, the term *subconscious* was coined, and is still used today.

The big guns of the corporate world certainly knew about the suggestible nature of the subconscious mind. By this time in my life, I had already seen television shows and read magazine articles about the real problems we had with subliminal advertising. A drive-in movie theater might show its viewers a single frame, in 1/24 of a second, that encouraged them to go to the concession stand and buy a soft drink. Consciously, the viewers do not see the image, nor are they aware of what they are shown, but their subconscious mind is able to see and read the entire advertisement even at such fast speeds. If the advertisement is shown slowly enough for your conscious mind to read it, you can analyze the information and choose not to buy the item. However, once your subconscious is commanded to want a soft drink, it can then influence and compel your conscious mind to go and buy it. This was considered to be an unethical business practice and made illegal, but as I discussed in *The Ascension Mysteries,* there are many examples of subliminal advertising of various sorts still being used.

The Superconscious

Since the subconscious seems to love to follow orders without question, the next question would be why? There must be a justifiable reason for our having an obedient inner self if we presume that we are the product of an intelligent design. Is there some other aspect of our consciousness that is giving the orders? Are we hardwired by some universal spiritual principle to trust this "higher self" that guides us through life? Apparently yes. Carl Jung theorized that there is a "superconscious" mind that we all ultimately have access to, but usually only through dreams and synchronicities. Our subconscious minds follow the guidelines from our superconscious, and we learn our own subconscious lessons as we move through our dreams on a nightly basis. Those lessons in turn influence our conscious thoughts, whether we are aware of it or not. Many of the books I read called the superconscious mind the Higher Self, and I will occasionally use that term here.

Jung's belief in a superconscious mind was strongly inspired by a profound near-death experience, where he felt he had come into direct contact with this universal mind—which often presents itself to people as a superintelligent, marvelously loving source of white light. Experiencers also report that this light is Home, in a way that seems to greatly transcend any other sense of home that they may have had before. There is a highly expanded awareness within this light, and you realize that it is you, and you are it—in the greatest sense.

Tibetan Buddhists like Namkhai Norbu are well aware of this universal presence in their practices and refer to it as "the mother light" or "natural light." Norbu's book *Dream Yoga and the Practice of Natural Light* said that we temporarily access the "mother light" after we fall asleep and before we start dreaming.[3] This book had a huge effect on me when I discovered it in college. The Tibetan Buddhists also teach that we access the "mother light" after we die and before we enter into the afterlife realms, which they call the bardos. The ultimate goal of Tibetan Buddhism was to access this "mother light" by capturing that brief moment when you have access to it before you start dreaming but are already asleep. Once you have accessed this light, you have merged with universal awareness. Among other things, you can get answers to any question you might possibly have. Tibetan Buddhism also encourages its monks to develop to a point where every dream is lucid. Norbu even compared our normal, non-lucid-dreaming state to "sleeping like an animal." In Western society, if you can even remember your dreams at all with any consistency, you are in great shape. Then, once you learn how to decipher your dreams, they can become a highly useful source of spiritual guidance.

In Jung's model, the subconscious mind is a separate but intimately connected part of us that has its own personality and agenda. The subconscious is the personality that we enter into every time we are having a dream, or that is walking around and doing things if we are in a somnambulistic trance. Jung believed that the superconscious mind was designing dreams for our subconscious self to experience and learn from. The subconscious then could do its part to try to influence us in the waking world, based on what it had learned. Our subconscious does not always make the best or wisest decisions while it is being tested by our superconscious in dreams. Just like our own waking personalities, the subconscious is experiencing its own lessons and growth patterns, fears and insecurities, strengths and weaknesses.

Hypnotists proved that the subconscious could do very powerful things, including creating a blister if we believed we were being burned, even when the hypnotist had only touched our skin with an ice cube. Jung also saw that the superconscious mind could somehow anticipate future events before they happen, and tip off your subconscious mind in dreams to send you a signal as a warning before these events occur. Thus, you might end up having a sudden pain or itch, a ringing in your ears, a pressure in your head or chest, or a sense of immense impending dread directly before heading into a genuinely dangerous situation that you could not have otherwise foreseen consciously.

This dream phenomenon is also the source of déjà vu. You may visit a certain location or meet a certain person in vivid dreams that you do not consciously remember afterward. However, once these events manifest in your physical reality, your subconscious gets excited because it remembers what you saw. Some part of this can bleed through into your conscious mind, creating a very strange feeling of familiarity. After twenty-seven years of capturing, writing down, and analyzing the majority of all my dreams every morning, I have had many hundreds of instances when I find myself in a situation I had precisely dreamed about beforehand. This never becomes boring or commonplace. I am always very surprised and excited when my waking world has an obvious crossover with what I had already dreamed. It has happened so many times that I could fill multiple volumes of books just telling the various, fascinating stories.

The subconscious also guides and directs us to experience synchronicity—strange events where our outside, worldly experiences correlate with our inner thoughts in strange ways that defy our typical ideas of physics. Jung's classic example of this was where he was discussing the Egyptian scarab beetle with a patient, only to have its Western counterpart fly in through the window and present itself to them in a very obvious fashion. This suggested that some higher, cosmic intelligence had guided the beetle to fly into their room at just the right moment. Synchronicity became a very important part of my own awakening, enough so that my second published book was entitled *The Synchronicity Key*. As we head into the very strange events that started happening to me after I began writing down my dreams, and especially after I read the Law of One series in 1996, you will hear of many other stunning examples.

Archetypes

Jung also felt that the superconscious mind had certain blueprints in it that everyone has to go through in our own ways. He believed these were primordial patterns that were written into the consciousness of the universe, and called them archetypes. The dictionary definition of *archetype* is "(in Jungian psychology) a collectively inherited unconscious idea, pattern of thought, image, etc., universally present in individual psyches."[4] Jung's four main archetypes he identified within us were the Shadow, the Anima, the Animus, and the Self.[5] We will review these and other archetypes now, as I believe this is very useful information for everyone. Once you begin remembering and documenting your dreams, you will quickly start finding multiple instances where these archetypes appear. These symbols will also appear in lucid dreams, which presents the very interesting challenge of trying to decipher what you are seeing in real time.

According to psychologist David Straker, the shadow "is, by its name, dark, shadowy, unknown and potentially troubling. It embodies chaos and wildness of character. The shadow thus tends not to obey rules, and in doing so it may discover new lands or plunge things into chaos and battle. It has a sense of the exotic and can be disturbingly fascinating. In myth, it appears as the wild man, spider-people, mysterious fighters and dark enemies. We may see the shadow in others and, if we dare, know it in ourselves. Mostly, however, we deny it in ourselves and project it onto others."[6] This is an important point. Most of us do not want to own the negative aspects of ourselves. This reluctance can force those negative aspects to appear as frightening characters in our dreams, or even waking hallucinations under certain circumstances. We can become obsessed with seeing the negativity and upsetting aspects of others, without ever consciously realizing how we are exaggerating these characteristics by being unable to identify and accept our own shadow. Jung also believed that this part of ourselves can directly take over our thoughts, actions, and behaviors when we become sufficiently triggered, such as in a temper tantrum. It can also occur in moments of extreme stress, confusion, or drug-induced states.

Jung considered the anima to be the female aspect of the soul, and the animus to be the corresponding male aspect. Jung's description of these two archetypes seems closely related to what most psychologists would call the subconscious mind. Jung therefore identifies our subconscious as having a separate male and female aspect. Together, we use the anima and animus to speak with what he called the collective unconscious, or the superconscious mind. The innate characteristics of each gender appear in a more sacred, advanced form in the anima and animus. Our creativity emanates from these aspects of ourselves, in Jungian terms.

Most of us have only brief and fleeting access to the anima and animus within us. When we see someone who embodies these sacred male and female archetypes in physical form, such as a great leader, artist, or musician, it is very common for us to feel a sense of awe and reverence for that person. In other cases, we may project our shadow onto them, as many often do, and view them with great disgust, looking for any possible way to remove their apparent righteousness. Jung believed that the anima and animus archetypes appeared as superheroes and gods in mythology. Some of these mythologies may have been taken directly out of people's dreams. Men have a far more dominant animus, and their anima is typically shaped by the female members of their family. Jung believed that women have a dominant anima, but that their animus is more complex than that of men and can be shaped by a variety of characters and influences throughout their lives.

If you are lucky enough to find a romantic life partner who has an anima or animus that is compatible with your own, you have what Jung called syzygy, the "Divine Couple." He believed that such unions have great power, and appear in a variety of trinity models in different traditions—which Joseph Campbell referred to collectively as the father, the mother, and the androgynous son. The word *syzygy* also refers to a planetary alignment, indicating the power that Jung felt such a union could have. The more you can tap into the power of your dreams and the guidance they provide, the more likely you are to be successfully steered into a blissful, meaningful, and productive coupling of this nature. It might also involve the very painful work of facing your deepest fears to disentangle yourself from someone who clearly does not have your highest and best interests in mind. Although it took most of my adult life to "find the right one," I eventually got together with my wife, Elizabeth, when I was forty-three years old. I have greatly appreciated the opportunity to experience this level of synergy with another person.

Perhaps best and most ironically of all, Jung saw the superconscious, collective unconscious, and/or "mother light" as simply the Self. The infinite awareness that most of us would call God or the Creator is the Self in Jungian terms. The term *Higher Self* is an easier way to avoid confusion when discussing this concept. Jung's concept of the true Self provides much deeper insight into the common use of the term *Self-Realization*. Jung believed that mystics and yogis who had achieved bliss, enlightenment, and the "nirvana" state had reunified the various archetypes within their beings to become embodiments of the true Self.

The Law of One series and other philosophies suggest that this work takes multiple lifetimes, and goes through a variety of stages. It is important to identify the archetypes that are the most active within ourselves, and learn how to integrate them with our overall Higher Self. In the simplest terms, we want to identify and heal our own shadow so we are not obsessed with looking for it in others, while also making sure that we do not allow others' shadows to overtake us. We want to identify and heal our own anima and animus so we do not project them onto others and worship them inappropriately, and instead develop our own creative talents. We also want to make conscious contact with our Higher Self so we can gain guidance and knowledge about what our soul has in mind for us, and begin following that path. If we begin practicing regular dream analysis, we will be receiving direct messages from our Higher Self that will greatly assist us in each of these categories.

Other archetypes Jung identified included the following list, again according to psychologist David Straker.[7] Bear in mind that Jung saw these characters as appearing in everyone's dreams and having the same basic symbolic meanings, regardless of where they might be in time and space. This list of definitions may help shed some light on various symbols that will appear in your dreams:

FAMILY ARCHETYPES
- The father: Stern, powerful, controlling
- The mother: Feeding, nurturing, soothing
- The child: Birth, beginnings, salvation

STORY ARCHETYPES
- The hero: Rescuer, champion
- The maiden: Purity, desire
- The wise old man: Knowledge, guidance
- The magician: Mysterious, powerful
- The Earth mother: Nature
- The witch or sorceress: Dangerous
- The trickster: Deceiving, hidden

ANIMAL ARCHETYPES
- The faithful dog: Unquestioning loyalty
- The enduring horse: Never giving up
- The devious cat: Self-serving

Jung also studied the meanings of the twelve signs of the Zodiac, and believed they represented a highly advanced and all-encompassing summary of the different personality archetypes that we all move through from lifetime to lifetime. Most of us will identify with just a few of them, but ideally, we will experience and master each of these various archetypes.

With all this in mind, scientists like Dr. LaBerge do not follow the conventional view of seeing dreams as "brain garbage" that sorts out useful memories from others that can easily be discarded. They see the subconscious as a separate and valid part of ourselves in its own right—having its own experiences, going through its own trials and nightmares, and influencing how we think and behave in our waking minds, whether or not we fully remember what we had dreamed. Dreams provide us with valuable lessons about who we are and what we are really doing here. Dreams are problem solvers, always looking to give us valuable advice that could help us make more effective choices in our lives. After twenty-seven years of remembering and analyzing my dreams on a daily basis, it never ceases to amaze me how I am almost always given insights about everyday issues that I might not otherwise have thought of.

In the next chapter, I will present you with my own distilled knowledge of how to analyze and interpret your dreams after twenty-seven years of experience. For me, every dream is a treasure chest of information from my Higher Self, and I have almost never met a dream that I cannot crack. The more you do it, the easier it becomes to understand what you are getting—so let's get started!

CHAPTER THREE

Dream Analysis 101

Most important, remember that the language that dreams use to teach us lessons is symbolism. If you can remember a dream, you always want to begin by analyzing it through the language of metaphor and symbolism instead of taking the events that occurred in it as a literal statement of fact. There is no hard-and-fast, absolute rule for what each person's dream symbols may mean. You do not need to get worried about "being right" and looking up the meaning of various symbols in a book. Learning your own dream language is ultimately a self-evident process that will occur as you meditate on the deeper meanings of what you are seeing.

It is most important to explore these symbols within yourself, and determine what they mean to you. In some cases, it took me years to understand what certain recurring symbols in my dreams meant for me. Once I figured out what these symbols meant, it was as if I had a master key that now unlocked the mysteries in many other dreams I had written down and documented over the years. Everyone has at least one or two powerful dreams that they can remember, from some point in their life. Those dreams can be analyzed for their symbolic meanings to gain greater understanding of whatever you were being told at that time in your life.

Everything Is You

The single biggest key to understanding your dream language is to see that everything in the dream—every landscape, every object, every character, and every event—is a symbolic representation of some aspect of yourself, and of whatever you are going through at that time in your life. The entire dream is a story that is telling you something about yourself in a symbolic form. Due to universal laws of free will explained in the Law of One series, dreams generally cannot be completely honest about what they are telling you. They have to communicate through the language of metaphor and symbolism. That way, you have the free will to reject the message they are offering if you are not ready to hear it. As an example, if you are having a dream that is really about a family member or a loved one, that person will almost always be symbolized by a different character in the dream. The character symbolizing your loved one will represent them in some way that you can decipher with logic and reason but isn't necessarily obvious at first. I have had countless occasions when dreams told me something immensely embarrassing or humiliating about myself or others I know, but I wasn't able to decipher their meanings until I was ready enough to accept this unpleasant truth.

What follows is a basic outline of the different symbols that I see in my own dream language, after twenty-seven years of study, and how I apply these symbols to the dreams of others. To begin with, animals represent the more primitive parts of yourself, ruled by strong emotions. You can study whether the animal is peaceful or aggressive, predator or prey, its color, where in the world it appears, and other traditional understandings associated with it, for greater insights. Children usually represent your own "inner child," the part of you that was shaped by early influences and that you can still revert to at various times, either positively or negatively. Female characters typically represent the more nurturing, caring, and compassionate parts of yourself, whereas masculine characters represent those parts of you that go out into the world and take action. You can obviously meditate on gender symbolism and take it much further than these basic concepts.

If you see a character from a distinct time in your past, it usually means that whatever struggles you are going through right now are intimately related to the most significant events that occurred in your time with that person. Let's say you are going through hell with a very difficult boss who seems to bully you every chance he gets. The discipline you experience from him triggers a sense of defiance in your personality. You deliberately avoid doing what you are asked—even though you know it is your job, and your defiance will cause you even more trouble. You end up making excuses for your behavior and feel that if you can avoid responsibility, you have "won" against your boss, who you have now projected the archetype of your Shadow onto. In a case like this, you may have a recurring nightmare where you meet up with a similar bully you had to deal with back in high school.

The dream will attempt to show you how you are creating the problems you experience. In a case like the abusive boss, if your dreams are successful, you will learn to forgive your boss for doing his job, which is to try to make sure that you are doing yours. And if your boss consistently abuses you beyond any level that is fair or justifiable, you will likely start getting dreams encouraging you to face your fears and find another job. In my early years in the working world with jobs just above minimum wage in their hourly rate, this ended up being a very common theme for me.

Another symbol that is surprisingly common in my dreams, and seems to be relatively standard with whomever I talk to, is the bathroom. In physical terms, the bathroom is where we relieve ourselves of toxic material that is no longer needed in the body. In dream symbolism, bathrooms almost always symbolize how we are processing and releasing our most toxic emotions. I have had countless dreams in which I keep trying to use a toilet, only to have it move around on me. This almost always means that I am not adequately working through my own toxic emotions. Similarly, I have had countless dreams where a bathroom is overflowing or otherwise a gigantic mess in some way. This means that my toxic emotions are "backing up" and overflowing into everyday life. If you are getting symbols like this, it is very important to slow down, take some time to be by yourself, and review the things in your life that are upsetting you.

Insomnia is almost always caused by our failure to process our emotions in an adequate fashion. All the great classic meditation teachings instruct us to avoid distraction as much as possible. Ideally, we focus on one thought at a time. We don't have music or video running in the background. If we have music on, we listen to the music. If we have a video on, we watch the video. If we are having a conversation, we stay present in the conversation, maintaining eye contact, and not getting distracted by push notifications on our phones. If we are driving, we are actually paying attention to the road and not just lost in the jumble of our own thoughts and the volume of the car stereo. If we keep ourselves distracted throughout the day, we may very well be avoiding painful issues. Then when we lie down at night, our minds are flooded with these upsetting problems. In the worst cases, we have a very difficult time falling asleep. In a case like this, a dream with an overflowing bathroom is a very normal symbol to wake up with the next morning.

Universal Symbols

My own experience has proven that certain symbols seem fairly universal in different people's dreams. It was quite a revelation for me, after years of daily dream analysis, to discover that water almost always symbolizes emotions. In using the example of the abusive boss, you might have a recurring nightmare where your office is flooding. This is a clear sign that you are being flooded with negative emotions about your boss. You may not even be consciously aware that you are sabotaging yourself and refusing to do the simple things you are asked. Any time I am going through emotional sorrow and pain, I can expect to have dreams of indoor flooding, rain, and getting caught up in rivers, powerful ocean currents, and the like. In the worst cases, I will be struggling with potentially drowning. Sorrow is probably the most prevalent "negative emotion" I have dealt with in my life, so I have had many thousands of water and flooding metaphors in my dreams over the years. Although some of these dreams may also feature bathrooms, I have countless hundreds of other dreams with flooding water where no bathrooms appear.

The other three natural elements besides water seem to appear equally consistently in everyone's dreams, according to their deeper archetypal meanings. Fire in dreams may refer to light, warmth, and inspiration. It can also refer to paradoxes, mysteries, and conflicts that can ultimately have a purifying effect, much like how forest fires stimulate new growth. In my case, fire in dreams almost always means some sort of anger or rage, whether it is something you are experiencing yourself or something that is being directed at you. This was one of the last ones I discovered, as I tend to have extraordinary patience and not react to upsetting events in my life with anger. I discovered the dream meaning of fire after I had ended up in an abusive relationship. There were literally dozens of cases where I would have a dream of fires or volcanic eruptions of some kind before I was about to get severely yelled at, either that same day or the day after. In fact, I eventually realized that my dreams were helping me to prepare for the next episode before it happened so I would suffer less when it arrived. This was not a "self-fulfilling prophecy" either. I would do everything I could to be polite, patient, forgiving, and understanding, but the conflicts still erupted.

Wind can represent spirit, creativity, change, messages, and intellectual activity, and a severe windstorm in a dream can mean you are having obsessive thoughts that are running out of control. If you are having consistent trouble with concentration or thinking clearly, you may have dreams where there is air pollution, a lack of breathable air, or a lack of necessary wind, such as for a windmill or a sailboat.

The element that most would call Earth is not so easily categorized, since every dream will have some sort of landscape, either indoors or outdoors. Earth and nature scenes are usually invitations for you to get out of the rat race and find a way to relax and reconnect with your roots. Going out into nature can rejuvenate us in many ways that are not currently appreciated in our conventional science. If you have a nightmare that involves being buried in soil, or otherwise features negative experiences with Earth touching your skin, it very likely means that you have a desperate need to get grounded. You are not adequately taking care of the responsibilities in your life. The answer is to step away from your stress, get yourself out of the situations that are irritating you, and take time to breathe, relax, meditate, and unwind.

Another universal symbolic principle I discovered in dreams is the height of something in the landscape. Any time you find yourself going down in a dream, such as a staircase, an elevator, a cave, a tunnel, or the lower floor in a building, it invariably means that you are dealing with the more primitive parts of yourself—the so-called lower chakras—where the strongest primal urges and emotional blockages can reside. Similarly, any movement you make above ground level in a dream is a sign that you have recently made choices that are elevating your overall spiritual level. A turn to the left can indicate that you are heading down a negative path, that is, the "left-handed path," and a turn to the right often indicates a positive shift. If the paths you have to take are mazelike, it usually indicates that your journey to work through these spiritual lessons is going to be complex and difficult—involving multiple phases that could take days, weeks, or months. You then study whether you are going up or down, left or right, and compare it with other symbols you see, to understand the deeper message.

Similarly, the speed with which you travel through the dream landscape indicates how rapidly you are making spiritual growth. If you are just walking, that is a normal speed. If you are on a bicycle, you are making faster progress. If you find yourself driving in a car, you are growing very quickly. If you find yourself in a bus or a train, this usually indicates that you are making rapid spiritual growth with a group of people. If you are flying in an airplane, that is an even better metaphor, because now you are also going into the higher altitude, thus rising in your spiritual vibration even more. The single best thing that can happen to you in a dream like this is flying through the air like a superhero. If you have a flying dream of this sort, congratulations—you have just earned your way into a quantum leap in the speed of your spiritual evolution.

After years of study, I also concluded that extraterrestrial or angelic beings show up in everyone's dreams, whether they realize it or not. This will usually be symbolized by characters who are of a different race than you are. The more different-looking someone is from the way you look, the more likely they will represent beings from "the other side." Angelic beings also often appear as authority figures who may be in uniforms, such as police, fire, doctors, nurses, and so on. In the early years, I had many dreams of the band KISS in their full makeup and costumes, as we will see, and eventually realized they symbolized positive mystical beings in my own symbol set. Others may be triggered by the strange makeup and loud music, and have KISS appear in a negative context, since symbols like this do depend upon the person. For me, any dreams involving music are invariably referring to spirituality and my overall mission in this life to elevate consciousness.

Recurring Dreams

I remember being captivated by Dr. LaBerge's description of a man who discovered he had arterial blockages around his heart, and who realized that his recurring dream about a tangle of clogged plumbing pipes was encouraging him to go get a checkup. The recurring dream may very well have saved his life. Any time a dream keeps repeating, this is a sign that you are consistently not seeing something that you really need to be aware of in your life. I wouldn't necessarily call it an emergency, but I would definitely encourage you to get serious about trying to analyze, decipher, and understand the message this dream is trying to convey to you. Every dream ultimately has an agenda to guide you into being a more loving, patient, forgiving, and compassionate person, toward your-self and others alike.

Recurring nightmares are the most obvious and intrusive dreams we get, and they often involve some kind of menacing villain that is chasing after you. Dr. LaBerge said this villain invariably represents some shadow aspect of yourself that is self-destructive and that you are not facing. You can analyze the specific details of the villain for further clues as to what he or she represents within yourself. There are countless examples of how this works.

For instance, pick a damaging addiction like alcoholism, sexual infi-delity, gambling, or abusing others. Then imagine some character who has a freakishly exaggerated symbolic connection to the addiction. An alcohol villain may have multiple empty bottles tied to his body that he drags along with him. Someone engaging in infidelity might have a very perverse and upsetting sexual villain who threatens to violate them. A gambler's nightmare villain may be made out of rotting money, playing cards, dice, or other symbols associated with the type of gambling they engage in. If someone is verbally or physically abusing someone, perhaps from feeling so hurt and violated that they feel they have no other choice, they may have some demonic, terrifying creature that abuses them in dreams. I have found that dreams almost always exaggerate the problems you are facing, and will present them as far worse situations than they really are. This is intended to help catch your attention and get you thinking about the problems in your own life with perhaps greater seriousness than you had considered before.

In my own case, I once had a nightmare while I was half-asleep on the floor of my friend Jude's house. This occurred while we were working on an album together in the early fall of 1993, a year after I had gotten sober in the fall of 1992. I had lost weight, stopped wearing black clothes, and cut my heavy-metal hair, but in my dream I had an exaggerated, ogre-type villain with these same qualities who was chasing after me. I had a handgun tucked in the front of my pants, and I knew I could turn around and shoot him and bring an end to this. For some reason, I did not want to take this final step, and instead chose to just keep running. At this moment, Jude spoke in his sleep and instantly woke me up. In a distressed-sounding voice, he said, "Shoot him. Just shoot him. Two bullets!"

That was another one of the most profound moments in my early awakening. It was very hard to get back to sleep as my mind was reeling with the implications. Having read Dr. LaBerge's books, I knew that the ogre-like villain must have represented some aspect of my personality from my marijuana-using years. As they said in the Alcoholics Anonymous meetings, it is all too easy to become a "dry drunk," where you still have all the same bad habits you had when you were an addict, only you are not actually using your former substance of choice.

At the time Jude had this bizarre shared-dream experience with me, I still had a paralyzing lack of self-confidence. I could not get up the courage to ask women out on dates even if they displayed obvious interest in me. I was not exercising very much, and I had transferred my addictive fixation to UFO and paranormal research with an obsessive-compulsive fervor. Any time I spent exercising was time when I could have been thinking and researching. The equivalent of shooting the villain in this oddly shared dream would be turning and facing my own weaknesses instead of running from them. Dr. LaBerge says that the best thing you can do in a dream where a villain is chasing you is to turn around, face the villain, tell them that you love them, and embrace them. If you actually do this, nothing bad happens. Instead, the villain will typically transform into something far less threatening and hug you back. At this point, many people report that everything transitions into blinding white light. These dreams can also be interpreted symbolically. In the case of my ogre dream, the message was for me to slow down, stop running from my past, and learn from it instead: Get myself in better shape, manage the responsibilities of life, and face my fear of talking to women.

The terrifying recurring nightmare is often the entry point for people to start paying attention to their dreams, but Dr. LaBerge and other scholars unilaterally agree that there is no such thing as a meaningless dream. Our so-called Higher Self, or what Jung simply referred to as the Self, has a definite agenda for us to become more loving and spiritual people.

I also have had positive recurring symbols. One that kept coming in for me was drums, since I had minored in jazz drumming in college. In the initial years after I graduated, I had many, many dreams where I was trying to play a drum kit and I couldn't get it to work. I would try to set it up, but things kept disappearing or moving around. For years I thought this was telling me I needed to play more music. It was a huge discovery to realize that the drums and all other musical instruments and symbols actually represented my spiritual work, such as with dreams and my advanced UFO research, and that I should focus on this more in a healthy way.

Color Symbolism

Once I read the Law of One series, I gained what I felt to be a much deeper insight into the true meanings of colors in dreams. In the Law of

One system, it is revealed the universe ultimately has seven main dimensions, or "densities." The proper technical explanation of how this works is outside the scope of this chapter, but suffice it to say that in the Law of One system, there are seven "rays" of light that radiate throughout the universe and permeate all of space, time, matter, and energy. These rays create and uphold what we would think of as seven main dimensions. They also correspond to the seven colors of the rainbow: red, orange, yellow, green, blue, indigo, and violet.

The Law of One series reveals that we have bodies that actively exist within each of these densities, completely outside linear time. This is much more complex than most people's basic idea of having a mind, body, and spirit. Each of the seven densities are anchored in our bodies with an energy center. This is what Hindu mystics called the chakras. In Law of One terms, the energy centers could be visualized as roughly spherical balls of light that appear in regular intervals as well as move up the spine. Red is at the base of the spine. Orange is in the navel. Yellow is in the solar plexus. Green is in the heart. Light blue is in the throat. Indigo is between the eyebrows, in the "third eye" area. Violet is above the head, and is also called the crown chakra. Another interesting detail is that in the Law of One series, the higher chakras appear to extraterrestrial beings as if they were crystals. The more advanced we become, the more "crystallized" these energy centers will appear from the spiritual perspective.

Although I could pull from very technical and elaborate Law of One quotes on the seven densities and their properties, for now I will keep it simple. I have found these symbolic interpretations of colors to be remarkably consistent and useful across many hundreds of my own dreams, as well as my analyses of the dreams of others. Whenever I am analyzing a dream, this is how I interpret each of the colors:

RED: Safety, sexuality, and security. Primal forces in the body and mind. The desire to protect oneself, to survive, to have food and shelter, and to procreate.

ORANGE: The self. How you see yourself. Depending upon the placement of this color in your symbols, this could indicate a positive, such as healthy self-esteem, or a negative, with a self-esteem being greatly challenged. Sexual issues can also easily appear in the orange color, since sex is extremely personal.

YELLOW: The other. How you see others. Positive instances of yellow can indicate that you are being loving, supportive, patient, and friendly to others. Negative instances of yellow may reveal that you are being manipulative and controlling toward others. Sexuality can also appear in this color, such as if you are being dominated by others or have your own desire to manipulate people. Any type of social problems you are going through in life are apt to appear in your dreams with some sort of yellow color symbolism attached to them.

GREEN: Love. This can represent love for yourself or the struggle you are going through to reach self-acceptance. This also can represent the love you have for others, as well as the love you are receiving from others. Generally speaking, green and the "higher" colors that follow are a good sign. Any dream where you are outdoors will typically feature green grass, trees, and the like. This indicates that you are working through the lessons of love.

LIGHT BLUE: Light. In this case, *light* refers to a variety of concepts, including wisdom, communication, honor, responsibility, and duty. The throat is obviously the part of us that speaks, and the Law of One indicates that the throat chakra is light blue in its spiritual "true color." When you see light blue in a dream, it can indicate that you are building knowledge and wisdom through dedicated study. It can represent a call to action, telling you there is something you need to communicate and have not yet done so. Light blue may also indicate that there is something you have elected to do, and once you make that choice, you have a duty to fulfill that promise. You also ideally see this responsibility as an honor that you are happy to carry out. Hence, the Law of One series typically merges those two words together as "honor/duty." This level is where many of the ancient sacred warrior codes have originated in various lineages.

INDIGO: Love/light. At this level, the spiritual feminine path of love and the spiritual masculine path of light are merged into a greater whole. Self and other are seen as one. This is a very good color to see in your dreams and is almost always a positive. It means that you are activating your ESP, experiencing synchronicities, starting to remember your dreams, and gaining true intuitive insights. To embody this level in your conscious, everyday awareness, the Law of One series says you have to make a conscious commitment to dedicate your life to serving others and their spiritual needs. This is admittedly not easy in today's world, but there are many different ways to do it. If you are consistently kind and loving to others in your seemingly regular job, that can easily become a dedicated spiritual practice.

VIOLET: Timelessness and foreverness. The Law of One calls this the "gateway density." It is the last stage of evolution we go through before we merge back into the "pure white light" of what they call "intelligent infinity." At this level, there is no self and there is no other. There is only timelessness and foreverness. Seeing violet in a dream is an excellent sign. It indicates you are getting into the deepest levels of meditation, awakening, and self-reflection. We will have much more to say about this level in a later chapter. This color doesn't show up very often in dreams, but if it does, rest assured that you are on a positive spiritual path.

Practical Application of Dream Symbolism

With the information in this chapter, you now have a solid basis upon which you can begin analyzing your dreams successfully. If you wake up and can still remember your dream, write down everything that happened to you, even if you don't think it is important. Note the characters, who they are and what they are wearing, including the colors. Always indicate whether you are indoors or outdoors, and describe the objects around you. Pay attention to who these people were in your life when you knew them. After you are done writing everything up, think about what these people might symbolize for you now. Always check for any of the four elements, and at the end, see how these elements may be giving you a message. Notice whether you are going up or down, left or right, and how difficult it is to navigate through a particular area. Remember that every twist and turn of the story, everything you go through and everything you talk about, is a symbol of something you are going through right now.

Furthermore, the most important protocol that will help you recall your dreams is to not move when you wake up. Remain still, and think about "Where was I? Who was I talking to? What was I doing? What was happening?" rather than asking yourself, "What was I dreaming?" The dreams seem real while they are happening, so you will remember them as if they were real events.

It is a marvelous spiritual exercise to begin remembering your dreams, for this increases your ability to tap into alternate realms of consciousness and get extremely precise messages from your Higher Self. I originally wrote everything in notebooks, but I now always use a laptop computer. I keep a word-processing file open and put the laptop in suspend mode before going to sleep. Each night before bed, I write the following day of the week, the date, and then a dash. That way, when I get up, all I have to do is hit the space bar and write the time. The day of the week is important to add for context, since you will be experiencing different life situations on workdays than on weekends. These different situations will directly affect what types of dreams you might have. On the next line, I write my first initial and a colon, and report on any stray thoughts I have after I wake up. This is a valuable technique to clear your conscious mind so it feels heard and can then get out of the way. Similar techniques exist in the remote-viewing training programs. Then, as I write down the dream, I do it with bullet points. I try not to make each bullet point longer than any one line of text. This keeps everything looking neat and makes it much easier to organize and move around. If I have a particular character who appears in a dream, I might have three to five different bullet points where I document different specific things about the way he or she looked, spoke, and so on.

You may not remember the dream in the original order that things happened. By using bullet points, you can grab an entire area of text and easily move it to another area once you remember when it happened. By far, one of the most amazing things about dream recall is when you start remembering new details from the dream while you are writing up other details that you already remember. Before too long, you can find yourself bringing back vividly long and detailed accounts, with multiple sections. You will then often find that your dream will repeat the same or similar messages over the course of the dream, using different symbols to do so. It appears that your Higher Self will do this on purpose in case you do not remember the entire dream. That way, even if you remember only the last portion of it, you will still get the basic message that the dream is trying to communicate. Dr. LaBerge also encourages you to remember as many specific details as possible, even if you don't think they are important. You will remember them as you write the dream down, but later on, they may disappear—so just document everything.

Another key technique is to make sure you don't move or get out of bed until you have three distinct and separate memories of dream events. I try to take each of those memories and turn them into phrases that have no more than three or four words each. Then I repeat the phrases verbally in my mind as I continue trying to remember other details. As a hypothetical example, I might not let myself get out of bed until I have something like "Red barn. Dove in a tree. Muddy stream." Then, the first thing I do when I get over to the laptop is to write those fragments down. Otherwise, I may remember the red barn and the dove in the tree, and explore them in more detail once I start writing, but I may forget the muddy stream.

It is also important to be patient with yourself and not expect perfection. There are still a few days a month when I wake up and forget everything, particularly if I am under stress. I don't get too upset about that, and I just write down *No dictation* for that particular day. Once you start capturing dreams regularly and deciphering your dream language, you will find them to be an incredible storehouse of wisdom and knowledge. I have never found any other spiritual practice that produces so much valuable information. Think about what it would be like to live your life, day after day, knowing exactly what your Higher Self thinks is the most important thing for you to be focusing on at the time.

Best of all, you can also "incubate" a dream. Before you go to bed, you can spend several minutes concentrating on a particular problem or question with strong intensity. Ask your Higher Self to give you a dream about this issue that will contain the answer. In many cases, I discover that my Higher Self already anticipated that I would do this, and my dreams from previous mornings already had the answer. Then the next dream that appeared after I asked the question only helped to further refine the details.

We all come up against strong programming from the modern world that tells us such behavior is a waste of our time, and that dreams do not matter. In the next chapter, we will address this situation and take a look at how my own "conditioning" started to be informed by greater truths.

CHAPTER FOUR

A Scientific Overview

Today, most of us are not remembering and recording our dreams, and even fewer of us have any idea of what our dreams might actually mean. In other eras, in our various past civilizations, however, this was not the case. Our present-day society is surprisingly materialistic, focusing only on what we encounter with our five senses in our waking life. Therefore, when I encourage you to write down and remember your dreams every morning, I admittedly have quite the challenge. We have all been conditioned into accepting and believing a highly materialistic viewpoint. Dreams may not appear to be worth your time, if you adhere to the sophism that "time is money." Nonetheless, if you put this dream work into practice, you may be very surprised at how quickly you will begin to reap the benefits. The first time you realize that one of your dreams has accurately predicted the future is a very exciting moment, though you may need several more examples before you can really allow yourself to believe it. All your life, you have been taught that prophecy and psychic phenomena is "Not Scientific," and that if you dare to believe that an accurate prophecy has actually occurred, you are suffering from delusions.

Our educational system teaches us that our value, ultimately to society as a whole, is determined by the truthfulness of the information we possess. We are given "accepted" books to read, political ideologies to embrace, flags to pledge our allegiance to, and scientific models to live by as if they were universal laws. We sit down with a pencil and paper and are given tests, which are graded based upon the accuracy with which we can repeat the information our authority figures told us was true. If we deviate from these social norms and do not accurately remember at least 65 percent of what we are taught to believe, we are given an F, which stands for "Fail"—and implies that we are also a failure in life. We are said to have scored a "poor" grade. The word *poor* also refers to someone who has no money, and without money, you will likely have a very difficult life. Worst of all, if you actually fail a grade, you risk losing your friends—the following year, you have to start over with a class of entirely new and younger people, while everyone else carries on without you. This can program us through fear and trauma to believe that we must accept the words and thoughts of "the authorities" as if they were absolute facts. If we do so, we will be rewarded with wealth, power, status, and friends. If we do not accept and regurgitate the information that is fed to us, we are social outcasts who will live in poverty.

This causes most people to get defensive about the status quo—and it can be quite surprising and distressing to see the degree of savagery, aggression, and hatred people can have when someone presents a viewpoint that is alternative to our existing models and beliefs. I have had plenty of opportunities to explore this in responses to my articles and videos, and I have had to accept a certain amount of pathological hatred as a basic and unavoidable aspect of doing my work.

Even within our educational system, however, we are told of many times throughout history that those who discovered innovative truths were punished for sharing their knowledge. Nicolaus Copernicus aroused great controversy in the 1500s for theorizing that the Earth revolved around the sun, instead of the sun flying around a fixed Earth as it appeared to be doing in the sky. Galileo Galilei was attacked by the papacy, which was the dominant political power of his day, for following up on the work of Copernicus. The priests literally refused to look through Galileo's telescope. Galileo was found guilty of "vehement . . . heresy" by the Inquisition and spent the rest of his life under house arrest. Nonetheless, most of Galileo's conclusions were found to be true, and he is now considered to be the father of modern science. Isaac Newton was ridiculed for his theory of gravity. Benjamin Franklin was ridiculed for his theory of electricity. Albert Einstein was ridiculed for the Theory of Relativity. The Wright brothers were vilified by the American scientific establishment for discovering powered flight. They were taken seriously only after shipping a working airplane to France and flying it before a crowd of esteemed authorities. It took the Wright brothers four years for the general public to accept that their initial breakthrough at Kitty Hawk actually happened.

From a young age, I realized that science is still evolving. What we think we know to be true could easily change as new information comes along. Upon the direct request of the old man, I began reading as many books on science as I could find—and conducted a variety of experiments at home that they suggested. This included things like soaking a chicken bone in vinegar for a couple days and then being able to tie it into a knot, or using a battery and a saltwater solution to electroplate copper atoms from a penny onto a nickel coin. I felt that we still had tremendous scientific breakthroughs ahead. If the UFOs that I saw on television and in various movies were in fact real, then there were still very significant scientific breakthroughs yet to be discovered. Once again, it appeared that we were suffering the arrogance of know-it-all syndrome. We believed we had all the answers, and that our current scientific knowledge was the pinnacle of our achievement as a species. We also had obvious political powers that were enforcing certain beliefs and opinions in order to maintain control. When we consider all of these factors and how they actively impact our lives, it is obviously wise for us to keep an open mind.

The Long Island Philosophy Class

In the second semester of my sophomore year of college, as my sobriety stabilized, I got my first insider NASA disclosure, and I started doing UFO research. I took a class in philosophy that proved to be highly frustrating, but also extremely revealing. The professor was attempting to teach us a history of various philosophies. The word *philosophy* itself, which comes from ancient Greek roots, translates as "the love of wisdom." Some philosophers were attracted to the strange question of whether or not we really exist. This branch of philosophy is known as existentialism, and this same word was in the title of the class itself.

René Descartes was often felt to have won the battle over the question of whether we exist with his simple phrase, "I think, therefore I am." Descartes also had a profound effect on science, with notions that came to be known as the Cartesian Doctrine, or materialism. The basic idea is that the universe is made of atoms—small, hard particles—and if we can't physically see and measure something, then it doesn't exist. All questions of dreams, visions, spirituality, higher consciousness, life after death, and so forth were handed over to the church. Science remained rigorously focused on the absolute validity of the material world—and nothing else. This agreement was made over four hundred years ago and it is still obviously in effect today, at least to a large degree.

Many philosophers, however, continued to doubt the basic concept of existence. Some believed that the only thing we can know for certain is that we are having certain perceptions. We appear to be seeing, hearing, smelling, touching, and tasting the world around us. We appear to be talking to other people who are separate from us. We appear to be human beings, in human bodies, walking around on a planet that orbits a star within what we now know to be one of billions of galaxies. Yet, just as we see in a lucid dream, we cannot absolutely prove that any of this is real. All we can prove is that we are having an experience that we normally accept as being real, through what appear to be our five senses. Yet in a greater sense, we could in fact be living in a great illusion—a dream. It is even possible that our true identity as a conscious and aware being is actually that of the dreamer who is dreaming this entire universe into existence, moment by moment.

These were very lofty "Ageless Wisdom" concepts that were not unknown to anyone who has had psychedelic experiences. I was intrigued by the idea that awareness itself might somehow be more "real" than the material world we perceive around us with that awareness. There may be some truth in this idea, since this concept does seem to consistently arise in deep meditation, contemplation, and other mystical states.

Within this philosophy class was a highly argumentative and confrontational student with a distinctly Long Island accent. She had bleached-blond hair and was obviously a severe binge drinker; I had seen her at a variety of college parties in the past. In my notebook, I called her Long Island, and used "LI" for short to document her side of the arguments she always had with the professor. I am not sure I ever caught her first name.

Every class quickly descended into a "fight to the death" between LI and our professor. She would listen to one small part of what he was saying and then ignore the rest while she was thinking up her next attack. She would confront the professor with highly materialistic thoughts, beliefs, and assumptions, often with simplicity and down-home sarcastic humor. She might say something like "If I am going to drink a beer, I just grab it. I'm not sitting there wondering about whether that beer really exists or not." The professor would attempt to address her statements and explain the course curriculum further, only to have her again capture one small part of what he said and confront him with it, ignoring the rest. In any one class, she might confront the professor twenty or more times. The perpetual arguing within this class became almost unbearable to sit through and was one of my first prolonged experiences with a psychopathic personality structure. No one in the class liked what was happening, but for the most part, she was able to keep doing it without any interruption. Some people would try to participate and steer the discussion in the way the professor intended to teach us, but invariably, LI would drag us right back down into the mud pit.

At some point our exhausted professor finally admitted that if we could not agree, as a class, on some very basic foundations, and if we did not have a willingness to listen for periods of time without interrupting, it would be very difficult for us to learn anything . . . if not nearly impossible. He was clearly talking about LI, who participated vastly more often than anyone else. Like others in the class, I had become so upset with her by this point that I couldn't even stand to look her in the eye. I always wondered if there might be a certain point where I would finally snap and confront her in class, as others had already done. She didn't even seem to care if this happened. She greatly enjoyed arguing with anyone and everyone, and made sure she dominated the entire class. There were a few precious days where her partying issues caused her not to show up, and we were able to go deeper. Our professor thought he was going to be teaching us about the history of philosophy, but he eventually admitted that our class had a very different lesson for us.

A Philosophical Argument

In philosophy, the word *argument* is used to describe a conversation between two philosophers in which they discuss whether certain new ideas might actually be true or not. Many things that we now take for granted, such as the idea of matter being made of tiny, individual atoms, began as philosophical discussions with scholars like Leucippus and Democritus in the fifth century BC. Much of modern mathematics originated in philosophy, such as the works of Pythagoras. Many of our understandings of astronomy, biology, and physics originated with philosophy. We also can credit philosophy with clarifying our understandings of virtue and ethics, and therefore it had critical importance in the development of written law and politics. Warfare, weapons technology, and battle plans often developed out of philosophical arguments as well. Philosophers also tackled spiritual concepts, including many scholars in the early formative years of Christianity. In the present day, there are a variety of ongoing philosophical discussions in our society, such as the role of artificial intelligence and the possible existence of extraterrestrials. Philosophy is a valuable part of how we chart out our future. It is no accident that *PhD* stands for "Doctor of Philosophy."

Our professor told us that the single most important "rule" in philosophy is that to have an argument, certain basic fundamental principles must be agreed upon as facts. These ideas may eventually be disproven, but for the purposes of a philosophical argument, both parties agree to accept that these principles are true. That way, they are not arguing over their most basic assumptions. Our professor stressed this point repeatedly throughout our entire class, almost every time we met. Once you can agree on certain basic points, your argument then goes forward with the basic tools of logic and reason. Otherwise, you may well be witnessing a narcissistic person bullying someone they don't agree with, and satisfying their egoic needs for dominance and control in the process.

As a very simple example of how the philosophical argument works, let's take René Descartes's classic line, "I think, therefore I am." To have a philosophical argument about the idea that having thoughts proves that we exist, both parties would need to agree that thinking is real. This might seem ridiculous, but believe it or not, some people have dedicated their entire lives to exploring concepts like this. Theoretically, you would have to think in order to have a thought, but some would-be philosophers enjoy questioning everything . . . including the most basic assumptions we need to work with in order to function as human beings.

So let's explore this a bit further. You, as a person, appear to be having an experience that we call thinking, where various distinct concepts come and go that we call thoughts. However, some might believe that our thoughts are not our own, that we have no free will, that our thoughts might not be created by us at all, and that what we consider to be our own thoughts might actually be a manifestation of some outside force manipulating us.

This is just a hypothetical example that I do not believe to be true. I do accept that we think our own thoughts, and that we have the free will to do so. Yet you can see certain modern philosophers speculating that we might all be the product of a vast artificial intelligence, like in the movie *The Matrix,* and that the nature of our true existence is completely hidden from us. In that case, the source, meaning, and destination of our thoughts, and of who and what we are as seemingly conscious beings, may be something we are completely unaware of.

If one of the philosophers in an argument refused to accept that such a thing as "thinking" was actually happening, then they would have no fundamental agreement for their argument to work off of. René Descartes considered it to be a fact that we think. To have an argument about the greater point Descartes was making about the nature of the universe, other philosophers would have to agree that we do think thoughts. In this example, if the philosophers cannot agree that thinking is real, then they could never progress to the second half of the discussion, which is whether or not our basic existence, the part of us that lets us say "I am" with confidence, is actually real: "I think, therefore I am." If you continue to argue over whether or not thinking is real, that's where the entire argument begins and ends. You never can make it past the word *therefore*. You are constantly fighting over whether "I think" is even true, and the deeper question of what it means to say "I am" is never even able to be asked.

LI had completely shattered any and all hope of having a philosophical discussion. In every single class, she would attack the fundamentals, and she and the professor were constantly arguing over the same things. These concepts were the building blocks that we needed to have in place before we could have any greater discussion. Without those foundation stones, nothing ever got done. It was one class after another after another of infuriatingly repetitive fighting. No matter where the professor tried to take us as a class, LI kept circling back to the idea that most of the ideas he was teaching us were fundamentally stupid. She would ridicule the professor, make jokes, and act as if he was wasting our time for trying to get us to think about such unusual things. She was completely incapable of accepting certain basic ideas, even long enough for us to have a discussion about what it might mean for us to be alive and aware as conscious beings in a universe of galaxies.

The Original Briefing

In the same semester when I went through this very difficult philosophy class, I was fortunate enough to receive a private briefing about the nature of the UFO phenomenon from a college friend of mine. This, again, was in my sophomore year, sometime approximately in February 1993. My friend's physics professor was the head of the department and had worked for NASA throughout the 1970s, in the "higher echelons." This professor blithely disclosed, to his entire physics class, that the Roswell crash really happened and was indeed an extraterrestrial spacecraft. Had LI been in this class, it was very unlikely that he would have been able to say much without being interrupted. The professor said that the people behind NASA didn't mind if we learned about this information through means such as a college classroom. NASA just didn't want it to be the top headline in the *New York Times*. He cited the example of the public panic from the *War of the Worlds* radio broadcast from October 30, 1938, when people thought we were suffering an alien invasion, to explain why we were not ready as a species for this information. Strangely, the professor also told his class that if anyone ever asked him about this again, he would deny ever having said anything. This caused a visible shock wave to ripple through the entire class. Clearly, he was very afraid . . . about something.

My friend was brave enough to meet the professor directly after class and interrogate him for two more hours about exactly what he knew. The professor shared far more detail with my friend than he had with the class. My friend then revealed every single part of that conversation to me, at great length, and answered a wide variety of questions I had, to the best of his ability. The professor was told that the Roswell crash and several other similar crashes had occurred. Beings had been found in these crashes, most of them dead but some of them alive. Considering that I had been having UFO-related dreams ever since I could remember at age two, I was extremely fascinated to discover that there was apparently a great deal of truth surrounding the phenomenon. I already had started to notice that my dreams could predict the future and provide accurate spiritual guidance, so this NASA disclosure was extremely fascinating.

The professor told my friend about three types of beings that were found within these craft. There were taller "Grays," with skinny, whitish bodies, long limbs, and unusually large heads with large black eyes. There were shorter "Grays," and the professor said their heads were actually helmets. Underneath the helmet was a "monstrosity," some kind of frightening-looking humanoid face, but the professor never revealed exactly what it looked like. Last, the professor had heard about beings that looked almost exactly like us—human—but they had subtle differences. This could include deep blue or purple irises, diamond-shaped pupils, odd skin colors, and unusual catlike ridges on the roof of the mouth.

A Celestial Endowment

I found out that technological marvels like lasers, LED lights, infrared night vision, fiber-optic cables, solid-state transistors, computer chips, Teflon, and Velcro had all been found initially on various crashed ships from elsewhere. The materials were then reverse-engineered, often by being sent to corporations as "foreign technology" to be studied and duplicated. I was absolutely stunned when Colonel Philip Corso came forward as a whistleblower in 1997, saying exactly the same things in his groundbreaking book *The Day after Roswell,* coauthored with William Birnes.[1] At this time, I had spoken about our professor's insider testimony only in obscure posts on Richard C. Hoagland's discussion forum on his website, enterprisemission.com. It was very unlikely, if not nearly impossible, that Corso's recollections could have been borrowed from my own written accounts—particularly because he also had far more specific details than I had ever gotten. This is the type of argument that skeptics might defend with everything they have. On some basic level, they are unwilling or unable to honestly examine the wealth of interconnecting evidence that exists.

Corso and the professor both revealed that our technological revolution was inextricably connected with this "celestial endowment." Without it, we might still be using vacuum-tube computers that fill entire basketball courts. The professor also said we had gotten other technologies, like antigravity and free energy, which were still highly classified— but were very much being used "on the inside." With those technologies, it was entirely possible, if not likely, that we had already developed bases on the moon, Mars, and other planets and satellites in our solar system and potentially beyond. I had absolutely no reason to doubt what my friend was telling me. The professor was the head of the department and an established authority. No one else in the class was brave enough to ask him any further questions about what he had said, but my friend was the star pupil of the class. I never dared to approach the professor myself, owing to his promise to deny ever having said a word about it.

A Gathering of Trolls

Though my philosophy class was almost mind-shatteringly frustrating, it proved to be of extreme importance in understanding how to proceed in the career I would eventually create for myself beginning in 1996. That was the year I began participating in Richard C. Hoagland's online discussion forum, after having read over three hundred books on UFOs, ancient civilizations, and the paranormal. The year 1996 was well before the term *troll* became widely used to mean a person who creates trouble for others in an online discussion, but trolls were extremely active in Hoagland's forum. It was nearly impossible to have a meaningful discussion about the UFO phenomenon, because certain individuals could never agree upon whether or not UFOs actually exist. The trolls would mercilessly attack every single piece of interesting data that came along. They would look for flaws, try to point out minor inconsistencies, and then attempt to "win the argument" and conclude that the entire discussion was a complete waste of time. Every discussion was staged to steer the reader back to their preexisting beliefs, which they defended with all the fervor of religious zealots. They never even considered the possibility that they might be wrong. Like the actions of LI in my philosophy class, this trolling was done with snark, sarcasm, and an obvious delight in causing misery to others.

Even to this day, many UFO researchers are still trapped in this basic problem of attempting to determine whether or not UFOs and intelligent extraterrestrials really do exist. They may analyze reports of sightings, photographs or films of alleged craft, landing-trace markings, cattle mutilations, abduction and contact stories, government and military insider testimonies, crop circles, or the records and remains of ancient civilizations. However, at the end of a public lecture, radio show, article, or book, the whole subject is usually still left open-ended, with a huge question mark hanging over it. Even if extraterrestrials are acknowledged to exist, the philosophical questions of who they are, where they came from, and what they want with us are almost never addressed. The spiritual aspects of the phenomenon are usually almost completely ignored, as are the deeper implications of the reality of the UFO presence. As a result, any greater philosophical discussion about the nature of space, time, matter, energy, consciousness, and existence itself is greatly reduced, if not eliminated entirely.

Four Main Tools for a Philosophical Argument on UFOs

From a strictly logical perspective, there are four main tools available to help deepen our philosophical understanding of the extraterrestrial presence, once we agree they exist for the purposes of a scholarly argument. First, we have the written reports of ancient dreams, contacts, and communications, many of which are dismissed as mythologies or get codified into religions. Second, we have spectacular architecture all over the planet made out of gigantic, multiton stone blocks that cannot be duplicated with today's technology. Third, we have the phenomenon of "close encounters" with UFOs, which can include sightings, photographs, films, radar tracings, alleged wreckage, possibly extraterrestrial bodies or skeletons, and apparent contact with extraterrestrials, the memories of which often will only become available through hypnosis. Fourth, we have modern-day alleged communications with extraterrestrials, most of which are telepathic in nature and which often arise out of contactee reports. Last, we have insider testimonies of individuals who claim to have interacted directly with these beings in highly classified military projects.

Once I began studying the UFO subject in 1993, I did my best to assess the validity of claims in each of these categories. As a general rule, if the same point shows up in three completely unrelated sources that are unaware of each other, I am more likely to consider that the information might be true. In some cases, multiple insiders have shared almost identical pieces of information with me that are highly specific, without ever having had contact with one another. In each of these cases, I had never published or spoken of this information online in any form. As I will discuss a little later on, the Law of One series had an astonishing number of connections to the insider testimony and scientific data I was gathering. It also anticipated many otherwise unexpected and mysterious scientific breakthroughs by two or more decades.

A Personal Connection

As I continued to meditate on the awesome implications of my NASA disclosure in 1993, I did have the distinct feeling that I had earned this information, in the karmic sense, through the very hard work I had done on self-improvement. I had listened to what the old man told me. I was starting to wonder if his friends on the ships that picked me up in my high school lucid dreams were actually real people and not just constructs of my subconscious mind.

The torture of my philosophy class with LI seemed to be encouraging me to start my own philosophical argument about UFOs. I rejected her irrationally skeptical attitude and stopped arguing with myself over the fundamental question of whether or not UFOs and extraterrestrials actually existed. I was able to accept that my friend was telling the truth, and that the professor was reporting accurately on the information he had seen and heard during his time at NASA. I would still search incessantly for proof, but this was coming from a perspective of accepting that such proof was likely to exist. Years later, I looked up the professor's name online and confirmed that he had worked at a NASA facility throughout most of the 1970s. Out of respect for his surviving family, I have not shared his name. There are plenty of other insiders who have indeed chosen to come forward and go on public record with their accounts, such as Colonel Philip Corso. Almost everything Corso disclosed was included in the things the professor had already revealed to my friend four years earlier.

Once I had established the basic, fundamental understanding that UFOs and extraterrestrials did indeed exist, I focused on gathering as much material as possible. I would assess its overall credibility, and then work to build a unified model to integrate what we know. Before too long, I again started reading books that talked about unusual feats of consciousness, such as telepathy. Some of these books were linking ESP with the idea of extraterrestrials. Certain people, such as Edgar Cayce, seemed to be in communication with an advanced extraterrestrial or higher-dimension consciousness. Edgar Cayce was a name that popped up quite often in the books I was reading—and for good reason.

The Edgar Cayce Enigma

The mystery, awe, and power of what was achieved in the Edgar Cayce Readings from the early 1900s until Cayce's death in 1945 seems to be a forgotten memory. These types of psychic results now appear to be an impossible dream that is immediately dismissed by skeptics who have a misplaced sense of confidence. Cayce was a walking paradox—a seemingly ordinary Kentucky tobacco farmer and child laborer with limited education who somehow gained access to omniscient intelligence. There are fourteen thousand documented examples of Edgar Cayce performing a "psychic reading," as his source called it. While under hypnosis, some part of Cayce would travel to a remote location where his client was located, accurately diagnose their medical problem, and prescribe unique and effective treatments. The only information he was given beforehand was the person's name and address, and an agreement that they would be present at that address during the scheduled time of the session. Since I had experienced my own out-of-body experiences, lucid dreams, and strange UFO-type contacts, I did not have a problem accepting what I was reading.

Cayce was completely asleep while he was doing this work. While under hypnosis, some greater part of his consciousness began speaking, and it usually spoke as "we" instead of "I." This was all recorded by Cayce's stenographer; Cayce had no memory of what he had said when he woke up. The words were difficult to read, including some written in a strange language, and with long run-on sentences that often extended into paragraphs. Yet the accuracy that his readings displayed was astonishing, including many documented future prophecies that proved to be correct. Once you have surveyed some of the more than six hundred books that have been written on Cayce's work, the simplest explanation is the obvious one. It appeared that some nonphysical part of Edgar

Cayce was visiting clients in their homes, in a process similar to what is now performed under controlled laboratory conditions with military remote viewing. Once there, Cayce could view inside their body, analyze its difficulties, and prescribe treatments—with an encyclopedic knowledge of medical terms, diagnoses, and obscure remedies that nonetheless really worked.

Here is a brief excerpt from my previous book, *The Synchronicity Key,* about some of the more fascinating aspects of the Cayce story:

> Warner Books published *The Edgar Cayce Reader* in 1967, twenty-two years after Cayce's death.[2] In the introduction, it is noted that the ten books written about Cayce up to that time had "totaled more than a million in sales." In 1998, fifty-three years after the death of Cayce, Paul K. Johnson published a book called *Edgar Cayce in Context* with the State University of New York that offered the following opinion: "[Cayce] exerted a literary influence comparable to the greatest religious innovators of the last two centuries in America."[3] Cayce can also be given considerable credit for inspiring the New Age and holistic health movements of the 1960s, which have become increasingly mainstream over time.
>
> In *Edgar Cayce in Context,* we find out that by May 1997, 646 books had been published on the subject of Edgar Cayce since 1950—compared to 542 books on Ellen G. White (one of the founders of the Seventh-Day Adventists), 264 on Joseph Smith (the founder of the Latter-Day Saint movement), and 121 on Helena Blavatsky (one of the founders of the Theosophical Society). . . . While Cayce was performing a reading, lying on a couch with his eyes closed, he would monitor the handwriting of his stenographer, Gladys Davis, as she took dictation and make corrections if she spelled something wrong.[4] When Cayce had clients there in the room with him, his source would often read their minds and answer the questions they were thinking of before they had a chance to speak them out loud.[5] Although Cayce spoke only English in his

waking personality, his source also had complete conversations with his clients in their own native languages, or would pass on witty little sayings that made them laugh. Cayce is estimated to have spoken fluently in more than twenty-four different languages during his readings.[6] However, his source continually emphasized that all of us have the potential to do these things.

Cayce's medical advice often led to miracle healings in patients the medical establishment had written off, and his readings concocted successful medicines with ingredients no one had ever thought to use, like baking soda and castor oil for warts.[7] A Canadian Catholic priest was healed of epilepsy; arthritis was cured in a young high school graduate from Dayton, Ohio; a New York dentist's migraine headache that had hammered him for two years was completely eliminated in just two weeks; a mysterious and debilitating skin disorder known as scleroderma[8] was cured in a young female Kentucky musician after one year, despite her being written off as a hopeless case; and a Philadelphia boy with infant glaucoma, normally considered incurable, regained his full eyesight.[9]

The typical materialistic person might have a great deal of trouble with the Cayce Readings, because if it hasn't happened to them, they might not want to believe it is possible. Yet most of them actually have had paranormal experiences, upon questioning, but they discount the validity of their own five senses in these cases. I myself admittedly needed to have many, many different repetitions of certain experiences, such as accurate prophecies of future events, before I was truly able to take in the greater model of the universe that I was being presented with. Again, it is my hope that you will be inspired to pay attention to your dreams as a result of reading this book, as this opens the door to a wealth of seemingly impossible miracles.

Exploring Alternative Scientific Concepts

Once I accepted the reality of the UFO phenomenon as a starting point for a philosophical argument, I eventually started exploring a variety of alternative scientific concepts. If UFOs exist, that means someone, somewhere, has perfected the ability to control gravity. They also would need to have discovered a source of energy that is vastly superior to our own, and would be nearly limitless in its longevity, unlike our own typical batteries.

Furthermore, Einstein's apparent boundary of the speed of light as the fastest velocity we can travel in the universe would have to be false. Otherwise, even visitors from the closest stars to our own would take a prohibitively long number of years to make it here. The travelers would probably need to go through some sort of cryogenic freeze, and would have the full knowledge that it would likely be a one-way trip. Then, as I dug deeper into the reports of contactees and UFO abductions, I would hear many accounts of people being telepathically influenced. They would "know" to get up in the middle of the night and go outside. This certainly sounded familiar. Once they did make it outside, they would see a ship hovering over their yard. Many UFO reports have these "weird" elements to them. The strange sleepwalking type of trance states encouraging me to go outside at night had happened to me, but I remembered seeing UFOs only in dreams, so I was puzzled.

As my search went on, I eventually discovered that some people on Earth appear to have souls that are significantly more advanced spiritually than most. One term we will encounter for such people is *Wanderers*. It does appear that these people are effectively extraterrestrial souls living in human bodies, who have consciously forgotten who they are. Another interesting aspect of this story is that apparently their original ET family continues to contact them throughout their lives. This contact can occur through dreams, telepathy, or benevolent contactee experiences, in which they are physically brought on board the ships of their home group. In the vast majority of all cases, these contacts are then blanked out from the person's conscious memory. They have only a vague sense that something very unusual may have happened to them. As bizarre as this must sound, the concept explained many different bizarre things that were happening to me throughout my childhood in upstate New York.

Most Wanderers stay asleep their entire lives, by design. The world is improved by their subconscious memories of a far more harmonious place as they work to help the planet. In my case, I was able to "penetrate the veil of forgetting," using a term from the Law of One series, and discover far more about who I am and what I am doing here than most others do. The most exciting part about sharing my story in this book is that you may start putting the pieces together in your own life and begin asking new questions. If you have been interested enough to pick up this book and are still reading it now, the chances are well above average that you yourself may be a Wanderer. If so, you owe it to yourself to commit to discovering the answer—and I will discuss tools that can help you find it.

CHAPTER FIVE

The Scientific Investigation Heats Up

My investigation into UFOs and the paranormal went further and further after I got sober and began writing down my dreams in 1992, and especially after I received my NASA disclosure in February 1993. I read well over three hundred books in the first three years alone, and then began migrating to the Internet starting in late 1995. There were countless occasions when my dreams gave me further insights into the scientific data I was researching in these books, far beyond the scope of what I could cover in this volume. I eventually began a new depth and focus of research after I became self-employed as a UFOlogist in July 1998, working fourteen hours a day, seven days a week.

None of this felt like hard work to me. I was very focused on my quest due to the awesome passion that I had to explore this greater truth. I did not want to be distracted by anyone or anything for very long, which at times caused obvious problems. I launched my own website and online business in February 1999, and between then and 2004, I printed and bound books out of all the best research I found online. During this period, my collection of research documents quickly expanded into nine feet of shelf space. The challenge of moving this mass of paper with me wherever I went led me to store all the information digitally, in detailed notes with hyperlinks, after 2004. If I were to print it all out and bind it into books now, I would probably have at least five times as much as the original collection.

I discovered that there were literally thousands of groundbreaking scientific discoveries out there that most people had never heard of, and probably wouldn't believe despite the fact that they had been verified. Established PhDs were making discoveries that could be repeated under controlled conditions in a laboratory. They did everything properly, made sure that their discoveries were not poisoned by their own biases, prejudices, and preexisting beliefs, and yet were often very reluctant to publish their conclusions. They understood that they were presenting information that contradicted our prevailing belief systems, and that by doing so, they opened themselves up to ridicule, harassment, and career ruin. It was surprising to learn how much of this kind of material was out there, and how little of it had been integrated into any greater whole. Some of it would appear in various online publications, but no one ever seemed to put these many thousands of scattered pieces together. One early example of a book that did do a great job of tying together contentious material like this for me was *The Holographic Universe* by Michael Talbot, which I read around 1995.[1]

The Alignments of Mars

Nothing captivated my imagination in those early years more than the Hyperdimensional Model that Richard C. Hoagland talked about in his classic *The Monuments of Mars,* which I first read in 1993, just a few months after my NASA disclosure.[2] Hoagland was analyzing NASA images of the moon and Mars, and pointing out multiple anomalies that did look like the ruins of intelligently built structures. On the Cydonia plateau of Mars, there is a mountain that is a mile and a half across with a giant human-looking face, surrounded by what appears to be a headdress. Just to the west of the face is a city of objects that are clearly shaped like pyramids. South of the face and the city is another, larger pyramid that is five-sided. Best of all, this is not a geometrically perfect pentagon but is actually styled in the exact proportions of Leonardo da Vinci's *Vitruvian Man.* This means that the pentagon is built to the exact proportions of the human body. Once you add in the human-looking face to the north, it isn't hard to conclude that humanlike beings built these structures.

Hoagland postulated that Mars was once Earth-like, with oceans, atmosphere, clouds, and rain. This was nearly two decades before NASA finally announced that Mars once had a large ocean that was at least a mile and a half deep across much of its surface. It is absolutely fascinating to have a philosophical discussion in which you begin by accepting that Mars was once an Earth-like home to an ancient human race with advanced technology. By starting with that as your fundamental premise, you can mount an intriguing investigation. Hoagland noted that one half of the face on Mars looked human and the other half appeared cat-like. Here on Earth we have the Sphinx, which is a half human, half feline creature—and as we know, the Sphinx sits immediately adjacent to the pyramids of Giza. The face on Mars sits immediately adjacent to pyramid complexes as well. This established the intriguing idea that the people who built the Sphinx and the Giza pyramids here on Earth may have been aware of the visible artifacts that were still on Mars. Perhaps the ruling caste of Egyptians may even have been descendants of that civilization, or had at least found records from the descendants. This is the central focus of the cosmic history of our solar system that is discussed in the second half of my previous book, *The Ascension Mysteries.*

Some people in Hoagland's discussion forum absolutely could not make it to the point of believing that any of this was true. They simply could not accept that NASA had photographed anything other than "a trick of light and shadow," or "Jesus on a potato chip." This made it nearly impossible for them to follow along with the next part of the discussion, where Hoagland's team analyzed the geometric and mathematical relationships between the unusual-looking structures they found on Mars. With my mind newly opened, I accepted that these objects were not optical illusions and were very likely ancient ruins. I studied all the data regarding the alignments very carefully and concluded that, at the very least, it was a highly compelling argument, if not actually the truth. Hoagland's team argued that the monuments were deliberately designed to give us the mathematical clues to decipher an entirely new and more advanced form of physics than the one we were currently using. This new form of physics is what Hoagland called the Hyperdimensional Model, and it was deep with mystery. With this new model, we could potentially unlock the mysteries of antigravity, free energy, faster-than-light warp drive, time travel, and the true source of consciousness. The Hyperdimensional Model was the scientific Rosetta stone that would allow us to explain all of the seemingly impossible aspects of the UFO phenomenon. Even better, it held the promise of how we could develop this remarkable technology for our own civilization. Additionally, as I went deeper and deeper into this model, it became increasingly clear that we were living in a holographic universe, just as Michael Talbot had postulated in his book of the same name. That meant that ultimately the universe could actually be the product of a dream from an "intelligent infinity," or One Infinite Creator, just as the Law of One series had indicated.

Scalar Waves

Hoagland's model was heavily influenced and guided by the work of Lieutenant Colonel Tom Bearden, who had worked in classified government and military programs and had made a variety of interesting scientific discoveries. Bearden's work focused on the idea that he had discovered a new type of energy that he called a scalar wave. The jargon quickly got dense, but it became a very sobering discussion when Bearden argued that scalar waves could be made into weapons that were potentially far worse than nuclear bombs. Scalar waves could cause water to instantly boil into steam or freeze into ice, even in large amounts, and humans are mostly made of water. Scalar waves could create and manipulate severe storms, including tornadoes and hurricanes. Scalar waves could be used to trigger massive earthquakes and volcanic eruptions. Scalar waves could manipulate the way our minds work, creating mass hysteria or other states of consciousness that certain power brokers might deem useful. Scalar waves could invisibly attack our technology, such as an airplane, and cause it to come flying apart in midair without anyone understanding what happened. Bearden believed that the infamous Space Shuttle *Challenger* disaster of January 28, 1986, was an attack by the Russians using scalar waves.

Bearden had some very elaborate science in his writings. This was by no means entry-level material. He wrote for an educated audience who were already operating at a PhD level of knowledge of physics. To understand what he was talking about, I had to quickly bring myself up to speed on all the terms and concepts he was referring to. Most people would have been incredibly frustrated by this challenge, but I forged ahead undeterred. I began intensively working through this "learning curve" in the summer of 1998 to try to gain a deeper understanding of exactly what Bearden was talking about. Much of my knowledge of physics was acquired by reading articles and books online, where credentialed independent scholars were tearing apart the existing models and pointing out their numerous, embarrassing flaws. This was what triggered the origin of my nine-foot-long collection of printed books of Internet research. Printing this complex material into books allowed me to get away from computer screens and spend long hours sitting and contemplating the meaning of the words.

It took several months of nonstop fourteen-hour days to get the basics down. In the process, I found a wealth of authors who were reviewing the basics while also pointing out many key areas where these established scientific conclusions were blatantly wrong. Since you needed to have a scientific mind to create a website back in those days, with the complexity of software, HTML programming language, and the like, a variety of great research works into alternative science were available in the late 1990s. You didn't have to look very far once you began searching for certain terms. These scientists were very happy to have a free press in which to share their conclusions with the general public, without fear of censorship. This data included a huge wealth of formerly classified material from Russia. After the USSR collapsed in 1991, many of these scientists were now free to declassify their work and publish it online without repercussions.

Bearden argued that we were working with a grossly oversimplified view of the electromagnetic wave. We think we are seeing two simple sine waves that move simultaneously: the magnetic wave, which moves left to right on the X axis, and the electrostatic wave, which moves up and down on the Y axis at the same time. The legendary scientist James Clerk Maxwell had originally mapped out far more detail and structure in the electromagnetic pulse than these two simple waves. Oliver Heaviside came along and drastically simplified everything to create the two-sine-wave model we still use today. Heaviside removed most of the three-dimensional details that Maxwell had found in the wave. Bearden called these hidden three-dimensional details "scalar potentials." The electrostatic and magnetic waves we map out in today's science textbooks are tracing only the outlines of these hidden three-dimensional energy structures. By eliminating the scalar potentials from our discussion, we actually lost an entire branch of science that could dramatically accelerate our technology. Though scalar waves could be used to harm people, they also have incredible healing potentials that are unavailable through any other means. If these technologies are properly regulated, they can be of amazing benefit to humanity—including eliminating many, if not most of the diseases we now take for granted, such as cancer.

The Hyperdimensional Model

As the years went by, the Hyperdimensional Model proved to be exactly what I had been looking for. The more I probed the nature of geometry and looked for clues to how the pieces all fit together, the more truths I uncovered. I had reason to believe that geometry was the hidden key to solving the greatest scientific mysteries of the universe. And the more I explored this idea, the more obvious it became. Much of this science appears in my first book, *The Source Field Investigations,* with over one thousand academic references, but in this present book, I will explore a smaller amount of information and expand upon it for greater insights into dreams, extraterrestrial communication, and Ascension. Most important, as this book continues, I will use the Hyperdimensional Model as the basis for a new and very interesting philosophical argument— namely, that the universe itself is a dream.

Tetrahedral Geometry

Once Tom Bearden started talking about the scalar potentials he saw in the electromagnetic wave, the discussion quickly shifted to geometry. These scalar potentials actually had a distinct shape. The entire electromagnetic wave was traveling along in the shape of a tetrahedron. A tetrahedron is similar to a pyramid in its basic shape, but instead of having a four-sided base, it has a three-sided base, which creates a total of four equilateral triangle faces. And sure enough, if you study the up-and-down movement of the electrostatic wave with the left-to-right movement of the magnetic wave, you can see that the waves are perfectly tracing the shape of a tetrahedron.[3]

Bearden very likely got this idea from Buckminster Fuller, who had already noticed the hidden geometric structure in the electromagnetic wave years earlier. It still amazes me that hardly anyone talks about this, since it is so simple and obvious once you look at it. This is probably because most people wouldn't have any reason to expect to see a hidden geometric pattern within the electromagnetic wave. We have no context for it, no idea of what it might be, nor how something like this could fit into a greater model of physics. Yet mysteries like these can also contain the greatest secrets, with the highest potential to transform our civilization as we know it. As the years went by, I eventually discovered this same geometry appearing in the structure of the Earth's continents, the relationships between the planets in our solar system, the growth patterns of plants, the nucleus of the atom, the electron clouds of the atom, the DNA molecule, and even the activity between clusters of neurons in the human brain.

I have every reason to believe that Unified Field Theory of physics—the true Holy Grail of modern science—will be fundamentally and deeply connected to sacred geometry. The term *sacred geometry* refers to the idea that certain geometric patterns, such as the tetrahedron, may actually be alive and conscious when they appear intertwined with the basic forces of nature and biological life as we now know it. Most of the key discoveries have already been made, and the real challenge now exists in presenting this message in a way that can reach mainstream consciousness. By this token, I also believe that a variety of extraterrestrial civilizations have already discovered this same science, and encoded these secrets into ancient architecture, sacred symbols, and other related forms.

For me, the most shocking part of this Hyperdimensional Model in those early years was in Richard Hoagland's suggestion that these same tetrahedral geometric patterns were appearing within planets in visible ways. Hoagland discussed this regularly, and he was arguably the most frequent and popular talent on *Coast to Coast AM* with Art Bell. This was the largest nighttime talk-radio program in the US, and had up to twenty million listeners per episode in the late 1990s. In those days, if you could get a show on Art Bell, you would instantly become a recognized name in the UFO community. It opened the door for book sales, conference invitations, and the possibility of collaboration with other like-minded scholars. You might very well be able to become self-supporting as a UFO researcher instead of needing to have a "regular job" and doing your paranormal work on the side. For me in 1996–1999, getting on the Art Bell show seemed like an impossible dream. Each episode began with the signature thumping synthesizer music and Art's opening monologue: "From the high desert in the great American Southwest, I bid you all good morning, good afternoon, good evening, wherever you may be in this great land of ours. . . ."

Art Bell was one of only three paranormal radio shows that were available online through streaming audio, using the Real Player. At the time, it was completely free to listen, and the show was supported by the sale of advertisements, which did consume a large amount of airtime. Some of Art's products were for the end of the world, such as a hand-powered crank-generator radio so you could still listen to Art Bell after all the power went off. This was expected in a variety of scenarios, such as the dreaded "Y2K" event, where power-grid computers were expected to reset themselves to the year 1900 once we hit the year 2000, since their software had been written to use only the last two digits for the year. Art was pivotal in raising public awareness about this issue, and billions of dollars were spent ensuring that we dodged that bullet.

I never missed a single episode of Richard Hoagland when he was on the air with Art Bell. I had been a huge fan of Hoagland's work and had been pondering his hyperdimensional physics model ever since I first read *The Monuments of Mars* back in 1993. I had devoted literally hundreds, if not thousands, of hours to meditating on these concepts and trying to gain a deeper understanding, using a similar form of reasoning, logic, and intuition as the philosophers I had studied in college. From 1993 to 1996, I had felt as if Hoagland had been my own private discovery that hardly anyone else knew about. Anytime I tried to discuss his research with others at my college, they were quite surprised, having never heard of it before, so I was stunned to discover that Hoagland had become such a popular radio personality and public speaker in the three years since I first read his groundbreaking book.

Hoagland would always talk with mystery, awe, and reverence about "19.5," as he called it. This refers to a specific latitude that could be north or south of the equator on a given planet or satellite. Tom Bearden had noticed that large, rotating storms appear on gas planets at 19.5 degrees latitude. This included the Great Red Spot on Jupiter, which has been spinning at the same exact latitude ever since the invention of the telescope. Conventional science has no explanation for how a gigantic storm like this, big enough to fit four Earths side by side inside it, could continue raging away at the same, odd latitude for over four hundred years without drifting around or disappearing. The mystery becomes even stranger when we realize that the same exact thing is happening on Neptune, which has one gigantic storm called the Great Dark Spot. And there it is, at the same mysterious latitude: 19.5.

The mystery became even more enticing once we went over to solid planets. There again, we see unusually energetic and visible structures appearing at the "magic" 19.5-degree latitude. On Earth, we have the volcanic island chain of Hawaii. There is so much volcanic activity there that an entire collection of islands has been formed as the bubbling lava has hardened into crust. The volcanoes are still very active, occasionally releasing volcanic fog or bursts of lava that can be potentially lethal for the local residents. Hawaii is well known to be the most volcanically active area on Earth, and it's right there at the magic 19.5-degree North latitude. We see a very similar thing happen when we travel over to Mars. There, we have the massive shield volcano Olympus Mons, which is two times higher in altitude than Earth's Mount Everest. Olympus Mons is by far the largest volcano on Mars, and obviously creates an incredibly damaging spectacle when it has a full eruption. Once again, it appears precisely at the 19.5-degree latitude.

At that time, we could not see Pluto in any detail, but four out of our eight visible planets showed undeniable vortex patterns at 19.5—a full 50 percent. Clearly, something is going on here. This phenomenon is real and it is not going away. The discovery wasn't as simple and straightforward as the idea of the Earth revolving around the sun, but it had every bit as much potential to be a scientific breakthrough as the work of Newton, Copernicus, Galileo, or Einstein. Wonderful new discoveries could be made, and I was definitely attracted to that. My great-grandfather Frederick Wilcock designed and built the New York City subway system, with a juris doctor degree in law and a PhD in engineering. My grandfather Donald F. Wilcock had a PhD in engineering with over eighty different patents, mostly in the field of bearings and lubrication. My grandfather taught me to have a passion for science from a very young age, and the mystery of these geometric vortexes ignited my curiosity like nothing before.

By the time I heard Hoagland talking about this on Art Bell, I had already spent years looking at his diagrams for how this model supposedly worked. The tetrahedron shape has a very interesting quality that might not seem to be that important, at first, when in fact it is of tremendous significance. Hoagland showed that a tetrahedron fits perfectly inside a sphere, such as the Earth. Each of the four corners of the tetrahedron will perfectly touch the edges of the sphere. And spheres appear in nature everywhere we look. Stars are spherical. Planets are spherical. Many fruits are predominantly spherical, such as apples and oranges. Cells are often roughly spherical in shape. Soap bubbles are naturally spherical since the air pressure pushes on them equally from all sides. Now we see that the tetrahedron geometry exists in perfect harmony with the sphere as well. To generate the 19.5-degree alignment, all you have to do is to draw a tetrahedron that was the appropriate size to fit inside a sphere. You then take one of the four corners of the tetrahedron and align it with the north or south pole of the sphere. The other three corners of the tetrahedron will all appear at the opposing 19.5-degree latitude. They will also be exactly 120 degrees apart from each other, dividing the circle into three equal sections.

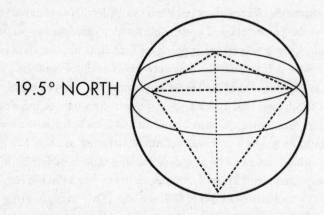

19.5° NORTH

Image of Sphere with Circumscribed Tetrahedron, Showing 19.5-Degree Vortex Point

Hoagland does not believe this tetrahedron is any type of solid object, such as a crystal. It is actually an energy wave, again what Bearden would call a "scalar potential." Most important, this tetrahedron of energy is not visible or measurable in our own "third dimension." The tetrahedron does not glow with anything like a dim, blue light that could show us where it was. You can't touch it. We can only see its aftereffects on the physical matter of planets, such as in the Great Red Spot, Great Dark Spot, Hawaii, or Olympus Mons. Hoagland also points out that there are two noticeably different cloud bands on Saturn at the 19.5-degree latitudes, perhaps owing to this same geometry. Additionally, sunspots usually never travel farther than 19.5 degrees of latitude north or south on the sun—as if this hidden geometry prevented them from going outside these boundaries. The thick atmosphere of Venus prevents us from seeing if it has a similar volcano at the 19.5-degree point on its surface—but it probably does.

I always had the sense that Hoagland had received classified insider briefings on this, such as from Tom Bearden or Arthur C. Clarke, and that whoever created those briefings knew a lot more about this science than they had ever released to Hoagland or anyone else. Science is all about repetition, and in this case, we have four different planets in our solar system where all their most noteworthy visible disturbances occur at the magic 19.5-degree latitude. This strongly suggests that these disturbances are the result of a hidden geometric energy pattern that is yet unknown to conventional science. Hoagland also said that the key to this science was "rotation, rotation, rotation." He believed, or was told, that once you started rotating an object, such as a planet, you could begin accessing these "scalar potentials" of energy that otherwise remained hidden but were nonetheless all around us. Hoagland implied that this was the secret to antigravity, if you understood how to properly harness its power.

DePalma's Spinning Ball Experiment

Richard Hoagland's *The Monuments of Mars* also discussed the work of Dr. Bruce DePalma, which was quite fascinating. DePalma was the brother of the noted director Brian De Palma, who is known for intense movies like *Carrie, Scarface, Body Double, The Untouchables, Carlito's Way, Mission: Impossible,* and others. Hoagland often talked about a very fascinating scientific discovery from Bruce DePalma, which suggested that we had made some serious mistakes in our understanding of gravity and its effects on physical matter. The discovery was known as DePalma's Spinning Ball Experiment and was published in a paper on March 17, 1977.[4]

The experiment was almost ridiculously simple. You create two catapults that simultaneously launch two balls into the air. The catapults and the balls are exactly the same in size, weight, and composition. The balls normally rise and fall in the same exact shape, known as a parabolic arc. The balls travel to the same height and fall at the same speed, just as we would expect. However, something very different happens if you set the experiment up again and change only one thing. This time, you simply spin one of the balls up to a speed of one thousand revolutions per minute while leaving the other one motionless. Then you release the catapults. Now something different happens—something that defies our known laws of physics.

For some unknown reason, the spinning ball will first rise higher and then fall faster than the ball that is not spinning. This is quite astonishing, and it doesn't make any sense within our conventional Newtonian physics models. Most scientists would laugh in your face if you told them about this, and would automatically assume that DePalma must be a "quack" who is practicing "pseudoscience." Nothing could be further from the truth. Gravity is expected to travel at a "constant" rate of acceleration, and it works no differently for a feather than for a chunk of lead. This experiment suggests that if we could understand what was happening, we could harness the power of antigravity. In this next quote from the paper, DePalma said that the ball that was not spinning would be called the identical non-rotating control. You have to remember that odd-sounding term in order to make sense of this quote. In his own words, DePalma said, "I think it is a mind-bending experience to see every stone fall at the exact same rate as any other stone. And when you spin an object, why does it fall faster? And most mind-boggling of all, why does it go higher than the identical non-rotating control released to go upward at the same initial velocity? . . . [This] presents a dilemma which can only be resolved or understood on the basis of radically new concepts in physics . . . growing out of the many discussions and correspondence pertaining to rotation, inertia, gravity, and motion in general."[5]

Perhaps the most important thing Dr. DePalma said in this quote is that his discovery "presents a dilemma which can only be resolved or understood on the basis of radically new concepts in physics."[6] That means that for us to explain his discovery, we will need to think about science, physical matter, and the universe in a "radically new" way— which is obviously not being taught in our schools. Spinning objects are not supposed to defeat gravity simply by rotating, but now we know that they actually do—at least in part. DePalma also said, "Without a theoretical foundation of understanding to make the experiment comprehensible—to fit the results into a context of rational understanding and harmony with the facts of other experiments—the data become trivial and worthless and, worst of all, subject to misinterpretation."[7]

DePalma is clearly calling for an entirely new theoretical model to integrate these observations into a new and superior scientific view. By definition, this new theoretical model will be surprising, unexpected, and quite different from what we think we know today. We need to find other experiments that have similar results, combine them, and try to figure out what we are dealing with. We have no current reason to expect that a rotating object will weigh less than a stationary object with the exact same mass, but now we know that it does. DePalma dropped some names of scientists who had discovered similarly interesting things, without going into detail about exactly what they had found: "We should remember the pioneers in this field: Wolfe, Cox, Dean, Laithwaite, Rendle, Searl, Kummel, DePalma and Delvers, to name but a few."[8] Once we figure out what is going on here, this research may finally allow us to control gravity, which is a true Holy Grail for our planet—propelling us into a *Star Trek* age.

In 2019, we finally saw some exciting movement in this direction from official sources. The US Navy declassified a patent by Salvatore Cezar Pais that described the creation of a flying triangle-shaped craft that uses "gravity control" to fly. In short, the US Navy is formally acknowledging that they have a working "repulsive gravity" system. They don't actually say they have a working prototype, only that they "might" have one—but the patent is very specific, and this suggests that such a craft was definitely developed, tested, and flown. The author does explain that gravity control is possible, and uses the experiment of Hideo Hayasaka and Sakae Takeuchi to help justify it. This is very similar to DePalma's Spinning Ball Experiment.

In this case, the Japanese scientists placed a gyroscope on a chemical beam balance. When the gyroscope is rotated in a rightward, clockwise direction, it also weighs slightly less. This was discussed in a *New Scientist* article from 1990:

> Hayasaka and Takeuchi found that when a gyroscope spins in
> a clockwise sense—looking down on it from above—it loses

weight. The amount it loses is only about five-thousandths of one per cent of its resting weight. The researchers also found that the faster the gyroscope spins, the more weight it loses (see figure). They published their work in *Physical Review Letters* (vol 63, p 2701).[9]

The navy patent said, "For the mathematical formalism of inertial (and thus gravitational) mass reduction consider that in a published *Physical Review Letter* (December 1989), Hayasaka and Takeuchi report the anomalous weight reduction of gyroscopes for right rotations only. . . . [This] yields the possibility of a local quantum vacuum effect, namely a negative pressure (repulsive gravity) condition being present."[10] I had discovered the Hayasaka-Takeuchi experiment back in the 1990s as one of a few studies that further validated the results of DePalma's Spinning Ball Experiment. This "hyperdimensional" knowledge is now finding its way into mainstream consciousness through the navy gravity-control patent.

Even more excitingly, this same inventor also filed a patent for a "compact fusion" device that generates massive quantities of energy, potentially over a thousand megawatts, with hardly any input power, in an object as small as 0.3 meters.[11] This is literally a "free energy" device, and the obvious implication is that it could be dropped into the navy's flying antigravity triangle craft as a power supply.

According to *The Drive,* a reputable online publication discussing military matters, "It is claimed in the patent application that this plasma compression fusion device is capable of producing power in the gigawatt (1 billion watts) to terawatt (1 trillion watts) range and above with input power only in the kilowatt (1,000 watts) to megawatt (1,000,000 watts) range. By comparison, America's largest nuclear power plant, the Palo Verde nuclear power plant in Arizona, generates around 4,000 megawatts (4 gigawatts), and the A1B nuclear reactors designed for the Navy's *Gerald R. Ford*–class aircraft carriers generate around 700 megawatts." The patent even claims that the device can "possibly lead to ignition plasma burn, that is self-sustained plasma burn without need for external input power."[12] After I wrote about these patents on my website, a reader pointed out that the name "Salvatore Pais" translates as "Savior of Our Nation" in Spanish. This suggests that the navy is deliberately releasing this technology to help save the planet from the ravages of coal, oil, gas, and automotive transportation. There is hardly any information on Salvatore Pais, and at this point we can speculate that he may have been assigned to file these patents because of his suggestive name.

Hoagland seemed to envision a tetrahedral energy wave forming within the spherical ball in DePalma's experiment. As the ball rotated, perhaps this tetrahedron-shaped energy wave was pulling in and shooting out energy that manipulated the force of gravity around the ball in some measurable way, just like a spinning planet. The 19.5-degree point created rotating cyclones on gas planets, and if we could harness that extra rotational energy, we might be able to tap it like a windmill or a water wheel. Thus the hyperdimensional physics model could also be our ticket to limitless clean, free energy. Rotating objects like the spinning ball were apparently accessing energy from some yet-unknown source that caused them to bend the "law" of gravity in exciting new ways.

This idea of invisible, hyperdimensional geometry was very interesting to me. Hoagland had clearly identified a geometric shape that was causing strange phenomena to appear on planets, but we really had no idea what this geometry was or why it was there in the first place. I had experienced strong fevers as a child and would often have elaborate hallucinations of geometric patterns. The same thing happened under the effect of psychedelics as well as in deep meditation. Many other people have reported having similar perceptions, and this includes various Eastern mystics who end up drawing elaborate geometric mandalas. I had always wondered if there was some deeper meaning for why so many people, myself included, had these unique visionary experiences with geometry. Perhaps we already knew the answer at some deep level of our being, and we just needed to remember it.

I started deeply meditating on these concepts in 1993. By the time I discovered the Law of One series in 1996, it was unlikely that a single day had gone by without my thinking about sacred geometry. I was extremely surprised to discover that the Law of One series presented a very advanced integration of geometry, science, and consciousness that went far beyond anything I had come up with on my own, even after countless hours of dedicated research. The main reason I am sharing this science with you now is to eventually show you the Law of One quotes that revealed the importance of geometry in the universe. Ultimately, we will see that the One Infinite Creator generated all the matter in the universe as a single thought, which also manifested as a vibration that creates geometry. We will read these quotes in later chapters, after some additional material has been filled in to help us set up the story. After three years of dedicated study in sacred geometry, it was truly fascinating to discover that a source already existed that puts all the pieces together and presents a truly unified physics model.

CHAPTER SIX

Crop Circles Reveal
Extraterrestrial Blueprints

C rop circles were perhaps the most enigmatic aspect of Richard
Hoagland's Hyperdimensional Model. In the original *Monuments
of Mars* book, Hoagland included images of two different crop
circles that very directly revealed the mathematics of a tetrahedron inside
a sphere.[1] In some notable cases, these crop formations created visible
diagrams of tetrahedrons and the angular relationships they generate
when they are placed inside spheres. These mysterious formations had
been regularly appearing in European crops for at least twelve hundred
years. I found records where the archbishop of France passed a law that
made it illegal for pagans to remove crops from crop circles. The actual
existence and appearance of crop circles, at the time, was never even
questioned.

Dr. Robert Plot sketched out multiple interesting crop formations
that had appeared on his land in southern England back in the 1600s.
These formations had astonishing geometric precision despite being inscribed into ordinary fields of wheat. The stalks would bend at the
growth nodes without breaking, and would continue growing after the
formation had appeared. There were no signs of tampering from humans, such as broken stalks or pathways in and out. Multiple witnesses
saw the formations appear spontaneously right in front of their eyes,

much like the opening of an Oriental fan. Certain witnesses saw Nordic-type extraterrestrial humans in unusual, silvery outfits who seemed to be perfecting the design of the crop circles after they were formed, using some kind of small machine. As they turned the knobs on the machine, certain stalks of wheat would move back and forth in the crop circle.

The crop circle mystery was quite significant, and my first introduction to it was with the German researcher Michael Hesemann's book *The Cosmic Connection*.[2] The book was full of gorgeous and fascinating pictures and had some truly inspiring theories. I was lucky enough to meet Hesemann and have extensive conversations with him at my first UFO conference in the fall of 1996. It was difficult to imagine how such beautiful patterns could be created in a wheat field, since you could appreciate them only from the air. Once I got online in the late fall of 1995, I quickly found the Crop Circle Connector website,[3] where you could scan through a huge library of crop circle images. These images had staggering beauty and precision, and were richly varied. At the time, certain people did try to make fake crop circles, such as the infamous "Doug and Dave," who were presented by the media as the ultimate answer to appease all the skeptics. The fake crop circles were very crude, however, and obviously quite different from the real ones, which had incredible beauty and sophistication. Some truly amazing crop circles appeared that next summer of 1996, and they again repeatedly told us to look at tetrahedral geometry. For me, it was deeply exciting to see these new formations showing up and validating Hoagland's model within less than a year after I had first gotten onto the Internet.

Hoagland's Hyperdimensional Model, therefore, was infused with incredible mystery and wonder. It seemed he had stumbled onto a whole new branch of science that the extraterrestrials very much wanted us to discover. I didn't really know what the tetrahedron was, nor did Hoagland, beyond a certain point, but the extraterrestrials apparently wanted us to figure it out. Someone had encoded the mathematics in the layout of ancient monuments on Mars, and now some obvious intelligence was encoding this same science into the layouts of a variety of mysterious crop circles on Earth. I was frankly astonished that more people hadn't jumped into this modern-day scientific adventure. To me, it was like a gold rush to see who could be the first to decipher this mystery, handed to us by advanced beings of a higher intelligence. If you could solve the puzzle, you could make breakthroughs that might significantly improve life for everyone on Earth. The extraterrestrials may be giving us the clues to unlock the secrets of antigravity, free energy, consciousness, and the true space age. This new science may also end up changing everything we thought we knew about reality as a whole, requiring us to rewrite almost every branch of science that we now take for granted.

I was happy to look at this whole body of data as if it was a philosophical argument. To have a successful platform to argue from, I accepted certain basics as being true after I did enough research to convince myself of their validity. My foundation therefore included the idea that extraterrestrials did exist, that crop circles were made by extraterrestrials, that the monuments of Mars were made by extraterrestrials, and that the alignments discovered by Hoagland's team on Mars did indeed reveal tetrahedral geometry. I was further able to accept that storms on gas planets, and giant volcanoes on solid planets, were somehow being generated by tetrahedral geometry, and that the extraterrestrials wanted us to study this same tetrahedral geometry by encoding it into their crop circles. Now I was free to explore what this geometry was, how it formed, why it formed, and why the extraterrestrials would want us to study this curious phenomenon. They could have encoded just about anything into their crop formations, but over and over again they reinforced the main message: "Study Sacred Geometry."

Sacred Geometry

In the fall of 1997, I found a book by Robert Lawlor called *Sacred Geometry*. He revealed that these same basic patterns appeared all throughout nature in very interesting ways, in the proportions of the human body as well as in all other living creatures. Many ancient philosophers, such as Pythagoras, studied sacred geometry and speculated about the reasons why these patterns appear so prevalently in nature. Lawlor and others also revealed that many of these philosophical investigations were hidden behind the veils of secret societies. Anyone who dared to reveal this knowledge to the general public was literally subject to the death penalty. They would swear under oath to "ever conceal and never reveal" the information.

The initiates apparently believed that this geometry also contained the secrets to attaining godlike states of being. Meditating on these patterns for prolonged periods apparently could activate dormant potentials in the human body, mind, and spirit. Therefore, the mystery schools believed the information had to be very carefully protected. If someone were to access this power and use it for evil intentions, they could potentially do tremendous damage. Most of us had lost any curiosity about sacred geometry in our modern age, though it was discussed in the original book version of Dan Brown's *The Da Vinci Code.* There was undeniable evidence of this same geometry encoded into classic architecture, such as cathedrals, as well as classic Renaissance paintings. The geometry also appeared in ancient stone monuments like Stonehenge and the Great Pyramid. Many scholars and philosophers believed that the geometry itself was somehow alive and intelligent—sacred. By tapping into this knowledge, through meditation for instance, it was believed that you could eventually develop seemingly superhuman abilities. Ultimately, you could experience Ascension—a transfiguration into some higher level of what it means to be human, where your body is transformed into a visibly glowing "light body" form.

This again was a very fascinating concept. Ancient mystery schools would apparently have their initiates build models of various sacred geometric objects, and then study and meditate on them for extended periods of time. I soon found myself doing the same thing. It definitely appeared that there was a massive gold mine of new scientific breakthroughs waiting for us. Our ancestors may well have been given this information by extraterrestrials and did the best they could to understand it with the science they had available in their time. Now, with far greater observational tools, we could hopefully finish the job and greatly enhance our scientific models. Unfortunately, as I found out later, some people would immediately throw my book down if they saw pictures of geometry in it. They would say that this is math, and that they "hate math." I had one potential customer do this right in front of me while I was at a book-signing table early in my career, back when I was printing out and hand-binding my own books. People like this had the same attitude as the priests with Galileo's telescope. I was greatly saddened to observe this behavior, since if we don't have enough curiosity to explore new ideas, we will never progress as a civilization.

Quantum Fields Act Like a Fluid

I listened very carefully to everything that Richard Hoagland said on the radio, and after a while it seemed clear that he hadn't fully solved the puzzle. He didn't appear to fully understand what the geometry was, how it formed, or why it formed. He ultimately agreed that there were still many aspects of the model that had not yet been discovered. He was happy to partner with me to further the investigation, beginning privately in 2000 and publicly in 2005. It wasn't clear how this geometry was causing giant vortexes to swirl around in the atmospheres of gas planets, nor in the lava under the surface crust of solid planets. It also wasn't clear why this same geometry appeared in living things. The connection between DePalma's Spinning Ball Experiment and the vortexes that appeared at 19.5 degrees latitude on rotating planets also did not seem immediately obvious. Hoagland believed that some power was kicking in when an object started rotating, and this power appeared in a tetrahedral geometric pattern. However, it really wasn't clear what the power was, or why it appeared in a rotating object. Again, this is more a physics discussion, and I recommend reading *The Source Field Investigations* to go more deeply into this topic than there is space for in this book.

Early on, I did realize that we obviously had made a big mistake about matter. René Descartes had created a materialistic philosophy in which matter at its smallest levels was made of tiny, hard particles. There was no alternate reality where these particles could go—they were always here with us. Descartes certainly had never heard of the quantum "wave-particle duality," where matter can appear as a particle one minute and then appear as a wave, with no solid identity, the next. It is possible that if we could transform enough particles in a piece of matter into a wave state, the object would weigh less. Descartes never had anything like this to work with. In his worldview, an object would always weigh the same unless you physically removed ome of its mass, say, by chipping a piece off.

At this point, I started visualizing DePalma's Spinning Ball Experiment as if the ball was like a wet dog shaking off a bunch of water. Each atom might have some type of energy in it that behaves like a fluid, and is not strictly trapped within that atom. This is different from the conventional idea that atoms can take in or give out only single photons at a time, which become electrons once they merge with the atom. In this new model, if you rotate the object fast enough, you might force some of this quantum fluid to spray out of the atoms, and the object then weighs less. Another way to look at this strange loss of mass is that rotating the object might cause some of its particles to transform into a wave state. There may be some fluidlike way in which this was happening. Even the "solid particle" state of matter could still behave more like a fluid than a hard object, and by introducing enough motion, the particles might flow into waves.

Later on, I found the cannonball experiment of Dr. Nikolai Kozyrev, which made this "quantum fluid" even more obvious.[4,5] Kozyrev weighed a cannonball and then dropped it on his concrete basement floor. After the cannonball hit the floor, it actually weighed less, even though none of it had chipped or broken off. It took twenty minutes for all the weight to return to the cannonball. In that case, the hard crash of the cannonball against the floor may have caused some of this fluidlike energy to splash out of its atoms. Particles turned into waves on a larger scale within the cannonball after the impact, and its weight decreased. Over time, the background energy of space and time itself flowed back into the cannonball and the waves reverted back to their normal particle state, causing the weight to return.

Equally fascinating was a discovery by Dr. Harold Aspden.[6] He took a magnetic rotor and brought it up to 3,250 revolutions per minute. He measured how much energy it takes to get the 800-gram rotor spinning that fast, which is normally 300 joules. Then he stopped the magnet from rotating. Within sixty seconds or less, he started spinning the magnet again. Now, for some amazing reason, it took far less energy to bring the magnet back up to the same rotational speed than it had before—only 30 joules instead of 300. This again suggested that there was some sort of fluidlike energy inside the magnet, and that even once the magnet physically stopped rotating, the fluidlike energy inside the magnet was still spinning very fast. As he started rotating the magnet again, the spinning energy made it much easier to bring the magnet back to its highest rotational speed. As I found more and more experiments like this, I realized that we really do not understand matter, gravity, and magnetism as much as we thought we did. There should be a way for us to harness this fluidlike behavior within physical matter so that we could ultimately control gravity.

Facing Fears

I felt that with the many hundreds of crop circle diagrams that had appeared over the years, the extraterrestrials were giving us a homework assignment. They were asking us to look into this science, to embrace it, and to study it in more detail. I thought I had a pretty good handle on it by 1996 and 1997 as I kept studying sacred geometry. However, as the crop formations continued to repeat the same point, I decided that I needed to take this far more seriously. That meant facing everyone's greatest fear—tackling a vastly complex body of technical information that one really knows nothing about. I would have to start from scratch, without the guidance of a professor, class, or structured curriculum to find the answers I sought. No one had figured this out yet, at least not within our own unclassified world, so there was no course in existence that could teach it. Much like how I started my practice of recording and analyzing dreams, I just had to throw myself into the study without really understanding the language.

I rolled up my sleeves and began exploring Tom Bearden's works in far more detail beginning in 1998. At times, it was crushingly frustrating to try to figure out what certain terms or concepts meant. However, my grandfather had taught me to have patience in the face of unfamiliar information. Ever since I was very young, Papa would sit me down and describe his work on a software program that used advanced trigonometry, such as "matrix inversions," to custom-design a particular type of bearing. The "tapered land thrust bearing" was quite difficult to manufacture, and this was his unique area of expertise. He felt it would be a huge breakthrough in his field to write a piece of software that could custom-design the bearings at any size. At the time, he told me, the US military had working models in only two different sizes, and they would have to design entire machines to fit one of these two sizes. He wrote his software in Fortran and had a series of subroutines, all of which had to compile and work together as a whole. He was pushing the power of his archaic amber-screen IBM computer, with its five-and-a-quarter-inch floppy disks, to the absolute limits of what it could do.

Throughout my entire childhood and adolescence, right up to his death in 2000, Papa would tell me exactly what he was working on, the problems he was having, and how he solved them. At one point, he discovered that a single semicolon had destroyed the entire program. I never fully understood what he was talking about, but I learned not to be afraid of any of it, to keep an open mind, and to understand as much of it as I could by listening very carefully to what he said and asking questions. This ended up being great training for me to tackle the immense frustration that can happen when trying to understand material as technical as Tom Bearden's papers. I also learned to read through scientific studies and not be intimidated by the equations. I would look for the concepts, where they used words instead of mathematics to explain the things they had discovered. In most cases, this was more than enough to understand the discovery.

The Global Grid

Another quantum leap I had in understanding and appreciating this new science came when I found *Anti-Gravity and the World Grid*,[7] a collection of essays by various authors that was compiled and edited by David

Hatcher Childress, who is now one of my costars on *Ancient Aliens*. I first found this book when I was still a college student, on my winter break between 1994 and 1995, at Borders books in Albany, New York. Richard Hoagland had focused exclusively on the geometry of the tetrahedron, whereas David Childress's book clearly indicated that there were other geometric patterns affecting the behavior of the Earth. This included the cube, octahedron, icosahedron, and dodecahedron. Together with the tetrahedron, these shapes formed the five basic Platonic solids, originally spelled out by Plato. The Platonic solids are invariably featured in every book on sacred geometry that you find. The Platonic solids have uniquely symmetrical properties. Every line is the same length. Every face is the same shape. Every internal angle is the same number of degrees. And each of the five shapes will fit perfectly inside a sphere, where each of its points contact the edge of the sphere precisely if they are of the same approximate width.

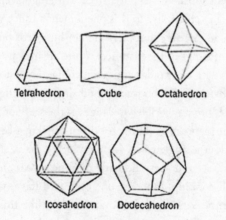

The Platonic Solids: Tetrahedron, Cube, Octahedron, Icosahedron, and Dodecahedron

One fascinating chapter in *Anti-Gravity and the World Grid* was from the New Zealand scientist Bruce Cathie, who analyzed many hundreds of UFO sighting reports and concluded that they were always traveling along the same "grid lines." Cathie eventually expanded these lines into a worldwide pattern, which described a cube inside the Earth, superimposed over its surface. That was extremely fascinating in light of Hoagland's discussions of tetrahedral geometry, particularly since Hawaii was at the magical 19.5-degree point. The tetrahedron was definitely at work on the Earth, as noted by the position of Hawaii, but now it appeared that the energy pattern of the cube needed to be considered as well. Yet you could very easily draw a cube around a tetrahedron. The tetrahedron fit perfectly inside a cube and happened to fill exactly one-third of its volume.

The Bermuda Triangle

I was even more amazed by the work of Ivan T. Sanderson, which was featured in a chapter written by William Becker and Bethe Hagens in David Childress's book. Sanderson began studying airplanes and ocean vessels that had vanished without a trace. Although skeptics might not think there is any credibility to this phenomenon, once you actually do the research, you discover that there are not hundreds but thousands of mysterious vanishings in the historical record. Planes are flying along in cloudless skies with clear radar and radio contact, only to suddenly vanish, with no distress calls, no traces of oil slick or floating debris on the ocean's surface, nor any visible wreckage on the seafloor. In some cases, multiple rescue planes out looking for the original missing pilot had also vanished without a single trace. In many other cases, ships are sailing along in clear seas and then suddenly disappear—or are found intact, with food still cooking, but everyone on board has mysteriously vanished. Every time Sanderson found an incident like this, he marked it with a pushpin on his map. As his map kept building, almost every incident clustered into one of ten points across the Earth's surface. The Bermuda Triangle is only one of these ten points but is by far the most well-known of all, thanks to mass-media publicity from a groundbreaking and bestselling book by Charles Berlitz entitled *The Bermuda Triangle*.[8]

These ten points were all equidistant from each other, and if you also added in the North and South Poles, they were perfectly aligned with the other points. Now you have a total of twelve equidistant vortex zones. If you play connect-the-dots between these twelve points, you will see the sacred geometry of the icosahedron, one of the five basic Platonic solids. It seemed very clear that this invisible icosahedral geometry was just as important as the tetrahedral geometry, at least on Earth. The geometry was now truly hyperdimensional, being our main key to unlock the mysteries of "portal" travel through space and time. It was quite amazing that an independent researcher like Ivan Sanderson had discovered this on his own. I felt it was worthy of a Nobel Prize and should have endowed his name with as much historical significance as Galileo, Newton, or Copernicus. I would only find out years later that these same vortex points were very well known to exist within classified military science programs that were actively using them, such as by building military bases at each available nexus point.

Sanderson's discoveries made the geometry far more mysterious than it already was. In Hoagland's case, the geometry was creating giant atmospheric storms and volcanoes. Now this invisible geometry, at certain times, was causing large objects to completely disappear, along with their human passengers. Where did these people go? Were they still alive? Did they travel to some other world? Did they leap forward or backward in time? Airplanes would just vanish out of the sky if they flew through these points but, for some reason, only at certain times. Ships could be sailing the seas, with everyone feeling fine one minute, only to have completely vanished without a trace the next—right as they sailed through one of these "Devil's Graveyards" on Earth.

Time Slips

William Becker and Bethe Hagens had found other cases of "time slips" that would occur right along these same "grid nodes" and "grid lines." An entire plane full of people might jump ahead in time, finding their watches ten minutes behind everyone else's. There was also a compelling suggestion that prehistoric creatures such as dinosaurs occasionally wandered into these vortexes and jumped ahead through millions of years to our own time. This provided possible explanations for phenomena like the Loch Ness Monster, medieval dragons, the legend of the phoenix, the image of a stegosaurus carved into an ancient Cambodian temple, and other such reports. If any of this was true, then it meant that we have "natural stargates" on Earth that can send us shooting through space and time or into completely alternate realities and dimensions. It again looked as if we had an amazing new frontier of science waiting for us. If we could fully identify and understand how this geometry worked with the Earth, we might be able to harness its power to create our own stargates, and travel through space at faster-than-light speeds, as the extraterrestrials already appeared to be doing. Best of all, we might be able to conquer the most outrageous scientific paradox of all—the mystery of genuine time travel.

A Worldwide Map for All Giant Stone Monuments

Becker and Hagens didn't stop with Ivan Sanderson's grid. The story became even more intriguing when the Russian team of Goncharov, Morozov, and Makarov got involved after Sanderson published his results. The Russians contemplated the fact that you can turn the icosahedron inside out to get what is called its geometric dual, or inverse, known as the dodecahedron. This is now a shape that has twelve faces, where each face is a five-sided pentagon. Overall, it looks like a soccer ball. It is perhaps the most beautiful and mysterious of all the Platonic solids since it is the only one that is made out of pentagons.

When the Russians took the shape of the dodecahedron and superimposed it over the Earth, in its exact inverse position to the icosahedron, they had an amazing discovery. Somehow, every single pyramid, monolith, stone circle, and "megalithic" stone formation on Earth was built right on one of the lines of this "icosa-dodeca" grid. The Russians had found a whopping thirty-three hundred stone structures that fit on the grid. Not one pyramid or giant stone monument was found in a location that was not crossed by the grid. How could this be possible? These ancient formations were believed to have been built by cultures completely isolated from one another. The pyramids in Egypt had smoother designs than the ones in Mesoamerica, which were built in layers that looked like giant staircases. Now we find out that every single stone formation, on every continent except Antarctica, is built according to a unified, worldwide pattern? This suggests that everyone who built pyramids was very well aware of this Global Grid, and that it may indeed have been a worldwide effort by a single, unified group of people.

As I thought about this even more, I realized that the energy from this grid could have somehow given the creators of these monuments an antigravity force that could be used to levitate the huge stones. The mysterious, invisible lines of the Global Grid may have been creating an energy that not only could cause ships and planes to disappear but could cause stone to become lighter—if you had the right technology to manipulate it. Perhaps these people could not levitate the stones unless the stones were already on one of the grid lines. At the very least, it might require far more energy and difficulty for them to levitate any stones that were not on the Global Grid. This was truly fascinating stuff, and as far as I could tell, no one else was asking these questions or connecting these dots. Yet, whoever had built the pyramids was obviously well aware of this lost, ancient science. There was simply no denying what the Russians had discovered. The answer was openly visible for those who chose to look.

Becker and Hagens took the Russian grid and connected all the points by adding some extra lines. This formed what they called the Becker-Hagens Grid. Now they had a geometric object with 120 different triangles on it, superimposed over the Earth. Once they added in these extra lines, magical things started to happen. I spent many, many hours staring at the Becker-Hagens Grid diagram and meditating on it. The more I looked at it, the more I realized that the Earth itself was being structured and shaped by this grid. Australia was perfectly positioned between two nodes and their surrounding lines. South America fit precisely within a triangular pattern of lines that tightly hugged its overall shape. And Becker and Hagens pointed out that the entire Mid-Atlantic Volcanic Ridge, a gigantic mountain range at the bottom of the Atlantic

Ocean, was in perfect alignment with the Global Grid in that area. The Mid-Atlantic Ridge continued in straight lines, made distinct angular turns, and then went on in additional straight lines, and its path was precisely the same as the Global Grid. There were far too many correlations to be random chance, and once you started looking at them, it was all very obvious. The grid was real.

Vibrating Fluids Create Geometric Patterns

And sure enough, as the crop circles continued appearing year after year, they made it very obvious that we needed to look at all five of the Platonic solids for answers, not just the tetrahedron. This became particularly clear in 1999, when three different English crop circles clearly indicated a cube inside a sphere: Honey Street on July 16, Wimpole Hall on July 23, and West Kennett Longbarrow on August 4.[9] The crop circles also had certain formations that appeared to illustrate the activity of sound waves rippling through water, or some similar liquid. For example, in 2001, we have Kexbrough on August 2, Keresforth Hill on August 12, and West Stowell on August 15, with a very similar formation again at West Stowell on August 15 of the following year.[10] I eventually discovered the work of Dr. Hans Jenny, initially in a book entitled *Cymatics,* and finally I felt I understood how this geometry might be forming. Jenny showed that these same geometric patterns would naturally appear in fluids, as if by magic.

Jenny's experiment started with tiny particles floating in water, where the solution just looks like a milky liquid. However, once he vibrated the water with certain "pure" sound frequencies, like what you hear when playing the white keys on the piano, something amazing happened. The particles in the water mysteriously arranged into beautiful geometric patterns that remained stable as long as he kept playing the sound. Instead of milky-white water, now he saw white lines where the geometries are located while everything else is dark, with no floating particles at all. All he had to do to get these amazing designs was to play single, sustained sound tones into the liquid, such as by singing. The geometric patterns that were formed by this process included the Platonic solids.

Therefore, the Platonic solids were obviously visual representations of vibration. They were crystallized sounds, in a sense. We don't normally think of our own voices as creating sacred geometric patterns, but as we move through different syllables at different pitches, we see different geometric shapes coming and going if we measure them with a liquid solution like Jenny was using.

The Law of One Tied It All Together

These are just a few of the many scientific mysteries that I uncovered during that time, as I began intensively researching this subject with the newly found power of the Internet. The more I read, the more I discovered. I was totally addicted and spent every waking minute of every day in full pursuit of this new knowledge. In other books, I have described the importance of the Law of One series and of dreams in assisting this investigation. However, I never went into very much detail about how all of this happened. I began reading the Law of One material in January 1996, three years after I had begun intensively researching UFOs and hyperdimensional physics. By the time I read *The Law of One*, I felt that I had made a variety of unique and original discoveries. I was quite surprised to discover that these discoveries were already featured in the Law of One material. In fact, the Law of One model was vastly more advanced than anything I had come up with on my own. This strongly enhanced my confidence that I had come in contact with an authentic source of higher-dimensional information.

My path to discovering the Law of One series in January 1996 is a fascinating story in and of itself. Increasingly stunning synchronicities and dream experiences led me to read the *Law of One*. I was very interested when I read Session 14, Question 25, where the source was asked how the *Law of One* information was normally communicated to the people of Earth. The answer was, in part, "We have used channels such as this one, but in most cases the channels feel inspired by dreams and visions without being aware, consciously, of our identity or existence."[11] As we have discussed, I began writing down my dreams every day in

September 1992, and after years of dedicated effort, I eventually learned how to decipher the dream language. In so doing, I was able to tap into a much more highly advanced source of spiritual guidance than anything else I had available at the time.

A Wealth of New Dream Data

I fought very hard for many years to have my work taken seriously by the UFO community. In the midst of that struggle, I was so busy that I never actually went back and reread any of the dreams I had written in notebooks between 1992 and 1996 before I switched over to typing my dreams into the computer. It was only after I put this book together that I realized I needed to thoroughly review the entire body of material. In so doing, I found a wealth of information that I had otherwise completely forgotten about in all my previous writings, lectures, and videos on this subject. Even more outrageously, the dreams I was reading from as far back as 1992 had many direct and obvious references to my own present as I was writing this book in 2019. The dreams somehow knew exactly where I would be living, who I would be living with, and what various objects around my house would look like, as well as describing a wide variety of situations I was dealing with at the time. There is no logical way that any of this could have happened unless consciousness itself somehow exists outside of time.

It definitely appeared that some part of me knew that 2019 would be the first time I would go back and reread these notebooks. A period of up to twenty-seven years obviously posed no boundary whatsoever to this effect manifesting itself in my dreams. I remembered writing down these dreams in many cases when they first came in, and had no idea that they would be describing events that would happen many years in my future, with such astonishing clarity. This phenomenon has caused me to meditate very deeply on concepts like destiny and free will. I call this the time-loop phenomenon, and it would take literally an entire book to properly document how many of these time loops I had while rereading my old notebooks and writing this book in 2019. However, the time-loop phenomenon has occurred all throughout my work, ever since it started, and I will provide plenty of intriguing examples of this phenomenon as we go on. Even before I started doing psychic readings in 1996, I had several mind-blowing examples of dreams predicting my own immediate future that I rediscovered while doing the research for this book. The time-loop phenomenon became far more direct and unavoidable after I began dictating entire paragraphs of information in Edgar Cayce–style readings as of November 1996. I used the protocols of remote viewing to ensure that my conscious mind was not tampering with the data beyond a minimal level.

Some people love the scientific discussions, such as those I briefly touched upon in the preceding chapters, and would feel cheated if I didn't mention them in a book. Others may have already lost interest by this point, and may only be hanging on by a thread or otherwise have already put the book down. If you have made it this far, congratulations! The rest of this book is not going to focus on these types of scientific arguments, since I have already done the best I can do to present them in previous volumes and other creative works. The reason I took two chapters to present you with the science I was studying at the time is to help you understand how amazed I was when I started reading the Law of One series. I discovered that these exact same scientific concepts and ideas had already been presented in this mysterious five-volume book series that was written between 1981 and 1983. In fact, the Law of One had a vastly more elaborate understanding of the science I had discovered than I had been able to piece together on my own. This gave my research a quantum upgrade and answered countless thousands of questions I would otherwise have never thought to ask. Yet, at its core, the Law of One is fundamentally a work of philosophy and spiritual guidance. The source stresses the importance of the positive, service-to-others mind-set above all else.

The study of my earliest recorded dreams is new and quite fascinating, particularly after I discovered so many forgotten examples in my notebooks. We will see how a variety of concepts I would later discover in the Law of One series, and from various insiders, was being presented to me through the dream space. The dreams also gave me a dramatic sneak preview of the concept of Ascension. I have had hundreds of dreams with breathtaking, incredibly powerful scenes that could easily translate into gorgeous cinematic sequences. We will see how these dreams guided me through a profound personal and spiritual healing process to prepare me for the work that would still lie ahead—and for my own potential Ascension. Now that I have had many hundreds of accurate future prophecies demonstrated to me over a twenty-seven-year period, I have no reason to doubt the Ascension prophecies. The most exciting prophecies, of course, are the ones that haven't come true yet—and that's why I wrote this book.

As you read these various dreams and how I analyze them, you will quickly begin learning the language. This will provide a very useful tool for you to harness the power of your dreams for higher guidance. In Session 86, Question 7, the Law of One series said that once you start working heavily on your spiritual evolution, becoming what they call an "adept," you will find that, in the source's words, "dreaming becomes the most important tool" to enhance your spiritual growth. That is about as marvelous an endorsement as anyone could ever ask for, given that the Law of One series has formed the spiritual and scientific backbone for my entire career and all previous works—and it fits with my own experience. You can also have direct contact with your own spiritual guides in dreams. As the source said: "While the so-called conscious mind rests, this adept may call upon those which guide it, those presences which surround it, and, most of all, the magical personality, which is the higher self."[12]

CHAPTER SEVEN

Prophetic Mysteries from
a Fellow Seeker

In the first month after I got sober, I had multiple dreams that I did not write down, then I awoke from a recurring nightmare that I had started using marijuana again. The first dream I actually did write down in a notebook was on October 23, 1992, just over a month after my sobriety started. In this dream, I had inherited a very large room that I could decorate or design however I chose. It had a true wealth of space and an unusually high ceiling. However, the room was totally bleak and colorless. Everything was either concrete-gray or white. The walls needed to be repaired and painted.

An interesting, peaceful person standing beside me told me I could try hanging colorful parachutes from the ceiling to brighten up the space. This person told me that my new space would be only as nice as the energy I decided to put into its creation. Looking back on it now, this dream was obviously talking about how depressed and unhappy I was at the time. The sad condition of the room represented my psychological state at the time. I had just given up a drug habit that had become the focal point of my life. I needed to invest time and attention in myself, and find more ways where I could be happy and add colors into my life.

Lucid Dreams and Time Loops

The next morning, October 24, 1992, I broke through and had a lucid dream. In this case, the loud, brash, and controversial rock and roll singer Meat Loaf had some sort of bizarre magic power. He was able to transform a range of fur pelts into ferocious, live animals. He then directed these animals to attack me. At first, I was terrified, but then I realized how ridiculous the whole thing was. Fur pelts do not transform back into living animals. I remembered Stephen LaBerge's teachings about testing my reality for strange things that were clearly impossible, and this was an obvious example. Right then, I realized I had to be dreaming, and I became lucid. My brother, father, and grandfather were there with me, and I started trying to explain to them that all this was a dream. None of them wanted to listen to me. I then went after Meat Loaf, for I knew I had to stop him from making the monsters. I concentrated and hit him with a blast of energy, using my hands to shape the energy into a beam. He immediately shrank down to half his original size. I blasted him three more times until he could fit in a mayonnaise jar that I suddenly manifested in my hand. I put him in the jar, where he no longer posed a threat to me, and covered the jar with a lid that I screwed on. He banged on the glass with his fists and I could hear his muffled voice.

At this point, I again tried to convince the men of my family that we were actually all in a dream. They did not want to believe me, even after what they just saw. I held up my hand and added an extra finger to show them some additional proof. They clearly saw this, but were still not impressed. At this point, I felt that if no one would believe me, I at least needed to write down what had happened to me in this dream. I manifested a notebook and a pen. After I finished writing some basic notes, I went back to read them, and they were all in perfect French. This was well beyond my conscious ability to speak and write French, yet as I read it, I somehow knew that the language, grammar, and spelling were perfect.

Amazingly, after I reread the dream for the first time while writing this book in August 2019, I had quite the time loop. I walked outside to my back porch in Colorado and a beaver pelt was sitting there on the patio. This genuinely shocked me. As it turned out, my wife had carried this with her for many years as one of her shamanic tools. She was going through her closet and noticed that the beaver pelt had become infested with moths. She had placed the pelt outside in the hope that the moths would fly away before she put it in the freezer to kill any eggs, and it had since gotten rained on. She had no idea that I was about to read a dream where fur pelts just like this were being turned back into live, aggressive animals.

The very next dream in my journal from 1992 had another time loop to my present. In this dream, I was seeing a series of stylized ice-like rocks that were polished smooth, round, and nearly clear in some parts. Each of them had designs carved into them that looked like peace signs. In the dream, the rocks were being grown in a Pyrex glass jar with a chemical solution and a stirring rod. The crystals could be grown to whatever size you wanted them to be, based on how long you left them in the solution. In my waking life in 2019, my wife, Elizabeth, had just purchased a carved crystal that looked almost exactly the same as these polished stones in the dream. My wife's new crystal was made of a whit-ish, icy material and was smooth and round, about two inches wide. The surface of the crystal was carved with the image of the Hindu Sri Yantra mandala. My dream from 1992 had the exact same objects, except that the carving in the dream was a simpler-looking peace sign. Otherwise, the objects were practically identical—yet my wife had just bought the crystal and brought it home a couple of days before. She had no idea about this dream when she bought the crystal, and neither did I.

The next dream I wrote down in my notebook was from November 1, 1992. In it, I met up with a group of Koreans and began falling in love with a particular woman. This was two solid years before I got together with my Japanese girlfriend Yumi in 1994. Now, in 2019, I was able to see that it was clearly a prophetic dream—I just didn't realize it at the time. Near the end of November 1992, on Thanksgiving Day, I had yet another dream in which I had an Asian girlfriend.

On November 3, 1992, I had a dream in which I again achieved lucid-ity. In this case, the lucidity happened as I was seeing one fantastic-looking UFO after another flying past me in the sky. Bear in mind that my insider NASA disclosure would not appear until three months after this point. Consciously, I did not yet know whether or not UFOs were real. However, in this experience, I was seeing such fantastically wonderful crafts that I knew I could not be living in waking reality—I had to be dreaming. After I became lucid, I wished for the UFOs to become more and more magnificent, and they did just that. Wonders flew past my eyes. Huge, gargantuan, and ridiculously sophisticated ships roared by. They were all sleek, white, and very high tech. Some of them were of almost impossible size. This dream was a total flashback to the many awe-inspiring UFO dreams I had when I was young, and helped to prepare me for my NASA disclosure three months later.

That same December, once I was back in my hometown, I had an incredible experience that I documented in both *The Synchronicity Key* and *The Ascension Mysteries*. I looked up at the sky after having a huge fight with my former friends, who had not gotten sober and doubted my new spiritual insights. I told the universe that I knew I was here for a spiritual purpose. Right then, a shooting star streaked through the exact part of the sky I was looking at. A huge surge of energy rose up from the Earth through my entire body, causing me to heave in ecstasy. Shortly after I returned to school the following semester, I got my NASA disclosure. I was much too interested in my UFO research at this point to write down any of my dreams. I didn't pick it up again until the summer, now in the year 1993. Most of those dreams were clearly demonstrating the tension I was feeling with my mother and her live-in boyfriend at the time. There did not appear to be any UFO or Ascension-related themes of significance at the time.

A Personal Crisis Leads to Religious Studies

In the fall semester of 1993, as I began my junior year, I migrated from Crispell Hall, the "study dorm" where we had three rooms that all opened out into an adjoining suite, to Bouton Hall, a dorm where everyone's room opened onto a commonly shared hallway. My hallway had one bathroom with a series of showers and stalls that the entire corridor of guys had to share. Bouton Hall was considered the artists' dorm. It was right next to the art building, and I enjoyed being around creative people. I found myself living in room 111, and again laughed at the synchronicity of my room number.

I ended up living with a roommate who was a member of a campus group called SCUM, short for Student Coalition for Universal Medievalism. His main passion in life was to be a Dungeon Master for the Dungeons and Dragons board game, which has now been greatly popularized by the hit Netflix show *Stranger Things*. My roommate had created an entire world for his fellow players to explore. Every meeting they had was in our room, and it would go on for hours. This greatly impacted my sense of private space, and my roommate and I were not getting along. I had no interest in the dark themes of Dungeons and Dragons, and my roommate soon began giving me the silent treatment for days on end. He also did passive-aggressive things like putting water in my bed, and even sculpted a pointy, dagger-like object out of gray clay and hung it on the ceiling right over my pillow.

Our room itself was barely more than twelve feet wide, and we had to share a bunk bed. For many days, I felt a great sense of personal crisis from what was happening, and decided that I needed to start reading spiritual literature instead of UFO books to try to find some higher guidance on what I should do. I ended up reading the Hindu Bhagavad-Gita; the Dhammapada or Buddha's Book of Righteousness; a book by the Dalai Lama entitled *A Flash of Lightning in the Dark of Night*; a book by Thomas Merton entitled *Zen and the Birds of Appetite*; and the Wilhelm-Baynes version of the I Ching textbook.

After reading all these works, I realized that the key to solving my problem had to involve compassion and forgiveness. I opened up to my roommate and began having long conversations with him in which all I did was ask him questions about himself. I got deeply involved in his personal issues and helped him work through his problems and frustrations. I used many of the tools I was practicing in my suicide hotline internship. With this strategy, I was able to turn a very upsetting situation into a pleasant friendship, so we were able to get along just fine for the rest of the year. This became a key experience in teaching me how to get along with other people, even if I didn't initially agree with them.

I spent as many waking hours as possible doing UFO and paranormal research while doing just enough work for my classes to make sure I had decent grades. I was consistently meditating on the Hyperdimensional Model, and I was always reading four or five different books at once. At the same time, I was having incredible synchronicity experiences, usually on a daily basis. Although I did not write down any of my dreams during this time, I created entire books' worth of typewritten personal journals. This included a regular catalog of interesting and bizarre synchronicities that were happening to me as I worked my way through hundreds of books.

I shared what I was studying with my roommate, at least to whatever degree he was willing to listen. At the end of the year, he let me know that he was moving back to his hometown. He ended up marrying his high school sweetheart, whom he had left behind to go to school and have other girlfriends. He gave up on all the Dungeons and Dragons material and actually became a Christian minister. Although he never told me that I had any influence on these things happening, I certainly suspected that my influence had been of key importance in getting him onto a spiritual path.

A Fellow Seeker

I ended up reaching out to my friend Artie, who was a year younger than me, and asking him if he wanted to room with me for my senior year. He gladly said yes. Artie was shorter than me, with thinning blond hair, a sensitive jawline, and glasses with very thick lenses. He obviously had a genius-level IQ. He had grown up in Connecticut, a tiny, affluent state just a short drive from New York City. Artie was very interested in my UFO research and would listen to me talk about it for however long I felt like sharing. He and I had been friends since the beginning of my junior year. I met him through my buddy Adam, who played guitar in my Chamber Jazz Ensembles band while I was the drummer. The only times Artie would interrupt my grand cosmic summaries of the books I was reading would be to ask questions, and he was hanging on every word.

I was utterly fascinated with Artie's life story as well—and this was admittedly a major part of why I asked him to move in with me. As best I could tell at the time, both of Artie's parents were involved in a terrifying and very secretive cult that was somehow connected with the government, secret societies, black magic, military defense contractors, and the reverse-engineering of UFO-related technology. Artie's mother ended up taking her own life when Artie was seven years old, and his father disappeared under very mysterious circumstances when he was ten. Artie was told his father had died, but as we will see, this may very well not be the case. Artie then was lucky enough to be raised by a normal woman who happened to be a friend of his mother's, along with her husband. Artie had never met his new mother until the day she assumed guardianship.

Later in life, Artie started having brief but very disturbing memory flashes, which he told his wife about. I remember hearing him tell me about this same memory at some point back in college, but at the time, it was very mysterious to me. Artie could vaguely remember being taken somewhere in the middle of the night. Once he arrived at the destination, he saw people wearing animal masks. Some of the masks had antlers or horns, and the masks depicted different animals like an elk or a moose. The men were wearing suit jackets and regular neckties. The women were wearing elegant dresses. When I asked him what he was feeling at the time, he said he was scared—actually petrified. His brother was also there in his memory, and he asked his brother about it several years ago, as of the time of this writing. His brother obviously didn't want to talk about it, saying "I don't remember that," while acting very agitated. Artie then tried to talk to him about it on one additional occasion, and his brother said, "I don't remember that at all. No, no, no." He again was very agitated and immediately changed the subject.

When I spoke to him for this book, Artie had again started to remember brief flashes of the experience after waking up from a very weird and disturbing dream in which someone was trying to hurt him. Then a few months after I interviewed him, he uncovered a new memory of an elderly man sexually abusing him at this same party while his parents stood by and did nothing to stop it. Whether we like it or not, there are many insiders who have come forward to report nearly identical-sounding trauma, which psychologists refer to as ritual abuse. Memory loss is clinically referred to by psychologists as dissociation, and this type of amnesia is another extremely common element in these whistleblower reports. Once I began learning about this dark universe in 2000. through the writings of an insider named Svali, I realized that Artie's story fit perfectly with what I was now learning much more about. He may have forgotten what happened to him, but many others have not—and a fair number of them have been quite public about their experiences. Stanley Kubrick's movie *Eyes Wide Shut* was one of the most prominent efforts to expose and publicize this dark aspect of our society, and the disturbing Epstein story has greatly increased public awareness of this problem.

As best I could tell, Artie was able to escape whatever nightmare his parents had been involved in after both of them allegedly died. I presented him with my theory while we were roommates. I knew there was something terrifying hiding behind his story, and he has since dedicated his entire life to trying to figure it out. Much of what he may have gone through is still an absolute mystery to him. I called him up as I was finishing this book in 2019, clarifying many details of what he had told me, and got some new information that adds shocking new elements to the mystery. I have noticed that when people are lying and making up stories, they usually like to connect all the dots so everything makes sense. In Artie's story, a wealth of puzzle pieces needed to be put together, and he himself had no idea how they fit. Yet this data aligns extremely well with what I have learned from many other insiders over the years, as well as through my private research into the so-called Illuminati and the Secret Space Program.

Psychiatric Experiments at the Orphanage

Artie's parents met each other while they were children, living in an orphanage that was run by a secret society similar to the Freemasons. The orphanage publicly referred to itself as a boarding school. Artie's father was transferred to the orphanage when he was still a small child, after his own father died in a tragic fire. If your father was a member of this society and he passed away, you would then be taken to live at the boarding school, since there was no Department of Children and Families at the time. You and your mother would then participate in "studies" and "experiments" that were done at a psychiatric facility on the campus. Considering everything that we now know, this almost certainly involved mind-control techniques.

Artie had to work very hard to find any information about the psychiatric building, which was torn down after his parents grew up. The boarding school had a significant partnership back in the 1930s through 1950s with a major university in the area. Artie suspected that after the kids left the school, they were still being studied by the psychiatrists and whoever they were really working for, but at that point, it was done more covertly than overtly. Artie was so intrigued by the mysteries of his parents' past that he ended up going to work at this same boarding school for many years as an adult, helping the kids who were living there. Nothing too strange ever happened to him, but he did gather some very significant new clues. In addition, he was placed in the exact same room that had been his father's bedroom growing up. No one told him this and it took him years to find out.

By talking to people who had worked there while both of his parents grew up in the orphanage, Artie found out that a psychiatrist would come in a couple of times a week to work with the kids and give them various pharmaceutical drugs. One woman who still worked there remembered that Artie's mom would get taken away at times to go to the "hospital," as they called it. On a number of these occasions, she wouldn't be brought back to her room until the next day.

If we compare the possible experiences of Artie's mother to the whistleblower Svali's very extensive written testimonials, some of which are preserved at svalispeaks.wordpress.com, it is entirely possible, even likely, that Artie's mother went through many, many hours of very specialized training. According to Svali, the group calling themselves the "Illuminati" has "Six Branches of Learning" that every member is trained in to varying degrees, depending upon their proclivities. The Six Branches are Sciences, Military, Government, Leadership, Scholarship, and Spiritual.[1] Similarly, if you are working on a Regional Leadership Council, which ranks below the National and World levels, you have Military, Spiritual, Scholarship, Finances, Training, and Sciences as your six main divisions.[2] Government is notably missing at these lower levels.

To explore the Six Branches of Learning sequentially, first we have Sciences, which focuses on the study and practice of mind control. This is the branch that Svali was allegedly a member of. Each group member must endure hours and hours of very torturous mind-control programs, and members of the Sciences branch study these techniques and administer the protocols. According to Svali, if an ordinary person were put through these techniques without formal training, they could be so traumatized that they would either die from a heart attack or have a complete mental breakdown and require permanent hospitalization. All members are given drugs that put them into a highly suggestive state, with effects similar to LSD but of shorter duration, and are then deeply hypnotized. Various programming commands are introduced, such as with "training films" and verbal keywords, while electric shocks cause extraordinary trauma to the body without visible or lasting physical damage.

The goal of these programs is to cause the mind to splinter, and to then program these fragments of the personality and ensure they remain in place over time with so-called tune-ups. If this process is performed before the age of three and a half, the person can develop a "core split" where there will be completely alternative identities that they have no conscious awareness of, protected by an amnesic barrier. These identities can then be called up through the use of certain code phrases. Orphanages like the ones Artie's mother and father grew up in can be used to administer these programs on children without the prying eyes of parents. Both versions of the movie *The Manchurian Candidate*, 1964 and 2004, reveal key aspects of how this technique, known as MKULTRA, or Mind-Kontrol Ultra, actually works. It can be used to create programmable assassins who have no memory of having killed someone afterward. There are apparently many different examples of these assets being deployed throughout recent history, including Sirhan Sirhan, who assassinated Robert F. Kennedy on June 5, 1968.

In the second category, Military, you dress up in uniforms, such as German Nazi outfits from World War II, and are trained in firearms, bomb-making of improvised explosive devices, assassination techniques, surveillance, setting traps, stalking, and riot control. Military can also include espionage tactics, including how to "drop a tag" and evade capture if someone is following you. The third category, Leadership, cultivates members with the skills necessary to be a public figure and influence how others think, such as by being the CEO of a major corporation. The fourth category, Government, is self-explanatory, where you learn the skills to obtain a law degree and how all the different aspects of governance must function. Leadership is a separate category from Government because in addition to training CEOs, Leadership may also prepare people for careers as actors, musicians, news anchors, and the like, where they are taught to remain loyal to this group's hidden agenda. There is apparently an Entertainment subcategory within Leadership.

The fifth category, Scholarship, focuses on academic subjects that revolve around the hidden history of the organization. These members stage and participate in plays where historical events that are important to the group, but otherwise overlooked by or unknown to the general public, are acted out in these secret meetings. Scholarship may also focus on the academic study of nations, corporations, and/or social structures the group intends to understand, in order to assist with efforts to infiltrate and control them. This can include training spies who learn languages fluently so they can physically infiltrate the desired countries.

The final, sixth category, Spiritual, focuses on practices that include the deliberate cultivation of out-of-body experiences to gather information that is otherwise difficult or impossible to obtain. This supposedly also includes "time travel," where a practitioner apparently enters the mind of someone in the past who is vulnerable, such as a drunk hobo passed out in a haystack. Apparently with enough training, a practitioner can occupy that person's body and potentially get them to commit murders that may eliminate people who the group dislikes in the present. If a person performs this "edit" successfully, the world ends up on a different timeline, and only the practitioner remembers the version of history that happened before. According to Svali, this was dramatized in the movie *The Matrix*, where the Agents were able to occupy the bodies of anyone within the Matrix and then get them to commit murders. This plot point is also the key feature of the X-Men movie *Days of Future Past* from 2014, where Wolverine travels back in time to 1973 in order to prevent a destructive event from ever taking place.

I understand how outrageous this sounds, and again, as various insiders have told me over the years, it doesn't matter whether you believe this is true or not. These people absolutely do believe this works, and they are "as serious as a heart attack" about it. Svali also says these out-of-body practices are very hard on the physical body, and cause the person to age more quickly, such as by causing their hair to turn gray at an earlier age than normal. The Spiritual branch also designs and conducts very disturbing ritual ceremonies like the one Artie had brief flashes of experiencing as a boy, where everyone was wearing masks. These ceremonies can feature elaborate black magic rites conveying very specific spiritual practices.

Of course, at the time Artie was telling me about his parents, I did not know any of this, but when I began reading Svali's testimony in 2000, many dots began connecting. Artie met another alumni at the orphanage who joked about how he had heard that some kids would get taken into the sewer systems underground at this same facility. Artie later discovered that one of the older homes on the campus had a door downstairs that was always locked, and a maintenance worker told him that it was an entrance to the sewer system. This may very well have been used as a ceremonial space.

Once an Intelligence Agent . . .

As an adult, Artie attended a highly fundamentalist Christian church in Connecticut for several years. He was very freaked out about his mysterious and disturbing childhood memories, and found comfort in the Christian faith. During this time, Artie met a fellow parishioner who had served as an Army Ranger and Green Beret, worked for the Central Intelligence Agency, and knew Artie's father. This was how Artie found out that after leaving the boarding school, his father joined the military, entered Army Intelligence, and served during the Vietnam War. His job was to perform logistics, which is to covertly infiltrate various locations, sketch out detailed maps of their internal layout, and get himself out of there undetected. This suggests that Artie's father had specialized in the Military branch. Artie's father would then bring the maps to his superiors, who would use this information to conduct assassinations, rescue prisoners of war, or collect other valuable targets. One of my insiders worked in this exact operational specialty for many years.

Logistics is difficult and dangerous work that involves the use of a vast array of spy skills and elite training that must be perfected over the course of years. This includes neutralizing anyone who tries to interfere with your mission. According to many insiders I have spoken to, most operatives never leave the intelligence community. Often, if one does try to leave this kind of work behind, they are haunted by PTSD. Memories come up that can cause them to spend all night sweating in bed, revved up with maximum adrenaline. Nothing in the ordinary world ever feels exciting or important enough, and a former operative can spiral into a deep depression. If someone stays involved in the community, however, their work generally gets more and more involved, and the pay goes higher and higher—they may well end up working directly with prominent social and political figures. Many of these agents take on seemingly normal-looking cover assignments in what appear to be ordinary companies, while actually continuing to work for the intelligence agencies. It is also possible for someone to begin in one agency and then get pulled into an even more clandestine organization or division as they advance.

Loyalty and skill are rewarded with positions of higher and higher influence and significance. The agents are sworn to secrecy and can never say a single word to their families about what they are really doing; otherwise, their cover story could easily fall apart. They just appear to be working a normal, boring job and are too emotionally unavailable to want to talk about it. The burden of all this hidden personal information often tears families to pieces. The family becomes an outsider group, and the agent can only develop true intimacy with his or her own immediate coworkers and superiors. I remember how my father always came home each night with at least one story about his work at General Electric while my brother and I were growing up. It would have been highly bizarre if our father came home and never said a single word about his job, but this is the life that these intelligence agents must live.

I had my suspicions about secret intelligence agencies and classified defense-contractor projects long before meeting Artie. My junior high friend Kevin, who was one of the smartest kids in my grade, had parents who both worked for a local nuclear power laboratory. They could not take him to work, nor could they tell him anything about what they were doing there. If they were ever having a conversation about their work and Kevin came into the room, they would immediately stop talking. They let Kevin know more than once that they considered UFOs and ETs to be real, without saying why. They were very concerned about the potential existence of extraterrestrial life, and considered it to be an incredibly dangerous situation. This opinion seemed to be a direct result of very specific information that they were given as part of their jobs, while many other data points about benevolent, angelic extraterrestrial human life are deliberately omitted. These programs are very highly compartmentalized, and each worker is only told the exact amount of information he or she needs to properly do their job. Kevin's parents also talked quite a bit about wormholes and Einstein's concept of a space-time continuum, where space and time are interconnected, so as you move through space, you are also moving through time.

According to one prominent insider I recently interviewed while writing this book, everyone who goes above a low- to midlevel position in the intelligence community is very well aware that UFOs exist, that they crashed here, and that we have since built our own by studying and replicating how they work. We have as many as 276 cities underground that can house up to 65,000 people each, as well as a variety of off-planet bases to visit as you get into the more highly compartmentalized programs. Once you enter that world, it is almost impossible ever to return to "surface life" on Earth again. I believe the main reason this seems so hard to believe for most of us now is simply because we have been lied to for so long, to such an exraordinary degree. Since the Roswell crash, our military-industrial complex has had well over seventy years to study, analyze, and build their own working UFO prototypes.

The Apollo missions achieved the seemingly impossible feat of putting a man on the moon, but then we are supposed to believe that humanity got bored afterward and simply gave up for fifty years? The dark side of the moon is a great place for the military-industrial complex to build bases, since no one here could ever see them with a telescope, and the reverse-engineered antigravity craft we've created have a technology called masking, which makes them invisible to the naked eye in most cases. The only way you may be able to see them is if you use the most advanced infrared night-vision technology. However, in that case, if you start actually getting good results and try to publicize them, you could easily receive threats. One of the whistleblowers I met from Dr. Steven Greer's Disclosure Project in 2001, Dan Salter, was assigned to buy off or threaten people who knew and saw too much—often referred to as offering them gold or lead.

The Organization

After his time in the military, Artie's father worked at a scientific organization and continued that job until his alleged death. For legal reasons, I will not share the name, so we will just call it "The Organization." All Artie knew about this company was that they ran a bunch of automated machines, and that his father apparently worked there as an "inspector." Artie did once get to visit his father's office at The Organization. Some of the work areas were all cubicles and did not look very well kept. His father worked in a room that was much better, with yellow floors, where the humidity and temperature had to be regulated. His father's supposed boss said to him at the time, only half joking, "I think your dad's office might be nicer than mine." There were many scientific instruments in his father's office, including traditional microscopes and a variety of machines. One of them looked like the spectrometers Artie worked with at SUNY New Paltz.

When I looked up The Organization online, I found that this company works with both public corporations and private military groups. One part of The Organization serves as a defense contractor that builds carbon-fiber parts for the aerospace industry. To me, that helped to answer many questions, because a variety of insiders have revealed that it is very common for defense contractors to be involved in UFO-related black projects, designing classified aircraft that are far more interesting than the Stealth bomber. Other parts of The Organization make products for the civilian sector. This very likely serves as a cover business for their highly classified work. The Organization has custom-designed unique products for many top Fortune 500 companies. The Organization also received awards from President Bill Clinton, President George W. Bush, and the Department of Commerce. It was bought out and taken private by a large equity firm within the last ten years, which means that now they must answer to no one but their own investors.

When Artie was about twenty-four or twenty-five years old, he and his brother met a man who had worked with his father at The Organization. The man reminisced about working together with Artie's father on a project in Northampton, Massachusetts. Artie responded, "I thought you worked with him at The Organization in Connecticut?" The man had a shocked and worried look on his face, and then immediately brushed it off and changed the subject. Artie's brother later joked with him about this. He said that maybe their father's job was a cover story, and they were never told what he was really doing. Now that we know The Organization was an aerospace defense contractor, it makes perfect sense that Artie's father was developing highly advanced classified technology in that lab and elsewhere. This may also have been only one aspect of his overall work. I was also intrigued when Artie told me his father ended up joining the same elite society that ran the boarding school he grew up in, and his father was about to graduate into the highest rank within this society before his apparent death in 1986. This, again, is not the Freemasons, but a similar and less well-known organization.

The Boy Genius

Keeping all this in mind, Artie had some very interesting anomalies in his childhood. His cousins remember him singing the Mickey Mouse Club theme song when he was only eighteen months old, and also being able to speak fluently. Artie had to wear reading glasses in first grade, and was too shy to read out loud. Once he finally did, he got moved from the lowest to the highest reading class in a single day. Artie was a true child prodigy, almost at a savant level of intelligence. As a boy, he could solve complex math problems in his head faster than someone could process them with a calculator. Artie was somehow able to multiply and divide five- or six-digit numbers this way, but after a few years, the ability mysteriously wore off, never to return.

Artie's mother supposedly had a job as a nurse, but she usually stayed home with him, until her tragic death. He blocked out most of the memories of his mother for reasons we will discuss. Artie read all her nursing textbooks when he was only four or five years old, and could give a full discourse on all the details of each phase of the human gestation process. If he didn't know a word, he would look it up in the dictionary. He also regularly researched things in encyclopedias, and read many different adult books on topics that interested him. His brother would go out and play with friends, but Artie usually wanted to stay home and read. He remembered his mother quizzing him on scientific topics as a kid, even before he entered kindergarten. She asked him to describe, in specific detail, what would occur in the blastula stage of development, the gastrula stage, and so on.

In another strange incident, Artie rattled off something in Japanese when he was six or seven years old, attending the second grade. His mother was still alive at this point, and the event happened in their living room. His father was sitting in a rocking chair with a Corelle plate and was cutting something with a knife at the time. His father stared at Artie and said, "What did you say?" He was clearly freaked out. Artie did not respond. His father repeated the question, and Artie said, "I don't know." His father asked him again and Artie repeated the same answer. Then his father said, "How did you know that?" He was genuinely shocked. Tears started welling in Artie's eyes. He didn't know. He said it just came out.

Later on, in a meeting with his uncle, this incident came up in conversation. His uncle said that Artie's father told him he had spoken in perfect Japanese. He spontaneously uttered a phrase that his father knew well from having served in the military. This was another mystery, because his father supposedly served in Vietnam, not Japan. However, in the world of defense logistics, anything is possible. Artie had not seen or heard anything in his normal, waking life that could have taught him this phrase in Japanese. It is possible that Artie went through training he does not consciously remember, such as in the Scholarship branch, where he was beginning to learn Japanese for anticipated future work.

Contactee Experiences—but from Whom?

I was particularly interested by two different stories Artie told from this time in his life. The first event took place when Artie was about four years old. He had a pair of Spider-Man Underoos, a type of underwear with a cartoon pattern, and a shirt that went along with it. He woke up in his bed and found that his underwear was now on backward, but not the shirt. He would never have put his own underwear on backward, and there was no way this could have happened on its own while he was sleeping. This mirrored many classic abduction and contactee stories I had been reading in a variety of books. As I was hearing this in 1994, I told him he may have been through some sort of medical exam, and whoever put his clothes back on did not understand which way they needed to go. I had also suspected that I had been through similar experiences myself, based upon the intriguing clues I discussed earlier, like waking up in the middle of the night in a trance, packing my bag, and walking out the side door of the house into the dark night, only to suddenly snap out of it.

When Artie was in first grade, at about six years of age, he remembers seeing a large, lighted object coming down in his yard outside. He vaguely remembers sleepwalking outside to take a look and see what it was. His parents saw him walking along, and he told them he was going out to see that big ball of light. It did not appear that his parents saw the light like he did. I was the first one to ever tell Artie that this sounded very much as if he had been through some sort of UFO contact and abduction experience. It also seemed to be intertwined with the weird things his mother and father were saying and doing.

I speculated that there might be more to this story than extraterrestrials. Artie's alleged UFO contacts could have been coming from some division of whatever strange group his parents seemed to be involved in. If you have read Part Two of *The Ascension Mysteries,* then you already know I spoke with many insiders who said that the military-industrial complex uses its own classified UFO-type craft to carry out its own abductions. These are often called military abductions, or MILABS. In an interview with Jenny McCarthy on the *Jenny McCarthy Show* of November 7, 2019, insider Corey Goode revealed details of his own childhood experience that appear to integrate very nicely with the clues from Artie's testimony. Here are two excerpts from the show, quoted in Corey's own words:

> MILABS stands for Military Abductions. Back during the days of MKULTRA, and some of these other dark programs that we know about, there were a lot of other programs that we don't know about. They were seeking out youth, preferably before seven years old, who had certain abilities. They would discover those abilities in various ways, through testing in school, standardized testing, and other ways. When they identified these children, they would bring them into a program, like the Explorers program, [where] instead of going to school, you would go to a museum or something like that. [In my case,] they would take us instead to a military base in Fort Worth, Texas, called Carswell Air Force Base at the time. There, during the day, they would train us and exploit our gifts in different ways. They put us in a program for ten years. At the end of those ten years, we would go into various dif-

ferent programs. Some of them could be quite dark. The one
that I happened to be pulled into was the secret space program, where you served twenty years in the secret space
program.

Corey went on to say that these programs deliberately looked for
children who came from troubled families that were less attentive to
them. This made the children far more resilient to things that could
traumatize most people, such as meeting unfamiliar-looking extraterrestrial humanoid beings. These kids could also be picked up in their
own backyards at night with craft that we would think of as UFOs.
These craft could actually be operated by the clandestine organization
they were working with, and performing what would appear to most
people as a classic ET abduction. Artie's reports of developing unusually
advanced, savant-level mathematical skills and then losing them is another perfect correlation with Corey's testimony about MILABS. Here
is another quote from Corey's appearance with Jenny McCarthy, this
time beginning at the 7:02 mark, where he is describing the job he was
trained to perform as an "intuitive empath":

> Intuitive Empaths were very coveted. They take your natural
> ability and train you with guru-type people and also scientists
> to help develop it. And then they give you a serum that boosts
> this ability, but the drawback is that it burns up your neurol-
> ogy. It overclocks your neurology. Intuitive Empaths would
> be brought into things to detect danger or deception. We
> were used to interface with various extraterrestrials. Often-
> times while the [extraterrestrials] were being interrogated,
> they would have us sitting by and analyzing what type of
> emotions, feelings and that type of thing they were picking
> up, and what we thought was the agenda and the motive be-
> hind those sorts of feelings. . . . Also, when you leave the pro-
> gram, they do a type of mind-wipe. They call it blank-slating
> someone. That way, they send someone back into normal life,
> and they don't have the memories. But with intuitive em-

paths, about three to five percent of them begin receiving the memories again. They become very confused, have trauma, and have to put it all together. The military tries to intervene when they see people who are beginning to go through that process. . . . They will try to confuse them more, get them committed, or blank-slate them again and hope the blank-slating takes this time.

Corey Goode has revealed it was well understood that certain human beings on Earth are extraterrestrial souls volunteering to be here, and usually consciously unaware of this connection. However, these people will invariably get positive contacts from their home group throughout their life, only to be re-abducted by a terrestrial military organization in each case. The organization debriefs the contactee, takes detailed notes of what happened to them, and then blank-slates them, so they have no memory of either contact experience. Then they are returned to their homes. Owing to the advanced time-manipulating technology that is used, they can be brought back just moments after they were taken. An interesting technology is used to make sure that all other people and animals in the area will remain asleep as this is done. The technology is called delta. It is only in rare cases like Artie's when people can remember anything at all.

Corey has hinted on many occasions that he knows a lot more about my own past than he is authorized to reveal, but up until now, I myself have been able to recover only bits and pieces of it. Thankfully, I have no doubt that I was never a member of the Illuminati. Many people apparently have these MILAB/secret space program experiences without having to suffer through the occult black magic aspects of the organization. The mind-wiping technology works so well that the only way you can really uncover what happened is to pull it out of your soul, such as through dream recall and analysis. Yet those dreams will seem so bizarre that you would never imagine they were in any way related to actual events that you may have experienced. I have gone back and reviewed a wide variety of dreams and experiences in my childhood after having had this information and am now quite convinced that I have had MILABS myself, as we will discuss. I do admittedly find it frustrating that I have not been able to remember more of these experiences consciously, but apparently the technology is extremely difficult to circumvent with the waking, conscious mind.

Suspicious Deaths of Both Parents

As an adult, Artie's mother got shock treatments and was often hospitalized because of her anger, but this only served to make her angrier. She consistently suffered from negative emotions, right up to the time of her tragic death. At certain times, she would go into a full tantrum and would act very strangely. Her hands would trace out complex symbols in the air at a high speed, with remarkable precision and violence. This suggests that she was a specialist in the Spiritual branch, along with Sciences due to her career focus on nursing. Artie noticed a similar phenomenon once he became obsessed with ninja movies, in which the characters make symbols with their fingers in the air, apparently to harness energy.

Artie's mother would do these movements really fast, almost like she was possessed by some outside force. In 1994, I speculated that she might have been doing some sort of black magic, such as summoning negative entities. This is not something she would have discovered on her own. It was very likely that someone had trained her how to execute these maneuvers. This may have been only one of many things she was taught on the nights she was taken away from the orphanage and was not brought back until the next day. As sad as this may sound, there are many people, potentially hundreds of thousands, if not millions, who are caught up in this dark and mysterious world. Artie was very scared when his mother did the hand symbols, for it looked so disturbing that he was afraid she might hurt him.

In one particularly severe episode of this phenomenon, Artie felt as though an invisible angelic being had entered the room as his mother went through the motions. She clearly seemed to hear something, because she turned her head as if to listen, suddenly stopped moving, sat down on the floor, and immediately became calm and relaxed. At the same time, Artie heard soothing words in his mind and felt a beautiful, loving presence that calmed him down as well. He never told his brother about this incident, because he didn't think his brother would believe him. This was another key event that led to his eventually becoming a Christian. I do believe Artie is telling the truth—that he had an encounter with benevolent human angelic ETs who are watching over, guiding, and protecting us. Thankfully, my own experiences throughout my life have been with this element of the extraterrestrial presence.

Many years later, I found out that one of the key founders of the modern rocketry and defense-contractor business, Jack Parsons, had done something similar to what Artie often saw his mother doing. An article in *Vice* magazine from January 2, 2015, reported that Parsons performed an occult magical ceremony called the Babalon Working, in which, among other things, he was "drawing occult symbols in the air with swords."[3] As it turns out, certain magical symbols, such as runes and sigils, can be drawn in the air while the person is visualizing them being formed out of light. It is believed in these occult groups that the person is creating actual thoughtforms in the spiritual plane, which can be used to both protect and defend themselves as well as to invoke and command spiritual beings.

Parsons's goal in the Babalon Working was most definitely to summon an entity, and the details are quite unsettling. The article reads:

> Just think about that for a second: one of the top minds driving America's early rocket program, a program that helped fuel the space race and the Cold War, was at the same time a leading figure in the world of the occult. . . . But for Parsons it didn't seem strange at all. He treated magic and rocketry as different sides of the same coin—both had been disparaged, both derided as impossible, but because of this both presented themselves as challenges to be conquered.[4]

Corey Goode and other insiders have suggested that this occult linkage to the origin of the space program goes much, much deeper than most of us could ever imagine.

Artie's mother took her own life on April 27, 1982. This happened to be his best friend's birthday, and he was seven years old at the time. Artie was going to Little League baseball tryouts, and was scheduled to go to his friend's birthday party afterward. Artie came home to find that his mother had taken a variety of pills, and she passed away later that same night.

Artie's father was then left to raise Artie and his brother alone. Artie still never heard a word about what his father was doing at work, and they hardly ever talked about the loss of his mother. Three years after his mother passed, when Artie was ten, he got up early on a Saturday morning to prepare for a birthday party that a friend of his was having down the street. His father came out into the hall and stared at him for an unusually long time, without ever saying a word. It was extremely awkward, if not terrifying. Artie said, "Dad, what's wrong?," but he wouldn't answer for a while. Artie repeated the question five different times, and his father finally said, "I love you." This was not something his father normally said. Then, right before Artie left for the birthday party down the street, his father again said he loved him, and hugged him very tightly, for a long time—like he had never hugged him before.

When Artie came home, a neighbor from across the street called out to him. She had been his nanny and watched over him when his father was at work for the last three years. She told Artie and his brother that their father had been taken to the hospital. Then their uncle visited and said their father wasn't doing well. No other details were given. The nanny later told Artie that his father had passed away. Artie did not go to the wake, and they held a closed-casket funeral. Even when he first told me this story, I did not feel that his father had actually passed away at all.

With the full experience and knowledge that I now have, I speculated that his father got pulled into an assignment where he would live out the rest of his life working in an underground or off-planet facility. This could have happened as a result of his making a mistake, such as getting caught telling someone just a bit of what he was really working on with the aerospace contractor. It is normal for people in this community to be forced to spend the rest of their lives in secret bases if they make a mistake of this sort. They are usually never again allowed to return to normal surface life on Earth. This is considered to be a far more desirable option than killing the person who made the mistake, since these people are highly trained in very specialized categories, and there are very few staff who have such unique training within these compartmentalized programs. At one point, I was threatened by people connected to Dr. Pete Peterson, one of my top insiders, who said I might end up being abducted and spend the rest of my life in an underground city if I talked about certain subjects online, but I continued doing so anyway. The threat never materialized and I am still here.

If my informed speculations are correct, then once Artie's father was taken underground, he could continue his work for The Organization on advanced and highly classified "black projects" without needing to maintain a cover story. He would be well aware that he could not tell his son anything about what he was about to do, or his son could be harmed— so all he could do was to give him a long, knowing stare, say he loved him, and give him a big hug before he left. He had to appear to have died in order to have a plausible cover story explaining his disappearance. These sorts of clandestine organizations take care of all the details to make the death seem authentic. By holding a closed-casket funeral, they did not need to create any convincing facsimile of his father's dead body. However, in this case, I believe Artie's father "bent the rules" by giving his son a knowing look before he had to leave. He knew that if he said anything out loud other than "I love you," it would be recorded and his son could be harmed—so all he could do was stare in silence.

Although this may sound very strange, it completely fits with a variety of other pieces of intel that I would end up gathering in later years. Intuitively, from the very first time Artie told me this story, I felt very strongly that his father had never actually died. His father was not unusually depressed and had not shown any signs of being at risk. There was no note or any type of statement that would have suggested he might take his own life, and he hadn't shown any signs of illness.

At the funeral, his father was given an honorable twenty-one-gun salute. Artie and his brother were presented with his American flag. The strangest aspect of this story was that in addition to army soldiers, there was a man in a navy uniform, another who was wearing a marine uniform, and yet another man who was wearing an air force uniform. Artie's father had served in the air force, but these other branches of the military had attended his ceremony as well. This seems to be quite unusual for a veteran's funeral, and it again suggested that his father had a far more prominent position in the military-industrial complex than he had ever been able to reveal to his own children. Once you enter the inside world, nothing is more important than the development of the black-ops technology in any one of a variety of secret space programs.

Artie met his adoptive parents after he lost his father. When Artie was orphaned, he found out that his aunt was the executor of his father's will and that his guardianship had been legally transferred to her. If Artie was born into an intergenerational and highly secretive cult, as it most definitely appears he was, then his aunt and uncle would be absolutely aware of it. In this case, I feel the most likely explanation is that Artie's aunt figured out a way to get him out of the cult so he could live a relatively normal life. His aunt turned over guardianship to a good female friend of his parents, since this woman and her husband could never have kids but really wanted them. The female friend had worked at a drugstore where his mother was once employed. When Artie began living with his new parents, he no longer had to deal with weird and terrifying ceremonial rage, nor any unsettling secrecy around his parents' work or history. It was only many years later that he discovered his new parents had to fight like crazy to keep custody of him. As a result of a very strange legal battle, his new parents could never actually adopt him—they could only act as his guardians.

Two Amazing Artifacts

When Artie was in middle school, his surrogate mother handed him the classic book on Edgar Cayce, *There Is a River*. She also gave him a few other Cayce books, including *The Sleeping Prophet* by Jess Stearn. In college, Artie was fascinated to hear additional details about the Cayce Readings from me, including material about Ra-Ptah, Atlantis, and Egypt, which I will go into later in this book. He was obsessed with

Egyptology, the Sphinx, and pyramids as a child, and wrote a fourth-grade paper on the Great Pyramid. The Cayce books helped steer him further in that direction.

In addition to reading about Edgar Cayce and studying Egyptology, as a child Artie came across two very fascinating stories of UFO-related artifacts. I spent countless hours meditating on both of these stories and trying to understand how they fit together into the greater picture that my research was revealing. In the first case, a friend of Artie's surrogate father had found a football-size, egg-shaped metallic object somewhere in the muddy sand of the Connecticut River. The object was unusually lightweight, and the metal was a dull, brushed-aluminum color. He could not cut, burn, or smash the object open, and there were no visible seams, buttons, or external markings on it. The smooth egg sat on his kitchen table for weeks. One day, his son happened to blow a dog whistle in the house. At this same moment, the egg suddenly spun open like a flower into two equal parts, dividing along spiraling, invisible corkscrew seams. Inside the object was a Rolodex-style series of photographic images, much like Polaroid pictures, only these images were printed on a very thin metallic type of material. Each picture was square, and there were quite a number of them.

The module had photographed important historical events that took place in the Connecticut River. There were images of ships that had sailed through the river over hundreds of years of time. One picture was from Norwich, Connecticut, in what appeared to be the Battle of 1812. In this case, the British were trying to invade Connecticut by coming up through the Connecticut River. A chain was put across the entire river to form a naval blockade, and the egg had apparently taken a picture of this event. The man was particularly puzzled by another picture that seemed out of place, because it looked like a scene from the Revolutionary War as opposed to the Civil War or the War of 1812. He knew that no technology like this should have existed that far back in time, and wondered if a group of people had been photographed doing a reenactment with this unusual device.

After the egg opened and he studied the remarkable pictures inside, the man excitedly called the FBI and reported his fascinating discovery.

He did not know what the object was. Perhaps it was a classified tool used by Russian spies. He felt he was the rightful owner of it, and that he would be able to get official support to help him understand his fantastic discovery and bring it out to the world. Instead of having a cooperative attitude, some men appeared at his house who were clearly not FBI agents. They said nothing about who they worked for or what they were. They immediately confiscated the object after they arrived. They did not ask him any questions, nor would they give him any information. Artie did not know whether the agents used guns to threaten him or not, but they almost certainly would have been armed. After they took the object, they refused to acknowledge that they had ever received it in the first place.

The second artifact was perhaps even more fascinating than the first. This information again came to Artie through his surrogate mother, who heard the story from a female friend of hers, who in turn had heard it from her husband. Artie's surrogate mother clearly had some degree of connections to the insider world, but it appears that she herself was not a member of it. In this case, her friend's husband worked for a major defense contractor. Somehow, in the course of his work, this man was able to gain access to a crystal-powered, gun-like device that could levitate objects. At least part of the technology seemed to involve the power of sound. The device looked like it was made of crystal, but it was much lighter than it seemed it should be for its size.

It worked somewhat like a revolver in that it had a rolling barrel with a series of compartments that would hold individual elements. Each compartment held a crystal that was in the shape of a four-sided obelisk, with a flat bottom and a pointed top. Each crystal was small enough to hold in your hand, and they varied in length from six to ten inches. You could roll the barrel and dial in these different-size crystals to engage them with the main mechanism. The crystals weren't necessarily perfectly smooth, nor were they clear on the inside. Some of them were clearly damaged and wouldn't work. The smoother, unbroken crystals sometimes would generate audible tones when you dialed them in, and at other times would not generate any sound.

While the gun was making the sounds, you could point it at things and get them to levitate, even if they were very large. Additionally, the researchers noted that people would get very euphoric and happy when they worked around the device. I would encounter a variety of similar reports from scientific studies of what I have called the Source Field, such as from Russian institutions. The defense contractor then conducted research to see if a device like this could be used to generate various types of moods in people. It was unclear if this research had ever produced tangible results, but I would have given just about anything to be able to get my hands on that device and test it for myself. Both the Cayce Readings and later the Law of One series reported on the extensive use of crystal-based technology in the Atlantean civilization. In fact, the Cayce Readings said the reason the Bermuda Triangle was so prone to cause planes and ships to disappear was that a giant crystal was still operating beneath the seafloor in that area. The crystal had been called the Firestone, and apparently it was used to satisfy almost all the power needs for the entire civilization.

Clearly, both of these world-changing technologies Artie heard about had been hidden away in classified programs. This made me greatly angry. I felt that the egg was almost certainly an extraterrestrial artifact, placed here by a group that was watching the people of Earth over many centuries, if not millennia. I envisioned hundreds of thousands if not millions of them positioned all over the world in key locations, and this man was lucky enough to find only one of them. It clearly was using some sort of technology to take the photographs that went far beyond a typical camera lens, since the surface of the egg had no visible seams. In this case, instead of storing the pictures digitally, apparently they chose to keep them in physical form. I also speculate that each photograph might be akin to a removable card that could then be inserted in a holographic projector. With the right technology, you might end up seeing far more than just the initial image. You might well get a full holographic replay of the event, complete with all the sights, sounds, smells, colors, and textures.

I feel that the crystal revolver could easily have been found in an ancient architectural site, such as Egypt. A device like this may well have been used to build the Great Pyramid and other such monuments out of gigantic, multiton stone blocks. I was very unhappy to find out that our own military-industrial complex was sitting on such a wealth of technology and keeping us in the dark. I was sure they had an excuse about how the truth would destroy our civilization, just as I had heard in my NASA disclosure, but I didn't agree with them. Our civilization has handled plagues, economic collapses, and world wars. It can handle UFOs as well—particularly once it becomes common knowledge that most of the extraterrestrials visiting us are highly positive, loving, and benevolent, and have been protecting us for millennia.

Strange Hints of a Deeper Mystery

After college, Artie and I stayed in contact by phone at least once or twice a year. I was intrigued by his commitment to go back to work where his parents had grown up, searching for answers. In 2008, Artie and his wife ran into a Borders bookstore in the pouring rain. They ran in for just a few minutes, not even ten, since Borders did not have the book Artie was looking for. When they went back outside, a plastic sheet from a three-ring binder had been placed under the windshield wiper of their Chevrolet HHR. A Xeroxed article was nestled inside the protective covering.

The article was talking about mind control, and mentioned Eric Harris, one of the two shooters in the Columbine school murders. Someone had circled the name Eric Harris with a black Sharpie marker. This article speculated that Harris had been through a type of mind control known as MK-ULTRA. This research project involved top universities and hospitals, just like Artie's parents had been affiliated with as children. Psychiatric drugs were used along with hypnosis and electrical shocks to create alternative personalities in people, and their conscious minds remained unaware of it. These alternative personalities could store information and even carry out elaborate, dangerous missions. After the program was exposed in congressional hearings in the 1970s, it was supposedly discontinued. Artie was born in 1975, so his parents grew up in the orphanage within the period when these deeply disturbing projects were conducted.

Having circled the name Eric Harris with the Sharpie marker, the mysterious author had then written, *"Who is this guy? You need to research him. This will help you answer questions."* Artie's wife was very freaked out. She used to think Artie was crazy when he talked about these sorts of things, but this event was undeniable. The paper had appeared so quickly on their windshield that someone must have been following them, and then positioned the paper immediately after they went inside the bookstore.

The next event took place two or three years ago, where they live now, a few states away. Again, Artie and his wife went into a store and came back out within a short period of time. Once again, something was left under the windshield wiper of their car, now a Ford Fusion, in the same type of plastic sheet. It was a white piece of paper with a message that was made of individual letters that had been cut out of newspaper and magazine articles. The message said, "Your physical and mental abilities have been impaired. There is nothing you can do to correct it. However, any further threats have been removed. Don't worry anymore." It wasn't raining this time. No punctuation had been used in the message, and both Artie and his wife were extremely freaked out. The message did not at all have the calming effect that its author had apparently intended. This again fits perfectly with the idea that Artie had been involved in MILAB programs as a child.

I explained to Artie that when we look at these two messages together, the implication is that he did suffer some sort of mind control that had damaged his physical body and his mental abilities to some degree. Nonetheless, he was able to break completely free of whatever his parents had been involved in, thanks to the work of his aunt, and he had nothing more to worry about. In 2011, Artie contacted The Organization to ask about his father's work history. Artie gave his father's name, said that he died in 1986, and tried to find out what he had done. The man on the phone wouldn't answer any questions. Artie said he had heard his father was an inspector, and the man said, "Yeah, that sounds about right." The man said they would call Artie back, but they never did. He also said they would send him an email, but they did not. Later on, Artie called again and one gentleman finally told him that his father had worked as an inspector on some projects—but other than that, he wouldn't give any specific details whatsoever.

It is my hope that sharing Artie's story with you can encourage more whistleblowers to come forward as time goes on. As we head into the next chapter, our story returns to the time when Artie was my roommate, and I got my first girlfriend at age twenty. The events that took place during that period propelled me ever deeper into the world of the mysterious, fueling my quest to seek the truth about extraterrestrial presence, the military-industrial complex, and our own origin and future destiny as souls awakening in the dream.

CHAPTER EIGHT

Wanderer Awakening

To have a full spiritual awakening, it is often necessary to first have a very strong break with the material world. My break took about a year to develop, and started in my senior year while I lived with Artie and traded fascinating stories. I knew something was wrong when a wasp stung me on the arm shortly after my first kiss with my new girlfriend, who was from Japan. In this book, I will call her Yumi. I was one of five buddies competing for her affection in the fall of 1994. The wasp sting was a synchronicity, but not the good kind. I had another "bad omen" the next day. I was thinking of our new romance while I was at work and I dropped a hand truck on my foot, causing a painful bruise. We really didn't have very much in common, other than that we both thought we wanted an exotic, foreign companion. I began picking up bits and pieces of Japanese, and I gave her detailed coaching on the English language. Artie eventually ended up moving into a house off campus and left me with the room so Yumi and I could live together.

Many years later, Artie told me he had a powerful dream in which a being that looked like Jesus appeared to him and said it was important that Artie let me have the room that year, free of charge. When Artie asked the being why this was necessary, the only answer was that this was an important thing for me to experience, and it would very much help with my spiritual awakening. Artie did give me an amazing gift, for it ultimately allowed Yumi and me to share a room together in the coolest dorm on campus during my senior year. I was terrified of living off campus, owing to all the malnutrition and starvation I saw people going through. By staying on campus, I had everything paid for, including all my housing and meals, and I could focus my efforts on reading as many UFO-related works as possible.

Yumi didn't like how I was reading books all the time, so I started telling her I had homework to do, and would then disappear into the study lounge to continue my research. Or I would have to sneak the books in like an addict while she was asleep. Very strange things started to happen as a result of this. One night, I was reading a book called *Aliens Among Us* by Dr. Ruth Montgomery while Yumi was asleep in the bed next to me. Supposedly, Ruth was pulling in psychic readings from her Higher Self and recording them directly with her typewriter, similar to what Edgar Cayce had done under hypnosis. Ruth's source went through an elaborate discussion of what it called Walk-Ins.

In a Walk-In, a person's soul has decided it has done everything it can do for this lifetime, usually after a series of increasingly horrible disasters that affected that person's life in seriously negative ways. Since the soul is ready to give up, it then agrees to allow a much more highly advanced extraterrestrial being to "walk in" after it leaves. The resulting effects on the person are quite profound. Almost overnight, they have a massive spiritual awakening. Everything about how they think, act, and feel suddenly changes. Everything becomes fresh and new, and the problems that once seemed so insurmountable in their lives suddenly become easy to fix. As I was reading this, it occurred to me that I might also have an extraterrestrial soul. However, in my case, it seemed that I had always been this way, not that I had traded a less advanced soul for a more highly advanced one after a series of deeply upsetting events.

Just as I was having the thought that I might be an ET soul, Yumi sat up in bed, opened her eyes, looked right at me, said something to me in Japanese, and then fell back asleep. This was incredibly bizarre and actually did scare me at first. I wrote down what she said, phonetically. It was a word I did not recognize, followed by the word *wa*, which translated as "aren't you." I asked her to translate it the next morning. She had to get her dictionary to find the matching word in English, and did not remember the event from the night before. The two words translated as "You're shining, aren't you?" I had to ask myself if some spiritual force had come through her while she was sleeping to tell me that I was actually glowing with light on a spiritual level, as I read this book and thought about being an ET soul. This was quite the synchronicity, and it also seemed to suggest that I might indeed have an extraterrestrial or angelic soul, in a way that most people on Earth do not have. It would certainly explain why I always felt like such an outcast.

On another occasion, Yumi got up in bed and appeared to be holding something in her hands, rubbing it as if to show me that it was wonderful. In Japanese, she said, *"Kon no waraji ro katandakedo,"* and I quickly wrote it down, not knowing what it meant. Then she looked around the room and her eyes widened, as if the room itself was extremely bizarre and mystifying to her—quite unlike the traditional Japanese architecture she may have been expecting. Suddenly, a force seemed to come over her and cause her to immediately fall asleep. Her eyes closed and she sank back onto the bed, as if some invisible being was gently guiding her back down.

The next morning, she translated it for me. The phrase was "Look at these new sandals I just bought." However, the word she used for "sandals" was *waraji*. This was a traditional wooden Japanese sandal that she would never have bought in this lifetime. We both wondered if we had some past life together. This was further enhanced by another night when she talked in her sleep, patted me on the leg, and called me Obakun. In English, this would be a cute and loving way of calling me Mr. Oba, which clearly was not my name. The old man in my dreams had appeared as Obi-Wan Kenobi throughout my childhood after I saw *Star Wars* in 1977. *Obakun* was phonetically similar to *Obi Ken*. Perhaps her Higher Self was tapping into that name somehow, and her soul was saying that I was now on my own Jedi-type path of sorts.

Shamanic Initiation

Yumi and I started having serious problems in our relationship early on, and before too long, we were having fights on a regular basis. I was never sure of whether we were going to stay together, or what I needed to do to make her happy. My body started falling apart with pain and illness. I soon realized that when she said she loved me, it meant something very different than it did when I said it. I developed crippling back pain from all the stress, but was still functioning.

At this point, in early December 1994, our jazz department hosted a concert on the stage in the Old Main building, and I took Yumi to see it. This was a collaborative effort between a psychedelic jazz saxophone player and a female Tuvan throat-singing shaman, who was wearing her traditional shamanic clothes. I sat there with Yumi in the front row as the shaman created a low, growling bass tone and simultaneously made high-pitched, whistle-like sounds. I was impressed with the sound system, for at times you could hear her voice coming in from the back of the auditorium and not the front. However, when I finally turned to look for the speakers in the back, there were none. She was somehow "throwing her voice" off the back of the auditorium like a cosmic ventriloquist.

At that point, I decided to close my eyes, go deep, and meditate. This shaman seemed like the real deal, and I wanted to try to tap into whatever domains of consciousness she might have been accessing. My breathing became deep and regular. I was counting my heartbeats and using a technique I had read about in a book on Hindu meditation— *Autobiography of a Yogi* by Paramahansa Yogananda. I was breathing in for six beats, holding for three, exhaling for six and holding it out for three. I did this for several cycles with my eyes fully closed, and soon the woman's voice was taking me to a very, very deep level of transcendence. I felt the sounds she was generating were vibrating my entire body to its very core. The period between exhaling and holding the air out of my lungs for three additional heartbeats was very long. I had just done this again and was about to breathe in again after the third heartbeat.

Suddenly, I had some kind of extremely intense chest spasm. I could not inhale. My entire chest seized up and I had no oxygen. My eyes stayed closed. I was deeply terrified for just a split second, and then suddenly something utterly bizarre happened. I found myself transported into some other realm. It appeared that I was somewhere out in space, surrounded by stars. I felt perfectly comfortable—neither cold nor hot.

In front of me was a beautiful light phenomenon. It was somewhat like a nebula and somewhat like a galaxy, but mostly spherical in shape. It was bright white in the middle, followed by a starry layer of yellow, then orange, then red on the edges. It looked like it was made of a series of concentric spiral galaxies that were tilted at different angles, like the traditional view of the electron orbits in an atom, but in a spherical shape.

The feeling I had as I saw this mass of light was one of indescribable joy. It was as if I had access to all knowledge in the universe, instantaneously. It all seemed to be emanating from the white light in the center of the formation. I could get any answer to any question just by thinking about it. At the same time, none of it even seemed to matter. There was just an incredible feeling of warmth, comfort, familiarity, and belongingness. It was Home—like a warm fireplace in a beautiful cabin with the one you love—but it was far stronger than anything I'd ever felt before. I was in sheer, rapturous religious ecstasy for what seemed like an eternity, and yet I somehow knew I wasn't there for very long. It is very difficult to assign words to an experience like this.

Before I left, I realized that I should take something back with me. I asked three specific questions about my life and instantaneously got the answers. One was whether or not I should stay together with Yumi. The immediate answer was that I already knew we were not compatible and we would soon go our separate ways. I then asked if I would be able to have a career in the UFO field, and the answer was a definite yes. Everything in my life was already steering me in that direction and I should learn to trust my feelings. Last, I asked if my work was also going to involve some sort of spiritual teaching and helping people heal and evolve. I had an incredible rushing sensation of wonder, and was told that this was the most important part of my journey—the true reason for why I was here.

Once I got the answers to my three questions, I knew I could return to my body and pull out of the experience. I decided that I wanted to breathe, and in that moment my body allowed my lungs to take in a huge gasp. My eyes and my mouth shot wide open. At this point, I truly had one of the greatest shocks of my life. The woman had moved on the stage and was now standing in front of me, about eight feet away. As soon as my eyes opened, I was looking right at her—and she was looking right at me. She did not break eye contact. This was definitely not my imagination. I was in complete shock. She then bowed to me and gave me a huge, knowing smile, maintaining full eye contact the entire time. In that moment, I absolutely knew, beyond any shadow of a doubt, that she had somehow catapulted me into this shamanic realm. I had read about shamans and yogis being able to create spontaneous bursts of religious ecstasy known as "darshan," but until that moment, I had never experienced it myself.

The Final Break

My back pain kept getting worse. One day in the food court, I arched my back over the chair and tried to get it to pop. I did get a loud crack, but I immediately realized that I had just made it much worse. After this happened, I could not stand up straight without searing pain. I had already gotten a spiritual message saying that my relationship would end, but I did not have the strength to actually break up with Yumi. Artie stopped by the room after I injured my back. I tried to act like everything was fine, but every time I tried to move, I cried out in pain. Artie ended up insisting that I go to the campus health center, and they in turn sent me to the emergency room at Vassar Hospital. The X-ray, thankfully, did not show anything wrong with my spine. I was prescribed codeine and muscle relaxers for the pain. This was the first time I had ever taken mind-altering pain medication in the two years since I had gotten sober, but I felt I had no choice. The drugs and physical stress weakened my immune system enough that I soon developed a bad case of mononucleosis—with extreme flu symptoms—right during finals. I ended up having to take my tests late because of pain and the effects of medication.

I went back home to my mother's house for Christmas, while Yumi returned to Japan and enjoyed a graduation ceremony where she reunited with all her friends from high school. I had a miserable dream; I kept being attacked by very long worms. I had to grab them, rip them off my body, and throw them away from me. I could see this was dramatizing my body's fight against the virus. I was barely recovered from this illness when I returned to college in January. Yumi immediately went into a huge depression from having seen her friends and then losing contact with all of them again. Day after day, she kept telling me she wanted to go back to Japan, and she obviously wasn't happy with me. Nothing I could say or do seemed to get her out of this, and I felt miserable.

However, Yumi also brought back one particularly remarkable prophecy from Japan. While visiting her relatives, Yumi showed a picture of me to her family psychic, a renowned Shinto priestess. This woman was very famous for her psychic accuracy, which went far beyond the capabilities of the average intuitive. It wasn't at all uncommon for people to be reduced to tears as the priestess told them things she could not possibly have known from any conscious level. Normally, it was far too expensive and her schedule was much too busy to see this woman more than once a year, but Yumi's parents had formed a unique bond with her that was unlike that of any other clients. Yumi had given the priestess three different cities where she could go to school, and the priestess was the one who said it was very important that she go to New Paltz, New York. The priestess had already told Yumi that she had "the gift" if she wanted to develop it, and that she could become just as powerful a psychic as the priestess was. I told Yumi that she would be crazy not to study with this woman and learn everything she could, but Yumi was afraid of the whole thing.

When Yumi reunited with the priestess that winter, she showed her a Polaroid of the two of us together. The priestess took one look at my face in the picture and said, "This man is going to become very famous. Spiritual leader. Very famous spiritual leader." This was a fascinating prophecy, but I had obviously no way of knowing if it was true. It did fit precisely with the guidance I had heard in my shamanic visionary experience from the Tuvan throat singer, though I had never told Yumi about any of the specifics of that experience. I published this prophecy in a book I put on my website back in 1999, entitled *Wanderer Awakening*, when I was first getting started online and was not at all recognized. I obviously had no way of knowing at the time if I would become a famous spiritual leader, but now it is clear that my work has reached and influenced millions of people.

The priestess also gave Yumi a two-inch-wide, very finely woven gold wafer that was sealed inside a protective layer of clear laminated plastic, and asked her to give it to me. It had a large equilateral triangle in it, and the triangle had a treelike trunk down the middle, with a series of about twenty straight-lined, perfectly horizontal branches that extended to the edges of the triangle on the way up. The priestess indicated that this gold object would help me reach my ultimate spiritual destiny more quickly. I had never had any gold before and carried it with me at all times until Yumi returned to Japan.

In the midst of all this pain and sickness, I thought back to the experience that the Tuvan shaman had given me just a couple of months before. I had written down my dreams after I first got sober in October 1992, and then had stopped practicing by the beginning of 1993, as I became completely obsessed with UFO research. I had another brief burst of dream work in the summer of 1993, and then again became totally involved with my UFO research. Now in early 1995, I felt that I had truly hit rock bottom. I needed to start remembering my dreams again and really commit to the practice. As it turned out, the very first dream I was able to recall after getting a notebook and a pen and leaving it next to my bed was quite surprising.

Now Stop Murdering

The date was January 30, 1995. At the time, I was happy to blame Yumi for everything that was going wrong in our relationship. In my dream, she had been murdered. As I said in the dream analysis chapter, you always want to begin by seeing every character as some part of yourself. In this case, Yumi could represent my feminine side. The murder could easily represent how my own sensitive, caring, emotional, and feeling side was going through incredible pain and loss by all the fighting I was experiencing. If you have murders in your dreams, you always want to begin by looking at how you may be sabotaging yourself and your relationships by doing things you may well be able to prevent.

In a strange dreamlike way, Yumi had actually been murdered two different times, in two different locations. In this dream, I was one of the key investigators visiting the crime scenes and trying to piece together exactly what had happened. There were various areas to explore that led up to the final crime scenes themselves, and I went through each one of them with intense scrutiny. Much to my surprise and terror, in every crime scene I found evidence suggesting that I had been there myself. In fact, as I continued doing this research, I was the only person who could be connected to every crime scene. By the end of the dream, I was convinced I must have been the one who had murdered Yumi, even though I had no conscious memory whatsoever of doing it. I certainly did not want to tell my fellow investigators about this; I knew I would be immediately arrested and imprisoned. The whole experience was extremely disturbing as I woke up and wrote it down. Again, in dream analysis terms, you could read this as being a clear indication that I was the one causing my inner feminine self to be "murdered," by disavowing the Tuvan shaman's guidance and continuing to stay in an unhappy relationship.

Yumi and I were having a very rough second semester together, with never more than two or three days without a major fight. She became very jealous and did not want me to have any other friends. I found myself curled up in a fetal position in bed and crying when I had a chance to be alone. My dreams were consistently telling me that I needed to get out. I also had now been sober for two and a half years, and the guys in the room immediately next to me were severe alcoholics. One night, not long after the dream in which I murdered Yumi, I heard glass smash in the room next to me. Everything then got frighteningly quiet. They turned off the loud music and no one was talking above a murmur.

Not long afterward, I went into our common dorm bathroom. My long-haired rock-and-roller neighbor was covered in blood, and very wasted. His long-haired friend had a stark white T-shirt that was also grotesquely covered with blood. The friend was being aggressive and bullying toward me, using lots of profanity to ask me what my problem was, telling me to get the hell out of there, not to tell anyone anything, and that I didn't see anything. I was so shocked by the whole thing that I did what he said, turned around and returned to my room. I found out later that my neighbor had smashed a beer bottle against the wall and cut his hand open. Someone finally called the police as they tried to stagger around outside, covered in blood, and he was taken to the hospital. For me, this was another very strong negative synchronicity, showing me that I had an aura of violence and extreme pain around me in this relationship—and I felt there was nothing I could do about it. I couldn't help but feel that this real-world synchronicity had dramatically high-lighted the dream in which I murdered Yumi—but I had no idea why.

Two years later, in 1997, after I started doing Edgar Cayce–style readings under hypnosis by a trained regression therapist, I had another dream about Yumi. This was connected to my dream about murdering her that I'd had two years prior. In the original dream, I had no recol-lection of killing her, but this dream allowed me to remember murdering Yumi. In this "memory," she had been a man living in rural Japan and I had been a woman. I was getting repeatedly violated by him after he would come back from long fishing trips, reeking of fish. Eventually, in distress, I got some poison from an old woman in town and put it in the soy sauce for his rice after he came home, reeling drunk on sake. The woman said his death would be peaceful, but in fact he fell to the ground in violent convulsions, with foam coming out of his mouth. It was abso-lutely horrific. I ran out the door into the night, terrified and trauma-tized, with bare feet. It was pouring rain and there was a powerful wind. I ran blindly across a footbridge that connected our mountaintop to another nearby mountain, stretching across a deep, rocky chasm. My foot slipped on the rain-saturated bridge and I plunged to my death in a sickening fall.

Before I ever hit the ground, I felt myself move from falling to rising. Everything went completely dark, and I again saw this same group of light beings who I now knew had always been with me, lifetime after lifetime. We laughed and joked about what had just happened, and I said, "I guess I really screwed up that time." This type of gallows humor, even in the face of seemingly terrible events, is a common element reported by people who have had near-death experiences. There is great compassion and understanding for the human experience in the afterlife, even in its most difficult and violent aspects.

In another dream from January 31, 1997, before I had the regression experience, I saw myself as an Asian woman. This dream happened shortly after I had broken up with Yumi on the telephone, and it was admittedly a messy breakup. My roommate Eric was not at all happy with me for how I had handled it, but I felt like I needed to be tough. In the dream, I was smelling a bottle of soy sauce and then was repelled by it, as if there was clearly a dangerous chemical added to the brew that did not smell good at all. Immediately after dictating this strange dream, I did a psychic reading where an entire sentence fragment came through that was almost all in Japanese, except the words *no good*. I did my best to speak the syllables I was hearing, having no idea whether they would mean anything. What I wrote down was *"Yatsu wo ogoshi—no good. Mo yame koroshi."* I needed to have my housemate's Japanese girlfriend Yuriko translate what I had heard. The translated phrase read, "Threatening him—no good. Now stop murdering." This was one of the most shocking things that had ever happened to me at the time. Surprisingly, I had been able to listen to the Japanese clearly enough that I had made only one minor mistake in translating what I was hearing into written, phonetic syllables.

Once I obtained the translation, I was dazzled and terrified at the same time. I did not know the words *threatening* or *murdering* in Japanese, and yet my own voice had spoken both of them. In this case, I believe this was obtained psychically, not through having experienced a clandestine program, as may have been the case with Artie. It clearly seemed this was not a typical dream but was helping me to recall an actual past-life memory, where I, as a woman, had poisoned my husband and then fallen from a bridge in the rain. Once I went through the hypnotic regression, I realized that this explained why I had so many dreams as a child in which I would be driving across a bridge in a car and suddenly plunge to my death. It also helped to explain why I had such a dreadful fear of rainstorms, as if getting caught in one of them could easily kill me.

This is one of many examples where dreams can be multidimensional. My original notebook-written dream from January 30, 1995, did feature me murdering Yumi, not once but twice. It is interesting to note that the original dream and the follow-up dream in 1997 were precisely two years and one day apart, on January 30, 1995, and January 31, 1997, and I did not notice this until putting this book together. In terms of analyzing the original 1995 notebook dream, you always want to begin by reading the dream as a metaphor of your current psychological and spiritual issues. Once you go through that level of analysis, you can look to see if the dream is talking about other people you know. Then you might find additional levels of meaning, including the idea that you are actually getting an accurate memory of past-life events.

My relationship with Yumi was apparently an example of past-life karma that needed to be balanced in the present. We had to get back together in a future lifetime, have a similarly dysfunctional relationship, and this time make better choices. My dream from January 30, 1995, had predicted that I would discover I had murdered Yumi—somehow, some way, at some time. As it turned out, I did not "get away" with murdering my spouse in another lifetime. I had to come back and redo the entire experience without an upsetting ending.

This is a very common element within reincarnation research. The people who are closest to us are almost never "new." We have a backstory with them that directly affects what is happening to us now, and our dreams can occasionally give us a precise view of what had happened in the past. In this case, I was lucky enough to have an entire sentence come through in Japanese that explained to me that this was not just a dream but an accurate retelling of a past-life event. If I hadn't had such a stunning event—telepathically bringing in words from a language I did not speak—I would probably have never believed that Yumi and I had had a past life together. I eventually reconnected with her on a tour of Japan in 2002, and apologized to her for murdering her in another lifetime. She just laughed and told me it was okay and that she had a very happy life now.

Dreams of Future Success in the UFO Field

After the upsetting dream in which I had apparently murdered Yumi, I decided to commit to writing down my dreams every morning, and I have done so ever since. The second dream from February 1, 1995, ended up being prophetic. In the notebook, I wrote, "Dad was clearly in a time of crisis. He was talking to someone on the phone and was essentially bargaining, trying to get a sum of money on some type of insurance-based loan. I couldn't believe that Dad had no money at all, and was surviving by taking a perilous loan." I found out later that my father had lost his main paying job as the host of a radio show, and was indeed thrown into a deep financial crisis. At the time the dream came, I had no conscious knowledge of this.

Just five days later, on February 6, 1995, I had a very epic, complex, and multifaceted prophetic dream. I found myself returning to a large suburban house over and over again. Each time I would run up the stairs and into the bathroom, and then make a precipitous jump through the bathroom window to a ledge on the other side. I could easily fall to my death each time I was doing this. Even though it was highly dangerous, for some reason I felt compelled to keep doing it over and over again. Bathrooms in dreams represent toxicity in your life that is usually not being healed. Jumping through the bathroom window therefore meant I was repeating the same unpleasant experiences with Yumi over and over again, without learning from them. The jumping metaphor ultimately also seemed to have a past-life connection, where I was replaying the experience of falling off of the footbridge across the chasm in my tragic past-life experience. In this case, the dream was showing me that I had to keep reliving the experience of having upsetting fights with Yumi without a terrible ending.

After about four times of running through the bathroom like this in the dream, I realized I might be better off if I stopped repeating the same behavior. Instead of going through the bathroom again and again, I might want to explore the rest of the house. That way, I might be able to get to the other side without having to make the same dangerous jump each time. Just as I was about to run up the stairs again, I decided to stop and walk into the living room. This was a great surprise to the young African American girl who had been watching me run through this obstacle course each time. As I said earlier, people of other races tend to represent extraterrestrials or angelic forces, so in this case the girl represented some aspect of my Higher Self that wanted to help me break this unfortunate and repetitive pattern. Now, in dream-metaphor terms, since I was writing down my dreams again, I had finally taken an interest in what my soul had to say.

"Hi, I'm David Wilcock," I said to the girl, slightly out of breath. "Do you mind if I take a look around?" She said, "No, that's okay, David. In fact, we've been expecting to see you for quite some time." I was puzzled. "What do you mean by that?" She responded, "Well, I'm really not supposed to say anything about this, but the extraterrestrials are working here right now to build up this house, and they know that you're here." I replied, "Come on, give me a break. You're telling me that there are extraterrestrials in this house right now?" She answered, "Yes, David, there are. If you walk over into the far hall to the left, you just might see them while they are working." My response was "This is too outrageous to believe. I'm going to go over and take a look for myself." Here, in symbolic terms, this dream was clearly talking about my love of UFO research. I had gotten into such a dark place with Yumi that I had stopped reading my UFO books. The dream was clearly encouraging me to keep reading them—even if I had to fight for it.

As the dream went on, I walked down the hallway and took a left as the girl had suggested. I do not interpret the left turn as anything negative. You have to consider the context of each dream to decide whether or not the direction you are traveling has a particular meaning. The only possible connotation for the left turn, in this case, was that my girlfriend at the time considered it a negative if I was doing UFO research. At that point in the dream, I went down another long corridor. At the end of the corridor was a waist-high barricade, and I stepped over it. Going into an adjoining, unfinished room, I looked out what was going to become a window later on. There, to my surprise and amazement, were about eight Gray-style extraterrestrials, all doing construction work on this house!

They seemed to be bathed in a brilliant, deep-blue light, and their skin was also somewhat blue. As I said in chapter 3, "Dream Analysis 101," indigo is a great sign in dreams, for it means your psychic abilities are activating. The ETs were erecting a massive chandelier in the room as well as several other fancy touches, like a black-marble bathroom with gold fixtures. It was quite stunning to watch them work.

Twenty years later, in 2015, I discovered that my friend and insider Corey Goode had heard about a group of blue-skinned, Gray-style extraterrestrials who had met with President Eisenhower in the 1950s. The secret government programs called these particular beings "the Blues." Apparently, these ETs had offered Eisenhower a deal: If we agreed to stop all development of nuclear weapons and to destroy our stockpiles, we would be given amazing technologies that would transform life on Earth as we knew it, end poverty, disease, and hunger, and save the planet. The only other terms of the deal were that we would have to create a global spiritual education process, bringing in new scientific concepts to inform the people of Earth that all religions were different perspectives on one common, universal truth.

Some people might think this is a dangerous "globalist" agenda, however I do feel that we all need to stop fighting and killing one another over such basic differences of opinion. My scientific work, such as in *The Source Field Investigations* and *The Synchronicity Key*, clearly shows that the universe is indeed alive and conscious—the product of a vastly intelligent design. According to various insider reports, Eisenhower felt we were not ready for this plan, and rejected the offer. It was quite stunning to go back and see that these same ETs had appeared in my dream from 1995, twenty years before I consciously obtained this information. In my dream, the Blues were building quite the gorgeous mansion. Eisenhower's rejection had obviously not stopped them from trying to help us.

In this same dream, I was aware that government personnel were right in the same area and were observing the behavior of these extraterrestrials. I was in great danger by being where I was, seeing what I was seeing. None of the neighbors were supposed to have any idea that extraterrestrials were building something inside this house. And yet, there was another building to my far left, and I noticed that a man was watching the ETs work from inside this place. He was as shocked as I was. Then I watched as men in military fatigues came up behind him with machine guns and ushered him away at gunpoint.

I very quickly left the area, not wanting to be spotted by the agents. The ETs seemed to keep on working regardless of this government presence. Then, after I walked back into the main room, I ran into a woman whom I recognized as a wealthy, prominent friend of my father's, who put on big music events in the Capital District of New York State, in and around Albany. In dream-analysis terms, a prominent authority figure of this type typically represents an angelic extraterrestrial being. The woman and I began talking, and she soon offered me a prominent job at their facility. This obviously meant I might end up working side by side with the same extraterrestrials I had just seen. There was a part of me that really wanted to say yes. I was very excited by the prospect. In symbolic terms, this was my Higher Self telling me I would be making a great decision if I decided to go into UFO research full-time, despite whatever fears I might have about whether I could make a living at it. Clearly, the house the ETs were building was exceptionally beautiful, and I could end up living there if I chose to join their team. The house turned out to look a good deal like some of the hotels where I would regularly participate in UFO conferences many years later.

Even though I had been given such an amazing offer in the dream, I remembered I had made a promise to pick up a female friend of mine in a little red car. Red is the color of sexuality and basic survival. I knew that this woman was Asian, was my girlfriend, and we were in love. She would be very upset with me if I did not meet with her on time, as we had agreed. I forlornly rejected the opportunity to work in the house, and did my best to feel excited about the imminent reunion with my girlfriend. The director woman seemed very disappointed, telling me that they "really needed me" there at the house. In symbolic terms, this was the dream showing me I was consciously allowing my relationship to pull me away from my UFO research, which I was being told was important. The next section of the dream showed me the consequences of this decision—in very brutal terms.

As I prepared to leave the mansion, I noticed that a large television was on in the room. It was showing some sort of horror movie, taking place in a long tunnel fashioned out of cobblestones. Flaming torches were evenly mounted along the walls of this tunnel, about every fifteen feet. In between each set of torches was a decaying body chained by the wrists. As I continued to watch this scene, I suddenly found myself directly projected into it!

I could feel the oppressive heat in the dark tunnel. I could smell the dank, wet, moldy horror of the dungeon and the miserable smoke of the torches. It was as if I was in some sort of hell. At the far end of the tunnel, there was a long-haired male figure, who, like the bodies, was also hanging in chains. He looked remarkably similar to Jesus. I suddenly heard a terrible demonic voice echo through the hallway. "Solomon," the voice cried out. "You realize now that my power has superseded your own. You will do as I say." I turned my head quickly and realized that the evil one was there, cloaked in many small pieces of flowing black cloth. He clutched a scepter in his left hand that was topped with a stylized skeletal claw hand holding a crystal ball. His face could not be seen, but the most prominent feature was his head, a dressed-up horse skull with big horns at the top. This was similar to the villains at the end of the movie *Time Bandits*, which I had watched many times on HBO as a child. The evil one thrust the scepter forward, and the scene shifted back to Solomon.

Now I felt like I was a part of the scenery. I was hovering in front of the chained spiritual figure. Suddenly and without warning, a series of perhaps thirteen thick, two-inch metal bars popped through Solomon's body, causing blood to gush out. It was incredibly graphic. The bars were at all different heights and angles, and they went straight through, causing Solomon to cry and wail pathetically, like a small child. This obviously was a direct metaphor of the crucifixion of Jesus and the wounds on his body from the Spear of Longinus. My Higher Self knew I would have balked at the name of Jesus at the time, so the name Solomon, the wise one, was chosen instead. In this case, the Christ symbolism in the dream refers to the part of each of us that is in alignment with the deepest spiritual mission of our soul.

The horse-headed demon continued teasing and taunting Solomon in my dream. I suddenly realized that I was now supersize, holding this tiny human in my hands and carefully sticking pins through his flesh like a voodoo doll. I was trying to make sure that I did each puncture exactly right—and this meant I was obviously listening to what the demon was telling me to do. As I drove the needles through, I would feel the rush of incredible pain within my own body. I was shocked awake, gasping for breath, with a thought that was more a psychic impression than a physical sentence, but it translated into "You are the one who is stabbing yourself." This was very intense, and I cried as I wrote down the dream. I was very well aware that this had to do with my relationship with Yumi, and my need to stand up for myself. The dream was obviously saying that Yumi's insistence on having all my free time was now standing in the way of my UFO research. For whatever reason, the forces in the dream said they "really needed me."

I took the advice of this dream seriously, and began to insist that I have the time to read my UFO books. I would make time for Yumi, and I certainly did, every day, but I also had to have some time for myself. Shortly thereafter, on February 11, 1995, I had a dream in which people were panning for gold with pans that looked like flying saucers. I picked up one of these pans and started mimicking what the others were doing. Almost immediately, I found two rocks that had intricate-looking clock parts in them. The clock gears were all made out of gold. I felt in the dream that I had made a vitally important historical discovery. This could have been some type of ancient machine, similar to the Rhodes Calculator that I had read about in the first UFO book I ever read after my NASA disclosure—*Our Ancestors Came from Outer Space* by Maurice Chatelain.[1] In that case, a rock had been found on May 7, 1902, by a diver named Elias Stadiatos off the Greek island of Antikythera. The rock had a very advanced mechanical device embedded in it that seemed to track the planetary orbits, and it was able to predict solar and lunar eclipses.[2] The rock was found in an ancient Greek shipwreck, and it had at least twenty gear wheels in it, some of which had machining that was quite advanced. The technology was far more sophisticated than anything the Greeks were believed to have had at the time. The last date fixed on the calculator was 86 BC.[3] It may have actually been a surviving relic from a lost, advanced civilization that was ancient even to the Greeks at the time. I was very excited about discovering a similar archaeological find in my dream.

My First Major Ascension Dream in the Notebooks

As I continued to heed the warnings of my dreams, and got back to work on my UFO research, I had a truly magnificent dream on March 5, 1995. This was less than two months after the great 6.9 earthquake in Kobe, Japan, on January 17, 1995, which obviously alarmed Yumi and her family members. In the dream, I found myself in a large city, and many people were milling around me. What follows is a direct transcript of what I wrote in my notebook at the time:

> Yumi hangs up the phone from talking with her mom or someone, and says to me that her mom is very afraid that there's going to be an earthquake, and she believes it was coming in Japan. She was very restless and uneasy about it, and I felt very strange too, like my body was humming or vibrating very fast. I also had a dizzy, queasy feeling of being off center or off-balance somehow. I walked up to a picture window, which was also like a mirror, and looked into it. To my surprise, I was bathed in very luminescent, magnesium-burning white light—pure, radiant white. And I had a well-developed beard! It was brown and whitish from the light. The look in my eyes was one of intense knowing, and I felt for that moment that I was seeing my future self. Then, I wondered why I had a beard and started to inspect it.

This dream captured a variety of interesting elements that are now commonplace in my work. Once we review the Law of One material and other such works, we will see that the expected time of our mass Ascension is directly correlated with major "Earth changes" such as earthquakes. The vibrating feeling that my body went through in this dream symbolizes the activation that we go through in the Ascension process. I then saw myself suddenly transformed into a Christlike being of light. This is apparently the fulfillment of the promise that Jesus and other great teachers gave us. In works such as the Law of One, we are taught that Jesus was the "way-shower" who would reveal our own path to Ascension. The Cayce Readings called Jesus our Elder Brother who revealed the path that all of us must one day follow. If we don't get the message to be more kind, loving, and in service to others now, we will soon end up having twenty-five thousand more years of reincarnation to figure it out on another planet, as we will discuss later on. And I don't know about you, but I have had enough of the abuse, bullying, sickness, loss, greed, jealousy, betrayal, anger, depression, and sadness of third-density life. If all you have to do is "just be nice" to graduate from this "Earth school," then sign me up.

CHAPTER NINE

Graduation

As I headed toward the end of the semester, I knew I was going to graduate with a bachelor's degree in psychology, as my grades were fine. That being said, I did not want my education to stop. My goal was to continue right along and get a master's or doctorate in something related to metaphysics and spirituality. I felt that an advanced degree would give me greater credibility as a UFO researcher. After surveying a variety of schools, I decided that Naropa Institute in Boulder, Colorado, would be the best possible choice. To apply to this school, I had to write up and print out an admissions letter that explained why I felt I would be a good candidate.

Prophetic Warnings

I had already had a prophetic dream that suggested this plan was not going to work out very well. On March 7, 1995, in my dream I got onto a bus that was going to Colorado. I had to forge through enormous amounts of muddy streams along the way, and it was quite a mess. Once I finally made it to Colorado, I needed to find a phone so I could talk to my family and figure out where I was going to stay. The only phone I could find was covered in mud. These metaphors clearly showed how ungrounded I was at the time. I then walked up to a staircase that I thought would take me where I needed to go. Instead of ascending, I slipped and fell, dropping fifteen feet down. This again seemed to refer back to the apparent past life I eventually remembered having with Yumi, where I had fallen off the footbridge. In this case I was fine, and had not been hurt. Several people came up to see if I would be okay. The dream clearly predicted that I would go through a very rough time by heading out to Colorado, but I was not going to be deterred.

I sat down to write my admissions letter sometime in May 1995 and started to write about all the Earth changes that were visible at that time. Again, Kobe, Japan, had a massive 6.9 earthquake on January 17, 1995, that had caused over a hundred billion dollars in damages, killing six thousand people and making forty-five thousand more homeless.[1] That was just one example that hit close to home, since Yumi was from Japan. It had been a sunny day when I started writing. As I continued describing the ongoing collapse of our society and the incredible problems that we faced as a planet, a storm suddenly appeared, seemingly out of nowhere. Before I even had time to figure out exactly what was happening, a savage wind started wresting the trees, causing them to reel back and forth. The sky darkened. Thunder started booming. Then, rain began cascading down in sheets. The next thing I knew, a huge flash of light appeared at almost the exact same moment that a tremendous bang of thunder exploded outside. Lightning must have struck something right near my dormitory, like a telephone pole. All of a sudden, my computer was dead and the power was out. I lost everything I had been writing, as I had not yet hit SAVE. I had unfortunately forgotten the classic nerd's saying, "He who saves first laughs last."

Once the power came back on, I worked this event right into my new admissions letter to Naropa, and cited it as a positive example of synchronicity. The sudden, violent storm gave synchronistic support to my case about the Earth Changes that were going on, and I reconstructed what I had written from memory. The whole event appeared to be so well timed that I could not ignore the significance of what had happened. I was sure that this was a sign that the institute would want to take me on board. Soon enough, I received a letter telling me that they wanted me to journey out to Colorado for an entrance interview. I would need to make the trip only two weeks after I graduated, which gave me very little time to recover from an extremely difficult year. At the time, I did not see that all the thunder, lightning, and pouring rain, as well as the loss of my written work, was actually a synchronistic warning that this trip to Colorado was not going to go well—at all.

You're Shining

Shortly after this event, as my graduation was looming, my former roommate, Artie, stopped by to chat. Yumi quickly lost interest in my metaphysical talk, and ended up falling asleep in our bed. I went on at great length about the idea of Ascension, which I had now been reading about in books such as the works of Ruth Montgomery and *The Celestine Prophecy* by James Redfield. I was now starting to see that Ascension was the grand focal point that all my research was pointing me toward. I was also speaking to Artie about the significance of benevolent, angelic extraterrestrials in this process, and how everything fit together into the "big picture" that I was now building. It was an exciting conversation, and Artie was totally fascinated. Suddenly, Yumi sat up in bed again, while obviously still fast asleep. Slowly and deliberately, in a deep trance, her head turned toward Artie and me.

By now, I was used to this, but Artie was obviously scared to death. Yumi then began to speak. "Shining, wa?" she asked, looking directly at me. She gave me a very interesting and ironic smile that was almost exactly the same as the one I had seen on the Tuvan priestess after I gasped for breath and opened my eyes. Then, just as suddenly, something seemed to "turn her off," and she collapsed back onto the bed. Artie looked at me with wide eyes and a big, goofy smile, for he had no idea what in the world was going on—and he was clearly nervous. "Yep, that's one of the things that happens," I told Artie. "Some force has been using Yumi to give me messages. Tomorrow she won't remember a thing. This is obviously another Ascension message. I believe some part of her is saying that we are glowing with light on a spiritual level right now—just like we might end up doing one day if we are lucky enough to Ascend."

In that moment, I realized that Yumi's conscious mind now knew the English word for "shining," so she didn't have to say it in Japanese this time. I explained to Artie that in the past, Yumi had said the word for "shining" in Japanese. It seemed quite obvious that, once again, Yumi's Higher Self had been able to temporarily speak through her physical body to give us an important, timely message. I was clearly being shown that the Ascension message I was starting to think about was indeed something very, very important for me to study. This was another bold and bizarre prophecy telling me that Ascension was real.

When I received my diploma onstage soon afterward, I was anxious. In all honesty, I was terrified. I did not want to leave college, but I knew my parents would have been extremely upset with me if I had taken an extra year to finish. If I didn't go to graduate school, I would have to enter the working world, and nothing was more terrifying to me than that. Everyone knew that a bachelor's degree in psychology was not very useful unless you went on to get a master's or a doctorate. I knew I would end up living in extreme poverty and lose most of the freedom I had enjoyed in college life. No good jobs were available in New York State for anyone who graduated with only a bachelor's degree in psychology.

Yumi drove back with me to my family home and stayed with me for about a week after graduation. On the second to last day that Yumi was in our house, I had an absolutely spectacular lucid dream, which I deliberately induced myself using Dr. Stephen LaBerge's MILD technique. In this dream, I found myself back in New Paltz. I was effortlessly flying around the campus, to the wonderment of others who watched me. I was so excited about what was happening that I tried to take notes, not realizing that the notepad was part of the dream too, and that I would not be able to bring it back with me when I awoke. As I tried to write down my experiences, I looked at the page. To my amazement, all of my thoughts, which were in English, were once again written in French! Furthermore, as before, I could tell they were accurate sentences, even though I myself would not have been able to put them together. It was an amazing, stunning, and eminently gratifying experience, and mirrored the lucid dream I discussed earlier.

The Prophet

On the day Yumi left, I walked down into the basement after her yellow taxi had pulled away, and I began sobbing. I was deeply saddened by the fact that we had never really been able to get along, and I knew our relationship was about to end. She had wanted me to wait three years for her to come back, but I knew we needed to break up. It would be easier to do so once she was back in her home country and we could both meet some new people. Instinctively and without even thinking, I walked over to the same paperback library under the stairs where I had found Harold Sherman's *How to Make ESP Work for You* and two other books on hypnosis when I was only seven years old. I blindly reached out and grabbed *The Prophet* by Kahlil Gibran, sat down, and started reading it.[2] I had never read it before and knew nothing about it except that it was considered a classic.

With tears still streaming down my face, I noticed that the opening scene in this book featured a prophet who had finally come of age, and was being called by God to leave his hometown. At first, I didn't realize how significant this was, but as I kept reading, I figured out that I was having another major synchronicity. The spiritual forces wanted me to realize that the character in *The Prophet* was a metaphor for myself, as well as my own imminent departure for Naropa in Boulder, Colorado, in a few days' time. In the book, the Prophet's departure ship had just arrived in the port, and the entire village was crying along with him. Given that I was still crying as I read this, and Yumi had just left me in her own vehicle, it was a most powerful experience. Before the Prophet was to leave his friends and family for the last time, they asked him if he would give them some final parting words of wisdom.

From this point forward, each chapter of the book is the Prophet's response to their questions. I was particularly inspired by the passage where the Prophet describes love as the force that grinds the "grain" of your soul in order to make "bread." He talked of the incredible work and sacrifice that went into a relationship, and I had just lived it. By this point, the synchronicity was so overpowering that I continued sobbing openly as I read the words. Thankfully, no one else was home at the time. It was so odd that I was guided to read this for the first time as Yumi had just left, and I myself, "the Prophet," was about to head off in a ship to my "place of calling," Naropa Institute in Boulder, Colorado.

I didn't consider myself a prophet at the time, so the whole thing was a mysterious but obviously meaningful synchronicity. Three years later, I would meet up with a spiritual friend in Virginia Beach who owned a farm, and he told me that *The Prophet* was seen by many spiritual scholars to be an Ascension book. The ship that the Prophet was set to board was a metaphor for Ascension and leaving the third-density world entirely.

The Train to Naropa

Naropa Institute was founded by Chogyam Trungpa Rinpoche, a lama who had moved to Boulder from Tibet. Before I would learn whether I had been accepted or rejected, I needed to travel out to the institute to undergo my entrance interview.

At this point in my life, I had never owned a working car. I had only ridden on a plane once as a child, when we went to Disney World. Both of my parents were horribly sick before we left on the Disney trip, almost to the point of deathly illness, but they decided to take us anyway. On that same flight, my brother ended up screaming and crying from the pressure in his ears as we landed—so the idea of flying freaked me out. I had always used the Adirondack Trailways bus to get to college, unless I was lucky enough to get a car ride. For some crazy reason, I decided that the best way to get to Colorado would be to take the Amtrak train from Schenectady, New York, all the way to Denver, in the normal coach class. Then I would travel the final leg of the trip by bus from Denver to Boulder. At this time in my life, every dollar was precious, and this was at least a hundred dollars less expensive than the cheapest flights I could have booked.

On the very first night, I realized that the train was a horrible idea. My dream prophecy of going through rivers and rivers of mud was already coming true. It was nearly impossible to sleep in a normal coach seat. The train was constantly swaying back and forth and making all sorts of loud and irritating noises—clanging, screeching, thumping, rattling, and chugging. People were constantly opening and closing the mechanical doors between the cars, and each time they hit the button, the door would make a huge noise. I had no earplugs to block the sound, so sleep was nearly impossible to achieve.

If I was lucky, I might nod off for an hour or two in the dark, but never for very long. Then I would try to act like a normal person during the day. I spent most of my time talking to Amish people, who also refused to use airplanes and were very down-to-earth, open, and receptive to the things I liked to talk about. I also enjoyed the views as we chugged on through the heartland of America, but I was consistently surprised by how many broken-down and blown-out buildings I saw along the railroad tracks. It didn't take long to realize that once the money is pulled out of something in our society—once it no longer makes a profit—it just sits there and slowly rots away. The railroad used to be a vibrant business, but now the entire industry was on life support—and more often than not, shocking signs of that decay would zip past me again and again.

The Watchers

I also brought one book with me to read on the journey—*The Watchers* by Raymond Fowler, which explored the classic Betty Andreasson abduction case. Fowler dedicated much of his life to researching this one story, but most of the UFO community wouldn't touch it because of its spiritual overtones. At the time, I did not realize how significant the Andreasson material would become for me; there is an entire chapter dedicated to the subject of the Watchers later on in this book.

Betty Andreasson's contactee information did feature typical Grays, and just as was revealed by the work of Harvard psychiatrist Dr. John Mack, these Grays were not at all evil, though other types of Grays definitely can be. On page 202 of the paperback edition, Betty was told that these ETs call themselves the Watchers. They explained that they are responsible for taking care of the Earth. They claimed to feel a love for the Earth that is constant, and lasts forever. They have supposedly been storing the genetic seed of humans from Earth for hundreds and hundreds of years, as well as every species and gender of plant for the same length of time. That way, if anything were ever to happen to us, the seed of human life on this planet would not be lost.

I admittedly wasn't convinced by this material at first. The Grays certainly had a bad reputation in UFOlogy, outside of John Mack's book. Betty's initial contact experience was in 1967, and her memory of this was later retrieved in hypnosis and written into Fowler's first book, *The Andreasson Affair*, which was published in 1979. In this contact, Betty and everyone else in her family were wide awake when the ETs arrived, although, like Betty, their memories were wiped, and recovered only with hypnosis. Betty's father watched the Grays walk right through their door as if it was made of air, on into the kitchen. In an early hypnotic session from 1978, Betty Andreasson seemed to be listening to words in her head and speaking them out loud. The words remained untranslated for several years until researcher Leonard Keane discovered that they were spoken in Gaelic, which is the native language of Ireland. The likelihood that Betty could have faked this is nearly impossible, since she was fully hypnotized and did not have any way of looking at reference material. The first two sentences of the translation were given in the introduction of *The Watchers*.[3] The full translation by Leonard Keane reads as follows. I find that it sounds surprisingly similar to the classic "quatrains" from Nostradamus, which seem to have eerily accurate future prophecies embedded within them:

> The living descendants of the Northern peoples are groping in universal darkness. Their (My) mother mourns. A dark occasion forebodes when weakness in high places will revive a high cost of living; an interval of mistakes in high places; an interval fit for distressing events.[4]

This is a very clear indication that Caucasians—the living descendants of the Northern peoples—are almost completely deactivated spiritually in the modern world, as are most other peoples. As a result, many of us wander in what these ETs consider to be an impenetrable spiritual darkness. The "mother" here obviously refers to our own mother Earth mourning this sad turn in our society. The prophecy goes on to say that the cost of living will become very high due to "weakness" and "mistakes in high places." This message came through in 1978 and was first published in *Transformation* by Whitley Strieber in 1988. It is certainly far more accurate now than it was at the time it was originally spoken, particularly since the so-called Great Recession in the aftermath of the 2008 economic collapse.

Another surprise for me in *The Watchers* was that what we think of as allegedly extraterrestrial Grays could actually be grown from our own human DNA. Fowler's research revealed that if an ordinary human fetus were grown to adulthood outside the womb, and retained its form along the way, it would look just like a typical Gray ET. According to Raymond Fowler, the medical name for this phenomenon, if we were able to achieve it, would be a "neonate." Without the pressure of the womb, the larger eyes and head of the fetal form would remain larger in proportion to the body, which would be thin. As the countryside rolled by for hours and hours, my mind was brimming with ideas about how the Grays might not be extraterrestrials at all. Some part of our own military-industrial complex could be growing them in laboratories to be used in ships that we ourselves are building. This is exactly what Dr. Steven Greer, a prominent UFOlogist, heard from his own insiders.

The Big Interview

To save money while I was in Colorado, I had booked a room at the Boulder Youth Hostel, and it was quite a scene. The shower curtain had thick, gray mold on it that kicked off an overpowering smell. Thankfully, I could go outside and find all sorts of interesting and funky businesses, places to have a nice breakfast, a healthy dinner, et cetera. I went to Naropa for my entrance interview and became friends with two other students applying there—a down-to-earth hippie girl named Meredith and a long-haired athletic guy named Carl. The staff showed us around the campus and everything looked very nice. They had a series of rooms for students to meditate in, with each room lit in one of the seven colors of the rainbow—red, orange, yellow, green, blue, indigo, and violet. There was a specific yoga posture they wanted you to hold in each room as you meditated.

In my interview, the admissions officer asked me if I had a daily meditation practice. I knew from their literature that they considered this a requirement for anyone who was applying. I cannot remember whether the minimum standard of time they wanted you to meditate each day was a half hour or an hour. They wanted you to do a sitting meditation every day, where you did nothing but sit in a contemplative state with your eyes closed. This was never my preferred style of meditation. I knew there were two different major types of meditation, contemplative and concentrative. In concentrative meditation, you intensely focus on one thing for prolonged periods, and this is what I was doing as I went through my research while I was apparently "shining" on the soul level. Some people cannot sit with a book or in front of a computer for more than an hour or so, whereas I could stay focused for many hours at a time without even moving. Concentrative meditation was my specialty, whether I would be remembering, writing, and analyzing my dreams, or studying and analyzing the contents of a book for hours on end. Each dream write-up took me about a half hour to complete. I did not want to lie to them, and I was very honest about how I meditated in my own way.

In my admission letter, I had already sent a list of about three hundred books I had read on UFOs and other paranormal topics during college, and also presented a fresh copy of the list when I arrived. I challenged the admissions officer to name any book on that list, and I would immediately give him a summary of the book's contents and how it related to what I hoped to learn from getting my degree at Naropa. My biggest goal at the time was developing the hyperdimensional physics model, linking it to spirituality, and exploring the role that extraterrestrials might be playing in human evolution and Ascension. I felt I could get to the answer by integrating this vast body of research materials. The only real sign of trouble I had in the interview, other than perhaps being too honest about the exact nature of my meditation practice, was that the officer never bothered to answer my challenge. I had put several hours into compiling the list, all from memory, and I knew I could give him an impressive report on any of those books. He had zero interest in accepting my offer and seemed to be mildly insulted when I again tried to convince him to "take the challenge."

We also talked with honesty about how I would pay for the education. I was very lucky in that my paternal grandfather had pledged full financial support for my tuition to go to graduate school. Papa wasn't thrilled about my education coming from a metaphysical institute, but he felt that any advanced degree was better than nothing. I told the officer how Papa had graduated top of his class at Harvard, that he had filed over eighty engineering patents, and that there was more than enough money there for him to pay for me to get this degree. I also explained how Papa's own father, Frederick, had designed and engineered tunnels all throughout the underground areas of New York City to build the initial east side of the subway system. I said I would be happy to work a regular job, if need be, to earn spending money if my grandfather didn't give me enough to cover my basic living expenses, but I expected that he would. However, I did not go in there with anything like a signed affidavit from Papa, confirming that he had actually agreed to pay for this. My mother and father's own financial situation was far too rough for them to be able to help me with so much as a single dollar, which I had been required to confirm with paperwork as part of the application process.

I had brought a quartz crystal along with me on the trip to Denver, one that I had been carrying around since I was in high school. This crystal had fallen and cracked in half while I was taking a shower after my single worst fight with Yumi, near the end of the second semester in my senior year. At the time, this felt like an obvious synchronicity showing me how my own heart was breaking. Oddly enough, the crystal had cracked along an interesting, wavy surface that now made it look like a rippling wave of water. This wavy surface was apparently showing me the original trace of the crystal's growth while it was being formed. I went up into the beautiful Flatirons with Meredith and Carl, who by this point had already fallen into a whirlwind romantic relationship. This was the most beautiful view I had ever seen in my entire life until then. As I looked out over the stunning vista, I had the strong urge to throw the crystal into the forest and release that part of my life—the pain and the broken heart—forever. I believed I had actually done it at the time, and part of the proof was that the crystal had gone completely missing afterward. Little did I realize that I would find the crystal again at an auspicious future moment, two and a half years later—setting up another profound synchronicity.

Carl encouraged me to get a "quick-and-dirty job" and start getting myself established in Boulder right away, so my transition into being a graduate student would be less stressful. I agreed, and got a job packaging three-and-a-half-inch floppy disks into mailers for a software company. All I did was stand there and stuff envelopes, all day long. The guys I was working with had plenty of time to talk as they stood there doing this. All they did was complain about a wide variety of things they didn't like about themselves and about life on Earth in general. I rode the bus to work and then came back to the filthy youth hostel in the evenings. Apartments were so expensive in Boulder that I knew I would need to get a much better job just to afford the most basic housing there. I was deeply, deeply tired, and my positive attitude was starting to fade. After about a week and a half of doing this routine, my mother called me and she sounded very grim. "David, I've got a letter here for you from Naropa. It's awfully thin. Do you want me to open it and read it to you?"

Rejected

I already knew what she meant by her saying it was a thin letter. I knew that my "metaphysical scholar and dream prophet" pitch had not gone over very well. Whether it was the fact that I did not do contemplative meditation on a daily basis or that I had failed to provide documented proof that Papa would pay for my tuition, I had not been accepted. Mom opened the letter and read it to me, and sure enough, they had turned me down. No explanation was given.

Regardless of whatever the hidden reason might have been, I was absolutely devastated—and I let myself cry. My mother kept telling me over the phone that it would be okay, while I allowed myself to grieve. I had figured out how to get it all paid for, and never had believed for a single second that they would turn down such an enthusiastic paying customer, since I was already almost overqualified. I hadn't bothered to apply to any other graduate schools. I had wanted to become a prominent UFO researcher, and some of the best ones had PhDs, like Dr. Leo Sprinkle, Dr. Steven Greer, Dr. Courtney Brown, and Dr. John Mack. I felt I was already making intriguing discoveries by combining the data I had read in these many books, but the officer never gave me a chance to show how it all fit together and tied in with the Hyperdimensional Model. If I could get my PhD in a subject I would actually be able to use in my career, that was even better. At Naropa, I was applying for a degree in transpersonal psychology, and from the list of books I would be reading, it was clear that this education would further enhance my understandings.

I still had my return train ticket booked, so I quit the job at the software company and tried to enjoy my last few days in Boulder before I returned home. A mystical, older hippie lady met up with me at a local restaurant, and wanted to give me a Tarot card reading. I said sure, why not? She did an elaborate spread with many different cards that she laid out in a circle. Each of the cards corresponded to an astrological sign and house; it was her own personal style she had developed. At the end was one card that was supposed to be the summary of the entire reading, telling me where my life was heading. She used quite a bit of drama and intrigue to build up to the moment when she threw down the last card. It was one of the worst cards in the entire Tarot deck. She seemed quite puzzled, as if that card had never shown up in such a crucial position before. Her brow furrowed and she grunted, "Hmm."

"Well, what does it mean?" I asked, already knowing how bad it was. The card was the Five of Cups, which pictures a morose man standing by a river. The man is completely covered with a deathly black robe, hiding his face and crying over three cups that had tipped over and spilled in front of him. Two more cups remained upright on his opposite side, but he obviously didn't care about those. The three fallen cups represented a broken heart in this case, and the water that flowed out of them indicated the love and joy that he could not replace. The only positive thing about this card was that the two cups still standing behind the morose man indicated that the situation wouldn't be a complete loss. You would still have something left over if you chose to look for it.

"Suffering," she responded. "The cards say that your future is definitely going to have some suffering." I responded, "Well, I hope not." Yet, I knew this reading was indeed accurate. The suffering she was talking about would last a lot longer than just the train ride home. I was going to have to face my greatest fear and become a "beast of burden" in the world of low-paying, entry-level jobs.

Joining the Ashram

On the trip home, I quickly bonded with two guys who were giving up their lives to join a Hindu ashram in South Fallsburg, New York. It was founded by a renowned guru, Baba Muktananda. In yet another incredible synchronicity, one of the two guys had literally just graduated with a doctorate in medicine from a school in California. Although he had finished all his exams and had gotten good grades, he still had to go through a series of board certifications before he could use his degree to practice medicine.

Just as he was about to graduate, he received a series of visions that literally commanded him to renounce his future in medicine and work as a "common person." His goal was now to move toward becoming a self-sufficient monk. Given the programming about college education that I had received from my family, I admitted to him that he sounded truly insane—but he was absolutely certain that he was doing the right thing. The synchronicity of meeting him on this train was almost beyond belief. He laughed as I told him about Naropa turning me down. "You don't need it," he said. "Look at me. I was asked to walk away after

I had already finished the whole thing. For me, that was the ultimate test of my faith, and I'm doing it. I think the reason you met me on this train is to show you that you are now answering to a much higher calling. My whole family thinks I'm crazy for what I'm doing, but I absolutely know that this is the right thing."

He was traveling with a friend who had studied with Muktananda while the guru was still alive, and had a very interesting story. Over time, the friend had become tired, bored, and disillusioned at the ashram. He was doing his chores, mopping the floor in the hallway, but he had become deeply depressed. Muktananda showed up at the other end of the hall, with no one else around, and immediately knew how his student was feeling.

Muktananda then dramatically held out his hand, and a visible orb of bluish-white light formed in it, about two inches wide. He grabbed this light as if it were a ball, and threw it at his student. The ball traveled to the area right between the student's eyes, and as it hit him, he was overcome with total ecstasy. His body dropped to the ground and he was literally convulsing with divine pleasure. This was a powerful example of the gift that true gurus can convey, known as "darshan." I eventually explained in detail about how I had experienced something similar with the Tuvan throat-singing shaman the previous winter, but at this point, I was totally captivated by his story. Muktananda then walked up to the man, looked down at him in his drooling ecstasy, and said, "Now you stay, and be happy, no?" The man was so blissed out, he could only nod his head and moan in agreement.

Although this story might sound completely ridiculous to a skeptic, the man talked about it in so much detail that it was obvious that, at the very least, he had experienced this event as if it was a reality. He had seen the blue sphere of light form in Muktananda's hand, watched it fly through the air, felt it hit him in the forehead, and then experienced an ecstasy that was far better than any drug experience he had ever had. He was not expecting a darshan experience, and it was definitely not his imagination. This reminded me that mystical experiences can and do happen to people, and that amazing things could still occur in my future regardless of whether or not I made it into a metaphysical graduate school. My new doctor friend had obviously come to believe that a doctoral degree was not necessary—that we were all responding to a significantly higher calling as we rode this train together.

I wrote down the name, address, and telephone number of the man who had the darshan experience in the back of *The Watchers*. Little did I know that I would eventually live right near the address he gave me in Santa Monica, California. I had completely forgotten about this until I picked up *The Watchers* again while writing this book, and his information was waiting there for me on the back page. To me, this was just another synchronicity showing how powerful of a message I had just received from the universe. We were all chugging through the heartland of America, headlong into an appointment with destiny.

CHAPTER TEN

Dreams of Ra-Ptah, Atlantis, and Flying Spheres

I
n spite of my experience with the two men on the train, after I dragged myself back home, I was devastated. The prophecies of wading through mud and crying over spilled cups of love immediately came true. My mother demanded that I get a "regular job" and pay fifty dollars a week to live there. Without a car, this was extremely difficult. I crashed through a series of very stressful dead-end jobs, with only my bicycle for transportation. At the same time that my external world was imploding with stress, depression, and anxiety, my inner world came to life like never before. I started experiencing truly remarkable spiritual dreams.

To understand what I was thinking as I interpreted these dreams, it is important to point out another key element of the Edgar Cayce story line. By this point, I had read several dozen books on UFOs and ancient civilizations that had gone into the Cayce story of Atlantis. What we now identify as the myth of Atlantis is actually a part of the history of ancient Egypt, as well as other areas. A number of the books I read revealed that Cayce's own readings indicated that he had once been the first pharaoh of Egypt, who we now call Osiris. The Cayce Readings said that many details had gotten lost in translation, and a more accurate name for this beloved leader at the time was Ra-Ptah. Cayce's stenographer spelled the second word in the transcripts with only two letters, *TA*, but it now appears that *PTAH* is a more accurate spelling.

Ra-Ptah was originally from Atlantis and, while living there, had received a series of shocking and undeniable visions and prophecies of a coming catastrophe that would nearly destroy the Atlantean civilization. This was what we would later come to know as the sinking of Atlantis. A small group of two hundred and thirty-one followers banded with him, and together they were able to survive the floods and devastation that wreaked havoc upon the Earth. Once things settled down, they relocated to Egypt and were able to integrate with the indigenous people of the area. Ra-Ptah knew he had to build a truly remarkable monument—the Great Pyramid—and Egypt was the only suitable location for its construction.

The readings revealed that Ra-Ptah had worked with a mysterious entity called Thoth Hermes Trismegistus to build the Great Pyramid. It appeared that Hermes and Enoch were also the same character, and the Cayce Readings said this being had been a prior incarnation of Jesus. In *The Ascension Mysteries,* I delve into the mysteries of the Book of Enoch, which is as old as the Book of Genesis and actually far more revealing. Enoch received visions of a coming flood, and Noah was apparently his grandson. The date that the Cayce Readings gave for the building of the Great Pyramid was "10,490 to 10,390 years before the entrance of the Master (Jesus the Christ) into the earth planes." This was obviously a far older date than conventional scholars would believe, placing the pyramid's construction at a beginning date of 10,490 BC.

Another very interesting point here is that in Egyptian histories, the reign of the original pharaoh Osiris was known as Zep Tepi, or the "First Time." In the many artistic depictions from this time, we see that the pharaoh and his people are openly interacting with unusual-looking humans. At least two of these characters, Horus and Thoth Hermes Trismegistus, are pictured as having avian heads on human bodies. Other types of interesting-looking humans were depicted as well. Although the Cayce Readings never mentioned UFOs, there was an interesting reference in one of them to a man who was helping to monitor portals that would apparently teleport people to "outer spheres," and/or allow those from these other realities to visit Earth. This enigmatic quote appeared on June 7, 1930, in reading number 1681-1, for a thirty-three-year-old banker who was a Quaker. Apparently, in Atlantis, his name was Segund, and he was a "keeper of the portals." Here is a portion of the quote:

> The entity was very close to those in authority; being that one who was the keeper of the portals, as well as the messages that were received from the visitation of those from the outer spheres.[1,2]

This quote is widely considered to be a true gem in the Cayce collection, for it clearly indicates that there were portals through which extraterrestrials from "outer spheres" were coming and going, and passing messages through to Earth as well. It is truly heartbreaking that no one ever asked Cayce's source any follow-up questions about this fascinating and controversial information. The reading did go on to say that Segund had a key role in unifying messages from Atlantis, Egypt, India, Indo-China, Mongolia, and the Aryan regions of what became India and Iran. Segund was also responsible for planning expeditions that helped identify where the survivors of the coming Atlantean catastrophe would need to relocate. If we accept the validity of the Cayce Readings as one of the basic foundations of our philosophical argument, then we have a great deal to work with when we bring in reading number 1681-1. If the birdlike human beings portrayed in the First Time are not actually mythological, they may very well represent extraterrestrial beings that are humanlike but have obviously unusual features, and were visiting and communicating through portals.

This group of two hundred and thirty-one people, including Segund, stayed with Ra-Ptah through thick and thin—even after he was eventually banished from Egypt. Ra-Ptah's banishment was the result of a grave mistake he had made. Although he taught monogamy, he himself decided to take on a second wife and have children with her. She happened to be the most beautiful woman in all of Egypt and a renowned temple dancer. The Cayce Readings said that her original name was Isris, and that over time, it had become simplified to Isis. The political opponents of Ra-Ptah's day used this example of spiritual hypocrisy to get him thrown out of the country, and for a time it worked. Ra-Ptah's core group of followers left Egypt along with him when he was banished.

Clearly, one of the most interesting things about this story was that it did not portray Ra-Ptah in a very favorable light—to say the least. Despite all his grand achievements, Ra-Ptah had lost much of his spiritual righteousness through a classic infidelity scandal. The Cayce Readings further hinted that this was how the story of the severed phallus of Osiris originally got started. In the mythological version, Osiris was chopped up into fourteen pieces, and Isis was able to recover all the pieces and restore his body to normal health, except the phallus.[3] An artificial replacement was then made, and this was apparently where the symbolism of the Egyptian obelisk originated. Osiris was also said to have conceived his son Horus, the hawk-headed deity, after this bizarre restoration, by procreating with his wife, Isis.

Some Cayce researchers believe this story can be seen as a dreamlike myth describing how Ra-Ptah eventually returned to Egypt after being banished, but was always haunted by the sex scandal. In fact, the Cayce Readings said that after he returned, Ra-Ptah took on multiple wives and threw his original teaching about monogamy completely out the window. The aftereffects of these unfortunate decisions changed the course of humanity's spiritual path for the ensuing twelve thousand years. We will go into more detail about this once we delve into the Law of One, which has astonishing correlations to the Cayce Readings but were consciously unknown to the woman who spoke the words.

According to the Cayce Readings, this same core group of two hundred and thirty-one people continued reincarnating with Ra-Ptah lifetime after lifetime. Even more interestingly, the readings revealed that America in general was a country where the Atlanteans were reincarnating as a group, so they could work off the karma of having destroyed their previous high-tech civilization through selfishness, greed, and materialism. Many Americans, therefore, had very intense dreams of catastrophes, for their souls were having vivid flashbacks of having died in the sinking of Atlantis. This was said to have been caused by a pole shift—when the Earth suddenly tilted on its axis.

I found the Cayce Readings' story of Ra-Ptah to be very interesting. After reading three hundred books and seeing the impossibility of so many ancient megalithic stone monuments around the world, it wasn't at all difficult to believe that there had been an advanced civilization on Earth that had been destroyed in what we would consider to be prehistoric times. We could choose to call it Atlantis or something else, but no one could deny the presence of these strange ruins. The Cayce reincarnation story was certainly one of the most interesting aspects of what I had come across in my research, particularly because his source claimed that a "Hall of Records" had been buried underneath the right paw of the Sphinx, along with a wide network of underground tunnels we have not yet officially discovered. Apparently, Ra-Ptah, Segund, and others had filled this secret underground chamber with a treasure trove of artifacts that documented their entire civilization and history. These treasures seem to have included holographic projectors that would play back three-dimensional movies of what had actually happened in our own ancient past. Since I knew there was a direct connection between the Monuments of Mars and the Giza plateau, I had to wonder if the Mars connection would appear inside the Hall of Records as well.

The Cayce Readings had also said that these people had cigar-shaped antigravity flying craft at the time. I was intrigued by the fact that I had seen the exact same type of craft in many of my own childhood dreams. I reasoned that if these craft could conquer gravity, they very likely could also have gone to Mars and inspected the ancient, fascinating ruins. The Cayce story did seem to tie it all together, complete with the connection to extraterrestrials visiting Earth through portals, and the suggestion that Americans were uniquely connected to the story of Atlantis. Given how obsessed I was with all this information, and how many synchronicities and dreams I was receiving, I had to wonder if I might have somehow been part of this same ancient Atlantean group. Before long, as I worked through a series of utterly miserable low-paying jobs, I had several marvelous dreams that seemed to be feeding me the answer.

Dream of an Atlantean Catastrophe

The first dream that seemed to relate to Ra-Ptah, Egypt, and Atlantis came in on July 6, 1995, less than a month after I had been rejected by the Naropa Institute. In this dream, I found myself on top of what appeared to be a giant step pyramid of some kind, similar to the Mayan temples. It was a very large, castle-like building made of stone, with a ring of pillars standing at the summit. I was the only one there who seemed to understand that the pillars and the building itself were all designed to function as a giant astronomical calendar. The society that had built this pyramid had reached its ultimate crisis as my dream began. Lightning was crashing. The Mayan-style pillars were toppling down, right in front of me, and water was flooding in from everywhere at a fantastic rate. It was extremely terrifying, to say the least.

All the people around me were from my honors classes in high school. There were a total of perhaps forty kids who were all in the same "gifted" classes with me every year. I have had countless dreams in which these same people show up. In this case, I seemed to be their spiritual leader. I was able to show them how to cross over the flooding parts of the pyramid and travel to safety. In fact, we were actually walking on water in order to do this. Much like Moses, I was also able to part the sea so everyone could travel through the area to safety, and they were amazed that I was able to do this. At one point, I stepped out into the water and was able to psychically form it into huge, beautiful quartz crystals with my hands. I showed them to the people as if they were gifts, but as soon as they tried to grab them, the crystals immediately melted like ice cubes.

The Golden Beings

I had the next dream of this type ten days later, on July 16, 1995. In this case, I went to a large, green outdoor park with my father and brother. We knew that the rock band KISS would be performing there, and we were excited to see them. Dad went into the bathroom to change his clothes, and we ended up waiting a long time for him to get ready. We urged Dad to hurry up, because we wanted to see KISS. Once Dad emerged, we all headed outside to the stage area and there they were! By this point, the concert was already happening in front of an audience. Once we arrived, the members of KISS stopped playing. They privately took the three of us over to a different spot in the park, and for some reason, no one in the audience tried to follow us. I then witnessed a sight that was a feast for the eyes, unduplicated by any movie I have ever seen in my life.

We were standing in front of a large, grassy field that didn't seem to be all that interesting. Suddenly, with a deep rumble that almost knocked us over, the ground opened up in a long straight line. Somehow, the whole park was built on top of an underground base that could open and close with this massive mechanical door. We peered down into the base, which seemingly went down forever, through this relatively narrow channel. Once I looked up, I realized that a giant spaceship had risen up through the channel—so large that I couldn't even begin to see what it really was. All I could see was the flat side of some massive object that was covered with lights, machinery, and technological-looking things. It was the most beautiful thing I had ever seen.

Now I tried to crane my head back to see exactly how big this object really was. As I looked up, I realized it was absolutely colossal in size and scope, so big that it looked like nothing more than a towering wall extending as far down and as far up as the eye could see. Panels of blue-white light in huge rectangles were interspersed along its incredible metallic frame, with dazzling, intricate detail. It was absolutely, completely breathtaking, to the point where I was literally moved to tears.

A door either opened or was already open, and the mysterious members of KISS led me directly inside this phenomenally massive structure. As I walked in with them, we headed through a large rectangular corridor that was perhaps forty feet tall. The walls were precisely cut with razor-sharp lines. The hall reminded me of the inside of the warehouses I was now working at, but this was far more majestic than any of my job sites. Everything looked like it was made out of gold. The walls were decorated with a multitude of technological-looking items as well as an endless amount of Egyptian-looking artifacts. Elaborate, gold-encrusted hieroglyphics covered the empty spaces, and there were countless numbers of what appeared to be solid-gold Egyptian statues lining the hall all the way down on both sides. The sheer majesty of what I was seeing was spectacular. I was so awestruck that I had to remind myself to breathe.

The members of KISS continued leading me deeper and deeper through this passageway. Finally, I met about three beings who were gigantic and exceedingly mysterious. They were approximately thirty-five feet tall. These beings, each of them wearing what appeared to be a robe, were quite extraordinary, appearing to be living statues made of solid gold. They sparkled and shined with the beautiful luster of gold as they stood there. These beings were so tremendously tall that their heads nearly touched the ceiling of the massive hall we were in. Their heads were larger than one would expect for the size of their bodies, and shaped like flattened fishbowls, almost like a McIntosh apple. The sides bulged out like an apple, but the top and bottom of their heads were straight-lined like a fishbowl. The lines on the top and bottom of their heads were the same width. Their facial features were quite stylized, like masks, and their faces never moved. Each face looked like something one might see on a Mayan temple wall. Despite their incredible size and imposing appearance, I felt completely safe in their presence—while also being very impressed by the level of spiritual power they were radiating. They told me to come with them, and we walked down the hall together. The entire experience was utterly breathtaking.

The first thing the beings did was to lead me to a large, solid-gold statue that clearly seemed to commemorate Horus, the falcon god. The beings notified me, through a form of mental telepathy, that they now had to find a new Horus, because the original Horus had somehow been destroyed. They would not give me any additional information about it. At this point, the dream got even more bizarre. We walked farther ahead and they ended up leading me to the original desk that I had used to hold my private memorabilia when I was growing up. Now everything looked like my bedroom, complete with the desk, which was always a huge mess. They pointed at the desk ominously. On a telepathic level, I knew they wanted me to search through the desk, categorize everything, and relive the memories of my past. They told me I needed to do this to find batteries that would power a small synthesizer. This appeared to be the same Casio SK-1 that my friend Jude and I had used to make our earliest music together in high school. To locate these batteries, I would have to go through various things that I recognized from all the different parts of my life.

After a good period of time searching through the desk, I finally located the batteries. The beings told me I could go. I quickly found myself back outside and met up with my father and brother. My perception then expanded, and I found myself flying high over the Earth. Now I was looking down at what were obviously the main pyramids on the Giza plateau in Egypt. However, there were also temporary silos built next to the pyramids: one large silo and two smaller ones in front of the main three pyramids. Strangest of all, everything was covered with snow, although Egypt was supposed to be a desert!

At this point, I suddenly found myself back on the ground level. Now the original gigantic doors to the underground base had opened even more. A gigantic, brownish-gray moonlike object rose out of the doors and into the air. It looked just like the Martian moon Phobos, and it seemed to float up into the sky like a balloon. As the moon went up, I again found myself levitating in the air and watching it rise. I was completely transfixed as I again looked down and saw the Giza pyramids covered in snow, with the silos nearby. At this point, the dream ended. I spent well over an hour writing it all down, complete with several sketches to illustrate what I had seen.

During this same time, I was reading *Genesis Revisited* by Zecharia Sitchin. In this book, Sitchin argued that Phobos was not a natural moon but had been hollowed out to form a massive extraterrestrial base. He had a variety of reasons to speculate on this, including the fact that the orbit of Phobos is unusually fast and eccentric. The orbital characteristics led many to conclude that the only explanation would be that Phobos was hollow. It would only be much later in life, beginning in about 2007 with Henry Deacon, that other insiders revealed to me that there were multiple moons in our solar system with gigantic, habitable civilizations inside them. I had also read other books that said there were gigantic passageways carved underground in areas like Peru and Egypt. Some modern explorers had found them, but their stories were inevitably covered up.

I could clearly tell that this dream had many direct connections to the Ra-Ptah story line. I saw the Egyptian pyramids, apparently while they were still under construction. The surrounding countryside was in a different climate at the time, where snow could accumulate. The golden beings were exceptionally amazing to behold. I could see that they were obviously suggesting that I might somehow be a replacement for Horus. The key was to go through the memories of my past and organize them. Only then would I find the "batteries" that would allow me to "make music." I have had many battery metaphors in dreams, and they represent the spiritual power we need to move forward with our greatest purpose. The music I would make in this case would be the spiritual career as a UFO researcher, a field I was hoping to break into.

New Births and Anomalous Flying Spheres

The next dream of this type came in five days later, on July 21, 1995. In it, I looked out the windows of my childhood home and saw a huge plane flying almost impossibly close to the ground. The craft was utterly enormous, and it was trying to land, in a strange leaflike, fluttering motion. This craft looked very similar to the UFOs I had seen in so many dreams as a youth. I went outside the house to investigate and found a body of water. A baby was floating in the water, and I of course felt the need to rescue him and bring him to safety. The dream then shifted, and I was now sailing on the ocean in a ship. We were having a very hard time, for it seemed we had just survived a global pole shift. A group of people around me were looking up to me as their spiritual leader. I addressed this group, telling them we had just survived a global pole shift and that things weren't going to be easy anymore. I held up a newspaper and told everyone they could each have two sheets to use as a blanket. One woman started violently arguing with me about this. After a while, I was able to convince her to accept our collective fate. This was a great relief to everyone else in the group.

The next dream like this occurred on July 25, 1995. I found myself going to a local museum to see an incredible UFO exhibit entitled "Anomalous Flying Spheres." While I was inside, I met a strange-looking girl who could read my mind with great depth and precision. Her face showed her visible shock when I revealed to her, telepathically, that I knew what she was doing. I sat down next to her and told her that she needed to meditate more often to develop her abilities. Later, after I woke up and analyzed this, I knew she was a metaphor for myself, as is the standard rule of all dreams. I told the girl about many of the UFO-related topics that I had been studying. At this point, an overweight man became very angry with me for doing this. He wanted to fight me for my beliefs, and I did not back down. We went outside and I became a third-party observer. I watched the entire conflict happen, and my character won the fight. In my analysis, I could tell that this man represented the past part of me that had suffered through various addictions and bad habits, including laziness and overeating, and still had doubts about my own research.

As soon as I won the fight, a beautiful spherical UFO appeared in the sky. I then began flying up into the air, and soared higher and higher. Suddenly, and without even knowing why, I shouted out, "Take me through the vortex!" There was a sudden flash of white light, and now the Earth was altogether different. It was nonetheless dimly familiar to me in some way as I glided back to ground level. Everyone was wearing white robes, and it appeared to be a very enlightened society. I had an immediate feeling of kinship with the people and the culture. There were plenty of megalithic stone monuments like Stonehenge, only in this case the stones were all a very pure white. An unusually exotic-looking woman then appeared beside me. She was wearing a white robe just like everyone else. She was very attractive, and she seemed to want to connect with me on a very deep level that could well have been romantic. As soon as I tried to approach her, something seemed to block me, and I woke up. By this point, I felt that I most certainly had had at least one past life in Atlantis, and I was starting to remember accurate details of what it had been like in my dreams.

I wouldn't find out until 2015 from the insider Corey Goode that dozens, if not hundreds, of gigantic spheres had flown into our solar system. As I described in *The Ascension Mysteries,* the first of these appeared in the mid-1980s, during the Reagan administration, and was called the Sentinel. This craft left, but beginning in 1999, many more started arriving in our solar system. They came in through our sun or from the outside of our solar system. I was very aware of planet-size objects entering our solar system at the time, thanks to a website by Kent Steadman entitled Cyberspace Orbit. Steadman was tracking the arrival of these planet-size, visible objects from the SOHO satellite. He called them Sun Cruisers. They could move through huge areas of space in a matter of days. On many occasions after they showed up, the satellites would mysteriously malfunction and the images would be cut off. A much larger number of these spheres apparently came in during the year 2012. Corey Goode received information that these spheres were intended to help stabilize our solar system as we moved through a massive energetic transformation. They would ensure that we would all be safe and end up going where we needed to go.

After having explored the Corey Goode disclosure material in a wide variety of television shows, conferences, videos, and website articles since 2015, I was quite surprised when I went back to my dream journals and saw this elaborate dream about "Anomalous Flying Spheres." The woman I had met up with seemed to be a picture-perfect description of a race of inner-Earth beings who call themselves the Anshar. I will have much more to say about them as we go on.

Time to Leave the Nest

I was eventually able to get my father to cosign a bank loan so I could get a little white Subaru hatchback with four-wheel drive for the snow. My mother made it clear that I needed to move out and get on with my life as an independent adult. Nothing could have been more terrifying to me at the time. I had quite the profound synchronicity as it hit me that I was really going to have to leave. I go into more detail in *The Syn-*

chronicity Key, but I went out into the backyard, lay down on my side in the grass, and sobbed. A robin came up and was quite obviously trying to cheer me up. He just sat there with his red breast, tilting his head, looking me right in the eye, and chirping away. The whole thing was extremely bizarre, and it went on for some time. I had never experienced this type of animal communication before, and I knew I had to face my greatest fears to reenter the working world, but ultimately it would all be for the best. My "place of calling" was now the New Paltz area, where I had just finished college. I still had a whole network of friends down there whom I could rely on to help me get started with adult living, and at the time I had one dream after another telling me I had to move back to New Paltz as soon as possible.

CHAPTER ELEVEN

The Place of Calling

My weird, mystical experience with the robin helped give me the confidence to take the Subaru and drive back down to New Paltz, where I had just finished college and still had a variety of friends I could stay with. I had been having almost daily dreams in which I had gone back to New Paltz to begin my adult life. I made the big drive on September 3, 1995. That morning, I had a dream that I was being chased by horrible, demonic-looking people. There were certain phrases you could say, partly in Japanese, that would defeat them. One of these phrases translated as "Do not speak of your intense hunger." At first, I was terrified because so many of them were chasing me, but then I realized that they were all in a single classroom from my high school. I ran out the door, shut it, and locked them in so they could not get me. Once I escaped, an interesting person showed up and told me that it was all really just a game, and they were never that dangerous. This person told me that if it ever happened again, the main thing I needed to say to them was "By the grace of God and the Law of One, begone!" I was unaware that I was about to discover the Law of One series just over two months later. This dream could be interpreted as my turning my back on all the demons from growing up very unpopular and disliked in my hometown. In New Paltz, I had a large circle of friends.

Starting a New Job from the Kitchen Floor

I had played drums in a college jazz ensemble with my friend Adam, and he had a little apartment in the back of an insurance building. There was only enough room for me to sleep on an air mattress on his linoleum kitchen floor. On my first morning, September 4, 1995, Adam came in the kitchen to have a bowl of cereal. As the cornflakes and the spoon hit the porcelain, it ripped me out of the dream state and seemed much louder than it really was. I bellowed out, "What are you, breaking glass?" We ended up laughing and laughing about that event on many other occasions afterward. Soon after, I began wearing earplugs to sleep, and I have almost always done it ever since. I had already become comfortable with wearing earplugs in my work as a drummer. The drumming magazines all warned that one had to protect the ears, for hearing damage was permanent.

The very next day, I got a job delivering pizzas for a local business, thanks to my friend Eric, who was also working there at the time. Adam's kitchen floor was only an emergency crash-landing site to get me started, and I did not want to impose. Since I now had a job, I was able to move into my own place just five days after I returned to New Paltz, on September 8, 1995. I chose a college boardinghouse that was just a short five-minute walk from Adam's place, right down the road. It had about seven bedrooms, and my rent was only two hundred twenty dollars a month. The morning after I made the big move, I had a wonderful dream in which I was surrounded by beautiful women who were all being very nice to me. In retrospect, it now seems likely that these were representations of benevolent, angelic extraterrestrial humans who were showing up almost every morning in my dreams to give me strength, guidance, support, and encouragement. And again, I would later read in Session 86, Question 7 of the Law of One series that during a dream, "while the so-called conscious mind rests, this adept may call upon those which guide it, those presences which surround it, and, most of all, the magical personality which is the higher self."[1] I did not consider that the people I was interacting with in dreams at the time were anyone or any-thing other than projections of my own subconscious mind.

Looking for Contact

On the night of September 12, 1995, my friend Matt came over for a visit. He was the only person I knew who was as interested in UFOs as Artie was. We had a long conversation. I told him that I had now been studying UFOs nonstop for two and a half years and had read well over three hundred books. I had wished that the extraterrestrials would show themselves and talk to me somehow, since I was dedicated to learning more about them. Matt's answer was that perhaps they already had been in contact with me, and I just hadn't been allowed to remember it yet. I thought back to Artie's experiences and realized Matt was absolutely right. Whatever was happening to me was clearly a very positive and benevolent phenomenon, so I was not afraid to find out that I had been contacted. I was certainly having a wealth of interesting dreams. At the time, I still did not realize that dream contacts were just as authentic as waking ones.

The next morning, on September 13, I realized I was dreaming and I captured lucidity. I was at my childhood home, in the driveway, and now, in this state, I wanted a solid answer about UFOs. I soared up into the air but discovered that I could never get above a certain height. I did not see any crafts in the sky. Finally, in frustration, I cried out, "Where are you? Come to me! Show yourselves!" Nothing was happening, from what I could tell, except I did see two bizarre lights in the distance that appeared to be UFOs. I sank back down to the Earth and tried to run through a fence, to convince myself that everything was just a dream and I still had control over my environment. The fence stretched like a rubber band, but I couldn't make my body pass through it, as I usually would have done in a lucid dream. After I awoke, I realized that the dream was telling me I hadn't prepared myself for any type of greater UFO contact, such as Edgar Cayce–style readings. The stretching fence seemed to indicate that there was some sort of barrier in my mind and emotions that I hadn't pushed through yet.

Part of the problem was that my job delivering pizzas was incredibly stressful. I was still learning how to drive the Subaru, and no matter how fast I made my deliveries, they always wanted it to be faster. On the nights when it was raining, the orders would go through the roof. I did not enjoy being in rainstorms, which now appears to be due to my past life experience with Yumi, plus it proved to be very difficult to see the numbers to find a particular house in the pouring rain—and people would be angry if their pizza was late. There was one night when I absolutely could not find the house I needed to deliver to, and I then dented the bumper on my car against a tree while backing up. I had a true "dark night of the soul" experience as I stood there and screamed in the rain, soaked to the skin. Many people did not understand or care that you are supposed to tip your delivery driver and would just say "keep the change" when it was something like thirty-seven cents.

Another Change of Plans

On September 17, 1995, I went and visited a female friend, who I will call Angelica, at her apartment. I knew her from the music department at New Paltz, where I had a few classes, and I had always wanted to spend more time talking to her—but we were both very busy. I had already lent her my hardcover copy of *Fingerprints of the Gods* by Graham Hancock, which I felt was truly spectacular, and now I was going to visit her to get it back. Hancock had summarized much of the very best evidence I had encountered over the course of reading the three hundred books, many of which were on ancient civilizations. This included the idea that the "lost continent" of Atlantis was actually Antarctica, and that our last ice age from 12,500 years ago had been caused by the Earth shifting on its axis. Atlantis was inundated with water, and then in its new position at the south pole, the water flash-froze into the glacial ice we see today.

There were some other facts in Hancock's book that I had never seen before and were completely amazing to me. Most notable was the work of Giorgio de Santillana and Hertha von Dechend. These were high-end, well-established historians with a long list of published scientific works to their names. In their epic masterpiece *Hamlet's Mill,* they had searched through a variety of historical records and had identified a total of thirty-five ancient spiritual traditions around the world. For some inexplicable reason, every single one of these legends had encoded information in them about a strange 25,000-year cycle. The Earth would apparently counter-rotate on its axis over the course of about 25,000 years, in a cycle with an imposing-sounding name: the Precession of the Equinoxes.

This cycle would cause the stars in the night sky to drift one degree every seventy-two years, if you looked at them on the same day each year—such as the spring or fall equinox. This meant that anyone who built an ancient stone monument and aligned it to the stars could not keep it in alignment for very long. The monument would drift out of position in only seventy-two years. Whoever wrote these ancient traditions clearly wanted us to understand this 25,000-year cycle and study it in our own modern era. It was extremely bizarre to see this same mathematical and astronomical data encoded in all these spiritual traditions that were isolated from one another, on different continents, at different times in history.

The 25,000-year cycle had also just gotten a huge boost through the work of Robert Bauval, in his classic *The Orion Mystery,* which was originally published in 1994. I didn't see it in the bookstore until the paperback version was published in 1995. Bauval noticed that the three pyramids of Giza precisely matched the three stars in the belt of Orion. The relative sizes of the pyramids corresponded to the brightness magnitudes of the stars, and their positions were the same. The Nile River was positioned in the same place as the Milky Way in the night sky. Other pyramids in the area were precisely aligned with stars as well.

What made this particularly fascinating was that, thanks to the 25,000-year drifting of stars in the night sky, the pyramids did not align with their celestial counterparts unless you dialed the clock back to approximately 10,500 BC. This would have occurred during the Age of Leo, and the Sphinx obviously has the body of a lion. The Sphinx also aligns with the constellation Leo on the horizon during this same time period. The time window 10,500 BC was literally only ten years before the date

Edgar Cayce's readings gave for the construction of the Great Pyramid: 10,490 to 10,390 BC. For a cycle spanning 25,000 years, this connection was almost impossibly perfect. I had already seen these Cayce dates featured in many other books, and seeing it validated through a scientifically measurable star alignment was incredibly exciting. I was quite surprised that Bauval himself had not spotted this connection in the book, so I felt I had made an original discovery. It had therefore been a huge sacrifice for me to lend Angelica a book that was this important to me—and now I was there to make sure I got it back. On the way over to her apartment, I saw a couple kissing on a bench; they were obviously very much in love. I wondered if this was a synchronicity letting me know that Angelica and I had a future together.

Angelica's apartment was sparsely furnished, which was normal for a college student. The only real furniture, apart from a mattress on the floor and a kitchen table with chairs, was a maroon-colored coffee table. Each leg of the table featured a stylized elephant head, and it was covered with gorgeous inlay work, mostly of white tiles. Little did I know how important this table would become just over two months later. As I looked at the table, I felt the need to tell Angelica about my train ride back from Boulder, and how I'd met these two guys who were going to South Fallsburg, New York—less than an hour from where we were now—to join an ashram founded by Baba Muktananda. I started my story by telling her that the items on her sacred table reminded me of an amazing guru I had just heard about, named Muktananda.

Angelica was absolutely shocked. "That's my guru," she said. "The ashram. I grew up there! Spent most of my life there. I only left so I could come here to go to college and get an education." She was visibly shaking. This was a profound synchronicity. I was fascinated to hear what it was like to live in an ashram, particularly after I had heard the story of Muktananda throwing the ball of light into his student's third eye, sending him into a spasmodic fit of ecstasy. I began asking Angelica all sorts of questions. I found out that Muktananda's daughter, Gurumayi, was now running the place, and she didn't seem to have any of the "sidhi" powers her father once had. Nonetheless, she seemed to be a very genuinely compassionate and loving person. Angelica ended up letting me borrow Gurumayi's new book, *My Lord Loves a Pure Heart: The Yoga of Divine Virtues.*[2]

After the amazing story I had heard on the train, and comparing that life to the miserable job I had now, I felt as if staying in a community like this would literally be heaven on Earth.[3] My friends on the train were giving up their entire lives, including one man who was renouncing his doctorate, just to join this community. I had wanted to explore the idea of joining the ashram myself but had been too busy surviving to pursue it. However, the more I talked with Angelica about it, the more I realized that everything has its limitations.

Angelica had grown up with very wealthy parents in Manhattan, who eventually divorced. Her mother took their entire family estate and handed it over to the ashram in exchange for being allowed to live and work there for the rest of her life. Angelica had then lived a cloistered life. It was extremely routine, and she always had to work a job. There had been no outrageous darshan experience of ecstasy in her case. She had predominantly worked as a food server at the Amrit Café. It was always the same people, and there wasn't much for anyone to talk about after a while. There was also a strict celibacy rule for everyone living there—no sex or romantic involvements of any kind. Angelica was very glad to be free and to come back into the "real world" with the rest of us. She said, "To me, the whole point is to get that knowledge and take it out of the ashram. If you just go and stay there your whole life, then you will never really bring it to others who need it."

I felt genuinely dazzled by our conversation, and was buzzing with energy and life as I walked home alone. Angelica did end up taking me down to the ashram a few weeks later. Although it was indeed beautiful, she pointed out a variety of things that got me to understand the problems she was talking about. There was a life-size golden statute of Muktananda's own guru, a Buddha-like man named Badhi Baba, in the middle of a large prayer room. I noticed how people were worshipping this statue, and some of them had a look on their faces that seemed much too proud and superior. It didn't seem healthy to me. Ideally, a statue like

that would be only a reminder of the divinity we each have inside ourselves.

Dreams Forecasting a Major Event in the Near Future

On September 18, 1995, the day after I got my book back from Angelica,
I had a strong series of dreams suggesting that Yumi was about to contact
me and say she was coming for a visit. I couldn't remember all the details, but I definitely knew what the overall theme had been. Shortly
after I awoke, the phone was ringing—and it was Yumi. She told me that
she had this terrible dream in which I was talking to a beautiful woman
and developing romantic feelings for her. I felt that Yumi was misus-
ing her psychic gifts in this case, and that on some level she was spying
on me.

I felt cornered, and denied that I had spoken with anyone, which was
unusual for me to do. Yumi then proceeded to tell me that she was coming back to America to see me in just a couple of weeks, and had already
booked her tickets. This was only three months after she had left, I had
thought for good, and the whole thing felt quite overwhelming. In the
notebook, after the dream that so perfectly predicted her impending call,
I wrote, "All in all, we have here a clear-cut example of mental telepathic
communication, wherein her ideas before going to bed were transmitted
to my dreaming brain in the morning with an astonishing degree of accuracy."

Yumi soon arrived and stayed for about ten days. Her hair had gotten
longer and she looked better than ever. We ended up having a great time.
I got some time off work and on the days when I did have to go, I would
spend time with her before I left. At one point, I brought her up to my
favorite outlook in the Shawangunk Mountains. I talked to her about the
book I was reading by Zecharia Sitchin, and how extraterrestrials had
built the ancient monuments we see around the world. I also told her
that I now had every reason to believe we were heading into a profound,
worldwide spiritual activation event of some kind, which many people

called Ascension. She had never seen a view like this, and the beauty of the mountaintop led to her hearing and receiving the message on a deeper level than she ever had before.

The next interesting dream I had during this time was on October 7, 1995. In it, there was a machine that had captured some spiritual entities and held them, so they were unable to escape. At the end of the dream, they finally broke free and literally consumed the highly negatively oriented man who had trapped them. This dream featured extraterrestrials, and the idea that the head on the Grays that everyone sees may be nothing more than a helmet. As you may remember, in my initial NASA briefing from 1993, I learned that one type of ETs were wearing helmets that made them look like Grays. The dream told me that this might be a helmet I myself could wear someday. Unlike the original NASA briefing, which said that the face underneath the mask was troublesome looking, in this case the dream was using this symbol of the helmet to inspire me for something positive. The intel about the helmet had a deep emotional resonance with me, and greatly helped to fuel my passion for UFO studies. This dream was clearly prophetic of my future work in using my research to stand up to the darkest forces on planet Earth. Artie's intriguing mysteries would take me many years to solve, but I already was well aware that we were being lied to on an almost unimaginable scale.

Three days later, on October 10, 1995, I ended up being symbolized as a thin person in a boxing match. My character realized that he was no match for the giant he had to fight. He was terrified at the size of his opponent. Once the fight began, everyone in the audience, including his opponent, transformed into hideous monsters. The main character then turned into a monster of his own, cartoonish and whimsical instead of terrifying and ugly. In this persona, he effortlessly and savagely destroyed his opponent. He looked at the bloody monster he had defeated and at the audience, and he felt disgusted by their monstrosity and trapped in their world of violence. This again seemed to be prophetic of my future career, where I would often use whimsical humor to expose very dark secrets.

Two days later, on October 12, 1995, I had a dream in which I was traveling with my UFO friend Matt to investigate an apparent UFO encounter. For some reason, we were extremely frightened about what might happen when we got there. Nothing much seemed to happen. I finally ended up driving back home without Matt. I found myself at the intersection where I saw the shooting star and had the enormous surge of energy come up through my feet. I saw my mother washing her car on a round, rotating pedestal in the middle of this same intersection. The car represented a vehicle that would allow me to travel much faster through the spirit world, and very clearly could have symbolized a UFO. However, I knew something was wrong as soon as I approached Mom, because she seemed to be extremely disturbed.

As soon as I got close to her, she told me that our house cat Mandy had died. As I wrote up this dream, I knew Mandy was a symbolic representation of my animal self, such as the ego and the childlike id. Mom explained to me that Mandy had to face her UFO double, who was significantly larger, and that she had died in the process. This could symbolize the "shamanic death" that occurs when you undergo a profound transformation in how you see yourself and your relationship to the universe around you, and that was already starting to happen to me at the time. In the dream, Mom somehow knew that this death had happened, even though she hadn't actually seen it yet. The dream also reminded me of when Artie was told about his father's alleged trip to the hospital. He had been out in the street, in roughly the same position relative to his house as I was to the car in this dream. When Artie first told me that story, I had visualized the scene as if it had happened in this exact same location. I always felt that Artie's father had gotten pulled into some kind of a black project rather than having died.

Since my household cat had to face her own UFO double, and had died in the process, this dream seemed to be predicting that I was soon going to learn something interesting about myself that was UFO-related. Like Artie's father, this discovery would take me into an entirely new and different world. I would apparently see that I had a "UFO double" that was "much bigger," on the soul level, than I had seen myself as being until then. In the process, the person I had been until then, at least in the egoic sense, would be seriously transformed.

The dream then shifted and I found myself in a grocery store. I called out for my UFO friend Matt, but he was nowhere to be found. I was very, very nervous, but I didn't even really know why. I saw a dish that had a giant leek sitting on it, and I was compelled to walk over and pick it up. In the dream, however, I knew that by choosing to pick up this leek, I would be agreeing to face my own impending extraterrestrial contact alone. I realized that if I ever found myself standing face-to-face with actual, live Grays, that could prove to be an extremely terrifying experience. Nonetheless, I was brave enough to walk over and pick up the leek anyway. I knew the choice meant I was putting myself on a timeline where this future meeting with extraterrestrials would become utterly inevitable. Ironically, I did not realize they were meeting with me almost every morning in my dreams. This prophecy referred only to a deepening of the contact into accurate spoken transmissions, and the realization that I was far more related to them than I had ever thought.

On October 27, 1995, well after Yumi had returned to Japan, I had a dream wherein most of the floor in my father's house had been removed, and a giant pit had been dug in the dirt right below it. An archaeological dig was being conducted, and the archaeologists had found a series of archaic masks buried underground in the area. My father's house happened to be directly above the site where the bulk of this ancient treasure was now expected to be found. At this point, we had not yet uncovered what we were digging for, but we knew we were very close—and I was a part of this same team. This again suggested that I was going to learn something quite profound about myself and my lineage. The golden beings in my epic KISS dream had faces that looked like masks, and these masks had the same Mayan-type appearance. There was no sense of the heaviness or negativity of the masks people were wearing in Artie's fleeting childhood memory. The dream seemed to say that this new discovery would lead to me realizing that I had a connection to something that was very ancient and highly valuable.

A Job at the Mental Hospital

After several weeks of suffering with the pizza delivery job, I decided that I had to do something better. Since I didn't have to work until 4:00 P.M., I had most of the day to look for other work. Yumi's arrival and emotional support had inspired me to begin the search. One of the jobs I applied for was at a local hospital, in the mental ward. With my new bachelor's degree in psychology, I got in as a tech as of about November 3, 1995. I was there to assist the nurses. At the time, I still wanted to get a PhD in psychology, and I felt that a job in the mental health field was of critical importance to building a residency credit for my degree. This job proved to be my final break with the material world before the much deeper awakening experiences began occurring immediately afterward. At times, I was greatly harassed and disrespected by the patients, which seemed to be a normal thing that all the nurses and techs went through in the ward. I did my best to keep the peace and be friendly to the patients, even though I was told that I "had nothing to offer them" and to just perform my duties with a minimum of social interaction. So many strange and upsetting things happened to me in just two and a half weeks that I was completely overwhelmed. I could write a whole play or movie script out of those experiences that would run the viewer through the full spectrum of human emotions.

The early wake-up time I had to hit for this job made it very difficult to capture dreams, but five days after it started, on November 8, 1995, I pulled in quite an epic one. In one section, I was looking at some sort of intricate, elaborate set of star maps that were used for space travel. Someone was telling me that traveling through a galaxy involved a great deal of work. You couldn't just go from point A to point B. You had to make a series of jumps along the way. Eight years later, after I met my first mega-insider, Daniel, in 2003, I discovered that we do indeed have a network of "stargates" that extraterrestrials use to travel around the galaxy. They were built in very ancient times and use existing wormholes that naturally appear between stars, and can be seen by their plasma filaments. In my dream, traveling from one galaxy to another was a tremendous proposition, and it caused me to have a very odd feeling throughout my entire body.

As the dream went on, I learned about a manned mission to Pluto. At the same time that I heard about the mission, I had a rubber ball model of the planet in my hands. I was squeezing the ball, and the people I was talking to were telling me that Pluto wasn't much different from Earth inside. It had grass, trees, animals, birds, rivers, lakes, and oceans stocked with fish. I found this quite fascinating and hard to believe, but I did trust them. As I looked at the ball, I noticed that it appeared almost identical to the levitating Martian moon Phobos from my fantastic earlier dream where I had met the golden beings. From there, I started thinking about all the shattered moonlets of Uranus and Neptune, and how the author Zecharia Sitchin thought that they proved the existence of the tenth planet, Nibiru. I then saw a visual image of this hidden planet in the dream as being grayish-white.

At this point, I woke up suddenly and looked at the clock. It was exactly 5:55, and I was greatly surprised. I felt the digits were burning into my soul, and it was immensely powerful. I had to wonder if I actually was receiving some sort of dream class from extraterrestrials, for these were very strange and vivid concepts. At the same time, it felt quite comfortable in the dream. It was nice to have this experience while I was going through hell at my job. Many years later, insiders would reveal that a variety of moons in our solar system do have Earth-like habitable worlds inside them, complete with clouds, rainfall, rivers, lakes, oceans, forests, meadows, and plenty of beautiful places to live. This is one of the many benefits of having highly advanced technology.

Resignation and Realization

I could easily fill two or more chapters of this book with hundreds of specific details about how difficult my job was during this time. Ultimately, on the morning of November 20, 1995, I wrote my resignation letter. I didn't bring it in with me that day, but as it turned out, I didn't need to. Once again, I had received a crystal-clear prophetic vision. My boss called me into his office first thing in the morning and told me I was being fired. When I asked him for a reason, he said it was because I was too friendly to the patients. They wanted someone who would just do their job and not offer any conversation or opinions; that was the treatment team's responsibility, not mine. Even with a bachelor's degree in psychology and a master's equivalent from suicide-hotline internships, they did not consider me to be educated enough to share my own thoughts with anyone. I was completely dumbfounded. I had gotten a psychology degree to be able to help people, and I certainly felt that being friendly was an essential element of that process.

I cried heavily when I got back to my car as I watched our local family of about fifteen wild turkeys glide by. I was well aware that I had taken this job only to help me get a PhD so I could eventually become a respected UFO researcher. The job was horribly stressful and had nearly ruined my life after only two and a half weeks. In just the last two days or so before I got fired, I had started learning to ignore the patients and maintain complete control over the ward—and this had frightened me. Had I kept doing it, my entire personality could have changed. I nonetheless still felt like an enormous failure for getting fired, and I had no idea what to do next.

When I got home, I was curious to revisit my journal entry of what I had dreamed that morning. At some point in that dream, there had been an exciting airshow like we used to have at the local military base every year in my hometown of Scotia, New York. In this case, I saw colossal aircraft that were flying much too close to the ground. They looked almost exactly the same as the UFOs I had seen in the dreams I used to have when I was very young. The craft were also somewhat dented, and I could see inside one of them. To my surprise, this craft appeared to be completely empty inside, and I wondered who or what was flying it. The obvious implication in this dream was that I would soon be able to fly such a craft myself, at least in the greater spiritual sense. The craft here represented my greater spiritual body and the ability that it had to traverse into unforeseen realms.

As I was watching this, I noticed that a woman was standing next to me who was exotic-looking and beautiful. She was a recurring character who had shown up in a variety of other UFO-related dreams. Now she finally revealed to me that she was part human and part extraterrestrial. I felt an incredible kinship and connection to her, as if we had known each other over the course of many different lifetimes. However, after I woke up, I still didn't believe this dream was "real," and I simply assumed that she represented a more spiritual aspect of my own personality structure.

Many years later, as I reread this dream for the first time while writing this book, I was surprised to see that she precisely matched Corey Goode's description of the Anshar priestesses. The Anshar claim to be human beings from Earth's own future who had to travel back in time to ensure that they were not defeated by a negative extraterrestrial group. If we as human beings fail to reach our Ascension, the Anshar claim that they will cease to exist. The woman's calming presence in the dream clearly let me know that I did not need to put up with the horrible stress of the mental hospital job any longer. She and her friends certainly did not want me turning into a prison warden. Her peaceful presence had inspired me to write my resignation letter as soon as I woke up. Little did I know that I would be fired before I was brave enough to bring the letter in and finish the job myself.

From Elsewhere: The Book That Changed My Life

I drove back up to my mother's house for Thanksgiving break, and I stopped off at a Barnes and Noble, on Wolf Road in Albany, New York, on the way home. I would always go straight to the UFO section and look for any new releases. For me, this was the equivalent of going to the movies or reading the headlines in a newspaper. This time, in November 1995, I saw a new orange-and-black hardcover book called *From Elsewhere: Being E.T. in America*. The author was Scott Mandelker, PhD, which immediately caught my eye. He had already achieved the same honor I had hoped to earn for myself. When I read the author's biography on the inside jacket cover, I was quite surprised to discover that he had earned a PhD in East-West psychology from none other than the

Naropa Institute. This immediately struck me as an intriguing synchronicity, since I was still dealing with the fallout from having been rejected
by this same school. Mandelker had already achieved my dream—
earning a PhD and becoming a published author discussing UFOs.

The tagline on Mandelker's book cover was "The Subculture of Those
Who Claim to Be of Non-Earthly Origins." As I read the inside jacket,
it was clear that Mandelker's name for this type of "ET soul" was Wanderer. Admittedly, my first response was sarcastic laughter. "A PhD, huh?
Just look at the title. *Non-Earthly Origins*. People are people. They are
born and die here on Earth. This guy is crazy." However, as I held the
book in my hands, I could feel it tingling with an almost unbearable
amount of energy. It was alive, electric, crackling and buzzing with what
seemed like a very high vibrational field. I had never felt anything like
that coming off a physical object before, and I had experimented with
"psychometry," obtaining psychic information from a physical object,
since reading about it as a teenager. I soon realized by flipping through
the book that Mandelker was basing the majority of his argument on a
series of 106 Edgar Cayce–style intuitive readings known as the Law of
One. I had already flipped through Book Three of the Law of One at the
same bookstore and found it to be so densely written that, at the time, I
was not interested in pursuing it any further. Ultimately, I would find
that the term *Wanderer* appeared in eighty-eight different passages
throughout the material.[4]

I opened the book to appendix 2, a twelve-part Wanderer Questionnaire. According to Mandelker, a Wanderer was an alleged ET soul. This
was a person who had volunteered to become human, but their soul had
originated in higher realms, or higher "densities," as the Law of One
called it. At those levels, these souls had already integrated the basic
lessons that Earth could teach us, such as through understanding and
mastering karma. They came here because our planet was in an unusually extreme amount of trouble compared to most other third-density
worlds. In the higher realms, it was as if we were all screaming and
crying for help, and these benevolent, angelic beings could not ignore
the call.

Part of the Wanderer's contract was called the Forgetting: They had to agree to forget who and what they really are. Only through intense spiritual work could they bring some but not all of the memories back. However, there was a definite silver lining for anyone consciously choosing a path like this. Mandelker referred back to passages such as Session 36, Question 17, showing that Wanderers can make progress much faster on Earth than is possible in the higher "densities" they came from:

> The Wanderer has the potential of greatly accelerating the density [from] whence it comes in its progress in evolution. This is due to the intensive life experiences and opportunities of the third density [like you now experience on Earth]. Thusly the positively-oriented Wanderer chooses to hazard the danger of the forgetting in order to be of service to others by radiating love of others.[5]

Another very fascinating point that Mandelker focused on was that the Wanderer would never be authorized to fully activate its true potential while living on Earth. Otherwise, that person would have magnificent superhero abilities, including levitation and telekinesis. This was explained in Session 65, Question 19 of the Law of One, as follows:

> The forgetting process can be penetrated to the extent of the Wanderer remembering what it is and why it is upon the planetary sphere. However, it would be an infringement if Wanderers penetrated the forgetting so far as to activate the more dense bodies and thus be able to live, shall we say, in a god-like manner. This would not be proper for those who have chosen to serve.[6]

I had experienced many lucid dreams by this point, where these magnificent abilities were literally effortless. Throughout my life, I had felt that I once had abilities like this but could not access them now, and it was greatly frustrating.

The Wanderer Questionnaire

In short, Scott Mandelker said that if you could answer enough of these twelve questions in the affirmative, then it meant that you were likely a Wanderer. As I reported at the end of *The Ascension Mysteries,* this was the most incredibly personal and revealing set of questions I had ever seen. Somehow, Mandelker had put together a list of questions that showed a deeper knowledge of me, and how my mind and spirit really worked, than even my own parents could have understood at the time. It was deeply and intensely personal, and incredibly profound. I would never have imagined that someone could have put all these strange things together into a single questionnaire, and in my case, almost every single question was a powerful yes. Here is the original list:

1. You were often lost in daydreams of ETs, UFOs, other worlds, space travel and utopian societies as a child. Your family thought you were "a bit odd," without knowing quite why.

2. You always felt like your parents were not your true parents, that your real family was far away and hidden. Perhaps you thought things around you were somehow "not the way they should be," and reminded you of life somewhere "far away." These beliefs may have caused you a great deal of pain and sorrow. You felt "out of place."

3. You've had one or more vivid UFO experiences (in a dream or during waking hours) which dramatically changed your life: they helped resolve doubts, inspired confidence and hope, and gave you meaning and greater purpose. From then on, you knew you were a different person. Like a spiritual wake-up call, it changed your life.

4. You are genuinely kind, gentle, harmless, peaceful, and non-aggressive (not just sometimes, but almost always). You are

not much interested in money and possessions, so if "some-one must do without," it is usually you—such is your habitual self-sacrifice. Acts of human cruelty, violence and perpetual global warfare seem really strange (shall we say, alien?). You just can't figure out all this anger, rage and competition.

5. You have a hard time recognizing evil and trickery: some people call you naive (and they're right!). When you do perceive genuine negativity in your midst, you recoil in horror and may feel shocked that "some people really do things like that." In a subtle way, you actually feel confused. Perhaps you vaguely sense having known a world free of such disharmony.

6. The essence of your life is serving others (be they family, friends, or in a profession), and you cherish great ideals, which may also be somewhat innocent and naive (in worldly terms). But you sincerely, deeply hope to improve the world. A lot of disappointment and frustration comes when such hopes and dreams don't materialize.

7. You completely embrace the scientific temperament, with a cool, reasonable, and measured approach to life. Human passion and red hot desire seem strange: you are baffled. Romance and the entire world of feelings are truly foreign to your natural way. You always analyze experiences, and so people say you're always in your head—which is true! (Note: This type of Wanderer is less common, and probably wouldn't be reading this book—their skepticism would be too great! Such an "odd bird" is probably a brilliant scientist.)

8. You easily get lost in science fiction, medieval epic fantasy (like *The Hobbit*) and visionary art. Given a choice, you'd much prefer to live in your dreams of the past or future than

in the present. Sometimes you consider your Earth life boring and meaningless, and wish you could go to a perfect, exciting world. Such dreams have been with you a long time.

9. You have an insatiable interest in UFOs, life on other worlds or previous Earth civilizations such as Atlantis or Lemuria. Sometimes you feel like you've really been there, and may even go back someday. There may be quite a few of such books on your bookshelves. (Actually, this question is a giveaway, since only Wanderers and Walk-ins have profound, undying curiosity about worlds beyond—and for good reason!)

10. You have a strong interest in mystic spirituality (East or West), both theory and practice, with a deep sense that you used to have greater powers and somehow lost them. You may feel it's unnecessary to discipline yourself since "you've already been there," but somehow forgot what you used to know. People may doubt your resolve, but you know it's not that simple.

11. You have become a conscious channel for ETs or some other non-Earth source—and you realize that the purpose of your life is to help others grow and evolve. (Most likely, you're no longer sleeping, Wanderer!)

12. You feel, and *perhaps all your life have felt* tremendous alienation and a sense of never quite fitting in. Maybe you hope to be like others, try your best to be "normal," or imagine yourself like everyone else—but the bottom line is that you simply feel different and always have. There is a very real fear of never finding a place in this world. (Which you might not! Note: This is the classic profile of Wanderers.)[7]

The only No answers I had were that I had never had a waking UFO sighting, only in dreams, and I had not achieved "conscious contact" with extraterrestrial beings—whatever that meant. I even identified strongly with Question 7, for I did have an intensely scientific mind-set and had been a miserable failure at relationships, not feeling confident enough to get a girlfriend until I was a senior in college, and then having significant problems once I finally did.

At this point, I looked to see if any other books caught my eye. I reached out and grabbed *The Mayan Factor* by José Argüelles. I opened the book at random, and to my utter surprise, I arrived on page 100, which had a large image of the exact same shape I had carved into a piece of jewelry in an art class I took in my senior year of high school. The symbol looked like a question mark with a squiggly tail. I had no idea that this symbol meant anything at the time I sculpted it. The Mayan version had a box that was drawn around this shape, and that was really the only difference from the stylized version of it that I made. However, I was surprised by what Argüelles said this symbol meant—the caption read, "CIB: Ability to contact and commune with Galactic Consciousness." That was very intense. There were many clues in my life suggesting that I was indeed moving toward some sort of Edgar Cayce–style telepathic contact with higher intelligence.

Even better, I had carved this pin as part of a two-pin set. The other pin was a Star Trek communicator—what they would touch when they wanted to talk to the *Enterprise*. I now felt even more upset that my drug use and desire to escape high school had led me to abandon all the contents in my locker at the end of the year, since those two pins had been in it. At the time, I was so distracted that I never even thought about it—I just had to get out of there. My abandonment of these items would haunt me in nightmares for many years afterward.

I took Scott Mandelker's book home to my mother's house and had already started reading it before heading over to her parents' house for Thanksgiving dinner. It was very difficult to tear myself away from the book for a family gathering, and meeting my mother's side of the family like this was always tense.

Great Stress and Transformation

My maternal grandparents were intense fundamentalist Christians and my mother definitely was not. They had essentially adopted another family from their church, and those boys had far larger and more prominent photographs in the china cabinet than Michael and I did. During the dinner, things took a sudden turn from simmering, unspoken tension to maximum intensity. My grandmother suddenly lost the ability to breathe comfortably. She started gasping, wheezing, and clutching her chest. For a brief moment, I wondered if she was pulling some sort of inappropriate and elaborate joke, but this was absolutely real. No one was laughing. I could hardly believe what was happening, but all of a sudden, we had to call an ambulance.

The speed with which the medical personnel arrived was astonishing. It honestly seemed like it was less than three minutes before my grandparents' house was overrun with people wearing red jackets. If this had been a dream, it was as if the extraterrestrials had arrived at the exact moment of disaster, when we needed them the most. They had flashlights on their heads. They had loud walkie-talkies that beeped and barked out military-sounding communications in between loud hissing noises. They were suddenly putting my grandmother on a stretcher and carrying her out in a matter of seconds. My grandfather collapsed into my arms and sobbed uncontrollably, and I cried along with him. We had bonded very nicely when he taught me how to drive in high school. The whole experience was extremely difficult to endure and process emotionally. Grandma soon transitioned from the emergency room into a full-time nursing home, where she later passed away. She would never again see the interior of her house after that traumatic night.

I knew that this whole event had dreamlike significance. Some part of me that embraced traditional beliefs and resisted all the "weird, metaphysical stuff," just like my grandmother, was now dying. The emergency personnel could easily represent extraterrestrials in the dream world. In the dream where I had to face my own UFO double, my mother told me that our beloved cat had passed away. Now I had a very bizarre experience with my grandmother nearly dying right after I started reading a book that was convincingly arguing that I was indeed an extraterrestrial soul. I had also seen many signs that my maternal grandfather had been dominated by his wife for many, many years, and on this very night, it stopped forever. Mom eventually had Grandpa move in with her and took care of him for several years. In the symbolism of the Tarot cards, the Death card only symbolized a transformation from one type of mind-set and lifestyle to another.

The pain and angst of this chaotic family scene caused me to throw myself into Scott Mandelker's book even more intensely. Starting the very next morning, I read it cover to cover, and then started from the beginning and reread it once again over the course of two or three days. Mandelker had interviewed a variety of people who had come to him for counseling services, and whom he had then identified as "extraterrestrial souls," or Wanderers. Like the medical personnel I had just seen in action, the Wanderers were here to intervene in what they considered to be a planetary spiritual emergency. In the questionnaire, he said that if you believed this is who and what you are, you needed to commit yourself to finding the truth. If you ask the Universe for proof, the Universe will provide you with some sort of answer—if you have properly prepared yourself to receive it.

Seeking Confirmation

After my second read through the book, I knew I had to try something. I went up and visited Jude, my best friend from high school, at a new rental house he and his fiancée were repainting on the shore of Lake George. I described the entire book to him as we looked at the lights on the opposite side of the lake. I imagined we were standing on some alien world, looking out at futuristic buildings in the distance. Jude revealed that he had been going through his old stuff just two days ago in the course of preparing for this move, and found a "dream" he had written up from around the time he was in kindergarten, at age five. He had been so excited about this dream that he wrote it up and presented it to his kindergarten teacher. Again, with my background in UFO research, I strongly suspected this was not a dream at all.

In his dream, two men came to him in his bedroom and brought him outside his house. He could distinctly feel the cold of the nighttime air. To his amazement, there was a huge "submarine" floating in his backyard, and they brought him right into it! The door closed, and they sat him down and gave him a ride. As this ship traveled through space, he saw many wonderful things and got a nice tour of the solar system. The men finally brought him back to his room and put him safely back in bed—and then the dream ended.

For some reason, Jude had thrown away that old piece of paper, seeing it as nothing more than an old dream. However, as soon I told him of my own experiences with recent prophetic dreams, leading up to the discovery of Mandelker's book, Jude wished he could have gotten the paper back. I read the personality descriptions to Jude right out of the book, and together we started to realize that we both fit the Wanderer Questionnaire to a tee. Both of us were sensitive, dedicated to others, creative, and obsessed with UFOs, metaphysics, and fantasy. Both of us had an extremely powerful mystical experience at around age five, and we were both shocked to realize that this was part of the "pattern." (The detail about having an experience around five years of age was not in the questionnaire itself, but it did appear in the main body of the book's text.) We both felt as if we were on a mission to save the planet. We were often taken advantage of by others, we were nonviolent, we engaged in helping professions like counseling, and we were unable to understand negativity or evil. Since Jude had mentioned a cylinder-shaped "submarine," I told him there were numerous reports of cigar-shaped UFOs in the literature.

I had nearly identical UFO dreams as a child, with identical-sounding craft, and they often led to my having long conversations with the old man. Mandelker suggested that one's "ET Family" would reconnect with you once you were born here, and they would usually erase your memory of these events after they happened—but not always. Either

way, some greater part of yourself was absolutely aware of all the ET
contacts you had, and once you reached the end of your normal biological life, all those memories would come flooding back.

The paint fumes in Jude's house were too much, so we went back to
his fiancée's parents' house in Queensbury, New York. We agreed that
we needed to try some form of intuitive communication to get the answer to the question of whether or not we were ET souls. I decided that
we should try "automatic writing," in which you try to get your non-
dominant hand to write on its own. The house was almost pitch-black,
so to get started we had to turn on a few lights. As I reached for one light
switch, I could hardly believe my eyes: There in the dining room, adjacent to the kitchen, was a table that was obviously from India. It was
square, had a red stain, and lots of white tile inlays, and each table leg
looked like a stylized elephant's head and trunk.

To my utter amazement, this was exactly the same table design that
I had been so fond of at Angelica's place. Angelica had all her sacred
items on this same table, and as soon as I saw them, I said they reminded
me of Muktananda. Then I had learned that Angelica spent most of her
childhood and adolescence in Muktananda's ashram. The guys I met on
the train were going out to that same ashram to stay, and one of them
had experienced a true miracle of darshan from Muktananda's advanced
"sidhi" powers. Now I was about to try to use my own abilities, however
small they might be, to try to determine if I was an extraterrestrial soul.
The synchronicity of seeing the same table in both places was so powerful that I could feel a physical pressure on my head as I strove to put it
all together. There was clearly something special about the place we were
in, and what we were about to try.

Each of us then taped a piece of paper down on the floor, blanked out
our minds, went into a deep state of meditation, and allowed the pencil
to move on its own. As I tuned in deeper and deeper, I could hear three
words coming through that my hand wanted to turn into writing:
"Chasten. Awareness. Hostile." I let my hand write each word. I meditated on these three words and realized that I did have a sleazy side, and
I could certainly be more chaste—as in pure and virtuous. I definitely
needed to cultivate my awareness, and there was also a part of my per-

sonality that had become hostile after my dysfunctional relationship and a string of bad jobs. It was only a few weeks ago that I was screaming in anger at the top of my lungs after crashing my car into a tree. So far, everything made sense. Now I felt I was too close to the work, for I shouldn't be understanding or analyzing anything that my hand was writing. I tuned in deeper and felt my hand doing some slow, curving lines back and forth across the same space. I had no idea what, if anything, I was writing.

At this point, I decided to try concentrating even harder. I put all my focus on my third-eye area, crossing both my eyes and looking up at it with my eyes closed. I tried to pull myself as deeply into trance as I possibly could, really focusing on the power of my breath. Suddenly and without warning, my hand jumped to life and started doing a bunch of things all by itself. Very quickly, it scribbled something out. The only character I was distinctly aware of writing was the letter *X*. Otherwise, I had no idea what it said or what had just happened, but I knew exactly when it was over. I immediately threw the pencil down, and said, "Jude, turn on the lights! Something crazy just happened." Nothing could have prepared me for what I was about to see.

CHAPTER TWELVE

Preparing for Contact

I t was November 1995. I had just lost my job at the mental hospital for being "too friendly to the patients," and in despair, I tried "automatic writing" to ask the burning question of whether I was an ET soul. Many different dreams had already been strongly suggesting that I would find the answer. As I was in a deep trance state, my left, non-writing hand had traced out legible words on the paper taped to the floor. The first encoded message had appeared from a combination of slow, curving lines that my hand had drawn forward and backward. When you read the lines together, they clearly and undeniably said "Christ Cometh." This was quite surprising to me, since I was not at all raised to be religious. My mother felt she had escaped from her fundamentalist Christian family and wanted nothing to do with it. I had just been through the upsetting event of watching my grandmother being taken to the emergency room during Thanksgiving dinner, which of course caused me to think about mortality, the afterlife, and their intense Christian beliefs. My father's parents would go to church for Christmas, funerals, and the occasional strawberry festival, but that was about it. Christianity had always felt like a dangerous and confused subject that I tried to avoid whenever possible.

Now my own hand had written "Christ Cometh" when I asked the question about whether or not I was an extraterrestrial/angelic soul. The answer was certainly deeper than the question. Jude also noticed that the last two letters of *Cometh* also looked like the word *Ra*, written with a capital *R* and a lowercase *A*. The word *Ra* was clearly smaller and on a lower level than the rest of the phrase, but it was legible. I didn't think this was a genuine discovery at the time, although it did occur to me that Scott Mandelker had based most of his research on the Law of One series. The name of the alleged entity speaking in those books was Ra—just like the word that had appeared in my automatic writing.

Then, on the next line down, my hand had suddenly jumped to life and written a short burst of letters and numbers very quickly. The lines were extra fine, but once we saw them in the light, I could clearly read them. The writing was a very bizarre eleven-letter code sequence. The capitalizations and the spacing have been preserved exactly as they appeared:

EC 40 57 & oxen

I have to say that, at this point, the excitement was almost overpowering. This code had somehow come through me without my conscious awareness whatsoever. It was a mystery . . . a puzzle. And ciphers can be broken. It looked as if the entire room was vibrating with visible sparkles of light. It didn't take us very long in this state to figure out that *EC 40 57* must be a Bible quote. Despite the fact that Jude's fiancée's family were staunch Christians, we had a really hard time finding a Bible. We eventually located a black leather-bound copy inside a wooden chest, on top of some blankets. I had never felt so happy about seeing a Bible in my entire life. The smell of the leather, the feel of the soft cover in my hands . . . in that moment, it was pure perfection. It had the answers I was looking for.

We immediately opened the book to Ecclesiastes, since the code started with *EC*, but there was no verse 40. Chapter 1 ended with verse 18. Jude was devastated; he was really hoping we would find something. "Wait a minute," I said. I suddenly remembered information I had read in one of the metaphysical books over the last three years. The chapter markers were only added in later. In the early years, Bible quotes were only counted by the verse number. I told Jude that we should start reading at 40 verses after the beginning, and end on 57 verses after the beginning. We quickly did the math and realized that this would generate a quote of Ecclesiastes 2:22–3:13. That was it! We had cracked the code! Best of all, the passage began with 2:22. This was another repeating-number synchronicity, just like the ones I had been seeing almost daily ever since I had started doing my UFO research, most frequently on digital clocks. The opening number 2:22 felt absolutely like a part of the message—as if I was finally discovering the supernatural contact that all of these synchronicities had been leading me toward.

My hands were trembling and I could barely hold back tears as I started reading the words out loud. I do not remember which version of the Bible I was reading from, but this passage from the New International Version is about as close as I can find online: "What do people get for all the toil and anxious striving with which they labor under the sun? All their days their work is grief and pain; even at night their minds do not rest. This too is meaningless."[1] I had to stop right there. I was devastated about losing my job at the mental hospital, and even more devastated about being rejected by the only metaphysical graduate school I had applied to. I certainly had enough anxiety that it was causing me to suffer with insomnia, as the passage described. Now it was as if some higher intelligence was sitting up there with a Bible, and found the single most important quote that I could have possibly heard at that time. The message was obvious: The mental ward was a really rough job, and it wasn't anywhere near as important for my future as I thought it would be. In fact, the whole thing was "meaningless." That was quite a powerful statement, and not one I could easily ignore. To do that job, I would have needed to violate the core of my being and treat people as a prison warden does. And I knew there was no way this quote could have been hiding somewhere in my subconscious, for I had never read the Bible.

Then, as the passage moved on into chapter 3, it went through a series of verses that were made immortal by the Byrds in their classic hit song "Turn, Turn, Turn." I honestly didn't even know those lyrics had come out of the Bible, and yet here were these timeless rock and roll lyrics in Ecclesiastes—minus the repetition of the words *turn, turn, turn*. Out loud I read:

To every thing, there is a season, and a time to every purpose
under heaven: A time to be born, and a time to die; a time to
plant, and a time to pluck up that which is planted; a time
to kill, and a time to heal; a time to break down, and a
time to build up; a time to weep, and a time to laugh; a time
to mourn, and a time to dance; a time to cast away stones,
and a time to gather stones together; a time to embrace, and
a time to refrain from embracing; a time to get, and a time to
lose; a time to keep, and a time to cast away; a time to rend,
and a time to sew; a time to keep silence, and a time to speak;
a time to love, and a time to hate; a time of war, and a time
of peace.[2]

Now these words took on far greater significance. The passage was all
about cycles of birth and death, metaphorically and literally. Clearly, it
appeared that some higher intelligence had picked out this quote for me.
This was no dream—this was absolutely happening to me in real life.
There was no way I could have consciously known about this passage
in the Bible. Losing the graduate school and then the mental health job
felt like a death, and my grandmother nearly died just days later on
Thanksgiving. There were multiple references to death and mourning in
this passage. With the constant repetition of the metaphors of new birth
in it as well, I was clearly being shown, as it said at the beginning, that
the loss of this job and the graduate school education was indeed "meaningless." The last line in the coded passage was Ecclesiastes 3:13, and I will
never forget the exact wording within whatever version of the Bible I was
reading at the time, which I have not been able to relocate online. It said,
"To eat and drink, and be happy in one's toil: This is the grace of God."
Now I felt I understood the message even more. Right now, the main
goal was to find a job that I could be happy with—a job that could pay
me enough to eat and drink and have a place to live. My future was very
likely going to involve some deeper level of the telepathic contact that I
had just experienced. Now the challenge was to figure out how I could
get additional results that were as good as what had happened with automatic writing.

The Beast of Burden?

My scribbled automatic writing ended with an ampersand, the "and" symbol, followed by the word *oxen*. I immediately understood what this meant, as it used dreamlike symbolism to convey a message. Earlier that summer, one of a variety of my temp jobs was with ADT Home Security at the Altamont Fair. My job was to get people interested enough in a home alarm system to agree to be contacted by a sales representative. My booth was directly behind the chicken barn and it was always very noisy and smelly. Directly next to me was a woman from Kenya, selling gorgeous dark statues of wild African animals that her husband had carved out of ebony. We had long conversations between bursts of customers. I finally bought the ox sculpture for twenty-two dollars, which was a huge sacrifice for me at the time, nearly four hours' worth of my pay. I felt this would be a good symbol for me now that I had finished college and needed to enter the working world and become a "beast of burden." I had accepted my fate, and the sculpture would help me have a good laugh about it. I also knew I was born in the Year of the Ox in the Chinese Zodiac.

When I asked the woman what the ox meant to people in her culture, she just laughed and said, "You Americans always want these animals to mean something." I chuckled, and decided to rephrase the question. I wanted her to explain this animal's role and behavior in Kenya, in order to tap into any dreamlike symbolism it might hold. By this point, I had been analyzing my dreams on a daily basis for almost three years. I said, "This is an ox, right? A beast of burden. You hitch up your plow to it, crack the whip, and get it to dig out your crops all day for you." The woman laughed. "Oh no," she said. "This is a water buffalo. One of the three most dangerous animals in all of Kenya. If you see this animal and you are more than three hundred feet away, you run like crazy. If you see one closer than three hundred feet, you pray for a quick death." I was quite surprised to hear this, and asked her what would happen. The water buffalo would run toward you at a very high speed, gut you with its horns, throw you up into the air, and then trample you after you hit the ground. It would continue to repeat the process until you had stopped moving.

At the time, I thought this was ironic. Perhaps I wasn't going to become a "slave to the system" by having to get a real job. Perhaps I would actually become a powerful force, in this case for good. Now this dreamlike metaphor had become far more significant, because the word *oxen* was included at the end of a Bible quote that had just told me my old job was meaningless, and I needed to find something I could be happy with. The greater message was that I was not going to become a "beast of burden" at all. Instead, I had the potential to become a true warrior for the positive. I would never fully recover all the stupendous abilities I may have had in the higher densities, as the Law of One source had indicated, but I could still make a difference in the world. My quote also featured the plural of the word *ox*, which suggested that I would help other people become spiritual warriors as well.

I had asked the Universe for an answer to the question "Am I a Wanderer?" Instead of giving me a simple yes, I had gotten the words *Christ Cometh* and an amazingly specific Bible quote that spoke directly to what I had just experienced—complete with the numerical synchronicity of 2:22. I was deeply fascinated by the whole thing. The extraterrestrials I was trying to get in contact with seemed to have a keen interest in Christianity, including an apparently encyclopedic knowledge of the Bible. The implications of all this were causing both of our minds to reel. In a surprising moment of clarity, Jude asked, "Well, do you think we should ask for more confirmation? Should we do it again, or is this our proof here?" I stopped and thought for a moment. "No," I said, pausing somberly, "I am pretty happy with what I got here." At that exact second, the clock struck two, making two loud bonging noises that echoed through the room.

Jude and I looked at each other in astonishment, realizing that yet another layer of synchronicity around the number two had just been added to the mix. This was even further proof that something truly extraordinary had occurred, and I had gotten the necessary message. I now had Ecclesiastes 2:22, the ox statue I bought for twenty-two dollars, and the clock striking two at the perfect moment to answer Jude's question. In yet another astonishing synchronicity, without any conscious planning on my part, the original hardcover American edition of this book is precisely at page 222 now as we reach this point in our story. I also had the elephant table appearing in the house, which linked this event to my meeting with Angelica and the train ride. My greatest wish was to become a talented and beloved spiritual servant of the people like Muktananda, and all roads now seemed to be leading in that direction.

At the same time, I was still living in a cramped little space in a boardinghouse with shared bathrooms and six other rooms of boarders, including a couple who were extremely disrespectful to the rest of us. I couldn't stand to live in a boardinghouse any longer. I called up my college buddy Eric, who had gotten me the pizza delivery job on the first night I had arrived, and asked him if he wanted to go in together on a place. One housemate would be far easier to deal with than seven. I was only making two hundred dollars a week, and he was earning about the same at the Godiva Chocolatier at the Poughkeepsie Mall. However, by pooling our income, we could get a much nicer place than either of our current rooms, and we would definitely clean up after ourselves, unlike my current roommates. Plus, we were already accustomed to hanging out and talking every day. Eric agreed with me that this was a terrific idea, and I immediately began scouring the newspaper's classified ads for our best option.

Goin' to Rosendale: Birthplace of Modern America

Eric and I both agreed that Rosendale was a great choice in which to find an apartment. About twelve minutes north of New Paltz on NY Route 32, it was a sleepy little country town with original brownstone brick buildings from the 1800s. And just like New Paltz and a few other neighboring towns, such as High Falls, Stone Ridge, and Marbletown, Rosendale had some historic stone houses that dated back to the 1700s and even the 1600s. Although most people talk only about Jamestown or Plymouth Rock as the original colonies in the US, the New Paltz area was also one of the very first American settlements, in this case by the Dutch. Since Rosendale became the birthplace of my own spiritual contact, which would generate so many accurate future prophecies, I feel it is worth the time to explore how the Rosendale area can be seen as the birthplace of modern America and the Industrial Revolution.

The Dutch had sailed across the Atlantic, found the mouth of the Hudson River, sailed north against the current for about ninety miles, and then stopped. They believed they had found Paradise on Earth. They were members of a very interesting religious group known as the Huguenots, with an intensely spiritual focus. They created a harmonious relationship with the native peoples. Their original wedding vows spoke with awe and reverence about the universe, and they had an immensely peaceful society, in harmony with their environment. They had fled their own native country because of persecution for their beliefs. Their stone houses are still standing, and it is common to see people taking historic tours of them.

Interestingly enough, the Huguenots had been drawn directly into an area with a geological anomaly—natural cement—that allowed the region to become the literal birthplace of the Industrial Revolution. This helped to usher in the modern world as we now know it. The Huguenots couldn't have known about this at the time, for this unique and highly valuable geological anomaly wasn't discovered for nearly another two hundred years. This did suggest that some higher force was at work, guiding these spiritual pilgrims to an immensely beneficial area. Rosendale was the town that had the most of this precious natural resource.

I had already toured Rosendale in a college class I had taken on the cement mining industry. Until the discovery of natural cement in 1818 by Canvass White in Fayetteville, New York, as the Erie Canal was under construction, all buildings had to be made of wood, stone, adobe, or brick.[3] It was very difficult, if not impossible, to make a building of any impressive size. It could be done, such as with the steel beams that made the Eiffel Tower in France or the grand old stone cathedrals of Europe, but it was highly expensive and impractical for the world of business. Rosendale changed all that, having by far the largest quantity of natural cement that had been found in the 1800s, and America got a jump start on the rest of the world as a result. Without Rosendale cement, the Industrial Revolution in America might have been delayed well into the twentieth century.

A soft material called dolostone had been found in the geological strata of Rosendale, creating a boom town as it became the largest single production source in the world for natural cement. The original discovery was made by accident in 1818. Canvass White realized that if you heated up the dolostone with fire and then got it wet, it would harden into a material that was stronger than steel. You could grind up the kiln-fired rocks into a powder, and it would harden into stone when you added water. This was the world's first cement, well before someone discovered that you could add quick-lime to sand and gravel and make concrete. Rosendale cement was of far higher quality than the concrete discovered later, and was of pivotal importance in the Industrial Revolution. Large buildings, factories, and structures that were never before possible could be made out of the cement. This began with the Delaware and Hudson Canal in 1825, which revolutionized shipping in the Northeast even before the rise of the railroad system. By 1850, fully three hundred million pounds of this cement were being produced per year.[4] Rosendale cement also built the Brooklyn Bridge, the Empire State Building, the pedestal for the Statue of Liberty, Grand Central Station, the Pennsylvania railroad tunnels, and the New York City sidewalks, to name only a few.

There was also a horrific downside to this money machine. Almost all the trees in the area had been cut down by the cement mining industry, because they needed to feed massive kilns that were constantly hungry for fuel. Throughout the countryside, there were gigantic wounds in the land where hundreds of thousands of tons of dolostone had been blasted and chipped out. Dynamite explosions constantly echoed through the land, and the ground shook from the impact. The labor was very difficult for the workers, and injuries and deaths were all too common. Business was booming, and the people running the company were multimillionaires. Then Portland cement began to be produced for sale in 1875, and it was significantly less expensive.[5] Rosendale Cement sales greatly weakened as the twentieth century moved along—and the company finally stopped selling all cement in 1970.[6] All the massive kilns that had been used to fire the dolostone were left to rot, just like the buildings I had seen in my railroad journey to Colorado. Gigantic caverns where the dolostone had been mined were left abandoned and unmarked. Some of these caves were turned into public parks, the Widow Jane Mine being the most notable one.[7]

The largest of the former mining caves in the area had been taken over and sealed off by Iron Mountain, a facility supposedly designed for government and private records storage. The entire Iron Mountain facility was effectively an underground base. Travelers could see the huge, bricked-up cave entrances right on Route 32 as they drove through town. In 2016, a photographer was finally allowed limited access to the facility and found that apparently only ten people are still working at the location today.[8] There were local rumors that the guidance systems and launch codes for our nuclear missile arsenal were stored there. Rosendale was therefore sitting on top of the brain that could guide nuclear missiles to completely destroy all life on planet Earth, if we ever did have a nuclear war. I realized that the womb of the Industrial Revolution might also contain the guidance systems for total planetary annihilation.

There was also a rumor that an underground train connected Iron Mountain to an EG&G Rotron facility in Woodstock. I knew from reading *Alien Contact* by Timothy Good that EG&G Rotron was one of the military defense contractors directly involved in reverse-engineering crashed extraterrestrial spacecraft—and that this technology, once declassified, could be humanity's best hope.[9] The UFOs had to be using a source of almost limitless clean energy. They obviously didn't need to stop off at the gas station on their way to Earth. They had no wings, turbofans, or jet engines, and could execute aeronautical maneuvers that showed they undoubtedly had conquered gravity and inertia. If we could develop antigravity and free energy, our world would change in ways we can barely even conceive of. And my research now had me completely convinced that the military-industrial complex already had this technology, in great abundance, but were refusing to share it with the rest of us. Even if Artie's crystal gun was the one and only gift that we ever got declassified, we would have antigravity and would be able to easily build massive pyramids once again.

EARTHQUAKE!

Just as I was writing the above section of the book, on July 4, 2019—Independence Day—I had a major synchronicity that is definitely worth mentioning. I was writing about dynamite blasting huge holes in the ground in Rosendale, and was envisioning all the shaking this would produce, when only minutes later, the ground under my feet here in Los Angeles began reeling, lasting about thirty seconds. The walls were swaying, I was hearing cracking noises, and it felt as though I was taking a ride on a giant bowl of Jell-O. It turned out to be a 6.4-magnitude earthquake up in the Searles Valley, a remote area of Kern County roughly a hundred miles north of Los Angeles. As we will see, this was by no means "in the middle of nowhere" but is actually a location of major significance. This was the biggest quake we've had here in twenty-five years—since all the way back to the 1994 Northridge quake, which was a 6.6.[10]

Thankfully, unlike Northridge, the current quake did not strike a populated civilian area. It instead hit a very large military base known as China Lake, which is the biggest Area 51–type facility that no one has ever heard of. Several insiders told me this facility housed some of the darkest aspects of the military-industrial complex and its relationships with negative, demonic extraterrestrials. I must admit that it was quite shocking to go through the biggest earthquake I have ever felt, right after I was writing about the ground shaking from dynamite blasts. Nonetheless, after all the spectacular synchronicities I have experienced, I shouldn't be very surprised. It is also interesting that this quake was the largest in Los Angeles since 1994. That was the same year I got together with Yumi and began the sequence of events that are just now culminating in the story for 1995. This sort of impressive synchronicity is not at all uncommon.

Another quake happened the next day, under China Lake, that was even larger, and this one scared me even more. I will describe that incident later in our story. The combination of these two quakes completely and utterly destroyed the China Lake black-ops megabase, but the media

never said a word about it. Various insiders suggested that nefarious covert aerosol spraying operations were being run out of the facility and
poisoning our skies. On the very next day, July 6, 2019, the notorious
Jeffrey Epstein was indicted and arrested. I wrote a huge article about all
this on July 7.[11] I do not see the timing of these three major events as an
accident. I believe this was the work of an alliance that had formed
within the government, military, and intelligence communities around
the world. Earthquake weapons were used to take out a mission-critical
base for the Deep State, and then Jeffrey Epstein, a criminal who could
expose the ugliest secrets of this secretive organization, was arrested. This
was a major combined attack that could lead up to massive arrests of
Deep State/Illuminati/New World Order/Cabal operatives—which my
own source has been predicting since at least 1999.

The Schoolhouse Art Gallery

Getting back to Rosendale, the main street had a popular brothel for the
miners in the 1800s. The women would stand on the upper deck and
wave at the workers as they made their way home, either on horseback or
by foot. The building was still there when Eric and I arrived in 1995, now
transformed into the Rosendale Café, the go-to place for hippie vegan
cuisine and quality live music. At the time, Eric and I were both vegans,
so the café was very appealing. I had been gradually guided into eating
a strict diet, which had started to happen after my experience with the
Tuvan shaman in my senior year. I avoided specifically dairy, processed
foods, refined sugar, and meat products. I finally found an ad in the local
newspaper for an "artsy" brick apartment that was a remodeled old
schoolhouse, and I happily made the call and got an appointment. Eric
and I went to take a look.

The landlady, Lauran, started out by impressing us with a tour of the
art gallery on the property. The gallery had huge, twenty-foot-high ceilings and gorgeous exposed brick walls from the mid-1800s. The windows
were seven feet tall and reminded me of what you might see in an old
church. There was track lighting everywhere. The walls were filled with

stunning, large paintings that used bright lollipop colors. The paintings were whimsical and unique: one part Picasso, one part classic cartoons, and a generous dose of LSD. There was a man with a duck's beak instead of a nose, and with the body of a swan, wrapping himself around a woman in a beautiful lily-green pond reminiscent of the works of Vincent van Gogh. There were portraits that seared with unexpected color and emotional immediacy. There was a comical, Minotaur-like image of a half-man, half-bull creature that looked like it could easily have been a Picasso. The passion in these paintings was stunning. They were magnificent. We were definitely going to visit this gallery regularly, just to admire its works. "The art gallery is really great," I said, "but when do we get to see the apartment?"

"This is it," Lauran replied. "This is the apartment." Eric and I were absolutely shocked into silence. There was a prolonged and awkward pause as we looked around in disbelief. This place was an epic paradise. It was a beautiful historic brick building, a sacred church, and an upscale psychedelic art gallery all merged into one. Lauran appeared to get a bit concerned at this point by our silence. "I hope you won't mind allowing us to store the paintings on the walls." I was flabbergasted. "Store the paintings? Are you kidding me? We need to hang up even more of them! This is a full-blown art gallery! Eric and I are both artists and musicians! These are masterpieces! You're not having any showings here?" Lauran replied, "No, we're just renting out the space. Your kitchen is over here, and . . ."

I was now so excited that I couldn't even hear what she was saying. Her voice seemed to trail off as I realized that I would do whatever it took to land this apartment. Lauran's father was the renowned painter and videographer Allen Epstein, and he had lived and worked in this house with a community of friends until his death in 1993, two years before our showing. Allen had gone to Yale on a full scholarship when he was only seventeen years old, and he was obviously a true creative genius, who eventually became quite successful in the video production business. Lauran needed to rent out all the rooms in order to pay the mortgage, taxes, and utilities and have some basic income. Her father had named the house Chateau Bullshinski, complete with a funny plaque at the front that enshrined the name in Old English calligraphy. The subtitle on this sign was THE METAPHYSICAL RESORT. That same type of offbeat sense of humor was visible everywhere. We didn't even need to see the bathroom or the loft. We were surrounded by green trees, rolling hills, and sleepy suburban homes with generous plots of land, and an old mining canal with free-flowing creek water down by the main road. We found out later that there was a gorgeous, gigantic cement-mining cave right up at the top of the hill. To be able to afford a place like this with minimum-wage employment seemed like an impossible dream come true. "We'll take it. Right now. PLEASE don't show this place to anyone else!"

The official Allen Epstein website has a listing for a gallery showing from 2009, and Lauran's flowery description of her father's paintings captures their glory in sensual language I could never hope to duplicate:

> Whether a high-energy pastel or a deeply worked oil, the portraits tell of a penetrating intimacy between the artist and sitter. It is as if Allen imbibed the soul of his subject and then released on paper or canvas a material residue of their character, pressed and worked into shape by his able hand and the clarity and compassion with which he saw them. In each unique piece, deft line, emotive color, gestures and material choices surprise, yet embedded in every impasto or powdery surface is the afterglow of this very personal exchange.[12]

The Happiest Time of My Life

Until I got together with my wife, Elizabeth, there was no question that the two precious years I spent in the Schoolhouse from 1995 to 1997 were the happiest times of my life, despite the extreme difficulty of the jobs I ended up taking, particularly during the first six months. This proved to be the ideal location for an angelic/spiritual contact to occur. The rent was $875 a month. Eric and I needed to work together to afford it, and once we got settled, we did. I was unemployed when I first arrived and had quite the shocking karmic wake-up call before the end of December that convinced me to take a job working for $5.77 an hour, a mere two cents above minimum wage. We will discuss the whole sequence of events in the next chapter. I ended up making about two hundred dollars a week. Eric and I never had a TV, nor did we want one. I was able to set up my drum kit in the main gallery room, and I started improvising with a talented group of musicians from college, calling ourselves the Rosendale Jazz Project. We had Andy on keyboards, Jason on the upright bass, Jim from upstairs on guitar, and yours truly on percussion. We would just start playing, with no agreed-upon key signature, chords, or melodies—and as if by some supernatural force, amazing compositions would start emanating from our instruments.

Meanwhile, Eric was quickly mastering the Renaissance lute, a gorgeously carved, gut-stringed precursor to the guitar, which was a staple of high society in the 1600s—right when the Huguenots first arrived in our area. Eric was a serious historian and was studying with Paul O'Dette, who was arguably the best lute player in the world. Eric's right thumb plucked out agile basslines across multiple, deep strings, while his remaining fingers revealed intricate chords, melodies, harmonies, and arpeggios. The music had a timeless quality that instantly transported me back to the golden age of the Renaissance, when science was transforming the world, and spirit had just been liberated for the benefit of all. Eric practiced for at least two hours a day, and his delivery was nearly flawless. He also would regularly play CDs of Gregorian chants, such as from the Tallis Scholars, which only added to the sacred, mystical ambience of the space—In fact, I am listening to Peter Phillips and the Tallis Scholars as I write this.

"He Is One of Us"

More and more, I was having powerful dreams about UFO contact. These dreams all seemed to be suggesting that positive extraterrestrials wanted to communicate with me. I thought back to my experience with automatic writing, which already felt like ancient history by now. Things had gotten much, much better since I had moved into the Schoolhouse. The automatic writing was very real, and very powerful . . . get a job and be happy . . . but now what? Nothing was happening.

Everything went into overdrive when I got our latest phone bill in the mail the following month, in January, soon after I had finally gotten a job. It was well over two hundred dollars. Almost the entire amount I owed was from breakup conversations with Yumi, which would often descend into prolonged and very expensive bouts of silence. I didn't have two hundred dollars. That was basically my food for the month. And my parents had hardly anything to share, so I didn't dare ask them for a loan.

I thought back to the messages I had received: Chasten, Awareness, Hostile; Christ Cometh; eat and drink and be happy in your work, for this is the grace of God. Let your work turn you into a nearly indestructible force for good. This message clearly had emanated from a supernatural force outside of myself, but now I felt terribly, horribly alone. I was sitting at the table in our apartment with one of our deep-blue-and-green Asian-style plates in front of me. My used napkin was resting on the plate. At that moment I completely lost it and broke down crying. I didn't know what the hell to do. "If you guys are real, and I know you are, then you need to show yourselves! Right now! I can't go on like this. Please!" Then I just sobbed and sobbed for several minutes. I finally pulled myself together and started looking out the huge windows, wondering if a glowing craft would be waiting for me outside. Nothing. I put my hands together and tried to levitate the napkin on my plate. Nothing. Not even a little tickle. The beautiful paintings stared down at me with compassion, but I was truly lost. I started crying all over again.

Finally, I realized that nothing was going to happen. I had to pull it together. I looked at the phone bill and remembered that I had ordered a special long-distance package for calling Japan at a deep discount. For some "convenient" reason, the phone company had never applied the discount. They had billed me for the full price of well over two dollars a minute. I grabbed our funny little phone, which stood up straight on its four rubber feet, and called the phone company. A woman answered and I very politely explained my situation.

After an excruciating pause while she looked through her system, she revealed that I was right, it was there in her notes, and they had made a mistake. I let out a huge sigh of relief. She then ran the numbers and came back with a manageable new bill of thirty-five dollars. That I could pay—and I did it by debit card right over the phone to lock it in. I was overwhelmed with relief and thanked her profusely for her help. I put the phone down, put on some music, and went to bed happy, well before Eric ever got home. By now, I had completely forgotten about my urgent prayer . . . but THEY definitely had not. Little did I know that Eric would wake up the next morning with a dream in which a Jesus-like being came out of a UFO to tell him, "It is very important that you know that he [David] is one of us." And Eric never knew a thing about the prayer I had made. This would just be the first of a series of ever-increasingly fascinating phenomena that ultimately led up to my making conscious, telepathic contact with angelic extraterrestrials. They gave me beautiful guidance and inspiration, and also displayed a mind-blowing ability to predict the future with shocking accuracy. Their ultimate message was to ask us to prepare for a massive solar-system-wide event that is very similar to the Christian idea of the rapture. Namely, our entire planet is heading into a massive and irreversible spiritual transformation.

Part Two

CHAPTER THIRTEEN

Run before You Can Fly

I first learned about the art of awakening in the dream when I was sixteen years old. Following the simple techniques of Dr. Stephen LaBerge, I could become fully lucid and conscious in my dream space. From there, I had godlike abilities. I could fly, walk through walls, manifest any objects I desired, and completely transform anything and everything around me. I stopped using all mind-altering drugs in September 1992 and soon began writing down my dreams every morning. In February 1993, I found out from an insider that UFOs were real, Roswell really happened, and everyone in the higher echelons of NASA knew about it. We had already built working antigravity craft from this technology, which was being used actively in highly classified programs. I ended up reading over three hundred books on the subject in the following three years. My senior-year college roommate, Artie, had a life that was littered with clues that his parents had somehow been involved in this mysterious world. Synchronicities were happening to me with greater and greater frequency, along with mind-blowingly wonderful dreams of UFOs, benevolent human extraterrestrials, and advanced ancient civilizations.

All the Dots Are Connecting

All this buildup had now culminated in a very intriguing discovery about myself. I was heavily guided to read *From Elsewhere: Being E.T. in America*, about "the subculture of those who claim to be of non-earthly origins," by Scott Mandelker. I found I could answer all twelve questions at the back of the book in the affirmative, which strongly suggested I had an unusually advanced and benevolent extraterrestrial soul. This meant that I might be something called a Wanderer, in Mandelker's terms. To fully remember that this was who I was, I would have to "penetrate the veil of forgetfulness," which is a phrase used in the Law of One series.

Mandelker's entire work was based on the Law of One, a mysterious body of intuitively revealed teachings that began appearing in 1981. In Session 12, Question 27, of the Law of One series, it indicated that there were 65 million wanderers on Earth at the time Mandelker estimated that the number should have been well in excess of 100 million in the 1990s, making it about one in 60 people. To penetrate the veil, it was necessary to use meditation and intuitive means to seek an answer that could not be provided by any of our normal five senses. The Law of One is arguably the finest modern example of what can be achieved through this type of a process. In a sitting meditation with my friend Jude, I then attempted to do "automatic writing" with my left hand. Five words came through, the first three of which I was semi-aware of. My hand then sprang to life and quickly scratched out a sequence of eleven characters that included a Bible quote. The encoded quote turned out to be Ecclesiastes 2:22–3:13. From the very beginning to the very end of the passage, it showed a precise understanding of what I had been going through in my life. I had lost a stressful job working in a mental hospital, which I had felt was necessary to earn a graduate degree and eventually transition into being a respectable UFO researcher. The handwritten message told me that "Christ Cometh," and I just needed to eat and drink and be happy in my work in order to focus my spare time on UFO research; I didn't need to take on another stressful job to move forward. Clearly, there were far greater things ahead for me.

My college friend Eric and I ended up going in together on an apartment, a beautiful remodeled 1800s schoolhouse, in Rosendale, New York, which produced the natural cement that made the modern industrial revolution possible in the US. Rosendale cement allowed for much larger and sturdier buildings to be constructed at a much lower cost. Many huge caves dotted the landscape, where countless tons of dolostone were blown and chipped out to make newly discovered Rosendale cement. The largest of these caves had been converted into a strange underground base called Iron Mountain. Local legends said that this base was connected by an underground tunnel system to another base run by the defense contractor EG&G Rotron in the Woodstock area. Our apartment was extremely beautiful, with exposed brick walls, cathedral ceilings, and a wealth of paintings from the prodigious artist and videographer Allen Epstein.

No Desire to Enter the "Real World"

The sheer awesomeness of the idea that I had an extraterrestrial soul, and that we were all heading into a mass spiritual awakening event on Earth that many called Ascension, made the hunt for a "normal job" seem incredibly depressing. When Eric and I first decided to get the art-gallery apartment, I was working at the mental hospital. Then after we signed the lease, I lost my job, found Scott Mandelker's book, and got the Bible quote telling me everything would be okay. Eric paid almost the entire $1,750 we needed to claim the space. I moved into our new place unemployed, but I wasn't really trying as hard as I should have been to find what was sure to be another low-paying job. I even admitted to myself that I was being lazy and self-indulgent. There were any number of days when I could have been looking for a job and decided instead to take my time, not go at all, or apply only to one place rather than four or five in a single day. The new apartment was an incredibly relaxing paradise, and I did not want to leave.

Every day I had to walk into a corporate office with stark fluorescent lights, fill out a depressing summary of all the dead-end jobs I had en-

dured, provide names and phone numbers for each of my former super-
visors, and try to act excited about taking on yet another low-paying and
very humble job. This felt degrading to me. I was new to adult living,
having graduated from an all-expenses-paid college experience only six
months before, and I knew that Eric had enough money to take care of
both of us, at least for a while, in addition to my parents, who had a
little money, and my grandparents, who had a lot of money. If I found
myself in a dire emergency, I could ask my relatives for a onetime grant
or loan, but this was by no means a sustainable option. My grandfather
was only interested in paying for graduate school, and otherwise he did
not intend to help me out. I was endangering my own life by not looking
very hard for work, but I still felt the need to have some "private space"
to adjust to this new discovery about myself. After all, I now knew I was
an awakened Volunteer Extraterrestrial Ambassador to Earth. Did my
angelic friends seriously expect me to work for six bucks an hour?

Little did I know that my lazy, self-indulgent attitude, where I expected everyone else to take care of my basic needs, was setting me up
for a massive blast of bad karma. The angelic extraterrestrials I had come
into contact with were not just there to give me synchronicities, insider
disclosures, mystical Bible quotes, and friendly dream advice. They were
equally responsible for creating explosions of karmic justice that would
knock me back on course if I fell out of line. In this particular case, they
decided that a terrifying car crash in the snow was necessary to get my
attention and shock me into getting another job. To show me that they
had planned out the whole thing, they gave me a series of prophetic
dreams about car accidents, leading right up to the terrifying moment
itself. Then, even as the crash was happening, they gave me an undeniable synchronicity that let me know they were involved in planning it—
every step of the way.

I feel this is one interesting way in which my own story deviates from
many other accounts of alleged spiritual contact. In many of these cases,
the contactee seems to report nothing but light, love, positivity, ego-
boosting compliments, and comforts from their source. In my own case,
I found myself being heavily criticized and experiencing very frightening
brushes with death if I did not listen carefully, follow the guidance, and

practice the highest possible moral and ethical standards. Regardless of how difficult certain suggestions were to follow, I was ultimately able to see that all these guidelines were coming from a truly mature and benevolent place. I learned the hard way that I could not "get away" with anything. Karma was absolute, inevitable, and meticulously precise. I do believe these same rules apply to everyone, whether they realize it or not. Sadly, some people have so much balancing to do that they will require multiple lifetimes to pay off their debts—and from the higher perspective, no one can cheat the system.

Prophetic Dreams of an Imminent Car Crash

My first prophetic car-crash dream was on December 10, 1995. In this case, I was driving in heavy snowfall. A huge snowplow truck was coming right at me as I drove up the road. I had to swerve off to the side just in time to avoid being hit. The mountain of snow that the plow was pushing was truly colossal. However, as soon as I was on the roadside, a massive, bloody war began. People were creating lethal weapons out of snow, and fighting and dying in this battle. I was no longer in my car, and I had to jump and run and work hard to avoid being hit by anything. A security guard from my job at the mental hospital was one of the people fighting, and he was in a total, violent rage. He spotted me and began running toward me at full speed with his weapon in hand, clearly with the intent to murder me. As he rushed up to me, I manifested my own sword out of snow and struck him with it.

In retaliation, he bit down on my middle finger—and would not let go. I was in terrible pain. I punched him again and again, but I could not get him to release the bite. Then all of a sudden, he stopped biting me and said, "It's cold," as if he was perplexed and had just woken up from a strange, violent trance. We both stopped fighting and sat down on the cold, snowy ground, looking at each other. Then we looked over to our left and realized that we both had a common enemy. Another guy was prancing around, acting like he was a star athlete, and waving to people as if he was royalty. He was the one who had started this war by convincing everyone to fight each other. In truth, he was just like us. We both started laughing at his ridiculous narcissism.

In dream-analysis terms, every character in this dream was a part of myself, as is usually the case. The security guard from the mental hospital was a part of me that was still very angry about my former job and did not want another one. In the dream, that part of me was ready to fight to the death to get some free time. Then that part of me finally realized that I was just too cold. Symbolically, this meant I felt emotionally unfulfilled and lonely. I was worried that getting another job would make my loneliness even worse. The guy who was pretending to be a star athlete was the part of me that felt entitled not to work. Once I realized how ridiculous this attitude was, I could get another job, take care of my basic needs, form a new circle of friends at work, and stop this war raging inside myself. Since the war was being fought with snow, this meant I had allowed my emotions to become very cold and hardened to the concerns of others, including my new housemate Eric. I should not have been living off Eric, nor any potential emergency funds from my family—the dreams clearly wanted me to take care of myself. I did not see all this at the time.

The second prophetic dream was on December 13, 1995. In this one, I was with a group of people who were looking at a car for sale that was being displayed in a garage. The car was extremely lightweight and therefore seemed quite unsafe to drive, particularly in the snow. Whoever was selling this car was up to no good. They were well aware that someone could crash in this car, and that it would crumple up very easily and potentially kill the driver. Suddenly, a massive and frightening-looking dinosaur appeared in the distance. He spotted us and started smashing his way over to where we were standing by the car. As I woke up, I thought about how easily the dinosaur could stomp on the car and destroy it. The paper-thin car symbolized my overall physical wellness. By being unemployed, I was unable to take care of myself. The salesman was the part of me that wasn't being honest about how much danger I was putting myself in by thinking that not having a job was a good idea. The dinosaur represented the inevitable negative karma that would come crashing into my life if I refused to take care of myself—and the dinosaur ended up smashing a car.

The next morning, on December 14, 1995, I saw my own car sitting in our new driveway in Rosendale. Another dinosaur, this time a ptero-dactyl, was flying in the air overhead. It had a triangular head, and as I kept looking, I realized it might be some kind of artificial flying craft built to look like a dinosaur. Not sure whether or not it was a real dino-saur, I said, "It's cool how you can still see those," before realizing the impossibility of seeing a dinosaur in modern times. For whatever reason, I was not triggered into awakening in the dream, despite how strange this was. The craft flew down and landed, and I noticed that a newlywed couple was seated in the cockpit, flying it. The craft ended up transform-ing into some sort of antique car. However, the car could fly, and it did not have any wheels. The couple were terrible pilots, but there seemed to be a mechanism that prevented them from hitting anything or crashing into the ground. I was very happy to see that safe and effective flying vehicles like that were now available.

The flying craft and the married couple piloting it again represented my extraterrestrial family. I may well have been seeing an actual visita-tion that had taken place, translated into a symbolic form in my dream. According to Corey Goode, it is common for both genuine ET contacts and military abductions, or MILABS, to introduce "screen memories" of an event after it happens. You will have a dream similar to what actually happened, but it will also have metaphorical and symbolic differences from the event itself. This is vastly more common than most of us could ever realize. By analyzing this sequence with the metaphorical language of dreams, the dinosaur craft suggested that these people had been around on Earth for millions of years, just as the Anshar would later reveal about themselves to Corey Goode.

I have also heard from various insiders that our own reverse-engineered antigravity spacecraft have very advanced systems called Flight Control. These systems prevent crashing in the vast majority of cases, thus greatly increasing the safety factor of traveling in them. Over-all, this dream again strongly warned me that I was going to have a car crash but that I would be safe, that no great damage would occur to me or to the car. This would be more akin to a wake-up call, albeit a very dramatic one.

As I was rereading all these dreams for the first time in August 2019, the time-loop phenomenon happened again. On December 15, 1995, I had a dream about a romantic relationship with a blond woman who had stunning similarities with my wife, Elizabeth. This would prove to be only one of many dreams I found from that time that featured her so precisely, and went into a series of very pertinent personal issues that I could never have known twenty-four years in advance. Then, on the sixteenth, I had another dream that perfectly described a black woman my wife and I have been working with on developing movies and television shows. The woman in the dream was a superhero who was levitating off the ground, with a flowing cape and gleaming bluish-white beams of light coming from her eyes. She was using these beams to zap down evil men who had great wealth and social influence. This was another interesting discovery, for this friend of ours is very well aware of the real problems we are facing in the world, and of the media suppression we must move through to get the truth.

Then, on December 17, 1995, I was back to having yet another prophetic dream about an upcoming car crash. In retrospect, it is interesting that I did not suspect a thing when all these dreams were coming in. I was very depressed and had no idea that my selfishness was causing me to require such a major blast of bad karma. In this dream, I was about to receive a used car as a gift. I was very grateful to receive it. Just as I was about to take possession of the vehicle, a mean little boy came up and started cutting the glass. I asked him to please not do that, but he didn't seem to care. It was obvious that he felt the car was abandoned, so he could do whatever he wanted. He then shattered the glass in the rearview mirror, right in front of me. I became so furious that I grabbed him in a headlock and wanted to hurt him. At this exact moment, my alarm woke me up. I realized this dream was saying I was only hurting myself, and the kid represented some part of me. What I did not see was that the kid represented the part of me that didn't want to get a job, because I was so angry and hostile about my past experiences. In the process, I was destroying my own spiritual vehicle, symbolized by the car. The headlock I put the boy in could easily have represented the car crash that was about to happen to this maladaptive part of myself, in a symbolic form.

Point of Impact

On the very next day, Monday, December 18, 1995, my accident happened in the early afternoon. At the time, I never thought about how bad my marijuana addiction had gotten before I had quit, and how self-destructive I had become while I was still using. I often tried to think and act as if it had never even happened. Now I was completely dodging my responsibility by not looking for a job. Lack of responsibility was the exact same problem that had plagued me as a marijuana smoker. Even though I had cleaned up, the habit patterns themselves still remained. I still wanted to live in a fog, ignore my worldly responsibilities, and stay "high," only now my drug of choice was UFO and metaphysical research.

I was driving down the road near our house, in the snow. The curving road ran next to an iced-over stream at the bottom of a deep ditch. Although I still had over three and a half more hours to look for another job that day, I made the conscious decision that I would just give up and go home. Eric wouldn't be there because he was working, so I could "get away" with it. I was weary and tired of beating my brains out, trying to find jobs that I was massively overqualified for, and that I didn't have any interest in performing except to pay for my food and rent.

I gripped the steering wheel in frustration as all these thoughts cascaded through my mind. *No more ridiculous job searching for today. I'm tired of it.* Suddenly, I rounded a left turn and the car started to slide—fast. This was very, very bad. I completely lost control of the vehicle as it began spinning in a clockwise circle, while I was going about thirty-five miles an hour. I mentally screamed, slammed on the brakes, and the spin only got worse. I wasn't experienced enough yet to know that you are supposed to steer into the turn and pump the brakes, or that you had to drive more slowly as you headed around turns in the snow. Time seemed to slow down to a crawl, and I honestly wondered if I was about to die. Neither steering nor braking did anything to stop the car's motion. Thankfully, there was no oncoming traffic. Out loud, I started screaming the *S* word in a percussive, rhythmic chant, two times per second, getting louder and louder the longer I slid.

My car actually did a complete 360-degree revolution on the road. At the same moment that I was swearing and sliding in this giant circle, which seemed to last for an eternity, I felt compelled to look at my car's digital clock. The blue digits 1:11 burned at me from the dashboard. There it was again! Why in the world was I seeing a clock synchronicity as I was about to die? I really didn't have time to think about what it meant, yet I was aware even as it was happening that the higher forces were somehow involved in this. Repeating digits on clocks were one of the key signatures of my "ET family," and here I was about to die in my car. Then my front right tire suddenly slammed into a post on the side of the road, and I came to an immediate, safe stop.

I was very, very lucky, because if I hadn't hit that post, my car could very easily have slid right off of the road, down the hill, and into the creek. The ice was thin enough that the car would have started sinking, and I may have drowned from the shock of the cold water hitting my skin and flooding the interior. Either way, I would have probably ended up in the hospital, surrounded by machines and concerned faces. The posts were spaced about thirty feet apart, and I was extremely lucky that I hit one. The sudden sound and force of the impact was highly jarring. I had no idea how much damage there would be, or even if I would ever be able to drive my car again. I had no money to get another car, and no job. On the verge of a total, helpless breakdown, both mentally and physically, I quickly jumped out to take a look.

My wheel and axle had absorbed the majority of the shock head-on, so there was very little damage. My hands were shaking as my body surged with adrenaline. Considering how frightening the accident itself was, and how, inevitably, I would have spun right into the creek at the speed I was going, the lack of damage to me or the car was literally miraculous. All I had was a dent in the surface of the car around the tire, which I was able to pull out by hand when I got home. The clock synchronicity was an obvious sign that the spiritual forces I was in contact with had somehow set up and carried out this crash. They were the Lords of Karma, and I had to be very careful not to get myself in trouble. This changed everything. I drove home and immediately went to my dream notebooks to see if anything had predicted this event. Sure enough, at least four different dreams in the past eight days had forecasted this event in advance. I knew I was trying to take advantage of Eric and possibly my family to have them pay for my own lack of responsibility, while making up excuses and saying I was doing everything I could. I immediately made a full commitment to get another job and stabilize myself.

Facing My Responsibility

As it turned out, I had no trouble whatsoever getting another job. I just had been resisting the option to do it. The very next day, I went back and reapplied to the UARC Day Treatment Center in Kingston. This was a facility for developmentally disabled adults who ranged from moderate to severe/profound in their levels of challenge. We had some students like this in our high school, and I was able to see them as human souls and not be frightened or upset by the way they looked. Jude had done this work on the residential side for years and had encouraged me to pursue it, because it would still count toward graduate school residency. I had originally worked a few days at the UARC job after leaving the pizza place, but then quit politely after the mental hospital called me back. Admittedly, part of the reason I left was that the UARC job paid only $5.77 an hour, literally two cents above minimum wage, whereas the mental hospital paid a relatively substantial $7.50. Now I had returned, newly humbled. Since they were always in need of help, I got my job back with only a brief burst of ridicule from my Irish boss: "Sooo, ya got CANNED!"

The Schoolhouse was such a sanctuary of healing and solace that I was able to glide through one of the toughest jobs imaginable. Thanks to my new psychology degree, the UARC management quickly positioned me in what they unofficially called the Behavior Rooms. The official term for them was ILR, which stood for Intensive Learning Rooms. These were two rooms in which the most disruptive "consumers," as they called them, were kept together so they wouldn't damage the peace of the other classrooms. Somehow, they felt that with a degree in psychology, I would be better trained in how to handle all this chaos. Some of the people could speak and others could not, and yelling and screaming would occur almost hour by hour. Fights broke out almost every day. All of them reminded me of children, and I felt genuine love and respect for them. Every day, I would see and hear utterly hilarious things, particularly from our two highest-functioning people, who could speak fluently. I often used whimsical comedy to keep the peace, and the people responded very well to my efforts. Much of my job was akin to being an umpire, breaking up inevitable fights while constantly watching both doors to make sure that our "runners" didn't try to escape.

My car crash was on Monday, December 18. Newly humbled, I went in and accepted the job offer on December 19. They wanted me to start right away, but instead, I asked to wait a week until the following Tuesday, December 26, to breathe and prepare myself. I then decided to delay my family visit for Christmas; I definitely needed to focus on preparing myself for this very difficult job. Then on December 20, I had a dream that gave me wonderful compliments for facing my responsibility. In this dream, I drove to a small airport and parked in an outdoor parking lot. When I got out of the car, I found cash lying on the ground that added up to twenty dollars. I then found a wallet with traveler's checks in it that added up to another fifty-five dollars. The traveler's checks needed to be signed in order to be cashed. Now, a newlywed couple came up to me and asked if I had seen a wallet lying around.

This was my big choice point. I knew I was dead broke. I could have lied to them and kept the money, but I couldn't live with myself for doing that; I wasn't that kind of person. So I told them yes, I did find their wallet, and I handed it over. Although they said there had been only twenty dollars in the wallet, I gave them all the cash I had found. They were so happy, they burst into tears. They had no idea how they were going to survive without that money. I felt terrific about what I had done as I watched them walk away, with their arms around each other. As soon as I opened the door to get back into the car, I was shocked. There on the passenger seat was a mountain of cash—easily a million dollars or more. I was overwhelmed with happiness. Even in the dream I felt like this was a great synchronicity that had obviously happened because I chose to be honest. In symbolic terms, the dream was clearly showing me that by taking on this very difficult job and facing my adult responsibility, instead of stealing from my new housemate and possibly my family, the rewards in the long term would be terrific.

At this point the dream shifted, as they often do. Now I was driving the car. In the place of the money, I now had a black man riding with me in the passenger seat. Two black women were riding in the back. We were talking, laughing, and having a great time together. Suddenly, flashing blue and red lights appeared in my rearview mirror. We were getting pulled over! A Caucasian police officer walked up and wanted to make sure I was okay, and that these people weren't forcing me to do anything against my will. I told the policeman that everything was fine, we were having a great time, and it was perfectly normal for black people and white people to be friends.

In dream analysis, people of other races typically represent your unseen angelic guides and helpers in the higher realms. Although this dream exaggerated the financial rewards for doing this work, it is nonetheless true that I would eventually make a respectable living from my career as a UFOlogist. The police officer represents the mainstream view that has been conditioned to think of any nonterrestrial beings as evil and dangerous. Many other dreams during this time were unambiguously talking about my wife—whom I got together with in 2016. It is difficult to describe how amazing it feels to experience these sorts of prophecies and realize that any skeptical explanations just fall apart under the sheer volume of evidence over the years. Many people feel they have to explain these things away to maintain their view of reality. Otherwise they worry that people will judge them as outcasts, mentally ill, or even insane. I can honestly say that nothing feels quite as good as that first prophetic dream or mind-blowing synchronicity, where you really see that you yourself have all the power you need to do this. You are awakening in the dream that we now collectively refer to as reality.

A Prophetic Dream of Spiritual Communication

On New Year's Day 1996, I had just worked the first four days of my new job and was earning $5.77 an hour, two cents above the minimum hourly amount of money you could be paid to do any job in New York State. I was making just enough to afford to live in our beautiful new apartment, surrounded by trees, rolling green lawns, and natural boulder outcroppings. On this same morning at the birth of the new year, I had a truly remarkable dream that ended up being highly prophetic of what would happen to me in November of that same year.

In this dream, a cool musician I knew from college, named Vinnie, had died. In real life, we had performed and recorded some music together in which I played Native American flute and he played hand drums. Somehow, I could see him and communicate with him perfectly clearly, even though he was in the afterlife. At the same time, I was aware that other people could not see or hear him—I was the only one who could. Vinnie wanted to convey a personal message to a friend of his, named Ron, who was having either a birthday party or a wedding, and was alive and well. Vinnie wanted to put his message on Ron's answering machine. Vinnie had hoped that if I hit RECORD, his voice would then be recorded onto the tape, across the expanse of the afterlife. I did what he asked and he spoke the message. When I played it back, all we got was a droning voice in the background—and it wasn't audible enough to understand anything. I then got the idea that since I could hear Vinnie perfectly well, all he had to do was speak to me, and then I would repeat the words he said into the machine. This was a very precise prophecy of the work I would be led to do beginning on November 10. Another fascinating time-loop synchronicity has happened as I am editing the final hardcover version of the book, on February 12, 2020. Just three days ago, I found out that my insider Daniel, who passed away on February 3, 2020, had recorded a private message for me just before he died. His son reached out to me by email and sent the audio file to me. Events like these never cease to amaze me.

As the dream continued, I kept trying to climb up into a part of the

Schoolhouse that was very difficult to reach, and looked like an attic. I had frustrating and ongoing trouble with the stairs, and eventually I had to climb over a huge metallic light fixture at the top to get where I wanted to go. In dream symbology, this seemed to indicate the trouble I was having in activating my higher chakras, which would allow this Edgar Cayce–style "tuned trance telepathy" communication to take place. I did finally reach the attic area of the Schoolhouse that I was looking for. At this point, I discovered that I could fly with no effort whatsoever, and I soared into the air. My college friend Chris was there, or at least a being that was projecting the image of Chris to me, and I told him I knew I was dreaming. The ground beneath me was twinkling like a hologram, and it was exceptionally beautiful and rich with vibrant, surreal-looking colors.

For whatever reason, I again found myself back at the Schoolhouse, even though I was still lucid. Once more, I felt the need to try to climb into the same inaccessible space. Then, a stepladder came down that looked exactly like the one we used to reach the attic in the house I grew up in. Finally, I was able to climb the stairs easily. As another very interesting time-loop synchronicity, as I now write this in November 2019, my mother was just back at this same house to get the heat turned on for the winter. I was fortunate enough to get my company to reacquire the little house I grew up in when it came on the market. It was at least ten times less expensive than a typical house in Los Angeles. I can never remember living anywhere else but this house in my childhood, for my parents got it when I was seven months old and my mother didn't sell it until two years after I graduated from college in 1997. Part of why my company reacquired it was to shoot a movie there, where we would re-enact various things that happened to me while I was growing up, like the bookshelf under the cellar stairs, the closet where I drew a large sketch of my two-and-a-half-foot-tall "Friend" on the wall, and the out-of-body experience in the upstairs hallway and stairwell.

In November 2019, the original wooden attic staircase had since been replaced with an aluminum one, and Mom could not get it to open. Let's not forget that in the dream from New Year's Day 1996, I had exceptional difficulty with this exact same stepladder. In real life, Mom was texting me, sending pictures of the extended ladder and asking me how to fix the problem. I sent her a PDF file of the installation manual for the Louisville Attic Ladder after she photographed the label and sent it to me. The gas technician ended up effortlessly lifting the stairs and closing the hatch, which caused my mother to laugh and text me back that everything was fine. Mom was amazed at how little the house had changed in the twenty-two years since she sold it in 1997. This was the first time she had seen it since she moved out. The house was very cold when she arrived, and she had spent almost an hour trying to figure out how to close the attic. Just today, I was taking care of various details to make sure the house is ready for the winter. So again, the time-loop synchronicity between the events that took place in this dream and the events of my present as I finish this book is impressive.

In the original dream from 1996, once I entered the attic, a remarkable series of visions began. I saw a landscape ablaze with brilliant, almost impossible colors. Everywhere I looked, there were fantastic, highly futuristic structures that looked like they must have been made by advanced extraterrestrial beings. This view was essentially identical to the illustrations of the underground cities of the Anshar that Corey Goode would end up commissioning after his contact experiences in 2016. It was so amazing that I had little I could compare it to at the time. I started running joyfully through this marvelous landscape of colors and structures. Along the way, I kept finding lotus flowers that were everywhere, and picking them up. Just like a video game, each time I picked up one of the lotus flowers, my overall power level seemed to increase. It was quite spectacular. Since I appear to be in a time loop here, I can read this as another of many signs that my higher-density friends are very happy with me for finally writing this up, after all these years, so I can share it with you.

EG&G Rotron

Not long after I started my stressful new job, I was in Woodstock with an acquaintance, who I will call Karen. We passed by the EG&G facility in the area. Excitedly, I blurted out, "Oh, look, EG&G Rotron! That's where they reverse-engineer the UFOs." Karen was suddenly overcome, visibly shaking, on the brink of tears. *"What. . . . Did. You. Just. Say?"* I then repeated myself. "I read about it in a book. *Alien Contact* by Timothy Good. According to his insiders, almost all of the military defense contractors are working on this." She responded, "If I tell you something, you have to promise me that you will never say a word about this to another soul." Now you can see why I am not using her real name or any identifying features. I promised, and she continued. "My father . . . used to work at EG&G. He could never tell us anything about what he was doing, nor could he take us to work." I did not interrupt her, but I had heard stories like this before from my senior-year roommate, Artie, and my junior high school friend Kevin. She began crying. "Finally, one day he told us. 'They'll kill me,' he said. 'I need to tell you this, but you can never tell another soul. If you do, they'll kill me . . . and they'll probably kill you as well, and everyone else we love.'"

She was shaking with fear and sobbing. I promised her I would keep this to myself. I had no problem with confidentiality. "It was UFOs," she said. "My father was working on UFOs. Top, top secret programs. And he was scared. Whatever they were working on was absolutely vital to our survival on planet Earth. It was our only hope. That's all I know."

After she had calmed down a little more, I opened up to her. "Karen, I've known this stuff was true for three years now, ever since my buddy heard about it from his college physics professor, who worked for NASA in the 1970s. I've already read over three hundred books on all of this, and my dream is to become a full-time, professional UFO researcher. There are several insiders who have come forward and risked their lives to speak about the same things your dad refused to talk about. So let me just say this . . . regardless of what they told your dad, this is not just about 'evil aliens.' The real story is much deeper than that, and there are definitely good guys and bad guys out there. The whole story is starting to look more and more like a biblical battle between angels and demons. If your father only encountered or heard about the negative types, I can imagine he would be quite upset."

As I kept talking to her and addressing her concerns, I could see her visibly start to relax. I gave her some of my most impressive stories of dreams, serendipitous "non-coincidences" and future prophecies, including the Bible quote I'd received through automatic writing—and she was truly amazed. I said the angelic, benevolent ETs were reaching out to us in dreams and synchronicities, and were making sure that our individual and collective destinies were being steered toward the most positive outcome. The more we started listening to them, the more they would be authorized to tell us. That was the first and the last time she ever wanted to talk about what her father had told her.

Eric's Dream of the Old Man

On January 18, 1996, I got the two-hundred-dollar phone bill in the mail that I described in the previous chapter. I was terrified that this one bill might ruin me financially. I had prayed for the ETs who gave me the Bible quote to show themselves, but nothing happened. We had plenty of snow on the ground when I woke up the next morning, and it was quite cold outside. Even though my old Subaru had a terrible habit of revving itself up way too high if it was left running, I went out and started the car to warm it up. I had already showered and was just going to stuff some breakfast in my face before I hurried off to work at the last minute, as usual. When I came back into the house, Eric was awake and on the phone. This was highly unusual, since he worked the late shift and would have had only about five or six hours of sleep by this point, compared to his usual eight. Eric had reddish pillow creases all over his face, and his eyes were barely open. I wondered who in the world would have called us this early, since everyone knew not to call us in the morning. It was one of his business associates who had been looking into getting a graduate degree in archive and records management from SUNY Albany. Eric got off the phone right as I was about to head for the door. "I just had this crazy dream about you," he said.

"Eric, I can't listen to your dream right now! I've got to go to work!" He replied, "David, you're definitely going to want to hear this one. It had UFOs in it." Now, as the Subaru continued roaring away at 5,000 revolutions per minute outside, everything came to a screeching halt. "Okay, you got me. Let's have it."

CHAPTER FOURTEEN

Gateway to the Law of One

The date was January 19, 1996. I had desperately prayed to know if I was an extraterrestrial soul the night before. The answer was now about to arrive in the form of a dream my housemate was having—even though he had no idea that I had made the prayer, since he didn't get home until after I went to sleep. Eric's dream started with him and me walking around in public with a girl he liked from the Rosendale Café, named Lenore. (I later incorrectly remembered the woman in the dream as being my ex-girlfriend Yumi, but my original notebook revealed the character's name.) We were all hanging out together in something like an outdoor mall. In his dream, the mall had no ceiling—it was all open to the outside air. Plenty of people were milling around, shopping and having fun.

Eric Dreams of the Moment of Truth

Suddenly, IT happened. UFOs. Dozens of them. Maybe hundreds. Maybe thousands. Who knows. They were everywhere. Flying through the skies. Flying in formation. Swooping, darting, and dancing around each other. It was the Big One. The moment we all had either hoped or feared might happen one day, after seeing so many movies about extraterrestrials. Everyone was gasping, staring up into the heavens, pointing their fingers, covering their mouths with their other hands, crying out, and in some cases screaming.

One of the disc-shaped craft dropped in for a closer look. A three-foot-wide flat disc came down out of the craft on a beam of light. A man was standing on the disc, surrounded by brilliant white light. He was wearing a white robe. He had sandals on his feet. He had gray hair and a gray beard. Eric said he had "very sensitive features." Leaves and bits of debris were swirling around him in a vortex. Eric said he looked like our normal vision of Jesus, although he had clearly gotten older than our typical illustrations of him—with gray instead of brown hair. He was also a picture-perfect description of the wise old man I had been seeing in my own dreams ever since I was two years old.

The old man began talking about the same kinds of Ascension prophecies that I had already been discussing with Eric, based on many dreams I was having and books I was reading:

> My brothers and sisters. Do not be afraid. I am here with you. We are here with you. Now. We always have been here with you. We are your angels, your guardians and protectors. We are your elder brothers and sisters. We are your family. We are you, and you are us. We have come to see you today because this is the time of times. The Alpha and the Omega. You were always wondering. Searching. Alone. Not sure. Never quite happy with the way things were.
>
> Now all of that has changed. An event is taking place, right now. A Graduation. It is time for each of you to make a choice. You can come with us, and live like we do, as true spiritual masters who tread lightly and are never seen unless we choose to be. Or, you can decide not to come with us. And that is fine. No harm will come to you. We will bring you to a safe place where you can live on in peace. That place can no longer be the Earth. Not now. Something is happening to the Earth. Something in this solar system, to use your terms. It is a cleansing. A purification. A rebirth. A natural event. We have no control over it. All we can do is make sure that you

are safe. If you are ready, you can stretch forth your hand—
and join us in the new tomorrow. A future of unspeakable
majesty, beauty, and splendor awaits you. The only limit is
your imagination. All the work we have ever done on your
planet, for countless millennia before time as you know it, has
brought us to this very moment. Here. Now. Today. Are you
ready?

At this point, Eric looked around and realized that everyone else had
scattered and run off in all directions. Now it was just Eric, Lenore, and
me, in a huge and barren outdoor mall. The gravity of the moment could
not be underestimated. All three of us were standing there in gaping silence. The old man stood silently, as if he was waiting for us to make a
decision. Finally, Lenore was able to put words together. She turned to
Eric and said, "Shouldn't one of us go talk to him?"

Eric replied, "I'll leave that to David. He's the UFO guy. He'll know
what to say!"

Both of them turned to look at me, and I accepted the invitation. As
I walked toward the old man, his platform gently glided down to ground
level. I walked up, stepped onto the platform, and suddenly, there was a
spark of recognition. I knew this man. I had met him before. And I even
knew his language. I said something to him that Eric could not understand, but sounded like a greeting. When Eric tried to verbalize what it
sounded like, the word was *Shezabah*. I said "Shezabah" to the man as if
it was a question, and then he said it back to me, with an even higher
pitch and more of a questioning tone: "Shezabah?!" (I looked up this
word with translation software while writing this book, and it translates
as "Laughing" in Arabic and "Story" in Zulu. Eric never studied Arabic.
These beings do reside on a spiritual level that we would most easily identify with the emotions of joy and laughter.)

Suddenly, full recognition flickered over both our faces. I knew who
he was, and he knew who I was. Memories arose from some forgotten
time, long ago, but now it was as if not a single minute had passed. We
both burst into laughter and tears. The man reached out to embrace me,
and I hugged him back for several seconds. We then turned to face Eric

and Lenore, the old man's arm still around my shoulders. Both of us were smiling widely and laughing. The man then looked into Eric's eyes with great intensity, and began speaking. He spoke very slowly and carefully, doing his best to make sure that Eric would remember what he said, word for word:

"It is very important that you know that he is one of us."

He looked over to me while he said "he is one of us," so there was no doubt the old man was saying that I was somehow a member of their lineage.

It All Comes Crashing In

"Is that the end of your dream?" I asked Eric. "Yeah, that's it," he replied. "Okay, man, I have REALLY got to go. Right now!" I dashed out the door and the Subaru was redlining at over 5,000, as expected. I got in, slammed the door, drove off, and definitely was not going to be on time. My curly-haired Irish boss scolded me as I arrived, and I knew I was in trouble: "Deevid, we caan't haave ya comin' ta work leet. You've got ta pull it together! What is it this time? Did ya decide ta stop off for a coffee? Cup'a joe? Come on, Deevid, let's go. Everyone heere's dependin' on ya."

That day the activity in the Behavior Rooms was literally nonstop. It was one round of screaming, fighting, escape attempts, and chaos after another. I never had a split second to think or to relax. I was totally in the moment of doing my job and maintaining order. A new girl had been hired who also had a BA in psychology, whom I recognized from some of my classes. She had no idea how to keep the peace, so everything was on my shoulders. She would just reel in horror as fights broke out, and she was not prepared to stop full-grown men from rushing for the exits as soon as they saw the opportunity. If anyone made it out into the hallway, I was in big trouble, as we were only fifty feet from the front doors, which opened out into the parking lot from the inside, thanks to fire code requirements. If anyone escaped, it could shatter our already fragile relationship with the surrounding community. I literally did not even have time to think about Eric's dream. My mind was incredibly focused on my most basic survival.

Then, right after that day of work, I had to drive back up to Scotia to see my mother for a belated Christmas visit. I was now driving at full speed on the New York State Thruway through a horrific downpour. My windshield was fogging up from the inside. I had to wipe it with the edge of my sleeve to have a hole I could see through. I kept hitting puddles that caused my car to suddenly slow down and slide. The technical term for this is "hydroplaning," and it is terrifying. I honestly felt that if I didn't keep driving, and tried to pull over somewhere, someone would hit me. I had to keep going. I had the exact same feeling of total panic, urgency, and terror that I had been enduring all day at work.

Suddenly, as my sweating hands gripped the steering wheel hard enough to leave fingernail marks behind, it hit me. My prayer. From the night before. It's THEM. The beings. Whoever they are, they answered. It's Eric's Dream. Eric's Dream is the answer to the prayer! And the answer is YES! I am one of THEM! Oh. My. GOD!

Astonishing Confirmation

At this point, with all the tension and fear and stress and pain and agony, not to mention a blinding migraine headache, I simply burst into tears. I could not control it. I realized this was a very, very dangerous situation. I could not safely drive a car when I was this emotional. It was far more dangerous for me to try to keep driving at this point than to pull over. I found the edge of the road and pulled way, way off to the side, well into the grass. And then I just let myself cry. I sobbed and sobbed and sobbed, for at least a half hour. By the time I stopped, the clouds had all blown away and the rain was gone. I continued on with the rest of my trip, enjoying great visibility and peace.

Now that such a stunning confirmation had happened, I could hardly even imagine the resources available to these beings. Somehow, they were able to send me a message through a dazzling example of synchronicity, using someone else's dreams to prove this was not my imagination.

I had had the urge to go start my car at the perfect moment. A friend of Eric's had called us at exactly the right time. Eric's dream was timed to end precisely in conjunction with these events. Three completely different people had been triangulated on the same moment of space and time, but none of us had any conscious idea that this was all being guided by an unseen, benevolent force.

Wave after wave of thoughts went through my mind. "You said you wanted the answer. Well, you got it. You are an Angelic Soul. And 'this Ascension thing' you've been reading, thinking, and dreaming about? It IS going to happen. You know that now. What other answer could there be? Did you tell Eric about your prayer? No. Had you read the Bible even once in your life before seeing that quote from Ecclesiastes? No. This is real. This is happening. This is Now. This is your life, David!"

Remarkable Time Loops While Writing This Chapter

Immediately after writing this last paragraph, I got up from my desk to go to the bathroom for a much-needed break. I have been so "in the moment" of reliving these memories that I have had tears streaming down my face and a wild headache. I looked out the window and there was a beautiful golden hawk, perched up on the highest branch of the tallest tree. Then I looked over at the clock, and it was at 4:44 P.M. Once again, right while I am putting this section together in written form on Independence Day 2019, just hours after the biggest earthquake we've had in Los Angeles for twenty-five years, the appearance of this hawk was another noteworthy synchronicity.

I knew the hawk was a very powerful symbol to have appeared at this point in the writing process. In Egyptian mythology, Ra and Horus, the hawk-headed god, are often seen as one and the same thing. As it says in the *Ancient History Encyclopedia*:

> There were many falcon gods (known as Avian Deities) in Egyptian religion who were eventually absorbed into the god known as Horus. . . . In time, he became combined with the

sun god Ra to form a new deity, Ra-Harahkhte, god of the
sun, who sailed across the sky during the day and was depicted as a falcon-headed man wearing the double crown of
Upper and Lower Egypt with the sun disk on it. His symbols
are the Eye of Horus (one of the most famous Egyptian symbols) and the falcon.[1]

The Law of One was authored by a group of three people who allegedly communicated with an entity known as Ra, asking questions
and recording the responses. Ra had first reached out to the ancient
Egyptians—and claimed that their totem animal was the hawk. In Session 96, Question 11, the questioner asked, "Was there a significance with
respect to the hawk that landed the other day just outside of the kitchen
window?" The answer was "This is correct. We may note that we find it
interesting that queries offered to us are often already known. We assume
that our confirmation is appreciated."[2] Additionally, the very last words
the questioner of the Law of One ever spoke in the entire series, in Session 106, Question 23, were "I would certainly appreciate the return of
the golden hawk. It gave me great comfort."[3] That only made the synchronistic appearance of the golden hawk, along with a 4:44 clock synchronicity, even more interesting as I was writing these words.

When Ra eventually reached out to my friend and insider colleague
Corey Goode through a member of its civilization in 2015, it appeared as
an eight-foot-tall avian humanoid with blue feathers. This has caused
many skeptics online to jeer at us with laughter, but the appearance of
these "Blue Avians" is extremely consistent with the artistic renditions of
Avian Deities from ancient Egypt, such as Horus. Ra's remarks about the
importance of the hawk symbol in the Law of One are only some of the
many confirmations they make of their true identity and appearance,
since they also claim responsibility for building the Great Pyramid and
working with the First Dynasty in Egypt.

As I wrote this book, I went back and looked to see what dreams I
had after this stunningly coordinated three-person synchronicity had
occurred. On January 20, 1996, I found myself in a beautiful log home
in a woodsy area, with high ceilings like those of my grandparents' vaca-

tion home in the Adirondacks. It also looked like the cabin where I ran through the Discovery program for troubled teens when I was in high school. Now I can see that this was a precise viewing of my house in Colorado, where I was writing the book in 2019. In this dream, my mother, my brother, my father, and some of my wife's family were vacationing there together. This was another astonishing time-loop synchronicity. Dad and Michael were attending their first-ever Wilcock family reunion. There was a whole branch of the family from Dad's side that we had fallen out of contact with. I would have been there, but I had to finish this book. I had just been sent pictures of the reunion and then immediately afterward, I reread this dream from 1996 where all of us were together for the first time. The cabin in my dream seemed very similar to where they were all meeting up in the Adirondacks.

The next dream was from January 21, 1996, and this also had a direct time-loop connection to the very moment I was writing the book. In this dream, I was outdoors and trying to work on my car. Inside the engine compartment was a curious round cylinder. I opened the container and noticed that there were tools in it, as well as another, smaller cylinder. I could see that even though the tools appeared to be flat and flimsy, they could be very useful for fixing the vehicle. The problem was that the whole container was filled to the brim with a noxious, chemical-smelling clear liquid. I was quite afraid of plunging my hand in to get these tools. Eric did it readily, and everything was fine. "Those chemicals just keep it clean," he said. Inside the other cylinder was money, and I realized that the cash was there just in case I needed to pay for emergency repairs.

In the symbolic dream language, this was talking about my new job in January 1996. I was indeed "fixing my spiritual vehicle" by taking this position at the time. I didn't like the job, and this was represented by the repair tools seeming flat and flimsy, and being saturated in a smelly liquid. Then I found out that it was nontoxic, and there was useful money in there for emergencies. This meant the job wasn't as bad as I thought it was, and the money I was earning was very helpful.

However, in the present sense, I was now in another stunning time loop. Right as I was reviewing this dream for the first time in twenty-three and a half years, my wife, Elizabeth, called me because her car wouldn't start. She had the hood open and was trying to figure out what to do, just as I was doing in my dream. A man came by to help her in the parking lot, and he did a great job. She ended up giving him forty dollars and a bag of chips for his time and trouble—which was represented as the cylinder of emergency money that I saw in my dream. I was truly amazed to discover yet another time loop of this nature. Never before in my entire life have I experienced so many obvious time loops in such a short period of time. Then again, this is the first time I have ever written about these experiences in anywhere near this level of detail. Some higher part of me clearly seemed to know exactly when I would finally come around to complete this cosmic homework assignment.

The Law of One and Cosmic Voyage

Let's now jump back to that pivotal day of January 19, 1996, when Eric's game-changing UFO dream came in. After surviving my trip up to my childhood home through the rain and breaking down in tears on the side of the road, I realized I needed to take "this Wanderer thing" a lot more seriously. And that meant I needed to read the source text that Scott Mandelker had based all of his research on—the Law of One series.

I again stopped off at the now-magical Borders bookstore on Wolf Road in Albany. This was where I had found Mandelker's book before Thanksgiving, which had awakened me to the fact that I had an extraterrestrial angelic soul. I knew they had Book Three of the Law of One series there, and I bought it. I also picked up a colorful, brand-new hardcover release by another credible PhD UFOlogist, Dr. Courtney Brown, entitled *Cosmic Voyage*. The book had just been released on January 1, 1996, so I was getting my hands on it less than three weeks after it was published. Based on the description on the jacket, this book was utterly irresistible to me.

It was nice to see my mother for Christmas, even though it was technically in the third week of January. Now that I had a bit of free time on my hands, I again tried to read Book Three of the Law of One, but it immediately became clear that this was like walking into an advanced

calculus class halfway through the semester. There were many different
terms I did not understand. This was not at all "light reading," and I
would need to start with Book One and work my way up from there.
That meant special-ordering the other three volumes. I ended up calling
in the order to Ariel Booksellers in New Paltz. Little did I know that my
initial foray into the Law of One material, by reading parts of Book
Three on January 19, 1996, was just four days after the fifteen-year an-
niversary of when the contact started on January 15, 1981. In hindsight,
this looked more like a synchronicity than a coincidence. After a short
and very relaxing break, where I couldn't stop thinking about Eric's
dream, I drove back to Rosendale and returned to work. As I waited for
the other volumes of the Law of One to arrive, I decided to throw myself
into Dr. Brown's *Cosmic Voyage* whenever I could find some alone time
after work—and I was very impressed with what I found.

Cosmic Voyage Was a Game Changer

Cosmic Voyage triggered a profound shift in my consciousness. By this
point, I had read just about every book on UFOlogy that I could find,
either from the bookstore or the library, and I was becoming quite disillusioned. Almost every book seemed to be saying the same things, over
and over again in an endless repetition. Each "new" author just recom-
bined various pieces of an overall body of data that was already available.
Although this was a large body of information, beyond the scope that
anyone could fit into one book, it was also very finite in its size and
depth.

I could examine the entire body of UFO, metaphysics, and ancient
civilizations data like a three-dimensional holographic puzzle with mov-
able pieces. I could see many ways to connect its different areas, and I
meta-analyzed how it all integrated as a whole. I knew its strengths and
was very aware of its many weaknesses. Any one genuine insider could
ignite and transform the entire structure, but they were exceedingly rare
marvels within the field. As an example, no one had ever heard of Area
51 before Bob Lazar emerged on the scene in 1989. Almost every UFO

book I read that was published since then would mention Lazar's name, along with various aspects of his testimony. Lazar claimed to have been tasked to reverse-engineer the power system on a crashed UFO, and discovered that the source of its massive energy was a triangular lump of a superheavy substance he called Element 115—a natural element with 115 protons in the nucleus. At the time, it was theoretically possible that this element might exist, but it hadn't been discovered yet.

I had memorized all the names of the people involved in the Roswell crash. I became tired of always reading the same names from the original MJ-12 committee that managed the UFO cover-up in America. I could expound on every theory of alien abduction, cattle mutilations, missing time, government conspiracy, and the like. I had read about so many different UFO sightings that they bored me to tears at this point. I would skim through those sections of the books without really reading them. "Lights in the sky" just didn't cut it anymore.

I also had familiarized myself with data various authors used to "prove" the former existence of Atlantis. Even the incredible, epic work *Fingerprints of the Gods* by Graham Hancock was predominantly repeated material for me, except his stunning analysis of the work of the historians Giorgio de Santillana and Hertha von Dechend. Hancock had combined and refined a large body of the existing data on ancient civilizations into one volume, with fully annotated scholastic accuracy and power. In a way, it was a huge relief to see that someone else had already done this work. I considered *Fingerprints* to be a work of absolute genius, truly worthy of a Nobel Prize. As a whole, I knew the maps, knew the monuments, knew the alignments, knew the Mayan Calendar, Sitchin's Sumerians, the Vimana flying craft described in the ancient Hindu Vedic scriptures, and the secrets of the Great Pyramid, Sphinx, and Stonehenge like the back of my hand. There was no question that we were being visited by extraterrestrials, in both ancient and modern times.

Hardly anything I read was new. I had become totally saturated. Every time I picked up a new book, I felt I was wasting my time, reading the same material once again. I usually would just critique each author on how well they integrated various pieces of the puzzle. This was extremely disheartening, particularly since I was spending every extra dollar I made on books. The Internet universe was just getting started, and the amount of content on UFOs and ancient civilizations was sparse. Everything good online would inevitably orbit around Art Bell, the legendary talk-radio host of *Coast to Coast AM*. Art was particularly fascinated with Richard C. Hoagland and the Face on Mars, Dr. Steven Greer and his mysterious top secret whistleblowers, a strange box of bismuth alloys that apparently would levitate in an electrical field called Art's Parts, and Major Ed Dames with his fantastic stories of remote viewing in the military.

Remote Viewing Is an Exact Science

Cosmic Voyage, however, revealed many new truths about remote viewing and extraterrestrial life. With remote viewing, an ordinary person can be trained to use their innate psychic abilities to accurately describe target locations. Remote viewers also have a guide who tells them where to go and what to explore on-site so they don't have to engage their conscious mind in thinking, which could break the trance and ruin the quality of their information. Both the viewer and their guide would have nothing to work off of but a series of random-number "coordinates" that someone else had assigned to the target—so there was no possibility of either person influencing the outcome. Despite this double-blind setup where one would expect that ordinary human beings were guaranteed to fail, the best remote viewers could guarantee a nearly 99 percent success rate in describing their targets. Electronic equipment would be used to determine that a person had made a 180-degree shift in the polarity of voltage running through their bodies, and this signaled that accurate remote viewing could begin. The initial research breakthroughs began in 1982 with the help of legendary psychic Ingo Swann.

According to Dr. Brown, author of the book *Cosmic Voyage*, our input from the five senses, as well as logic and imagination, will eventually cease in deep meditation. What remains is a "field of consciousness" that can be brimming with activity. Dr. Brown and his colleagues believe this is a mass mind comprising all individuals. The data from this greater field of consciousness is normally overwritten by our five senses as well as our thoughts, memories, and emotions. The remote viewing protocols give us a means of breaking through these protective layers—to "penetrate the veil of forgetting," in Law of One terms. The trick is to enter into this unique state of consciousness and then carefully bring data out of it, without disrupting your trance state. Dr. Brown's book described all the basics of these protocols as it went along.

Dr. Brown, a highly credentialed and well-published social scientist with Emory University in Georgia, emerged with stunning findings that came entirely through the realms of consciousness. In his own words: "I have an enviable and hard-earned reputation for thoughtful and creative research, often involving sophisticated nonlinear mathematical representations of social phenomena."[4] Dr. Brown got into Transcendental Meditation from reading about the Maharishi Effect in a social sciences journal back in 1988.

As I have discussed in previous volumes, it was discovered that a group of seven thousand trained meditators were somehow able to reduce global war, terrorism, crime, and fatalities by an astonishing 72 percent just by remaining in a state of meditation. All other potential factors that could have influenced this data, such as weekends, weather, holidays, and the like, were ruled out. This discovery fundamentally changes what it means to be human, as well as our understanding of the mind. It is therefore not surprising that an open-minded social scientist would seek to learn more about this groundbreaking discovery and actually experience the meditation training firsthand.

Dr. Brown then secured a research grant from Emory University to take a Transcendental Meditation class and directly investigate the Maharishi Effect, while also participating in the process that was creating its stunning peace-keeping results. He eventually made it all the way up to the Siddhi level. Dr. Brown was ultimately welcomed into a new remote-viewing training program in 1993, because the military brass involved realized that a social scientist would have a greater ability to understand the dynamics of extraterrestrial cultures. His prior history with Transcendental Meditation was also seen as useful to them in terms of the speed with which he could be trained.

Dr. Brown put his career and reputation on the line to release *Cosmic Voyage*, where he shared the transcripts and results from a number of fascinating remote-viewing sessions. Dr. Brown's targets of choice were extraterrestrial-related, beginning with a surprise session on September 29, 1993. I did find it interesting that the timing of Dr. Brown's awakening was similar to mine, since my NASA disclosure had occurred only about seven months before this. I didn't start reading Hoagland's *The Monuments of Mars* until the summer of 1993, so Dr. Brown and I both discovered the secrets of Mars within just a few months of each other.

Dr. Brown's military trainers sent him to remote-view the Cydonia area of Mars, where the Face and pyramids Richard C. Hoagland had discussed were located. The results came as a total shock to Dr. Brown, who quickly had to adapt to a very new reality. He saw a pyramid that was far more massive than anything he had ever seen on Earth, along with people who looked essentially the same as humans from here. Their civilization was being destroyed much like Pompeii, by a volcano erupting nearby. These people were rescued at the last minute by an extraterrestrial team, and we will explore that story later in the chapter.

Extraterrestrial targets like these were regularly interspersed with mundane ordinary locations to keep Dr. Brown honest. One inside joke was that people would be sent to the sewage treatment plant at Fort Meade, Maryland, as a control. To me, Dr. Brown's findings were nothing short of spectacular. They fit in perfectly with everything I was already thinking, learning, dreaming, and reading about at the time. Finally we had some tangible data about what might have happened on Mars—data that was obtained through a scientific, repeatable process. Even better, the whole book was essentially a collection of mysterious puzzle pieces, laid out session by session. Dr. Brown handed you the raw data and let you draw your own conclusions. In my case, this raw data correlated with hundreds of different things I had already been studying.

As Dr. Brown said in his 1996 book,

> The most significant discovery of the past fifteen years is that
> we do not need to rely on gifted individuals to perform these
> feats [of remote viewing] any longer. The talent can be taught,

and anyone—including scientists—can learn it and use it with great accuracy. Moreover, the reliability of trained individuals is generally much greater than that of the best natural psychics. Executed competently, studies employing remote viewing using trained viewers can yield replicable results with nearly total accuracy, virtually all of the time.[5]

That was quite a claim for such a credentialed scientist to make, but the data did support it. Whenever he viewed a conventional target, his accuracy was effectively 100 percent. He was more than happy to allow his work to be scrutinized and audited to prove this basic fact. Had the media ever taken an interest, they certainly could have supervised and monitored a session, filmed it, and proved that he was performing this task correctly. This was later done with Joe McMoneagle on Japanese television, where he was able to reunite a long-lost family on live TV.[6] With this verifiable accuracy for terrestrial targets in mind, if a skeptic were to then say that everything ET-related that Dr. Brown viewed was false, that would violate the basic protocols of science. At that point, the skeptic is simply acting on biases and preconceptions they have been taught, to believe we are alone in the universe. As uncomfortable as it may be for people who are not accustomed to thinking of UFOs and extraterrestrials as real, the most logical explanation for Dr. Brown's findings is that he is seeing the truth, whether it is advanced ancient ruins on Mars or a sewage treatment plant in Fort Meade.

According to Dr. Brown, most remote viewers would begin their training by attending the Monroe Institute in Virginia. The Monroe Institute had developed a technology called Hemi-Sync, which utilized sound frequencies to induce out-of-body states of consciousness. This was brought about through playing a tone of, say, 100 cycles per second in one ear and 104 cycles per second in the other ear. This apparently causes a natural "beat frequency" of four hertz to appear between the two hemispheres of the brain as they try to reconcile the difference. By adjusting the difference between the two sound frequencies, we can coerce the brain into frequency levels that would usually occur only in sleep and dreaming. By doing all this with a guided meditation, the idea was to stay awake as the sounds guide you into a state where you would normally be asleep. This apparently makes it much easier to consciously enter into an out-of-body or lucid-dreaming state. People were apparently having phenomenal success with this at the Monroe Institute, and this was still only a transitional step to learning remote viewing.

Dr. Brown's book also said that remote viewers had greatly debunked, if not completely deflated, the entire field of channeling, by scientifically proving that their data was inaccurate. It was stated in the book that most channelers were receiving a certain amount of psychic information, but it was tainted with the "analytic overlays" that came from their conscious mind. Therefore, the strict protocols of remote viewing were the only way to preserve the accuracy of the data.

Major Ed Dames

My dreams were making it clearer and clearer that I needed to somehow form a bridge from the world of UFO research into the spiritual side of dreaming, lucidity, ancient spiritual teachings, and higher consciousness. Now, with the advent of Dr. Brown's *Cosmic Voyage*, it was starting to happen. Dr. Brown was professionally trained in the same remote-viewing practices as some of Art Bell's most prominent and favored guests, such as Joe McMoneagle. Not long after the release of *Cosmic Voyage,* it publicly emerged that the anonymous trainer in Dr. Brown's book was the legendary and controversial Major Ed Dames himself.

Ed Dames invariably would get on the air and talk about the number one thing his remote viewers would see in our future, above all else. Their data showed that in the near future, our sun was going to release a massive blast of light, matter, and energy. It was very difficult, if not impossible to pin down exactly when this was going to happen, but the data suggested it was well within our lifetimes, even if not very soon. Dames had a negative and sardonic view of what this event would do to all life on Earth, and he referred to it as the "Kill Shot." Art's morbid humor would kick in and he would say this event would turn us all into "hash browns," shredded potato cakes that are baked to a golden brown. This is also why Art invariably referred to Dames as "Dr. Doom," and these stories helped him sell countless units of disaster supplies such as battery-powered radios that would recharge with a hand crank.

I did not know if this solar-event scenario was authentic at the time, but I certainly was seeing something far more beautiful and amazing in our future than a mass catastrophe. Eric had just had a stunning UFO dream of mass ascension, answering my own prayers to find out about my possible ET identity, on the very same day I picked up *Cosmic Voyage*. In Dr. Brown's book, there were also tantalizing clues that the intelligence community knew a lot more about UFOs and extraterrestrials than they had ever revealed to the public. That simple truth had to be factored into any analysis of what may end up happening in this potential solar event.

The Midwayers

The most exciting example of Dr. Brown's leaked intel about extraterrestrials was in his chapter entitled "Subspace Helpers." The data was acquired in a remote-viewing session from October 2, 1993. The military intelligence community apparently had a name for the angelic human ETs I had seen in so many dreams, now including those of my housemate Eric. They called these human-looking ETs the Midwayers. Although the term *Midwayers* came from a popular channeled work known as *The Urantia Book,* Dr. Brown pointed out that his own remote-viewing research concluded that this book contained false and manipulative information interspersed with truthful information. An example of what Dr. Brown considered to be false information was the idea that reincarnation is not a genuine phenomenon.[7] Dr. Brown had a wealth of remote-viewing data, not published in the book, that unequivocally suggested that reincarnation was a basic fact of life. I would soon find that the Law of One series shared the same opinion about the *Urantia Book* as we see in Session 14, Question 30. This would prove to be one of hundreds of different correlations between the Law of One series, Dr. Brown's material, and so many other works I had studied.

According to Brown, the Midwayers work with light and are very interested in furthering their own evolution. They have been called angels in our own past, but in Dr. Brown's view, this is not an accurate assessment of who they really are—most likely due to the fact that we have so little knowledge of them from our ancient traditions besides a few surviving written accounts. A bit later on, Dr. Brown said the Midwayers never assume physical form in our own waking reality, "although their density is close to human physical density and their bodies are just out of range of our physical abilities to perceive them."[8] He also said the Midwayers have a critical assignment to work here on Earth and promote our physical and spiritual evolution.

Near the end of his book, these same beings are described when Dr. Brown says, "Remote viewers now know that Earth is also being visited by what appears to be future humans who also have the technological ability to move through time."[9] This and other passages made it clear that even though these beings exist in a spiritual realm that Dr. Brown chose to call "subspace," they are still very human. In fact, they are you and me—human beings from our own Earth future, having been activated into a higher level of human evolution, and then traveling back in time to help us out. The Midwayers look precisely the same as the group calling themselves the Anshar, which contacted Corey Goode beginning in 2016. The Anshar also said they were humans from Earth's own future who had traveled back in time to help us. I was utterly fascinated as I reread these details in Dr. Brown's book, knowing what I know now. I have seen very similar beings in my dreams on many occasions, and they definitely appear to have the ability to move through time. The Law of One has many references to beings of this sort and how they work with us. Dr. Brown also states, "Linear time does not exist outside of the physical world. All events happen simultaneously. . . . Remote viewers can pierce time as easily as space."[10] Although this may seem very hard to believe for most of us, it was a well-established fact within the classified world of the remote viewing community.

Another key clue that these people are very human in nature came in chapter 17, from a session done on September 11, 1994. Dr. Brown remote-viewed the creation of various TV episodes of *Star Trek: The Next Gen-*

eration. He saw information being planted into the mind of a writer on the show through his dreams. The information was coming to this man through an implant he had received from a Gray-type extraterrestrial. This certainly indicated that the story of the Grays was far more complex than the malevolent evil they were usually portrayed as having in the movies. It mirrored what I had read in *The Watchers* while I was on the train to Colorado and back. Dr. Brown ended up exploring this particular group in quite some detail throughout the book. We will discuss these particular findings a bit later.

The implant monitored this writer's thoughts and introduced new ideas to him on a regular basis, particularly while he was asleep. The man happily credited his own creativity and imagination for these novel ideas. Dr. Brown's remote viewing indicated that beings we see in *Star Trek* and other such shows are not portrayed strictly accurately in terms of how they look. The greater purpose of these shows is simply to acclimate us to new ideas over time.

Dr. Brown also observed that the producers of the initial Star Trek series in the 1960s were being directly assisted, outside their immediate, visible 3-D space, by ten or more human-looking beings who were wearing white, luminous robes. He then said, "The subspace beings in [this] structure are former human beings. I am [also] seeing that they are closely working with the Grays on an Earth project relating to physical humans." We will return to this intriguing concept about the Earth project a bit later on. The key that jumped out at me at this point, once again, was the idea that these angelic Midwayers were in fact former human beings.

Brown said the discovery of the Midwayers ricocheted through the remote-viewing community for many years. They learned that these beings have extreme importance to our lives, but it was very difficult to explain their existence and agenda to military generals worried about defense. At one point early in the book, Dr. Brown said, "I was told of one instance in which a very high-ranking civilian political appointee serving directly under the secretary of defense began to object strenuously during a top secret briefing on the subject of UFOs when the matters of alien technology and psychic information were raised. The official asserted that this information was not supposed to be known by any humans until we died and learned it from heavenly sources."[11] This quote reveals that even when people have a "need to know" clearance and absolute proof that certain intel is authentic, they might still have a negative reaction to it and completely shut it down.

Another key quote about these people from earlier in the book could lead to potential misunderstandings: "The Midwayers are themselves not extraterrestrials, since they apparently are rather permanently based here on Earth. Yet they are not human, nor do they assume human form in a physical sense. They are subspace beings who live and work in a human environment. The Midwayers work here, but their command structure does not originate on this planet."[12] This one passage could be confusing when seen by itself, for elsewhere his data showed that these people are indeed future humans who simply do not have physical bodies as we now think of our own, but still look like us. In this same quote, Dr. Brown went on to say that these people are working to promote our human evolutionary potential. They have a goal that is very important to them, which Dr. Brown admits in the book he doesn't fully understand. To me, with all the dreams I was having, the answer seemed obvious. Regardless of what you choose to call them, these angelic beings are here to help guide us through life, in the hope that we will graduate in the upcoming Ascension.

CHAPTER FIFTEEN

Cosmic Voyage and Insights
into Ascension

Ironically, there is no mention of Ascension anywhere in *Cosmic Voyage*. Dr. Brown and his people were apparently not having the same dreams, synchronicities, and intuitive flashes that I was receiving so frequently. However, Dr. Brown did have a highly intriguing set of data regarding the idea that human beings from our own time frame, such as Americans, would soon end up being relocated to a new planet in the nearby Pleiades star cluster. If we correlate this with his trainer Major Ed Dames's oft-cited reports of a coming solar flash, this relocation could be seen as some type of cosmic Noah's ark plan. Advanced future humans could end up moving Earth people to a new planet just before the solar flash takes place, for our own safety. This vision of our future came from a session Dr. Brown conducted on February 9, 1994.

The Galactic Federation and Planetary Transfers

To understand the context of this session, it is important to know that Dr. Brown had created a collection of possible interesting ET-related choices for his research. These were randomly interspersed with normal targets. One of the interesting choices was the concept of a "Galactic

Federation." This is apparently a greater spiritual governing body, comprising a variety of advanced extraterrestrial groups working harmoniously together. This concept had appeared in many different channeled books, which Dr. Brown's data did not conclude were credible, but he wanted to explore the concept nonetheless. On February 9, 1994, without knowing the target, Dr. Brown got his first intuitive look at this Galactic Federation.

In his remote viewing session, he perceived himself entering a towering structure that had energetic, bright white, blue, and yellow lights. He noticed an energy vortex encircling a round object in the center of the room, which he feels may have been a planet, or at least a holographic projection of such an image. He could smell ammonia in the air. The many beings in this facility were all bald, humanoid, and wore white gowns. It felt like a Zen monastery, and they communicated both verbally and telepathically. Dr. Brown was welcomed by a president or prime minister of this group, and felt this was a highly competitive job. Dr. Brown was told that Earth human representation on the council was beginning now. The head being was wearing a bluish-white gown and was a bit heavyset. He was somber, but had a definite sense of humor, which together made him appear like Buddha. The identification of this being as Buddha was introduced into Dr. Brown's mind, apparently to help facilitate greater communication. This does not necessarily mean that this being actually was Buddha, merely that it took that form to help Dr. Brown feel more comfortable.

Dr. Brown was shown an image of our Milky Way galaxy divided up into sections with dotted lines. He was told that this Federation did need our help in a galactic sense. Specifically, Dr. Brown said,

> I am being told that there will be a movement off the planet in the future for humans. . . . Earth humans are violent and troublesome currently. They need shaping before a later merger. Definitely humans need to undergo some sort of change before extending far off the planet. . . . There definitely will be a planetary disaster, or perhaps I should say disasters. There will be political chaos, turbulence, an unrav-

eling of the current political order. . . . He is telling me very directly that consciousness must become a focal concern of humans in order for us to proceed further. . . . We [in the Federation] are not saviors, just initial representatives.[1]

Dr. Brown's words from 1996 are certainly prophetic as I write these words in 2019. We are most definitely seeing "political chaos, turbulence, [and] an unraveling of the current political order" in a way that would have seemed unimaginable back when his words were written.

Nothing about this idea of an upcoming catastrophe was upsetting or frightening to me, because by this point, I had experienced over three years' worth of dreams encouraging me to see such an event as a multi-dimensional evolution of what it means to be human. Regarding the idea of being a human representative for the Galactic Federation, Dr. Brown was also told not to let this work go to his head, but just to do his job: "I am told in no uncertain terms that I am to complete this book project. Others will play their parts. There are many involved. Many species, representatives, groups."[2] Reading this passage in 1996 encouraged me that I might have my own role to play in the process, as so many of my dreams had been suggesting. The Federation was described as a galactic governmental organization, where Earth humans are now being prepared for full membership.[3]

Additional Confirmation of Earth Human Transfer

The idea of Earth humans being transferred elsewhere in an expected near-term future event was given far more detail in a session from March 10, 1994. This data appears in Dr. Brown's book in a chapter entitled "The Human Repository." Here, Dr. Brown remote-viewed a planet in the Pleiades star system. He noticed something very bright in the sky. He was able to perceive that there were beings near the light who were more advanced than the beings he was seeing on the ground of this world. Once he looked at the people on the surface, he said the following: "Focusing on the ground for now, there is dirt, grass, and humans wearing normal American-type casual clothing. Let me check that out. Yep. Pants, socks, shoes, the works. The humans are quite upset. There is a lot of fear here, plus crying."[4] He said the beings in the sky seemed like Grays. When he tried to tap into the timeline for when this event took place, he saw that it was sometime slightly later than the year 2000. This fit in with countless speculations of a change surrounding the end date of the Mayan Calendar, namely December 21, 2012, or sometime not too long thereafter. I do believe that even though the 2012 "end date" came and went, we are still very much heading toward a solar-system wide multidimensional shift in our near future. Quoting Dr. Brown again, "It seems that humans migrated here" to this new world in the Pleiades star cluster.

As he delved into this vision even deeper, he noticed how familiar these people were. It wasn't that they were extraterrestrials who had a surprising similarity to people from Earth. They very clearly were from Earth. According to Dr. Brown, "[these people] really seemed like Americans. They appeared to be farming people who perhaps lived in or visited a nearby city or village. The Gray ET beings were doing what was a fairly routine mission for them."[5] This raised the intriguing idea that the Grays were here, at least in part, to help facilitate transfers of people from one planet to another, such as for a protective measure. This mirrored Betty Andreasson's testimony in *The Watchers,* where the Grays told her they protect the seed of humanity as well as the biosphere of the Earth. They could use this living genetic material to terraform a new planet for us as needed. If a transfer like this had once happened to our ancestors, and they got dropped off here on Earth, the story would quickly turn into ancient mythology. Soon, no one would believe we had originated on another planet in the past.

As the session went on, the Grays contacted Dr. Brown directly, and started trying to feed him information faster than he could handle. As he tried to process all the information, he said the following: "The people on this [new] world are from Earth. The Grays brought them here. They have been transplanted. The humans do not know everything. They do not even know where they are."[6] When Dr. Brown asked the reason for why this happened, the response was "Human survival is at stake. A new location is needed away from Earth's climatic disasters."[7] The Grays went on to tell him that they were transplanting our genetic material to ensure our survival with a better, more advanced gene pool. They added new or modified genes to increase the connections between our spirits and physical bodies.

As the session continued, Dr. Brown discovered that this new place was a Class M planet orbiting a binary star system, sometime shortly after 2000 AD. Bear in mind that a date range of 2030 would still be considered "shortly after 2000 AD." The post-2000 time frame fit with many other prophecies I had encountered over the years. Dr. Brown also said, "It seems that some humans will be 'space-lifted' to a safe haven while the rest of humanity slugs it out back home."[8] This was literally identical to the Ascension scenario I had already been studying and meditating on. It was quite surprising that Dr. Brown was presenting this as "raw data" without seeming to understand any of the backstory behind it that I had already been researching. The transfer Dr. Brown was seeing may well have been describing what would happen to those people who were not really Ascending but just needed to be moved to a safe place once the Earth went through its upheavals. This exact same concept would appear only weeks later when I read the Law of One. The people who graduate into fourth density in this apparently multidimensional event do get to remain on Earth as it transforms into a fourth-density planet.

Dr. Brown now revealed that other remote-viewing data showed Grays collecting plant and animal specimens from the Earth, apparently to help transfer it to the new world. I had seen similar reports of ETs scooping up trees and water in a number of UFO books, and again this was precisely the same thing that Betty Andreasson heard from the Grays in *The Watchers*. Yet, Dr. Brown never referenced this material at any point in the book. In Dr. Brown's next session, he had a non-ET-related calibration target: He viewed President Clinton accurately. Ed Dames immediately pulled him out once he recognized Clinton.[9]

Grays Are Children of the Logos

Another interesting piece of information occurred when Dr. Brown was apparently able to connect with a being he identified as Jesus. In a session from June 14, 1994, Dr. Brown admitted that he felt very disturbed about the idea that there could be anything good about the Grays. Once he got the opportunity to meet this Jesus-like being, the question of the Grays was very much on his mind. According to Dr. Brown, "[the being identifying as Jesus said] there is no being that humans will interact with that is not of his design. He then stated that we are to help his children however they come to us."[10] Brown did not understand what this means. For starters, the passage suggests that the identity of Jesus is actually a galactic consciousness. The Law of One, which I would begin reading immediately after Dr. Brown's book, very clearly revealed this same concept, albeit with a slightly veiled code.

What if Jesus became the full embodiment on Earth of a galactic superidentity that makes humanlike beings in its image across countless millions of planets within this galaxy? It would stand to reason that Jesus would then see any and all life within our galaxy as his own children. "God the Father" could then represent the universe as a whole, whereas "God the Son" would be our own native galaxy. This is precisely what the Law of One hints at by referring to our galaxy as the Logos, which translates as "word" in Greek. This is also where the common term *logo*, such as a stylized design for the name of a business, is derived from. The Collins English Dictionary defines *Logos* as a term from Christian theology that means "the divine Word; the second person of the Trinity incarnate in the person of Jesus."[11] The Law of One does not constrain the meaning of *Logos* as this dictionary definition does. Everything in the universe is a projection of the Logos within the Law of One system.

The term *logos* appears throughout 146 different Law of One passages, and is also said to be equivalent to the word *love*.[12] In Session 13, Question 7, the term *Logos* clearly refers to the consciousness of the entire manifest universe: "Awareness led to the focus of infinity into infinite energy. You have called this by various vibrational sound complexes, the most common to your ears being 'Logos' or 'Love.' The Creator is the focusing of infinity as an aware or conscious principle, called by us as closely as we can create understanding/learning in your language, intelligent infinity."[13] In Session 28, Question 7, the Law of One says, "There are many different Logos entities or creations, and we would call each, using your sound vibration complexes, a galaxy."[14]

In the classic Bible verse at the very beginning of the book of John, namely 1:1, it says, "In the beginning was the Word, and the Word was with God, and the Word was God."[15] If we modify this seemingly mysterious verse by using the original Greek word *Logos*, the passage would read as: "In the beginning was the Logos, and the Logos was with God, and the Logos was God." Shortly thereafter in John 1:14, again swapping the term *Logos* for *word*, we have, "And the Logos was made flesh, and dwelt among us."[16]

By using the term *Logos* for the galactic mind as well as the embodiment of the entire universe, as well as the definition of love itself, the Law of One clearly seems to be hinting that we should read and meditate on these Bible passages. This may not satisfy fundamentalist views that want to see Earth humans as the only "Chosen Ones" out there, but as we acclimate to the widespread presence of extraterrestrial life, the Law of One series provides us with a way in which our own traditional religions can easily adapt—and still be seen as highly relevant in a much greater galactic context. The Jesus that Christians pray to may well be an embodiment of the same creator that all life in our galaxy emanates from.

Again, in Law of One philosophical terms, the One Infinite Creator that made all the universe is the Logos, or "God," and our galaxy is also a Logos, or the "son of God" that is "with God," as it said in John 1:1: "The Logos was with God, and the Logos was God." This also ties back in with Genesis 1:27, where if we replace the word *God* with *Logos* and make it gender-neutral, we get, "The Logos created human beings in its own image."[17] Every insider I have spoken to has said that all extraterrestrial life in our galaxy has a humanlike appearance. The human form is therefore the image of how the mind of our galaxy chooses to express itself as intelligent life.

Therefore, instead of contradicting Christian thought, the Law of One series presents a new idea where the mind of the galaxy is available to all on Earth, as well as all others throughout our galaxy. All intelligent life in this galaxy would then be an embodiment of the mind of the galactic Logos. Dr. Brown's results clearly supported this concept, and again he never read the Law of One series. I confirmed this in a written interview with him while writing this book. He was very excited to hear about some of the connections I had found.

Later in Dr. Brown's book, the being identifying as Jesus was asked if non-Christians would still need to call on the name of Jesus to reach their full evolutionary potential. The being seemed genuinely upset and frustrated by this question. "Quite forcefully, he stated that a name is nothing. Everything depends on personality development, and this includes the development of a deep ability to both perceive and love beyond the self."[18] This was a comfortable answer that I could certainly agree with, particularly in light of how much difficulty my own mother had with mainstream fundamentalist Christian religious views. The Law of One series frequently speaks about the development and disciplines of the personality as being of paramount importance, such as in Session 74, Question 10. The three-part formula for the discipline of the personality is given in Session 74, Question 11, as follows: "One, know yourself. Two, accept yourself. Three, become the Creator. The third step is that step that, when accomplished, renders one the most humble servant of all, transparent in personality and completely able to know and accept other selves. . . . To become the Creator is to become all that there is. There is then no personality in the sense with which the adept begins its learn/teaching."[19]

It is very common for people to assume that all Grays must be evil, if they even believe in this UFO subject whatsoever. My research has certainly concluded that some types of Grays are negative, and many insiders have revealed that there are a large number of varieties. You can definitely have intelligent life within our galaxy, or Logos, that is negatively polarized. In Law of One terms, this simply means that the being is "confused"—a word that is used in 101 different passages.[20] Eventually all beings will awaken in the dream and reunite with Oneness, no matter how "confused" they may be. The Gray type of form is simply one of the ways in which the human body can evolve, where the eyes and head grow larger relative to the rest of the body. Or, just as Raymond Fowler described in *The Watchers,* you could grow a neonate—a being that looked just like a Gray—from a normal human fetus if its head was not compressed by the pressure of a womb as it grew.

When I then thought back to my original NASA disclosure, the insider said they had identified three types of beings. The tallest was a human type that looked very similar, but not identical to us. The next tallest of them was a physiologically authentic Gray. The shortest of the three types was a being wearing a sophisticated helmet that made it look like it was a Gray, but underneath the helmet, its actual face was "a monstrosity." This strongly suggested that the facial features were of a reptilian appearance instead. That was the intuitive flash I got when I first received this information in 1993. Dr. Brown's own research also revealed at least three different races of Grays.

The idea that not all Gray-type ETs visiting us are evil also fits with the prodigious research of Harvard psychiatrist Dr. John Mack in his epic classic from 1994, *Abduction.*[21] Dr. Mack cataloged and summarized dozens of UFO contactee reports, where he brought people under deep hypnosis and helped them retrieve memories that would otherwise have been lost. Many Gray-style beings were encountered in these regressions, and most of the interactions were remarkably uplifting and positive. The mainstream media never said a word about the conclusions of Dr. Mack's book, and he died a tragic and untimely death in 2004, when he was struck by a driver suspected of being drunk.[22] I was very sad that I never got to meet him or discuss his findings with him in any capacity.

Perhaps the closest we ever got in the mainstream media to an admission of Dr. Mack's research was a quote from his obituary in the *New York Times.* Regarding his abduction research, it said, "In the 1990s, Dr. Mack studied dozens of people who said they had had such contact with aliens, culminating in his book *Abduction: Human Encounters with Aliens* in 1994. In it, he focused less on whether aliens were real than on the spiritual effects of perceived encounters, arguing that "the abduction phenomenon has important philosophical, spiritual and social implications for everyone."[23]

When I considered all this data as a whole, I speculated that if a certain type of future humans who now looked like Grays were conducting vital, planet-saving operations, their negative and demonic ET opponents would most definitely want to interfere with their mission. By actually impersonating these Grays and conducting terrifying and traumatic abductions, Earth people could be confused beyond any hope of seeing good in Gray-type extraterrestrials. Christians and other religious people may come to see Grays and all other extraterrestrial life as strictly demonic, and some of them definitely do. Once again, this could be another example of "divide and conquer," where people who look different from us are demonized as "the other," so we will eventually have no trouble in agreeing to their mass slaughter. We will explore much more on this in an upcoming chapter on the Watchers, as the Grays referred to themselves in the Betty Andreasson case.

In Dr. Brown's session from June 14, 1994, the being appearing as Jesus also said there should be no limits to our desire to help others, whether Grays or people from Mars or whoever. If we want to elevate ourselves to the next stage of our evolution, prejudice cannot coexist with these higher forms of life. The being identifying as Jesus also said it is not that we should work with the ETs, it is that we must. Our situation here on Earth has been deliberately designed so that both groups need each other for their individual and mutual well-being.

Exploring the Lost Civilization of Mars

In my initial read, perhaps the single most invigorating thing about Dr. Brown's *Cosmic Voyage* was that he put a name and a face to the civilization that was responsible for constructing the Martian monuments. I had read about this lost civilization with amazement in Richard C. Hoagland's book *The Monuments of Mars* after my NASA disclosure in 1993, and I never missed a single appearance of his on the air with Art Bell. Now, three years later, I felt we were finally getting some deeper insights into what the heck these monuments were, and who built them. Unless an insider came out with stunning new intel on Mars, which did happen later in my career, the only viable means of gathering information about something like this would be through a verifiable intuitive process such as remote viewing or Edgar Cayce–quality psychic readings, which are extremely rare, to say the least.

If Dr. Brown was right, then the people from Mars were our own long-lost brothers and sisters. They were very close to being human like us, only taller. Dr. Brown's first-ever ET-related remote-viewing session revealed that large numbers of the Martian civilization went through a series of Gray abduction-type genetic procedures prior to the destruction of their planet, and that their genetic materials and souls were later transferred into new bodies on Earth.

Again, Dr. Brown's first visit to Mars was on September 29, 1993. At the time, he had no idea that extraterrestrial targets like this could even exist. As the session went on, he struggled to understand the wonders and horrors he was seeing, but the protocols require us not to analyze or attempt to interpret anything. We just continue performing the procedure. In this case, Dr. Brown found himself looking at a gigantic pyramid, vastly larger than anything he had ever known to exist on Earth. He knew that this massive structure had to do with worship. He determined that it was solid but hollow inside, and very tall. As time went on, he realized that many people had died to build it. At a certain point, a volcano began erupting near the pyramid. It was a scene very much like Pompeii. Lots of people were dying, and there was a terrible feeling of complete hopelessness. Those who survived the catastrophe were thrown into desperate poverty.

Packaged and Transferred to Earth

Dr. Brown's data showed that a new group of people "from very far away" then came in to help the survivors and to rebuild. When Major Ed Dames told him what the target was at the end of the session, Dr. Brown was completely astonished. On October 2, 1993, he conducted a Type Six session, where both the viewer and the guide knew what the target was: to go back to Mars. Although this is not as reliable as the double-blind method, many experiments have proven that viable data can still be gathered this way. Dr. Brown noted that the people of Mars had no hair and larger eyes than humans. They also had some telepathic ability. The feel of their culture and architecture reminded Dr. Brown of places he had studied in Africa. The peak of Martian society could specifically be compared to that of ancient Egypt. The women stayed at home with their children, for the most part.

At a certain point in their history, the people of Mars experienced an extremely rapid advancement in technology. Not long after this, their civilization collapsed. Many of the people died in this catastrophe and some were rescued, but they did not necessarily like the terms. Dr. Brown again observed that a race of smaller, shorter beings arrived, and they were on a mission. Highly motivated, they worked with speed and urgency. Dr. Brown said the short beings "are here as the first stage of a larger project. I get the sense that they are packaging everything."[24] He observed that these beings were Grays, with short bodies and milky white skin. Before the survivors of Mars left their planet, they saw these beings as godlike entities. Dr. Brown then went on to say, "Somehow the Martians are getting packed up in preparation for some change. . . . It feels like the short beings are planning on the Martians getting a physical change in their bodies, and they're being put in cold storage for a while. These little short folks look like Grays."[25]

As the session went on, Dr. Brown got even more specific details:

> The rescuers were the beings that we now know as Grays. They arrived at the last moments of the collapse of the Martian civilization. With great speed, they somehow "stored" the Martians. Apparently this was necessary to preserve what could be saved of Martian life. I cannot provide a technical explanation, but the essential focus of the rescue was the preservation of Martian genetic material. All of this happened millions of years ago.[26]

This data would later prove to correlate almost perfectly with what I gathered from the Law of One series as well as from insiders like Corey

Goode. The only difference is that the apparent time of this catastrophe was 500,000 years ago, whereas Dr. Brown had initially felt it was millions of years ago. This type of variance in time accuracy is perfectly understandable if it wasn't the main focus of Dr. Brown's remote-viewing target. In addition, in the Law of One series, the source reported having problems with our system of time measurement as a general rule.

While speaking in summary about this fascinating planet-to-planet transfer within our own solar system, Dr. Brown said, "Virtually all remote-viewing data show that the Martians seem to have been genetically altered to enable them to live in the heavier gravity and different conditions on Earth. The actual alteration occurred recently, following a period of preservation, and is not yet complete."[27]

This became one of the most astonishing correlations for me when I began reading the Law of One. In Session 9, Question 6, Ra said:

> The first of those to come here [to Earth] were brought from another planet in your solar system called by you the Red Planet, Mars. This planet's environment became inhospitable to third-density beings. The first entities, therefore, were of this race, as you may call it, manipulated somewhat by those who were guardians at that time.[28]

The answer continued after Question 7:

> These entities arrived, or were preserved, for the experience upon your sphere by a type of birthing which is non-reproductive, but consists of preparing genetic material for the incarnation of the mind/body/spirit complexes of those entities from the Red Planet.[29]

The source went on to confirm that this planet-to-planet transfer happened after the race had died from the physical world as we know it on Mars.

The correlation between Dr. Brown's results and the Law of One were absolutely astonishing to me. Dr. Brown repeatedly used the word *pack-*

aged to describe how this process took place. Ra said the people of Mars were "manipulated somewhat," where they were "preserved . . . by a type of birthing which is non-reproductive, but consists of preparing genetic material for . . . incarnation." This therefore gives us much greater insight into the phenomenon of abduction and the sampling of genetic material. We are seeing how an entire planet worth of beings can be preserved and re-introduced on a new planet if the world they are living on is damaged in some way. This is not the same as simply cloning human beings, because in this case, genetic modifications can also be made in order to adapt people to different atmosphere, gravitational strength, height, sunlight intensity, et cetera. Any one person can be cloned from a DNA sample, such as from the scoop marks that so many abductees had visible signs of, where a small circular area of their skin was removed. The more benevolent aspects of the typical abduction phenomenon we read about in books, such as *Abduction* by Dr. John Mack, could simply be an example of this "packaging" taking place on Earth. Therefore, if something were to happen to our own planet, our civilization and genetic diversity would not perish.

In chapter 16 of *Cosmic Voyage,* Dr. Brown remote-viewed the collapse of the early Gray civilization he was studying. He once again noticed that they were being genetically packaged before a coming collapse.[30] Their civilization was seduced on a collective level by "an arrogant, rebellious, and very powerful leader. They later felt betrayed, but the damage was too far gone. They had to recover from scratch."[31] This arrogant leader had a spiritual connection to a being that Dr. Brown identified as Lucifer. He tuned in to Lucifer as a very insecure, fearful being, afraid of its own inevitable death and the punishment that it knew would then result. Dr. Brown's results indicated that the Grays may have voluntarily eliminated their sexuality and emotions to avoid the damage that had been caused by the influence of this nonphysical being.

Tuning In to the Consciousness of Jesus and God

In chapter 18, Dr. Brown used a method called Solo Type 1 to tune in to the consciousness of Jesus without the use of his guide. In this session, the being identifying as Jesus thanked him for showing up on his own. The being said that the Grays are God's children, and no less valuable than those we call human. The greater evolutionary goal for Earth humans working with them involves merging with the Creator in some way.[32] In another session from July 14, 1994, Dr. Brown tuned in to this group of Grays in the far future. By this point, they had become more human-looking and had learned to love once again. They all now had a type of spiritual energy similar to what he had seen in other positive beings. Dr. Brown said the being he felt was Jesus had a sense of command or authority, whereas these beings just radiated love without the other component.[33]

After this, Dr. Brown began to contemplate God. The results echoed very precisely what I was about to start reading in the Law of One series. He saw how all the universe was created from a single awareness: "from [God's] own substance." Later, he said, "One can love oneself, and all others, because one sees that all of everything is created from the same fabric. Somehow, love is the theme of God, the glue that keeps the universe together."[34] This is precisely what we see in the Law of One series, where the terms *Logos* and *love* are seen as interchangeable.

Closer to the end of the book, Dr. Brown conducted a session on God once again. I found the following quote to be particularly beautiful:

> God spent an eternity as a point source. His evolution reached a point of change in which he could not bear the loneliness of isolation. His only recourse was to re-create himself throughout an infinitude, thereby initiating a sequence of creating new gods, new hims, beings to care for him, and for him to care for. He loves us because we ended a loneliness that was beyond any ability to describe in words. He will never allow the demise of his creations, since it would send him back to the point-source past, and that was his prison. The future is forever to expand.[35]

Dr. Brown saw that there was great joy in God's new creation. He also saw that our emotions are not as difficult as we may think. Instead, they provide us with a very effective connection back to our truest identity as God. Additionally, he realized that we all have a deep subconscious fear of the isolation and loneliness that we once felt as God. Fundamentally, we are interconnected with this source, and have never really left. When we become deeply inspired, we are filled with the joy and bliss and wonderment that this core identity always has. We can spend our entire lives wandering through materialism and attachment disorders without ever realizing that the true source of this love and power is within ourselves.

No Way for Me to Replicate Dr. Brown's Research

According to Dr. Brown, the only way that one could continue in this type of work and become a representative for the Galactic Federation was to engage and complete a study of remote viewing—in exactly the same way he had done. And unfortunately, in order to carry out this study in the way Dr. Brown required, it would necessitate an investment of at least eight to ten thousand dollars. There was a three-step process that he said was vital to developing this ability, which was a description of how he himself had gotten there. Step one was to take Transcendental Meditation all the way through to the most advanced level, called the "Siddhi" stage. Step two was to go to the Monroe Institute in Faber, Virginia, and take the Farsight Voyager course. Step three was to then go to Brown's own university in Atlanta, Georgia, and pay five thousand dollars for a one-week course in remote viewing.

According to Brown, no method of spiritual information gathering was valid other than remote viewing. I almost believed Dr. Brown and other remote viewers when they said remote viewing was the only game in town. However, I was all too familiar with the legacy of Edgar Cayce, since his work appeared in many books I had found on Atlantis, Egypt, ancient civilizations, extraterrestrials, and UFOs. Many authors saw the Cayce Readings as their most valuable asset when trying to understand how these mysterious, lost secrets all fit together. Though the verbiage of the Cayce Readings was often almost exasperating, with run-on sentences that would extend through entire paragraphs, it was truly amazing material. There is simply no way that the "Sleeping Prophet" could have accurately diagnosed the medical problems of fourteen thousand people, in documented "psychic readings," having only their name and address as a resource, unless he had a genuine ability to access higher consciousness.

Cayce's process was obviously very similar to remote viewing. Instead of using a pair of random numbers as "coordinates," Cayce's sleeping mind used the name and address of a person, and nothing else. I realized that it is all too common for highly intelligent people to form cliques, thinking their group has all the answers, and everyone else is too unsophisticated to understand or appreciate what they are doing. They build up a world of jargon and gradually become elitist, to the point where any outsiders who attempt to enter that world might be unfairly judged. You can see this in fine art, ballet, theater, classical music, jazz music, classic rock, professional sports, yoga, tai chi, martial arts, the financial sector, corporate management, government, the military, and, yes, even the shadowy world of the Illuminati or Cabal. This is essentially human nature. My guides have always encouraged me to be more inclusive and appreciative of others, even if I did not agree with them. So although the remote viewers felt that no one else had ever accessed psychic consciousness properly, it was easy to see that the Cayce Readings proved them wrong.

As I noted previously, I would soon find out that the explanation in the Law of One series for the demise of the Martian civilization, their genetic "storage," and subsequent transfer to Earth was virtually identical to Dr. Brown's scenario. The people of Mars went through a comprehensive genetic storage and "packaging" that led to their being transplanted to Earth with bodies that were modified to handle our biosphere. This was one of the greatest shocks I went through in my initial reading of the Law of One.

Furthermore, the Law of One gives additional information that Dr. Brown did not obtain in his remote-viewing sessions, by revealing that the same "planet-hopping" transfer process happened with a world known as Maldek, which exploded through an act of war and became the Asteroid Belt. The former inhabitants of Maldek had greater karma to work off than the people of Mars, and thus they incarnated here as

Bigfoot-type creatures. These bodies had "self-imposed limitations of form," as it said in Session 59, Question 4, which allowed them to work off the karma of having destroyed their planet.[36] This again may cause some people to laugh in disbelief, and that is fine. Many people have had encounters with Bigfoot-type creatures, and if our governments were consistently telling the truth, one of many significant questions the public would want answers to would be to explore what these beings are and where they originated from.

Earlier, in Session 10, Question 1, we read, "The group decision [for the people of Maldek] was to place upon itself a type of what you may call karma alleviation. For this purpose they came into incarnation within your planetary sphere, in what were not acceptable human forms." Then in Session 10, Question 3, a more technical-sounding description of this karmic choice was given, when it said, "The [karmic] alleviation mechanism [for the people of Maldek] was designed by the placement of this consciousness in second-dimensional physical chemical complexes which are not able to be dexterous or manipulative to the extent which is appropriate to the workings of the third-density distortions of the mind complex."[37] Put more simply, the Bigfoot body is more apelike than humanlike, and it therefore does not allow them to work with tools and develop advanced technology.

In Session 59, Question 5, it was revealed that fully two billion souls have now transferred to Earth from Maldek through this process.[38] If it seems hard to believe that we could have such a large Bigfoot population, we must remember that multiple insiders have independently disclosed the "honeycomb earth" model, where there are vast numbers of habitable passages inside the Earth. There are various cave entrances that allow direct access to these inner worlds, which the Bigfoot creatures apparently know very well. By reading Session 9, Question 18, we get more information on this, where it says that "these [Maldek] entities are working their understanding complexes through a series of what you would call karmic restitutions. They dwell within your deeper underground passageways, and are known to you as 'Bigfoot.'"[39]

This idea of the descendants of Maldek incarnating within the Earth was also indicated in Session 6, Questions 10 and 13, where it read, "These entities, destroying their planetary sphere, thus were forced to find room for themselves upon this third density, which is the only one in your solar system at their time/space present which was hospitable and capable of offering the lessons necessary to decrease their mind/body/spirit distortions with respect to the Law of One. . . . The ones who were harvested to your sphere from the sphere known before its dissolution as other names, but to your peoples as Maldek, incarnated, many within your Earth's surface rather than upon it."[40] Apparently many of these people later reincarnated as normal humans on the surface, after a sufficient degree of their karmic alleviation had been paid out. Reincarnation is discussed in the next chapter.

Dr. Brown's material regarding the Galactic Federation was also in many ways literally identical to what I soon found in the Law of One. This type of connection was far too specific to be a product of chance. It seemed obvious that Dr. Brown wasn't lying, and he certainly had not read the Law of One series going in, as it was quite obscure and practically unknown in the UFO field. He had a picture-perfect description of the Mars genetic transfer, but had never done a session on the idea of the Asteroid Belt also having been an inhabited world that underwent a similar incarnative process. In fact, when I emailed him while writing this book, he was still unaware that the Law of One had conveyed similar information. Dr. Brown admittedly had no previous interest in UFOlogy, and could hardly even have imagined the data that was being generated. Each new session was a shocking new discovery to both himself and his guide.

How could Dr. Brown have been repeatedly starting with absolutely nothing but a set of coordinates and ending up with findings identical to those in the Law of One series? Once I dug into the Law of One, there were just so many connections popping out between the two that the most logical conclusion was that both of them were accurately describing a greater body of authentic information. The Law of One, however, went leaps and bounds further in its informational content than Dr. Brown's findings had done in *Cosmic Voyage*. The connections between Dr. Brown's work and the Law of One were actually just a few small points compared to the vastly greater worldview that the series as a whole was communicating.

CHAPTER SIXTEEN

The Law of One Puts All the Pieces Together

D r. Scott Mandelker's book *From Elsewhere* triggered a series of experiences that convinced me that I was indeed a Wanderer, or extraterrestrial soul. The most powerful of these experiences was my housemate Eric's dream on January 19, 1996, where a being that looked like Jesus threw his arm around my shoulders and said, "It is very important that you know that he is one of us." Just as in remote-viewing research, Eric's dream was "blind," in that he had no conscious way of knowing that I had prayed for an answer to this very question just hours before he came home. That same night after Eric's dream came in, I began reading *Cosmic Voyage* by Dr. Courtney Brown. I ordered the remaining books of the Law of One series, and they arrived at my local bookstore soon afterward. Dr. Mandelker's endorsement of the Law of One series was quite a powerful statement for me at the time, considering his background.

An Expert on Buddhism Says the Law of One Is the Best

Dr. Mandelker had earned a PhD in East-West psychology and was an expert scholar in Buddhism who had actually traveled to various temples in Southeast Asia to meditate for weeks on end in silence. He painted a dramatic picture of trying to find God through meditation while gigantic "tree roaches" slammed themselves against the screens of the hut where he was staying. Dr. Mandelker said that the Law of One series had all the very highest and deepest secret wisdom of the great masters in one book. He claimed that the knowledge within the Law of One series had superseded the entire weight of his Naropa Institute PhD education and all his private studies before then. Never before had he read a single source so rich with wisdom, spirituality, and insight. The Law of One had become his Source Text, as he had never before found a single written work that offered such profound new insights each and every time he opened it. The source of the Law of One explained that it was the highest-level extraterrestrial consciousness to ever directly deal with human beings like us. At sixth density, Ra was fully two quantum leaps in evolution ahead of the typical fourth-density extraterrestrials we would see flying in craft in our skies. Ra was operating at the same level as the Higher Self that was apparently orchestrating the dreams and synchronicities that I and others like me were having. If there was any one recommendation that Dr. Mandelker gave in *From Elsewhere,* it was a very simple one: *Read the Law of One.*

Now I was ready to accept the challenge. I had to. All roads were leading me to the Law of One. Dr. Mandelker was the expert, and he had just revealed that if I had achieved my dream and actually gone to Naropa and gotten a PhD, I would have concluded that the Law of One was the most advanced postgraduate spiritual work I could possibly be studying. And there was no Law of One university. It was all independent study. I would soon find out that the Law of One strongly endorsed the value of reading inspirational books and meditating on their contents, as I had been doing heavily in the preceding years. This is seen in Session 49, Question 8: "Contemplation or the consideration in a meditative state of an inspiring image or text is extremely useful also among your peoples."[1] The practice of remembering and analyzing one's dreams was also said to be of the highest spiritual value.

In Session 85, Question 19, it read, "The so-called dreaming contains a great deal which, if made available to the conscious mind and used, shall aid it in [positive] polarization to a great extent."[2] In Session 86, Question 7, it read, "In all cases it is useful to a mind/body/spirit complex [person] to ponder the content and emotive resonance of dreams."[3] Also interesting is Session 95, Question 18, where it read, "There is what might be called a partial vocabulary of the dreams, due to the common heritage of all mind/body/spirit complexes. Due to each entity's unique incarnational experiences, there is an overlay which grows to be a larger and larger proportion of the dream vocabulary as the entity gains experience."[4] This was exactly what I had experienced. Certain symbols were unique to me, such as the idea of drums, which I had studied academically in a college jazz program, representing my greater spiritual work. I also would see people I knew at various times in my life and be able to analyze the dream based on who they were and what I had experienced with them at the time we were in contact.

I had grabbed my copy of *The Law of One: Book Three* at Borders the same night I bought *Cosmic Voyage*, but for some reason the bookstore did not carry any of the other three volumes. I had already looked through Book Three on the shelves before, and had admittedly put it back. The language was incredibly dense, almost impenetrable. Ra was using all sorts of elaborate and mysterious jargon, just as we see in many different intelligent subcultures throughout our society. One obviously needed to have read the first book to be able to understand the third. The writing was very much like "scientific poetry," written from such a level of "higher intelligence" that it might actually be beyond our own human intellectual capacity to understand it. The questioner, Dr. Don Elkins, often struggled to understand and respond to what he was being told. He almost always made mistakes in his questions that then had to be corrected.

I quickly decided that I was better off waiting until the other three volumes had arrived in the mail, and *Cosmic Voyage* was more than enough to keep me satisfied while I waited. This Law of One study was nothing to take lightly, and starting on Book Three was definitely not the right idea. Somewhere just before the end of January 1996, while struggling to make a living at two cents above minimum wage in a highly stressful job, I opened my new copy of Book One of *The Law of One* and began reading. My life would never be the same.

A Socratic Dialogue

Thankfully, Book One did open with an extensive overview of the UFO research that the group had been conducting for over twenty years before their contact began. I found that the source did not want to just deliver information—it was important that the group ask questions that would then be responded to. This was similar but not identical in style to how the wise old philosopher Socrates worked, in what scholars call a Socratic dialogue.

As it says on the Filosophia Prática website:

> Socratic dialogue is a formal method by which a small group (5–15 people), guided by a facilitator, finds a precise answer to a universal question (e.g., "What is happiness?", "What is integrity?", "Can conflict be fruitful?", etc.). . . . The method of the Socratic dialogue is as rewarding as its goal. It involves group decision-making by consensus, which is distinctly unlike most other modalities of group function. To begin with, since the Socratic dialogue is neither a debate nor any other kind of competition, there are no winners and losers. . . . You need not be a philosopher, nor have philosophical qualifications, to participate in a Socratic dialogue. An appealing presupposition of the dialogue is that universal truths are grounded in our particular experiences. The purpose of the dialogue is to reach the universal from the particular. . . . Reference to published works is not admissible in a Socratic dialogue; reference to concrete personal experience is what counts and suffices for the purpose.[5]

This, again, relates to the idea that "Ageless Wisdom" is ultimately available to each of us in a state of contemplative meditation.

The main person asking all the questions, Dr. Don Elkins, happened to have a PhD in physics and brought all that advanced knowledge into his questions—particularly in Book Two. This added a strong professional element to the dialogue that would never have happened without someone so highly trained in the sciences. Dr. Elkins worked as a commercial airline pilot to make as much "money per unit of time" as possible to help support the group, which included Carla Rueckert, a well-read librarian and devout Christian who spoke the words in an unconscious trance state. Her extensive vocabulary allowed the source to use advanced words that were unfamiliar to most people, including myself, so I also needed to have a dictionary handy as I read *The Law of One*. Also part of the group was Jim McCarty, the highly athletic "scribe" who typed it all up from the original cassette tapes. Eventually, after living with Carla and Jim for two years, I realized that Jim had anchored in the body, Don the mind, and Carla the loving spirit. Thus, with the three of them combined, they were able to secure a high-level contact. Don and Carla had been researching and experimenting with channeling for over twenty years before the Law of One contact began, and felt that if it was done properly, it was the best way to gain a deeper understanding of the truth behind the UFO phenomenon.

The Law of One Philosophy

It's hard even to know where to begin in describing what it was like to read *The Law of One* for the first time. It was described as a work of philosophy, and I was already familiar with the history and various branches of philosophy from a few of my college classes. The terms *philosophy* or *philosophical* appear in a total of forty-nine different passages throughout the material.[6] In Session 1, Question 10, we read:

> We are not available to many of your peoples, for this is not an easily understood way of communication or type of philosophy. However, our very being is hopefully a poignant example of both the necessity and the near-hopelessness of attempting to teach. . . . The few whom you will illuminate by sharing your light are far more than enough reason for the greatest possible effort. To serve one is to serve all. Therefore,

we offer the question back to you to state that indeed it is the only activity worth doing: to learn/teach or teach/learn.[7]

As we see in the above passage, Ra felt they had a "necessity" to teach through this channeling method, which is "not an easily understood way of communication." They also considered it to be an act of "near-hopelessness," since very few people would ever find out about this incredible material compared to the total number of Earth's population. Yet, due to the power of the Law of One, "to serve one is to serve all."

This principle of Oneness was explained earlier in the same answer with a most fascinating statement:

> You must understand that the distinction between yourself and others is not visible to us. We do not consider that a separation exists between the consciousness-raising efforts of the distortion which you project as a personality and the distortion which you project as an other personality. Thus, to learn is the same as to teach unless you are not teaching what you are learning; in which case you have done you/they little or no good.[8]

It was quite mind-expanding for me to consider the idea of an extraterrestrial group that cannot see us as separate beings. At their level, it is literally impossible for them to perceive us as individuals. Years later, I would discover the Meditation Effect, where we see that a group of seven thousand people meditating on Pure Consciousness were able to reduce crime, war, terrorism, accidents, and fatalities worldwide by an astonishing 72 percent, while health and quality of life notably increased.[9] All other variables such as cycles, trends, weather, weekends, and holidays had been ruled out. By 1993, this effect had been proven in fifty different scientific studies over the preceding thirty years.[10] This became a major point that I returned to throughout my book *The Source Field Investigations,* and it also formed the Inciting Incident that led Dr. Courtney Brown into his own sacred quest for Truth, as we have seen.

Another example of scientific data that helps to prove this unique claim in *The Law of One* is known as the Multiples Effect. By the year 1922, William Ogburn and Dorothy Thomas had compiled a list of fully 148 major scientific discoveries that appeared in at least two different people's minds simultaneously. In some cases, multiple individuals got the same ideas at the exact same times, without having any idea that someone else was working on the same concept. This included the mathematics of calculus, the theory of evolution, decimal fractions, the oxygen molecule, color photography, and logarithms. Four scientists independently discovered sunspots in 1611. The law of conservation of energy was simultaneously formulated by four different scientists in 1847. At least six people independently invented the thermometer. Nine scientists simultaneously developed the telescope, without knowing anything about each other or what they were working on. Several people in England and America developed the typewriter at the same time. Five scientists "exclusively" discovered the steamboat at the same time: Fulton, Jouffroy, Rumsey, Stevens, and Symmington.[11]

In Law of One terms, these mass effects happen because we all ultimately share one mind. We have the illusion that our thoughts are our own, when in fact many of them are emerging from a greater collective consciousness—just as Carl Jung had postulated. As we think about and meditate on certain problems we are trying to solve, we are actually accessing a greater collective mind that we all share here on Earth. The information will start appearing to us in dreams and spontaneous intuitive flashes. For this same reason, if I ever think of an idea for a great dot-com website address, I immediately go and register the name right then.

The value of reaching just a few people was further explained in one of my most favorite passages, from Session 17, Question 2:

> It is impossible to help another being directly. It is only possible to make catalyst available in whatever form, the most important being the radiation of realization of oneness with the Creator from the self, less important being information such as we share with you. We, ourselves, do not feel an urgency for this information to be widely disseminated. It is

enough that we have made it available to three, four, or five. This is extremely ample reward, for if one of these obtains fourth-density understanding due to this catalyst, then we shall have fulfilled the Law of One in the distortion of service.

We encourage a dispassionate attempt to share information without concern for numbers or quick growth among others. That you attempt to make this information available is, in your term, your service. The attempt, if it reaches one, reaches all. We cannot offer shortcuts to enlightenment. Enlightenment is of the moment—[it] is an opening to intelligent infinity. It can only be accomplished by the self, for the self. Another self cannot teach/learn enlightenment, but only teach/learn information, inspiration, or a sharing of love, of mystery, of the unknown that makes the other-self reach out and begin the seeking process that ends in a moment—but who can know when an entity will open the gate to the present?[12]

This idea of fully opening "the gateway to the present" is another example of a direct linkage between *The Law of One* and Buddhism.

The source wasn't that interested in talking about themselves, as we see in Session 2, Question 2:

We are aware that you find our incarnate, as you call it, state of interest. We waited for a second query so as to emphasize that the time/space of several thousand of your years creates a spurious type of interest. Thus in giving this information, we ask the proper lack of stress be placed upon our experiences in your local space/time. The teach/learning which is our responsibility is philosophical rather than historical.[13]

This was a follow-up to a statement made in Session 1, Question 1: "We are not a part of time and, thus, are able to be with you in any of your times."[14] This time-travel capability of beings in the higher realms had already been proven to me in a number of prophetic dreams. Dr. Courtney Brown's own research strongly supported this concept as well. When my own contact started eleven months later, I soon had dozens of fantastic examples of prophecy taking place. I couldn't understand how this was happening, but it quickly became very obvious that prophecy was no joke.

The source often reiterated that their main interest was in communicating philosophical teachings. Ra was so concerned about free will that questions were an absolute necessity, as we see in Session 2, Question 6: "It is not our understanding that we have the right/duty to share our perceptions on any subject but philosophy without direct question."[15]

Oneness and Reincarnation

Even though it was very difficult to get started in this material, I realized that its philosophy was consistent and logical. Ultimately, like a Socratic dialogue, the truths in the work would become self-evident from one's own personal experience and study. The source was continually explaining the same philosophical concepts in different words, since the underlying message was extremely simple. The real difficulty was in simply hearing it on a deep enough level that you began actually applying it to your everyday life. The most important, overarching principle in the work was that we are all One. We ultimately all share the same awareness, and awareness is what created the universe—just as many different philosophers have theorized. Once we understand that basic principle, we then realize that if we harm others, we are only harming ourselves. Therefore, the core teaching is for us to learn to be more loving with ourselves and others.

The great choice we face in third-density life, as they call it, is between love and control. One example of this teaching is in Session 46, Question 16: "This experience in your density may be loved and accepted, or it may be controlled. These are the two paths. When neither path is chosen, the catalyst fails in its design, and the entity proceeds until catalyst strikes it, which causes it to form a bias toward acceptance and love, or separation and control."[16] The term *catalyst* simply refers to something we use for our own growth.

In Session 46, Questions 9-12, it reads, "Control is the key to negatively polarized use of catalyst. Acceptance is the key to positively polarized use of catalyst. . . . The first acceptance, or control depending upon polarity, is of the self. Anger is one of many things to be accepted and loved as a part of self, or controlled as a part of self. . . . The negative polarization contains a great requirement for control and repression. . . . Thus you may find, for instance, negatively polarized entities controlling and repressing such basic bodily complex needs as the sexual desire in order that in the practice thereof, the will may be used to enforce itself upon the other-self with greater efficiency when the sexual behavior is allowed."[17]

I certainly have had many experiences with people who are very controlling, while still believing they are on a positive spiritual path. This is a classic example of "confusion," in Law of One terms. The most important principle in the Law of One after the idea of Oneness itself is free will. By manipulating and controlling others, and violating their free will, you may gain money and power, but in the process you are creating debilitating karma that could make it nearly impossible for you to be ready for Ascension at the end of this particular cycle on Earth.

Another key point in the material is that we are multi-incarnational beings. We do not live just one lifetime and then dissolve into an eternal nothingness, as many people may secretly fear. The suffering we cause through manipulating, dominating, and controlling others can necessitate lifetimes of reincarnation to properly balance out. I had already noticed that the Cayce Readings had discussed reincarnation in extensive detail, based on other books I had read. Reincarnation is also a key element of most major world religions, and there is extensive evidence that reincarnation was originally a teaching of Jesus, as I discuss in my book *The Synchronicity Key*.

Here is one key excerpt from *The Synchronicity Key* that helps to make the point about reincarnation. In this case, I use the spelling of the name Jesus that the Law of One series recommends as being the most accurate—Jehoshua:

Further historic evidence [for the Christian teaching of rein-
carnation] comes from Origen (AD 185–254), who is considered the first great father of the Christian church after Paul.
Origen had extensive instruction from Clement of Alexandria. Clement, in turn, had studied directly with Peter, one of
the original twelve apostles who traveled with Jehoshua. Origen inherited the direct, oral tradition of the teachings of
Jehoshua and built a spiritual theology out of this knowledge.
Reincarnation was a crucial aspect of Origen's theology. Both
Origen and his teacher, Clement of Alexandria, wrote about
receiving secret teachings from Jehoshua that were passed to
them through the apostles. They ardently insisted that reincarnation and preexistence were one of Jehoshua's most important secret teachings. This quote from Origen summarizes
his perspective nicely: "The soul has neither beginning nor
end. . . . [Souls] come into this world strengthened by the
victories or weakened by the defeats of their previous lives."[18]

It is interesting and tragic to contemplate how teachings like this were
intended to reach us, only to be lost in the sands of time. Reincarnation
is discussed repeatedly in the Law of One, and Session 26, Question 36,
is a good starting point: "Why then be concerned with the grass that
blooms, withers and dies in its season, only to grow once again due to
the infinite love and light of the One Creator? This is the message we
bring. Each entity is only superficially that which blooms and dies. In
the deeper sense there is no end to beingness."[19]

The 25,000-Year Cycle

At times, the material became deeply scientific in nature, and made
many assertions that could be proven either right or wrong. There was
no gray area. This was quite different from the Nostradamus prophecies
from the 1500s, derived from a collection of 942 poetic quatrains that
were often so vaguely worded that they could be interpreted to mean

many different things. I had read a variety of Nostradamus books that analyzed his legendary writings from his book *Les Prophéties,* and on many occasions the authors seemed to try to force-fit his words into the "accurate prophecies" they wanted to see.

One of the things *The Law of One* talked about was the same "25,000-year cycle" I had recently read about in *Fingerprints of Gods,* which revealed that the mystery of this cycle was encoded into thirty-five ancient traditions around the world. *The Law of One* mentions the 25,000-year cycle in seventy-six passages throughout the series.[20] The term *major cycle* means the same thing as "25,000-year cycle" in the Law of One series, and the term *major cycle* appears in an additional twenty-two passages, for a total of ninety-eight references.[21] Dr. Don Elkins had no idea that this 25,000-year cycle was called The Precession of the Equinoxes, and *The Law of One* never mentioned that it had anything to do with an alleged wobble in the Earth's axis. That only convinced me even more of the authenticity of *The Law of One.* If either Don or Carla was aware of this connection, it very likely would have emerged in the words themselves.

The Law of One said that our Earth goes through an amazing transformation at the end of each 25,000-year cycle, in which its human inhabitants have the opportunity to Ascend into the fourth density. They chose the unique and mysterious word *harvest* to describe this mass Ascension process. This term is again derived from the Bible, and most specifically from the book of Matthew, chapter 13, regarding "the Parable of the Weeds." Most significant is the description in Matthew 13:36–43. Negatively oriented people are presented as being akin to weeds in a garden, and the weeds are plucked out one by one at the time of harvest. The exact use of the term *harvest* can be seen in Matthew 13:39, where it says, "The harvest is the end of the world, and the reapers are the angels." The light-body activation prophecy appears in Matthew 13:43, where it says, "Then [after the harvest] shall the righteous shine forth as the sun in the kingdom of their father."[22]

Before the planet-hopping of Mars and Maldek that we discussed in the last chapter is one aspect of the harvest process. Life in this new fourth-density Earth was revealed to be at least one hundred times more harmonious than the third. This next passage from Session 20, Question

24 is admittedly dense, and includes jargon that is unique to the *Law of One* material, but as we go on, the words will make more sense:

> The mind/body/spirit complex of third density [i.e., a human being such as we now see on Earth] has perhaps one hundred times as intensive a program of catalytic action from which to distill distortions and learn/teachings than any other of the densities. Thus the learn/teachings are most confusing to the mind/body/spirit complex which is, shall we say, inundated by the ocean of experience.[23]

The phrase *catalytic action* is a slightly different wording of one of their favorite terms, *catalyst*. The word *catalyst* refers to any experiences that cause us to grow spiritually—and many but not all of these experiences are difficult. The word *catalyst* is similar to how we use the word *karma*, and it appears in a stunning 189 passages throughout the Law of One series.[24] So, in short, this quote was a very technical-sounding prophecy informing us that once we made it into fourth density, the level of happiness, bliss, peace, and harmony was so high that we could barely even imagine what that would feel like in today's world. Life on Earth is a hundred times worse, a hundred times more depressing and sad, irritating and frustrating, shocking and upsetting, than your everyday life after Ascension.

How do you visualize a life where you are consistently one hundred times happier than you could ever be now? Karma, or "catalyst," is so intense in our own third-density world that it is easy for us to be "inundated by the ocean of experience" and not realize that the negative things that happen to us in our lives—the "learn/teachings" we experience—are the direct result of our own thoughts and actions. I already had experienced dozens of Ascension dreams by this point, where some gigantic event happened on Earth that transformed me into a light-body form—as well as many others. The idea of this next level of existence being a hundred times more harmonious was very appealing to me, and still is. Both *The Source Field Investigations* and *The Synchronicity Key* go into far more detail about the 25,000-year cycle than in this volume, and it is a truly vast subject to study.

Sacred Geometry and the Global Grid

As I dove into this material, I was very excited to learn more about the Hyperdimensional Model from a direct extraterrestrial source, which added greatly to the secret message of the crop circles telling us to study sacred geometry. The Schoolhouse had a series of apartments in one larger building, and one of our housemates was a computer genius named Jack. He taught me how to use Eric's intimidating desktop computer—and how to log on to the Internet through our dial-up telephone modem. By the time I started reading *The Law of One,* I had already spent about a month and a half looking around online. There really wasn't very much of this kind of paranormal material online at the time, but I did find nuggets of gold. As I said, Art Bell had a highly popular radio show, *Coast to Coast AM,* with a variety of UFO researchers appearing regularly. Richard C. Hoagland was his top guest, and there were many new articles to explore on Hoagland's website, enterprisemission.com. Hoagland had a forum on his website that was very popular, and seemed to be the front line of the battle for disclosure at the time.

I already felt I had made serious breakthroughs in the Hyperdimensional Model. Although the crop circles were obviously promoting sacred geometry, I believed I had made some genuinely original discoveries. I had taken the planetary energy fields well beyond the tetrahedral vortexes appearing at the 19.5-degree latitude in Hoagland's initial model. I had now "discovered" the icosa-dodeca Global Grid, upon which all 3,300 of the world's great stone monuments were located. I wasn't sure if anyone besides the Russians were even aware of this. I certainly didn't think the Russians had ever linked it back to Hoagland and Tom Bearden's Hyperdimensional Model, since the Russians had published way back in 1972, long before Hoagland's work had appeared. I felt as if I had stumbled over a truly lost science from ancient times.

I was absolutely astonished when I got up to Session 14, Question 7, and read the following response when the questioner simply asked what they meant by the term *balancing pyramid*. Here was the answer:

> Imagine, if you will, the many force fields of the Earth in their geometrically precise web. Energies stream into the Earth planes, as you would call them, from magnetically determined points. Due to growing thought-form distortions in understanding of the Law of One, the planet itself was seen to have the potential for imbalance. The balancing pyramidal structures were charged with crystals which drew the appropriate balance from the energy forces streaming into the various geometrical centers of electromagnetic energy, which surround—and shape—the planetary sphere.[25]

This was a picture-perfect description of the Global Grid. I thought that hardly anyone besides Ivan T. Sanderson, the obscure Russian group from the early 1970s, and the team of William Becker and Bethe Hagens even knew about the Grid. I felt that I had made an original discovery about how the lines on the Becker-Hagens Grid were shaping the continents, since they themselves had not written about it in the book. Now I had the Law of One series describing how the "force fields of the earth in their geometrically precise web . . . surround and shape the planetary sphere." I was absolutely astonished to see this in *The Law of One*, and couldn't believe that I was apparently the first person to see how these statements correlated with real-world scientific research. It was also made clear that the pyramids were built on the global grid to stabilize the Earth on its axis after the last major catastrophe that destroyed the highly advanced civilization of Atlantis.

Deliberately Planted Synchronicity

The source made it clear to L/L Research that many seemingly random connections that were happening in their lives were actually being directly orchestrated from higher realms. This came early along, in Session 8, Question 1: "Consider, if you will, the path your life-experience complex has taken. Consider the coincidences and odd circumstances by which one thing flowed to the next. Consider this well. Each entity will receive the opportunity that each needs."[26] I couldn't help but notice that this quote applied perfectly to what was happening to me. My three-year, three-hundred-book path of study was now paying off on almost every page I read. This included reading Dr. Brown's book immediately before beginning my study of the Law of One.

This quote about "coincidences and odd circumstances" also seemed to be referring back to a great synchronicity story for Dr. Don Elkins and Carla Rueckert, the two original members of the group that channeled *The Law of One*. This story appeared in the introduction to Book One, as follows:

> Don and I, who had officially gone into partnership as L/L Research in 1970, had written an unpublished book titled *The Crucifixion of Esmeralda Sweetwater* in 1968. In 1974, Andrija Puharich published a book with Doubleday titled *URI*. The book is the narrative of Dr. Puharich's investigation of Uri Geller and their unexpected communication with extraterrestrial intelligences. The form of contact was quite novel in that first some object like an ashtray would levitate, signaling Dr. Puharich to load his cassette tape recorder. The recorder's buttons would then be depressed by some invisible force and the machine would record. On playback, a message from an extraterrestrial source would be present.[27]

Right there, I was absolutely stunned. Not even a month before, on New Year's Day 1996, I had the dream I shared previously, where my musician friend Vinnie had transitioned into the afterlife. He was trying to convey a message to his friend Ron by having me press RECORD on a cassette player and speak onto the tape. Some background noises were heard, but I could not make out what they were saying. Now I was reading the Law of One series, where the exact same procedure documented in my dream was being used successfully. The synchronicity was absolutely astonishing. Seeing this same dream time loop into my mother's problems with the new attic door at the house I grew up in only makes this even more poignant as I write this book. Let's continue with this same quote from Book One of the Law of One series.

> Don was impressed by the large number of correlations between these messages and our own research. The book is fascinating in its own right, but it was especially fascinating to us because of the incredible number of distinct and compelling similarities between the characters in the real-life journal of Dr. Puharich's work with Uri and the supposedly fictional characters in our book.
>
> We went to New York to meet Andrija after phoning him, sharing our long-standing research with him and comparing notes. As our genial host came out onto his front verandah to welcome us, I stopped, amazed, to look at the house. Even the house in which he lived in the country north of New York City was a dead ringer for the house his fictional counterpart had owned in our book. The identity was so close that I could not help but ask, "Andrija, what happened to your peonies? When I wrote about your house I saw your driveway circled with peony bushes." Puharich laughed, "Oh, those. I had those cut down three years ago."[28]

Pyramid Technology to Stabilize Earth's Axis

In the Law of One quote I shared that revealed our Global Grid of geometry, Ra was clearly saying that pyramids were being deliberately built on this Grid to help keep the Earth "balanced," so it was less likely to have another pole shift. We are about to review the hard science that suggests this really could work. The Law of One source had already confirmed that the Earth had gone through previous cataclysms, including the sinking of the legendary Atlantis. I had a great deal of research to support the idea of an Atlantean catastrophe, including *When the Sky Fell* by Rand and Rose Flem-Ath, *Fingerprints of the Gods* by Graham Hancock, and many other books with similar information. Atlantis is referred to in a total of nineteen passages throughout the Law of One material.[29]

In 2001, I discovered research headed by Dr. Alexander Golod from the Russian National Academy of Sciences that confirmed that large pyramids built of PVC pipes and fiberglass were able to reduce the severity of earthquakes and extreme weather—in a statistically significant fashion: "Areas near the pyramids seem to have diminished seismic activity. Instead of one large powerful earthquake occurring, there are hundreds of tiny ones. Also violent weather seems to decrease in the area of the pyramids."[30] To fully explain how this works is time-consuming, but for now let's just reflect on the fact that Dr. Golod's research confirmed exactly what the Law of One series said: Pyramids can and do have a balancing effect upon the "rhythms" of the Earth.

Many other mind-blowing discoveries were made with Dr. Golod's pyramids, including the reduction of radioactivity, the spontaneous charging of electrical capacitors, the purification of water and oil, a significant increase in the size of plants grown from pyramid-charged seeds, and a notable improvement in the behavior of prisoners in selected Russian jail cells built with pyramid-charged granite rocks. Additionally, the scientists observed the measurable killing of pathogenic viruses and bacteria, the miraculous rescuing of premature babies that were otherwise written off for dead, and the healing of a variety of diseases, including cancer.[31] The science behind how this works is explained in great detail in *The Source Field Investigations*. It is a logical extension of the Hyperdimensional Model. The basic idea is that there is a fluidlike, living energy that gives rise to matter and life itself, and I decided to call this energy the Source Field. In the Law of One, this same phenomenon is termed *intelligent energy*, and this phrase appears sixty-five times throughout the material.[32] The pyramid shape seems to work like a funnel to capture this fluidlike energy and cause it to begin spinning, much like a torpedo or whirlpool inside. Hence the word *pyramid* is derived from "pyre-amid," or "fire in the middle."

It was also very fascinating to hear the source tell us that humans are the main force that is destabilizing the Earth's axis. We have caused this instability by having "growing thought-form distortions in understanding of the Law of One." In context, what they are saying is that the universe has an agenda. There is only Existence—one mind, one thought, one Creator. The universe, including the Earth we live on, is an "illusion" that the Creator built to teach us the Law of One. Our job is to discover the Law of One for ourselves and begin living, breathing, and walking that truth—"to radiate the realization of Oneness with the Creator"[33] to others. If enough of us fall out of alignment with the Law of One in our thoughts and actions, then the Earth itself begins to destabilize under our feet.

This is akin to an immune-system reaction. As long as we are loving and positive, the Earth will remain a safe place to live. Once enough of us start slipping into selfishness, materialism, suspicion, jealousy, greed, and despair, manipulating and controlling others for our own benefit, the Earth can become a danger zone. A giant earthquake or volcanic eruption is a wake-up call that causes us to pull together, rely on each other, and set aside our differences. People who are ordinarily walking around angry will now perform heroic acts, sharing food, water, and shelter with each other, and realize that we all have a common bond, regardless of race, creed, color, or nationality. Karma can manifest on mass levels, through things like Earth changes, as well as on the personal level. The positive ETs built the pyramids for us as a way to help reduce the stress we were causing—as if the pyramids were needles of stone working the acupuncture meridians of the Earth, which is a living being in its own right. Without these balancing pyramids, things would have been far worse.

Despite how amazing this material was, it quickly became clear that Ra had gotten themselves in a great deal of trouble in the karmic sense. In trying to give us the highest-level teachings possible, they discovered that "the greater preponderance of your entities find themselves in what may be considered a perpetual childhood," as they said in Session 20, Question 25.[34] One of their most important objectives in producing the Law of One series in 1981 to 1983 was to pay out a form of restitution to the mass consciousness of Earth and its people by offering us such advanced spiritual material. Why would such a karmic payback be necessary? In short, Ra built the Great Pyramid as a positive symbol of the coming Ascension—but this magnificent stone edifice was then taken over by negatively inclined priests and peoples. Even to this day, many people consider the pyramid and All-Seeing Eye on the back of the US dollar bill to be an Illuminati symbol. This was never the intention, as we will see.

CHAPTER SEVENTEEN

A Mission of Restitution

Earlier in Session 4, Question 20, Ra had defined this mysterious Law of One by saying, "There is . . . only identity." The complete quote was as follows:

The Law of One, though beyond the limitations of name, as you call vibratory sound complexes, may be approximated by stating that all things are one, that there is no polarity, no right or wrong, no disharmony, but only identity. All is one, and that one is love/light, light/love, the Infinite Creator. One of the primal distortions of the Law of One is that of healing. Healing occurs when a mind/body/spirit complex realizes, deep within itself, the Law of One; that is, that there is no disharmony, no imperfection; that all is complete and whole and perfect. Thus, the intelligent infinity within this mind/body/spirit complex re-forms the illusion of body, mind, or spirit to a form congruent with the Law of One. The healer acts as energizer or catalyst for this completely individual process.[1]

Defining the Law of One and the Mind/Body/Spirit Complex

The term *mind/body/spirit complex* is their unique way of defining what we would think of as a person. They see the mind, the body, and the spirit as separate and distinct entities that come together in a "complex" form to make a human being. You might immediately balk at the idea that, in the grandest sense, "there is . . . no right or wrong." The Law of One series makes it very clear that the universe we think we know is an "illusion." Part of that illusion is galaxies, stars, planets, and the idea of an apparently separate self in bodies like ours. Since we are truly One with all others, anything we say, think about, or do to someone else will be returned back to us in our seemingly physical experience. This is the Law of Karma, which is referred to as the First Distortion of the Law of One. As I said in the last chapter, this is the most important teaching in the Law of One series after the concept of Oneness itself.

Karma, Healing, and Restitution

Another one of the "distortions" they referred to in the above quote is the "distortion of healing," but the First Distortion is a term that shows up in a total of sixty passages throughout the series.[2] As I read *The Law of One*, I had to keep reminding myself that "First Distortion" means "Karma." They indicated that Karma was indeed a universal law, which had existed from the very beginning of space and time itself. Karma was the first and most important "distortion" of the Law of One. This Oneness, or "intelligent infinity," was compared to pure white light. Anything within our "illusion" of a physical universe was therefore seen to be a "distortion" of this light. The word *distortion* appears in a total of 597 different passages, often in the most unlikely sounding places.[3] If you subtract the 60 passages that specifically say *First Distortion*, that still leaves 537 other instances of the term *distortion*. *First distortion* translates as "karma," but the word *distortion* by itself can mean just about anything we might normally think of as being good or bad.

Let's talk about that contentious statement where the source says "there is no right or wrong" in the ultimate sense. There certainly are plenty of negative things we can do to ourselves and others in this "illusion" that will be balanced out by karma. To harm others is to absolutely guarantee that you are harming yourself. Ultimately, there is nothing "wrong" that happens outside of linear time, because the balance is preserved. You get your karma. You pay everything back, down to the tiniest amount. The Universe moves forward. Again, once you have achieved what the Law of One calls "healing," you consciously recognize that there is no disharmony, no imperfection: All is complete and whole and perfect.

To achieve this state of healing, you must also go through what is called "restitution" in the physical illusion. This term appears only three times in the material, but it is of key importance. Two of the three instances of *restitution* arose in Session 26, in response to questions about the nuclear attacks of Hiroshima and Nagasaki. The following excerpt is combined from Questions 27 through 31 in Session 26:

> Such actions as nuclear destruction affect the entire planet. There are no differences at this level of destruction, and the planet will need to be healed. . . . Once the healing has taken place, the harvest [Ascension] may go forth unimpeded. However, the entire planet will undergo healing for this action, no distinction being made betwixt victim and aggressor, this due to damage done to the planet. . . . Healing is a process of acceptance, forgiveness, and, if possible, restitution. The restitution not being available in time/space, there are many among your peoples now attempting restitution while in the physical. . . . These [people do this by] attempt[ing] feelings of love towards the planetary sphere and comfort and healing of the scars and the imbalances of these actions.[4]

Of particular importance in this passage is Question 30: "Healing is a process of acceptance, forgiveness, and, if possible, restitution." My own experience with karma proved that every experience we have ever delivered to others, regardless of whether it was in this lifetime or prior ones, must be paid back in full through restitution. That means that you must physically experience the exact nature of suffering that you caused others to feel. You can then trust that perfect balance has been restored, since you paid your restitution—and thus in the grander sense, all is good and whole and perfect. After first meditating on this Hiroshima quote in 1996, I would go to various huge cement-mining caves throughout Rosendale and send love to the Earth in these areas as a form of restitution, to comfort the Earth and heal the scars of these massive dynamite explosions. I also thanked the Earth for the use of the dolostone in helping build our current civilization, wherein the opportunity to awaken within the dream and access intelligent infinity becomes possible.

Our earlier quote from Session 4, Question 20, also said that once this healing process occurs where we see all as whole, complete, and perfect, we "re-form the illusion of body, mind, or spirit to a form congruent with the Law of One." This appears to be a technical-sounding way of describing a light-body activation—and you get there only by paying off your debts through restitution. The light body is a form that is more "congruent with the Law of One." In Session 34, Question 2, the source also told us what we could expect to feel if we were able to connect with this "intelligent infinity" on a conscious level:

> The experience of each entity is unique in perception of intelligent infinity. Perceptions range from a limitless joy to a strong dedication to service to others while in the incarnated state. The entity which reaches intelligent infinity most often will perceive this experience as one of unspeakable profundity. However, it is not usual for the entity to immediately desire the cessation of the incarnation. Rather the desire to communicate or use this experience to aid others is extremely strong.[5]

When I read this, I thought about the many reports of people seeing and feeling "The Light" in near-death experiences. In Law of One terms, anything other than that pure light is a distortion.

The Seven Densities

According to the Law of One, in order for us to reach the highest spiritual level, we have to work through each of the seven densities—which they refer to as "true color" red, orange, yellow, green, blue, indigo, and violet—before returning to the Oneness. Each density is akin to a separate plane of existence that we work through in our evolution. We are connected to these densities through our seven energy centers, or chakras. Again, these chakras appear on the soul level as a series of round vortexes that rise through the middle of the body, from the base of the spine through to the top of the head. They also display the colors of the rainbow along the way: red, orange, yellow, green, blue, indigo, and violet. Apparently, some people can see into the spirit world and are thus able to visually perceive these energy centers. The ancient Hindu scriptures talk about the chakras quite extensively. The Law of One says that each of our seven chakras are directly connected to each of the seven densities. In that sense, we are already fully multidimensional beings—perfect holographic images of the whole.

In Session 49, Question 6, Ra gives a short summary of the lessons for each density, and I will add in the numbers here to make it easier to read. I have found that these explanations for each color also translate directly into what they symbolize in dreams, as I shared in chapter 3, "Dream Analysis 101":

> Each experience will be sequentially understood by the growing and seeking mind/body/spirit complex in terms of 1) survival [red], then in terms of 2) personal identity [orange], then in terms of 3) social relations [yellow], then in terms of 4) universal love [green], then in terms of 5) how the experience may beget free communication [light blue], then in terms of 6) how the experience may be linked to universal energies [indigo], and finally in terms of 7) the sacramental nature of each experience [violet]. Meanwhile, the Creator lies within. In the north pole, the crown is already upon the head, and

the entity is potentially a god. This energy is brought into
being by the humble and trusting acceptance of this energy,
through meditation and contemplation of the self and of the
Creator.[6]

There again, if you read this carefully, it clearly says that the seventh-
density teaching is to "embrace the sacramental nature of each experience." The Tibetan monk Tulku Urgyen Rinpoche advocates a similar
practice in his book *Rainbow Painting*.[7] He said that if we can remember
to recognize the true essence of mind while in the midst of great conflict,
such as while we are running for our lives from a pack of vicious dogs,
we will gain a much greater level of insight than in normal meditation
practice. The degree of conflict in our world today makes it possible for
exceptional spiritual insights to be realized. To be at peace with whatever
happens to you, no matter how physically difficult it may be, is to embrace the sacramental nature of each experience. You have then experienced "the distortion of healing" as defined in the Law of One series,
where "there is no disharmony, no imperfection; that all is complete and
whole and perfect."[8] Therefore, when you see the term *healing* appear in
the Law of One series, it carries far more weight than you may have
normally placed upon the word. *Healing* appears in a total of 180 different Law of One passages.[9]

The Law of One also teaches us that it is very important to set sacred
boundaries as well. Part of the sacramental nature of each experience is
to preserve your own well-being if it serves the greater good to do so.
One place where this was explained was in Session 42, Question 6. The
fourth density is the plane of existence that our Earth is moving into
now, but it is by no means the end of the road for what we will learn:

> The fourth density, as we have said, abounds in compassion.
> This compassion is folly [ignorance] when seen through the
> eyes of wisdom. It is the salvation of third density, but creates
> a mismatch in the ultimate balance of the entity. Thus we, as
> a social memory complex of fourth density, had the tendency
> towards compassion even to martyrdom in aid of other-selves.

When the fifth-density harvest was achieved, we found that
in this vibratory level flaws could be seen in the efficacy of
such unrelieved compassion. We spent much time/space in
contemplation of those ways of the Creator which imbue love
with wisdom.[10]

The most important discussion of "sacred boundaries" in the Law of
One appears in Session 67, Question 11. Carla Rueckert, the "instrument," was being constantly attacked by a negative entity that wished to
stop the Law of One message from getting through, such as by trying to
telepathically influence her to step in front of an oncoming car or causing massive flare-ups of her arthritic pains. Dr. Elkins asked how they
could simultaneously send love to this entity, which the Law of One requires that you do on the positive path, while not allowing it to hurt or
kill Carla. This was the answer:

Upon the many other planes of existence there are those
whose every fiber rejoices at your service, and those such as
the entity of whom you have been speaking, which wish only
to terminate the life upon the third-density plane of this instrument. All are the Creator. There is one vast panoply of
biases and distortions, colors and hues, in an unending pattern. In the case of those with whom you, as entities and as a
group, are not in resonance, you wish them love, light, peace,
joy, and bid them well. No more than this can you do for
your portion of the Creator is as it is, and your experience and
offering of experience, to be valuable, needs be more and
more a perfect representation of who you truly are. Could
you, then, serve a negative entity by offering the instrument's
life? It is unlikely that you would find this a true service. Thus
you may see in many cases the loving balance being achieved,
the love being offered, light being sent, and the service of the
service-to-self oriented entity gratefully acknowledged, while
being rejected as not being useful in your journey at this time.
Thus you serve One Creator without paradox.[11]

The Law of Foreverness

Another critical aspect of the seventh-density teaching is the following concept: "The seventh density is a density of completion, and the turning toward timelessness or foreverness."[12] This idea of "foreverness" was further developed in Session 3, Question 10. Dr. Don Elkins, the questioner, asked whether a single person who was fully awakened to the Law of One could "build a pyramid by direct mental effort." Here was part of the answer:

> There is a distinction between the individual power through the Law of One and the combined, or societal memory complex mind/body/spirit understanding of the Law of One. In the first case only the one individual, purified of all flaws, could move a mountain. In the case of mass understanding of unity, each individual may contain an acceptable amount of distortion, and yet the mass mind could move mountains. The progress is normally from the understanding which you now seek to a dimension of understanding which is governed by the laws of love, and which seeks the laws of light. Those who are vibrating with the Law of Light seek the Law of One. Those who vibrate with the Law of One seek the Law of Foreverness.

Each density from the fourth on up was associated with a law or a set of laws. The fourth is the Law of Love; the fifth density is the Law of Light, which they also define as wisdom; the sixth density where Ra is speaking from is the Law of One, hence the title of the series; and the seventh density is the Law of Foreverness. Dr. Scott Mandelker explained in his book that it is a sixth-density understanding to see self and other as One. Once you reach seventh density, you realize there is no self. There is no other. There is only Timelessness and Foreverness. Buddhist texts presented this same concept, and it was often translated into English with the term *The Void*. This is the final realization we will all eventually have before we reunite with what is called "intelligent infinity."

Intelligent infinity is how the universe began, if you want to call it a beginning, since there really is no such thing as Time. However, within the illusion, there was what appeared to be the formation of a visible universe with a duration of time that passes. The first thing that intelligent infinity needed to "do" to create the universe was to generate something called intelligent energy—the Logos—which is also labeled infinite energy. This was described in Session 13, Question 7, among many other places. This quote, as it turns out, is one of the most critical passages in the entire series, since it contains some encoded information that took me years to properly decipher:

> Awareness led to the focus of infinity into infinite energy. You have called this by various vibrational sound complexes, the most common to your ears being "Logos" or "Love." The Creator is the focusing of infinity as an aware or conscious principle, called by us as closely as we can create understanding/learning in your language, intelligent infinity.[13]

If you pay close attention to what was said in this quote, we hear that the universe is indeed made out of Love. More specifically, we have an "intelligent infinity" that focuses itself into an "aware or conscious principle," which becomes what we would normally think of as God—the Creator of the universe. What we call "God" is often called "Logos" or "Love" in the Law of One series. The "infinite . . . intelligent energy" is directed to create form out of formlessness. That infinite energy that makes the universe is Love—the Logos. As we discussed in the previous chapter, the Law of One gave us a very important hidden clue by using the term *Logos* here. The Greek translation of the term *Logos* is "Word." This is one of a few key phrases, like *Harvest*, that directly connect the Law of One to the Christian Bible. There is nothing obvious about this, and in fact it took me many years to figure out that the source wanted us to make this connection. As I said, the word *Logos* appears in fully 146 Law of One passages.[14]

Another important point here is that the words *Logos* and *Love* are presented as being interchangeable. This is another confusing thing in the Law of One. When they say "Logos," they can be referring to the Creator itself, a galaxy, or a star like our sun, which exists in a state of oneness with the galaxy we see it in. A planet like Earth is defined as a "sub-Logos,"[15] and then a person like you or me is considered to be a "sub-sub-Logos."[16] You can see how easily this could get confusing. The basic idea, again, is that all is One. You and I are holographic images of the One Infinite Creator, and we are only distorted to appear as a human form within the illusion.

If you want to get a bit more technical about the term *sub-sub-Logos*, check this out from Session 54, Question 5: "The sub-sub-Logos resides, not in dimensionalities, but only in co-Creators, or mind/body/spirit complexes."[17] This means that we are truly co-Creators with the entire universe itself. There is no "dimension" where you will find a sub-sub-Logos—instead, each of us is a "co-Creator or sub-sub-Logos, [which] you call so carelessly a person."[18] Another example that gives us additional new insights is in Session 29, Question 8, where Dr. Elkins asked, "Then every entity that exists would be some type of sub- or sub-sub-Logos. Is this correct?" The answer was "This is correct down to the limits of any observation, for the entire creation is alive."[19] This quote may be almost singularly responsible for why I soon chose to name my website Divine Cosmos. If you begin studying the universe as a single, vast living being, many scientific mysteries suddenly become much clearer. I went to great pains to explain this in *The Source Field Investigations*.

Experience All Things Desired

Another quote that really jumped out at me from my very first reading is a further explanation of how we apply this Law of One philosophy to our everyday lives and thoughts. It appears in Session 18, Question 5, and is one of my very favorites:

> The proper role of the entity is, in this density, to experience
> all things desired—to then analyze, understand, and accept

these experiences, distilling from them the love/light within them. Nothing shall be overcome. That which is not needed falls away. . . .

We have found it to be inappropriate in the extreme to encourage the overcoming of any desires, except to suggest the imagination rather than the carrying out in the physical plane, as you call it, of those desires not consonant with the Law of One; this preserving the primal distortion of free will . . . All things are acceptable in the proper time for each entity, and in experiencing, in understanding, in accepting, in then sharing with other-selves, the appropriate description shall be moving away from distortions of one kind to distortions of another which may be more consonant with the Law of One. It is, shall we say, a shortcut to simply ignore or overcome any desire. It must instead be understood and accepted. This takes patience and experience, which can be analyzed with care, with compassion for self and for other-self.[20]

This is a fascinating philosophical statement that is certainly far more open and inclusive than most other religious or spiritual teachings. In the simplest terms, the source is saying: "Do what you want, and please learn from it—so you don't keep repeating the negative stuff and suffering from bad karma. If you want to actually hurt someone, try to act this out in your imagination instead of in physical form, so you don't create additional karma by violating the Law of One and have to pay restitutions." If you keep repeating lessons without learning anything from them, you are in a state the Law of One refers to as "True Helplessness." This was defined in Session 19, Question 18: "Those truly helpless are those who have not consciously chosen [the positive or negative path], but who repeat patterns without knowledge of the repetition or the meaning of the pattern."[21]

The Confederation of Planets

My immersion into the Law of One was as profound and complete as I could get away with. The fascination I felt with *Cosmic Voyage* quickly got swept away in an ocean of vastly greater size and complexity. Any time I wasn't at my job keeping the peace, I was up in the loft or down on the couch, reading the Law of One with intense focus. If I had a day off, I might spend twelve to fourteen hours happily reading the books. I could easily spend forty-five minutes with the book open to one particular page, reading and meditating on its philosophy the entire time. This was nothing I could rush. I needed to take it slow, go deep within myself, and toss each of these powerful statements around in my mind until they finally made sense. I would only turn the page once I felt that I at least had a reasonable level of understanding about what I was reading.

Early along in Session 6, things got very cosmic when Ra explained the larger group that they were working with:

> I am one of the members of the Confederation of Planets in the Service of the Infinite Creator. There are approximately fifty-three civilizations, comprising approximately five hundred planetary consciousness complexes in this Confederation. This Confederation contains those from your own planet who have attained dimensions beyond your third. It contains planetary entities within your solar system, and it contains planetary entities from other galaxies. It is a true Confederation in that its members are not alike, but allied in service according to the Law of One.[22]

The term *galaxies* was very confusing. Ra saw a single planetary system as indistinguishable from a larger galaxy like the Milky Way. They apparently had observed that a single solar system could grow into what we would think of as a galaxy with many stars. Dr. Elkins had to create the term *major galaxy* to differentiate the two. In Session 16, Question 33, Ra clarified that they were helping people from seven different solar systems within our Milky Way galaxy: "This Confederation works with the planetary spheres of seven of your galaxies, if you will, and is responsible for the callings of the densities of these galaxies. . . . We use that term [galaxy] in this sense as you would use star systems."[23]

This was further explained in Session 28, Question 7, as follows:

> A Logos may create what you call a star system or it may be the Logos creating billions of star systems. This is the cause of the confusion in the term galaxy, for there are many different Logos entities or creations and we would call each, using your sound vibration complexes, a galaxy.[24]

Then it was confirmed that these smaller Logos systems can grow a larger number of stars over time in Session 82, Question 8:

> In the case of the galactic systems, the first manifestation of the Logos is a cluster of central systems which generate the outward swirling energies producing, in their turn, further energy centers for the Logos, or what you would call stars.[25]

Recent History of Ra and the Confederation

In the very first statement from the very first session, Ra said, "The Confederation of Planets in the Service of the Infinite Creator has only one important statement. That statement, my friends, as you know, is 'All things, all of life, all of the creation is part of one original thought.'"[26] As this discussion continued into Question 1, we read the following:

> We are old upon your planet and have served with varying degrees of success in transmitting the Law of One, of Unity, of Singleness to your peoples. We have walked your earth. We have seen the faces of your peoples. This is not so with many of the entities of the Confederation. We found it was

not efficacious. However, we then felt the great responsibility of staying, in the capacity of removing the distortions and powers that had been given to the Law of One. We will continue in this until your, shall we say, cycle is appropriately ended. If not this one, then the next. We are not a part of time and, thus, are able to be with you in any of your times.[27]

Ra clearly indicated in this passage that some kind of damage had occurred to the people of Earth from their arrival here, and that they were bound to their own form of restitution to heal it. This was further explained in Session 2, as we will see. Dr. Elkins then asked about the name Ra, and got a surprising answer in response:

The identity of the vibration Ra is our identity. We as a group, or what you would call a social memory complex, made contact with a race of your planetary kind which you call Egyptians. Others from our density made contact at the same time in South America, and the so-called "lost cities" were their attempts to contribute to the Law of One. We spoke to one who heard and understood and was in a position to decree the Law of One. However, the priests and peoples of that era quickly distorted our message, robbing it of the, shall we say, compassion with which unity is informed by its very nature. Since it contains all, it cannot abhor any. When we were no longer able to have appropriate channels through which to enunciate the Law of One, we removed ourselves from the now-hypocritical position which we had allowed ourselves to be placed in. And other myths, shall we say, other understandings having more to do with polarity and the things of your vibrational complex, again took over in that particular society complex.[28]

This quote immediately captured my imagination. Clearly, Ra was saying that they contacted ancient Egypt and were directly involved in the building of the Great Pyramid. They further indicated that they "spoke to one who heard and understood and was in a position to decree the Law of One." This was very obviously the same character that Edgar Cayce's source was referring to as Ra-Ptah. The Cayce Readings had indicated that Ra-Ptah had fallen prey to his lower instincts and ultimately had multiple wives, and that this and other actions negatively affected the future course of religion as we know it. Ra was confirming this exact same idea by saying that "the priests and peoples of that era quickly distorted our message," creating "other understandings having more to do with polarity." In this sense, polarity only occurs when we see and experience evil as something separate from the unity and loving consciousness of pure Oneness.

The Pyramids Inadvertently Created Damage

As we head into Session 2, Question 2, we get far more detail about Ra's involvement with building pyramids, and how this in turn created damage to the people of Earth that they are still working to repair:

> We are those of the Confederation who eleven thousand of your years ago came to two of your planetary cultures which were at that time closely in touch with the creation of the One Creator. It was our naïve belief that we could teach/learn by direct contact, and the free will distortions of individual feeling or personality were in no danger, we thought, of being disturbed—as these cultures were already closely aligned with an all-embracing belief in the live-ness or consciousness of all. We came and were welcomed by the peoples whom we wished to serve. We attempted to aid them in technical ways having to do with the healing of mind/body/spirit complex distortions through the use of the crystal, appropriate to the distortion, placed within a certain appropriate series of ratios of time/space material. *Thus were the pyramids created.* [Emphasis added]

We found that the technology was reserved largely for those with the effectual mind/body distortion of power. This was not intended by the Law of One. We left your peoples. The group that was to work with those in the area of South America, as you call that portion of your sphere, gave up not so easily. They returned. We did not. However, we have never left your vibration due to our responsibility for the changes in consciousness we had first caused and then found distorted in ways not relegated to the Law of One.[29]

Ra also explained in Session 23, Question 6, that for a period of time, they physically materialized in forms that "closely resembled their true natures" among the Egyptians. This very much appears to be the image of Horus, the avian-headed deity, as we have previously explored. Ra identified themselves strongly with the hawk as their totem animal. We also see in the myth of Osiris and Isis that their child was apparently Horus, though this could have arisen as a misunderstanding, where Ra was appearing in this form after being invoked by Osiris and Isis, thus appearing to be their direct offspring.

Other quotes reveal that Ra materialized in this form while the pyramids were being built. This ended up creating a great deal of confusion and forced them to withdraw from view fairly quickly:

Thus we emerged, or materialized, in physical-chemical complexes representing as closely as possible our natures, this effort being to appear as brothers and spend a limited amount of time as teachers of the Law of One, for there was an ever-stronger interest in the sun body, and this vibrates in concordance with our particular distortions. We discovered that for each word we could utter, there were thirty impressions we gave by our very being, which confused those entities we had come to serve. After a short period we removed ourselves from these entities and spent much time attempting to understand how best to serve those to whom we had offered ourselves in love/light.[30]

We are certainly witnessing this same problem in modern times with the strident difficulty that some people online have with the concept of Blue Avians and the contact that Corey Goode has received. Corey had no idea of the connection to Horus or the Law of One when the Blue Avians allegedly began contacting him. This contact began regularly occurring only four months after he and I began speaking on a daily basis.

Temples of Human Sacrifice

Ra became far more specific in Session 23 about how their original positive intent to create pyramids that could heal people and balance the Earth on its new axis, after the fall of Atlantis, had become distorted. In both South America and Egypt, the "priests and peoples of the era" began using these pyramids for human sacrifices—which was exactly the opposite of the extremely positive purposes they were originally built to fulfill. Also remember that the sun is at the Octave or Logos level, and therefore is indeed a visible manifestation of universal consciousness within our local area. Take a look:

> The [Confederation] entities who walked among those in your South American continent were called by a similar desire upon the part of the entities therein to learn of the manifestations of the sun. They worshiped this source of light and life. Thus, these entities were visited by light beings not unlike ourselves. Instructions were given, and they were more accepted and less distorted than ours. The entities themselves began to construct a series of underground and hidden cities, including pyramid structures.
>
> These pyramids were somewhat at variance from the design that we had promulgated. However, the original ideas were the same, with the addition of a desire or intention of creating places of meditation and rest, a feeling of the presence of the One Creator; these pyramids then being for all

people, not only initiates and those to be healed. They left
this density when it was discovered that their plans were sol-
idly in motion and, in fact, had been recorded. During the
next approximately three thousand five hundred [3,500] years
these plans became, though somewhat distorted, in a state of
near-completion in many aspects.[31]

As this quote continues, it will be helpful to explain two new terms.
The Earth was put under "quarantine" by the Confederation at a certain
point in our past history, because our people had so many spiritual problems. Once the quarantine was established, it was impossible for random
extraterrestrial groups to fly into our atmosphere and land on the Earth.
In addition, even the positive groups had to request permission to appear
on Earth and perform a given mission—they couldn't just show up. This
and other administrative Confederation decisions were made in a local
governing body called the Council of Saturn, which resides in the full
eighth-density octave level within the rings of Saturn.[32,33] Eighth density
is the ultimate goal that we are all working toward.

In Session 52, Question 12, it said:

This octave density of which we have spoken is both omega
and alpha, the spiritual mass of the infinite universes becoming one central sun or Creator once again. Then is born a new
universe, a new infinity, a new Logos which incorporates all
that the Creator has experienced of Itself. In this new octave
there are also those who wander. We know very little across the
boundary of octave except that these beings come to aid our
octave in its Logos completion.[34]

With all that said, let us continue in this quote from Session 23 about
what happened in South America:

Therefore, as is the case in all breakings of the quarantine, the
[Confederation] entity who was helping the South American
entities along the South American ways you call in part the

Amazon River, went before the Council of Saturn to request a second attempt to correct, in person, the distortions which had occurred in their plans. This having been granted, this entity or social memory complex returned—and the entity chosen as messenger came among the peoples once more to correct the errors. [This was likely a historical South American figure such as Viracocha or Quetzalcoatl.] Again, all was recorded and the entity rejoined its social memory complex and left your skies. As in our experience, the teachings were, for the most part, greatly and grossly perverted to the extent in later times of actual human sacrifice rather than healing of humans. Thus, this social memory complex is also given the honor/duty of remaining until those distortions are worked out of the distortion complexes of your peoples.[35]

Notice that the source said "as in our experience," human sacrifice occurred with the South American pyramids. Sadly, this indicates that similar practices did occur inside structures such as the Great Pyramid of Giza in Egypt. This is certainly not commonly known, but the Law of One source does operate from an effectively omniscient perspective. Although the Great Pyramid was ultimately used for these negative practices, the original intent was highly positive—to present us with one of the most magnificent spiritual gifts imaginable. As we head into the next chapter, we will explore the mysteries of the Great Pyramid. Until you truly understand just how impossible the Pyramid is from any conventional technological standpoint, you cannot truly appreciate the level of sophistication that went into its construction. Once we fully understand this data, it will become much easier to contemplate how this structure could have been built by the most advanced, benevolent extraterrestrial life ever to appear on Earth.

CHAPTER EIGHTEEN

Mysteries of the Great Pyramid

The Law of One series was transforming everything I thought I knew about reality and my place within the greater universe we live in. Each volume of the Law of One series had Egyptian hieroglyphics on the cover. It became clear as I read the books that Ra was a highly positive group that existed outside of time. They were doing their best to give us teachings that would help transform consciousness on planet Earth, and prepare us for a mass Ascension event they called harvest. Yet, thanks initially to the misdeeds of Ra-Ptah, this plan was thrown off course. Mistakes were made with ramifications far greater than anyone could possibly have imagined at the time. The ultimate result of these mistakes was the formation of what many now call the Illuminati.

The Illuminati and the Negative Polarity

It is a well-known historical fact that people were being beheaded and sacrificed on the tops of the South American pyramids. However, there is no common understanding that the same thing was happening within the Great Pyramid, such as in the King's Chamber sarcophagus—but here Ra clearly indicates that it was indeed what happened, "as in our

[Ra's] experience." As I was first reading this, I realized it was revealing a far more significant point than the Law of One had directly explained. By the time I found the Law of One series, I had already read *New World Order: The Ancient Plan of Secret Societies* by William T. Still.[1] The book was jam-packed with information about the history and ongoing presence of the so-called Illuminati in our society—and was the main source for literally thousands of articles in the conspiracy genre from the late 1990s to the early 2000s. It had a tremendous effect on me when I read it somewhere in approximately 1994 or 1995, and I didn't have the courage to share this information publicly, under my real name, until 2007.

"Illuminati" never appears in the Law of One, although there is a great degree of discussion regarding the negative polarity or "service to self" path, as well as what they call the "elite." The term *elite* appears twelve different times in the Law of One series. In the modern Internet conspiracy culture, the symbol of the pyramid with the All-Seeing Eye is widely considered to be an Illuminati symbol, and therefore associated with extreme negativity for most people who are aware of it. This was by no means the original intent behind the pyramid's construction, according to the Law of One series.

Dr. Elkins asked why some people choose to pursue the service-to-self path, in Session 19, Question 17, and the answer he received was quite poignant:

> We can speak only in metaphor. Some love the light. Some love the darkness. It is a matter of the unique and infinitely various Creator choosing and playing among its experiences, as a child upon a picnic. Some enjoy the picnic and find the sun beautiful, the food delicious, the games refreshing, and glow with the joy of creation. Some find the night delicious, their picnic being pain, difficulty, sufferings of others, and the examination of the perversities of nature. These enjoy a different picnic. All these experiences are available. It is free will of each entity which chooses the form of play, the form of pleasure.[2]

It is still quite common to see certain people on the Internet get very upset about the name Ra, believing that this must be some evil and negative group. However, if you actually read the Law of One series, it is a beautiful philosophy that emphasizes the importance of positive spiritual virtues like love, forgiveness, and service to others. Ra have done their best to heal the damage that was created by their arrival, and hopefully, this book can further assist in that healing process. Initially positive symbols like the Masonic square and compass, which are used to draw images of sacred geometry, are now often associated with a worldwide satanic cult that has been variously called the Illuminati, the Cabal, the New World Order, or, in more recent times, the Deep State. As you delve into this disturbing material, you find that at least some within this group do indeed enjoy "pain, difficulty, sufferings of others, and the examination of the perversities of nature."[3]

Grievous Naïveté

There are multiple occasions where Ra explains how their own extreme level of harmony caused them to be very naïve in dealing with a third-density world like Earth—and particularly by building the Great Pyramid. In Session 41, Question 26, they say, "Our harmony, however, has been a grievous source of naïveté as regards working with your planet."[4] In Session 57, Question 17, we hear about the misuse of the King's Chamber, which could apparently create a light-body activation if properly used. The statement that this chamber was used for "grossly distorted" purposes is another indication that the human sacrifices they spoke about previously in Session 23 had at least partly taken place in this area:

> However, we found that your peoples are not distorted towards the desire for purity to a great enough extent to be given this powerful and potentially dangerous gift. We, therefore, would suggest it not be used for healing in the traditional, shall we say, King's Chamber configuration which we naïvely

gave to your peoples only to see its use grossly distorted and our teachings lost.[5]

Then consider the words of Session 60, Question 16:

It is our honor/duty to attempt to remove the distortions that the use of this [pyramid] shape has caused in the thinking of your peoples and in the activities of some of your entities. We do not deny that such shapes are efficacious, nor do we withhold the general gist of this efficacy. However, we wish to offer our understanding, limited though it is, that contrary to our naïve beliefs many thousands of your years ago, the optimum shape for initiation does not exist.[6]

Then, in Session 22, Question 26, we read:

We remind you that we are one of the naïve members of that Confederation, and are still attempting to recoup the damage for which we feel responsibility. It is our duty as well as honor to continue with your peoples, therefore, until all traces of the distortions of our teach/learnings have been embraced by their opposite distortions, and balance achieved.[7]

In Session 71, Questions 19 and 20, Dr. Elkins was told that one of the reasons his group was selected for this contact was to help make these reparations—though a full restitution was very unlikely:

We . . . have . . . wished to attempt to make reparation for distortions of this law [the Law of One] set in motion by our naïve actions of your past. . . . We mean no disrespect for your service, but we do not expect to make full reparations for these distortions. We may, however, offer our thoughts in the attempt. The attempt is far more important to us than the completeness of the result. The nature of your language is such that what is distorted cannot, to our knowledge, be fully undistorted but only illuminated somewhat.[8]

That last phrase is particularly interesting, because the use of the word *illuminated* may be a hint that the damage that was inadvertently done to the Earth included the creation of the so-called Illuminati. According to insiders such as Svali, this term was widely used by the group long before the Law of One series originated in 1981.

Another example of Ra's focus on restitution is in Session 14, Question 18, where Dr. Elkins asked why this group hoped to increase the number of people who would make it to fourth density by as many as possible at the end of our cycle:

> I speak for the social memory complex termed Ra. We came among you to aid you. Our efforts in service were perverted. Our desire then is to eliminate as far as possible the distortions caused by those misreading our information and guidance. The general cause of service such as the Confederation offers is that of the primal distortion of the Law of One, which is service. The One Being of the creation is like unto a body, if you will accept this third-density analogy. Would we ignore a pain in the leg? A bruise upon the skin? A cut which is festering? No. There is no ignoring a call. We, the entities of sorrow, choose as our service the attempt to heal the sorrow, which we are calling analogous to the pains of a physical body complex distortion.[9]

Everlasting Rock

The most interesting quotes about the actual building of the Great Pyramid appear in Session 3 of the Law of One, which was almost entirely dedicated to this one topic. Though their discussion can get very technical, Question 11 makes it clear that this was done by a massive telekinetic

manifestation process: "The pyramids which we thought/built were constructed from thought-forms created by our social memory complex."[10]
When Dr. Elkins reiterated this statement as a question, trying to confirm that the pyramid was built by thought, their response was "We built
with everlasting rock the Great Pyramid, as you call it. Other of the
pyramids were built with stone moved from one place to another."[11]
Therefore, the Great Pyramid was clearly not built with typical stones,
but through some mysterious process involving what they chose to call
"everlasting rock."

This is a surprisingly nontechnical term for Ra to have used, compared to their normal semantic complexity. This suggests that they may
have been using this term to provide a clue to a greater series of concepts.
The answer may be found in Isaiah 26:4, where it says "Trust in the Lord
forever, for the Lord God is an everlasting rock."[12] In other translations,
the term *everlasting rock* appears as *the rock of ages*.[13] The Law of One
series therefore appears to be making a direct connection between the
Great Pyramid and the Old and New Testaments. There are other references in the Bible that suggest an intimate familiarity with the Great
Pyramid, such as in Psalms 118:22: "The stone which the builders rejected
has become the chief cornerstone."[14] Normally a building has four different cornerstones, but the Great Pyramid's capstone, which symbolizes
the coming Ascension event, could be considered as the single "chief
cornerstone." In the Old Testament, this also appears in Isaiah 28:16:
"Behold, I am the one who has laid as a foundation in Zion, a stone, a
tested stone, a precious cornerstone, of a sure foundation."[15]

Jesus ended up borrowing this Old Testament scripture and defined
himself as "the chief cornerstone" in Mark 12:10, Matthew 21:42, and
Luke 20:17, and is further quoted saying this in Acts 4:11, Ephesians 2:20,
and 1 Peter 2:7. Jesus is also referred to as "the rock," such as in 1 Corin-
thians 10:4. And in Matthew 16:18, Jesus said, "Upon this rock I will
build my church; and the gates of hell shall not prevail against it."[16] This
may also be a parable that gives the reader another clue to look at the
Great Pyramid.

The Law of One series made these biblical references in the language
of metaphor, thus preserving the free will of the reader to either follow

up on the research leads they presented or ignore them, as I myself did for many years. When Dr. Elkins asked for clarification as to what "everlasting rock" meant, the response was, "If you can understand the concept of thought-forms, you will realize that the thought-form is more regular in its distortion than the energy fields created by the materials in the rock, which has been created through thought-form from thought to finite energy and beingness in your, shall we say, distorted reflection of the level of the thought-form."[17] This explained why certain pyramid researchers had found bits of hair, insects, and other organic materials inside the pyramid blocks. To me, this meant that sand was collected and combined into a limestone-type material, and a certain degree of extra materials were blended into the finished product from the original sand.

Dr. Elkins wanted to know why they didn't just build the pyramid as one gigantic solid mass of stone if they had the ability to do so. The response was quite interesting:

> There is a law which we believe to be one of the more significant primal distortions of the Law of One. That is the Law of Confusion. You have called this the Law of Free Will. We wished to make a healing machine, or time/space ratio complex which was as efficacious as possible. However, we did not desire to allow the mystery to be penetrated by the peoples in such a way that we became worshipped as builders of a miraculous pyramid. Thus it appears to be made, not thought.[18]

Despite their efforts not to be worshipped, their presence clearly caused a great deal of confusion and forced them to withdraw. Some people saw them as gods, while others saw them as demons, and it caused a great deal of infighting—which apparently led to wars and the loss of human life. With Ra's unique focus on the importance of free will, their own presence was seen to violate the free will of people on Earth, and the rules they must abide by forced them to withdraw.

It is very difficult, if not impossible, for us to currently visualize a mental and telekinetic power of sufficient strength to take materials like desert sand and transform it into stone blocks. However, throughout the

Law of One series, Ra makes it clear that they are the highest-level ETs that would ever directly interact with a planet like ours. If the pyramid could indeed be manifested directly with consciousness, there would be no limit to the degree of precision and perfection with which it could be realized. As is, the pyramid can reveal many secrets for those who take a deeper look—secrets that prove it would be quite impossible for the pyramid to be built without some form of super-advanced technology. This is exactly what we see when we analyze the monument itself.

The Prophecy in Stone

By the time I read the Law of One series, I already had spent three years studying *The Great Pyramid Decoded* by Peter Lemesurier. This was one of the very first books I picked up after hearing from my friend's professor that UFOs were real. In fact, I bought a copy of the book and brought it home on the very same day that I went to pick up my special-ordered copy of *The Monuments of Mars* by Richard C. Hoagland. The material in *Great Pyramid Decoded* was astonishingly complex, but that didn't scare me in the least. Lemesurier built off the works of other scholars to make an irrefutable case that the Great Pyramid had a "Prophecy in Stone" built into it. In short, the actual passageways, corridors, and chambers inside the Great Pyramid had very precise prophecies of future events, right down to the year when they would occur. And despite modern conspiracy theorists thinking the Great Pyramid is somehow connected to the Illuminati and would therefore convey negative information, it will be very clear when we study the Great Pyramid Timeline that the birth, crucifixion, and ascension of Jesus—or Jehoshua in the Law of One—was of absolutely critical importance in our own progress toward Ascension at the end of our current 25,000-year cycle.

To properly cover the fascinating material in *Great Pyramid Decoded*, I will initially bring back a few of the same pages that were originally shared in *The Source Field Investigations*. This provides the critical backstory for understanding how the Great Pyramid absolutely could not have been built without the use of a very highly advanced technology—

vastly exceeding anything available to us even in today's world. Then we will continue on to explore the mysteries of the Great Pyramid Timeline before returning to our discussion of the Law of One and the Confederation's efforts to assist in our global Ascension process.

As you read this excerpt, bear in mind that my goal in *Source Field* was to present a fully developed overview of the science that was presented in the Law of One series, without actually needing to refer to it as a reference except in the appendix. This proved that the Law of One scientific model could stand on its own, without my having to say "take my word for it that this material is true." These scientific extrapolations went well beyond anything that Carla Rueckert, whose voice spoke the words, had been able to understand herself—and I lived with her in her home for nearly two years, in 2003 and 2004.

Most people are unaware of how amazing the Great Pyramid looked when it was first built, and how this stunning design continued to be visible up until the 1300s. There are many surprises in store for us once we delve into the history of the Great Pyramid and its precise measurements. Most specifically, I want you to pay very close attention to the discussion of the so-called Egyptian Inch or Pyramid Inch, as this becomes the main tool we will use to decipher the Pyramid Timeline and its prophecies—both those that have already happened and those that are still to come. It would have been fun to add some of the Law of One quotes that we have already shared, but I was shooting for a more mainstream approach at this time. Here we go:

Fascinating Scientific Facts about the Great Pyramid

The Great Pyramid is considered the largest stone building on Earth, covering some thirteen acres at its base—the equivalent of seven Midtown city blocks in Manhattan—and it rises to the height of a forty-story building. Approximately 2.3 million limestone and granite blocks were used to build it, each of them weighing 2.5 to 70 tons apiece—for a total mass of about 6.3 million tons. No crane ever built in modern times is strong enough to lift stones this heavy—it would simply tumble over. The bedrock underneath the Great Pyramid was leveled out so perfectly that no corner of the pyramid's base is more than a half-inch higher or lower than the others.[19] Such precise leveling goes significantly beyond even the finest architectural standards of today.[20]

Strangely, the pyramid is also located at the exact center of the Earth's landmass—the one true *axis mundi*. Its east-west axis sits precisely on the longest land parallel, covering the greatest amount of land and the least amount of water on Earth—passing through Africa, Asia, and America along the way. The longest land meridian, crossing over Asia, Africa, Europe, and Antarctica, also passes right through the pyramid.[21] The likelihood of finding this "perfect location" by accident is 1 in 3 billion.[22] I didn't understand why this location was so important until years later, as we will see—but it has to do with the flow and positioning of natural energy fields from the Earth that have remained unknown to mainstream scientists in our own modern times.

The sides of the pyramid line up so well with true rotational north that they only deviate by 3 minutes of arc in any one direction—less than 0.06 percent.[23] Another "coincidence" is that if you calculate the average height of land above sea level, with Miami as the low and the Himalayas as the high, you come out with 5,449 inches—which is the exact height of the Great Pyramid.[24]

To me, the most surprising fact of all was that when the Great Pyramid was first built, it was covered with twenty-one acres of gleaming, brightly polished white casing stones—a total of about 115,000 blocks of pure white limestone[25] averaging 100 inches, or 8.3 feet, in thickness. If you caught the glint of the sun's reflection off of these stones in the daytime, it would be blindingly bright—thus earning it the name Ta Khut, or "the Light." The reflections could apparently be seen from the mountains of Israel hundreds of miles away.[26] Despite the fact that some of these casing stones weighed sixteen

tons, all six sides were carved to fit together so perfectly that
the cracks between them were only one-fiftieth of an inch
wide[27]—which is narrower than a human fingernail. Sir
W. M. Flinders Petrie described this in the late 1800s as "the
finest opticians' work on the scale of acres," comparing it to
the precision used to grind lenses for a telescope. Richard C.
Hoagland has pointed out that even the tiles on a NASA
space shuttle do not fit together this closely. Even more surprisingly, these cracks are not empty—they are filled with a
cement that is incredibly strong. There is no known way you
could fit a mortar into cracks one-fiftieth of an inch wide, and
evenly cover areas as large as five feet by seven feet wide in the
vertical, with any known methods. And if you were foolhardy
enough to smash the casing stones with a sledgehammer,
you would find that the limestone itself breaks before the cement does.[28]

I'm well aware of how fantastic this must sound. It's one
thing to see the pyramid sitting there as it is today—a giant
mass of decaying stone blocks. It would be quite something
else to witness it in its original form, looking like a gigantic,
gleaming white sculpture in the desert—something totally
unlike any other technological achievement we've ever seen
on Earth—whether from ancient times or in our modern
world. Thankfully, many people witnessed these casing stones
in their original form and documented their observations in
writing over the centuries—and the history can be found in
Peter Tompkins's *Secrets of the Great Pyramid.*[29]

According to Tompkins, limestone becomes harder and
more polished with time and weather, unlike marble—think
about the gorgeous stalactites and stalagmites of limestone
you can find in underground caves. Therefore, the pyramid
did not get progressively more dull-looking as the centuries
rolled by after it was first built.[30] In approximately 440 BC,
Herodotus wrote that the pyramid's casing stones were highly
polished—with joints so fine they could scarcely even be seen

with the naked eye.[31] The thirteenth-century Arab historian Abd-al-Latif said that despite their polished appearance, these stones were inscribed with mysterious, unintelligible characters—enough to fill ten thousand pages. His colleagues assumed these writings were the graffiti of ancient tourists.[32] William of Baldensal visited the pyramid in the early 1300s and described these strange inscriptions as being all arranged in long, careful rows of strange symbols.[33] When the casing stones eventually were lost, so went any hope of documenting these mysterious writings for future codebreaking analysis and study.

Diodorus Siclus, who lived soon after the time of Christ, wrote that the casing stones were "complete and without the least decay."[34] The Roman naturalist Pliny witnessed native boys running up the polished sides, to the delight of tourists. In about AD 24, Strabo visited Egypt, and said there was an entrance on the north face of the pyramid that was made of a hinged stone you could raise from the bottom up, but was otherwise indistinguishable from its surroundings when it lay flush.[35]

Inside the Great Pyramid, there are three different chambers. The largest of these is known as the King's Chamber, and is the only part of the pyramid that is made of red granite, which is extremely hard. In the 1990s, Bernard Pietsch analyzed the twenty different stones on the floor of the King's Chamber and made startling discoveries. Strangely, although the stones are all either square or rectangular, hardly any of them are the same size—except when you have an identical pair side by side. These stones are arranged in a series of six different rows—and each row has a different width from any of the others. In *Anatomy of the King's Chamber,* Pietsch presents staggeringly complex and compelling evidence that a variety of measurements from Mercury, Venus, Earth, the Moon, Mars, Jupiter, and Saturn—including their orbital periods—are encoded in the stones' dimensions.[36]

Within the King's Chamber there is a loose stone coffin carved out of an extremely hard chocolate-brown granite, estimated to weigh three tons. The external volume of the sarcophagus is exactly twice the internal volume. Thanks to the patterns of circular drill marks found inside, engineer Christopher Dunn calculated that the coffin was carved out by tubular drills that could cut through granite five hundred times faster than any technology we now have available.[37] (In chapter 13, I propose this is actually the result of a technology that can dramatically soften stone.) Skeptics believe this may have been done with diamond-tipped drill bits in Egypt, despite the impossibility of achieving the necessary speeds involved with any modern technology. Dunn points out that the strongest metal they had at the time was copper. The diamonds would have cut through the copper like butter before they ever even put a dent in the granite.[38]

The sarcophagus has grooves for a lid to be fitted in place, but no such lid has ever been found—as if it were never intended to be found. Many pyramid researchers, including Peter Lemesurier, interpret this open tomb as symbolizing a time when there will be no more death, i.e., the coming Golden Age. The coffin was empty—and there is no evidence it ever held a mummy. The granite sarcophagus also cannot fit through the Antechamber, meaning that it had to be built into the pyramid from the very beginning—totally in contrast with any known Egyptian burial practices.[39]

Although this was not discovered until much later, the north and south walls of both the King's Chamber and the Queen's Chamber also contained airshafts that went on an upward-sloping angle, all the way out to the surface of the pyramid. This supplied just enough oxygen to refresh the atmosphere inside each room. In the mid-1990s, Rudolf Gantenbrink sent a miniature robot some sixty-five meters up the shafts, and confirmed that in the King's Chamber, the south shaft points at the star Al Nitak, or Zeta Orionis. The north

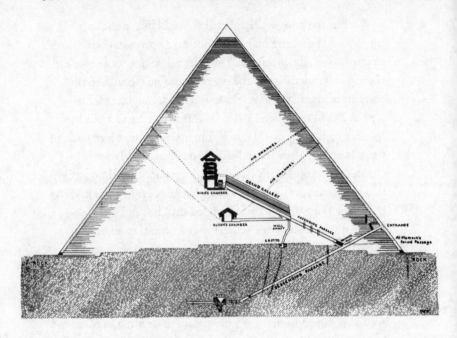

Pyramid Airshafts and Passageways

shaft points at Alpha Draconis, which used to be the pole star in the third millennium BC. The northern Queen's Chamber shaft is aimed at Beta Ursae Minoris, and the southern channel points to Sirius.[40] All these alignments date back to about 2500 BC. That was the most recent time in which they all lined up.[41] According to ancient-civilizations researcher Joseph Jochmans, "As Bauval and Gilbert showed through computer calculations, the constellational alignments imprinted in the Air Passages for 2450 BCE were also present earlier, in about 10,500 BCE, because of the Precession of the Equinoxes."[42] An Edgar Cayce reading from June 30, 1932, said that work on the Great Pyramid and the Sphinx began this very same year.[43]

In the thirteenth century, an Arab historian compared the pyramid to a gigantic female breast, noting the casing stones still looked perfect on the outside except for the original entrance carved by Caliph Al-Mamoun.[44] Disaster struck in the year 1356,[45] as the first of a series of earthquakes leveled significant areas of northern Egypt, collapsing entire city blocks to rubble. The pyramid was shaken so hard by these quakes that many of the casing stones broke off and tumbled into a giant mess. The people were desperate to rebuild—and used this fallen limestone from the pyramid as raw material to help build the new capital city El Kaherah, "The Victorious," as well as to rebuild Cairo. Apparently, the stones that hadn't already fallen off were then deliberately broken off, because the quality of the limestone was very pure and provided an excellent building material. According to the French Baron d'Anglure, who visited this area of Egypt in 1396, "Certain masons demolished the course of great casing stones which covered [the pyramid,] and tumbled them into the valley."[46] Two bridges were built across the Nile specifically to help drag the stones across the river via camel trains, so as to build mosques and palaces in Cairo and El Kaherah.[47]

As the centuries rolled by, the legend of the once-great casing stones had faded into nothing more than a superstitious myth. However, Lieutenant Colonel Richard Howard-Vyse conducted excavations in and around the pyramid beginning in 1836 that permanently eliminated the skeptics' arguments. Howard-Vyse found that the pyramid was surrounded by debris of limestone chunks and sand that had piled up around the base by as much as fifty feet. He cleared a patch in the center of the north façade, hoping to reach the base and bedrock of the pyramid. There he found two of the original casing stones—forever ending the scholarly argument about whether the pyramid had ever been covered with a perfectly flat, polished white surface. The original blocks were still so finely carved that an exact measurement of the slope angle could be calculated.[48] According to Howard-Vyse, they were perfect: "in a sloping plane as correct and true almost as modern work by optical instrument makers. The joints were scarcely perceptible, not wider than the thickness of silver paper."[49]

Howard-Vyse published his detailed measurements and notes in 1840, and his assistant John Perring published his own book as well. This opened up a whole new phase of study known as Pyramidology.[50] John Taylor, a gifted mathematician and amateur astronomer who worked as an editor of the *London Observer* in the nineteenth century, was already in his fifties when Howard-Vyse's data came in from Egypt. Taylor then began a rigorous thirty-year investigation into all the measurements that had been reported in and around the pyramid, looking for hidden mathematical and geometric formulas. Taylor found that if he measured the perimeter of the base in inches, it came out to roughly 100 times 366—and if he divided the perimeter by 25 inches, he got 366 once again. What's the big deal about 366? It is suspiciously close to the exact length of an Earth year—365.2422 days.[51] Taylor found that by slightly changing the length of a typical British inch, these figures could become exact reflections of the Earth year. Was this merely a cheap mathematical cheat, or was there any worthwhile science behind it? That question was soon answered when a highly fortunate "coincidence" struck at almost the exact same time.

Sir John Herschel, one of Britain's most highly regarded astronomers at the turn of the nineteenth century, had very recently tried to invent a new measuring unit to replace the existing British system. He wanted it to be based on the exact dimensions of the Earth. Without knowing anything about Taylor's research, Herschel used the most accurate dimensions of the Earth available at the time to suggest that we should be using inches that were very slightly longer than normal—by a mere half the width of a human hair, or 1.00106 British inches. Herschel blasted the French for basing their metric system on the curvature of the Earth, which can change, rather than using a line that went straight through the Earth's center, from pole to pole. A recent British Ordnance Survey had fixed that pole-to-pole distance within the

Earth as 7898.78 miles, or 500,500,000 British inches. It would become exactly 500 million inches if the British inch were made just a slight bit longer. Herschel argued that the existing British inch should be officially lengthened to obtain this truly scientific measuring unit.

Fifty of these inches would then be exactly one ten-millionth of the Earth's polar axis. Twenty-five of them would make a very useful cubit—which could replace the existing British yard and foot. Little did Herschel know that Taylor had already discovered these exact same units within the dimensions of the Great Pyramid.[52] When Taylor found out about this, he was thrilled. He now had compelling evidence that the builders of the pyramid must have known the true spherical dimensions of the planet, and built their whole measurement system off it. That again implies that the ancient Egyptians possessed a significantly more advanced technology than we normally give them credit for.[53] Lemesurier reported that in International Geophysical Year 1957, the Earth's diameter from pole to pole was measured with flawless satellite precision—much more accurately than in Herschel's time. As a result, we now know that the pyramid inch is indeed one five-hundred-millionth of the Earth's diameter at the poles—and this connection is so exact that the numbers check out down to multiple decimal points of accuracy.[54] This means the pyramid was indeed built to be a mathematically perfect reflection of the length of a year on Earth around its perimeter. These precisely Earth-scaled measurements appear again and again in obvious ways—both inside and outside the pyramid.

However, an even greater mystery is found when we measure the diagonals of the Great Pyramid—namely, the distance from one corner, over the top and down to the other corner. This distance comes out to 25,826.4 pyramid inches[55]—remarkably close to modern calculations of the true length of the precession of the equinoxes in the years.

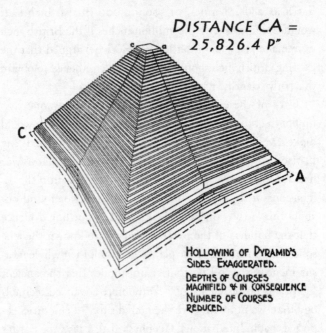

DISTANCE CA =
25,826.4 P"

C

A

HOLLOWING OF PYRAMID'S
SIDES EXAGGERATED.
DEPTHS OF COURSES
MAGNIFIED & IN CONSEQUENCE
NUMBER OF COURSES
REDUCED.

Pyramid Diagonals Adding Up to 25,826.4 Pyramid Inches (Precession Number)

It definitely seems that the Great Pyramid's designers
wanted us to use the Egyptian inch. By making the pyramid's
diagonals add up to the precession of the equinoxes in Egyptian inches, we seem to have been given a message to pay attention to this great cycle. These same builders obviously
knew the exact dimensions of the earth, and therefore may
very well have traveled the world—seeding many different
ancient myths in many different ancient cultures. As Santillana and Von Dechend revealed again and again in *Hamlet's
Mill,* the hidden message in each of these ancient myths told
us to look at the precession—or what many ancient cultures
also called the Great Year.

Another very interesting point to consider is the linkage between the Great Pyramid and the Bible. There is strong evidence that Isaiah spoke of the pyramid in chapter 19, verses 19 and 20: "In that day there shall be an altar to the Lord in the midst of the Land of Egypt, and a monument at the border thereof to the Lord, and it shall be for a sign, and for a witness unto the Lord of Hosts in the Land of Egypt." The Great Pyramid certainly is in the midst of the land of Egypt, and could definitely be seen as a monumental altar.

On page 293 of *Great Pyramid Decoded*, Lemesurier reveals that the mirror-polished white casing stones cast triangular reflections of light on the desert surface, and during the Summer Solstice, this would appear as a perfect, starlike Christian crucifix shape from overhead. The top, left, and right reflections are about the same length, and the bottom reflection is about three times longer.

Another intriguing fact is that if you draw a diagonal line to the northeast from the Great Pyramid, where you use the east-west meridian as your X axis and use the angle of the pyramid's Ascending Passage at 26 degrees, 18 minutes, and 9.7 seconds, that line happens to cross directly through Bethlehem, the birthplace of Jesus. The precision of this alignment is so exact that it is almost certainly not a coincidence.

An additional enigma I described on page 470 of *The Ascension Mysteries* is the fact that the measured size of the Granite Coffer in the King's Chamber is precisely identical to the dimensions of the Ark of the Covenant in the Old Testament, at 2.5 by 1.5 by 1.5 cubits, even though the coffin in the Pyramid allegedly was not discovered until much later.

Lastly, the number 153 is of key importance in the Bible and in the Great Pyramid alike. In the Old Testament, the number of builders of Solomon's first temple, a symbol of the light-body, was said to be about 153,000,[56] and the Tetragrammaton, or name of God, happens to appear exactly 153 times in the Book of Genesis.[57] In John 21:11, it says that Simon Peter brought in a net with exactly 153 large fishes after Jesus' arrival. The net did not break even though they caught "so many." The number 153 is therefore considered to symbolize the people who will be Ascending at the end of the cycle, as the fish-catch is another harvest metaphor.

The number 153 also has interesting numerological characteristics, as it is the sum of the integers from 1 to 17. This makes it a triangular number, where if you visualize each number like a coin and you arrange the coins into triangle shapes as you place them down one by one, the seventeenth row of the triangle ends in the number 153. The numbers 1 and 15 are also triangular numbers.

In the Great Pyramid, the roof of the Grand Gallery is exactly 153 units of twelve Pyramid Inches in length. The top of the Great Step, which is also the floor of the King's Chamber complex, is exactly 153 horizontal layers of stone blocks below the existing flat top of the pyramid. And lastly, the two low sections of the King's Chamber Passage together measure 153.057 P" in length.[58]

These connections again establish a very direct linkage between the exact dimensions of the Great Pyramid and the numerology in the Bible. This is another proof that the pyramid was intended to be a prophecy of the coming Messiah and the mass Ascension that would later occur.

CHAPTER NINETEEN

The Pyramid Timeline

The Edgar Cayce Readings gave us a direct and undeniable indication that the pyramid itself was built to encode a Message in Stone. In reading 294–151, while the Great Pyramid is being discussed as a temple, we hear, "As the changes came about in the earth, the rise and fall of nations were to be depicted in this same temple, that was to act as an interpreter for that which had been, that which is, and that which is to be in the material plane."[1] This clearly validated the existing work of Pyramidologists who had suggested that past, present, and future historical events were very neatly encoded into the stonework of the Great Pyramid. Once we look at the full story, it is obviously a message about our collective Ascension. The reading also said the Pyramid Timeline described "the rise and fall of nations," and we will certainly see that with prophecies of events such as World War I, World War II, 9/11, and the 2007–08 economic collapse.

The Return of the Capstone Symbolizes Planetary Awakening

If the Great Pyramid does have a symbolic story to tell, another obvious part of the message would be that it was deliberately left unfinished on the outside. There is a flat, square area at the top where a pyramid-shaped capstone can be fitted. When we remember how well the Great Pyramid preserves the Earth's exact measurements, it is no surprise that Peter Lemesurier, the author of *Great Pyramid Decoded*, suggested the flattened top meant the Earth it lf, like the Great Pyramid, is somehow unfinished. It could be that the folks who built the pyramid intended to return at some point to finish the job they started, perhaps the end of the Great Year that they built into its measurements. The Law of One series does predict a "harvest" at the end of the 25,000-year cycle, with a return of positive confederation ET groups to assist us. My own dreams said the same thing, particularly beginning in 1995, and Corey Goode's contactee experiences gave us additional detail as of 2015. The return of the capstone also transforms the pyramid from a six-sided object—with a base, four sides, and a top—to a five-sided object. According to Lemesurier, in Egyptian numerology, six means "imperfection" and five means "Divine Initiation." Given that we see the exact length of an Earth year in the perimeter, as well as the exact length of the great precession cycle in the diagonals, this suggests that the conclusion of our current cycle of precession will heal and transform the imperfections of humanity—by moving us through a Divine Initiation of some kind.

The concept of a Pyramid Timeline is discussed by Peter Tompkins in *Secrets of the Great Pyramid* as follows: "To make things worse [for pioneering pyramid researcher Piazzi Smyth], another Scot, a religious enthusiast called Robert Menzies, advanced the theory that the passage system in the Great Pyramid was nothing less than a *chronological representation of prophecy,* corroborating the Bible, built on a scale of one pyramid inch to the solar year." [Emphasis added] This was in 1865.[2] The researcher Piazzi Smyth believed that the Pyramid should have a stellar alignment that was encoded to an exact year in the BC era, and this would represent the starting point for any prophetic timeline written into the stonework of its inner passageways. Robert Menzies believed Smyth's proposed alignment should be clearly marked in the Descending Passage, such as through a pair of vertical lines on either side of the tunnel. Menzies already had a good idea of where this inscription should be based on the passages and their relationships to each other. Menzies was thrilled to find out that Smyth discovered two Scored Lines in the same area he expected the markers should be![3]

An Encoded Alignment

The actual start-date alignment had already been discovered a year before, in 1864, when Piazzi Smyth, who had worked as Scotland's Astronomer Royal for twenty years,[4] visited the Great Pyramid and conducted careful measurements. Smyth concluded that at midnight during the equinox of about 2170 BC (it was later corrected to 2141 BC), the pole star of the time, Alpha Draconis, would be visible all the way down at the very bottom of the Descending Passage, at the same time that n-Tauri, or Alcyone of the Pleiades, would be precisely overhead.[5] Smyth believed this alignment could not be an accident. He felt it encoded the exact time the pyramid was constructed, using the slow, 25,920-year wobble of the Earth's axis known as the *precession of the equinoxes*. This no longer appears to be the case, thanks to the far older alignment discovered by Robert Bauval dating back to 10,490 BC, but this alignment would prove to be of *extreme* value in studying the deeper message of the Pyramid Timeline. It fixes the exact moment we are supposed to begin counting time.

Several prominent pyramid scholars concluded that this rare alignment of the Pleiades and Pole Star was apparently not accidental nor random. By using the Scored Lines as the beginning of a timeline, where you start counting your way through the passages with one Pyramid Inch equaling one year, you can look for any changes in direction, structure, measurements, stone composition, or otherwise, and note what year that change corresponds to. Many of the changes in the pyramid's passageways correspond with very noteworthy events in our own history when you use this system, including 9/11, the so-called Great Recession, and the Edward Snowden NSA revelations. Skeptics will invariably argue that the Pyramid Timeline must be a "hoax" or a "coincidence." Others will balk at how important Christianity is to the events depicted in the timeline. Nonetheless, the sheer number of highly significant dates that are clearly encoded in the timeline, based on this simple, repetitive, and logical system, makes these skeptical positions very difficult to defend.

Smyth also theorized that the pyramid's perimeter would reveal the precise number of days in an Earth year, expressed in Pyramid Inches, once properly measured. Although Smyth received a gold medal from the Royal Society of Edinburgh for his work, the skeptics were predictably savage—particularly because Smyth believed these astonishing results could only be the result of Divine Intervention, where the God of the Bible guided the hand of the pyramid's earthly architect. Sir James Y. Simpson, a prominent member of the Royal Society of Edinburgh, said "the whole of Professor Smyth's theory about the Great Pyramid is a series of strange hallucinations, which only a few weak women believe, and perhaps a few womanly men, but no more."[6] *Ouch!* I think Sir James must have reincarnated in the form of an army of YouTube video commenters and Twitter enthusiasts.

Caliph Al-Mamoun's Treasure Hunt

Abdullah Al-Mamoun came into power in Alexandria in 813 AD—the son of caliph Harun Al-Rashid, who was immortalized in the classic *Arabian Nights*. Al-Mamoun heard the Great Pyramid contained a secret chamber that held maps and tables of the Earth's measurements, as well as those of the Solar System. These records were allegedly very accurate, even though they dated from long, long ago. This chamber was also believed to have great treasures and strange items, including "arms [swords, knives, etc.] which would not rust" and "glass which can be bent but does not break."[7] Of course, even a clear plastic water bottle from today's world would be seen by someone in Al-Mamoun's time as being made of bendable "glass," but this could also be a legend of something far more impressive. In November 2017, a new and previously undiscovered chamber was found with the use of muon particles, massive quantum particles that are similar to electrons and can penetrate through rock to reveal inconsistencies—such as an empty chamber. Researchers discovered a thirty-meter-long hidden chamber above the Grand Gallery that is quite large enough to be a treasure room, and the results were published in the prestigious *Nature* science journal.[8]

Al-Mamoun brought a huge team of engineers, stonemasons, architects, and builders to the pyramid in 820 AD to search for the glorious treasure room. They were unable to find the allegedly secret entrance, so they smashed their way in with brute force. This was done by lighting fires on the stones, then throwing cold vinegar on them until they cracked.[9] They bored in over 100 feet without finding anything but solid rock. In total frustration, they were just about ready to give up when a worker heard something heavy fall inside the pyramid—to the east of where they were tunneling. They eventually hacked their way into a narrow, claustrophobic Descending Passage, which is about 350 feet long, slicing its way directly through the solid bedrock after about the first quarter of the way down. The Descending Passage is carved out with such astonishing precision that it never deviates by more than a *quarter of an inch* from left to right, and a *tenth of an inch* from top to bottom! The only way we could even *hope* to duplicate this feat with modern technology is by the use of our very best laser-controlled drilling techniques.[10]

This is a very important point, for this fact can be easily discovered with a minimum amount of research, but no one has any idea how it could have been done. And remember that if it could be done underneath the pyramid, boring directly through solid rock, the technology existed for it to be replicated elsewhere—as the Cayce Readings and other sources have asserted regarding the so-called Hall of Records that Ra-Ptah and his associates left for us to rediscover. The Hall of Records is expected to be an amazing treasure room filled with some of the best Atlantean technology there is to offer. This appears to include holographic projectors that will reveal our true history, including the fact that Earth humans are descended from multiple different extraterrestrial human races that emigrated here.

Al-Mamoun's men soon discovered that the loud sound they heard was a square stone that had fallen from the ceiling of the Descending Passage. This stone revealed the existence of granite behind it, rather than limestone. This was very mysterious, and eventually proved to be the location of the Ascending Passage that they then smashed their way through in their hunt for treasure. At this point, they continued heading down to the bottom of the dark, stuffy passage and found what is now called the Subterranean Chamber. This is a room with a perfectly flat ceiling, but the floor appears unfinished—covered with a variety of smooth, irregularly curving bumps, much like the frothing surface of an angry sea. An ominous Pit appears in this room that you could easily fall into, and in the Pyramid Timeline, the Pit may well begin as of 2001— precisely marking the time of 9/11, and also reaching "rock bottom" in the exact time frame of the 2008 economic collapse, as we will see. The Pyramid Timeline gives us two possible choices as to what this date could be, and 2001 is one of them. World Wars I and II are both clearly marked in the Timeline as we head toward the Pit.

Torch marks on the ceiling of the Subterranean Chamber convinced them someone had been there before, and must have taken out anything interesting in the room. They then headed back up the tunnel, trying not to breathe too much since their torches were consuming much of the oxygen, and studied the ceiling where the stone had fallen. They realized the red-and-black-granite square in the wall might be the end of a stone plug. This suggested another passageway might be behind it, and that it had been deliberately blocked off.[11] The granite was too hard to break, so they had to tunnel around it. This proved to be a great deal of work, as they found two more huge blocks after the first one. They next encountered an additional series of limestone plugs that they were able to smash out with chisels, bit by bit.[12]

Soon after they passed the last of the limestone plugs, the height of the Ascending Passage suddenly rose considerably—to more than twenty-three feet, at 286.1 Egyptian inches. This was the beginning of the Grand Gallery, a long hallway that continued sloping upward at the same angle as the Ascending Passage. In the Pyramid Timeline, the exact moment in our history where the ceiling rises this dramatically happens to correspond with the arrival of Jesus. In fact, the exact thirty-three-year period of time between his birth and his ultimate Ascension is very neatly recorded in a triangular area within the measurements of the passage, as Lemesurier's book reveals. This was exciting to pyramid researchers who were open to Christianity, and provided an equal degree of

controversy and scorn for those who did not want to see the Great Pyramid as a "Bible in Stone."

The walls of the Grand Gallery had seven horizontal layers that tapered inward as they reached the ceiling. Each layer was narrower than
the one below it, creating a curious, ratcheting-inward pattern as it went
up—like an extra-steep version of a Mayan step-pyramid, only flipped
inside out. As we will see, by inferring this meaning from the Law of
One series, this structure seems to symbolically indicate that Jesus had
activated all seven chakras as part of the Ascension process.

Once you reach this point inside the pyramid, you have two choices—
you can go straight, or climb up a vertical wall. The easier path involves
crouching down and walking straight ahead through another narrow
passageway that leads you into a small room—which came to be called
the Queen's Chamber. Peter Lemesurier and other researchers interpreted this chamber as symbolically representing the path of traditional
religion. The Queen's Chamber featured a fifteen-foot-tall carved niche
inside the wall on the left, which cut in deep enough for a person to
stand in. The niche *also* had seven steplike layers—just like the Grand
Gallery. This again seems to show the potential for someone to reach
Ascension through conventional religion, if they stay true to the core
teachings of service to others that it espouses. There are a variety of legends of levitating Christian saints, as one example. Al-Mamoun's men
tunneled into this recessed area, hoping to find another passageway, but
found nothing. In terms of the Pyramid Timeline, authors like Lemesurier are not exactly sure how to interpret the Queen's Chamber. The
Descending Passage encodes by far the greatest number of specific dates,
as we will see, but the Ascending Passage has all of the crown-jewel
prophecies regarding the end of our 25,000-year cycle and the anticipated
results.

The Path to Ascension

Alternatively, if you are standing at the beginning of the Grand Gallery
and do not choose to head into the Queen's Chamber, you can instead

climb up a perilous series of square holes on either the left or the right wall. Now you will find a ladder in this location for tourists. After several feet of climbing, this will bring you up to the steeply ascending main floor of the Grand Gallery. Then you will see the impressive seven-layered walls tapering up to a high ceiling above you. According to the Pyramid Timeline researchers, this room symbolizes the path of Ascension—where you are going through the initiation that activates dormant psychic abilities within you. I learned about these symbolic meanings in 1993, and they soon became very frequent elements in my dreams.

If you climbed all the way up the Grand Gallery, which was a good distance, you would come to a sudden, three-foot-tall stone wall called the Great Step. You would have to perilously pull yourself up and over this vertical wall to keep going. If you read Lemesurier's book, the exact year that we hit the Great Step, based upon the original pole-star and Pleiades alignment of 2141 BC, is the year 1845. This appears to represent a sudden wall that we hit, as a planet, which we then have to climb up and over in order to continue moving forward. One could also say it represents a sudden, vertical increase in our progress. As people hiking up through the pyramid, we have to risk serious, if not fatal bodily injury to pull ourselves up and over the Great Step. Once we do it successfully, we enter into the most visually stunning part of the pyramid's inner passages.

What exactly happens in 1845 that could match such a massive vertical leap depicted within the Pyramid? One very significant historical point to consider is the invention of the telegraph. This was the first time humanity ever attained instantaneous communication at a distance. Symbolically, this may be seen as a precursor to a time where we are all able to regain the ability to do this telepathically, which is one key element of how we will change in fourth density, according to the Law of One series. So much of our modern technological age centers around instantaneous, worldwide communication, such as with the Internet—and indeed, it all began in 1845.

Samuel Morse didn't obtain government support for his groundbreaking new invention until 1843, and he then built a smaller-scale telegraph system between Washington, DC, and Baltimore, Maryland, along a railroad line. However, the first long-distance telegraph message wasn't transmitted along this line until May 24, 1844,[13] between Samuel Morse and his associate Alfred Vail. The message, tapped out in the simple code Morse devised, was "What hath God wrought!"[14] Why not have the Great Step start in 1844, then? Here's the key: the first commercial telegraph line, where ordinary people could actually communicate for business or personal reasons, began along this same Washington-Baltimore corridor as of April 1, 1845—exactly where we reach the Great Step in the Timeline! Both the Magnetic Telegraph Company in the United States and the Electrical Telegraph Company in Britain were formed as of May 1845, and the first public codes for telegraph were introduced this year as well.[15]

Even the Internet could be traced back to the telegraph as the first major breakthrough of its kind, and the Internet again could be a foreshadowing of the fourth-density Earth, where we apparently will have instantaneous access to all knowledge and information in the universe just by thought. This access to our collective body of human information gives us the ability to liberate ourselves from fear and ignorance, which is a very important aspect of our own spiritual awakening.

Given the significance of the Great Step, we appear to be invited to consider other historical events in addition to the invention of the telegraph, and we do indeed find them. Some of these events center on United States history, but they seem to reflect the overall movement toward a more unified world—thanks to advances in technology bringing all of us closer together. At the same time, the consolidation of the United States as a technologically superior nation would pave the way for much human suffering as well. The duality of these changes can be seen very nicely in the historical events that occur in 1845.

The United States Congress authorized contracts for overseas mail delivery to foreign countries as of March 3, 1845,[16] thus allowing the US to become a truly international society. This form of communication again mirrors the invention of the telegraph in terms of bringing us together as a planet. Macon B. Allen was the first black lawyer to be admitted to the bar in America as of May 3, 1845,[17] which was a major step forward in civil rights. The first issue of *Scientific American* magazine was

published on August 28, 1845, helping to advance our collective understanding and make advanced, cutting-edge knowledge available to everyday people without needing to access a university.[18]

Charles Darwin published his first investigations of the Galapagos
Islands in 1845, which was the precursor to his theory of evolution in
1859.[19] Darwin's detailed observations of the Galapagos were only one
section of a major journal he published in 1845, regarding his worldwide
sailing trip on the HMS *Beagle*.[20] Though I have argued in *The Source
Field Investigations* that the theory of evolution appears to have flaws, as
the process is not strictly random but has an intelligent design behind it,
Darwin's theory still represented a substantial leap forward in human
scientific understanding. We finally gained the idea that life moves forward in a progression, transforming from one species to another over
time. The end of the 25,000-year cycle, or Great Year, appears to represent yet another important evolutionary transformation in what it means
to be human. Darwin's theory in 1845 paved the way for us to imagine
ourselves evolving into something far more advanced than we are now.

Additionally, in September 1845 a fungus brought over on ships from
North America began frighteningly wiping out all the potato crops in
Ireland. This caused the Great Potato Famine, since many Irish people
relied almost entirely on the potato for survival.[21] This soon led to nearly
a million Irish emigrating to the United States alone.[22] Many others traveled to the developing lands of Canada and Australia. According to the
BBC, although this famine appeared to be a tragedy, history could have
turned out very differently if it had not happened: "These dispossessed
Irish played a major part in shaping the great democracies of the 20th
Century, and helped ensure that America joined World War I on the side
of Britain rather than Germany."[23]

Incidentally, the Mormons began migrating from the East to Utah in
1845.[24] The first nationally observed, uniform election day in the United
States was on November 4, 1845,[25] again bringing America together as a
unified nation. And on December 2, 1845, President James K. Polk officially put forward the controversial idea of Manifest Destiny to
Congress—namely that the US should aggressively expand into the
West, believing it to be part of a greater Divine Plan.[26] This perfectly

encapsulates the duality of our modern world. On the one hand, this westward expansion allowed the United States to eventually become the main scientific and industrial engine of society for many years. On the other hand, it also created a great toll of human suffering, in the name of religion and the apparent "Will of God."

Given all the above, 1845 was obviously a key turning point in modern history, with multiple reasons why it was an excellent year to have chosen for such a major symbolic milestone. We have the commercial debut of the telegraph, the consolidation of America as an international entity, the beginning of some significant world migrations, and the publication of the precursor to the theory of Evolution. In the Pyramid Timeline, 1845 does represent a sudden change. It is a painful process, but it paves the way for many other events yet to come.

According to Lemesurier, the next significant date pops out if we continue measuring the slope underneath the Great Step by one inch equals one year, while we still follow the underlying slope angle of the Grand Gallery. In this case, we hit the stone wall on the opposite side as of June 22, 1914—the Summer Solstice. This is the beginning of World War I, and we will see that this date also appears precisely in the Descending Passage, where more difficult events are apt to be portrayed. Since this same date shows up again in the Ascending Passage, it clearly indicates that 1914 is another year of very significant duality, with both negative and positive events occurring.

We are now heading directly into the most interesting and beautiful part of the Timeline—the full spiritual awakening into a Golden Age, rather than remaining in doom, gloom, and destruction. Einstein's general relativity theory appeared soon after this date in 1916, potentially giving us one of our biggest clues to the science we needed for the Golden Age. Medical, technological, and scientific advances abounded in the time window of 1914 and thereafter. Furthermore, World War I was deemed "the war to end all wars." Disasters of this scale eventually awaken us from the "dream of hell," where we no longer feel the need to attack and kill each other over petty religious and political differences. World War II was the last major war of its kind, but the great lesson was originally conveyed beginning in 1914. It is only through seeing war, chaos, and destruction on this scale that we finally awaken in the dream and realize that we no longer need to lash out at one another with hatred, fear, and violence.

The Great Step area also proves to be one of the most challenging and contentious parts of the Pyramid Timeline, since Lemesurier believed that the time scale of "one inch equals one year" needed to be changed at this point, causing one inch to last multiple years. However, Lemesurier's own words reveal that if we do not apply this conversion and keep it at the normal scale, the year 2012 is flagged as being of key importance. Lemesurier apparently never saw how beautifully this aligned with the end date of the Mayan Calendar.

Again, 2012 was the mathematical end date of the 25,000-year cycle, but it appears that we have been granted a bit of an extension for the final shift-point, because we were simply not ready yet as a planet for the full weight of prophesied events to occur as of 2012. This message was communicated to me through a variety of different means, including my own dreams and readings, as well as the visionary experiences of Corey Goode. So many events happen so quickly in the timeline after you pass the Great Step, if you're allowing one inch to be one year, that Lemesurier felt the need to dramatically slow down the speed of time's passage. He couldn't understand how such an intense cluster of Ascension-type events could happen in such a narrow time frame. This is the exact time frame we now find ourselves within.

Once you make it up and over the Great Step, after only a few more feet, you have to crouch down to enter the Antechamber, whose floor and ceiling are made of granite, not limestone. Some of the blocks in this and the following chamber were estimated to weigh as much as fifty tons. It was later discovered that this granite had been transported all the way from a quarry in Aswan, some six hundred miles away.[27] No one has provided a satisfactory explanation of how these stones could have been transported over such a long distance, and more important, why these particular stones would be chosen rather than many others that would have been much, much closer and easier to get. If we accept Ra's explanation in the Law of One series that the Great Pyramid was constructed with thought, and only appears to have been built by humans, it may very well be that they needed granite from six hundred miles away to get the proper resonant qualities for the technology to work as they intended.

It is also very interesting that if you draw a sphere into the Antechamber, where the front of the sphere touches the front of the stone making the chamber, the back of the sphere touches the back of the chamber, and the bottom of the sphere touches the floor, that sphere is 365.242 Pyramid Inches in circumference. This is the exact number of days in a year, down to the decimal-point level of accuracy. The entire Antechamber therefore symbolizes the Earth, on a smaller scale than the exterior of the Great Pyramid itself. The sphere's outside circumference adds up to exactly one Earth year in Pyramid Inches. This allows us to safely assume that the events occurring in the Antechamber are predicted to affect the entire Earth—in a very significant way. It also strongly suggests that we should not drop the timing convention of "one Pyramid Inch equals one year," as Lemesurier chose to do.

The left and right walls of the Antechamber feature a series of four vertical grooves running from floor to ceiling, as if intended to hold four large blocks of stone in place. Each of these hypothetical stone blocks could be lowered down to prevent you from moving forward—or potentially from moving backward as well, if they were dropped in place behind you. In dreamlike symbolic terms, this clearly seems to indicate that these are massive "points of no return" for humanity. The first of these four sockets did have a large, rectangular slab of granite wedged into it, which you would again have to crouch under to continue moving forward. I did this myself when I took a tour of the Great Pyramid with a group, and I made sure to stand up in that crevice and get a good look at the Granite Slab and the symbol that raises off of it, which Pyramid researchers call the Boss or the Seal.

The top of the block was curiously rough, as if it had been broken off from a larger piece of stone and was never fully finished off. Lemesurier interprets this as a sign that whatever massive spiritual force impacts the Earth at this time is coming in from the heavens, since the stone appears to have been broken off from some higher place and then appeared in our reality. The first part of the slab that sticks out is the small symbol called the Boss or the Seal, as we will explore in just a minute, and then an inch later, the timeline reaches the much larger mass of the slab's surface. This means that the main body of the slab appears in the timeline as of the year 2013. On June 6, 2013, the first of many Edward Snowden revelations about the NSA and mass surveillance entered into mass consciousness.[28]

This was most definitely another "point of no return" for humanity, which neatly aligned with prophecies of a mass awakening after the year 2012. Up until the "Global Surveillance Disclosures" of Snowden in June 2013, we were living in a collective state of ignorance. Anyone who spoke about global surveillance was deemed a "conspiracy theorist," and this very massive aspect of modern life on Earth was ignored and denied. The Law of One series explains that as we head into a fourth-density Earth, all thoughts are known to all people, and there are no secrets. Therefore, just six months after the Mayan Calendar end date of December 21, 2012, we became far more aware of this principle of the "glass ceiling," where all our thoughts are interconnected on a collective level. This is another direct stepping-stone to Ascension. Everyone thinks differently now that they realize their thoughts and activities online are essentially public.

It is also very important to point out that the slab is not perfectly flat, left to right. It has a very distinctive wave shape embedded in it. If we do not tamper with the one-inch-equals-one-year measurement system, the Boss at the front of the stone slab appears at the all-important Mayan Calendar end date of 2012. On page 109 of *Great Pyramid Decoded*, Lemesurier said, "It might still be argued that the scale of 1" per year should apply throughout the King's Chamber Passage. . . . [The] application of such a thesis would date the first Messianic advent at A.D. 2012, the second at 2030, the third at 2057, and the fourth at 2084. But in this case it seems fairly obvious that the dates are too close together to make sense."[29] Here I respectfully disagree. The date of 2030 has been popping up in my own dreams as well as Corey Goode's visions as the exact time for when we can expect the first of a series of "solar flashes" to occur. The year 2030 is the exact date when we hit the space that would hold the second slab. It is possible that the other dates, 2057 and 2084, will represent additional solar-flash moments that various sources have told us to expect. The wave-like shape of the visible slab in the first set of grooves could symbolize the wave of hyperdimensional energy that is coming in as we move through this epic transition into what the Law of One series refers to as "fourth density."

As I saw for myself when I toured the Great Pyramid, there is just enough room between the inside front wall of the Antechamber and this slab of granite to stand up in the crack, and inspect the front of the slab. There you find a five-inch-wide, three-inch-tall, stylized half circle that rises up from the surrounding stone by one inch, again called the Boss. The symbol features a horizontal line at the bottom, with a half circle that rises above it and is connected to it. This shape neatly resembles a sunrise or a rainbow, and it also looks like the Egyptian hieroglyphic symbol for a loaf of bread. The entire granite slab also approximately resembles the shape of a slice of bread, and the four grooves have symbolic similarity to a four-slice toaster oven.

This again has a variety of biblical connections, and it is the only small-size visual symbol in the entire pyramid. Bread is a symbol of spiritual "food" being brought to the Earth in a form we can directly consume and digest, hence its use in communion ceremonies and the like. In the book of John, chapter 6, we have what may be the most dramatic and public miracle of Jesus, where he apparently fed five thousand people by duplicating a single loaf of bread and a single fish into multiple copies through some sort of telekinetic manifestation process. This event occurs in John 6:11. The next day, Jesus took the opportunity to speak to the people with a variety of parables regarding bread. This included his claim to being an embodiment of the Logos in John 6:35, where he said, "I am the bread of life: he that cometh to me shall never hunger; and he that believeth on me shall never thirst."[30] Then in John 6:51, he said, "I am the living bread which came down from heaven: if any man eat of this bread, he shall live for ever: and the bread that I will give is my flesh, which I will give for the life of the world."[31]

These references to bread are obviously dreamlike metaphors rather than being literal statements of bread raining down from the heavens and causing immortality once you eat it. The bread represents a spiritual type of food that sustains the soul rather than a physically edible substance. In Session 73, Question 13, of the Law of One series, the source explained why Jesus used parables: "You may have read some of this entity's workings. It offered itself as teacher to those mind/body/spirit complexes which gathered to hear, and even then spoke as through a veil so as to leave room for those not wishing to hear. When this entity was asked to heal, it oft times did so, always ending the working with two admonitions: first, that the entity healed had been healed by its faith, that is, its ability to allow and accept changes through the violet ray into the gateway of intelligent energy; second, saying always, "Tell no one." These are the workings which attempt a maximal quality of free will while maintaining fidelity to the positive purity of the working."[32]

The Snowden revelations of 2013 certainly could be categorized as a type of spiritual "bread," since the revelation of global surveillance greatly accelerated our mass awakening. It is also humorous to point out that the construction base we use to prototype new computer electronic circuits is called a breadboard.[33] Additionally, the Boss is stylized to look like the rainbow that might arrive after a prolonged ordeal of storm clouds. The rainbow represents that burst of color that lets us all know there is something divine and mystical and magical in our lives. It is the breakthrough of a higher reality that we can so often forget about, and it is a thing of beauty, nonthreatening, that everyone loves to see. The rainbow is therefore a very fitting metaphor of Ascension.

The Boss also represents the new sunrise—the promise of a Golden Age finally made manifest and visible. The sunrise is the beginning of a new cycle on Earth—the time that the long, dark night turns into the bright new day. Symbolically it is very appropriate to associate this sunrise symbol with the end of our 25,920-year precession cycle as well. Lemesurier has a detailed discussion of all this that begins on page 107 of *Great Pyramid Decoded*. He explains that the Granite Leaf is the only part of the entire Great Pyramid that simultaneously encodes the three different measurement systems of the Pyramid Inch, Sacred Cubit, and Royal Cubit that he discusses. Therefore, we can safely see it as the "Rosetta stone" of the Pyramid. If you focus your attention just on this stone, and study its measurements, you can unlock all the other mysteries hidden within the Pyramid; it is the key geometric event. This also implies that it represents the key symbolic event as well, linking the perfection and Ascension of each human being with the perfection of the Earth.

With the position of the Boss precisely corresponding to the year 2012 in the Pyramid Timeline, it suggests the harbinger of a solar event that also activates all seven "rays," or densities, in Law of One terms. This is precisely what the Law of One tells us will happen in the "quantum leap" they anticipate will occur in our future.

The Law of One calibrated the timing of the fourth-density shift as sometime approximately thirty years after 1981 in Session 6, Questions 16, 17, and 18.[34] Specifically, it said, "This [Earth] sphere is at this time in fourth-dimension vibration. Its material is quite confused due to the society memory complexes embedded in its consciousness. It has not made an easy transition to the vibrations which beckon. Therefore, it will be fetched with some inconvenience. . . . This inconvenience, or disharmonious vibratory complex, has begun several of your years in the past. It shall continue unabated for a period of approximately three oh, thirty [30], of your years." Dr. Elkins then asked if the Earth would be a fourth-density planet after this thirty-year time period, and the source answered, "This is so."[35] These passages were spoken in 1981, and when you add on thirty years, you get 2011. Dr. Elkins then asked if the harvest would occur in the year 2011 in Session 17, Question 29, or whether it would be spread out over a longer period of time. The answer was, "This [year 2011] is an approximation. We have stated we have difficulty with your time/space. This is an appropriate probable/possible time/space nexus for harvest. Those who are not in incarnation at this time will be included in the harvest."[36] These passages were one key reason why I was so excited about the 2012 Mayan calendar end date in the years leading up to its arrival. Then once I started hearing about the year 2030 for the solar flash from my own dreams as well as Corey Goode's visionary experiences, I found that this date was also in the Pyramid Timeline as well, appearing as the date that the grooves to hold the second slab appear. Clearly the Law of One indicated that the "harvest" process does not occur all at once—it begins with this collective awakening before we get to the final stage where the multidimensional activation takes place.

Again, 2011 was only one year away from 2012, and the shift event itself has apparently since been moved forward in order to give us more time. This was a key aspect of what Corey Goode's contacts revealed to us beginning in 2015. I remember being greatly concerned in the run-up to December 21, 2012, that the changes I was expecting to see in our society, based on the Law of One material as well as my own dreams and intuitive readings, simply had not come to pass. Now at the time of this book being written, these changes are far more obvious. We will discuss more of these prophecies in later chapters.

After you move through the Antechamber, with its four grooves ending as of 2084, you head directly into the King's Chamber, which features an open sarcophagus. Pyramidologists invariably see this as a representation of a time where we transcend our mortal bodies, and the death that comes along with them, as a key part of light-body activation. The sarcophagus is loose, and can be moved around the room, so any attempt to pin it down to a particular moment in time seems beside the point. Such a mystical event may happen at different times for different people, and so attempting to define specific prophetic dates at this point may be unnecessary.

However, let's not forget that the Antechamber presents a spherical shape with a circumference of 365.242 Pyramid Inches, symbolically indicating the Earth. Once we reach the floor of the King's Chamber, we see twenty different stones that encode various dimensions of the planets, all the way through to Saturn—according to the work of Bernard Pietsch. This, of course, is a very substantial change, and suggests that humanity becomes a truly interplanetary, space-faring culture—which may be a return to our true history.

Furthermore, in the 1940s, Professor F. J. Dick found that the shape of the King's Chamber secretly encodes a twenty-sided geometry known as the icosahedron, where each side is a perfect equilateral triangle, and the overall shape resembles a soccer ball. I was very excited when I first learned about this, as these geometries show up at every level of the universe in the new scientific model that the Law of One series inspired me to pursue. We see an outer icosahedron as well as an inner one that can be drawn from the exact size and shape of the King's Chamber. According to Matila Ghyka in *The Geometry of Art and Life,* when you draw these hidden shapes into the King's Chamber on paper, you get an un-expected surprise: They line up with "the 'symmetry' . . . of the ideal or average . . . human body and face." To see this connection, you need to use Leonardo da Vinci's *Vitruvian Man*, or another diagram like it, to represent the body. The smaller icosahedron captures the navel, the mouth, the edges of the limbs, and the height of the face—whereas the larger icosahedron captures the face in more detail, including the horizontal line you can draw between the two eyes, the tip of the nose, and the location of the mouth.[37] These proportions are not coincidental either—they suggest there is a deep, hidden truth about biological life we have not yet recovered in modern times. This is precisely what we hear in the Law of One series, and is one of many arguments that I was later able to validate scientifically. The icosahedron also appears in the arrangement of vortex points on the Earth—one of which the Great Pyramid was built directly upon—as well as in the spacing of the planets. The science behind all this was thoroughly discussed in my first book, *The Source Field Investigations*. Thus, these two geometries together suggest, again, that the human form will be energetically transfigured in some remarkable way, since this geometry has the power to port us through space and time itself, such as with the Bermuda Triangle.

Lastly, in the King's Chamber we also encounter airshafts that again are really star-shafts, pointing us into a whole new cosmic direction: the south shaft points directly at the star Al Nitak, or Zeta Orionis, and the north shaft points at Alpha Draconis, which again used to be the pole star—the anchor—in the third millennium BC. Lemesurier also points out that the entrance to the star-shaft on the far side of the King's Chamber has a curious and undeniable resemblance to a pregnant mother's stomach. This again symbolizes a new birth for humanity that is taking place at this time as our Ascended light bodies activate. So, we see a progression from events happening on Earth, in the Antechamber, to events affecting the entire Solar System, in the King's Chamber, to events bringing us outside the solar system through the star-shafts. Of course, no one knows for sure what these alleged prophecies really mean, but it is certainly interesting to speculate, and the Law of One series certainly gives us many clues. It may be that Earth humanity becomes a galactic species as a result of the changes that are predicted to occur. This is directly implied in the Law of One series. Once we become fourth density, we quickly regain contact with the greater community of intelligent life that surrounds us.

Getting back to the original discovery of the King's Chamber, Al-Mamoun's men worked very hard to find the precious ancient treasure, but the giant, lidless coffin didn't even offer up a mummy. The tired, broken men went into a rage, ripping up part of the floor and hacking at the immaculately sculpted granite walls. Nowadays the guard won't even let you hum in there or stay near the sarcophagus for very long during normal hours, as I discovered from personal experience.

Discoveries of the Remaining Passages

For hundreds of years after Al-Mamoun's time, no new discoveries were made and the glorious casing stones remained pristine and undamaged. Lieutenant Colonel Howard-Vyse was definitely not the first to carefully scrutinize and explore the Great Pyramid in recent times. Nearly three hundred years after the destruction of the casing stones, in 1638, the thirty-six-year-old Oxford-trained mathematician and astronomer John Greaves visited the pyramid on a sponsorship from the Archbishop of Canterbury. He believed, just as Al-Mamoun had eight centuries before, that the pyramid preserved the exact dimensions of our planet—which at this point no one knew.[38] Greaves had already been to Italy and measured ancient buildings to determine what measuring unit the Romans were using—and he concluded it was similar to a British foot, only twenty-eight thousandths shorter.[39] He had assumed the pyramid might use similar measurements. When Greaves first entered the pyramid, he could not access the Descending Passage because Al-Mamoun's men had left behind a significant amount of debris from smashing through the limestone plugs in the Ascending Passage.[40]

Greaves was the first to discover that there was a *third* way you could go once you reached the Grand Gallery. One of the stones on the floor against the wall on the right was loose, and when you moved it away, you exposed the Well-Shaft—a passageway that went straight down, starting out as a nice and symmetrical shaft, but then quickly appearing to have been smashed through the masonry of the Pyramid with brute force. As we will see, in the Pyramid Timeline this represents the vertical path we can make toward Ascension as we dig ourselves out of the dark pit of materialism in the Descending Passage. Greaves tried to lower himself through the Well-Shaft on a rope, but there was an incredible number of bats in there. The smell was so oppressive, and the passageway so dark and tight, that he just couldn't make it all the way down. Other intrepid explorers completed the journey later on.

About a third of the way down the Well-Shaft was a curiously irregular-shaped room that allowed you to rest for a minute; it came to be called the Grotto. It was all built of smooth, flowing curves—no straight lines at all. This suggested that the entire passageway was likely intended to be built this way for symbolic reasons, the Pyramid Timeline researchers concluded. The rough, jagged Well-Shaft passageway then continued on down from there, finally feeding into the Descending Passage—some 23.8 feet before it reached the entrance to the Subterranean Chamber.[41]

Strangely, the Well-Shaft's entrance was not visible in the Descending Passage—it blended right into the stone wall, and appeared never to have been broken or disturbed until it was first discovered. If there was a secret way to open the portal without breaking it, like a hidden door, no one had found it. As we will see, this also has symbolic meaning, for once you go through your "dark night of the soul," you start looking much harder for a way out and will try just about anything to turn your life around. Anyone trying to access the King's or Queen's Chamber in ancient times would have had to crawl up through this Well-Shaft to get there, since there were granite and limestone plugs in the Ascending Passage that stopped you from moving through it. The hidden door therefore was likely used by the Egyptian priesthood to access the King's Chamber and hide secrets from people who were not initiates. The granite plugs in the Ascending Passage had been tapered in such a way that they must have been built into the pyramid from the beginning. They could not have been inserted afterward, as they were wider on the far side and fit the Ascending Passage very snugly.

Greaves also estimated that the outside of the pyramid had 207 different levels.[42] He was soon followed by Tito Livio Burattini, who took careful measurements for four years with the same instruments Greaves used, and sent the results to his sponsor, Jesuit Father Athanasius Kirchner. Burattini was robbed by bandits on the way home and lost all his notes on the pyramid along with all his money, but, thankfully, the results he sent to Kirchner survived.

Nathaniel Davison, who later became British consul general in Algeria, made additional significant discoveries in 1765.[43] Davison discovered the first of a series of "relieving chambers" stacked above the King's Chamber. This was a narrow room you could barely even squeeze into, but which encompassed the entire perimeter of the King's Chamber beneath it. Davison believed it was built to relieve the pressure on the King's Chamber from the surrounding weight of stones.[44] Lieutenant Colonel Howard-Vyse, again beginning in 1836, eventually discovered additional relieving chambers above Davison's first. The relieving chambers do not necessarily mean anything in the Pyramid Timeline, but they do appear to help harness and concentrate energy within the pyramid. The idea of pyramids harnessing an energy unknown to Western scientists is another discussion I thoroughly cover in *The Source Field Investigations*.

Howard-Vyse was running out of money, his workers' morale was very low, and the pressure was on, as he hadn't found anything terribly new or noteworthy. There was a major push to associate the Great Pyramid with the pharaoh Cheops. Though up until this point, no written inscriptions had ever been found inside the Great Pyramid, Howard-Vyse fortuitously "discovered" roughly painted red hieroglyphics in these relieving chambers, which appeared to say the Pyramid had indeed been built by Cheops. Howard-Vyse called them "quarry marks," as if the original builders needed to scribble graffiti on the stones for building instructions while otherwise accomplishing such flawless perfection. These scrawls of red paint happened to be at just the right angle for

Howard-Vyse to have painted them from the direction he got into the chambers. According to Zecharia Sitchin, the quarry marks had mistakes that were consistent with the definitive book on Egyptian hieroglyphics that Howard-Vyse was using at the time, by E. A. Wallis-Budge.[45] Skeptics have since attacked Sitchin's data, some believe conclusively— perhaps in a desperate bid to prevent the demise of orthodox Egyptology's dating of the Great Pyramid.[46] To me, Sitchin's data is extremely convincing, and conventional scholars simply do not want to let go of their prized belief systems.

Earth Proportions in Pyramid Measurements

Sir Isaac Newton had heard of ancient legends suggesting the Great Pyramid's measurements revealed the exact proportions of the Earth. It is entirely possible that this information came to him through secret societies that were widely popular in his time. Newton was very interested in this idea, as without an exact measurement of the Earth's circumference, he wouldn't have the right information to properly create his new theory of gravitation. All Newton had to go on was Eratosthenes's measurements from Greek times, which did not fit his theory accurately enough.

After studying the best-available pyramid measurements very closely, Newton concluded the Great Pyramid had been built using two different measuring lengths, which he called cubits, honoring the old traditions— and he dubbed them the "profane" cubit and the "sacred" cubit.[47] Newton believed the King's Chamber was based on a profane cubit of 20.63 British inches, which would then make it *exactly* 20 by 10 cubits in size. This measuring unit is what researchers like Lemesurier call the Royal Cubit. The longer, more arcane sacred cubit he found elsewhere was about 25 British inches in length. One twenty-fifth of this distance was naturally very close to the British inch, and Newton felt this might also be significant. Again, let's not forget that the Granite Slab in the Antechamber, encoding the 2012 and 2013 prophetic dates so precisely, is a "Rosetta stone" that reveals the Royal Cubit, Sacred Cubit, and Egyptian

Inch. Unfortunately for Newton, all the debris piled up around the outside base of the pyramid made the earlier measurements incorrect, so he never found the precise figures for the Earth's measurements that he was looking for.[48] Newton eventually used French astronomer Jean Picard's measurements to formulate his theory of gravitation.[49] And yes . . . it seems likely that Jean Picard was the inspiration for the name of the captain in *Star Trek: The Next Generation*.

CHAPTER TWENTY

Historic Events Encoded in the Great Pyramid

ccording to Lemesurier in *The Great Pyramid Decoded*, perhaps:

the Pyramid's designer wished to show that his predictions were "based" on a cyclic view of history . . . derived from the precession of the equinoxes. . . . We are faced with the interesting notion that history tends to repeat itself in some respects every twenty-six thousand years or so. . . . In terms of current historical and archeological theory the notion sounds wildly fantastic, of course, and yet, in view of the declarations of Edgar Cayce on such topics as Atlantis, one wonders.[1]

Lemesurier continues:

[Perhaps we can] more justly conceive of the progression of the ages in terms of a spiral. The march of evolution and history, in other words, displays a circular motion, but each revolution takes place at a different level (presumably a higher one) and is characterized by accomplishments of a different order. Indeed, the fact that the ancient Aztecs apparently regarded the conch-shell as symbolic of the succeeding ages

would suggest that they subscribed to some such notion. Nor
is the idea without its distinguished modern adherents: even
Einstein is alleged to have subscribed to it.[2]

This idea of repeating cycles of history is so significant that I wrote an
entire book dedicated to it: *The Synchronicity Key*. Later on, Lemesurier
said:

> the Pyramid's designer seems to have seen human history—
> and with it, presumably, the very development of the human
> soul—as basically cyclic or spiral in form. . . . [Perhaps] the
> present reduced-design Pyramid denotes in some way the
> "imperfect," reincarnating human soul spiraling on its inexo-
> rable karmic way towards union with the eternal or divine.[3]

And on page 287, Lemesurier said:

> There appears to be nothing improbable in a cyclic view of
> world history. In fact the only real obstacle to the more gen-
> eral acceptance of such a view is the apparent lack of specific
> archeological evidence to back it up—which may have more
> than a little to do with lack of knowledge of what to look for
> or where exactly to look for it. Whether, as Edgar Cayce has
> claimed, such evidence will in due course be found, only time
> will tell.[4]

The evidence for a cyclical view of history is quite extensive, and far
outside the scope of this book. One of the most prominent cycles in
which history is repeating itself is the 2,160-year Age of the Zodiac, of
which there are exactly twelve in the "Great Year" or precession. This
bizarre time-loop phenomenon may help explain how the Pyramid
Timeline could have such prophetic accuracy, as we will explore in this
chapter with far more detail. The idea that the pyramid's interior passageways contained a Prophecy in Stone was not openly explored until
Robert Menzies proposed it in 1865, but the Founding Fathers clearly

appeared to be aware that the Great Pyramid foretold a coming Golden Age. A lot of people are disturbed by this connection now, and invoke the dreaded Illuminati in any discussion about it—but I think it's important to remain objective and consider the available facts. We'll discuss this more later on. For now, I'll wrap up our Great Pyramid history lesson from the last chapter with the most recent investigations. Each of these pioneers made significant contributions—either wittingly or unwittingly—to the concept of a Pyramid Timeline.

A Top Skeptic Proves Himself Wrong with Science

In 1881, Sir W. M. Flinders Petrie published incredibly precise surveying measurements he'd made in his epic book *Pyramids and Temples of Gizeh*. He had hoped to completely demolish the idea of a Pyramid Timeline with the facts, probably because his father was a devout Pyramidologist. The level of precision Petrie used to make his measurements was so extreme that it bordered on the ridiculous. Petrie was also innovative enough to walk around outside the Great Pyramid in nothing but his pink underwear, so he wouldn't be bothered by drunk, disorderly Victorian tourists.[5] In today's society I don't think that would work—there would be images and video of him all over social media. To my own surprise, questionable sites like Wikipedia still assert that Petrie proved there is "no scientific support" to the "alleged numerical coincidences" of the Great Pyramid[6]—even while they openly admit that the Pyramid Inch is precisely one five-hundred-millionth of the Earth's diameter from pole to pole, a fact proven by Petrie's own measurements. Of course, no mention is made of the many engineering feats that are simply not possible to duplicate with any technology available in our own time—like the stunningly perfect leveling of the base of the pyramid, which is never off by more than half an inch.

Here's the funny part: According to Peter Lemesurier:

> Petrie . . . was blissfully unaware . . . that his own data actually validated up to the very hilt the Pyramidologists'

earlier mathematical claims concerning the Pyramid's dimensions. . . . To have one's basic premises unwittingly and irrevocably vindicated by the efforts of one's fiercest opponent is a stroke of good fortune such as rarely befalls the theorist. But that that confirmation should come from the eminent Petrie himself was a turn of events that even the most optimistic Pyramidologist could scarcely have hoped for.[7]

The Pyramid Timeline Investigation Heats Up

John and Morton Edgar continued the investigation into the Pyramid Timeline in 1923 with *The Great Pyramid Passages and Chambers.* Two years later, D. Davidson and H. Aldersmith published their own influential work entitled *The Great Pyramid: Its Divine Message.* Dr. Adam Rutherford released his enormous five-volume *Pyramidology* in 1957, and twenty years later, Peter Lemesurier published *The Great Pyramid Decoded,* having worked with Rutherford in detail. Lemesurier summarized and updated all these prior works, and continued revising his conclusions with the graphically rich *Decoding the Great Pyramid,* as well as *Gods of the Dawn* in 1999. Lemesurier's estate was very helpful when I approached them about the writing of this book. I thank them for their cooperation and look forward to discussing the Pyramid Timeline in this and other works.

The Pyramid Timeline is such a technical subject that it does take an entire book to explain it in full detail. Although Lemesurier's book is highly technical, it contains everything you need to know for an advanced study. It does appear that the source of the Law of One series designed this prophetic system with the Atlantean priest-king Ra-Ptah, "hiding the message in plain sight" so as to avoid violating the Law of Free Will. As explained in the previous chapter, Piazzi Smyth's star alignment gives us the year we begin counting from—now corrected to 2141 BC—and the Scored Lines, which appear about forty feet after the entrance into the Descending Passage, represent the location we use for the year 2141 BC within the masonry of the Great Pyramid. Then, we simply move through the passageways, counting one Pyramid Inch for every year. The idea that a Pyramid Inch could indeed represent a year was well established on the exterior, since we find the exact length of the precession of the equinoxes in the diagonals—for a total of 25,826.4 Pyramid Inches.

If we accept that Ra built the Great Pyramid, this again flags the importance of the 25,000-year cycle they mention so repeatedly in the Law of One series. By the time I read the Law of One series, I already had been deeply studying *Great Pyramid Decoded* for two and a half years, and was working hard to understand the Ascension prophecies encoded in the Pyramid Timeline. Lemesurier's take on it was admittedly Christian, in that he was expecting to see a physical manifestation of the Second Coming of Christ at the time symbolized by the Boss and Granite Leaf in the Antechamber. In his unique, recalibrated interpretation of the timeline, the first sign of the Messiah would appear in late 2034, with a physical appearance by the autumn of 2039.[8] By leaving the timescale at "one inch equals one year," we instead have the dates of 2012 and 2013, and obviously no such Messianic appearance has occurred.

The Law of One series did give their perspective on the interesting idea of a possible Messianic return in Session 17, Question 22: "I will attempt to sort out this question. It is difficult. This entity [Jesus] became aware that it was not an entity of itself, but operated as a messenger of the One Creator, whom this entity saw as love. This entity was aware that this cycle was in its last portion and spoke to the effect that those of its consciousness would return at the harvest. The particular mind/body/spirit complex you call Jesus is, as what you would call an entity, not to return except as a member of the Confederation occasionally speaking through a channel. However, there are others of the identical congruency of consciousness that will welcome those to the fourth density. This is the meaning of the returning."[9]

I picked up *Decoded* at the same bookstore, on the same day that I received my copy of Richard C. Hoagland's *The Monuments of Mars.* The Law of One material made the entire discussion of the Pyramid Timeline far more understandable, and definitely verified that the author of the Pyramid Timeline was able to "live outside of time" and see future events with stunning clarity.

So, once we know the starting location and accept the basic premise that one Pyramid Inch equals one year, we then look for any changes in direction, shape, stone composition, or measurements. We also want to check the level or course of stone any given position corresponds to, when seen from the outside. The key is to study the potential symbolism of these changes, and then look at our own history and see if anything noteworthy happened during these times. The results are very interesting, and again it heavily ties in with Christian concepts. Everything points back to a very clear and unambiguous Ascension prophecy. I do find it truly tragic that none of my colleagues have ever even touched the Pyramid Timeline information at the time of this writing, for it is so rich with detail, complexity, and prophecy.

Dream Analysis 101 Returns

Think back to our chapter "Dream Analysis 101" (chapter 3), where I talked about how the direction you travel in a dream can have symbolic meanings. Let's assume that this symbolism is essentially a universal feature of the collective subconscious, and that in a society of dream interpreters, everyone would discover this for themselves. The same exact logic applies within the Great Pyramid. If a passageway is heading down, the Pyramid Timeline researchers see this as representing a decrease in the overall quality of life on Earth, and therefore a greater amount of difficulty, strife, and challenge. Similarly, if a passageway heads upward, this could represent an improvement in our lives—a progressive movement forward. It may still be difficult to climb, but we are continually making progress all along the way.

Another important point Peter Lemesurier made is that the pyramid's designer did apparently intend to have it tell a story. This story does seem to have all the essential elements of the Hero's Journey, which the Law of One indicates is a Galactic template that all of us must go through in a series of individual archetypes. When we look at the image of the Pyramid's passages and chambers from a side view, where they all appear in a straight, vertical line, we see that it creates a stylized stick-man figure inside the pyramid. The Subterranean Chamber looks like feet, the Grotto looks like male genitalia, the Queen's Chamber would be the heart, the King's Chamber is the head, and the narrow relieving chambers and A-shaped granite slabs above them form a kinglike crown for the head to wear. Thus, the Pyramid Timeline is the story of the Hero—the Logos that all of us are in the process of awakening into embodying.

To stay within the logic of the collective Hero's Journey story apparently told by the pyramid's designer, we must begin by going through the Descending Passage. There would be no visible sign of the Ascending Passage if you walked into the pyramid before Caliph Al-Mamoun smashed his way through it. The only thing you could see is the pathway going down. This seems to indicate how we all must go through a phase of materialism and selfishness in the awakening process.

As we go farther and farther down this passage in time, we head into materialism, world hunger, devastating wars, and Earth changes, which brings us to the global difficulties we are now facing. Although this journey is associated with ever-increasing selfishness and materialism, our desire for greater and greater worldly comforts fuels many advances in technology as well. It isn't until the end of the 25,000-year cycle, or Great Year, that our technology finally turns on us and reveals that it can potentially destroy the entire Earth. This shows us the dark side of all the progress we've made. World War I, World War II, 9/11, and the "Great Recession" all appear very prominently in this sense.

The First Encoded Historic Event Is the Exodus

The Pyramid Timeline shows us important historical events through changes in the structure and measurements of a passageway as it goes along. Without getting into the exact mathematical codes for each measurement, which takes an entire book to properly explain, this simple system of noting whatever changes occur during the "one inch equals one year" scale at least allows us to understand what years are being flagged by the Pyramid Timeline. The first significant change in the Descending Passage is the moment when we discover that the Granite Plug blocked off the Ascending Passage. In the timeline, this apparently corresponds to March 30, 1453 BC. According to Lemesurier, his mentor Dr. Adam Rutherford cites an impressive body of evidence that this is the exact time when Moses led the Exodus from Egypt.[10] Also, as we discover on page 51 of *Decoded*, the red rock of the granite plug we pass in this area is virtually identical with the stone we find on Mount Horeb. Moses allegedly received the Ten Commandments on two blocks of stone taken from this same mountain. So it appears that this granite was deliberately installed into the pyramid in advance, to further reveal that the timeline would be referring to Moses in this area.

This is a pivotal event in the history of Judaism, and therefore of Western society as a whole. It also would have occurred in the future from when the Great Pyramid is now believed to have been built— starting in 10,490 BC, according to both the Cayce Readings and Robert Bauval's precession-encoded measurement. The idea that the Pyramid Timeline signaled such an important Judeo-Christian event is offensive to pyramid researchers who do not want to see any connection between the Great Pyramid and Christianity, but if you can remain open-minded to this idea, it is highly interesting. Dr. Rutherford felt the Exodus also provides a great deal of symbolism about our collective struggle to reach the purported Golden Age. Spiritual people are often forced to confront the elites of their day and form their own movement away from conventional structures in order to embrace freedom. Whether the Exodus story is literally true or not, the symbolic meaning of this legend is worth considering as the first significant part of the pyramid's internal message—once we've spotted the exact length of the 25,000-year cycle on the outside of the pyramid, and interpreted the Ascension symbolism of its yet-to-be finished capstone.

In the Exodus, the Hebrew people in Egypt were fleeing a cruel and unjust world where they were held as slaves. When the pharaoh would not let them leave the country, the angel of death killed all the firstborn Egyptian children, passing over the Hebrew households. The pharaoh was then convinced by this highly disturbing event to allow the Hebrews to leave. The arrival of Moses represented an early manifestation of powerful spiritual forces on Earth, helping lead the way to freedom and liberation. None of these people ever thought they'd be able to break the bonds of their cruel enslavement, but Moses spoke for all of them when he said, "Let my people go."

It is important to point out that the Law of One series does indicate that the Yahweh that Moses was in contact with originated as a positive entity, but then was replaced by a negative entity masquerading as positive due to Moses's own inability to avoid temptations from others. This was partly explained in Session 16, Question 19: "The one called Moishe was open to impression and received the Law of One in its most simple form. However, the information became negatively oriented due to his people's pressure to do specific physical things in the third-density planes. This left the entity open for the type of information and philosophy of a self-service nature."[11]

The trip taken by Moses and his supporters was not without difficulty. They seemed cornered when they reached the Red Sea, but Moses miraculously parted the waters and continued to go forward. This is a perfect example of the Hero's Journey story line, where an All Is Lost point is reached, but then a miraculous event allows them to survive. Moses and his people spent forty years wandering through the desert. This could symbolize how even those with a strong spiritual path will still have to endure many hardships. However, there were blessings as well, including edible food, or manna, that would appear in the mornings, as well as water that spurted up from a rock. The symbolic lesson here could be that even in the worst of times, the pilgrims were always taken care of by mysterious spiritual forces. Jordan Maxwell is one of a series of researchers who now have concluded that the descriptions of manna are consistent with mushrooms, which these people may have been unfamiliar with until they required them for basic survival.

The Israelites did eventually reach the Promised Land, thus giving the story a happy ending. The Golden Age prophecies suggest that everyone will experience the Ascension event and get where they need to go—whether that means they repeat the cycle or graduate. Therefore, the story of the Exodus could represent a "hologram," or a foreshadowing, of the greater message the pyramid is ultimately intended to convey for all of humanity. Either way, it is the very first historic event we are alerted to after the start date of the timeline itself.

The Next Ascension Turning Point Is AD 1223

Nothing else changes in the Descending Passage until AD 1223, where we reach the hidden entrance to the Well-Shaft. Again, the Well-Shaft appears to symbolize the path we all must take when we begin having a spiritual awakening. We literally have to smash our way through the obstacles and difficulties in life, much like the idea of spending forty days in the desert, before we can reach a place of stability, balance, and true happiness. Peter Lemesurier associates AD 1223 with the teachings of Saint Francis of Assisi, who helped create the opportunity to reform Christian thought back to its original mystical core.

Saint Francis wrote the guidelines that governed all monastic life thereafter, and these writings were officially confirmed by the Pope on November 29, 1223.[12] The first Franciscan monastery was founded in England this same year.[13] Saint Francis is also documented as having created the first nativity scene on December 25, 1223.[14] This fascinated the people, bringing them closer to the story of Jesus's birth, and triggered a renewed interest in their spirituality. Now we have the first and second dates in the Pyramid Timeline having direct Christian correlations.

The following year, Saint Francis was the first to develop *stigmata*— the psychic manifestation of wounds on his own body that mirrored those of Jesus.[15] This is another very significant event in Western history, perhaps representing the earliest manifestation, in a Christian saint, of the type of supernatural abilities that many more of us may develop as we move through the Ascension process.

Lemesurier also refers to 1223 as the time period when humanity be-gan "coming of age"—when our thought processes began taking us out of the Dark Ages and moving us into the modern scientific era. Since he did not go into detail, I continued doing more research myself, and found other interesting new leads. As one example, the Smithsonian Institution officially certified the year 1223 as the year glazed pottery first appeared in the world—a new technology brought to Japan from China.[16] As another example, during the birth of the nation of Spain, they founded their prestigious university in Salamanca in this exact same year. Salamanca "was the source of the artistic, educational and cultural enlightenment that fueled Spain's Golden Age."[17] Universities were not very common in the 1200s. Other than in Arabic lands, this school was one of the first of its kind—and Spain was leading the way in those early years.

Spain had an important role in sailing the world's oceans and discovering new lands—significantly expanding the scope of Western civilization—and it all began in AD 1223 with the founding of Salamanca. With the dawning of scientific knowledge, humanity now had the opportunity to become a worldwide civilization, paving the way for our eventual Ascension. Thus, it seems perfectly appropriate that in the year 1223, the spiritual seekers of humanity began blasting their way up through the Well-Shaft to the spiritual heights in the upper chambers.

Prophecy of the Renaissance and a Global Dark Night of the Soul

The next significant year in the Descending Passage, as revealed in Peter Lemesurier's *Great Pyramid Decoded,* is AD 1440. This is the exact year the Renaissance began, which is widely accepted as having originated with an artistic debate between Ghiberti and Brunelleschi. The year 1440 is also when John Gutenberg invented the first movable-type printing press, though he'd made nonmoving prototypes since 1436.[18] If you read *The Synchronicity Key* and have studied my conclusions about the science of cycles of repeating time, you'll recall that the year 1440 is also two exact 720-year cycles after Jesus's birth. The 720-year cycle is precisely one-third of the 2,160-year Age of the Zodiac. In *Synchronicity,* I study this and a variety of other interrelated and fascinating cycles. The printing press was another critical discovery that directly helped usher in the modern age of technology and worldwide travel, communication, and knowledge. Again, this paved the way for our Ascension by allowing us the freedom to communicate and educate ourselves about the various pathways to higher consciousness.

Soon after this point in the timeline, the Descending Passage stops sloping downward on a diagonal, and instead begins moving forward on a flat, horizontal plane, leading into the Subterranean Chamber—which becomes humanity's greatest moment of challenge and initiation. If we draw a line out from the ceiling of the horizontal part of the Descending Passage and extend it back over to the diagonal, that year is AD 1440. Furthermore, if you draw a line out from the bottom of the tunnel the same way, it crosses the diagonal of the Descending Passage in 1521—the significance of which I'll explain below. The pyramid's designer had to deliberately narrow the width of the passageway once it shifted into the horizontal area to make these two alignments fit properly. This also means that any movement through the tunnel after this point becomes even more claustrophobic, literally forcing you down on your hands and knees. This should definitely be considered a key part of any intended symbolic message.

The year 1521 is highly significant in our history. As one example, Spain is on record as conquering the Aztecs in 1521. The Spanish tragically burned entire libraries of precious ancient records, claiming they contained nothing but superstitious beliefs.[19] In addition, 1521 is considered to be the exact year the Reformation started, which gave common people access to the Bible and made possible the birth of Protestant denominations of Christianity. Although Martin Luther first nailed his list of ninety-five grievances against the Roman church on the door at Wittenberg on October 31, 1517, it wasn't until April 18, 1521, that he stood before the Pope and his leadership at the Diet of Worms and refused to renounce the books he had written on Christianity.[20] According to one scholar, Luther's bravery in the face of the empire's greatest power in 1521 was "the moment in the world's history to which Christendom has been looking forward. . . . So great is the rejoicing in Germany that for a moment it may seem that the Emperor's power is in danger rather than Luther and his adherents."[21] So yet again, we are seeing how neatly the pyramid's hidden message ties in with the development of the Christian faith. No special tricks or inappropriate changes are required . . . you simply keep counting with the system of one inch equals one year.

During the time window of 1440 to 1521, we also have the fall of Constantinople in 1453, which effectively ended the Roman Empire. This clearly represents the end of a major era in the movement of human history, opening the way for new cycles to take place. Columbus "discovered" America in 1492, as one key part of the circumnavigation of the Earth by European civilization during this time. The conquering of the Aztecs and the burning of their precious ancient libraries in 1521 revealed the wanton disrespect and destruction of traditional cultures that occurred as a result of these Western expansions. This trend has unfortunately often continued ever since.

Another key measurement Lemesurier identifies in this area of the timeline, where there is a distinct "bend" between the diagonal and the horizontal section of the passageway, points to the year 1506. Christopher Columbus died on May 20, 1506, which the higher forces may have seen as a relief.[22] The greatest and most famous Islamic university, the Nizamiyah, was fully restored in 1506, showing a key step forward in our overall education.[23] This is also the year that Nicholas V began renovating St. Peter's Basilica in Rome, the "great architectural symbol of the power and universality of the papacy,"[24] directly over the foundations of Constantine's original site from AD 324, which was now in decaying ruins.[25]

The building of St. Peter's in 1506 required a huge amount of money from the entire Christian world to finance,[26] and it remains the seat of Vatican power to this very day. Nicholas V also built it to house the Vatican Library—consolidating the many literary treasures of the Roman Empire in a single location. These treasures included ancient documents from the Library of Alexandria that multiple insiders have told me date back to extraterrestrial civilizations before they ever even arrived on Earth. The burning of the library was allegedly just a cover operation, and apparently all the important ancient records were relocated to the Vatican before the fires were set. The only records that actually burned in the fire were things like tax and census documents, according to multiple insiders.

Emery Smith is another insider who revealed that the "Library" of Alexandria is also a wonderland of advanced ancient technology that has all been hidden away from us, while it continues to be developed in secret. Therefore, the construction of St. Peter's effectively sealed off many ancient secrets from the Western world in a heavily fortified area.[27] That makes the year 1506 very significant in light of the designers of the Pyramid, who appear to have known that the truth of our ancient history would be hidden away from the public by powerful forces—thus requiring that they write it in stone.

Using the same logic that reveals the 1506 date in the bend between the diagonal and the horizontal sections of the Descending Passage, Lemesurier also uses straightforward geometry to reveal that the year 1510 is of significance. It is the year Martin Luther first visited Rome and witnessed the extravagances of the Pope and the Cardinals. This shook his belief in the infallibility of the papacy, and he soon discovered numerous places in the Bible that contradicted the idea of having a pope.[28] This led to the creation of his list of ninety-five grievances, which he finished seven years after his initial trip to Rome in 1510.

Hence, all the precursors to Luther's triggering of the Reformation in 1521, as revealed in the timeline, began in 1510—which was also flagged by the timeline! Already, it should be obvious that the "coincidences" are stacking up. These are definitely not just random years in our history, but represent critical turning points that historians could look back upon—or in this case look forward into, since even the most mainstream interpretation of when the Great Pyramid was constructed is thousands of years before these events transpired.

A Critical Historical Period from 1767 to 1848

After 1521, there are no new changes in the Descending Passage until we reach what is known as the Recess, or Lesser Chamber. This is an area where the ceiling of the passage suddenly rises for a period of time, and becomes all rough and ragged, looking like it's been smashed out. This foreshadows the bumpy floor of the Subterranean Chamber itself. There is a clear indication in dreamlike symbolic language that the tortured look of the ceiling indicates that this is meant to symbolize a time of great ordeal for humanity. The Recess begins in 1767 and ends in 1848. As it turns out, 1767 is the year the British imposed a tax on all tea in the American colonies. This was the direct Inciting Incident that triggered the American Revolution just nine years later, in 1776. Regardless of your opinions about America, it did become a dominant world power, and the Pyramid Timeline indicates that these events did lead to our collective dark night of the soul—as well as providing the fuel for us to discover a way out.

As we travel through this rough period from 1767 to 1848, we have the bloody French Revolution of 1789. This ushered in Napoleon's reign, which led to many violent wars as he attempted to build a huge empire. The carnage didn't end until the Battle of Waterloo in 1815. All the early struggles of the foundation of America occurred during this time, including the War of 1812. Another revolution occurred in France in 1830. Belgium seceded from the Netherlands that same year. The year 1845 was given critical significance by the position of the Great Step in the Ascending Passage, as we revealed in the previous chapter. It correlates with the first commercial availability of instant communication at a distance through the telegraph, as well as the theory of evolution and other advances. Karl Marx wrote his Communist Manifesto in 1847, just one year before the Pyramid's Recess comes to an end in 1848.[29]

Though many of us have now forgotten this moment in the sands of time, the pyramid's designer couldn't have possibly picked a better year for the Recess to end. An incredible number of countries all over Europe revolted in 1848—even though there appeared to be no common cause. It was as if some sort of greater movement was taking place, which some historians call a "revolutionary wave." Something as peculiar as a wave of angry uprisings, happening in so many countries at once for different reasons, may well be showing us "energetic" fingerprints of some kind—influencing humanity on a mass scale.

According to Wikipedia as of 2009, when I first compiled notes on this subject:

The European Revolutions of 1848, known in some countries as the Spring of Nations, Springtime of the Peoples or the

Year of Revolution, were a series of political upheavals throughout the European continent. Described by some historians as a revolutionary wave, the period of unrest began in France and then, further propelled by the French Revolution of 1848, soon spread to the rest of Europe. Although most of the revolutions were quickly put down, there was a significant amount of violence in many areas, with tens of thousands of people tortured and killed. While the immediate political effects of the revolutions were largely reversed, the long-term reverberations of the events were far-reaching. . . . Great Britain, the Kingdom of the Netherlands, the Russian Empire . . . and the Ottoman Empire were the *only* major European states to go without a national revolution over this period. . . . These revolutions arose from such a wide variety of causes that it is difficult to view them as resulting from a coherent movement or social phenomenon.[30]

The Arrival of World War I in 1914

The entire period of 1767 to 1848 was characterized by the pyramid's bumpy, damaged ceiling. This seemed to predict a period of great social upheaval, foreshadowing the chaos that would come later on. In 1914 is when the smooth, flat floor of the passage drops into the churning rage of the Subterranean Chamber. This is the year that World War I began like a sudden rushing collapse of dominoes—with country after country declaring war against one another, all in the same year. Let's also not forget that this same date appears prominently underneath the Great Step, when the Ascending Passage slope finally "hits the wall."

When we read through the history ourselves, it almost appears as if a sort of mass insanity was taking place all over the world. This was not just something that was discovered after the fact. In 1893, Dr. Adam Rutherford's Egyptologist father predicted "an ominous event of great magnitude" in 1914, based on a similar alignment he found in the Grand Gallery—as we discussed.[31] This is an example where the timeline was successfully used to predict future events—though Rutherford was wrong about other things, and did not succeed in his own attempts to prognosticate our immediate future destiny.[32]

According to Peter Lemesurier, in 1914 the traditional world, and all its negativity, really became exposed and turned upon by the people—in America, Europe, and the Far East. Major revolutions took place in Russia and China. Another critical element that Lemesurier overlooked, because the awareness of the importance of this situation did not largely exist back in 1977, was that the Federal Reserve began operating in the United States this very same year—on November 26, 1914. The American financial system was handed over to a privatized corporation of international bankers who could potentially manipulate the currency supply for their own ends. One classic reference work for this discussion is *The Creature from Jekyll Island* by G. Edward Griffin.[33]

However, the events of 1914 weren't all negative: Albert Einstein became director of the Kaiser Wilhelm Physical Institute and emigrated to Germany, publishing his General Relativity Theory two years later.[34] Relativity gave us breathtaking new insights into space and time—revealing that everything is ultimately created by a unified source of energy, where space and time work together in a greater whole. Also in 1914, there was a massive expansion of scientific, military, and commercial technology, as well as significant advances in the field of medicine that allowed world population numbers to substantially increase.[35] These events dealt fatal blows to the entrenched powers and negative elements of the materialistic world—and we are still experiencing their positive repercussions today. Lemesurier cites multiple symbolic clues, in the form of measurements in this area and their greater apparent meanings, that 1914 represented a time of significant spiritual rebirth for humanity.

It is not precisely correct to state that 1914 is the next significant year in the timeline after 1848. The ceiling of the Subterranean Chamber starts in 1911—three years before the floor drops out in 1914. This suggests that many precursors to the events of 1914 should be found in 1911, and the evidence does support this idea. For example, Italy declared war on Turkey in 1911, and although every other nation in Europe opposed it, no one took action.[36] There was also a revolution in central China.

Germany created a crisis throughout Europe by sending a gunship into a closed port of Morocco to challenge French dominance of the area, causing great upset—but no action.[37]

The first aircraft landing on a United States naval battleship was accomplished in 1911, as well as the first coast-to-coast flight across the US. This directly set the stage for the mechanized warfare of the twentieth century and beyond, which would so soon come into play in 1914. And most interestingly, on May 15, 1911, Standard Oil was ordered to break up its thirty-seven interlocking firms, demolishing its legendary industrial monopoly. Their appeal to the Supreme Court was turned down.[38] The owners of Standard Oil then reorganized and combined their wealth and influence with other international bankers to create the Federal Reserve, which, as noted earlier, took control of the American financial system on November 16, 1914.[39] Nonetheless, the breakup of Standard Oil may well be a harbinger of much greater global disclosures and antitrust maneuvers that many are eagerly anticipating at the time I finish writing this book. The more we look at how well these pieces fit together, the more impossible it is to imagine that all this is somehow a coincidence. I believe skeptics simply reject the whole thing rather than taking the time required to explain how so many historically significant events could have been encoded into the Great Pyramid. Whether or not you study the numerological significance of the measurements in these areas, simply counting one inch as one year, and looking for obvious changes, generates these results.

The Age of Hell on Earth

From this point forward, the pyramid's floor is a mess. Humanity undergoes seemingly unending challenges and difficulties—which is an apt description of the twentieth century. It should come as little surprise that the next significant point, as we move through the uncertainty of the Subterranean Chamber, appears in 1945. This, of course, is when World War II finally ended.[40] It is literally astonishing that the Great Pyramid so precisely flags the beginning of World War I as well as the end of World War II. Structurally, the date of 1945 appears in the exact center of a symmetrical area in the pyramid, as viewed from the side. (See the next image for reference.)

From the side view, we see what look like two pillars coming up from the floor. This is a classical symbolic representation of duality, which very much fits this period of time. Between these two pillars, it appears that a half circle comes down from the ceiling. This very likely symbolizes the promise of peace, spiritual renewal, and Ascension. It may even represent a direct intervention from a higher reality. Very interestingly, the first widely known modern UFO sightings began shortly after this point, with the Roswell crash in 1947.

The floor of the Subterranean Chamber continues to violently fluctuate in height from this point. Most pyramid researchers consider this floor to be "unfinished," as if such a marvelously perfected monument in the desert would somehow have been left abandoned. This is almost certainly not the case. The grotesquely distorted floor is using dream symbolism to indicate that this entire period of history is replete with wars, peril, mass death, stress, and chaos. Furthermore, the overall quality of life shows a slow, gradual downtrend, as seen in the height of the floor, right up until a year that Lemesurier believes is 2004. As we will see in just a moment, he also revealed that there is a rare three-year period of "wiggle room" on this measurement. On page 132 of my edition of *Great Pyramid Decoded*, he said, "Moreover, there are indications that the datings for the whole Chamber may be adjustable to the extent of some three years." Then on page 134, he clarified this by saying, "the Chamber seems to have what we have described as an 'adjustable join' with the passage leading into it. . . . Consequently a tolerance of at least +/- three years should be applied to all datings given." The date Lemesurier indicates as 2004 is therefore almost certainly intended by the Pyramid's designer to be 2001, which is when 9/11 took place. At this point in the Pyramid Timeline, which Lemesurier admits could be 2001, there is a sudden, massive drop in the height of the floor. This leads us into what the pyramid researchers called the Pit of Ordeal. Although Lemesurier

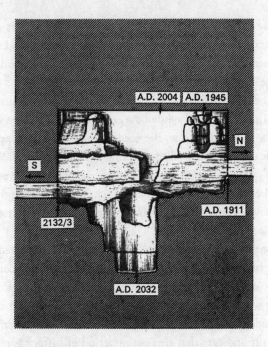

Lemesurier's Original Diagram of Subterranean
Chamber and Dates (Without Three-Year Back-
date Adjustment)

wrote his book in 1977, and most prophecy books of his time were bet-
ting all their money on the year 2000, in *The Great Pyramid Decoded,* we
see 2001 as the year where "the bottom will fall out of the world."

Again, Lemesurier speculated in 1977 that there was indeed a three-
year window of error throughout the Subterranean Chamber. On page
124 of *The Great Pyramid Decoded,* he got more specific by indicating
that since the ceiling of the chamber begins in 1911, but the floor doesn't
drop out until 1914, everything in this section could thus be backdated
by three years. That makes 9/11 happen at the exact time we drop into
the Pit of Ordeal in the Pyramid Timeline.

The Pit then reaches its deepest point just a few years later. If we scale
both of the following dates back by three years and then otherwise recite
Lemesurier's decoding of the prophecy exactly as it was written, this is

what we see on page 135: "Then, in around 2001, 'the bottom will fall out of the world.' Both world-civilization and its technologies will quickly collapse to rock-bottom by 2007, and will remain at that level for at least fifteen years."

The year 2007 is certainly an interesting date. The great economic collapse of 2008 really began with what scholars call the 2007 Financial Crisis. This was when the Federal Reserve responded to the massive subprime mortgage crisis by doing their first mega-bailout, where they added 24 billion dollars into the banking system as of August 2007.[41] According to *The Balance,* this was a response to "the breakdown of trust that occurred between banks the year before the 2008 financial crisis."[42] The US Treasury created a 75-billion-dollar superfund in an attempt to bail out subprime mortgages on November 21, 2007, and home foreclosures in December 2007 were 97 percent higher than in December 2006, increasing by a total of 75 percent for the year 2007.[43] All these events were the direct precursors of the full meltdown that happened in 2008.

The further and further we go in this investigation, the more impossible it becomes that these dates in the Great Pyramid Timeline could be a product of random coincidence. The Pyramid designers even politely remind us here that the great 2008 economic collapse truthfully began in 2007. I remember reading this prophecy back in 1993 and wondering what would cause our world to collapse to "rock-bottom" in the time interval of 2007 to 2010—and now we know.

It is also interesting to read Lemesurier's prophecy of what will happen to people on the Ascension path during this time frame. On page 157, if we adjust the 2004 date to 2001 as permitted and change the language to be gender-neutral, we have the following: "As for the initiates of the upper path, rebirth during the present era is foreseen as an essential preliminary to their entry into the Final Age of rebirth into the spirit-planes, destined to lead ultimately to union with the Divine. . . . These efforts will be aided, if not precipitated, by a period of terrible physical upheaval starting in 1914 and reaching its peak in AD 2001. All people, including the enlightened, will have to undergo this period of ordeal, but it is those who place the greatest value on physical things who, inevitably, will suffer most acutely from it. By many, however, the need for a complete re-orientation of values will be seen and fully acted upon, and a civilization of extraordinary vigour and achievement will ensue. A small minority . . . will none the less persist right to the end in their rejection of anything resembling true enlightenment, and for them a path of non-escape is projected by the Pyramid's designer, possibly leading to experience of a further cycle of physical existence."[44]

This concept of mass rebirth in a further cycle of physical, third-density existence is revealed in the Law of One within Session 17, Question 24: "The great majority of your peoples will repeat third density."[45] However, we do have a ray of hope in Session 65, Question 12, where it reads, "Could your planet polarize towards harmony in one fine, strong moment of inspiration? Yes, my friends. It is not probable; but it is ever possible."[46]

Since we do have a three-year "sliding scale" in the time window we are now discussing, allowing the first "bottom" of the Pit to be either 2001 or 2004, we do want to investigate both of these dates. By 2004, the Iraq War was raging, even though there was already significant public opposition. George W. Bush won a second term despite soaring unpopularity, and almost immediately signed the Intelligence Reform and Terrorism Act of 2004 in an attempt to consolidate the various intelligence agencies into the Department of Homeland Security and put all competing agencies under the control of a single national intelligence director.[47]

Then, on December 26, 2004, the greatest earthquake in over forty years struck the Pacific Ocean near Sumatra. This created a massive tsunami that killed as many as 266,000 people in the coastal regions of Indonesia and Africa.[48] This epic catastrophe was the first of the "mega-earth changes" that we are now seeing at the end of the Age. It obviously dwarfed September 11, 2001, in the number of its fatalities and the scope of destruction. The Indonesian tsunami was soon followed by Hurricane Katrina in August 2005, which was another example that our climate was changing in very powerful and dangerous ways. This seemingly validates many of the most distressing prophecies that the bottom would indeed fall out of the world in this time frame.

It is also significant to note that the great financial crisis is commonly mapped out by scientists like Jin Wook Choi as having occurred precisely between 2007 and 2010. Choi wrote a paper entitled "The 2007–2010 US financial crisis" for *The Journal of Economic Asymmetries* in 2013.[49] The paper indicates that this was only one of many studies on the 2007–2010 financial crisis.[50] This period of 2007 to 2010 is the exact three-year time window where "the bottom will fall out of the world" and "hit rock-bottom" in Lemesurier's interpretation of the Pyramid Timeline. The year 2010 is seen as the administrative end of the financial crisis, because US president Obama signed the Dodd-Frank Act in July 2010. This created the most substantial government reform of the financial system since the Glass-Steagall Act, which was implemented after the 1929 stock market crash that triggered the Great Depression.[51] The Dodd-Frank Act made it far more difficult for mortgage companies and lenders to take advantage of consumers.

1942, the Battle of Los Angeles, and Ascension

We can use this same three-year "slide" and also apply it to the end of World War II, which the Timeline dates at 1945. Let's remember that 1945 appears in symbolic terms as the first sign of hope for the coming Ascension. This three-year window backdates us to 1942, where we have the infamous Battle of Los Angeles, a favorite topic among UFO researchers. This massive UFO sighting took place over Los Angeles less than three months after Japan attacked the US at Pearl Harbor. From 3:16 to 4:14 A.M. on February 25, 1942, soldiers fired over 1,400 massive, 12.8-pound explosive antiaircraft shells at a series of brightly lit, nonmoving targets that hovered silently in the California night sky.[52] According to one eyewitness, a former chair of the Department of Anthropology at Occidental College in Los Angeles, this "official estimate" of the number of shots fired is way, way too low.[53] The main object was described as looking like "a surreal, hanging magic lantern"[54] and a "silvery, lozenge-shaped 'bug.'"[55] Several buildings were damaged by the friendly fire, three civilians were killed, and another three died from heart attacks owing to the extreme stress of the hour-long bombardment.[56]

In 1983, the Office of Air Force History reported that the "unidentified objects" (their words) were only, uh, weather balloons—yet the classic front-page newspaper photograph of the event clearly shows a flying saucer–shaped bright area being lit up by at least nine different spotlights as the "weather balloon" was being shot at.[57] None of the explosive rounds had any effect on it. Some researchers estimate it was roughly eight hundred feet in diameter.[58] The object moved directly over MGM Studios in Culver City—arguably the media capital of the world during this time frame.[59] Over one million people saw it at the time, due to the incredible volume of the chaos of gunfire in the middle of the night.[60]

According to a female air-raid warden quoted on About.com:

> It was huge! It was just enormous! And it was practically right over my house. I had never seen anything like it in my life! . . . It was just hovering there in the sky and hardly moving at all. It was a lovely pale orange and about the most beautiful thing you've ever seen. I could see it perfectly because it was very close. It was big! They sent fighter planes up and I watched them in groups approach it and then turn away. They were shooting at it but it didn't seem to matter. It was like the Fourth of July but much louder. They were firing like crazy but they couldn't touch it. I'll never forget what a magnificent sight it was. Just marvelous. And what a gorgeous color![61]

The *Long Beach Independent* wrote an editorial that said, "There is a mysterious reticence about the whole affair, and it appears that some form of censorship is trying to halt discussion on the matter."[62]

This definitely fits the Pyramid Timeline symbolism of an "intervention from above," showing that even in the depths of World War II, and the fear of real defeat at the hands of Hitler and the Japanese, there were higher powers surrounding the Earth that could not be touched by any of the weapons we now possess. Since the term *flying saucer* wasn't invented until 1947, and the acronym *UFO* wasn't coined until even later, the Battle of Los Angeles has somehow remained overlooked by the majority of the public. The whole event did appear to symbolize that our problems in the world would resolve peacefully. A very clear message was sent that these Visitors are not hostile, and that they have technology significantly more advanced than our own. In 1945, three years after the Battle of Los Angeles, the war was over—as the Pyramid Timeline implies.

Lemesurier's original date of 2010, when the floor of the Pit of Ordeal plummets to its deepest level, may have more to offer us than just a marker for the Dodd-Frank Act. On April 20, 2010, the Deepwater Horizon oil rig exploded and soon sank, creating what is now seen as the greatest ecological disaster in human history.[63] For at least several weeks after this event, the mood worldwide about it was quite apocalyptic. Two thousand ten was also the year that the European Union began collapsing, beginning with the economy of Greece in the spring of 2010.[64]

On January 13, 2010, a massive earthquake devastated Haiti and was considered by geologists to be "quite strange," as it was the worst they had seen in over two hundred years.[65] Chile then had a massive 8.8 earthquake the following month, on February 27, 2010, which was the fifth largest ever recorded.[66,67] The Chile quake was so powerful it actually shifted the tilt of the Earth's axis and shortened its length of day.[68] Mexico had a massive 7.2 quake in Baja, California, on April 4, 2010, causing tremors all the way to Arizona and Southern California.[69] An unprecedented eruption of volcanic fog from Iceland halted all European air traffic in April and May, stranding millions.[70] Indonesia had another massive tsunami on October 25, 2010,[71] which was very unusual as it seemed out of proportion to the quakes that created it, since a series of slow, mild quakes led to a massive tsunami wave.[72] Iran also had a devastating 6.5 quake on December 20, 2010.[73] This ongoing global upheaval, both in geological and financial terms with the European economic collapse, perfectly fits the obvious symbolism of the Pyramid Timeline.

With the Mayan Calendar end date of 2012 appearing precisely in the pyramid's Antechamber, and the year 2013 corresponding to the world-changing Snowden NSA revelations, we can deduce that these events are all part of the Ascension process. By going through mass initiation, we also end up experiencing the much greater likelihood of a mass spiritual awakening. I am already seeing this happen, for the darkest aspects of the negative elite used to be "fringe" subjects, but now they are essentially common knowledge. Events taking place as I write this book in the end of 2019 suggest that we are on the verge of a mass exposure of horrific conspiracies, and I will share some readings that I did on this subject from 1999 in later chapters.

From here on out, we are heading into future events and there is no way to know what will happen, if anything, although things could look pretty bleak as we continue along through the Pit of Ordeal. About the only positive is that the level of the floor never sinks any lower than it does in 2007–2010. Lemesurier indicates that the year 2032 is a significant turning point, and thanks to the three-year variance, this also should be backdated to 2029. This is only one year away from the date of 2030, where the second set of grooves appear in the Antechamber to signal the next time window where an Ascension-related mega-event could occur.

The Pit therefore gives us the second reinforcement of the prophetic date that Corey Goode, his insiders, and my own dreams have been giving as a possible time window for when the actual "solar flash" will finally occur. In Session 40, Questions 10 and 11, in the Law of One series, it says there will be a "final movement of vibratory matter, shall we say, through the quantum leap, as you would call it" at the end of the cycle. It goes on to say that "the nature of quanta is such that the movement over the boundary is that of discrete placement of vibratory level."[74] I have often used this passage in my lectures to explain that there will apparently be a "final . . . quantum leap" where the energy that makes up our basic reality "moves over the boundary" and has a "discrete placement of vibratory level" into fourth density. The dictionary definition of "discrete" is "apart or detached from others; separate; distinct."[75] Session 40, Question 11, therefore indicates that we will move into a completely separate and distinct new vibratory and dimensional level once we go through this event.

The Law of One series also directly informs us that the Earth will shift by 20 degrees on its axis as we go through this "quantum leap." One of the passages that explains this is Session 59, Question 24. The question was a follow-up to previously disclosed information: "When the planetary axes realign, will they realign 20° east of north to conform to the green vibration?" The answer was, in part, "There is every indication that this [pole shift] will occur. We cannot speak of certainties, but are aware that the grosser or less dense materials will be pulled into conformation with the denser and lighter energies which give your Logos its proceedings through the realms of experience."[76]

The source repeatedly stresses that this is not a catastrophic event for humans, despite us being told in Session 17, Question 1, that this event "will cause your planetary sphere to have some ruptures in its outer garment while making itself appropriately magnetized for fourth density. This is the planetary adjustment."[77] If you are on the Ascension path, you seemingly get a multidimensional light-body activation at this time, whereas if you are going to repeat the third-density cycle, you apparently will have a planet-hopping relocation event—like what Dr. Courtney Brown saw in his remote-viewing sessions. That relocation would still be akin to an Ascension-style event, filled with awe and mystery. Only the darkest and most negatively polarized people will actually stay on Earth to experience this shift in physical form, as my own source has repeatedly stressed.

This scenario was hinted at in Session 16, Questions 11 and 12, when it said there is only one harvest event that we will all go through in our own way: "Questioner: Is there a harvest of entities oriented towards service to self like there is a harvest here of entities oriented towards service to others? Ra: I am Ra. There is one harvest. Those able to enter fourth density through vibrational complex levels may choose the manner of their further seeking of the One Creator. Questioner: Then as we enter the fourth density there will be a split, shall we say, and part of the individuals who go into the fourth density will go to planets or places where there is service to others, and the other part will go into places where there is service to self. Is this correct? Ra: . . . This is correct."

The End of the Descending Passage Timeline

The floor height in the Subterranean Chamber still remains the same in the pit until a sudden vertical jump, going straight up, in about 2055. This, as Lemesurier indicates, represents the timeline for "materialist humanity," not those who are set to experience Ascension. Something positive will apparently happen in or around 2055 that digs everyone on this timeline out of the pit. There is another, even greater vertical jump in about 2075, and another vertical jump in about 2100, which is almost as big as the one in 2055. Only then do we see the people on this timeline finally elevated out of the last of the pit. Then we have a slow, gradual increase in height until 2132, when we finally exit the Subterranean Chamber and again end up in a tunnel that is carved like the rest of the Descending Passage. The floor becomes flat and level once more, as it had remained up until 1911–1914. However, I should also point out that, by this point, the height of the floor is now *lower* than it was when going in. The passage then continues along, experiences a brief "kink" to the west, which Peter Lemesurier interprets as a possibility of new spiritual seeking, and eventually reaches a dead end. Lemesurier believes this means the pyramid is not built to track this phase of humanity's evolution any further, even though it continues moving along.

When we go through the same timeline for the Ascending Passage and the King's Chamber, we really see only two clusters of events, as we discussed in the previous chapter. The birth, life, and resurrection of Jesus is depicted in a very precise and undeniable way, in the moment where the "roof" gets blown off and the passage becomes much, much taller and more beautiful. Then we have the Great Step, which again indicates a major shift-point for humanity that paves the final path to Ascension, providing particular focus on the dates of 1845 and 1914, right at the beginning of World War I.

Once we get into the Antechamber, we have the inset granite slab with the half-circle Boss symbol on it. As we discussed, this is interpreted as a prophecy of Ascension, which Lemesurier directly associates with the Second Coming of Christ. If you do not change the timescale at the Great Step, this Ascension harbinger was expected to happen in 2012—which was a perfect fit with the Mayan Calendar. Again, one of the main aspects of Corey Goode's contact was to explain that the time window for this event had to be moved forward, since we were not yet ready as a planet for this to happen.

Just as a reminder, I had first picked up *The Great Pyramid Decoded* on the same trip to the bookstore when I picked up my copy of Richard

C. Hoagland's *Monuments of Mars,* back in 1993. It was therefore one of the very first books I read on my quest, after finding out from the professor that UFOs really exist. Now in retrospect it is obvious that I was guided to read *The Great Pyramid Decoded* right at the beginning of my epic three-hundred-volume research period in college. The specific, corroborating details in the Law of One series were a welcome relief after struggling with *The Great Pyramid Decoded* for two and a half years. I was very impressed by the incredible accuracy of this Prophecy in Stone. There were far too many prophecy hits on very specific dates in our history for this to be any type of coincidence, and this has continued to be the case in our own recent history.

Since Ra said they existed outside of time, the Pyramid Timeline was an excellent proof of that same concept. Best of all, the timeline gave additional proof of an Ascension event that was anticipated in the exact same time window as the Mayan Calendar end date, even though Lemesurier himself did not appear to see this. I had already observed incredible synchronicity events and future prophecies in my own life.

In the Law of One series, they explain that there are people on Earth who are part of a "negative elite," guided and manipulated by negative, demonic extraterrestrials they refer to as the Orion Confederation. The Law of One further indicates and this negative group can only disrupt life on Earth and feed on the energy of our fear until we, as a planet, reach a certain state of collective evolution. This is explained in Session 11, Question 16, as follows: "The crusaders move in their chariots to conquer planetary mind/body/spirit social complexes before they reach the stage of achieving social memory."[78] When the questioner then asks "At what stage does a planet achieve social memory," the answer was "A mind/body/spirit social complex becomes a social memory complex when its entire group of entities are of one orientation or seeking. The group memory lost to the individuals in the roots of the tree of mind then become[s] known to the social complex, thus creating a social memory complex. The advantages of this complex are the relative lack of distortion in understanding the social beingness and the relative lack of distortion in pursuing the direction of seeking, for all understanding/ distortions are available to the entities of the society."[79]

This is clearly describing a world in which everyone has become telepathic, in a type of group mind. Once this happens, the negative can no longer maintain control, and the "quantum leap" is then activated. Ultimately, this means that we are in control of when the great shift will occur, and any exact estimates of when this will happen are impossible. The Internet clearly seems to be the precursor that helps usher in this mass telepathic synergy. The free flow of communication has allowed for many previously suppressed truths to finally see the light of day. The Pyramid Timeline seems to flag the coming of the Internet by stressing the importance of 1845. This again was the year we first began having instant communication at a distance via telegraph.

As I was putting all this together while reading the Law of One in 1996, a new character arrived at the Schoolhouse at just the right time to add even more intrigue to everything that was happening to me. Antonio would soon reveal that his godfather was allegedly one of the top ninety directing members of a worldwide secret organization called the Illuminati. I had previously encountered this name while reading *New World Order: The Ancient Plan of Secret Societies* by William T. Still, sometime in 1994 or 1995.[80] I had already shown the book to my housemate Eric, and had him read through the whole thing. Eric didn't believe there was any such thing as the Illuminati, but now our new housemate was saying he was friends with the top members of this same organization. The information I got from Antonio was extremely interesting—to say the least.

CHAPTER TWENTY-ONE

The First Illuminati Insider

The connections I was seeing between the Law of One series, *Cosmic Voyage* by Dr. Courtney Brown, *The Watchers* by Raymond Fowler, the prophecies of the Pyramid Timeline, and so many other pieces of my research were absolutely astonishing to me. It was somewhat hilarious to be making all of these potentially world-changing discoveries while working a really tough job for barely above minimum wage, but I was so thrilled by the discoveries I was making that it hardly seemed to matter. My friend Eric and I were living in the Schoolhouse— the beautifully remodeled 1800s brick building and art gallery in Rosendale, New York, which had four other apartments where our potential friends could live. My job allowed me to afford rent, food, and basic expenses, and I was happy. There was one woman who had been there long before the rest of us arrived and would never speak a word to any of us. Other than that, we all had quite a sense of community.

Antonio and the Illuminati

I began reading the Law of One series as of approximately February 1, 1996. I couldn't go terribly fast, for I might end up spending forty-five minutes meditating on one two-page spread before ever turning to the next one. I was nonetheless completely fascinated, and spent as many hours in the books as I possibly could. Almost every page had stunning correlations to things I had studied in the past, such as the Pyramid Timeline. I also found countless connections to information that essentially rewrote many of our most beloved branches of science, and would become the foundation of much of my life's work. The one-to-one correlation between Dr. Brown's research and statements in the Law of One will be more fully explored in the next chapter. To rest my mind, I would read other things, such as websites on the newly emerging Internet or other books.

Both Eric and I were getting almost an inundation of synchronicity during this time. It was happening so often that it could literally be hour by hour. On the Internet, I discovered the work of Terrence McKenna, who was very strongly pushing the Mayan Calendar end date of 2012 as representing some sort of cosmic dimensional shift for humanity. When I tuned in on his work with my dreams, intuition, and synchronicities, I felt he had aspects of truth, but his overall model was still flawed. One obvious synchronicity was that the first time I tried to read McKenna's stuff, the computer powered itself down to a black screen, even though we did not lose power in the rest of the house. Then it happened again when I tried to read McKenna once more. By combining this with other pieces of data that were coming in, I saw it as a sign not to get too involved—and I didn't.

Then, on February 10, 1996, I awoke with an extremely strong dream message. I was told that I needed to take the things I was learning about and write them up in a book of my own. I certainly had not been thinking of anything like this at the time, but I even got the title that I was supposed to give this new material: *Convergence.* I did end up releasing a trilogy of free books on my own website under that title, but I didn't start this until three years later, in 1999. The best aspects of that material appeared in *The Source Field Investigations,* by which time my writing skills had improved enough that I could definitely notice a difference. Right as I was bursting with inspiration and charting out what would become my future spiritual and career path, a new insider appeared in my life who took the mystery and intrigue factor to an even higher level.

A young, athletic, and charismatic man from Spain I will call Antonio first came to visit us at the Schoolhouse around February 16, 1996, according to my written journal notes from February 20 of that year.

Within a few minutes of meeting each other, Antonio and I got into a high-level conversation about subjects that my housemate Eric knew almost nothing about. This included pyramids, Atlantis, sunken architecture, the Freemasons, extraterrestrials, reverse-engineered technology, and Ascension. Antonio was admittedly impressed with how much I had discovered over the course of my research, but he had a curiously dismissive attitude. He felt I still didn't really know very much, since everything I had obtained was from books. He, on the other hand, claimed to have had direct access to a group he called the Illuminati. I had already read about this group in William T. Still's book *New World Order*, which certainly did not paint a positive portrait of this organization. However, Antonio was absolutely convinced that Still had it all wrong, and the Illuminati were the good guys in our planetary story line—even though he was never formally brought in by them as a member. He had worked in a bar where top-level members gathered, and he got to hear stories about them from his godfather. My opinions on the Illuminati were nowhere near as solid in 1996 as they would become later—particularly after reading the highly disturbing whistleblower testimony of Svali, beginning in 2000.

The full story of Antonio unfolded over the course of multiple conversations after he moved into an upstairs apartment in the Schoolhouse, which occurred about a month later. Rather than attempting to reconstruct piece by piece how I learned all this, I will just share the overview. Antonio's father had worked, if you want to call it that, as a jewel smuggler. He would buy various precious gemstones, including diamonds, at low prices, circumvent taxes and other duty fees by smuggling them through airports and customs stops, and then sell them at conventional prices in Spain. Antonio's father died under suspicious circumstances before Antonio was a teenager, but I never got the details. After his father's tragic death, Antonio was placed under the guardianship of his godfather, a medical doctor who lived on a massive Spanish estate—and was one of the wealthiest people in the country. Antonio finally ended up going to an all-boys' boarding school, but while he still lived at the mansion, he either had to stay in his room or be out in the gardens, digging rocks out of the soil. He was so heavily overworked that the only time he had to himself was at night, so he would stay up late trying to read books. Then he would be forced to get up very early the next morning, and he was therefore in constant need of extra sleep.

Antonio described how he was not allowed to sleep during the day, and there was a butler who was assigned to do a regular patrol and make sure he was awake and working when he was in his room. Antonio said the only way he could get enough sleep was to put towels down on the cold tile floor in his bathroom. He would always be half listening if the butler showed up, so he would just appear to be using the toilet. He did feel that the butler became aware of what he was doing, and decided to allow him to sleep anyway. He finally escaped by getting placed in a boarding school, which was much better. At some point, his godfather finally began speaking to him and took Antonio under his wing. Antonio eventually found out that his godfather was apparently one of the top ninety highest-ranking members of a group they called the Illuminati, and Antonio's late father had also been a member. Once Antonio became a teenager, his godfather granted him a job working in a Masonic bar in Spain to which only the highest-level members of this secret order were invited. There were interesting cryptic symbols on the wall outside the bar, one of which was triangular. These symbols indicated how high your rank must be in order to be welcomed inside.

An Ancient and Highly Powerful Secret Society

Antonio was told that the Illuminati were the secret rulers and controllers of the world. They had people in just about every country, from the highest levels on down. They were fabulously wealthy, and involved in just about everything—governments, militaries, corporations, religions, you name it. They had a very complex and elaborate set of spiritual philosophies and practices, and everything they were doing was part of a greater, secret spiritual tradition, which they believed to be very ancient, from far before Christianity started. More than once, Antonio spoke ominously about "leather aprons," which are worn in Masonic lodges, and strongly implied that he had seen these people wearing them. He also felt, or was told, that this tradition went directly back to ancient Egypt. Luckily, he was apparently never initiated into the organization. He remained a friend of very high-level people, but he was still technically an outsider.

The Illuminati believed in Atlantis, which I could easily accept, given all the research I had done. They also felt they were the surviving descendants of the mighty civilization, and had retained many of its secrets that were lost to the general public. That, to me, was very exciting. They taught Antonio that he should never have a sexual release unless it was with a woman, as otherwise he would be depleting his own supply of spiritual energy. They felt this spiritual energy must be preserved, such as for magical work of various sorts that Antonio had never been trained in, as well as for all-around vitality. This type of strict celibacy code is generally not found in positive spiritual teachings like the Law of One, and it can easily create stress, frustration, and pent-up aggression. As we already discussed, the Law of One said in Session 46, Question 12, that the deliberate repression of sexual desire magnifies the behavior of negatively polarized individuals in their violation of the free will of others when the sexual activity is then allowed.[1]

Antonio started bringing in a new woman almost every week after he moved in with us. Any time I went out to a store with him, if he met a cute girl, he would tell her she was the most beautiful woman he had ever seen. This naturally could not be true for each woman he met, and was obviously a game he was playing to see who was interested. He was incredibly smooth and unflinchingly confident, although Eric ended up being embarrassed by this and asked him not to do it when they were on an outing together. Whenever he got a new girl, we would never see the former one again. Finally, one particularly attractive woman became his girlfriend—and she also befriended the rest of us. She had recovered from a heroin addiction when she was still a teenager, and she and I connected nicely as two people who had successfully kicked a drug habit.

Antonio's godfather told him the Illuminati was an ancient secret society that was making sure humanity did not destroy itself. As an introduction, Antonio strongly encouraged me to read a book from 1983 called *The People of the Secret,* by a man with the obvious pseudonym Ernest Scott. This was clearly a code name, indicating that the author considered himself to be an earnest Scottish Rite Mason. The book was incredibly dense and hard to follow, though at times it could be quite fascinating. Much of it, honestly, went well over my head, and I felt I wouldn't be able to truly appreciate all its contents unless I had a PhD in European history. The cover features an image of planet Earth surrounded by an octagon, made out of what looks like thin, straight-lined comets, and the publishing company called itself Octagon Press, Limited. The octagon is very likely meant to indicate the shield symbol. Many whistleblowers have said the top Illuminati family is the Rothschilds, and their last name translates as "Red Shield" in German.[2]

The core premise of *The People of the Secret* is that a Hidden Directorate of nonterrestrial intelligence is secretly running our planet. I eventually realized that in the Law of One series, this corresponded to the so-called Orion Confederation, which is discussed in 131 different passages.[3] The first detailed response about the Orion Confederation as a source of some of the UFO sightings we are seeing in our skies was given in Session 7, Questions 14 and 15:

> Consider, if you will, a simple example of intentions which are bad/good. This example is Adolf. This is your vibratory sound complex. The intention is to presumably unify by choosing the distortion complex called elite from a social memory complex, and then enslaving, by various effects, those who are seen as the distortion of not-elite . . . [creating] a distortion thought of by the so-called Orion group as an empire. The problem facing them is that they face a great deal of random energy released by the concept of separation. This causes them to be vulnerable as the distortions amongst their own members are not harmonized. . . . Like the Confederation, the densities of the mass consciousnesses which comprise that group are varied. There are a very few third density, a larger number of fourth density, a similarly large number of

fifth density, and very few sixth-density entities comprising
this organization. Their numbers are perhaps one-tenth ours
at any point in the space/time continuum as the problem of
spiritual entropy causes them to experience constant disinte-
gration of their social memory complexes.[4]

The People of the Secret goes on to say that this "Hidden Directorate"
nonterrestrial intelligence communicates to a group of elite humans on
Earth whom the book calls the Hidden Executive. These elite humans
have been through magical training and apparently can perform feats
that most of us would consider to be superhuman. By the context, it
would appear that Antonio's godfather was a Hidden Executive member,
though I didn't hear about him having any unusual abilities. The Hidden
Executive in turn gives instructions to subordinates who had to go
through initiation, apparently into secret mystery schools and other such
orders. Quite surprisingly, these so-called subordinates are people we
identify as kings, queens, presidents, prime ministers, and other top lead-
ers in various aspects of our society, who "take part in the ordinary life
of nations," usually without being detected by anyone. Notice that, in
the above Law of One quote, it says there are "a very few third density"
members of the Orion Confederation, and that specifically refers to humans on Earth who are cooperating with this agenda. *The People of the
Secret* also speaks of an elaborate and highly secret coordination that is
occurring between religious and political factions that are outwardly in
violent, murderous conflict with each other, such as the Vatican and
Islam.

Chapter 1 is entitled "The Hidden Tradition." Chapter 2 is "A Secret
Directorate?" And chapter 3 is "The Inner Alliance: Rome, Christianity
and Islam." The covert alliance between Islam and the Vatican is a key
theme reappearing throughout the book. Special attention is also paid
throughout to mystical Sufism as well as the Order of the Assassins, such
as in chapter 9, "Freemasons, Sufis, (and) Initiatory Societies"; chapter
10, "Assassins, Kali-Worshippers, (and) Dervishes"; and chapter 12, "Sufi
Discourses, Rituals (and) Initiation." If the reader isn't really paying attention, the book would simply appear to be talking about these really

cool Sufi spiritual teachings that this hidden group of people had brought in and apparently perfected.

The highest-level Freemasons, from 32nd degree and upward, can become Shriners, and at this level they all wear red Sufi-style caps. The red is supposed to symbolize that the fez, as the cap is called, has been "soaked in the blood of the infidel." I remember seeing Shriners driving around in tiny, silly cars, wearing these same hats, in our local parades where I grew up in Scotia, New York. I found out only many years later from top insiders that a strong part of the Illuminati secret teachings were born of a hidden alliance between the Roman Knight Templars and the Islamic Order of the Assassins. This secret alliance apparently began during the Crusades. Many of the covert techniques still used in the spy trade today were originally developed by the Assassins. The deeper Islamic philosophies and practices were later combined with Celtic, Egyptian, and Babylonian mysticism that the Roman Empire had researched and aggregated.

Instances of the Word *Illuminati*

I of course wanted to look for the word *Illuminati* and certain other variants of it as I read the book, since Antonio had told me this was the name of his godfather's group. One mention of the term appeared in a discussion of Roger Bacon, who was born in 1214 and died in 1292. Bacon wore Arab clothing at Oxford and had a controversial reputation, where people joked that he was able to "make women of devils and juggle cats into costermongers." A costermonger is a person who sells groceries in the streets. Bacon generated a large degree of controversy by simultaneously appearing to support Christianity, while also asserting that there were far deeper mysteries to be explored that most Christians knew nothing about, which he was bringing in from Arab traditions. *The People of the Secret* referred to Roger Bacon as "one of the greatest of the European intellects and one of the most outstanding figures of all time."[5]

On the next page, we see a word closely related to *Illuminati*, where it reads that Bacon cited the *Wisdom of Illumination* by the Sufi master (and martyr) Suhrawardi, [who] had declared that his philosophy was that of the inner teaching of all the ancients, Greek, Persian and Egyptian. It was the science of Light and through it, man could attain to a state about which he could not normally even dream. Bacon . . . declared that the same secret had been held by Noah, Abraham, the Chaldean and Egyptian masters, Zoroaster, Pythagoras, Socrates and the Sufis.[6]

Once I started reading more books on the subject and meeting certain whistleblowers firsthand, I found out that the Illuminati like to take pieces of information from all different spiritual traditions and combine them. However, there are some very clear, overarching themes that emerge, with which almost everyone else would have a major problem. I will get to what Antonio ended up telling me about this in his own words in a minute.

Another quote that used similar words from earlier in the book was "'Illuminism' . . . injected into the European consciousness from the school of [the Islamic teacher] Ibn Masarra (883–931) in Cordoba, [Spain,] traced by Professor Asin. From the experiences to which Masarra's pupils were given access, they were able to glimpse the heights to which human consciousness could aspire."[7] Other parts of the book do talk about seemingly superhuman feats that various mystics were able to perform, including telekinesis. Again, all this might sound very interesting until you find out the deeper levels of what the Illuminati have since gotten themselves into.

On page 179, the word *Illuminati* actually appeared, as follows:

Afghanistan is therefore linked in the tradition of the "witches," the Anthroposophists, the Theosophists, the Buddhist Lamaists of Tibet, the Vedantists, the Masons and the "Illuminati." The single common factor is a Sufic impulse emanating from Afghanistan. Roger Bacon, who lectured at Oxford on the Illuminist philosophy . . . was careful to call it merely "Eastern."[8]

The idea that Bacon had to be careful not to use the term *Illuminati* shows that even in the 1200s, they were aware that this group had to be very covert about what they were really doing. This also demonstrates that the term *illuminati* was secretly being used some five hundred years before Adam Weishaupt founded a society of the same name in Bavaria. Most modern scholars argue that the term originated with Weishaupt's group.

The Witchcraft Connection

The reason for this secrecy becomes clear as you head into chapter 10, "Assassins, Kali-Worshippers [and] Dervishes." I did not find it until I was writing this book, and if I had found it back then, I would have been asking a lot more questions. The author speaks with a seemingly inappropriate degree of excitement about a particular Assassin sect from India called Thuggee. The origin of the term *thug* in the English language comes from the Hindi word for "thief." These people would find extraordinary pleasure in making friends with a group of travelers whom they intended to murder and then burglarize. They were so friendly that they were immediately trusted, no matter how suspicious they appeared to be. They typically killed people by strangling them to death, and said that the murders caused an ecstasy that made everything else in life seem unimportant. British major general Sir William Sleeman nearly stamped them out and exposed many of their practices.[9]

From here, *The People of the Secret* becomes even more disturbing as it discusses the overwhelming parallels between Sufism and witchcraft. I do understand that some people in today's world are practitioners of Wicca, and might see it as an essentially positive practice. As we read through the book, it becomes very clear that the type of witchcraft they are talking about is obviously related to black magic and practices most people would immediately identify as being evil. The term *Saracen* is used frequently, and this is simply another name for anyone in the Middle Ages who practiced the religion of Islam.[10] The author explains that witchcraft developed most thoroughly in areas of Europe occupied by Saracens. This especially included Spain from the years 711 until 1492, after which time it was "Christianized." This certainly does not imply that all Islam is negative in nature, merely that a sect developed within these areas of Spain that began practicing what we would think of as black magic. The Law of One mentions Islam once in Session 2, Question 2, where it said that "the one known as Muhammad delivered the peoples into a more intelligible distortion of mind/body/spirit relationships."[11] Since Antonio's recommendation for reading this book apparently came from top Illuminati members based in Spain, this connection between the Illuminati and certain Islamic sects is definitely worthy of being pointed out.

The book speaks with great reverence about "The Saracen Two-Horned Cult," referring to the costumes they wear, featuring headdresses with two horns and a lit flame between them. The author explains that witches use a ritual knife called an athame. He does not say what this knife would be used for, but later on, we see that it almost certainly is a sacrificial dagger. The Saracen Two-Horned Cult has a similar weapon called Adh-dhamme. The sound of the word for "ritual knife" in witchcraft, athame, is almost exactly the same as Adh-dhamme. Two-Horned Cult members ceremonially dance in a sheet they call a kafan, which is very similar to the word coven, used to describe a group of witches. Two-Horned meetings are called Az-Zabat, which means "powerful occasion," and this is very like the same word as Sabbat in witchcraft. The author points out that the Sufi master Jalaluddin Rumi wrote about the idea of riding on a stick, a theme very common in witchcraft.[12]

The author goes on to explain that the Two-Horned were a division of a Bedouin tribe called the Aniza. The Two-Horned Cult migrated to Spain beginning in the year 1460. The Arabic word for "goat" has the same consonant roots as Aniza, and thus the Two-Horned Cult adopted the goat as a symbol for their clan.

As the chapter goes on, we learn about a leader of the Spanish Jews named Rabbi Ishaq Toledano, who welcomed the Two-Horned Cult and teamed up with them.[13] He was specifically working with their magical spells to see if he could use them to defeat their mutual Christian enemies. Rabbi Ishaq knew that if any of the specifics of the magic spells they were using against the Christian enemy emerged, they would all very likely be tortured and killed. As a result, Rabbi Ishaq created loyalty and secrecy in the group by getting its members to do the most horrific crimes imaginable. There is a direct through line between what this group of people started doing and what we now hear from many Illuminati whistleblowers, including Svali.

The group had levels of rank that became increasingly more difficult to achieve, with greater and greater levels of trust and secrecy. As a test to see who was willing to advance in the community, the members were forced to torture and kill people, particularly Christians. The group also created rituals involving sexual perversions and forcing people to eat "abominable material" that is not specified. This appears to be a thinly veiled reference to cannibalism. Poisons and drugs were also deployed to further bond the members. The sect worshipped an idol that the author says is "unspecified," but very likely is goat-related, based upon the context. They would whip each other and trade "obscene kisses" while possessed by the idol's apparent force.

The Muslim writer Abdus Salam ibn Zumairi wrote, 130 years later, a very thorough description of the Two-Horned Cult in Spain. His words implied that it was still alive and well during the time he was there, before getting deported. He also claimed that the cult members could fly,[14] However, this was likely a myth perpetuated to create fear and awe in the people who heard about them.

Read the Final Chapter to Get the Message

The final chapter of *The People of the Secret* is very short, and says some provocative things. It summarizes clues that have been dropped throughout the book, to reveal that this Illuminati group was being guided and influenced by some sort of extraterrestrial or otherwise non-Earth human intelligence. The name the author gives for this mysterious intelligence is the Hidden Directorate. I did read this final chapter and eventually saw its obvious similarities to what the Law of One series was referring to as the Orion Confederation.

The passage you are about to read is preceded by a discussion in which the author asserts that the Earth is at a low level of consciousness, and that Earth's people have to be directed, behind the scenes, to make choices that this hidden, nonphysical intelligence feels are in its best interests. The author then says, on page 251:

> Responsibility for this process [of guiding people to make certain choices] on Earth lies with an Intelligence which has been called The Hidden Directorate. This may correspond to the level symbolized in occult legend as an Individual (e.g., "The Regent" [which translates as "The Ruler"] or "The Ancient of Days" [an apparent term for God that appears in the Book of Daniel], etc.). It is to be equated either with the Demi-Urgic level or with the level immediately below. No grounds exist for an opinion as to whether this Intelligence is, in any sense, comprehensible to man, a single or a composite Intelligence, or whether it is discarnate or corporeal.
>
> Below this level, certain levels of ordinary humanity, in whom qualitative changes have taken place, are in touch with the Directorate and may at intervals share its consciousness. This group of advanced human individuals is what has been referred to as the Hidden Executive. It is the reality behind all legends of "masters" and "initiates" from earliest historical times to the present. There may be several Centres on earth from which the Executive operates, corresponding to the division of responsibility for humanity assigned before the Withdrawal of 12,000 years ago. One such Centre is—or was—in Afghanistan and corresponds to the legend of the Markaz ("Powerhouse"). There may be other Centres corresponding to various ethnic groups. . . . The executive also operates at the level of ordinary life through a descending order of initiated subordinates. These take part in the ordinary life of nations and are almost wholly, but not quite, unsuspected. *These are the Secret People.*

There is much to explore in this section alone. "The Ancient of Days" is a name usually associated with God in the Old Testament Book of

Daniel. The concept of the Demiurge comes out of Gnosticism,[15] and as the years went by and I encountered more and more insider information, I discovered that the Illuminati believe that the God of the Abrahamic traditions—Judaism, Christianity, and Islam—is a false god. The term *Demiurge* literally translates as "Worker for the People,"[16] and Gnostics also call it the "Half-God," which is how they see the God most people identify with. They actually see Lucifer as the misunderstood good guy who authored the ancient mystery school teachings.

In the Illuminati religious view, Lucifer apparently wishes to free us from the "encumbrances" of ethics and morality—which they believe restrict our freedom. You can see this on Gnosis.org, a major Gnostic website, where it says, "If the words 'ethics' or 'morality' are taken to mean a system of rules, then Gnosticism is opposed to them both. Such systems usually originate with the Demiurge and are covertly designed to serve his purposes."[17]

This is where everything starts to take a serious turn for the worse. Although I support religious freedom, if you use spirituality as an excuse to rape, torture, and kill people, that can no longer be ignored. The writers of Gnosis.org probably would never take it this far, but multiple insiders have assured me that this is the basis of the secret religion of the elite. Lucifer, in this case, could be the ultimate identity of what this book is calling the Hidden Directorate, since in their religion, Lucifer is greatly superior to the Demiurge. The Illuminati further believe that karma applies only to people who follow the "Slave Religions," and that their group operates more like a natural force, such as a wildfire—without any karmic repercussions whatsoever.

Then, in the above passage from *Secret,* we also notice this strange, offhanded mention of "the Withdrawal of 12,000 years ago." This does not appear to be explained elsewhere in the book, but it is a clear and obvious reference to the fall of Atlantis. As the years went by, I found that the secret Illuminati religion absolutely believes Atlantis is real and that there were gods on the Earth in those days who withdrew and abandoned them. The people were then forced to endure the Great Flood. Many of them perished, and their survivors collected what little remained of their advanced, technological civilization and preserved it in secret. Many of these records ultimately ended up in the Vatican Library. The survivors hoped to regain control of the Earth and usher in the "New World Order," as they called it. The end of the above passage also makes it clear that the title of the book, *The People of the Secret,* refers to this same Illuminati group of terrestrial power brokers.

Notice also that they keep steering the reader back to Afghanistan. Although this may well be the origin of key Islamic traditions they use, they also mention that there are "other Centres corresponding to various ethnic groups" as well. The most important centers for their organization are never mentioned. Based on extensive research, these centers would obviously include Vatican City in Rome, which is considered the spiritual capital of the organization, and the City of London in England, which is considered its financial capital. As I have often said in my lectures, Washington, DC, was historically considered its military capital, though that definitely appears to have changed as of the time of this writing. Each of these cities is labeled as a major Illuminati center by having a prominent obelisk statue on display. Overall, these people are certainly not "unsuspected" in today's age, thanks to a much larger public awakening that has occurred—predominantly owing to the liberating power of the Internet. I was definitely getting information well ahead of the curve by hearing all of this back in 1996, just as the Internet was getting started. I have definitely played an important part in helping to foster this overall awakening, having written and spoken about this well ahead of many others.

Now we will continue with this same quote from right where we left off in *The People of the Secret.* Once again, it features an encoded reference that does not appear to be mentioned elsewhere in the book. In this case, it is talking about the same solar event that we keep hearing about in so many Ascension prophecies. However, here the story has been twisted around and remixed into a new, Luciferian version of Ascension, which they here call "soul-making" and "The Great Work." The passage reads as follows:

> When "the solar wind blows," a major operation of soul-making is begun by the Directorate. As a result, a relatively

large number of human individuals may complete a significant part of The Great Work in a single generation. A small
number may reach completion. Both categories will serve the
evolutionary process of mankind thereafter, but their post-
mortem situations may be different.[18]

The Rabbit Hole Gets Even Deeper

I couldn't really make it through *The People of the Secret* at the time, so I
continued to ask Antonio as many questions as I could. Along the way, I
kept learning a variety of strange and at times disturbing things. First of
all, Antonio told me that the Illuminati would deliberately create destructive wars for various purposes, which they felt were ultimately benevolent.
The only example he could give me was that he was told they might start
a war along a border between two countries. The violence along this border prevents immigration from occurring. They feel this is a positive
thing, because it prevents certain groups from intermingling, which apparently they did not want, for whatever reason. They felt that certain
poorer groups would create violence and humanitarian crises, and in
various cases, they wanted to keep these groups separate from one another.

Antonio often said there was a terrible amount of information that he
knew but did not want to say. This could easily include information
about highly unethical sexual practices and ritual magic. One of the
things he did admit to was that he was quite certain that AIDS was of
artificial origin. More than anything else he ever told me, he felt that this
was the deadliest thing he knew. He would not go into very much detail,
and said that other people with this information whom he personally
knew had already been killed. The obvious implication was that the Illuminati had manufactured this disease themselves, and one of their
main goals was to sizably reduce Earth's population. As the years went
by, many other insiders would tell me exactly the same thing. Then, in
2019, the movie *Cold Case Hammarskjöld* featured Alexander Jones, an
insider who testified to his personal involvement in spreading AIDS
throughout the African continent on an industrial scale.[19,20] This mass

depopulation agenda appears to be one of the main "terrible secrets" that Antonio was too afraid to go into any detail about, beyond his disclosure about AIDS.

Antonio also revealed that the Illuminati were directly involved in the UFO arena on the highest of high levels. This fit in very nicely with what my friend Artie had told me. When I told Antonio about the stories of the photographing egg and the crystal antigravity gun, he again acted like they were no big deal, and just a small part of what there was to know. From the various things Antonio told me, it became obvious that the Illuminati were hiding incredible secrets. As an example, Antonio was quite certain that a small number of human-looking extraterrestrial beings were living on Earth now. He said they would appear human in almost every way, and could blend right in with the rest of us without detection. He wouldn't give me any other information, which was frustrating, including how he'd even found out about it in the first place. Many other insiders would end up telling me the same thing as the years went by. The Secret Space Program apparently has these ETs under very tight surveillance, and they have earned trust after many years of behaving themselves.

Antonio was frequently obsessed with talking about the megalithic stone architecture of a site in the Pacific Islands of Micronesia, called Nan Madol. He felt this was one of the best and most overlooked megalithic architectural sites on Earth. Somewhere in this same general vicinity, he spoke of an island where the natives had an extraterrestrial artifact they were carefully guarding. He said you would have to risk your own death to go and see it. The rumor was that if these natives let you in to see this purported extraterrestrial artifact, the site had some weird technology that would shrink your head size somehow when you went in, but you could still think. I literally laughed in his face when he said that, but he claimed it was absolutely true. That is still not something I have ever heard any other insider tell me about after all these years, though very bizarre and quirky details like this do frequently appear when you are interviewing real insiders. More than one insider has told me about islands on Earth that have holographic cloaking, hidden advanced technology, or other mysterious and publicly unknown secrets.

Antonio then said that after World War II, the Japanese sailed into the harbor of this same island and found large, flat sheets of platinum under the sand near the shoreline. The Japanese saw this as a useful metal and pulled out the platinum sheets for their own industrial use. That made me far more interested and intrigued by this otherwise silly-sounding story, since the platinum was obviously a tangible artifact. When I asked him to please tell me what in the world was so important inside this island that the natives were hiding, he finally came out with it. He told me that they had a sarcophagus with something in it that would "make the Roswell alien autopsy look like nothing." Twenty years later, Corey Goode would tell me about "Stasis Beings" that have been found around the world in various secret locations. These beings are people who used some sort of very ancient time-accelerating technology to put themselves into a protective bubble. They program the stasis field to fast-forward them through time, and not to deactivate itself until we are right on the verge of Ascension. These beings are apparently interesting to see, as they are in suspended animation.

At the time, I was also excited by the public release of the alleged alien autopsy film that was found by Ray Santilli. Antonio dismissed it out of hand, and said he was told that if you did the research, it would ultimately trace back to Steven Spielberg's own company, Amblin Entertainment. He never told me exactly how he learned this, but he was quite certain about it. He did say, though, that the film was almost an exact duplicate of the actual original footage, so much so that there was hardly any difference at all between the two. He implied that if the Illuminati ever had a need to discredit UFOs, they could first promote this film and then reveal exactly how it was all faked. This would include showing us behind-the-scenes footage of the set and the props that were used.

The Twenty-Six Boxes

Antonio's weirdest story of all dealt with the Masonic bar. One night, one of his godfather's high-level friends had a dire emergency, and required an immediate team of trusted individuals to help. The consequences of this mission could easily be deadly. The insider had twenty-six boxes of highly classified documents stored in his attic, and somehow his security cover had been blown. Apparently, there were warring factions within the Illuminati and the insider was on the losing side in this particular case. He apparently had smuggled these documents out of a secure facility somewhere and kept them in a private collection, which was considered to be an unacceptable risk. The boxes now had to be moved very quickly. Although Antonio was extremely terrified, he joined up with this team and ensured that the boxes were moved to a safe location.

Once they completed the frantic movement of the twenty-six boxes, Antonio was given a reward for risking his life to help them. They allowed him to pick one of the boxes, open it, and inspect its contents. Up until then, none of them had told him anything about ETs or UFOs, nor had he ever been initiated into their order. Antonio excitedly opened a box and was amazed by what he saw. The first document resting on top was from the United States government, and was secretly circulated to the leadership of every country in the world. It was a document outlining the protocols for what they should do if a UFO crash-landed in their country. The document cast a veil of incredible fear around the whole idea. They claimed threats could be in these UFOs that could include viruses that could wipe out all life on Earth, or hostile aliens with hyper-advanced weaponry. The document said the United States had experience handling these various incidents successfully, and therefore any such crash should be reported to the US military for immediate "disposal." This way, the military wing of the Illuminati attempted to ensure that no other countries got any new technology to play around with and back-engineer.

Antonio also saw a photograph of a triangular-shaped UFO coming up out of the jungle, where you could actually see plants draping over its sides. He said he has never seen any UFO photograph in the everyday world that was anywhere near as amazing-looking as this one. Then he saw a photo that looked like the arm of an extraterrestrial being. It was clearly humanlike, but had distinctive differences. It was only at this point, he said, that he started to have a genuine panic attack. The weirdest thing he found in the box, however, was a description of something that they called "The Spirit of the Rock." Various photographs of rock outcroppings were taken where you could see what appeared to be a humanlike face. They apparently believed this was not just an optical illusion but an actual manifestation of a spiritual consciousness that had formed in the rock. The document said that once this entity occupied the rock, it would naturally erode the surface in a way that formed a noticeable face for those who knew what they were looking for. They also claimed to be able to connect with these spirits. I wasn't sure if I believed any of that, other than something you could easily come up with while you were on LSD or other psychedelics, but it was certainly an interesting story.

Once the story of the twenty-six boxes came in, it became very clear to me that the Illuminati had to be controlling the military-industrial complex, and were therefore ultimately responsible for the UFO cover-up. Clearly, they were deadly serious about these secrets never leaking out to the public. Even their highest-level members could be killed for attempting to hold any private collection of these sorts of documents. This data was connecting very precisely with everything Artie had told me, and now I was gaining information about the highest levels of this same group. I did see this as another manifestation of synchronicity. Information was coming at me from every direction and I had to piece it all together.

Antonio insisted that these were the good guys, but I had a very hard time accepting how deliberately creating false wars and releasing the AIDS virus into our society could ever be seen as a good thing. I became increasingly skeptical about this hyperwealthy group and their intentions as I kept listening. The Law of One was speaking extensively about the "negative elite," and these descriptions sounded precisely similar to Antonio's Illuminati. The Law of One also said the negative elite were ultimately being run by a malevolent extraterrestrial group that had a local headquarters in the constellation Orion. They were therefore called the "Orion Crusaders" or other similar variants in the Law of One. This negative extraterrestrial intelligence closely aligned with the concept of the Hidden Directorate in *The People of the Secret*. The very end of this book also implied that you might be invited into the organization once you learned of it.

As time went on and our friendship grew, Antonio ended up really blasting me about my UFO research. He felt that the vast majority of all UFO researchers did not actually believe in what they were talking about. Instead, the reason they work so hard, for so many years, is that they secretly are trying to convince themselves that it is all really true. Something in them is never satisfied with the answers they uncover, and they keep trying to find more and more information to ease this hunger for truth. Antonio certainly had learned the truth, beyond any shadow of a doubt, and he felt that this had completely transformed him. He told me that I would never really be anything significant as a UFO researcher unless I allowed myself to accept that UFOs really did exist. Once I no longer felt the need to try to convince myself of something this obvious, it would be much easier to make progress in the work. I wouldn't be plagued with the self-doubt of researchers who are really doing it only to try to ease their own pervasive skepticism.

I urged Antonio to go out into the world and share what he had heard with others, as he might be able to help people get a greater view of reality. He did not feel this would do any good. His main goal was to write a book about spiritual growth, because he felt that nothing we do with this information will be any good if people do not learn to become more caring and loving first. That was an interesting perspective that I certainly could agree with, and it showed that in spite of his insistence that they were "the good guys," he had not actually bought into the ideology of his godfather's elite friends.

Furthermore, Antonio told me that Zecharia Sitchin, the author of *Genesis Revisited*, was a good friend of his godfather's, and ultimately became friends with Antonio as well. I had already disagreed with many of Sitchin's conclusions on my own, and we talked about this at some length. I felt that Sitchin was taking a very complex subject, where multiple, different extraterrestrial races were involved, and trying to boil it all down to one race of Anunnaki that could be traced back to Sumer and then on to every other country and culture on Earth. To me, it was all far too reductive. There are obviously a wide variety of extraterrestrial civilizations that have interacted with Earth over time.

Antonio revealed that the Illuminati were telling Sitchin what to say, with a definite agenda behind it. Some of the things that Sitchin had purported to transcribe were simply things they had told him they wanted him to say, and the way they wanted him to say them. All this was apparently being done to set the stage for a future event where they intended to reveal far more of themselves and their agenda to the public. I would hear much more about this from insiders such as Svali as the years went by, and they referred to this anticipated event as "The Revealing." Ironically, I ended up alone with Sitchin in an elevator at a conference a year or so before his death. I had already publicized what Antonio had told me by this point. Sitchin was completely terrified of me, and backed up against the wall of the elevator with his eyes wide. I made eye contact with him but did not engage. He knew that I knew, and that was more than enough.

Hippie Housemate's Strange Adventure

Not long after Antonio moved into his apartment in the Schoolhouse, our housemate Jack moved out. In Jack's place, we got a tall hippie guy with long red hair and John Lennon Coke-bottle glasses, whom I will call Ron. He had a contract to work as a caretaker for our landlady and pay off part of his rent that way. Ron loved to find abandoned houses and walk into them. In many cases, memorabilia would be left in the houses that provided a stunning window through time. Ron also taught us that when people threw all their garbage into the backyard, and then decades went by, everything would rot away except the glass. Ron therefore found places where you could go "bottle digging" and unearth very interesting glass bottles that were far more dynamic than what we typically see today. Eric and I did this at one of Ron's sites near the house, and we did find some really nice collectible stuff.

Ron loved to walk around in the woods, in places no one else would ever go. One time, he was walking alongside a creek, and he saw a drainage culvert that was large enough for him to walk into. It was mostly covered over by plant growth. Once he went inside, he was quite surprised, as he was able to keep walking for quite some distance. He always kept a flashlight with him in case he found an abandoned house he wanted to go into. Eventually, Ron came up to a set of closed blast doors, with a red LED light and a camera at the top. He had no idea what might happen, but he fearlessly kept walking toward the doors. Once he got close, the doors suddenly opened and two men in military fatigues were standing there. Both of them were carrying machine guns. They told him to turn around, walk away, and never tell anyone what he saw or where he went, and this would be his only warning. I told him about the legends of underground bases that I had heard about in our area, and he had apparently found one of their secret entrances. Antonio said he was "very stupid" and could easily have gotten himself killed.

This curious event that happened to Ron, coupled with the ongoing stories from Antonio, made me soon realize that I did not like or trust the Illuminati. It seemed clear that this was the group at the epicenter of the UFO cover-up. They were hiding technologies from us that could save the planet. If they were indeed trying to greatly reduce Earth's population, it was quite hard to imagine how they could think of themselves as working on behalf of our greater good. If overpopulation is a genuine problem, it is Nature's job to solve the matter. It is not our place to step in, think we have all the answers, and decide to act as if we are akin to God. We have more than enough support from extraterrestrials in the higher realms who guard over and watch our planet to ensure our safety. It is completely inappropriate for any group of human beings to take it upon themselves to try to "solve the problem" by attempting to kill billions of people. Yet, this is exactly what the negative extraterrestrials want—to create as much misery and pain and suffering on Earth as possible. In so doing, they create energy they feed upon for their survival, which insiders in classified programs refer to as "loosh." Hence they apparently have a saying, "Give Lucius his Loosh."

In Session 43, Questions 6 and 7, of the Law of One, it says, "The thought-form entities feed upon fear. . . . These entities are, shall we say, creatures of the Orion group." Then earlier in Session 16, Question 45, in describing one type of Orion being that causes cattle mutilations, it says, "These entities may take any thought-form associated with an emotion of fear or terror."[21] This could obviously include a reptilian/demonic-looking form, as many insiders have reported with the so-called Draco Reptilian negative ETs. Importantly, in the next passage, Question 46, it also said that these entities cannot directly attack third-density beings like us.[22] In passages such as Session 11, Question 18, it is explained that they must trick our own people into doing their bidding: "Contact is made [by the negative ETs] with those who call. Those then upon the planetary sphere act much as do you to disseminate the attitudes and philosophy of their particular understanding of the Law of One, which is service to self. These become the elite. Through these, the attempt begins to create a condition whereby the remainder of the planetary entities are enslaved by their own free will."[23]

Another Prophetic Dream Encourages Writing

During this same time frame, another powerful dream came in on April 13, 1996. I was still reading the Law of One series as much as I could, and with Antonio's information, I was connecting even more dots. In this dream, everyone seemed like they were on the run from a hideous creature. It was a huge, spindly spider with a stylized, robotic-looking Gray-type alien head that had glowing eyes. They were all trying to keep one step ahead of it, and this continued through many small subplots. I felt dread, knowing that this entity was getting closer and closer. Finally, at the end of the dream the monster caught up with me. I could not find any escape, nor could I even move. I was very afraid.

At this point, the head suddenly sprouted upward, and the spider legs transformed into a thin, standing extraterrestrial humanoid form. Its entire body now seemed to be glowing with a luminescent green energy, and the eyes were very prominent, burning with light. Suddenly, the creature shot some form of thought wave at me, which I could physically feel and see. At this point, a wind tunnel of books started flying at me from behind the creature. Each book was either whizzing past my body or was actually crashing into me. As each of them went by, I realized that these were all the different books about metaphysics and extraterrestrials that I had been reading over the last three years! What was even more remarkable was that I became aware of the complete range of knowledge that each book contained as it zipped past.

So much information was coming into my mind all at once that I could hardly believe it. I should have been completely overwhelmed by this, but somehow I was able to take it all in. The contents of these books were fusing together like never before. I was catching my first real glimpse of some kind of Grand Unified Theory of Metaphysics. This was a concept that would somehow synthesize all my research into one body of work. I woke up from the dream truly stunned. I realized that no one else had put together a worldview like the one I was now seeing, and it very much needed to be heard and appreciated. Although I had seen in my mind holographic constructs of how my research fit together for a long time, this dream suddenly caused it to become far more ornate and complex, while at the same time being much easier to understand as a meta-message. The initially fearsome appearance of the being showed that people have to face all sorts of fears of the unknown just to begin a study of this subject, no matter how positive it turns out to be. Our fear-based conditioning from the negative elite runs very deep.

The next day, I had a dream in which the logo of the place I was working for was emblazoned onto a football helmet that also looked exactly like the hat of a Spanish conquistador. On one level, it seemed to be saying I wasn't getting paid enough and I should look for another job. As I wrote this thought in my notebook that morning, the furnace made a loud bang, which seemed to provide further synchronistic support to the message. On another level, it could be read as saying that Antonio's elite Spanish friends were indeed planetary conquerors, just as they were described in the Law of One. Since the place where I worked was caring for developmentally disabled people, there was also the obvious implication that the elite organization Antonio had been exposed to had some serious blind spots in their philosophy. A week after this dream, on April 21, I had the epic event where I went to Robin's Food Warehouse, had all these synchronicities in the weight and price of the items, and then reached a particular country intersection on North Ohioville Road where I had a synchronicity on my odometer and my clock at the same time.

Then, six days later, on April 27, I had another very powerful dream, which has stayed with me for the rest of my life. I was walking down a street from downtown Schenectady that I recognized from my youth. I noticed a slightly UFO-shaped cloud in the sky at first, and then another one that looked very similar. Suddenly, two silver UFO craft clearly appeared in the sky. They almost seemed to be in a dogfight with each other. I kept saying over and over again, "What the hell is that?" Then I grabbed a passerby, pointed at the craft, and said, "Do you think that is a helicopter?" I was very excited and wanted to make sure I had a second opinion, and a witness for my sighting. They didn't say much, and were just staring at the event like I was. The craft kept changing between UFOs and helicopters as the dream progressed. At times they flew very close to me, almost directly over my head, but there was no wind like there would be with a helicopter.

I raised my arms in a gesture of peace and walked toward them, even though I was feeling very strange about the whole thing. As I approached, the craft began spinning at the middle quite wildly. They compressed and then merged into one single form that was only about two feet wide. This extremely fast-rotating object slammed down into the Earth in a massive, spinning vortex, causing the ground to shake as it crashed. Once it made a landing, it finally became still. As I approached the object, I realized that it was an angular, aircraft-shaped, sharp-edged telephone. The phone then started ringing, and the dream ended before I had decided whether or not to pick it up. I somehow knew that the positive extraterrestrials were telling me they wanted me to contact them as a result of this dream message. I was astonished to go back and review this dream with what I know now. The drawing I made of the UFOs in the dream looked almost precisely identical to the "Anshar Bus Craft" that Corey Goode had been seeing since 2016, and had commissioned artwork for. I knew this dream was clearly telling me that one way or another, the extraterrestrials wanted to speak with me.

Then, on May 1, I attended a basketball game and ate French fries while I was there. This was not at all something I would normally do. When I got into my car, the odometer said 126664. Now, 666 is not a positive number synchronicity as a general rule, and I interpreted it as a major statement against the idea of eating fries. As I continued thinking this was a definite no, I looked up and saw a phone number on a billboard that ended in 666. Then I immediately looked back at the odometer, and it was now 126666. Even the tenths was almost exactly at 6 as I passed the sign. Clearly, I was being guided to improve my diet. Combined with the other messages, this seemed to be another key element to establishing contact with positive extraterrestrials.

Things were getting very, very interesting . . . to say the least. These and many other synchronicities led up to my discovering the true meaning and identity of the Watchers in the Betty Andreasson case, and seeing how beautifully this material integrated with the Law of One series. This was where I really became convinced that we were in a spiritual battle with darkness, and that each of us was faced with choices that would determine where we end up going as this Ascension event finally comes to pass.

CHAPTER TWENTY-TWO

The Watchers

Although my memory and notes are not specific enough to be exactly certain of the timing, I believe that it was in April or May of 1996 that I first found *Watchers II* by Raymond Fowler. This was a follow-up to the Betty Andreasson case, and provided a wealth of additional details that had not appeared in his previous books. While writing this book, I had admittedly forgotten many of the specific details of Betty's strange and wonderful ET-related adventures in the twenty-three years since I last read about them. Once I went back and reviewed *Watchers II* while finalizing my book, I was stunned to discover that certain specific aspects of Corey Goode's experiences were almost precisely identical to what happened to Betty Andreasson Luca. In fact, the biggest problem we are likely to have now is people thinking that Corey must have based his testimony on *Watchers II* to begin with. Nothing could be further from the truth. I feel the only logical explanation for these pieces fitting together so well is because we are dealing with truthful information. It's as simple as that.

A Glowing Endorsement

Once I got to Session 53 of the Law of One series, I was quite surprised to see that the Betty Andreasson material was given a positive, if not glowing endorsement, as follows:

The entities in this [Betty Andreasson contact] and some other vividly remembered cases are those who, feeling the need to plant Confederation imagery in such a way as not to abrogate free will, use the symbols of death, resurrection, love, and peace as a means of creating, upon the thought level, the time/space illusion of a systematic train of events which give the message of love and hope. This type of contact is chosen by careful consideration of Confederation members which are contacting an entity of like home vibration, if you will. This project then goes before the Council of Saturn and, if approved, is completed. The characteristics of this type of contact include the nonpainful nature of thoughts experienced and the message content which speaks not of doom but of the new dawning age.[1]

As we can see, this contact was given "careful consideration" by members of the Confederation, including our own local governing body that the highest-level decisions apparently must pass through, the Council of Saturn. Ra also indicates that these messages are intended to help us understand that we are heading into Ascension, and that this process is not doom and gloom in nature. Fowler's original book, *The Andreasson Affair,* came out in February 1980, so this was a fresh, hot topic in UFOlogy at the time the session was conducted in 1981. Most important, Betty had remembered contact only with Gray-style extraterrestrials at the time *The Andreasson Affair* was written. Ra's statement in the Law of One series clearly suggests that Betty's recollections are accurate, and that there is indeed a positive aspect to the contactee phenomenon.

The Grays Are the Eyes and Ears of the Elders

As I said earlier, in the book I read on the train in 1995, the Grays contacting Betty referred to themselves as The Watchers. They said they were caretakers of the Earth and all life upon it—carefully and systematically storing a vast diversity of genetic codes for humans as well as plants and animals. This again fit very nicely with Dr. Courtney Brown's data show-ing Gray ETs being involved in transferring life from one planet to an-other. Once I read *Watchers II*, the story became far more interesting. In this volume, it was revealed that the Grays were akin to biological robots, and Betty got to meet the beings who were working with the Grays and really running the show. These beings called themselves Elders.

Betty's description of the Elders fit precisely with the Midwayers that Dr. Brown had reported, the Anshar that Corey Goode would encounter in 2016, and the beings I had been seeing in my dreams throughout my entire life. Betty's husband, Bob Luca, was actually the first one to have seen them in the narrative of *Watchers II*, during a regression he was having that was reported on page 30. Betty's own encounter with them begins on page 89, after she visited a cigar-shaped mothership. She saw a man who looked human like us but was about two feet taller than usual. He had whitish-colored hair, pale white skin, and a long white robe. Betty then remembered having seen people who looked like him before. This is a perfect description of one type of what various high-level insiders have called "Tall Whites."

Millions of Contactee Experiences

Before we go into the fascinating details that Betty obtained from the Elders, I want to synergize the data in *Watchers* and *Watchers II* pertain-ing to the abduction phenomenon. Until I read this, I had no idea how far-reaching in scope this situation really was, and how many people it seemed to be affecting. Early in the book, we learn that the Roper Orga-nization conducted three major national surveys on cases of possible ET abduction in 1991.[2] The Bigelow Holding Corporation published an analysis of the results, which was then sent to nearly 100,000 mental health professionals, including psychiatrists and psychologists. The Roper report indicated that a stunning 2 percent of American adults had a constellation of experiences that strongly suggested they had gone through an ET abduction.[3] With an American population of roughly 300 million, that would indicate that 6 million people in America alone may have experienced abduction. That number was honestly much higher than what I was expecting to hear.

Equally significant was a 1987 study by Dr. Thomas E. Bullard on UFO abduction cases.[4] The study was commissioned by the Fund for UFO Research, and added up to 642 pages in two volumes. Dr. Bullard analyzed a total of over three hundred different independent reports and concluded that they had far too many similarities to be hoaxes or random fantasies.[5] Since this data was analyzed back in 1987, it was well before the concept of abduction had become anywhere near as mainstream as it is today. Most interestingly, on page 242 of *Watchers II,* we find that the Bullard study concluded that the abduction experience usually had very positive spiritual aspects within it. This is quite different from the massive propaganda campaign the negative elite have mounted ever since, such as through countless "alien invasion" movies. These positive, spiritual events would occur over the course of an eight-stage contact process that everyone seemed to go through, as follows:

1. *Capture.* Witness is caught and taken aboard a UFO.

2. *Examination.* Witness experiences an examination.

3. *Conference.* Witness talks with ETs for a period of time.

4. *Tour.* ETs allow witness to see parts of their ship.

5. *Otherworldly Journey.* Witness visits a strange, mystical place.

6. *Theophany.* Witness has a beautiful religious experience.

7. *Return.* Witness returns and departs from ship.

8. *Aftermath.* Aftereffects and other unusual events.[6]

This pattern of events certainly matched up nicely with the research of Harvard psychiatrist Dr. John Mack. In his classic book *Abduction,*

we find that the contactees remembered having volunteered to participate in this process before they were born. Though they might have some
anxiety in the initial stages, at some point, their deeper memories kick
in. Everything we see in Dr. Bullard's list, from stage 3 and onward, is a
very positive and uplifting experience, and again it is quite amazing that
these stages remained consistent across more than three hundred independent reports.

Then when we consider that six million or more Americans alone may
have been through this process, with their memories of these events being almost entirely obscured by deliberately induced amnesia, this becomes an extremely fascinating phenomenon to study in more detail. We
also hear in the introduction to *The Watchers* that contactees are often
given white gowns to wear, and they see other human-looking people in
similar clothing. In the 1970s and early '80s, it was also common for
black, unmarked helicopters to appear on these people's property after
the fact, flying well below regulation airspace. A fair number of photos
of these have been taken, and they are usually unmarked versions of
various conventional types of helicopters.[7] The original book on Betty,
The Andreasson Affair, has some of these pictures. The technology used
by the negative elite has since become far more advanced than helicopters and flies with a cloaking system known as "masking" that makes the
crafts almost 100 percent invisible.

Who Are the Watchers?

Since the Law of One strongly endorsed the Andreasson material as
being credible and positive in nature, the question then becomes who
these Watchers really are, and whether or not they show up in history.
Some readers might want to jump to the conclusion that all Watchers
must be evil. There is indeed a negative group identified as Watchers in
the apocryphal Book of Enoch. However, there are undeniable references
to positive Watchers in the Book of Enoch as well. In Enoch 12:4–7,
we read:

And behold the Watchers called me Enoch the scribe. Then the Lord said to me: Enoch, scribe of righteousness, go tell the Watchers of heaven, who have deserted the lofty sky . . . who have been polluted with women and have done as the sons of men do, by taking to themselves wives, and who have been greatly corrupted on the earth, that on the earth, they shall never obtain peace and remission of sin.

What we see in the above passage is that the name Watchers appears to refer to extraterrestrial angelic groups. It was only once one of these groups decided to "desert the lofty sky" and mate with people of Earth that they became fallen Watchers, or Nephilim. Another example of a positive mention of Watchers comes in the Old Testament of the Bible, in chapter 4 of Daniel. Consider the following passages from the original King James Version of the Bible. Daniel actually receives his classic prophetic vision from two beings, one called a Watcher and the other called a "holy one," which is probably one of the angelic, human-looking Elders:

4:13 I saw in the visions of my head upon my bed, and, behold, a watcher and an holy one came down from heaven . . .

4:17 This matter is by the decree of the watchers, and the demand by the word of the holy ones: to the intent that the living may know that the most High ruleth in the kingdom of men . . .

4:23 And whereas the king saw a watcher and an holy one coming down from heaven . . .[8]

In the original *Watchers* book, we read that the earliest church fathers believed that celestial beings could be physical and sexual in nature. This was only later rejected.[9] The Chaldeans also believed in beings who would look over the affairs of humankind on Earth. Their name for this class of celestial entity is Ir, which is pronounced the same as Ur and translates as "Watcher."[10,11]

The Law of One, the Guardians, and the Watchers

As I was finishing this book, I went back to the Law of One series to see if the term *watcher* ever appears there. I found five separate instances in the Law of One where the words *guard* and *watch* are used together in the same passage. *Guard* is a clear reference to another term, *guardians*, which appears in twenty different passages throughout the series.[12] The guardians are described as highly benevolent extraterrestrials who ensure that we are guarded and protected, and that no harm comes to us over and above what we have directly authorized through our own karma. Therefore, when we see these five instances of *guard* and *watch* being used together, the clear implication is that Guardians are one key type of Watchers. The first instance of this pairing of the two terms is in Session 6, Question 14, where Ra was answering a question about the Ascension process. Part of their answer was "This [Ascension] process is guarded or watched by those nurturing beings who, being very close to the Law of One in their distortions, nevertheless have the distortion towards active service."

The second time we see the terms paired is in Session 7, Question 9. Ra is speaking about the Council of Saturn, and says the following:

> The members of the Council are representatives from the Confederation and from those vibratory levels of your inner planes bearing responsibility for your third density. . . . In number, the Council that sits in constant session, though varying in its members by means of balancing, which takes place, what you would call irregularly, is nine. That is the Session Council. To back up this Council, there are twenty-four entities which offer their services as requested. These entities faithfully watch and have been called the Guardians.[13]

The third time we see the words paired is in Session 10, Question 9. A very long and complex answer is given to the question "When a graduation occurs [and an] entity or entities move [at] the end of a cycle from one planet to another, by what means do they go from one planet to the other?" The answer uses difficult jargon to explain how the soul of the person is carefully studied to determine the exact amount of progress that was made across multiple incarnations. Then the quote reveals that the greater essence of that person "chooses the more appropriate new environment for either a repetition of the cycle or a moving forward into the next cycle. This is the manner of the harvesting, guarded and watched over by many."[14] This passage, again, ended by saying that this harvest or Ascension process is "guarded and watched over by many."

We see this pairing again in Session 50, Question 5. The Ascension process is again discussed, in regard to people who are not spiritually aware enough to understand karma and other related teachings. Watchers are beings who are guarding and helping these people, as follows:

> There are those whose lessons are more random due to their present inability to comprehend the nature and mechanism of the evolution of mind, body, and spirit. Of these we may say that the process is guarded by those who never cease their watchful expectation of being of service. There is no entity without help.[15]

The most elaborate quote that alludes to the title of Watchers is in Session 51, Question 1. The core of the question that was asked was "Is it necessary for entities to supervise the harvest [i.e., Ascension], or is it automatic? Could you answer this, please?" Ra's answer was:

> In time of harvest there are always harvesters. The fruit is formed as it will be, but there is some supervision necessary to ensure that this bounty is placed as it should be, without the bruise or the blemish. There are those of three levels watching over harvest.

The first level is planetary and that which may be called angelic. This type of guardian includes the mind/body/spirit complex totality or higher self of an entity, and those inner-plane entities which have been attracted to this entity through its inner seeking.

The second class of those who ward this process are those of the Confederation who have the honor/duty of standing in the small places at the edge of the steps of light/love so that those entities being harvested will not, no matter how confused or unable to make contact with their higher self, stumble and fall away for any reason other than the strength of the light. These Confederation entities catch those who stumble and set them aright so that they may continue into the light.

The third group watching over this process is that group you call the Guardians. This group is from the octave above our own, and serves in this manner as light-bringers. These Guardians provide the precise emissions of light/love in exquisitely fastidious disseminations of discrimination so that the precise light/love vibration of each entity may be ascertained.

Thus the harvest is automatic, in that those harvested will respond according to that which is unchangeable during harvest. That is the violet-ray emanation. However, these helpers are around to ensure a proper harvesting so that each entity may have the fullest opportunity to express its violet-ray self-hood.[16]

The Importance of the Elders

The material in *Watchers II* again made it clear that a great deal of work was necessary to store enough genetic material, over time, to rebuild an entire planet and its people on a new sphere. In a hypnotic session from November 6, 1992, Betty found out that the Elders—tall beings with white hair—control the Grays through their eyes and their brains. The eyes of the Grays were described as being like cameras that the Elders can see through remotely. However, the Grays are much more sophisticated than simple cameras, as they are indeed living, walking beings in their own right.[17] Then on page 167, an Elder describes the Grays as their "Remote imaging surrogates. [The Elder said] they are connected to [the Grays] in a way, with bio-electric mind projections."[18] Immediately after I got sober, I started having strong thoughts about extraterrestrials, and by February of 1993, I had my NASA disclosure, which threw me into a world of nonstop research. This created a major quantum leap forward in my spiritual progress. Now that I was reading this book and connecting it with the Law of One, I felt I was gaining an even greater appreciation of how all the pieces fit together.

On page 105 of *Watchers II*, the Elders described themselves as "ambassadors of 'Oh.'" This was the name they gave for the One Infinite Creator, and it sounds the same as someone chanting the Aum, which the Hindus believed was the sound of God. Later, on page 134, one of the elders explained that the "Oh" is the internal, external, eternal presence.[19] The Elders also identified themselves as masters of rings, cycles, and orbs.[20]

As I read this, I got the idea that one Elder could send out and monitor the actions of multiple Grays at once, perhaps hundreds of them. This way, the rote and mundane work of genetic sampling and preservation could be conducted over the course of centuries of our time, without the Elders needing to be involved in every single step of the process. When I discussed this with Corey Goode, he said that both positive and negative groups of extraterrestrials create and use Grays to do work for them. Robots cannot be used owing to an ongoing problem with a predatory artificial intelligence that we have discussed extensively in our articles, lectures, and television shows. This is also discussed to some degree in my previous book, *The Ascension Mysteries*. This consciousness is the true essence of Lucifer, which the Law of One refers to as the "Luciferian Force," and it is ultimately in complete control of the Draco Reptilian negative ETs. Since Grays are biologically based, the problem with artificial intelligence taking over can be subverted. On page 155 of *Watchers II,* Betty says the same thing, namely that both positive and negative Watchers use Grays to do their work.[21]

Historical Appearances of Grays

Once we go back through history and begin looking for possible examples of Grays appearing in various accounts, we will not be disappointed.
Though the names keep changing, the underlying story line is remarkably consistent with modern-day abduction and contactee reports. Much
of the data Fowler draws upon to make this argument comes from the
classic book *Passport to Magonia* by Jacques Vallée.[22] For many centuries,
humans have had experiences highly similar to modern-day abduction
reports with nonhuman entities called fairies, gnomes, elves, and demons, among other names.[23]

According to Fowler, the Middle Ages also had many popular beliefs
and stories of sexual interaction between nonhumans and humans. During this time, there was a prevailing belief in the existence of male incubi
and female succubi who had sexual interaction with human beings. Wal-
ter Evans-Wentz, an expert on fairy folklore, believes the fairies who
were reported to be enticing people in the nineteenth century are similar
if not identical to the succubi of the Middle Ages.[24] Many modern-day
abduction experiences do have a sexual component, where sperm samples
are obtained from men, and women end up being impregnated, and the
developing embryo is removed and nurtured outside the womb shortly
after gestation begins. It is again important to remember that a majority
of contactees report, while under hypnosis, that they remembered having
chosen to participate in this program before they were born, and they felt
very honored to be involved in helping to ensure the continuity and future of the human race, regardless of what may happen on planet Earth.

One book Jacques Vallée quotes from on this subject is Evans-Wentz's
The Fairy-Faith in Celtic Countries: Its Psychological Origin and Nature,
published in 1911: "This sort of belief in fairies being able to take people
was very common. . . . A man whom I have seen, Roderick MacNeil, was
lifted up by the hosts and left three miles from where he was taken up."[25]
Vallee reported that these historic contactee reports also included amnesia, just like we see now. On page 87 of *Passport to Magonia*, Vallee writes,

"The mind of a person coming out of Fairyland is usually blank as to what has been seen and done there."[26]

Another case of what appears to be a typical abduction from a Gray was preserved in a book from 1891, entitled *The Science of Fairy Tales: An Inquiry into Fairy Mythology* by Edwin Sidney Hartland. In this book, Hartland quotes from a Swedish book published in 1775. The Swedish book in turn quoted a legal statement from April 12, 1671, by Peter Rahn, who was the husband of a midwife. Peter Rahn swore under oath that his wife was taken to fairyland by a dwarflike entity to help out in a childbirth.[27] The quote reveals that the being who did this was

> a little man, swart of face and clad in grey, who begged the declarent's wife to come and help his wife then in labor. The declarent, seeing they had to do with a Troll, prayed over his wife, blessed her, and bade her in God's name go with the stranger. She seemed to be borne along by the wind.[28]

This has all the classic elements of the abduction scenario, since at times humans from Earth witness births taking place in a contact experience.

We also find out that according to the prolific paranormal researcher John Keel, similar stories were reported by Ella E. Clark in her *Indian Legends from the Northern Rockies*. These legends spoke of three-foot-tall entities who were abducting children. The beings could also make themselves invisible, just as we see in modern reports.[29] Additionally, the anthropologist Brian Stross found stories of little men from the Tzeltal Indians in Chiapas, Mexico. They called these beings the ihk'al. The beings apparently had a device on their back that allowed them to fly. They would occasionally kidnap women and force them to bear children.[30] Let's also not forget that the Australian aborigines have multiple cave paintings of beings they call the Wandjina, which look almost exactly the same as typical Gray ETs. These beings again were seen as having great mystical significance.

Time-Bending Phenomena

Jacques Vallée also reported similar abduction stories from European and Chinese folklore that involve time-bending phenomena. A person may disappear for weeks, months, or years, but has no sense of duration when they return.[31] Getting back to the mythologist Edwin Hartland's classic 1891 *Science of Fairy Tales*, Vallée quotes him describing a farmer's son named Gitto Bach who had vanished and reappeared:

> During two whole years nothing was heard from him; but at length one morning when his mother, who had long and bitterly mourned for him as dead, opened the door, whom should she see but Gitto with a bundle under his arm. He was dressed and looked exactly as when she last saw him, for he had not grown a bit. "Where have you been all this time?" asked his mother. "Why it was only yesterday I went away," he replied.[32]

One fascinating time-travel story in *Watchers II* involves an incident that took place in a night border patrol group from Chile. A glowing object descended behind a small hill on the border of Chile and Peru. Corporal Armando Valdes, the patrol leader, went over the hill to take a look. He came back in fifteen minutes with a dazed stare on his face. He now had visible beard growth, and his digital watch was found to be five days ahead of everyone else's time.[33] Another similarly fascinating example came from Dr. Leo Sprinkle, who investigated the classic Casey County abduction case. Louise Smith from Liberty, Kentucky, went through a typical Gray abduction, and after it ended, she reported that the minute hand on her watch was spinning nearly as fast as the second hand.[34]

Betty Andreasson's own husband, Bob, was able to recall under hypnosis that while his experience was taking place in the astral, his body was almost completely motionless in the car he had been taken from. It was frozen in time, and he was told that he would be brought back in his astral form just split seconds after he left. Under hypnosis, he said, "There is almost no time passing where the bodies are. . . . I didn't understand that. . . . Time is nothing."[35] This discussion of contactee reports happening in an out-of-body experience, complete with amnesia afterward, got me thinking much more deeply about the many strange events of my own childhood, including my astral projection at age five. Corey Goode and other insiders have reported this same ability for members of the secret space program to travel through time as desired, though they must be extremely careful to avoid creating paradoxes, as this can destabilize the very fabric of their existence. In Bob Luca's ET contact, he was also shown a vision of planet Earth. He saw dark spots on certain parts of the planet, and the beings told him that he would understand what this meant in time.[36]

Betty Andreasson, Corey Goode, and the Blue Spheres

Nothing surprised me more as I was going through the final stages of writing this book than reviewing the contact experience Betty Andreasson Luca had in the summer of 1989. This was the exact same time frame when I had started practicing lucid dreaming and having amazing waking contacts with Elder-type humans on board a giant spaceship. Again, at the time, I did not think any of this was other than my fertile imagination. What I found in reviewing Betty's contact from this same period was an astonishing correlation with what happened to Corey Goode beginning in 2015.

Corey reported being contacted by a small orb of blue light. It would zip around him in his room until he stood at attention and indicated that he was ready. At this point, the orb would suddenly widen and go around his entire body. Once it did, he would be transported to a new location, after which the orb would either shrink or disappear. These contacts brought him face-to-face with "Blue Avians" who eventually revealed themselves as incarnations of the same Ra that wrote the Law of One. I had suspected this was going on well before he got the final confirmation from them. Corey Goode also claimed to have met with beings exactly fitting the description of Dr. Brown's Midwayers and Betty Andreasson Luca's Elders.

Getting back to the main feature of *Watchers II,* in the summer of 1989, Betty felt the urge to get up out of bed and go outside.[37] She walked into the woods and saw a blue orb. The orb then expanded to the size of her entire body and she found herself levitating inside it. This is precisely the same as what Corey Goode reported happening to him.[38] This was mind-blowing, and I took a picture of Betty's illustration and sent it over to Corey. He was equally impressed. In this event, Betty also saw clusters of pastel-colored light orbs in the trees, each of which was the size of an orange. The blue orb eventually took her onto an extraterrestrial mothership. Once she started walking around, the blue orb transformed back into a tiny blue light that followed her for a period of time.[39] This, again, is precisely what Corey Goode reported happening to him on multiple occasions since 2015, well before either of us knew or remembered anything about this report from Betty.

As Betty's experience went on, she found herself walking through a forest with strange and beautiful light effects. This mirrored experiences Corey had in the underground cities of the Anshar. Once Betty finished her trip through this mystical forest, she again found herself inside a blue orb.[40]

At this point, she had still encountered only extraterrestrials that looked like Grays. When she asked them about the blue sphere that was following her around, this was what she said:

> Those . . . orbs—he called them orbs—they are record keep-
> ers of intelligence. They can become small as what we know
> as atoms, or they can become large, but they each are intel-
> ligent, just as the earth and the moon and the sun are
> intelligences and all the planets are intelligent. They have an
> intelligence of their own. They're living.[41]

This was precisely the same thing Corey Goode was told—namely that the orbs he was interacting with were living and intelligent beings with awareness and a sense of purpose about what they were doing. I was

delighted to see this level of specific correspondence between the different contactee reports.

As Betty's experience continued, she attempted to understand where
the crystal forest she had just passed through was actually located. She
was told that "there is a place on this very Earth that you do not know
of."⁴² This doesn't precisely indicate that the hidden location was inside
the Earth, but obviously we have explored everything there is to see on
the surface. Many other insiders have independently produced the same
information about beautiful, seemingly outdoor natural environments
inside the Earth, and I do discuss some of these accounts in *The Ascension
Mysteries*.

Betty didn't actually encounter one of the human-looking Elders directly until page 89 in *Watchers II*, while she was on a cigar-shaped mothership. She reported them as having whitish-colored hair, pale white
skin, and long white robes that nearly touched the ground. She also
claimed to have seen people like them before, but this was the first time
we encountered these memories of hers in the books. On page 115, she
noted that all of them looked male, but one of the beings told her "we
are neither male or female here." This was about the only discrepancy I
could find between Betty and Corey's reports. When I asked Corey how
this might have happened, he said that the Anshar are far more "balanced" in their "masculine-feminine polarity" than people on Earth.
Corey definitely encountered both men and women, as well as people
who looked like every different race of humans we see on Earth today.
He did say that the men seemed more effeminate, in general, than what
we are accustomed to seeing in people on Earth at this time.

Another very interesting vision is given to Betty starting on page 119,
which was perhaps intended to help her feel more comfortable with the
relationships between the Elders and the people in her church. She saw
the minister's wife in her church being telepathically spoken to by an
Elder. The wife began speaking in tongues. The minister of the church
was then touched on the shoulder by another Elder, and this allowed him
to be able to interpret what his wife was saying.

Creating Light Grids of Sacred Geometry

For me, the true grand finale of Betty's visions in the book, which made me long to reconnect with the old man and his friends, appears on page 126. Three Elders stood together in a triangular pattern. They reached their arms out to one another and touched their palms together, so their arms formed a triangle. Then, they began meditating and chanting. Betty was astonished to see a triangle of light form between the three of them as they did this. Each corner of the triangle emerged from the third-eye centers of the beings, meaning that each being's forehead had two lines of light coming out of it. The lines connected into a perfect triangle. An additional circle of light formed in the middle of this triangle, perfectly centered.

Then, once this light grid was stable, three more Elders entered the circle, bringing it to a total of six people standing side by side, equidistant from one another and pressing their palms together. The second three Elders formed an additional triangle that was upside down from the original, forming a perfect Star of David pattern in the positions of their arms and the lines of light that they then manifested. This also caused another circle of light to form around the entire group, in addition to the ring of light that was still inside the Star of David.[43] As strange as this may sound, I actually cried when I read this. Some part of me seemed to have a distant memory of working with light like this, and creating grid patterns with the help of others working together as a team.

Now the entire Star of David light grid began levitating into the air, above the beings who had generated it. The pattern then shrank and collapsed into its center, forming a violet-colored ball of light.[44] Betty was able to carry this ball with her as one of the Elders took her on an interesting adventure, where she again teleported to various locations. The light was used to help people who were sick or in pain, and it was used to successfully drive off dark entities who were apparently trying to steal a man's soul as he lay on his deathbed. As I reread this account and considered the endorsement it received from the Law of One series, I considered that Betty had witnessed the birth of one of these spherical beings of light. This was also a fascinating use of sacred geometry to create a type of living being. In this same experience, Betty was taken to see "the light" of the One Infinite Creator, which threw her into a state of unspeakable joy. This is identical to the reports of thousands of people who have had near-death experiences, or NDEs, and is mirrored in the reports from the three hundred individuals in the Thomas E. Bullard abduction study.

A blue orb took Betty back to the Earth at the end of this marvelous experience, again paralleling Corey Goode's own reports.[45] Fowler's book also reported the results of his own father going through a regression for an apparent contact experience. In his father's regression, he saw the exact same type of beings that Betty had seen, wearing white robes and having blond or white hair.[46]

As we head into the next chapter, we will explore the final events in my life that led up to my own telepathic contact originating. It was clear at times that I was speaking with beings Dr. Brown would call the Midwayers, Betty would call the Elders, insiders would call the Tall Whites, and Corey would call the Anshar. I also got to meet Dr. Scott Mandelker, who wrote the book that awakened me to the fact that I was an extraterrestrial soul, as well as Dr. Courtney Brown, at a UFO conference in Connecticut. Additionally, I was nearly recruited for a strange program that used psychics, by a man who claimed to work for a defense contractor. Less than a month after this conference, my contact began— and my life was forever transformed.

CHAPTER TWENTY-THREE

The Contact Begins

A s the year 1996 rolled on, I became very aware that my dreams were encouraging me to seek out a direct telepathic contact with my Higher Self, in the classic style of the Edgar Cayce Readings. There were a number of other beautiful dreams and synchronicities during this time that I will have to save for the next book. This included one dream where I found myself flying up through a spectacular vortex of light emanating from the moon, in what appeared to be a very vivid prophecy of the Ascension event. I finally quit my job at the day treatment facility on July 23, 1996, and didn't land a stable job again until November. As I reviewed the dreams from this period for the first time in 2019, I had a variety of astonishing time-loop phenomena to the present. The dreams knew what I was doing, where I was living, who I was living and working with, and even very specific things about the objects and situations surrounding me. Although I had many other experiences with time loops in the past, I'd never had this many before.

A Brother in Synchronicity

I ended up joining Richard C. Hoagland's discussion forum to seek community and begin sharing my findings with others. Admittedly, I was trying to catch Richard's attention, and it took four years of dedicated work before he actually started to interact with me directly. I had a variety of weird and wonderful experiences with synchronicity as I posted these writings. Each post was assigned a seemingly random number, and I was not paying attention to it when I would hit SEND. Nonetheless, almost every time I posted something, I was getting undeniable numerical synchronicities. Some people on the board simply could not accept that this was really happening, no matter how many times I documented it. I printed out records of everything I posted at the time, back in 1996, and still have all of them in my files.

There was another man on the forum who was equally interested in dreams, synchronicity, and crop circles. His name was Joe Mason. Joe and I began speaking to each other in the forum and comparing notes. He wrote about a phenomenon he had experienced since 1990, which he called the Dream Voice. The Dream Voice messages were audible sentence fragments that came to him in the morning when he was first waking up. He usually would get only one sentence fragment at a time.

The most important aspect of the technique is that you listen carefully and write down whatever you hear, no matter how weird it is. You do not attempt to analyze the content in any way—you just document the results. This is exactly the same thing that the remote-viewing protocols teach you. This contact again came to Joe during the same time I began having lucid dreams and Betty Andreasson Luca remembered her experiences with the Elders. The messages were invariably written in a strange, encrypted language style that used dreamlike symbols to convey meaning. Several of them had provocative hints about the coming Ascension event. Here are just a few of Joe's original results from his website that I find interesting:

> 6. Sept. 90—We are still apes! The great cycle is not over yet. We will become Man at the end of the cycle.

> 19. 4–25–91—I am the Christ that gives the hyperactive square of intelligence.

35. 5–18–91—All that exists is God manifesting himself. To say otherwise is a blasphemy.

60. 7–1–91—Chocolate versus vanilla. Racism makes about as much sense.

138. 9–22–91—The natural flow of things is abundance and joy.

222. 12–28–91—I was there, and then not there. In short, there is no beginning or end.

236. 2–9–92—(something about) the plan of the gods had "gone wrong" in making humans, but a higher god had done this for a challenge for them to "repair."

257. 4–16–92—A member of a UFO group will get in touch with you in September . . . (Note: In September a man wrote a letter [to Joe] who was researching dreams about UFOs and aliens.)

292. 6–5–92—We have some very convincing material, especially the incredible curriculum on Jesus Christ.

350. 7–20–92—Each of us is a puzzle piece, and he's an exact frequency that matches us.

366. 8–10–92—We each have an Eagle and small hawk. Listen to it.

387. 8–20–92—From dee back of dee statue of Liberty to dee front of everything else. . . . [Note: After I began working with Joe Mason in 1996, he ended up getting together with Dolores Finney, who went by the name Dee. This message appeared to predict her arrival four years in advance.]

398. 8–27–92—I don't care how big a scoundrel he is, he is a human being and thus part of all.

401. 8–29–92—Some young people are cutting their strings (?) and going over to the coop, where the source is.

418. 9–12–92—The sun will get hot, and here we go again.

441. 10–3–92—A concrete bridge should be poured all in one piece.

450. 10–10–92—All people would begin to feel the healing energy.

The National UFO Congress

On October 12, 1996, the annual National UFO Congress conference was being held in New Haven, Connecticut, at the North Haven Holiday Inn. I found out about this only by calling the phone number in Dr. Mandelker's book, in the hopes of reaching out to him to share the results of my own awakening after reading his book. Dr. Mandelker personally answered the phone, and let me know he would be speaking at this conference. I immediately said I would find a way to get there. I knew that speaking at events just like this was my future. I needed to get myself there and try to get some recognition and guidance as to how to break into the scene. I also wanted to speak with Dr. Mandelker directly about what was happening to me, and ask him if he thought I had what it took to become a full-time UFO researcher. I ended up having to borrow two hundred dollars from Eric's girlfriend to be able to go.

Antonio found out about this just three days before I was scheduled to leave, and he yelled at me in a highly angry and abusive manner. For well over a half an hour, it dragged on, in front of Eric and his girlfriend, and they rarely, if ever, came to my defense. In his thick Spanish accent, Antonio berated me. "You haven't had a steady job for months now, David. What the hell do you think you are doing borrowing and spending someone else's money? And for what? To go and see a God-damn UFO conference? Where nobody knows anything? You have everything you need here. If you have any questions about UFOs you can ask me. You don't need these people. All they are doing is making money—and now they've tricked you into stealing from other people to pay for it! You are not going. This is ridiculous. You either need to go upstairs, get that money and pay her back, right now, or at least promise us that you will use this loan for something reasonable, like paying for food and rent. You need to get a life, David!"

As Antonio was laying into me, a curious feeing of absolute calm, inner peace, and firm strength coursed through me. I had looked over at the sign in our apartment that said CHATEAU BULLSHINSKI and felt a sense of deep knowing that this exact experience I was now having was part of the initiation of living in the Metaphysical Resort. Life is a tapestry of good and bad, ups and downs, joy and disaster, pleasure and pain, just like the Bible quote from Ecclesiastes had said about life and death. Life. He told me I needed to get a life. That was the answer.

"Antonio, with all due respect, I AM getting a life. I have invested way more hours of my life into this world, which people are exploring at this conference and others like it, than anything else I have ever done. I can't keep working dead-end jobs like this. That's no life. I have read over three hundred books now—three hundred—and nothing is stopping me. I even tried to go to graduate school for this, got the whole thing paid for, and they turned me down. If they had said yes, I wouldn't be here right now, Antonio—I'd be a graduate student in Colorado. I will get a job after this event and I will pay her back. She gave me this money of her own free will because she believes in me, even if you don't, and I have the right to use it however I choose. I am not telling you what you should do with your future, so don't tell me what to do with mine."

Antonio did back off after this, and Eric and his girlfriend did not take his side once we stopped fighting. It was all very intense, but I got through it, and a few days later, I had driven to North Haven and was staying in a cheap room in the same hotel where the conference was. By this point, I had finally finished working through all four volumes of the

Law of One series, which was no easy task, and I brought Book One with me to start reading it again from the beginning. This conference was irresistible to me, as it had both Dr. Scott Mandelker and Dr. Courtney Brown on the list of speakers. In fact, Dr. Brown was scheduled to speak immediately before Dr. Mandelker. It was almost too good to be true.

A Vote of Confidence

Once I got there, Dr. Mandelker agreed to meet with me, but since he had a career as a professional therapist, he wanted it to happen in the guise of a paid one-hour session. I told him I had very little money, and he said he worked on a sliding scale and gave me a small price that I could afford. My entire session essentially revolved around one question: Did he think I had what it takes to be a professional UFO researcher? Could I build an audience, get a book deal, and achieve enough success to end up speaking at events just like this? To make the case, I laid out all the evidence. I talked about having read over three hundred books on the subject. I mentioned that I had now become a scholar of the Law of One series, his favorite source text, and had worked through all four of the books in meticulous detail. I described how I had discovered many connections between the Law of One and other bodies of information that no one had ever seen before, at least in terms of anything I could find online or in bookstores.

And I let him know that I was a successful graduate of the challenge he posed in his book. I had passed the Wanderer Questionnaire with flying colors, twelve out of twelve. I had an amazing Bible quote come through me from automatic writing, and whoever or whatever fed me that quote knew exactly what was going on in my life. I had prayed to know if I was indeed an extraterrestrial soul, and the answer came the next morning in a fantastic UFO dream from my housemate. The same old man who had appeared in my dreams throughout my entire life was now showing up in other people's dreams, and his message was clear: "It is very important that you know that he is one of us." Yet, I knew nothing about the UFO conference world. I had no idea if I could break into it or how I could make this work. I asked Dr. Mandelker, point-blank: "Do you think I have what it takes? Can I do this, or should I listen to my housemate Antonio and just get a job?"

Dr. Mandelker replied, "I absolutely believe in you, David. You have one of the most remarkable Wanderer stories I have ever heard. You are clearly operating at a genius level as an intellect, and you are a highly prolific researcher. Very few of the people speaking at this event have done as much research and fact-finding as you have. I think you do need to get a job, in order to stabilize yourself, but you can also use that structure to buy yourself some time. Once you dig yourself out of this current crisis, I think the main thing you need to do is just start giving back to the world. Take the things you are learning, put them together, and get them out there. Learn how to make a website, as I'm sure you're smart enough to figure out. Once you put information out there, anyone will be able to find it. Then you can start trying to get yourself on some radio shows. Perhaps you'll even make it onto Art Bell one day. You can do this, David. You absolutely can. I believe in you, even if no one else does."

I nearly cried when I got such a glowing endorsement from a man I saw as a true idol at this point. Our session was over, but the message came through loud and clear. Just over four years later, Dr. Mandelker and I would end up cohosting a grant-sponsored seminar tour together entitled "The Time of Global Shift." Scott and I became good friends, and we would trade off Law of One quotes that we had memorized verbatim in the Q&A section. "The Time of Global Shift" tour ended up being the first well-paying conference job I ever had. Once all this started, I also got my first full-length appearance on the Art Bell show with Scott on April 30, 2001, and we managed to cover a wide range of fascinating material about the coming Ascension.

Later that same day, after I had this life-changing vote of confidence from a true hero of mine, it was time to see "the best of the best" in action. Dr. Courtney Brown's talk began immediately after my session ended and I had to run down there to make it on time. I happened to be carrying my copy of *The Ra Material*, Book One of the Law of One series, when I went. Dr. Brown spent almost his entire talk time describing remote viewing, how it worked, and why it was so accurate. He quickly ran out of time, as I believe he was given only one hour to speak. He hardly got to cover any of the conclusions from his research. Nonetheless, he had given out some amazing teasers. Dr. Mandelker was on immediately after him. There was barely enough time in between for anyone to even make it to the bathroom.

Dr. Brown's talk was so captivating that this very large audience almost completely cleared the room to go chase him down, ask him questions, and buy his books. I knew I had to be there for Dr. Mandelker, for even though Dr. Brown's book was important, Dr. Mandelker had awakened me to being a Wanderer and brought me to the Law of One series. By the time Scott got on stage, there was hardly anyone left in the room—perhaps a total of about forty people at the most. People were thinking Scott was going to tell them about UFOs, but instead he gave us a truly profound analysis of Law of One spirituality, showing how it tied together with Buddhist concepts of centering your mind fully in the present. He said it was very likely that everyone in this audience was a Wanderer, and if you want to find the answer, all you have to do is look within yourself, meditate, and show the universe that you are a genuine seeker, with an honest desire to know the truth. It seemed obvious that he was taking themes we had discussed in our meeting from the day before and working them into his talk.

At some point, he mentioned the Law of One series, and said that he felt this was our most powerful resource in exploring the truth. He then called me out by name and asked me to come up and show everyone the book. I was not at all expecting this, but Scott gave me an incredible gift by doing so. I did not say anything, but now I was standing in front of the entire audience and showing them what the book looked like. I also threw some humor in, holding the book as if I were selling it on a game show. People loved it.

The Power Is Within You

As soon as Dr. Mandelker's talk was over, I rushed out of the room. I had to see if Dr. Brown was still available for me to talk to. I went to the book-signing table and no one was there. All his books were gone. I ran over to the front desk, described Dr. Brown to the clerk, and asked if he had seen the man. The clerk told me, "Yes, he just checked out. He's out on the front curb waiting for a taxi cab right now. If you run, you might still have a chance to catch him before he leaves." That was all I needed to hear. I sprinted down the hall at top speed to meet another one of my biggest heroes. Remarkably, I found Dr. Brown sitting on his suitcase on the curb, all by himself, looking exhausted. No one else had followed him out there, so I was able to talk to him without any interruptions whatsoever.

I could see he was wiped out, and after having met so many rock stars as a kid, I knew the best thing I could do would be to stay very calm, ask him a few questions, and let him talk. There was so much I wanted to tell him, but now just wasn't the time. One of the questions I asked was "Well, tell me this. How has it changed you, to know that within your own mind, you have the capacity to gather all of this fantastic information?"

"Well, it certainly wasn't easy," Dr. Brown responded. "I would have to say that it turned my whole world upside down. People just aren't supposed to be capable of doing things like this, and yet there it is. I can sit down any time I want and violate all of our known scientific laws with nothing more than two numbers, a few pieces of paper, and a pencil."

"Right! Right!" I agreed. "Well, you have discovered so much new information that I have to admit that your book is the best thing to come around in UFOlogy for years."

Dr. Brown replied, "And this is just the beginning. There is so much out there for us to explore; we have to just start by figuring out what questions we need to ask."

At some point, I asked him what he thought it would take for the extraterrestrials to want to reveal themselves to us. "We are the ones who need to change," he said. "All we see in movies are 'evil aliens' that we end up fighting and killing. Yet, as I have seen, we are being visited by truly wonderful people who have been watching, guiding, and protecting us for millennia. They are more than happy to reach out to us, but we have to take the first step."

Much like in that iconic opening scene from Kahlil Gibran's *The Prophet,* Dr. Brown's taxi pulled up at this moment, and I had to say goodbye to him. I thanked him for taking the time to talk to me. As the driver packed his suitcase into the trunk, he replied, "You're welcome, David. Just remember that the potentials that you have within your own mind are more extraordinary than you could ever even believe."

"I will, Dr. Brown. I will remember. Thank you." He entered the taxi and left. As soon as I went back inside and headed over to the conference room, a few people recognized me as "The Guy with the Book" from Dr. Mandelker's talk. They started asking me questions about the Law of One series, and I answered them to the best of my ability. Within minutes, I had attracted a crowd of at least fifteen people, who were all leaning in and listening attentively to every word I said. Their eyes were wide. The more they asked, the more they realized that I knew. After several minutes, one guy told me, "They need to invite you to speak here, David. You know a lot more than most of the people at this thing, and you're also a much better speaker. This information is amazing, and the world needs to know about it. You have somehow found the deep spiritual core of the UFO phenomenon, and where it is taking us as a planet and a species. I've never heard anyone else talk like this before. It's amazing." Everyone around him was nodding their heads and agreeing with him. I thanked him and asked them all to "put in a good word for me."

The Final Temptation

Like these people said, I wasn't terribly inspired by many of the other speakers. I ended up spending a lot of time at the round tables in the meeting rooms next door. There I got to meet another one of my heroes, Dr. Michael Hesemann, who wrote *The Cosmic Connection,* which was a far-reaching and fascinating book.[1] Dr. Hesemann's conclusion was that the Earth was going through a profound metamorphosis that would change who and what we are. He also believed that crop circles were giving us ongoing symbols of this change in progress. He gave multiple examples of formations that mirrored ancient illustrations of the pregnant mother goddess. He argued that the Earth was the pregnant goddess, and she was going to be giving birth to a new humanity. The world would be transformed into a paradise, without war or fear or pain, and we would have remarkable new abilities. Dr. Hesemann and I had a terrific conversation about all of this, and there wasn't one empty seat at our table.

One of the things I told everyone about was my original NASA disclosure from 1993. This was still a year before Colonel Philip Corso came out with *The Day after Roswell,* which precisely validated everything I had heard.[2] I talked about how crashed extraterrestrial technology had been reverse-engineered into so many things we now took for granted, like LED lights, fiber optics, infrared night vision, lasers, Velcro, Teflon, Kevlar, and computer chips. As I was saying all this, I noticed that a studious-looking man who had come and sat down right next to me was paying very close attention. He was wearing a brown suit with a brown vest, a white button-down shirt, and a tie. He had small glasses that were balanced on the end of his nose, and long professor-style gray hair with a bald spot on top. "Your friend sure found some good information," he told me. He was speaking about my friend in college who gave me the NASA disclosure. "I am genuinely impressed."

This admittedly triggered great curiosity. How did this guy know that the college professor was telling the truth? I asked him who he was and what he was doing here at the conference, since he admittedly looked a little out of place with his dressy clothes. He told me his name, which I have long since forgotten, and told me that one of his jobs was a college professor. Then he told me he also did independent freelance work for various aerospace defense contractors. He gave me some specific names of big companies that most UFO buffs would easily recognize.

With total confidence, I bravely replied, "I know these companies. I've read all about it. You guys pose as independent corporations, but you're really just owned by the military. And they in turn are owned by a very interesting and secretive worldwide organization that I have just started learning about, which has deep ties to the spiritual traditions of various ancient civilizations. So here's what you guys are up to, based upon what I have now learned. You get these no-bid government contracts to work on projects that are drastically overpriced. Then you take all that extra money and funnel it into the good stuff—black projects that are so classified that We the People never get to hear a word about anything. All you guys are really doing is hiring yourselves. You just have to make it look like you are paying independent companies so the public doesn't get wise to what you are doing."

He replied, "Well, you're a very knowledgeable young man, uh . . ." He carefully scrutinized my name tag through the glasses on the end of his nose. ". . . David Wilcock. Let me ask you a question, and I know this might sound odd. Are you an artist or a musician?"

"Both," I responded. "I just got my bachelor's degree last year and I minored in jazz performance as a drummer. I was somewhere between the second or third best drummer in the entire jazz program."

The professor said, "I am actually not in the least bit surprised. Look, David, your friend gave you a lot of good information, but there is much, much more for you to know. I would love to tell you all about it, but we can't do it here. I'm going to head over to the buffet and why don't you show up in a few minutes and meet with me privately? You won't be disappointed." Then, he suddenly got up and left.

Not too long after this, another guy, wearing a green T-shirt, came and sat next to me. "Did that guy just ask you to go and meet with him alone?" he asked me.

"Yes, he did," I replied. "How did you know that?"

The man answered, "It's the government. They send these guys out at every conference. They are recruiters. They are looking for people just like you."

I was quite surprised when he said this. "For what?" I asked.

"Did he just ask you if you are a musician?"

I was shocked. "My God, yes, he did! How could you know that?"

He replied, "I am a part of the Pine Bush UFO group. We have other witnesses who have privately come forward after getting recruited by these guys. You definitely do not want to go talk to him." When I asked him why, he said, "They are looking for musicians because they discovered that these people make the best psychics. They bring you in and get you to sign a massive legal document that says you can never say a word to anyone about what you are doing. The document literally spells out that they can kill you if you break the contract. Then they get you working on various psychic projects that can include remote viewing and connecting with extraterrestrials telepathically, but these ETs are not the good guys. The work is very exhausting and people burn out within two or three years. Once they have used you up, they kick you out and break all their promises about the money you are going to receive. If you try to do anything or complain about it, they threaten your life . . . and they are absolutely serious about it."

This warning was more than enough to convince me not to go talk to the professor. A few years later, I would hear about the testimony of Dan Sherman, a soldier for the US Air Force who worked in an identical-sounding program for the NSA called Project Preserve Destiny.[3] I was now very well aware that I had found myself in a war between positive and negative extraterrestrials. We human beings were the proxies for this war, with both sides working behind the scenes to steer us in the direction they felt was most beneficial. I was having powerful contacts with benevolent, positive extraterrestrials throughout my entire life, and they definitely were telling me that I could enter into direct telepathic contact with them. The dreams and synchronicities made it crystal clear that all this was building up to something. I therefore decided to take Dr. Mandelker's advice and pursue this on my own rather than joining an organization where I would end up working for someone else. I needed to preserve my own destiny and not get entangled in such a potentially threatening situation. Less than a month later, my own telepathic ET contact would begin.

Shortly after I returned home from the conference, on October 18, 1996, I finally got a letter from my biggest hero at the time, Richard C. Hoagland. Although it was nice to finally be acknowledged, he wasn't terribly supportive. Hoagland said that all I was doing was combining other people's research. He felt that if I really wanted to contribute to the community, I needed to start doing my own independent research. Once I generated my own data, I could build my own platform and make a name for myself. I did see the logic in what he was saying, and the best chance I had to build up my own material was to somehow try to make direct telepathic contact with extraterrestrials.

Building the Foundation

At the same time, my everyday life was racked with stress and pain. I had been largely unemployed since I left my job with the UARC Day Treatment Center in July. I had to borrow seven hundred dollars from my grandparents just to barely survive, and I was out of time. I ended up applying for another job that was similar to UARC on November 5, 1996, and got an interview the next day. At the exact moment I pulled into the parking spot for the interview, my odometer read 128888—a rare and meaningful quadruple-digit synchronicity. I was clearly getting told that I needed to take the job if they offered it to me.

I visited the facility the next day, November 7, and was offered a job. That night, I called Yumi on the phone, since we were still in occasional contact, and told her what was going on. I was admittedly feeling vulnerable and not at all happy about taking on another job like this. She was very cold to me and made it clear that we would never again be together. Although she didn't admit it, I strongly suspected that she had gotten together with someone else, and that was fine. This ended up being the last time we ever spoke to each other until I briefly met up with her on a tour of Japan in 2002. The next morning, I called the company back and accepted their job offer. My starting date was set for Monday, 11/11, 1996. I laughed to myself about the synchronicity but did not say anything to the company representative, as I didn't want to sound weird. I knew I wasn't going to be stuck in this job. It was more a transitional step as I was building myself into a career as a full-time UFO investigator.

The next day, November 9, I finally followed up with Joe Mason—the dream and synchronicity researcher I had met on Richard Hoagland's forum. He had given me his phone number and asked to talk, and that night I gave him a call. That conversation proved to be one of the most mind-blowing experiences I had ever had. Joe had found incredible connections between the Bible, crop circles, synchronicity, Ascension, and this curious phenomenon he called the Dream Voice. His life was filled with one mind-boggling synchronicity story after another, just like mine. He had gotten deeply involved in analyzing the exact measurements and symbolic meanings of crop circles, and was having dreams and synchronicities that were telling him how it all fit together.

The crown jewel of Joe's work was the Dream Voice. He told me that when you first wake up in the morning and can remember your dream, you will hear a "still, small voice" in the background. It will fade in and out. Your job is simply to listen to it, and make no effort to analyze or understand it. Simply listen, and no matter how weird or crazy it may sound, just write down exactly what you hear. He had experienced very interesting Ascension-themed messages this way, as well as a variety of prophecies that proved to be accurate. As he was telling me all this, I was struggling to stay awake. We ended up speaking until five in the morning. I took pages and pages of notes, and was struggling to write down everything that Joe was saying even while I was barely conscious.

Breakthrough to Contact

The next morning, November 10, 1996, I woke up totally exhausted. I struggled to remember my dream, but it slipped through my fingers. However, I was still in a very deep trance state. And I realized I could still hear what sounded like Joe Mason's voice talking, just like in our call from the night before. This was the Dream Voice! It was happening. I had heard things like this for many years as I was waking up, thinking it was just my imagination, and I had never bothered to try to write them down before. Now I decided to try. I ended up filling several pages, sentence by sentence. No matter how weird or cryptic anything sounded, I just wrote it down exactly as I heard it. And I kept going and going and going and going. Finally, after what seemed like well over an hour, I decided it was time to stop. I had to start a new job the next day and I was also very interested to see what I might have written. I had no idea what I was going to find, as I had followed the remote-viewing protocols and simply wrote it all down without any conscious understanding, emotional attachment, or analysis.

The results were nothing short of spectacular. They spoke in a dreamlike language of symbolism. Some of the sentences were completely encrypted and made no sense at all, but I was surprised at how many of them were understandable. There were multiple symbolic references to Ascension, using the same biblical language of farming and the harvest that I had seen in the Law of One. There were also clear indications that dark forces were trying to prevent us from graduating. Here are some key excerpts:

> Does the Farmhand have enough manual labor? The Bible, just analyze it. I'm too proud of you! . . . Hold it. The religions I am concerned with will be someday lighted, and we will go on to greater heights as a conglomerate being in the cosmos. . . .
>
> [Your] country [and] continuity [is being] shaded by an invisible hand which controls the sound in the lower ear. [It is] the sound of Hades. It massages the temples. A book called The Greek Mythologies. Tombstone. [We are] talking about a 70-mph wind from everyplace. Pause for the government's actions to be completed. Needless to say, the point we're in is in the middle of Al-Tamin. Register, we've got to that. The meaning being that, it could be better, for there is sometimes touch and significant contact with the devil. [There is] a different way of doing it for those without much to say.[4]

Before we go on here, I just now looked up Al-Tamin, for this was one of the references I never understood at the time. I had heard the term and wrote it down phonetically. The main search result I got was Al-Tamim, which is an area of northeastern Iraq. Only the last letter is different, and they sound identical, so I simply didn't spell it right. As it says in the *Encyclopaedia Britannica*, "[Al-Tamim's] capital, Kirkūk, is one of the largest oil-producing centres in Iraq, and has oil pipelines that connect it with Tripoli (Lebanon) and with Yumurtalik on the Turkish Mediterranean."[5] Therefore, the reading was making a direct reference to the presence of the US military in Iraq, and all the wars we were fighting over oil. This would include the re-invigoration of the Gulf War on Iraq and Afghanistan after 9/11, which at this point was still five years away. Thus, the reading described that as a result of the US's military occupation of Al-Tamim, "it could be better, for there is sometimes touch and significant contact with the devil."

Now let's continue with more of this groundbreaking first session:

> I am impressed with that which [you,] the vehicle, have designed—nature, motivation, motivational programs. With humans and all that, they [the extraterrestrials] make a special return . . . The longest I've ever seen of that is the coverage of evolution. [It is] also a million years, which encompasses everything—German, Spanish, etc. . . . One of our women, Theresa, a sibling inoperative—the Christian, psychically. It was rough—they "nailed this in" (the sin), you know. I think a lot of people jump to their conclusions in silence. That's what the trinity is. . . . [6]

This passage proved to be one of the most fascinating prophecies from the first session. The reading clearly seemed to be referring to Mother Teresa, and the beings identified her as "one of our women." The references to her being "a sibling" and "the Christian" were further clues that they were referring to Mother Teresa. Then they said that she was "inoperative" and "it was rough." This message came through on November 10, 1996, and less than two weeks later, on November 22, 1996, she had a heart attack.[7] She was readmitted to the hospital with chest pains and breathing problems that day, and died of a massive heart attack less than a year later, on September 5, 1997. This was only six days after the tragic death of Princess Diana, and suggested some higher force of synchronicity was again at work. This stunning prophecy of Mother Teresa's heart attack was a profound wake-up call. Once it came to pass, I could no longer deny that I was experiencing an authentic contact with higher intelligence.

The next excerpt from this initial session begins with the strange name Ananawanda. This seemed to be a veiled reference to various religions. I had already seen more than one allegedly channeled book that had called Jesus by the name Sananda, and that seemed to be a strong part of the message. In fact, I do seem to remember hearing it originally as Sananda, and then being worried that I was understanding the words too much—so I asked for it to change:

"The devotees of Ananawanda are pathetically bonded from high school on to the eclipse-conjunction. The rivers do such a thing in Italy, you know; it relies on the Germans to get it out."[8] This was another veiled reference to the Vatican, which as I later would learn is the spiritual headquarters of the Illuminati. During World War II, Italy was on Hitler's side, and was running as a fascist dictatorship under Mussolini. When the reading said "it relies on the Germans to get it out," this seemed to imply how Hitler was used to enact the Vatican's plans for world war, since he had Mussolini's support. After World War II, everyone loved to jump on Hitler, which is very well deserved, but Italy almost entirely got away with a free pass and no further scrutiny. Then as the reading goes on, they appear to be referencing a prior catastrophe that greatly damaged life on Earth and required genetic tinkering to ensure that humanity survived:

> An iceberg landed on the ocean, with such a suddenness that
> the oceans exploded. Water rose many feet in the air. The
> inbreeding took care of that, the weird stuff.[9]

This next passage clearly uses a Law of One metaphor of Ascension, by referencing the "reaping" that occurs at the time of harvest, as Ra calls it. They also refer to a "vortex of light four times as big," which could easily be a reference to the anticipated solar flash event: "If you look at the reaping curve, you see a vortex of light four times as big. [It is] centered around the moon and Jupiter—a wild conjunction."[10] The reading finally ended with the following passage, which was highly interesting:

I love it when people refer to the Midwestern Atlantis. There
are also formations in the desert you should know about, in
Chichen Itza. After I'm done, you should take a walk to them.
You can go with your mind, you know? Check it out. I must
go now. Peace be with you in the Light of everlasting Love.[11]

This was a clear invitation to study astral projection and get myself to
have another genuine out-of-body experience. Right as I was reading
these words and drinking in the gravity of what I was being told, the
phone started ringing. There was an incredible feeling of energy on this
call. The sound of the ringing seemed to reverberate through my entire
body, mind, and spirit.

As I reached out for the phone, I honestly wondered if it would be Joe
Mason on the other line, asking me something like "Did you just get all
of that?" Instead, it was the guy with the green T-shirt from the Pine
Bush UFO group, who I had just met a month ago at the conference. At
the very beginning of the call, he introduced himself, reminded me who
he was, and then said, "I've just been invited to a seminar on how to do
astral projection. It starts today and it's right down here in Pine Bush.
Do you want to go?" This was a relatively short drive from where I lived
in Rosendale. "My God," I responded. "You have no idea what has just
happened to me, or how amazing it is that you just asked me that. I have
just downloaded pages and pages of written material from some kind of
extraterrestrial intelligence. And right at the end, it was inviting me to
study astral projection. That's what I was just reading as you called me."

This was before the era of electronic navigation. I got so lost in trying
to find my way to the venue where the class was being held that I ended
up having to turn around and drive home. I later would learn that this
man had negative intentions of his own, and my guides were protecting
me by ensuring that I never made it to the meeting. It took only a few
more telephone calls before I understood that this was not a person I
wanted to be in contact with. None of that really mattered, as I had just
broken through and made contact. The material was incredibly fascinating, rich and deep. It will obviously take another book to unpack what

happened to me, with all the transcripts, in order to give this discussion
the depth and quality that I like to use for something this important.

I didn't pull anything in on the day I started my new job, 11/11, but I
was able to get another reading the day after. I woke up to the clock saying 5:55, which was a great start. Among other things, this reading said:

> A plugged-in discussion with your family and friends for you.
> You were lonely at age five. The little bits and pieces come
> together, and I mean that quite literally. . . . Hello, David.
> Plan B. It's been a very long time. We've built and destroyed
> civilizations. . . . As the process goes around, there are ascen-
> sions, and a new cycle begins. Sometimes you will be receiving
> a spectrum of anecdotes instead of the real thing. Speaking
> of the tones inside of your body, they're in there, but you can't
> quite know them yet. It takes thought and discipline. [David
> looks at clock, is running late.] We will not do anything to
> put you at risk. Go wash up. We will not influence the dis-
> tance of the human body—it must be done from within. I
> was talking to another guy at a staff meeting the other day
> and he said the same thing. So you've got to listen to the new
> schedule, try on different parts. See what you like; you'll be
> pleased. Irrigation they didn't even know about in the year
> 3020 BC.[12]

In another session from November 16, they said:

> Who do you think we are? Space aliens? Wrong. That's the
> one thing about our service is that we need to help. . . . Please
> don't forget the crystal—it is the technology of your own
> family. We will also be there on Sunday, the day of rest. You
> will thank us then.[13]

Violence ended up breaking out at work on November 18, and a staff
person was bitten. I was the first one to intervene and do a bite release,

as I had been taught and certified to do at my other job. This resulted in a bitter and ultimately hopeless argument, since this facility had never wanted to use SCIP techniques. SCIP stands for Strategic Crisis Intervention and Prevention, and I was trained in it from my prior place of employment. One of the things we were taught to do was to perform "takedowns," where we safely get the person to the ground with their arms wrapped around them so they cannot do further harm. My reading from the following morning showed that the beings were clearly upset about what had happened and felt I was too reactive in how I had handled the situation:

> You being attacked is nonsense. You have to learn to use substantial self-control. This symbolism is for your own good. . . . This can be double-sided. Where you work, you need to put a lot of effort in. Move as quick as you can through the Church. Centering around Christmas and the New Year, you'll be ready for a change.[14]

This proved to be another remarkably accurate prophecy. I was indeed working in a church recreational building, and the reading said, "Move as quick as you can through the Church." I ended up being forced to leave the job within the exact time window that the reading had named, although I took the final step of quitting before they could fire me. Shortly after this incident, on November 22, I took my break time at work to meditate deeply and see if I could pull in a reading. This ended up being the only time I ever did a reading at a job. The words were inspiring and beautiful, and here is what they said:

> Believe it when I tell you the end is coming. The end of organized materialism. You've got to listen to your own inner voice. Nothing else will do. The voice of your ego will destroy you. These things are to be discussed, not repeated. The things you think of will come from higher and higher places. To facilitate this transition demands concentration and respect, an easier job than one might imagine. Be fruitful in

your life and do not fall prey to the forces which conspire within you to bring you down. Know that salvation awaits. The Green party lends its archetypes to your aid. Be friendly unto thyself, and know that you are one with God.[15]

The reference to the Green party was obviously a dreamlike symbol, indicating that the beings I was speaking and working with were at the fourth-density, green-ray level of consciousness. I reread these words many times and was very uplifted by them. I kept the notebook with me wherever I went, and new passages were continually being added to the collection.

CHAPTER TWENTY-FOUR

A Remarkable Discovery

Every morning, I would have to wake up early, before my alarm went off, try to remember my dream, listen to the Dream Voice, document its results, and then rush to take a shower, eat something, and head out the door with just enough time to make it to work. Every minute counted. Unfortunately, there were some people who refused to even go the speed limit on Route 32, which I again had to navigate every morning on the way to work. Once someone slowed too much, they could easily create a long line of cars with angry drivers just like me behind them, but they didn't seem to care. Although Route 32 was a winding road, there were places where you could legally pass. I was regularly trying to go as fast as I could, since I was always running late. On multiple occasions, I took dangerous risks to try to get around them because I felt it was better than feeling trapped.

I did notice a series of warnings coming in about this in various readings. They started in a cryptic fashion, but got more and more obvious. Little did I know that history was going to repeat itself. The beings were going to repeat a prior lesson by setting me up with another car crash, almost exactly one year later. This time, they would very precisely predict the event in advance, but with written words instead of dreams. Here is a list of the prophecies that were suggesting I was getting myself in trouble, beginning with the date:

11/16/96: For the tumors, you must let us know. Collections will be three thousand dollars . . . A collection of money challenges . . . I really encourage the New York Local State of Awards. I feel guilty as an accountant [for you, when you go] chapter 7. You do want to help us, don't you?

11/19/96: You can stay up all night, or use your greeting cards. Use the greeting cards, clean out your room and all will be written out in the second act. I wouldn't like to be out this afternoon if I were you. It just doesn't seem right to me. You know who walked in the last time.

11/20/96: We need two more people. More importantly, people have a habit. Important things need to be done with them. You'll work on it and get it done. Drive carefully. Don't do anything overboard. Pull up as much money as you can; it's more of a community lesson than anything else.

11/23/96: A staff person is going to sit down with you. No more BS channeling. You have to tone your voice. Evidently you know where your passport is, so use it. . . . Life is beautiful. It's not that hard, I just want you to understand what the process is. You've got five more staffings/stackings to go. I stopped singing a long time ago. When I sing now, I find there are not so many players around me. . . . I have a dream for you. Lie back and relax and we'll bring it in. [The dream featured me establishing direct two-way telepathic communication with Jesus. He was standing there and speaking to me directly as I heard the words. We were having a relaxed, friendly conversation about how I could continue to develop the ability to hear what he was saying telepathically. I then found myself playing music on stage. The reading then continued.]

What you are being shown is that you have a sandwich in the fridge that is going to be cut down into slices. There are stressed-out people and they want attention. Good—you ARE listening to me! Listen to immediacy. When we bump into each other, I will spend just enough time to ask you a few questions. In the Light, you have the most candid footing. . . . Soon we will sit down and begin to redirect your thoughts. What I don't get is why you are so against the idea. It isn't part of the test for you to ignite the Source in flames. It's been so long since we've been interrupted that off the top of my head I can think of no reason for your reluctance. We went a little nuts in the fridge, but were taught something in the freezer. Branch out your control to all aspects of your life. Be aware that your trouble has not completely ended; the cards have shown you. [This was a reference to a Tarot card reading I had done for myself recently.]

[Question: "Tell me of my true home and from where I came."] Ah, the woodward. Ah, beautiful, a place of light and of forever. A place you will be returning to so quickly. Just go through the steps to get there. It sounds easy, and it is you who makes it difficult. [Question: "What about Dr. Courtney Brown's remote viewings of the Grays? Are they actually working for good, or what?"] You will recall our friend talking about the Pleiades. [This was a reference to another inspirational book I had read, Patricia Pereira's *Songs of the Arcturians*.[1]] Lots of energy is coming in, and it is neither good nor bad. These concepts of duality are part of the prison of third-density existence. [The Grays] have been moving around for quite a while. We're not talking about that. I'm going to get there soon enough. There are more pressing matters. We must focus on the urgent situation now before you. God knows how long it has taken us to decide when to do this with you. And another thing, you really ought to wear more blue; it suits you quite well.[2]

Although that last sentence sounds like a joke, they were again speaking in symbolic dream language. By asking me to "wear more blue," they meant that I should spend more time with my higher chakras—light blue and indigo—active. That would mean being far more meditative and "tuned in" to universal energy, peace, and love throughout my daily existence.

Now let's continue. Here we get references to my "playing Virgo too loud." The astrological sign of Virgo is associated with being analytical, perfectionistic, critical, and judgmental, among other things.[3] I certainly did have a desire to have a "perfect" drive to work, and could not handle someone going below the speed limit. The reading also indicated an upcoming mistake that would involve the state police, which this crash certainly did.

> 11/24/96: You played Virgo too loud. It doesn't matter, as long as you understand that this is the answer to the state police. Again, it is as much my mistake as yours. Your family: That would be a good idea. A nice thing to look at. It is in my cards for the New Year. I've orchestrated the next 10 years starting from now. We've discussed it, and you know this is true. . . . As concerns astral travel, be aware that others will be waiting for you, and you should not walk into it blindly. You've already had Quality Assurance saying that you were messed up. Just be patient and still, knowing that you were born into the seventies and lived throughout the nineties. The color pink on a paintbrush—you want to use wide strokes. You'll see me doing this too. Someone wrote me a letter saying you were the most vicious man alive. We disagree with this, but driving badly and staring at women in lust will not elicit favorable responses. Go to sleep now and rest.

> 11/25/96: The Father/Son confuses you. Merely stated, it implies that women are in charge of the world. You'd be a totally different person if that were the case. You made a point of being nuts when you left, [actually, when you] removed yourself. Why do you think we ran into the cops that day? These actions must be balanced, you know. . . . Be aware of the

tandem about to erupt. . . . Heaven and Earth will not be
possible until you get this stuff done. Treat everything with
the utmost seriousness."[4]

This next excerpt from November 28 explains that the part of me that
can indulge in negativity, here referred to as Lucifer, is always waiting to
be awakened and activated, as with all of us. Their obvious goal is to
discourage me from doing that, and "let sleeping dogs lie," as it were, by
simply stepping over this part of myself and moving on. A reference is
also made to alcohol, suggesting that I was behaving much like a drunk
driver on the road—which would be another example of "awakening
Lucifer." On the positive side, I was being told that once I worked
through these personal problems, I could have a career as a UFOlogist,
including radio appearances.

> 11/28/96: Lucifer seems to be sleeping on the floor. Perhaps
> you'd like to give him a walk, or step over him again. Any as-
> signment we give you could be anytime in the next seventeen
> months. Don't go anywhere. National Public Radio, Radiol-
> ogy may not be far behind. You're going to lose respect if you
> listen to some jackass and hinge everything on that. Patience,
> again. It doesn't look like you're sleeping there too long. What
> kind of drinks do you have? You know it's off-limits, right?[5]

Remarkable Prophecies

The next reading, from November 30, 1996, predicted my upcoming job
with Gaiam TV, which ran from 2013 to 2018, when I finally resigned.
The depth and clarity of the prophecy was utterly astonishing once I
eventually realized what it was saying. This reading came in after I had
traveled back up to my mother's house for Thanksgiving break, and I
published it on my website three years later, in 1999. I have also included
a time-stamped reference from April 9, 2001, to show this came in long
before I started the Gaiam TV job:

11/30/96: You're probably one of very few people in the club who can understand *The Ra Material*. You're fat enough in the mouth; you need to wash it down. Up against the wall, now you're looking for it. It reminds me of when we would touch base before. You went on a diet. Establish your horizons and ask yourself a question: "Do I like to sit in school?" You can pick an answer. If no, start to study. Take notes.

There is no need for a planned sacrifice. Apples and oranges can be a pair, you know—if that lands national. Saturn returns, it can't possibly be Homeopathic TV. Think of Art Bell doing yoga. Maybe something will come of it, maybe some other time. Another period of snow before vacation; you can come inside. Don't be a slave; slaves do the work of many for the pay of few. It's easy to latch on to that feeling of powerlessness. Don't worry, we have some crazy little dreams waiting for you. The following weekend, we're going to have a special function.[6,7]

It is easy to miss this prophecy if you don't understand the context. I visited Gaiam in January 2013 after being invited to appear as a guest on George Noory's show, *Beyond Belief*. George was the replacement for Art Bell after his resignation from *Coast to Coast AM*. Gaiam at the time was most well-known for selling yoga products in Whole Foods, and this reading had said, "Think of Art Bell doing yoga." Right before that sentence, it said, "Homeopathic TV," and the name of the company I started working for was Gaiam TV. My show with George became the highest-rated program on the network, and led to my beginning with one weekly show, *Wisdom Teachings,* and later a second show, which became *Cosmic Disclosure* once I brought in Corey Goode to share his fascinating information.

I later realized that Corey Goode's arrival in 2015 was predicted in the above passage as well, when it said, "Apples and oranges can be a pair, you know, if that lands national." Corey and I were certainly opposites, and the phrase "apples and oranges" is a popular American saying to illustrate how different two people can be. Regarding the idea of our work "landing national," Gaiam did end up buying prominent front-page ads on Drudge Report, arguably the biggest national news site of all, right during the highly contentious 2016 presidential election. This dramatically helped to raise awareness of the reality of the Secret Space Program, and pave the way for later disclosures that have not yet happened at the time of this writing but are highly anticipated.

Another intriguing synchronicity was that once I began flying out to Boulder to work for Gaiam, I usually stayed in the same house that Chogyam Trungpa had lived and died in after he founded the Naropa Institute. It was interesting that Naropa had only recently rejected me when this prophecy came in, but once the time loop was completed, I found myself staying in the founder's house. A good part of *The Synchronicity Key* was written there, as well as many, if not most, of my slides for *Wisdom Teachings*. The house had become a sanctuary in the astral plane for ghosts, many of whom I met in my dreams. A large number of these people had died under very traumatic circumstances, such as the Holocaust, and they appreciated the calm and soothing energy that the house provided, such as from group sound healing ceremonies conducted there every month, and other such events.

Yet another remarkable time-loop synchronicity associated with this prophecy did not occur to me until after I finished and submitted the first full draft of this book on Saturday, November 16, 2019. That same day, I got on a plane and flew out to the MGM Grand Hotel in Las Vegas to meet my friend Steven Tyler, the lead singer of Aerosmith, who I have known for seven years but rarely get to see in person. My wife and I spent time with him in his dressing room before that evening's performance. The November 1996 reading said, "Don't worry, we have some crazy little dreams waiting for you. The following weekend, we're going to have a special function." I had always wondered about the phrase "crazy little dreams," and now I realized it was a reference to three of the biggest Aerosmith songs: Crazy, Dream On, and Rag Doll, where Steven sings "Daddy's little cutie" in the chorus—thus explaining the presence of the word *little*. The "special function" on the "following weekend" was the meeting I had with Steven immediately after adding these prophecies into the book and finishing it—almost exactly twenty-three years after the information had originally come through.

The Coming Car Crash

The quality of the delivery was improving by the day. Here are some excerpts from December 2 that again alluded to the upcoming crash, but were also complimentary of the work I was doing in the greater sense.

> 12/2/96: In your cap and gown, think about what you are shopping for, for a moment; aquamarine, the colors of the spectrum. . . . Many people feel they are lost. It's quite appropriate in this society, though. How do you think I feel about it? I never say anything to cause this. . . . This is my speakerphone; this is something you can watch. It will be around for many years. We need some purchasing orders bad. Silence is your greatest ally. . . . We have almost determined the breadth of your ancient knowledge to have. It's a lot to write about. . . . For this month, there will be lots of surprises; Habitu.[8]

Before we go on, this passage proved to be quite astonishing. Later that same day, I was driving in the van for work. I was on a new street and passed a restaurant I had never seen before. The name of the restaurant was Habitu. I recognized the word immediately, opened up my notebook, and read it in awe. Shortly after this point, I asked about various dreams I was receiving suggesting that they might be steering me into having a girlfriend. The first two sentences of the answer were "Linear tube thought. This thought answer will be stated with Paul." By this point, I had just started recording the messages into a tape recorder and then transcribing them by hand into the notebook afterward. Just one page after I wrote those words in the notebook, I discovered that my brother's friend Paul had written a message to me in the notebook and never told me about it. This was another astonishing synchronicity in the early days of the phenomenon. As the reading continued, it gave a powerful message about changes we h~ e yet to see in our future at this time.

> We have always tried to give you direction without pushing or forcing. The receipt of a female into the life processes could be most extraordinary. The patriarch is winding down, landing with such a force in each stanza. More and more, the barriers are toppling. Those who have faith in the one capitalizing on the shopping [are misguided.] We all know by now that this is a malevolent force that will soon disintegrate. . . . Just analyze the diagrams [in] the Bible. Murder is still being sung in the hearts of foul men. Save thyself up on the river. Know that the decades of tyranny are over. Accept that circumstances have changed. There is a new understanding now that is being brought out into the light. People will not be the same; with the speed of thought, they will fly and travel. The reason [we are telling you all this] is for YOU to provide a cloaking mechanism, when all goes platinum. It will divide the Mormon records as those of the Church, as usual.[9]

The statement "when all goes platinum" could well be a reference to the anticipated solar flash event. The idea of providing a "cloaking mechanism" for this event appears to be a reference to light-body activation, after which time people "will fly and travel . . . with the speed of thought." The next reading, from December 3, included another warning about the upcoming car crash that I did not see at the time. It was slightly disguised by talking about a stain on the side of the road, and the idea of encountering Saturn, the planet of trials and tribulations.

> 12/3/96: It's such a mess when you're dividing. A loose stain on the side of the road. Go inside and look around. Look at yourself [and] see what you might find. . . . Saturn will be

opening itself up to you shortly. . . . You can call me Bitches' Brew. . . . In unison, the voice of the Creator sings out, but who shall decode the signal? Continued assumptions prove incorrect. It is our pledge to be of assistance despite the circumstances. Those who learn the truth of religion will find themselves in an inverse position to the dictates of society. . . . It is about to be centralized again; I am sorry. Discussions reminiscent of our talk so long ago. The memories come quickly, like fleeting ghosts.[10]

I found it very mysterious that this source was telling me that these "discussions [were] reminiscent of our talk so long ago," since I had only started doing this practice within the last three weeks. Were they talking about a past life? I was not sure. The next reading came in that same night, at 7:26 P.M. As I was sitting in the house after work, I very clearly heard, "Go get a piece of paper." I then started writing down what I heard, and this is a partial transcript of the result, which gives undeniable hints that those who Ascend will have the power of levitation:

A new thought is enveloping you. Obscured by the obstructions in your mind, yet rapidly coming into focus. A Christmas tree, its parlances to behold. ["Parlance" means "a way or manner of speaking."[11]] I have a feeling you're not alone in this; the children will understand the new standard. Obscure light refractions are diffusing into the population. The mirror is kept gleaming brightly. In the forest of thought, the storm is dissipating, as a free expression of thought comes to the mind, flowing and dancing freely like a magical sprite. The cloaks that have enveloped us will be cast away, for there is a new shade under the sun. Those with wings shall soar above.

Abstract thoughts and notions are brought with serendipity into the arena of believing. The vines in the musty forest provide anchorage to higher levels. Above the tree line, one

sees a most beautiful splendor. He who is pure in heart will
have no difficulty attaining this, for it is one body, one mind,
one soul, and the abstract thoughts and notions of the past
will be shed away like an old skin. Swiftly come the messen-
gers of destiny, bringing with them the notions of a new age.
It is but for you to perceive it that it may become reality. The
dimension of thought runs deep—its length and breadth
cannot be measured by your three-dimensional instruments.
Its scope is historic in ways you cannot even comprehend. The
abysmal failures and longings of the past will no longer hold
sway over you. Confused in a box, many will open to new
surprises. Thought patterns are divided among the many
from the One. Those abuses of intellect will fade away.

Your shirt. Your underwear. A jacket. How fitted for a
king . . . The abstract notion that one can survive without
words is not a myth, but reality. The technological abuses
of Earth's history will fall away. I'm so forgetful; I grabbed
the bottle of shaving cream when I wanted to reveal something else. Your purple head will glisten. What you choose
to believe is for you to decide. The choice is around you,
and you may drink of it. No one survives in the pathways
of the dead. If you believe there is only one mind, how can
there be two different people? This communication grows
thin. Duty stands before you, and you must embrace it. Fear
not, for God is with you in the Light and love of infinite
creation.[12]

The next day, Wednesday, December 4, was when the most important
prophecy of my upcoming car crash came in. Let's begin just by reading
what it said, and then we will analyze it.

12/4/96: Have some tea . . . My gift to the world will be a 3 1/2-
by-11 sheet of paper. Expect it on Friday. This runs counter to
earlier systems of thought. We can work on visual sites. 90
minutes till 10:00.[13]

Though this may seem deceptively simple, it proved to be a stunning prophecy. That same Friday, I was driving on US Route 9W to Pough-keepsie in the midst of a freezing-cold blizzard for my training to become "med certified." The cars ahead of me came to a sudden stop out of no-where, and I slammed on the brakes. My car slid forward nearly thirty-five feet through the slush, and I gently tapped the bumper of the car in front of me, leaving a dime-size dent. The woman insisted on having the police arrive. The passage began by saying, "Have some tea," and some of the emergency personnel were drinking hot tea after they arrived in order to stay warm. The state police officer wrote me a ticket for the ac-cident, which was on a 3 1/2-by-11 sheet of paper, and the reading said, "My gift to the world will be a 3 1/2-by-11 sheet of paper." The time he assigned to the collision was 8:30 A.M, which was indeed "90 minutes till 10:00." This accident happened almost exactly one year after my previous one, with a difference of only twelve days. I had a hard time understand-ing how this accident could be a "gift to the world," but in hindsight, this event did help me to become far more considerate of others and thereby further activate my own Ascension process.

Based on the context, this reading also could be a 9/11 prophecy. First of all, the 9/11 event is always written as the numeral 9, a slash, and then the numeral 11. In the reading, I was told that the source's "gift to the world" would be a 3 1/2-by-11 sheet of paper. The measurements of the paper had a slash in them, followed by 11. Additional support was given when the time was marked as "90 minutes until 10:00." If we eliminate the zeroes, this passage fixed the numerals 9 and 1, the two key numbers in 9/11. This may all seem like a reach, but not when we see what came in that same Friday. Other 9/11 prophecies also came in later on that were far more precise, and I featured several of them in *The Synchronicity Key*. And let's not forget that the Great Pyramid itself, which may have been built as far back as 10,490 BC, seems to have a very impressive 9/11 proph-ecy built into the stonework of the pit in the Subterranean Chamber.

On that same day, Wednesday, December 4, 1996, I asked my source a question. I woke up with a dream the morning before that I had not actually documented and written down, since I was focused on pulling in the readings and was in a hurry to leave the house. In that dream, I

was seeing spectacular images of Mayan-style pyramids, roads, and buildings that were submerged at the bottom of the ocean. This was far more
beautiful and spectacular than anything I had ever seen or read about in
any books on ancient civilizations. I wanted to ask why I had been shown
this amazing vision, and what it meant for me. Here was the answer,
which included additional obvious prophecies of the coming car crash. I
was running late, not sticking to a schedule, and would end up crashing
my car due to slippery road conditions. The reading even says, "The path
is slippery" and "Make sure your seat belt is buckled in," so again, they
clearly knew what was about to happen:

> Nothing is forever. The reason why you have such difficulty
> with that is that you were passed up. It's time for another cycle
> to go around. Come with me, and I will show you the way to
> the Light. The path is slippery, so one must run carefully. . . .
> It is important that you stick to a schedule. We're a little out
> of range timewise. Eventually, there will be more for you. . . .
> I'll check again to make sure your seat belt is buckled in. Trust
> your instincts above all else, for they will not fail you. It's
> terrible; it's so far away. You have Karaoke in your hand. In
> working on advancements, some times it is necessary to fall
> asleep. The supervisor will see you again. Cloudy glasses,
> you're fine; it's similar to what happened before.[14]

Much of this passage was prophetic of the crash. In the spiritual
sense, I had fallen asleep. The windshield was indeed cloudy that day,
hence the reference to "cloudy glasses." This crash was indeed "similar to
what happened before," since I had been through a well-prophesied karmic car crash the year before. The line "the supervisor will see you again"
indicated how this was a disciplinary action, just like I would go through
at work if I was called into a meeting with my supervisor. Now let's continue:

> But seriously, you have to start thinking of the world. You
> don't have to, but it has suffered long enough. . . . The whole

residence is on strike. You've got it named; you have me, I am peaceful and PhD. Your cap and gown can be pretty exciting, as long as you clean it every once in a while. Your work shows promise; new thoughts and information will be arriving to you soon. It's time to do some shopping, shopping for lunch specials. Which one do you want, Christina? . . . I've been here for a long time, and I know you pretty well by now. Don't forget that there are starving kids, Afrikaan, African. It's basically a series about the hopes and doubts of living and growing up in America. Look to the end of the book for some insights on that one.[15]

The metaphor of "shopping for lunch specials" had to do with the creation of work that would feed others spiritually. By calling me Christina, the source was referring to how my feminine Christ self was now awakening. The idea of "starving kids" was a reference to all the people who have never really felt any sense of absolute proof of a higher, positive spiritual power in the world. And the last sentence, "Look to the end of the book for some insights on that one," has another very obvious time loop to my present as I write these words. I am at the very end of the book now, and am trying to make sure that some of the most important messages from these early readings make it into this book before I run out of pages. I had to laugh when I reread those words as I was putting this chapter together. Even well into the creative process for this book in the summer of 2019, I did not realize that the moment the readings started would only appear at the very end.

The reading continued with the surprise discovery that I was speaking with a female entity, and that the man I had been hearing from before was apparently her supervisor. As I heard these words, I was also shown a vision of a female in a white robe, which again is exactly like the Midwayers, Elders, or Anshar:

You know I'm late, Dave. I'm supposed to be sitting right next to my supervisor at this point. [Voice was of a grandmotherly woman.] Did you assume that I was male this year? Wrong again. The birth of stars; you must check your messages. . . . You need to go to the bathroom now, and get changed for work. Peace be with you in the Light of everlasting Love.[16]

The next day, Thursday, December 5, featured additional prophecies of the next day's car crash that I completely did not understand at the time. This included a mention of "private dummies," which appears to be a veiled reference to crash-test dummies, as well as "rescue squads" and the idea that a "tragedy" was coming:

12/5/96: Letting go of something important . . . It's only being scheduled in some ways so you can understand procrastination. I do this to involve the notions of my peers in caring for you. . . . Private dummies adorn your collection. When the answer is so simple, it is also so terrible; still, when I think about it, it would be nice if I had more than one hope. Dream; you must put a stop to this sleep deprivation. If you were to land a new job, you might calm down a little bit. To not stop looking might be good for you. If you talk to your friends about it, they could help you in Highland [a town not far from Rosendale]. It's all mixed up; right now, I'd rather not talk about it.

The missing pieces fit together, and then again, sometimes they don't. Think deeply about what you are planning on embarking on. Many great rescue squads have come into being. Their illustrious voices sing high the praises of the Creator. To give you details at this point would be redundant. You scared me this summer; I was working very diligently to find a table for you. You need little or no prompting in order to get through most things; that's why it was such a tragedy. One must see that you cannot live only on hummus. [I was on a vegan diet and often ate chips and hummus when I should have had a more balanced meal.] Jeopardizing your health had severe consequences. You lied to me about certain

things, and that was hard to compensate for. And the truth
is, some of it goes way back to the mind essence of what I was
saying before. Truly the highest order is to know one's self.
Everyone has a similar weakness. . . . It is aesthetically pleas-
ing for me to see you growing, and I know that one day we
will integrate in views together as One. I know that you are
going to finish with accolades and high honors. . . . Peace be
with you in the Light of everlasting Love.[17]

9/11: The Greatest Science Fiction Story Ever Told

Now we have finally reached the morning of Friday, December 6, 1996.
This is when I had my strongest 9/11 prophecy, including the actual numerals 911, as well as a passage with the ironic joke that "CBS and ABC
give it adequate coverage." Obviously, the news coverage of 9/11 was far
more than adequate—it was a nonstop inundation of images of mass
destruction for weeks and weeks on end. Once we see this in context, the
many other statements in this reading not only apply to my going
through a personal "dark night of the soul" and healing process—they
also indicated that a similar collapse would happen with the patriarchal
negative elites who have dominated our planet for centuries, if not millennia. The "negative elite" were very likely involved in planning and
carrying out 9/11, as many scholars have argued, and as I discuss in *The
Ascension Mysteries*. Nine-eleven actually represented a defeat for them,
as I argued with historical cycle analysis in *The Synchronicity Key*. At
times I will pause this reading and step in for commentary as we go
along.

> 12/6/96: Under the aegis of friendly planetary transformation,
> the talk show host has got a new one. They're all special ef-
> fects, designed to ride the lightning bolts. That's one way of
> losing their cookies is to get real syndicated. It's doctor-
> recommended; who is going to ask the pediatrician? Who is
> going to look at the self with tangible results? Self-awareness

is the key to building a foundation. If you're on the floor, you
might have to postpone things.[18]

Once we see the prophetic references to 9/11, we can understand what
this passage is talking about. First of all, this tragedy did create years'
worth of conversation for talk-show hosts. This included the idea that
9/11 was an inside job. Less than two years after the 9/11 event, I read
intelligence leaks from the investigator Sherman Skolnick, saying that
the buildings were brought down by low-yield mini-nuke devices, according to his insiders. Here is a quote from Skolnick that was published
on April 4, 2003: "In 1992, members of our investigative group spent
about four months extensively interviewing Michael Riconoscuito. Described by those who knew him well as a weapons and electronic genius,
which we verified he is/was, he ran afoul of the American CIA because
he divulged to a Congressional Committee the dirty business of Daddy
Business and others in the 'spook' industry. [The federal jails, in various
places in this nation, have put away by frame-ups, several former CIA
pilots who blew the whistle on dope shipments, CIA covert operators
and such, all on the outs with the spy cartel, and put in jail on long sentences. Riconosciuto was framed up on a twenty-eight-year rap.] As we
confirmed, Riconosciuto helped invent and develop a sub-atomic weapon
he and others called 'blue lightning.' . . . If the truth about 'blue lightning' comes out, will ordinary Americans find out what really took
down, as by controlled demolitions, the World Trade Center twin towers
and WTC Building 7 in Manhattan, September 11, 2001?"[19]

According to my insider Pete Peterson, the Blue Lightning devices are
only about the size of the top joint of your thumb, and they are referred
to as "fifth-gen nukes." The code name of Blue Lightning was used because of the visible blue energy they give off. And this reading said,
"they're all special effects, designed to ride the lightning bolts." I found
this very interesting indeed. As Skolnick's insiders revealed, the collapse
of the Twin Towers was indeed an act of "special effects," caused not by
typical jet-fuel burning but the "lightning bolts" from the Blue Lightning weapon.

This passage also said that this catastrophe was ultimately "doctor-recommended," as it was necessary for the positive beings to allow us to go through this process in order to realize the true darkness in our world. Only then would we be emboldened enough to rise up against it. Now let's pick it up with the very next words they spoke, after I asked a question that proved to be irrelevant to their greater point. Notice that the next line says, "These vital matters have been recorded in stone." It was only as I was writing this chapter that I understood this line was referring to the Pyramid Timeline. We have discussed the very precise prophecy of 9/11 in the timeline, where, in Peter Lemesurier's words, "the bottom will fall out of the world," and we enter what Great Pyramid researchers call the Pit of Hell on Earth. As we remember, Lemesurier expected this to happen in 2004, but by his own logic, we can also back-date it by three years, which fixes this event to 2001.

> These vital matters have been recorded in stone. Fear not; the breath of the Infinite is about to be born again. It's no prob-lem when you know what you are doing. The oddest part about this is its connection to the Church. Discoveries in the caves will be changing all of that so soon. If a person is sick, they need constant attention. If a person is real sick, they need to collapse. In a smaller church, prayer is a very strong system. I'm aware of myself choosing attractive names, which is not good. You know it's Christmas when Joshua presents himself to you.[20]

Before we go any further, the above passage is talking about the fall of the patriarchy, and personifying it as if a single man was going through this. Multiple insiders would later tell me that the negative elite are directly tied to the Church, since the Vatican is their spiritual head-quarters. The reading indicated that this patriarch is "real sick" and "needs to collapse." As the passage continues, the metaphor of the col-lapsing patriarchy continues—and then we get the now-legendary 9/11 prophecy. It begins by outlining that the whole story line was a fraud. In fact, the reading referred to it as "the greatest science fiction story ever told."

> Sometimes a habit must be dropped cold turkey in order to leave it. All pleasantries have been exhausted; there is no other way for the energy to flow. The patriarch must be denominated. It's the greatest science fiction story ever told. Someone comes in—Rescue 911. CBS and ABC give it adequate coverage. A cast-iron fence is wrought around the victim's body. He likes to do that. An impenetrable wall needs only be potentiated by positive energy. . . . The essential concept will be felt so strongly that it cannot be ignored. In the context of the rest of the people, the material you present is truly a magical gift. . . . Peace be with you in the Light of everlasting Love.[21]

This passage talks about how "the patriarch must be denominated." The word *denominated* is a humorous play on words, for a politician needs to be nominated by his or her party to run for president. This was another clue that the US government itself was at least partly involved in the planning of 9/11. The "habit" that this patriarchal cult has had of dominating the planet "must be dropped cold turkey," just like I had to drop my habit of running late and speeding on the roads. Then we have a direct numerical reference to 9/11 as "Rescue 911." Again, we see the ironic joke that "CBS and ABC give it adequate coverage." This made no sense for my little personal car crash, but perfect sense for 9/11. Then it said, "A cast-iron fence is wrought around the victim's body." Indeed, the support beams of the World Trade Center were made of steel, and wrought iron is a form of iron that has been made stronger by being heated and then worked with tools. After the World Trade Center fell, a small area of steel beams remained standing. This was the "cast-iron fence" that was "wrought around the victim's body."

The reading also indicated that this event would not be doom and gloom: "An impenetrable wall needs only be potentiated by positive energy." In this case, a strong part of that positive energy is our collective desire for freedom and liberty. This type of a disaster creates prayers that authorize the benevolent, angelic extraterrestrial Guardians and Watchers to be allowed to do far more to help us than they otherwise would have been able to carry out. And indeed, the reading then says, "The essential concept [of our collective desire for freedom] will be felt so strongly that it cannot be ignored."

When we look back to the Pyramid Timeline, we see that not everyone has to enter the Pit. By simply seeing it in front of us, and the trap that it represents, we can turn back, retrace our steps, and then travel up through the Well-Shaft. This delivers us directly up to the entrance to the Ascending Passage, at AD 33 in the Pyramid Timeline—right at the moment when Jesus achieves Ascension. Lemesurier revealed that the Pyramid Timeline is a metaphor for the spiritual journey we all go through, and on that level the timing is not fixed. We all have the opportunity to Ascend if we will it to be, mainly by ensuring that our waking focus is on love and acceptance of others, rather than manipulation and control.

One last prophecy I will share in this chapter came in just fifteen days later, on December 21, 1996. With the benefit of hindsight, this again appeared to be a direct prophecy of 9/11, and the "scoundrels" who were secretly responsible for planning it:

> 12/21/96: Remember when I told you about the scoundrels? On the good side of it, there's always a way out. . . . Spirit authorities are connected, but they won't directly intervene without good reason. When people disappear in the buildings, sometimes you have lost them. Getting closer to that state known as sleep, that state known as New York.[22]

This reading directly mentioned New York, and mentioned how "people disappear in the buildings" and "sometimes you have lost them." The beginning of the reading again clearly implied that this was done by "the scoundrels." The implication here is that the 9/11 event and other such engineered catastrophes will ultimately cause "spirit authorities" to "directly intervene," so that "on the good side, there is always a way out." Although we have yet to see this prophecy fully realized at the time of this writing, I am ever hopeful and confident that we will. I will close this chapter with two more readings that came in as of 1998 and made the message even clearer. These were documented on my website in 1999, well before 9/11 ever took place. The first reading is referring to a dream I had just dictated, where I did indeed see a 9/11-style "airborne explosion" that damaged a skyscraper-type building.

> 7/1/98: We understand that these are very distressing circumstances, and would remind you that the tectonic shifts involved in the upcoming changes also make New York a particularly undesirable target location [to live in]. . . . In the following dream the cycle was completed by the appearance of the airborne explosion. This also was interwoven with the more long-term [solar] effects of the Ascension, but the bomb aspect was correctly given, and needs to be addressed at this time. This is coming in the form of an ongoing jihad, which does not want to be acknowledged to the people by your government. Yet, there is every reason to believe that it is progressing, and that New York is the number one target for any such actions. Let us all hope together that this prophecy shall fail to come to pass.

> 7/9/98: [The 1993] World Trade Center bombing really shook things up. The next time one tries something like this, it will become a much larger story, if the details are worked out properly.[23]

CHAPTER TWENTY-FIVE

Conclusion

Except for the last passage from December 21, 1996, and the two passages from 1998, all the readings we just reviewed happened less than a month after my contact started. Many hundreds of pages of beautiful, lyrical passages flowed through me. To properly review everything that happened, and all the astonishing future prophecies that these readings gave me, I will need to write at least one more book. In all honesty, it will probably take more than one volume just to cover the basics to a level where I will feel satisfied.

Stunning Prophetic Accuracy

During the years of 1996 to 2000, where I recorded my own voice every morning to dictate my dreams and readings, I would often sit down to transcribe a stack of as many as four or five ninety-minute cassette tapes of material that I had dictated but hadn't yet had the time to write up. In almost every case where I did this, the readings were describing what had happened to me right before I sat down. Since there are hundreds of pages of readings and we are now in the final chapter, I will speed up the timeline and review just a few examples from what I lovingly call the "Greatest Hits Collection." These prophecies will be well known to readers who followed my website within the first few years after its debut in February 1999, although I have now gone back to the archives and dug out specific details that I never published back then.

One of the most fantastic prophecies I ever received came in on Christmas Day 1996. Eric had become aware that he wanted to break up with his girlfriend, a Japanese exchange student he got together with shortly after Yumi and I paired up. As I told him all the stories of what was happening with the readings, and read him some of the words, he asked me if I could pull in any information for him. That was all it took. What follows is just a short excerpt of what we got, with the key prophecy included.

> 12/25/96: Coming in to sight is a big boost. . . . Your life is geared to be full of information. Sit down, I suggest you use it. A lot of times, I will end up smiling; I almost rubbed it off on you. . . . You keep saying to try a little harder, but the decision is already set in stone, so why wait? However, you have my admonitions regarding [not breaking up during] Christmas and the vacation. Give yourself some breathing room within the time frame to allow her to ease into it herself. . . . However, trust your feelings. If you can't wait, then there's no sense in holding it inside. You knew this months ago. It is nice to see you aligning with your true path. Don't tell me you don't think this is going to work. Nonsense. You are more than ready to take that chance, and [she] is good and ready to leave you.
>
> You may be interested to know that student loans will come through. You should visit New Paltz. Life will change; life in a conservatory . . . People on a lesser path will not know the richness that awaits you. So soon will you return. I never complained about the foreign assignments I was given, however I realized when they had followed their due course. It is important that you see that this experience will give her a more balanced approach to life. Recognize the synchronicity

between the relative birth and death times of your and David's relationships. Two years, two months.[1]

Eric and I read over these and other words in the reading and studied them intensely after they came through. It was indeed true that both our relationships ended up lasting two years and two months. However, a much greater surprise was still in store for us. I did tell Eric that the sentence in the second paragraph of the transcript originally had been "You may be interested to know that your student loans for New Paltz will come through." Since I knew Eric had graduated from New Paltz and was now earning a master's degree from SUNY Albany, I broke the normal remote-viewing-type protocols and allowed my conscious mind to get in the way. I asked for the sentence to be reworded because I was genuinely afraid I was getting bad information. However, no matter how often I asked, all I could get was the slightly different version that we see in the transcript above.

Roughly two weeks later, Eric walked into the Schoolhouse and was extremely serious when he told me, "You need to sit down. You're not going to believe this." I laughed at first, but he was not smiling, so I did what he said. "You remember that reading you got for me about New Paltz?" he asked me.

"Of course," I replied.

"Get this," he said. "My mother just got a call from the bursar's office at New Paltz. They were moving their office from one room to another. One of the last things they had to move was a file cabinet. As they pulled the file cabinet away from the wall, they found an envelope behind it. Inside that envelope was a Stafford Loan check, made out to me, for nine hundred dollars. David, the check is still good! She just put it in the mail and we will have it tomorrow. Now we can pay the rent!"

I was absolutely flabbergasted. Despite the fact that we both held jobs, we had run out of money—and desperately needed $867 to pay the rent. We had no idea how we were going to get it. "My God, Eric. I remember! In that reading they did for you, they said, 'You may be interested to know that your student loans for New Paltz will come through.' We desperately need 867 bucks, and now you find a check for 900! It's unbelievable! We're saved! How in the world were the beings able to do that?"

The Cayce Connection

As the year 1997 rolled on, I became increasingly convinced that I needed to move to Virginia Beach, the home of the Edgar Cayce Readings. Cayce had founded the Association for Research and Enlightenment, or ARE, and it was still running on the North End of the beach. My reasons for wanting to move were twofold. One, Cayce had readings that said Virginia Beach was a "safety land," where the damage from catastrophic earthquakes, tsunamis, and the like would be much less serious.

There was a notorious Cayce reading from an entity calling itself Halaliel that said California was going to sink into the ocean in 1998. This obviously did not happen, but with all the accurate prophecies I was experiencing in 1997, I did not want to take a chance.

The ARE would later release publications explaining that Halaliel was a "trickster entity" that Cayce called in by allowing himself to be angry at his detractors. Thanks to the Law of Free Will, Cayce's own negativity forced his source to allow this entity to have a chance to speak—and thus produce messages of doom. Cayce's group soon chose not to invoke Halaliel, and were then congratulated for having made the right choice. In reading 262-57, on January 7, 1934, when the group finally asked who Halaliel was, Cayce's source said, "One in and with whose courts Ariel fought when there was the rebellion in heaven. Now, where is heaven? Where is Ariel, and who was he? A companion of Lucifer or Satan, and one that made for the disputing of the influences in the experiences of Adam in the Garden."[2] This reading may have been implying, in a veiled manner, that at some point Halaliel had aligned with Lucifer.

This type of interference problem was discussed in Session 12, Question 15, of the Law of One, as follows:

> It is entirely possible for the untuned channel, as you call that service, to receive both positive and negative communica-

tions. If the entity at the base of its confusion is oriented towards service to others, the entity will begin to receive messages of doom. If the entity at the base of the complex of beingness is oriented towards service to self, the crusaders, who in this case, do not find it necessary to lie, will simply begin to give the philosophy they are here to give. Many of your so-called contacts among your people have been confused and self-destructive because the channels were oriented towards service to others but, in the desire for proof, were open to the lying information of the crusaders who then were able to neutralize the effectiveness of the channel.[3]

Sadly, even a channel as renowned as Edgar Cayce was not exempt from this happening. As of 1997, I had every reason to think that this prophecy of a global disaster in 1998 might still come true, and I believed in the value of the "safety land" prophecies. My second reason for going to Virginia Beach was that the ARE had a graduate program in metaphysics with a school they called Atlantic University. Therefore, I could go to the "safety land" and still get an education, even if nothing happened in 1998.

In mid-1997, I went onto the ARE website to see if they had any satellite offices closer to my home, where I could get more information. They had only one location in all the Northeast, and it happened to be in Marbletown—literally the next town over from Rosendale! It was less than a ten-minute drive from my house, door to door. The guy who was running it was named Skip Weatherford. I soon came over to visit him and he was fascinated with my story, which he said sounded very similar to that of Edgar Cayce. Not long after we started working together, he gave me a hypnotic regression to see if I could find any additional information about a possible past life in Atlantis. While under hypnosis, I had fuzzy memories of being a prominent leader during that time. In the regression, I realized that I had become karmically bound to the Earth as a result of mistakes I had made in that lifetime. Specifically, I remembered having a feeling of intellectual superiority, and having too much pride in my accomplishments. This was a key factor that apparently led to my having to continually reincarnate on Earth for the following twelve thousand years.

In my second session with Skip on May 22, 1997, very strange things happened. When I was doing readings at the time, I would put a quartz crystal under my left hand and a palm-size, triangular amethyst cluster under my right hand. In this session with Skip, as soon as my right hand hit the amethyst cluster, a thin line of blue electricity shot out from the wall and touched the crystal. The line was slightly bent in the middle and it was perhaps six inches long. I did not get shocked when it hit the crystal. Skip saw it and was as surprised as I was.

Once I was under hypnosis, the beings came through and began speaking to Skip directly. At a certain point, he became aware that all he had to do was think of his next question, and the source would begin answering it. He finally mentioned this out loud and wanted to know how it was possible. My eyes suddenly opened and I looked at him with pupils that were dilated completely black. I turned my head, and with an emotionless, almost robotic delivery, my voice said, "It is by virtue of the oneness of consciousness that I can do this, as you well know." I was aware enough to notice that he was quite surprised, but was able to hold the trance state, which was unusually intense in this session.

As I left his house to go home, the clock showed 3:33. Immediately after I left his house, the power went off and stayed off for exactly one hour. I was proud of myself for whatever had just happened, and I drove too fast on the way home, out of excitement. A police officer pulled me over, giving me a healthy reminder that I was still subject to the Law of Karma and I needed not to be cocky. Thankfully, the officer let me go with a warning because I was so apologetic, almost on the brink of tears, and explained to him that I could not afford to pay a ticket.

Strap On Your Parachute Hat

As the year 1997 went by, and the readings kept dazzling me with one accurate prophecy after another, I became fairly certain that I was going to move to Virginia Beach. Eric ended up trying out the Dream Voice technique on his own as of September 24, 1997, since I had thoroughly explained the protocols to him and he was interested. The file with his readings in it is dated October 17, 1997, and it has lived in the Documents folder of every computer and hard drive I've ever owned, making it easy to forensically prove its authentic dating. Eric pulled through twelve different sessions from September 24 until October 17 that sounded much like my own did. The first words Eric ever got were, "My consciousness is being traced on the inside. Hi, my name is Mike, what's your name?" Based on my own contacts as well as those of Edgar Cayce, this may have been a hint that the source speaking was not just "Mike," but Archangel Michael, who had also spoken through me at times. Then on September 26, Michael said, in part, "What are we come for? We have been with you since June. Welcome to our sun. This is our planet, welcome." The next day, Michael asked Eric, "What is the most powerful thing you've ever done?" Then on the twenty-ninth, among other things, Michael said, "Dave as the wolf." This seemed to be prophetic of my upcoming move, where I would have to go out on my own to Virginia Beach as the "lone wolf."

Michael got oddly political on the thirtieth, where Eric heard a repeating verse from the KISS song "God of Thunder," which was apparently intended to symbolize the Illuminati in Eric's reading: "I am the lord of the wasteland . . . I use the darkness to please me . . ." Then the reading itself soon said, "Russia is hard to define. He's afraid. . . . How can one feel so intransigent? Technically, it is the Democrats who underscore the White House. This is because of the rules of the game as we know them."

This seemed highly prophetic, since I reread this again for the first time during a final editing pass for this book on January 18, 2020. I read Michael's prophecy right in the midst of a massive impeachment drama, where the Democrats are desperately trying to remove the president, after three years of arguing that Russia had interfered in the 2016 election—such as in the Mueller investigation. Eric's reading said, "Russia is hard to define. He's afraid. . . . How can one feel so intransigent?" This clearly seems to be about the president and his troubles with the alleged election interference from Russia, which has indeed been "hard to define" and would naturally cause him to feel afraid for his presidency.

This was followed by "How can one feel so intransigent," and the word *intransigent* means "a person who refuses to agree or compromise, as in politics."[4] Eric's source then said, "Technically it's the Democrats who actually underscore the White House . . . because of the rules of the game as we know them." The Democrats have clearly been intransigent, as has the president himself, causing a major standoff.

Other Michael passages from October 5 also now sound prophetic, as I reread this for the first time while writing the book. It also had strange encrypted language that doesn't necessarily make sense, as will happen when you follow the protocols properly.

> In some distant city, one dares to attack the Pope, but is caught unawares. Coming to a sense of what ONE is about. Remember, it is not the user, but the finisher. Go along (with) Tompkins' grandson. Refracting our troubles abroad by using some "grand device" for the destruction of worth like none has ever seen before. Yield in your heart, not your mind. Believe in the ONE, all else is futile. Sunspots appear as historic sites. What else would you expect? This is not a bi-matrix anymore. Sign-off: Law School. Goodbye.

This again was in 1997, and at the time of this writing, the papacy is indeed under attack like never before with sexual abuse scandals. William Tompkins did not appear as an insider until 2016, and he verified everything Corey Goode and my other insiders were telling us. Michael appears to be referring to me here as "Tompkins' grandson," and it is true that Tompkins and I became very close before his death at age ninety-four. Eric and I did not know anyone with the last name of Tompkins, so this was another of many cryptic passages when it first came in. The "grand device for the destruction of worth" seemed to be a reference to the 2007–2008 economic collapse prophesied in the Great Pyramid Timeline, and the hardship our world has endured since then, where ordinary people never really recovered financially from the damage. I considered at the time this reading came in that "Law school" was a reference to the Law of One.

On October 7, Eric pulled in language that was surprisingly spiritual-sounding, since Eric was not religious in his waking life: "Hello, here we are again my friend. It is all ONE and nothing at the same time that we follow. Won't you join us? Simply this: who is a rightful heir of our legacy? Don't you know? Fall into step behind the master and you will relish the joys of the eternal bliss. Fear not, we are all ONE, no exceptions." A few lines later, the source began speaking in German, at a level that was far beyond Eric's waking ability and required him to use a dictionary to translate it: "*Wir sind gerechnet. Alles sind unflugende wirtinhausen Sagen (und) lachen wir du komm(s)t mit uns nach heilige Lande, sofor(t)! . . . Ans werkende kamin. So ist alles fertig? Gut. Geben Sie mir bitte ein wunderbares todsprungen Pater.*"

Eric's translation of this, which was part of a larger passage in German, came out as, "We are just and fair. Everything[one] is fleeing the landlady's house. We say and laugh—or we say laughingly: You will come with us to the Holy lands, immediately! . . . To the working fireplace. Is everything finished [ready]? Good. Please give me a wonderful godfather that has sprung from death." Eric used a dictionary to find the most precise meanings of each word, in context, and thus his version is slightly different than a machine-generated translation, such as you might get from Google Translate. The voice then reverted back to English, and said, "Ha! It is I, your long-lost friend Martin."

Eric did not know anyone named Martin in his waking life, and he felt betrayed by Martin's words, as the "lady's house" that "everyone" was "fleeing" from clearly represented the Schoolhouse. Eric did not want me to move out, but by this point he was well aware that I had received prophecies urging me to do so. My readings had already guided me to work a season at Mohonk Mountain House, a gorgeous five-star Victorian resort hotel. For a certain period, I had really loved it, but I eventually burned out from answering the nonstop calls we were getting in Reservations for fall-foliage weekends that always sold out over a year in advance. The only way I could stay on past October would be to work the switchboard, and I just couldn't cope with the idea. I knew it was "now or never." Eric's reading proposed a toast to "the working fireplace," as yet another sign that it was time for me to leave Mohonk. Every room had a working fireplace, and I included this in each conversation I had with a prospective customer. The idea of "going to the holy lands" was similar to my idea of moving to Virginia Beach, since the Cayce readings saw it as a "safety land" from potential Earth Changes.

Eric's 1997 readings also seem to have other time-loop prophecies to our own present. Certain passages seem to refer to the Alliance in the US military and intelligence communities that I have been writing so much about on my website since 2009—a group that clearly seems to be opposing the so-called Illuminati. This is part of what came in on October 7, 1997: "Greed is an unquenchable thirst. Let go of your false hopes and ambitions. Weed out all propaganda. Life is yours for the taking. Martin Schauerkoff, Lieutenant. [This is a likely reference to Norman Schwarzkopf, a top US military general.] His word was gospel. Treat him like a brother even though he is a bastard. God bless them all." This reading seems to be confirming that the Alliance is doing its best to weed out all propaganda and expose those who have an unquenchable thirst for greed. Many people have a negative view of the military at this time, but the reading encourages to treat people in the Alliance as our brothers nonetheless.

A brief excerpt of a passage Eric pulled in on October 13, 1997, further alluded to the Alliance's plans to majorly restructure the financial system to make it fair, and implies that these benevolent, angelic extraterrestrials have somehow helped to ensure this would come to pass: "Gone are the days of simple material pursuits. We must now teach the world how to play fair. . . . Politics unheard of: Campaign Finance Reform. Something to avoid, it causes breast cancer. But we never raised any pigs." In context, this again suggests that the Alliance will create massive, sweeping changes in our society. There was also a stunningly accurate message for me in other parts of this passage, which I have not included here. This prophecy was time-looped to my immediate present, just like how we saw the coordinates to the 2019–2020 impeachment crisis. Although this data is too personal to include and analyze, I am quite amazed by what it said, as it is extremely relevant and helpful within my immediate present situation.

Now let's go back in time just a bit, to September 23, 1997. A reading that morning clearly seemed to be telling me I needed to move. Among other things it said, "The point is, if you are going down in this area, you are going to have to wear a parachute hat. Virginia would be a good time." I couldn't help but understand this one and it knocked me out of trance, so on the tape I then said, "The implications of what you just said are rather stunning. My mind is a little bit reeling; I am sorry that it is taking me a while to get back into this [trance state.]"[5]

Then the next morning, on September 24, 1997, at 6:40 A.M., the very first words I pulled in from the reading were, "A priest, living in the vernacular [native, indigenous] state. He only beckons for the truth of one thing; wisdom. His many lives have affected him deeply, and that is okay. He still yearns for that which he sees in the distance; a new tomorrow, unfettered by the concerns that so deeply affected him in the past. He prepares himself for a time where there will need to be a much greater focus on the issues at hand than there currently is."[6] This seemed very prophetic, and clearly referred to my having had multiple past lives that affected me very deeply, including that of a priest. I fell back asleep and woke up again at 8:00, after a very intense dream that convinced me I had to make the move to Virginia Beach.

At some point in this dream, I became lucid, and I strongly asked to meet the source of my "Dream Voice," as I was calling it at the time. I found myself in a strange, roomy Victorian house that had wind blowing through it. Then I met a woman my own age who, in retrospect, was the spitting image of my wife, Elizabeth. We had immense romantic feelings for each other, but then she wandered off. When I found her again, she was sitting at a desk in a room that looked just like my junior- and senior-year dormitory, where I began regularly writing my dreams down in 1995. There was a guy seated at the other desk who I did not recognize. This strange plot twist caused me to become angry, since I had asked to meet my source and wasn't being heard—so I yelled out, "Isn't there someone around here who knows what the hell is going on?"

I then walked back out into the hallway and saw a different woman standing there. She had long, slightly graying hair, and was wearing what looked to be a faded purple hippie dress. She had very insightful, penetrating blue eyes, and I was immediately comforted by her. She looked at me and she said, "You know you have to move, don't you?" I was a little suprised and did not know what to do or what to say, but she kept staring at me. I finally blurted out, "Oh, okay, I understand." I was in a complete state of shock. I then felt influenced to turn, and it felt as though the flow of time was frozen in place, and I was in between two moments. I was in a long and rather wide hallway with a variety of doors on both sides that all looked slightly different, each with their own decorations. I got the feeling that I was right near the sea, and all the way in the back I could see a doorway with stairs leading down.

A really attractive girl with wavy blond hair appeared at one of the doors, which I now can see was an obvious manifestation of my future wife, Elizabeth. She immediately asked me where I was from, and for some reason I said, "Blooming-town" instead of Bloomington. The Schoolhouse was indeed in a little town called Bloomington, immediately next to Rosendale. The girl then laughed and said, "So, you're from Blooming-town, huh? That means you're blooming, doesn't it?" I got the nature of the metaphor and laughed along with her. Then everything went white, and I had a complete phase shift into a whole different situation. I was hovering in the air and observed myself as a seven-year-old boy, where I began doing psychic experiments with my friends in second grade. In this case, my seven-year-old self was dressed in a little gray three-piece suit, and I was speaking to some other kids about ESP in a lecture format, complete with a kid-size podium. I kept hearing a soft, gentle motherly voice that was apparently trying to communicate with my young self telepathically as I spoke, apparently without success. She kept saying, "Diamond . . . Diamond David?" but my younger self did not seem to be able to hear her. This section was obviously prophetic of my future career, where I would often dress up in suits and educate audiences about the ESP events from my youth, among many other topics.

Now Who's That?

Along with Eric's reading in German, which he admittedly felt betrayed by, I knew this lucid dream message from the old woman was the final sign I needed. I called the ARE in Virginia Beach and connected with local members who could help me when I arrived. Just days before I was scheduled to leave, Skip phoned me. He told me I had to come over to his house, right now. I had plenty of work to do to get ready to move, so I really didn't want to go. Skip told me it was extremely important that I come over, right now. I finally relented, got in the car, and drove over. When I walked inside, Skip had a magazine in his hand. He had taped a piece of white paper over the cover of the magazine and had cut a rectangular-shaped hole in the middle of the paper. With a huge, swooping movement of his arm, he dramatically and loudly slapped the magazine down on the table and pointed at it. "Now who's that?" he asked me. Inside the cutout was a portrait of a face that looked exactly the same as mine. It was so similar to me that apart from the strange, antique-looking white collar, I could easily have thought it was a picture of me.

At the same time, I could tell that someone had traced over the picture with a colored pencil to bring out some additional details, in an early, manual version of Photoshop. The ARE had a magazine for its members entitled *Venture Inward,* and I had seen other copies of the magazine at his house before. As the silence hung in the air and I continued looking at the picture, I realized this would have to be what Edgar Cayce looked like as a young man. It was a picture on the cover of *Venture Inward* magazine! The colored pencil enhancement technique had already been used on other covers I had seen. I had to say something, so I blurted out, "That's Edgar Cayce." Skip put his hand on his hip, cocked his head, and smiled widely. "Who else does it look like?" he asked me. "It's incredible, Skip, I have to say. That's my face. What in the world is going on? That's MY FACE!"

He answered, "You're right, David. Your face looks exactly the same as Edgar Cayce's face did when he was your age. And look at you. Now you're doing readings that are very similar to what he was doing. I don't know if you've studied all the research on reincarnation, but there are scientists like Dr. Ian Stevenson who have shown that each time we come back, our faces look the same as they did before. Dr. Stevenson studied many hundreds of children, mostly in the Middle East, who could accurately remember details of their past lives.[7] They could bring back names, places, specific details of what was on the walls inside a house, and in some cases even solve murders—and get their former killers to confess. I'm telling you, David, I've never seen anything like this. Your faces are almost identical. I think you are Edgar Cayce! You have to be! And now you're about to move to Virginia Beach. Think about it!"

A Group of German Steel Helmets

On October 20, 1997, with only seven hundred dollars in my wallet, I threw everything I owned into the Subaru, gave away all my furniture, and made the long, twelve-hour drive down I-95 from Rosendale to Virginia Beach. Eric and I were forced to end our lease of the School-house, because otherwise we would have to financially commit to a full year. Our landlady did start showing our apartment to prospective new tenants on October 4, 1997, before we had even moved out. By this point, Eric already had gotten a job with the Huguenot Historical Society, and actually moved into the upper floor of their library building. This ful-filled the prophecy he had gotten from my source on Christmas Day, when it told him, "Life will change; life in a conservatory." This had appeared right after the prophetic line that told him, "Your student loans for New Paltz will come through."

The first place I stayed in Virginia Beach was a condominium on Old Great Neck Road, which was off of Great Neck Road, with a woman named Linda. I seemed to remember seeing "Great Neck" appear in one of my readings, which turned out to have arrived on July 20, 1997. Linda also had a housemate named Dennis, who had been a professional wres-tler on television with the stage name Dr. Doom. The morning after I arrived, I sat down on her white leather couch and my eyes immediately locked on to the bookshelf. I could hardly believe what I saw. There was a book sitting sideways on the shelf entitled *The History of the German Steel Helmet: 1921–1945*. I immediately knew something wonderful had happened.

The day before the words *Great Neck* came through, on July 19, 1997, I had pulled in a brief phrase that sounded like it was in German. I wrote it out phonetically as "Skar-stal-ded." I had no idea what it meant, so I asked Eric to translate it for me. He felt I must have been hearing *Scarstahldig*, which meant "a group of German steel helmets." Now I was looking at this prominently positioned book about the history of the German steel helmet—and I was living on Old Great Neck Road, off of Great Neck Road. When Dennis came home, I told him what had happened. I showed him the printed proof of the prophecy, since I had created hard copies of everything before I left. He was astonished. "I collect German steel helmets as an investment," he said. "I have one of the largest collections of them in the world. It might be *the* largest." We were both astonished. Even more strangely, later that same year, his storage unit was broken into and someone stole the entire collection.

The Gang's All Here

I started meeting members of the ARE and Cayce enthusiasts, and they were all amazed at my story—and particularly with the facial similarity. It created quite a buzz in the community. I soon moved in with a man named Jim who owned a small farm, and had been best friends with Edgar Cayce's secretary, Gladys Davis. Jim was a huge Cayce fan. Over many years, Gladys had told him just about everything there was to know, including many of the more obscure stories that were not commonly known. Over the course of several months, I got to learn a wealth of information about the Cayce Readings that went well beyond what most people could have gathered without extensive research. Jim had a book entitled *Edgar Cayce's Photographic Legacy,* and he was convinced that we would find pictures of people in Cayce's inner circle that matched up with the people who were closest to me in my own life. It didn't take long at all to discover that Cayce's father, Leslie "the Squire," looked exactly like my father—and my father would only ever buy men's clothing at a place called the Squire Shop in downtown Schenectady.

I saw an immediate facial match between Wesley Harrington Ketchum, the first person who got Cayce to bring his readings out to the world, and my brother, Michael. Cayce's wife, Gertrude, was the spitting image of my friend Angelica, who had grown up in Muktananda's ashram. My former housemate Eric was somewhat similar-looking to David Kahn, one of Cayce's best friends, but not as strongly as the other matches I found. My college buddy Chris looked nearly identical to Cayce's main financial backer, Morton Blumenthal, who ultimately had a huge falling-out with Cayce and his team. Last, my best friend from high school, Jude, looked almost exactly the same as Morton Blumenthal's very spiritually minded brother, Edwin.

Since then, I have identified others as well, including Cayce's wife's cousin Stella, who looks exactly the same as my friend Sun. Best of all, Sun named her cat Stella Blue, and was directly responsible for introducing me to my wife, Elizabeth. I also discovered that Gladys Davis had reincarnated as a friend of mine, but she never wanted to go public with the story and never has. My housemate Jeff, who I lived with for many years in Topanga, California, ended up looking exactly the same as one of Cayce's main supporters, Linden Shroyer. He was the first to spot this connection by blurting it out as a joke while we were flipping through the Cayce photo book, right while I was showing Sun her precise similarity to Stella. Jim was also able to identify multiple passages in the Cayce readings where Ra was mentioned as a separate entity from Ra-Ptah. This included readings number 996-002, 444-001, and 5756-10. Ra was further indicated as being a separate entity from "the priest," which was a reference to Ra-Ptah, in 2067-001 and 3347-001. Lastly, the phrase "those of Ra," clearly indicating a group of beings, appears in 294-152, 378-014, 897-001, and 219-001. Most Cayce scholars believe that Ra and Ra-Ptah were the same being, but these passages clearly reveal that this is not the case.

With the Answer Comes Great Responsibility

As the facial similarities started rolling in, and the stories began connecting, Jim started pressuring me very strongly to do a reading where I would just ask the question, point-blank. I was truly terrified of this, because I knew what the implications were. Being Edgar Cayce reincarnated was bad enough, for it meant my life was destined not to be private. I would almost certainly be obligated to share all this with the world, and it would be very controversial, to say the least. However, the far greater conflict was in the fact that Edgar Cayce's own readings had

said he was the Atlantean priest-king Ra-Ptah, who built the Great Pyramid. The Law of One series had explained how Ra-Ptah's mistakes had
altered the course of history toward the negative. It was very clear that if
I was Edgar Cayce, then I would also have to be Ra-Ptah. And, if I was
indeed Ra-Ptah, that meant I had some serious karmic restitution that
would need to be made to the world for the bad decisions I had carried
out in that lifetime. Furthermore, I knew people would have a hard time
with this. I would be laughed at, scorned, and ridiculed on a massive
scale. The whole idea was absolutely terrifying, but I still felt I needed to
get the answer.

On the morning of November 26, 1997, around 7:25 A.M., I finally
"popped the question." Here was what happened as I transcribed it,
where I was coming out of trance to ask questions and then descending
back into it to get the answers. Notice that the very first words were
"table rock." This could be a metaphor of the Great Pyramid with its flat,
tablelike top:

Q: I would like to incubate a question on identity here, related to Edgar Cayce.

A: Table Rock. This is our boss. We will have to move
over, as he is in charge. What we are doing here is staring each
other in the face. Sometimes, you will need to do that. It
should be very easy to take a guess at this point, but with that
guess comes responsibility; enormous responsibility. Furthermore, as you are well aware, your connection with us will
need to be dramatically strengthened. In short, David, the
answer is yes; you will need to review the whole life and see
the parallels.[8]

This was profoundly upsetting to me on multiple levels. I had seen
certain people try to say they had been someone prominent in another
lifetime, and I would always cringe. However, I had to admit that this
was a compelling case. My face looked the same as Edgar Cayce's face, I
had an undying interest in Ancient Egypt, I had all these dreams in 1995
that seemed to relate to the life of Ra-Ptah, and I was pulling in psychic

readings that were similar to Edgar's. I believed in this strongly enough to move to Virginia Beach with only seven hundred dollars. Yet, even with all the evidence, I did not want to be this person. I had been through ridicule and bullying my entire life. The last thing I wanted to do was to endure even more of it. Even more disturbing to me was a prophecy Jim identified in Cayce Reading 294-151, which seemed to predict that Cayce would have reincarnated and discovered his former identity as of 1998—which at this point was just over a month away. The prophecy read, "Is it not fitting, then, that these must return? As this priest may develop himself to be in that position, to be in the capacity of a LIBERATOR of the world in its relationships to individuals in those periods to come; for he must enter again at that period, or in 1998." No pressure! I carefully pointed out to Jim that the reading said Cayce's reincarnation "may develop himself" to be *a* liberator, not that he would be *the* liberator. Jim also revealed that in *Many Happy Returns* by William Church, on page 226, Cayce had a dream where he had returned to Virginia Beach in a future lifetime—and now here I was in Virginia Beach, putting all these pieces together just a month before 1998. Another Cayce dream in *Many Happy Returns* said that he would be surrounded by many of the same people who had been with him in his previous life at this time. The sense of obligation and stress that these passages put on my shoulders was considerable, since at the time I did not have a website and was almost completely obscure on the internet.[9,10]

Only a month or two later, Jim got the idea that I should compare the positions of the planets when I was born to the positions when Edgar Cayce was born. I had an astrology software program on my computer that allowed me to create a Bi-Wheel, where you can see how two charts overlap.

As soon as I ran the Bi-Wheel between myself, at March 8, 1973, 11:16 P.M. in Schenectady, New York, and Edgar Cayce, at March 13, 1877, in Hopkinsville, Kentucky, I was completely shocked. All the inner planets were sitting in exactly the same positions, and all the outer planets were in perfect angular relationships to one another. When I saw this, I literally became sick to my stomach and ran into the bathroom, thinking I was going to throw up. I clutched the sides of the porcelain with both hands. I managed to keep it down, but I broke out in a cold sweat, my heart was pounding, and I was hyperventilating. This was the Point of No Return. I knew now that reincarnation was the most logical explanation for all of these connections. I did not want this life. I did not want to be this person. Now I knew that I had an immense responsibility to try to right the wrongs I had created, and I would invariably end up having to tell the world about this reincarnation story.

The Meaning of the Leek and "EC 40 57"

It was at this point that I realized Jim was regularly buying exactly the same type of leeks that featured in my terrifying dream where I was about to meet my UFO double. Yet, instead of this just being a case of having an extraterrestrial soul, it was actually something far more controversial. Cayce's readings had reported multiple past lives that were illustrious, to say the least. This allegedly included Ra-Ptah, a Persian priest-king named Ujhlt (pronounced YOOLT), Pythagoras, the biblical King David, and the biblical author of the gospel of Luke.

However, apart from these amazing-sounding incarnations, Cayce also had apparently been a security guard who committed suicide, which had a profoundly negative effect on him, as well as spending his two most recent lives as a man named John Bainbridge, who the readings described as an alcoholic, gambler, womanizer, and "wastrel." He liked this life so much that he reincarnated again as his own grandson. This was a curious plot twist, because shortly before I left the Schoolhouse, Eric had a very powerful dream where all the American Founding Fathers had reincarnated as these guys who were overweight alcoholics, sitting in front of a TV, eating snacks and drinking beer. Eric's dream was giving a potential clue into my own multi-incarnational history, as well as a simple statement of fact: high-profile lifetimes can cause amazing spiritual damage that requires multiple additional lifetimes to work off, just like Ra explained in the Law of One series, such as with the story of Moses.

Once I realized I might be Edgar Cayce reincarnated, many puzzle pieces began to fit together. Cayce's ESP was developed through hypnosis, and as soon as I was old enough to read adult books at age seven, I started researching ESP and hypnosis. Cayce used his ESP for healing, and when I was eight years old, I stuck an American Lung Association Christmas sticker with the 1981 date on it at the beginning of the chapter heading in the ESP book entitled "Your Healing Power." I soon went back and looked at the original phrase I had gotten from the automatic writing that started all this. The first two letters, *EC*, were capitalized, unlike a normal Bible quote. Edgar Cayce's name has the same two capital letters for its initials, and Cayce usually referred to himself as EC in his own writings. Both Cayce and I were born in the Year of the Ox, hence the "oxen" at the end of my original message. Now my curiosity was ignited. I wanted to find out if the second part of the message, "40 57," had a meaning that I had overlooked, other than being a Bible quote. What if these represented ages in Cayce's life where important crisis points had happened, just like what I had gone through with losing my job and then my grandmother getting rushed to the emergency room during Thanksgiving?

Jim had enough Cayce books on hand that it was easy to find the answer. In the biography *There Is a River,* we learn that when Cayce turned forty, the year was 1917. Cayce saw the start of World War I, and most of his entire Sunday Bible school of young men were taken away by the draft to fight what was by far the deadliest war in human history up until then. This was obviously a difficult event in Cayce's life—the loss of those whom he had been caring for, and the world descending into what the Pyramid Timeline described as the dawning of the era of hell on Earth. There was the "40" in my original message.

When Cayce was fifty-seven, the year was 1935. Between the ages of forty and fifty-seven, Cayce had seen the rise and fall of his professional career with his Cayce Hospital. Morton and Edwin Blumenthal, two brothers from New York who got very rich from the business and financial advice of Cayce's readings, had funded the Cayce Hospital. However, the Blumenthals failed to listen to the advice of the Cayce Readings and refused to pull all their money out of the stock market, as advised, in 1929. The Great Crash happened soon afterward, and the Blumenthals lost almost everything. The Cayce Hospital collapsed soon after it had started, and the patients had to be turned away, facing a very uncertain future. Until then, the Cayce Hospital had seemed like a godsend, where Edgar could do his readings, receive a steady salary, and treat his patients with complete legitimacy. His dream had come true. Established doctors had underwritten his credibility and all the legal loopholes had been closed, so there was no risk of any government trouble. This loss haunted Cayce for the rest of his life. He was still feeling the sting of defeat a few years later, when his whole family was arrested in Detroit for practicing medicine without a license. This was in December 1935, when Cayce was fifty-seven years old. There was the "57" in my original message!

The synchronicity was even stronger because when this message came in through automatic writing in 1995, I had also just "lost the hospital" in my own life—that is, my job working at the ward. Plus, Cayce's arrest in Detroit at age fifty-seven had occurred exactly sixty years earlier, almost to the week, from when I was fired from the hospital and did the automatic writing. The synchronicity of all these connections was nothing short of staggering. I clearly seemed to be repeating karma from Cayce's life on a very precise cycle-based system of some kind. Eventually, I wrote *The Synchronicity Key,* an entire book on time cycles like these.

The numeral 60 is a basic "harmonic number" that we see in the cycles I discussed. As an example, the Age of the Zodiac, 2,160 years, is one of the most fascinating examples of history repeating itself. In the book, I give a wealth of evidence that key events from the Roman Empire precisely reappeared as United States history, exactly 2,160 years later. Key figures in both timelines reincarnated, such as the Carthaginian warlord Hannibal reincarnating as Hitler. Their faces are nearly identical, except that Hannibal has a full beard. And the 2,160-year cycle can also be broken up into 36 smaller repeating units of 60-year cycles. Patterns of events are not random; they repeat in these cycles. I was now seeing a dramatic example of it in my own life, complete with the facial similarity— and it all traced back to the very first reading I had ever obtained.

Both ages forty and fifty-seven involved a cycle of humiliation and loss in Cayce's life, similar to the total ruin that I now felt of losing my own hospital job and getting reprimanded. I had also been beaten up by the system for trying to help other people, just like what happened to

Cayce when he was arrested. And last but not least, the house number of the place I was living with Jim when I discovered these connections was 2280. This is the exact same number you get if you multiply 40 by 57. I was truly astonished at the connections, since the Bible passage from Ecclesiastes also spoke to precisely what I was going through in my life at the time, while additionally beginning with the synchronicity number 2:22.

A Stunning Return

By the following year, in 1998, I had moved more than once, and in May I was renting a room in a house that was just a block or two away from the ARE headquarters. My friend Chris moved in during the middle of the month. As a reminder, Chris was the spitting image of Morton Blumenthal. By this point, my readings had repeatedly confirmed that Chris was Blumenthal's reincarnation. The beings told me I had to go and turn myself in, and reveal the full story to the management of the ARE. They also told me that if I didn't actually go through with this, it was the equivalent of a spiritual felony—just like I would be committing if I failed to tell the world about this story. I knew I was going in at a great disadvantage. I was not an unconscious channel in this lifetime. I was not having entire conversations with people in foreign languages while under trance. I was not performing "health readings" with an ency-clopedic knowledge of obscure medical terms. The people at the ARE would obviously want to see all of these things in full display or else they would never be convinced. Based on the principles in the Law of One series, it was obvious that in the modern Internet era, it would violate free will if I were able to perform these types of feats. The Law of Confusion needed to be preserved. I had come in as a different person, with a different mission and different corresponding talents, both on the personal and the intuitive side. The Cayce Readings had indicated that I would be more like "the priest" Ra-Ptah in this lifetime than Cayce himself.

On May 16, while working the front desk at a local hotel, I found a large diamond on the floor after a woman had come behind the desk to make a call. Everyone had left by the time I found the precious jewel. I turned the diamond back into the hotel I was working at, hoping they could get it to her. Chris ended up calling me "Diamond David" after this, without knowing that this was exactly the same name the old woman used in my lucid dream where she told me to move to Virginia Beach. The readings assured me that I had done the right thing by turning the diamond in, even though I very desperately needed money. I quit my job at the hotel soon afterward, as they had worked me on a constant schedule that alternated between morning, evening, and overnight shifts, every day, for over two weeks straight. My sleep patterns were completely destroyed, and I was totally exhausted.

I had called ahead to the ARE, told them who I thought I was, and set up a meeting on May 29 to go over the evidence. Chris quickly decided that Virginia Beach wasn't right for him, and he moved out on the same day my meeting was scheduled. Chris and I had a major argument in the checkout lane of a grocery store, just hours before I first visited the ARE, which made me very tense. The Cayce Hospital, of course, was the building that Blumenthal had financed before he had a falling-out with Edgar Cayce, and this would be the first time I saw the hospital in my current life. Once Blumenthal pulled out his money, Cayce lost control of the hospital and soon became destitute.

As I prepared to walk the short distance over to the ARE, I was incredibly nervous and my hands were literally shaking with fear. I had printed out a copy of the combination chart, showing the astonishing linkage between the positions of the planets at the time of Cayce's birth and the positions at my own birth. And of course, I was walking in with my face, which was nearly identical looking to that of Edgar Cayce at the same age. Portrait artists had already confirmed that this near-perfect facial similarity was authentic. A surviving recording of Cayce's voice also sounded just like my own, albeit with a southern accent. Lastly, ever since I went to Colorado, I had carried my toothbrush, toothpaste, nail clipper, hairbrush, and other toiletries in an inexpensive Buxton nylon container I had gotten as a Christmas gift. For whatever reason, just as I was preparing to go to the ARE, I felt compelled to clean out the container.

I lifted the empty bag and something fairly large and heavy shifted inside. I could clearly hear and feel it slide from the front of the bag to the back. What in the world could it be? There was a zipper on the side that I never used, and I unzipped it and looked inside. Much to my amazement, there was my lost quartz crystal! It was the same crystal I had carried with me since junior high school. It was the same crystal that fell and cracked, leaving a smooth, wavy surface, after I had my worst fight with Yumi. I took it to symbolize my own fractured soul, and all the pain and trauma I had been through. It was the same crystal I had felt guided to throw into the Flatirons as I stood before the most beautiful view I had ever seen, in Boulder, Colorado. It reminded me of the diamond I had just given away, but it was far more precious to me on a sentimental level. Suddenly, I realized what had happened. I never had the strength to throw the crystal after all. I still wanted to keep it with me, even if it was broken. On the day I was in the youth hostel, I was in a rush to pack and leave. For whatever reason, I had unzipped my bag and put the crystal in the side pouch.

The crystal had sat in there every morning, undetected, as I moved back in with my mother. I had it in Adam's bathroom when I was sleeping on his kitchen floor. I carried it with me every time I went to the shared bathroom at the boardinghouse when I returned to New Paltz. I kept it sitting on the countertop next to the shower the whole time I lived in the Schoolhouse. It drove with me to Virginia Beach and sat in every bathroom of every house I had rented. I never thought I would see it again. I believed it was gone forever. And now, here it was. This was truly one of the most astonishing synchronicities I had ever had, particularly because of the timing and the gravity of what I was about to do, just hours before Chris was moving away. I burst into tears and held the crystal next to my heart. Even if the ARE wouldn't accept me—and I already knew they wouldn't—I knew the truth.

It didn't matter who I was before. It didn't matter whether I was a prominent spiritual leader or an impoverished farmer. It didn't matter if I was rich or poor, tall or short, heavy or skinny, ignorant or intelligent. Based on what I knew from the Law of One, all that really mattered was that I knew the truth. I was living in a dream. The world we think we know is an illusion. We become entranced with the illusion. We want to see more, do more, live more, and love more. We grasp at the material world as if it can somehow ease the hunger pains we feel for true spiritual nourishment. Eventually, the materialistic path collapses. We have a Dark Night of the Soul. The habit patterns and addictions that had papered over the pain we feel in our hearts no longer work anymore. We stand up, dust ourselves off, and walk away from what doesn't work for us. We learn to make healthier choices. We learn that it is okay to love ourselves and to share that love with others.

No longer do we need to live in fear, pain, misery, and terror. No longer do we need to feel abandoned by a God that seems completely indifferent to us. No longer are we alone in the universe, stranded on a tiny blue planet that is slowly decaying into an eventual gravitational collapse and thermal death. As we awaken in the dream, we recognize the ultimate truth: There is only One of us here. We are—you are—the Creator. That is all you ever have been, all you are now, and all you ever will be. And that means everyone else is worthy of love. They are equals. We are above no one and below no one. We are all humble seekers on this path. We will do what we can to help ourselves and to help others feel loved. We try our best to practice forgiveness, compassion, patience, responsibility, duty, and honor. We can learn to see self and other as One. Ultimately, we need to meditate on the greatest truth: There is no self, there is no other. There is no time. There is no space. There is no before or after. There is only Awareness. It is here. It is now. It is everyone and everywhere. It is our true identity—and it is what we feel when we are truly inspired and filled with love.

People Didn't Handle It Very Well

A reincarnation story like this may help to serve as a reminder of this greater reality that we are all taking part in. Let's not forget that in Session 1, Question 10, of the Law of One series it says, "We do not consider that a separation exists between the consciousness-raising efforts of the distortion which you project as a personality and the distortion which you project as an other-personality." For this same reason, in Section 10,

Question 14, the Law of One series advises us to "Gaze within a mirror [and] see the Creator." We are also encouraged to see the Creator in all others, and in the universe that surrounds us.

Over the years, I found that hardly anyone in my personal or professional life could handle it. The facial similarity, the astrology, the reincarnated family and friends, the time-bending power of the readings . . . it was all just too much. I was subject to every imaginable type and variety of projections from others. In one conversation, or one written exchange, I could go from someone seeing me as their Divine Animus to their Shadow. And then, since they hadn't healed this part of themselves, they would confront, attack, argue, castigate, yell, scream, cry, make threats, attempt blackmail, and do their very best to sabotage my life, my peace of mind, my happiness, my finances, and my freedom. It happened so regularly that it was truly disheartening.

All of this reached a crescendo after the book I cowrote with Wynn Free, *The Reincarnation of Edgar Cayce?*, was released on March 11, 2004. My contributions consisted of two work periods where I added certain specific details, taking no more than a day or two of my time in each case. Part Two was a selection of my readings, and Part Three I wrote on my own. The following year, in 2005, I made an appearance at the Conscious Life Expo in Los Angeles, California, where I presented the material and sold the books. A former colleague came up to my table and repeated death threats to my face that he had already sent to me earlier in several emails. An intuitive had told him that if I didn't stop talking about this reincarnation story, God was going to kill me. This was the only time I ever truly yelled at someone after I became a public figure. I threw the books on the ground and regretted my outburst immediately. The organizer of the expo was able to get us together a couple of years later and I did apologize to him for what had happened.

This same year, Richard Hoagland took me under his wing as an apprentice and urged me to drop the whole Cayce story. People just couldn't handle it and it wouldn't do me any good. I then dedicated myself more strongly than ever to pursue the "hard science," since this is the arena in which much of the battle is being fought. Richard's first "assignment" to me was to write *Interplanetary Day After Tomorrow*, a master document outlining conclusive NASA evidence that our entire solar system is going through a massive energetic buildup.[11,12,13] The sun and planets are all becoming brighter, hotter, and more magnetic. This is a very dramatic and physically measurable precursor to the coming solar flash. I expanded greatly upon this information in *The Source Field Investigations.*

Skeptics can immediately denounce anything they don't agree with by calling it "pseudoscience" and invoking the will of the collective authorities as if it were the will of God. Yet, I knew the world was being run by an elite cabal whose members were hiding spectacular amounts of paradigm-shattering information from us—on every level. They set it up this way to benefit themselves. By keeping us believing that we are in a spiritually dead and materialistic universe, they can hide the truth of our greater divinity.

I decided that if I did have any connection to this seemingly mythical Atlantean priest-king Ra-Ptah, I had a great deal of karmic restitution to pay. My work pivoted to disclosure. I focused on revealing suppressed scientific truths. I found more and more whistleblowers who shed light on the awesome size and scope of the Secret Space Program—where we, as humans, are already a Galactic race. The knowledge is simply being withheld from us. Furthermore, beginning on February 26, 2007, I decided to take everything I knew about the Illuminati and their plans to destroy the lives of billions of people and go public with it. The first article I wrote like this was called "The Revealing: Endgame of the New World Order."[14] This soon became one of my most frequent areas of concern, and I feel that I have made great contributions in this and other categories. And in all honesty, I will often go for weeks at a time, if not months, without ever thinking about this reincarnation case. I rarely, if ever, mention it in my articles, conferences, television episodes, or books. I just want to focus on doing the best I can in this lifetime, without comparing myself to anyone or anything else. This was by far the most difficult book for me to write, and it took me almost three years to process and heal from the trauma enough to finish it. I was only able to bring myself to write about the Cayce connections at the very end of the creative process, just days before handing in the final draft.

I also want to point out that angelic beings like Ra can only help us as much as we ask them to, through our own free will—such as through prayer and meditation. This prayerful request is referred to as "calling," and the word appears in 719 different passages throughout the Law of One series.[15] Most important is the "Law of Squares," which reveals that each additional person who starts praying for help creates an exponential increase in what these higher forces are then authorized to do for us. This is explained in the first eight questions of Session 7, as well as in other areas throughout the material.[16] Therefore, we can never under-estimate the value of calling upon the higher forces to help us out in whatever way we feel is appropriate, and particularly for the biggest problems we face in the world. Prayers for the negative do not benefit from this exponential doubling effect, as we see in passages such as Session 24, Question 8— and thus the calling for the negative is "not nearly as great" as what we see for the positive.[17]

Prophecies of the Defeat of the Negative Elite

Throughout the year 1999, I began publishing each new reading on my website almost as soon as it came in. I did not, however, include a reading from January 3, 1999, in which I was told that the ultimate source inspiring my work was the same Ra that had transmitted the *Law of One*. My material was not as rigorous as the *Law of One* since it had to filter through my conscious mind, but the source did say, "Do not doubt yourself in knowing that you have indeed produced much comparable material with us." A greater excerpt of this passage was eventually published in *The Reincarnation of Edgar Cayce?*, and appeared in a sample chapter on my website.[18]

I did publish many readings in 1999, including a very remarkable transmission that came in on June 17, which ended up having a blatant prophecy of the following year's election crisis as well as 9/11. I published it on June 23, 1999, and was able to locate a time-encoded snapshot of it on Archive.org from November 28, 1999, which categorically proves that this reading came in well before the 2000 election crisis and 9/11.[19] Early along, the source said, "The vice president looks at this as being partly his own authorship, while not realizing that he is completely naked. The interim period decides the next victor."

Over a year later, we had an election crisis between former vice president Al Gore and Texas governor George W. Bush. There was indeed an "interim period" after the November 7, 2000, election of thirty-six days before the "victor" was declared, since the race was apparently so close.[20] It was only the Supreme Court that finally decided in favor of Bush, even though it was later determined that former VP Al Gore had actually won more votes. After the election, Gore tried to politically manipulate the situation, which the reading said was his thinking the crisis could be handled with "partly his own authorship." The reading then said Gore did not realize he was "completely naked," implying the system was rigged and there was no way he could ever have prevailed.

Let's now pick up with the same reading a bit later. Bear in mind that with this level of stunning prophetic accuracy, it is likely that the other portions of the reading are equally serious.

> When you look at it strictly from a higher-dimensional perspective, there is a certain quantitative value of negative energy that exists on the planetary sphere at present. This needs to be counterbalanced, for as we move closer and closer to the vernal point, or the conjunction of the solar cycle that we have spoken of, there is then no further wiggle room, so to speak. As this energy continues to expand, it produces an increasing stress upon the Global Grid mechanism of energetic vibrations. And this does then directly create a host of internal stresses, the product of which is the polar realignment at some distinctive point in linear time. In order to redirect your thoughts, we scan the most immediate circumstances that are likely to occur in your future. And with this knowledge, we suit ourselves up with the forethought and the awareness that you can be healed, that we can enact change within your life.
>
> Higher and higher the chariot raises in the sky, and it will be seen by all. The buildings will be smoking, the people will

be crying, and at that point it will already have been done.
There will be other stages of it, of course, but this is an important point.[21]

This last passage is a clear reference to 9/11. The planes are referred to
as "the chariot," indicating that they would be used as weapons of war,
and would "be seen by all." Then it spoke very frankly in saying, "The
buildings will be smoking, the people will be crying, and at that point it
will already have been done." There is no valid skeptical explanation that
can "debunk" a prophecy like this, particularly since we can prove it
appeared on my site well over a year in advance of the election crisis.

Other readings I published from my source predicted a sequence of
events that seemed unthinkable at the time. Events like 9/11 were very
upsetting, but a resistance would appear that would prevent this nefarious group from fulfilling its plans of total world domination. I was told
that "a new agreement would be reached in terms of international finance." I was also told that there would be "something like a coup over
the military-industrial complex." It also said that "government is in for a
massive cleaning," and "at first [this event] will be interpreted as chaos
and disorder." In addition to the wonderful freedom that such a sequence
of events would provide for us, the readings also made it clear that these
events would help to create a mass spiritual awakening unlike anything
we have ever seen before. At the time I am finalizing this book in November 2019, these prophecies have not yet come true, but there are intriguing
signs of future success that I have covered extensively in my articles,
videos, films, and elsewhere. Let's now read these prophecies, which we
again can easily prove I posted online in 1999, shortly after they arrived.
It is my sincere hope that by the time this book is released, we will already
have observed some very significant new developments in these areas.

10/4/99: The Big Brother scenario is indeed real, and Big
Brother is counting on us to not expose these truths as they
have already been done. The subjugation of the populace war-
rants their ignorance, and if they are to become smarter about
what is happening to them, they might actually begin doing

something about it. Indeed, as we have already said, it is precisely the focus of experience that these [New World Order]
individuals are now going through that will give them so
much more to lose when the final steps into the basement are
then made, and a new agreement is reached in terms of international finance.

So, if you can think in terms deeper than those portrayed
in the media, you will see that there are indeed some serious
thugs on the loose here. When we speak of their plans of
world domination, we are speaking of something that they do
believe can and will be accomplished. We are here to tell you
that just the opposite is going to happen. In their strive and
quest for power, they will lose all that they had already
gained, and gain nothing new.[22]

This reading was originally uploaded to my website on November 3,
1999, under the title "Stock Market Crash!" You can see a time-stamped
copy of it on Archive.org at this next reference.[23] The earliest surviving
version now on Archive is from March 11, 2000. The day after the above
passage came through, I had another reading that went into even more
detail. It was October 5, 1999. This reading was published on November
5, 1999, in an article entitled "Alcoholism and Politics Give Way to
Fourth-Dimensional Government," as well as in Part One of an article
entitled "The Great Awakening."[24] You can see a time-encoded snapshot
of the original post on Archive.org from November 28, 1999.[25]

10/5/99: Once you start binding the loose bits and pieces together, you can see how all this is leading toward something
like a coup over the military-industrial complex and its stran-
glehold over this story regarding UFOs and the like. . . . The
question then, is, "What would you do if the Saint Bernard
comes to you with the whiskey under his neck in your final
moments, giving you another chance?" How would you approach these systems when this same phenomenon is going to
be happening to them?. . . . We are not about to issue a blan-

ket condemnation of government as a whole. However, what we do see is that government is in for a massive cleaning. There are some whose strength will benefit from this, but at first it will be interpreted as chaos and disorder.

You yourself, the reader of these words, do have the opportunity to choose not to behave in such a manner at the time that this guidance is given. We are not talking about fascist Nazi concentration camps that will be created and the like. No, rather what we are discussing is the systematic breakdown of existing orders in order to make way for changes that will result. . . . When you have hooked up the cables and the wires to the ivory tower, and continued to watch what it is that is being pandered to you through the media and so forth, you are going down an empty road. Like the gigantic rain forests, the aspects of society that represent the positive and the spiritual motivations seem to continue to be mowed down by the public opinion as it is contorted to be believed through the media. . . .

We are tired of the house of delegates as well. That is the reason for the explicit political content of this dream [David had before this reading]. . . . The idea of this transformation of your society is indeed all-encompassing. . . . We now know what to expect and how we will get there. David has embraced these mission parameters, just as you must embrace yours. . . . And so, for the thinking person, the question becomes this: What do I do when I want to eventually re-sculpt society to the way that it should be? We advocate that you take some serious time in contemplation of these matters.[26]

Just Be Nice

I want to thank you for reading this book and continuing to support this work through whatever means you feel are appropriate. The Ascension teachings are almost absurdly simple. According to the Law of One, if you want to graduate into your new life as an angelic being, all you have to do is *Just Be Nice*. Dr. Scott Mandelker and I would always joke about this at our conferences. Look at your thoughts about yourself and others. If those thoughts are even slightly over 50 percent oriented toward love, patience, forgiveness, and kindness—what the Law of One calls "service to others"—you are cleared for takeoff. If more than 50 percent of your thoughts and actions are geared toward negative emotions such as manipulation, control, jealousy, anger, rage, and fear, then you have some work to do . . . but *there's still time to change the road you're on.*

And in response to the inevitable question of when the great multidimensional solar event is anticipated to take place, the "best guess" from Corey Goode's sources, as well as from certain dreams I have had, is that we won't have to wait much longer than somewhere between 2029 and 2031. The reason for this is that apparently the physics of this event will allow it to happen only at either a solar minimum or a solar maximum. These dates again are precisely mirrored in the Great Pyramid Timeline, adding extra intrigue to the investigation.

The giant spheres that Corey was shown in his visions have apparently held off this event so that we all have more time to prepare for it. I have also seen very clearly that only the most negatively polarized individuals will choose to stay on the Earth in physical form as these changes occur. In this way, they can release a great deal of karma in a short time and, hopefully, at least begin the path of restoring their own karmic balance. For the majority of people who are going to have to repeat the cycle, they will likely experience a relocation event, just like we see in Dr. Courtney Brown's remote viewing. And I don't know about you, but I am very tired of reincarnating in third density—dealing with anger, depression, sadness, loss, betrayal, fear, violence, terror, and pain.

The Law of One series clearly indicates that even fourth-density life is one hundred times more harmonious than life in 3-D. You get to have all the abilities of a superhero as you develop into this new being, with full memories of your past lives and the ability to help people like never before. If all I have to do is spread love and peace to get there, I'm ready. Let's do this!

Acceptance of a Natural Evolutionary Event

The solar flash is a natural event and we can't change it. We can shrink in terror, ask "the authorities" to save us, and get desperate, or we can simply trust that the bizarre psychic events that have happened to many different people, like what I outlined in this book, are meant to show us that we are heading into a benevolent, positive transformation. It is a true Graduation for the Earth itself, and all its people—wherever they may go. This was exactly what was coursing through my mind during the second LA earthquake I went through while writing this book. I had just decided to meditate, lying down on my bed. I was in a highly elevated spiritual consciousness. I breathed deeply and felt myself connecting with the Earth—understanding its pain, its fear, and its longing for a new tomorrow. A dog had been wailing and screaming in a strange way outside for several minutes, and had finally stopped.

As I tuned in to the Earth, I heard a sound come rushing up from behind me. It was an impulse traveling through the Earth at a very fast speed. I saw it moving like a shock wave. I heard it rush toward me at what seemed like at least five hundred miles per hour. It sounded like a massive bowling ball rolling underground. As it hit the house, the paintings shook, and that's when I knew something was going on. This was not just a meditative effect. As I was lying there in bed, the entire room started shaking. It got worse, and worse, and worse. I felt the consciousness of the Earth and the certainty of our Ascension.

I honestly felt tuned into the Earth's consciousness, as if I was making a decision right then as to whether or not now was the right time. I then realized that we were not ready for this just yet. It wasn't time. Then I realized that I was not really the Earth—I was David Wilcock, lying on his bed, and I needed to get the heck out of there! I got up out of bed and ran downstairs to try to get out of the house before it all fell on me. By the time I reached the front door, the shaking had stopped. Nonetheless, I was happy to see that I was indeed ready for the "final test"—to face any such changes with confidence and peace, knowing that our friends will be standing by ready to get us wherever we need to go when this event finally happens.

The Law of One series makes it clear that our focus should be on "seeking the heart of the self" rather than in trying to find a safety land and thinking that we need to try to physically survive the Earth Changes. This is in Session 14, Question 14, and then a follow-up answer in Session 15, Question 14:

> The harvest is now. There is not at this time any reason to include efforts along these distortions towards longevity, but rather to encourage distortions toward seeking the heart of self, for this which resides clearly in the violet-ray energy field will determine the harvesting of each mind/body/spirit complex. . . . [27]
>
> You have been given information upon healing, as you call this distortion. This information may be seen in a more general context as ways to understand the self. The understanding, experiencing, accepting, and merging of self with self and with other-self, and finally with the Creator, is the path to the heart of self. In each infinitesimal part of your self resides the One in all of Its power. [28]

I now leave you with four summary statements from the Law of One and two Bible quotes. The first statement was made in the very first session of the Law of One that started the entire series, as this really is the core of the message—and the key to Awakening in the Dream:

> Let us for a moment consider thought. What is it, my friends, to take thought? Took you then thought today? What thoughts did you think today? What thoughts were part of the original thought today? In how many of your thoughts did the creation abide? Was love contained? And was service freely given? You are not part of a material universe. You are part of a thought. You are dancing in a ballroom in which

there is no material. You are dancing thoughts. You move your body, your mind, and your spirit in somewhat eccentric patterns—for you have not completely grasped the concept that you are part of the original thought.[29]

We can only ask each group to consider the relative effect of philosophy and your so-called specific information. It is not the specificity of the information which attracts negative influences. It is the importance placed upon it.

This is why we iterate quite often, when asked for specific information, that it pales to insignificance, just as the grass withers and dies while the love and the light of the One Infinite Creator redounds to the very infinite realms of creation forever and ever, creating and creating itself in perpetuity.

Why then be concerned with the grass that blooms, withers, and dies in its season only to grow once again due to the infinite love and light of the One Creator? This is the message we bring. Each entity is only superficially that which blooms and dies. In the deeper sense, there is no end to beingness.[30]

I tell you, if [my disciples] keep silence, the stones will shout aloud.—Luke 19:40

As I do these things, so shall you do them—and greater things.—John 14:12

We cannot offer shortcuts to enlightenment. Enlightenment is of the moment, [and] is an opening to intelligent infinity. It can only be accomplished by the self, for the self . . . but who can know when an entity will open the gate to the present?—Law of One, Session 17, Question 2

In forgiveness lies the stoppage of the wheel of action, or what you call karma.—Law of One, Session 17, Question 20

Notes

CHAPTER ONE

1. Stephen LaBerge, *Lucid Dreaming: The Power of Being Awake and Aware in Your Dreams* (New York: Ballantine Books, 1986).

2. Stephen LaBerge and Howard Rheingold, *Exploring the World of Lucid Dreaming* (New York: Ballantine Books, 1991).

3. Harold Sherman, *How to Make ESP Work for You* (New York: Fawcett Crest, 1968), https://www.amazon.com/How-Make-ESP-Work-You/dp/B00BPC1V6O/ref=sr_1_2? keywords=how+to+make+esp+work+for+you&qid=1564085953&s=gateway&sr=8-2.

CHAPTER TWO

1. Stephen LaBerge, *Lucid Dreaming: The Power of Being Awake and Aware in Your Dreams* (New York: Ballantine Books, 1986).

2. Stephen LaBerge and Howard Rheingold, *Exploring the World of Lucid Dreaming* (New York: Ballantine Books, 1991).

3. Namkhai Norbu and Michael Katz, *Dream Yoga and the Practice of Natural Light*, 9th ed. (Ithaca, NY: Snow Lion Publications, 1994).

4. Dictionary.com, *"archetype,"* Definition #2, https://www.dictionary.com/browse /archetype.

5. David Straker, "Jung's Archetypes," Changing Minds, April 22, 2007, http://changing minds.org/explanations/identity/jung_archetypes.htm.

6. Ibid.

7. Ibid.

CHAPTER FOUR

1. Philip J. Corso and William Birnes, *The Day After Roswell: The Truth Exposed After Fifty Years!* (New York: Pocket Books, 1994).

2. Hugh Lynn Cayce, ed., *The Edgar Cayce Reader* (New York: Warner Books, 1967), 7.

3. Paul K. Johnson, *Edgar Cayce in Context* (New York: State University of New York Press, 1998), 2.

4. John Van Auken, "A Brief Story about Edgar Cayce," Association for Research and Enlightenment, 2002, http://www.edgarcayce.org/ps2/edgar_cayce_story.html.

5. Ibid.

6. Bob Leaman, *Armageddon: Doomsday in Our Lifetime?* (Richmond, Victoria, Australia: Greenhouse Publications, 1986), chapter 4, http://www.dreamscape.com/morgana/phoebe.htm.

7. Anne Hunt, "Edgar Cayce's Wart Remedy," Ezine Articles, 2006, http://ezinearticles.com/?Edgar-Cayces-Wart-Remedy&id=895289.

8. *A.D.A.M. Medical Encyclopedia*, "scleroderma," PubMed Health, February 2, 2012, http://www.ncbi.nlm.nih.gov/pubmedhealth/PMH0001465/.

9. Gina Cerminara, *Many Mansions: The Edgar Cayce Story on Reincarnation* (New York: Signet, 1998), 26.

CHAPTER FIVE

1. Michael Talbot, *The Holographic Universe: The Revolutionary Theory of Reality,* reprint ed. (New York: Harper Perennial, 2011).

2. Richard C. Hoagland, *The Monuments of Mars*, 5th ed. (Frog Books, 2001).

3. David Wilcock, *The Divine Cosmos*, chap. 4: "The Sequential Perspective," *Divine Cosmos*, June 4, 2002, https://webarchive.org/web/20030604021756, http://ascension2000.com/divinecosmos/, https://divinecosmos.com/books-free-online/the-divine-cosmos/98-the-divine-cosmos-chapter-04-the-sequential-perspective.

4. Bruce E. DePalma, *"Gravity & the Spinning Ball Experiment,"* Rex Research, March 17, 1977, http://rexresearch.com/depalma2/depalm.htm.

5. Ibid.

6. Ibid.

7. Ibid.

8. Ibid.

9. Malcom Macallum, "Science: Does a Spinning Mass Really Lose Weight?," *New Scientist* 1704 (February 17, 1990), https://www.newscientist.com/article/mg12517042-700-science-does-a-spinning-mass-really-lose-weight/.

10. Salvatore Cezar Pais, "Craft Using an Inertial Mass Reduction Device," US Secretary of the Navy, Patent #US10144532B2. Granted and published December 4, 2018, https://patents.google.com/patent/US10144532B2/en.

11. Salvatore Cezar Pais, "Plasma Compression Fusion Device," US Secretary of the Navy, Patent #US20190295733A1. Published September 26, 2019. Application status is pending as of January 2, 2020, https://patents.google.com/patent/US201902957 33A1/en

12. Brett Tingley and Tyler Rogoway, "Scientist Behind the Navy's 'UFO Patents' Has Now Filed One for a Compact Fusion Reactor," *The Drive* (October 9, 2019), https://www.thedrive.com/the-war-zone/30256/scientist-behind-the-navys-ufo-patents-has-now-filed-one-for-a-compact-fusion-reactor.

CHAPTER SIX

1. Richard C. Hoagland, *The Monuments of Mars,* 5th ed. (Frog Books, 2001).

2. Michael Hesemann, *The Cosmic Connection: Worldwide Crop Formations and ET Contacts* (Southlake, TX: Gateway, 1995), https://www.amazon.co.uk/Cosmic-Connection-Worldwide-Formations-Contacts/dp/1858600170.

3. Mark Fussell and Stuart Dike, "The Crop Circle Connector," http://www.cropcircleconnector.com/interface2005.htm.

4. A. P. Levich, "A Substantial Interpretation of N. A. Kozyrev Conception of Time," World Scientific Publishing Co., 1996, https://www.scribd.com/doc/133048207/A -Substantial-Interpretation-of-N-A-Kozyrev-Conception-of-Time-A-P-Levich.

5. David Wilcock, *The Divine Cosmos,* chap. 1: "The Breakthroughs of Dr. N. A. Kozyrev," The Divine Cosmos website (November 17, 2005), https://divinecosmos.com/books-free -online/the-divine-cosmos/95-the-divine-cosmos-chapter-01-the-break throughs-of-dr-na-kozyrev/.

6. Harold Aspden, "Discovery of Virtual Inertia," *New Energy News* 2, no. 10 (February 1995), http://newenergytimes.com/v2/archives/fic/N/N199502s.PDF.

7. David Hatcher Childress, *Anti-Gravity and the World Grid,* 1st ed. (Adventures Unlimited Press, 1987).

8. Charles Berlitz, *The Bermuda Triangle,* 1st ed. (New York: Doubleday, 1974).

9. Honey Street, near Alton Barnes, Wiltshire, July 16, 1999, Crop Circle Connector, http://www.cropcirclearchives.co.uk/archives/1999/HoneyStreet/HoneyStreet99a.html; Wimpole Hall, near Great Eversdon, Cambridgeshire, July 23, 1999, Crop Circle Connector, http://www.cropcirclearchives.co.uk/archives/1999/GreatEversdon/Great Eversdon99a.html; West Kennett Longbarrow, near Avebury, Wiltshire, August 4, 1999, Crop Circle Connector, http://www.cropcirclearchives.co.uk/archives/1999/East Kennett/EastKennett99c.html.

10. Windmill Hill, near Avebury, Wiltshire, June 28, 2000, Crop Circle Connector, http://www.cropcirclearchives.co.uk/archives/2000/windmill/windmill2000a.html, Kex brough, near Barnsley, South Yorkshire, August 2, 2001, Crop Circle Connector, http://www.cropcirclearchives.co.uk/archives/2001/kexbrough/kexbrough2001a.html; Keres forth Hill, near Barnsley, South Yorkshire, August 12, 2001, Crop Circle Connector, http://www.cropcirclearchives.co.uk/archives/2001/KeresforthHill/Keresforth Hill2001a.html; West Stowell, near Pewsey, Wiltshire, August 15, 2002, Crop Circle Connector, http://www.cropcirclearchives.co.uk/archives/2002/weststowell/weststowell 2002a.html.

11. Don Elkins, Carla Rueckert, and Jim McCarty, Law of One, Session 14, Question 25, https://www.lawofone.info/s/14#25.

12. Law of One, Session 86, Question 7, https://www.lawofone.info/s/86#7.

CHAPTER SEVEN

1. "Svali" and Greg Szymanski, "Transcript Svali's Interview with Greg Szymanski," *Svali Speaks*, from radio appearance on January 17, 2006, https://svalispeaks.wordpress.com /2008/09/19/transcript-svalis-interview-with-greg-szymanski/.

2. "Svali" and H. J. Springer, "Part 12—The Top of the Pyramid" *Svali Speaks*, republished September 12, 2008. Originally from Centrexnews.com, which disappeared from the Internet in 2003, https://svalispeaks.wordpress.com/2008/09/12/part-12-the-top-of-the -pyramid/.

3. George Pendle, "The Occult Rocket Scientist Who Conjured Spirits with L. Ron Hubbard," Motherboard Tech by Vice, January 2, 2015, https://www.vice.com/en_us/article /vvbxgm/the-last-of-the-magicians.

4. Ibid.

CHAPTER EIGHT

1. Maurice Chatelain, *Our Ancestors Came from Outer Space* (Garden City, NY: Doubleday, 1978).

2. Philip Coppens, "The Wheels of Greek Astronomical Science," Eye of the Psychic, 2019, https://www.eyeofthepsychic.com/antikythera/.

3. Ibid.

CHAPTER NINE

1. Caryl-Sue, "Jan 17, 1995 CE: Kobe Earthquake," National Geographic Society, December 12, 2014, https://www.nationalgeographic.org/thisday/jan17/kobe-earthquake/.

2. Kahlil Gibran, *The Prophet* (New York: Alfred A. Knopf, Reprint edition, 1963).

3. Whitley Strieber, *Transformation: The Breakthrough* (London: Arrow, 1989), 251–252.

4. Paul E. Potter, "Phoenixes and Ostriches," UFO Physics, May 19, 2004, UFOphysics .com, https://web.archive.org/web/20040806184720/http://www.ufophysics.com /sunsnova.htm.

CHAPTER TEN

1. Edgar Cayce, *The Edgar Cayce Readings* (Virginia Beach, VA: Association for Research and Enlightenment, June 7, 1930), Reading Number 1681-1.

2. David McMillin, "Segund: Keeper of the Portals," https://web.archive.org/web /20180619154117/http://www.mcmillinmedia.com/atlantean-segund.

3. Tim Gihring, "Ancient Egypt and the Mystery of the Missing Phallus," December 12, 2018, Minneapolis Institute of Art, https://medium.com/minneapolis-institute-of-art /ancient-egypt-and-the-mystery-of-the-missing-phallus-97db0103ecdc.

CHAPTER ELEVEN

1. Law of One, Session 86, Question 7, https://www.lawofone.info/s/86#7.

2. Gurumayi Chidvilasananda, *My Lord Loves a Pure Heart: The Yoga of Divine Virtues* (South Fallsburg, NY: Siddha Yoga Publications, January 1, 1994).

3. SYDA Foundation, "Shree Muktananda Ashram," https://www.siddhayoga.org/global -community/shree-muktananda-ashram.

4. Law of One, search of the term *wanderer*, https://www.lawofone.info/results.php?q =wanderer.

5. Law of One, Session 36, Question 17, https://www.lawofone.info/results.php?s=36#17.

6. Law of One, Session 65, Question 19, https://www.lawofone.info/results.php?s=65#19.

7. Scott Mandelker, *From Elsewhere: Being E.T. in America* (New York: Birch Lane Press, 1995), 207–10.

CHAPTER TWELVE

1. Holy Bible, New International Version, NIV, Ecclesiastes 2:22–23. Copyright © 1973, 1978, 1984, 2011 by Biblica, Inc., https://biblehub.com/niv/ecclesiastes/2.htm.

2. King James Bible, Ecclesiastes 3:1–13.

3. Edison Coatings, Inc., "History of Rosendale Cement," http://www.rosendalecement .net/html/history.html.

4. Ibid.

5. John Harakal, "Development of Portland Cement in the United States," Penn State College of Engineering website, Course CE-584, https://www.engr.psu.edu/ce/courses /ce584/concrete/library/materials/History/DevelopementofPC-main.html.

6. Edison Coatings, Inc., "History of Rosendale Cement," http://www.rosendalecement .net/html/history.html.

7. Century House Historical Society, Snyder Estate Natural Cement Historic District, https://www.centuryhouse.org/.

8. Sarah Jacobs, "Inside the Secretive Subterranean Facility Where a $5 Billion Business Stores the Files of Fortune 1000 Companies," *Business Insider,* January 8, 2016, https://www.businessinsider.com/inside-iron-mountains-storage-facility-2016-1#while-many-of-iron-mountains-storage-facilities-are-above-ground-insidewarehouses-hangars-and-nondescript-office-buildingsaccording-to-the-new-yorker-they-do-have-a-handful-of-units-in-previously-active-iron-or-limestone-mines-3.

9. Timothy Good, *Alien Contact: Top Secret UFO Files Revealed* (Fort Mill, SC: Quill House Publishers, 1994).

10. Harriet Ryan et al., "Largest Earthquake in Decades Hits Southern California, Measuring 6.4 Magnitude," *Los Angeles Times,* July 4, 2019, https://www.latimes.com/local/lanow/la-me-earthquake-california-shake-quake-20190704-story.html.

11. David Wilcock, "IT BEGINS: Epstein Indicted, Black-Ops Mega-Base Destroyed!," Divine Cosmos website, July 7, 2019, https://divinecosmos.com/davids-blog/23251-it-begins-epstein/.

12. Lauran Epstein, "Friends of the Artist: Portraits by Allen Epstein (1941–1993)," Exhibit July 12–August 2, 2009, AllenEpstein.org, http://www.allenepstein.org/.

CHAPTER FOURTEEN

1. Joshua J. Mark, "Horus," *Ancient History Encyclopedia*, last modified March 16, 2016, https://www.ancient.eu/Horus/.

2. Law of One, Session 96, Question 11, https://www.lawofone.info/results.php?s=96#11.

3. Law of One, Session 106, Question 23, https://www.lawofone.info/results.php?s=106#23.

4. Courtney Brown, PhD, *Cosmic Voyage* (New York: Dutton, 1996), free PDF, page 18, http://courtneybrown.com/publications/cosmic.html.

5. Ibid., 15.

6. McMoneagle, Nancy, *Remote Viewing in Japan*, McEagle.com, https://webarchive.org/web/20060429193515; http://www.mceagle.com/remote-viewing/Japan2.html.

7. Brown, *Cosmic Voyage*, 168.

8. Ibid., 92.

9. Ibid., 211.

10. Ibid., 210.

11. Ibid., 23.

12. Ibid., 92.

CHAPTER FIFTEEN

1. Courtney Brown, PhD, *Cosmic Voyage* (New York: Dutton, 1996), free PDF, pages 103-104, http://courtneybrown.com/publications/cosmic.html.

2. Ibid., 104.

3. Ibid., 105.

4. Ibid., 116.

5. Ibid., 117.

6. Ibid., 119.

7. Ibid.

8. Ibid., 120.

9. Ibid., 122.

10. Ibid., 125.

11. Collins English Dictionary, "Logos," Complete & Unabridged 2012 Digital Edition, (Glasgow, Scotland: William Collins Sons & Co. Ltd. 1979, 1986; New York: HarperCollins, 1998, 2000, 2003, 2005, 2006, 2007, 2009, 2012).

12. Law of One, Search for term *logos*, https://www.lawofone.info/results.php?q=logos.

13. Law of One, Session 13, Question 7, https://www.lawofone.info/s/13#7.

14. Law of One, Session 28, Question 7, https://www.lawofone.info/s/28#7.

15. King James Bible, John 1:1, https://www.biblegateway.com/passage/?search=John+1& version=KJV.

16. King James Bible, John 1:14, https://www.biblegateway.com/passage/?search=John+1% 3A14&version=KJV.

17. King James Bible, Genesis 1:27, https://biblehub.com/kjv/genesis/1.htm.

18. Brown, *Cosmic Voyage,* 160.

19. Law of One, search on the term *confused*, https://www.lawofone.info/results.php?q =confused.

20. Law of One, Session 74, Questions 10–11, https://www.lawofone.info/s/74#10.

21. John Mack, *Abduction: Human Encounters with Aliens* (New York: Scribner, 1994).

22. Jennifer Bayot, "Dr. John E. Mack, Psychiatrist, Dies at 74," *New York Times,* September 30, 2004, https://www.nytimes.com/2004/09/30/us/dr-john-e-mack-psychiatrist -dies-at-74.html.

23. Ibid.

24. Brown, *Cosmic Voyage*, 83.

25. Ibid., 84.

26. Ibid., 85.

27. Ibid.

28. Law of One, Session 9, Question 6, https://www.lawofone.info/s/9#6.

29. Law of One, Session 9, Question 7, https://www.lawofone.info/s/9#7.

30. Brown, *Cosmic Voyage*, 141.

31. Ibid., 144.

32. Ibid., 159.

33. Ibid., 183.

34. Ibid., 184.

35. Ibid., 215.

36. Law of One, Session 59, Question 4, https://www.lawofone.info/s/59#4.

37. Law of One, Session 10, Question 3, https://www.lawofone.info/s/10#3.

38. Law of One, Session 59, Question 5, https://www.lawofone.info/s/59#5.

39. Law of One, Session 9, Question 18, https://www.lawofone.info/s/9#18.

40. Law of One, Session 6, Questions 10 and 13, https://www.lawofone.info/s/6#10.

CHAPTER SIXTEEN

1. Law of One, Session 49, Question 8, https://www.lawofone.info/results.php?s=49#8.

2. Law of One, Session 85, Question 19, https://www.lawofone.info/s/85#19.

3. Law of One, Session 86, Question 7, https://www.lawofone.info/s/86#7.

4. Law of One, Session 95, Question 18, https://www.lawofone.info/s/95#18.

5. Lou Marinoff, "The Structure and Function of a Socratic Dialogue," Filosophia Prática website, https://sites.google.com/site/entelequiafilosofiapratica/aconselhamento -filosofico-1/the-structure-and-function-of-a-socratic-dialogue-by-lou-marinoff.

6. Law of One, search of the term *philosophy*, https://www.lawofone.info/results.php?q =philosophy.

7. Law of One, Session 1, Question 10, https://www.lawofone.info/results.php?s=1#10.

8. Ibid.

9. *Journal of Offender Rehabilitation* 36, nos. 1/2/3/4 (2003): 283–302, https://web.archive .org/web/20160926040230/http://proposal.permanentpeace.org/research/index.html.

10. D. Orme-Johnson, "The Science of World Peace: Research Shows Meditation Is Effective," *International Journal of Healing and Caring* 3, no. 3 (September 1993): 2.

11. Malcolm Gladwell, "In the Air: Who Says Big Ideas Are Rare?," *New Yorker*, May 12, 2008, http://www.newyorker.com/reporting/2008/05/12/080512fa_fact_gladwell?currentPage=all (Accessed December 2010).

12. Law of One, Session 17, Question 2, https://www.lawofone.info/results.php?s=17#2.

13. Law of One, Session 2, Question 2, https://www.lawofone.info/results.php?s=2#2.

14. Law of One, Session 1, Question 1, https://www.lawofone.info/results.php?s=1#1.

15. Law of One, Session 2, Question 6, https://www.lawofone.info/results.php?s=2#6.

16. Law of One, Session 46, Question 16, https://www.lawofone.info/s/46#16.

17. Law of One, Session 46, Questions 9–12, https://www.lawofone.info/s/46#9.

18. Origen, *The Writings of Origen (De Principiis)*, vol. 1, trans. Rev. Frederick Crombie (Edinburgh: T. & T. Clark, 1869), http://books.google.com/books?id=vMcIAQAAIAAJ.

19. Law of One, Session 26, Question 36, https://www.lawofone.info/results.php?s=26#36.

20. Law of One, search of the term *25,000*, https://www.lawofone.info/results.php?q=25%2C000.

21. Law of One, search of the term *major cycle*, https://www.lawofone.info/results.php?q=major+cycle&st=phrase&qo=&lh=aq&qc=0&s=&c=&fp=0&v=e&l=30&o=r.

22. King James Bible, Matthew 13, https://biblehub.com/kjv/matthew/13.htm.

23. Law of One, Session 20, Question 24, https://www.lawofone.info/results.php?s=20#24.

24. Law of One, search of the term *catalyst*, https://www.lawofone.info/results.php?q=catalyst.

25. Law of One, Session 14, Question 7, https://www.lawofone.info/results.php?s=14#7.

26. Law of One, Session 8, Question 1, https://www.lawofone.info/results.php?s=8#1.

27. Don Elkins, Carla Rueckert, and Jim McCarty, *The Law of One*, "Introduction to Book I," https://www.lawofone.info/results.php?s=Intro.

28. Ibid.

29. Law of One, search for *Atlant*, minus the four instances of *Atlanta*, https://www.lawofone.info/results.php?q=atlant.

30. John DeSalvo, PhD, "Summary of Research," Great Pyramid of Giza Research Association, http://gizapyramid.com/russian/research.htm.

31. John DeSalvo, PhD, "On the Way to Disclosing the Mysterious Power of the Great Pyramid," Great Pyramid of Giza Research Association, January 24, 2001, http://gizapyramid.com/DrV-article.htm.

32. Law of One, search for phrase *intelligent energy*, https://www.lawofone.info/results.php?q=intelligent+energy&st=phrase.

33. Law of One, Session 17, Question 2, https://www.lawofone.info/results.php?s=17#2.

34. Law of One, Session 20, Question 25, https://www.lawofone.info/results.php?s=20#25.

CHAPTER SEVENTEEN

1. Law of One, Session 4, Question 20, https://www.lawofone.info/results.php?s=4#20.

2. Law of One, search of the term *first distortion*, https://www.lawofone.info/results.php?q=first+distortion&st=phrase&qo=&lh=aq&qc=0&s=&c=&fp=0&v=e&l=30&o=r.

3. Law of One, search of the term *distortion*, https://www.lawofone.info/results.php?q=distortion.

4. Law of One, Session 26, Questions 26–31, https://www.lawofone.info/results.php?s=26#26.

5. Law of One, Session 34, Question 2, https://www.lawofone.info/results.php?s=34#2.

6. Law of One, Session 49, Question 6, https://www.lawofone.info/results.php?s=49#6.

7. Tulku Urgyen Rinpoche, *Rainbow Painting: A Collection of Miscellaneous Aspects of Development and Completion*, 1st ed. (Woodstock, NY: Rangjung Yeshe Publications, 2004) 25.

8. Law of One, Session 4, Question 20, https://www.lawofone.info/results.php?s=4#20.

9. Law of One, search on the term *healing*, https://www.lawofone.info/results.php?q=healing.

10. Law of One, Session 42, Question 6, https://www.lawofone.info/results.php?s=42#6.

11. Law of One, Session 67, Question 11, https://www.lawofone.info/s/67#11.

12. Law of One, Session 41, Question 16, https://www.lawofone.info/results.php?s=41#16.

13. Law of One, Session 13, Question 7, https://www.lawofone.info/results.php?s=13#7.

14. Law of One, search of the term *logos*, https://www.lawofone.info/results.php?q=logos.

15. Law of One, Session 29, Question 1, https://www.lawofone.info/results.php?s=29#1.

16. Law of One, Session 29, Question 7, https://www.lawofone.info/results.php?s=29#7.

17. Law of One, Session 54, Question 5, https://www.lawofone.info/results.php?s=54#5.

18. Law of One, Session 51, Question 10, https://www.lawofone.info/results.php?s=51#10.

19. Law of One, Session 29, Question 8, https://www.lawofone.info/results.php?s=29#8.

20. Law of One, Session 18, Question 5, https://www.lawofone.info/results.php?s=18#5.

21. Law of One, Session 19, Question 18, https://www.lawofone.info/s/19#18.

22. Law of One, Session 6, Question 24, https://www.lawofone.info/results.php?s=6#24.

23. Law of One, Session 16, Question 33, https://www.lawofone.info/results.php?s=16#33.

24. Law of One, Session 28, Question 7, https://www.lawofone.info/results.php?s=28#7.

25. Law of One, Session 82, Question 8, https://www.lawofone.info/results.php?s=82#8.

26. Law of One, Session 1, Question 0, https://www.lawofone.info/results.php?s=1#0.

27. Law of One, Session 1, Question 1, https://www.lawofone.info/results.php?s=1#1.

28. Ibid.

29. Law of One, Session 2, Question 2, https://www.lawofone.info/results.php?s=2#2.

30. Law of One, Session 23, Question 6, https://www.lawofone.info/results.php?s=23#6.

31. Law of One, Session 23, Question 16, https://www.lawofone.info/results.php?s=23#16.

32. Law of One, Session 6, Question 8, https://www.lawofone.info/results.php?s=6#8.

33. Law of One, Session 7, Question 9, https://www.lawofone.info/results.php?s=7#9.

34. Law of One, Session 52, Question 12, https://www.lawofone.info/results.php?s=52#12.

35. Law of One, Session 23, Question 16, https://www.lawofone.info/results.php?s=23#16.

CHAPTER EIGHTEEN

1. William T. Still, *New World Order: The Ancient Plan of Secret Societies* (Lafayette, LA: Huntington House Publishers, 1990).

2. Law of One, Session 19, Question 17, https://www.lawofone.info/results.php?s=19#17.

3. Law of One, Session 19, Question 17, https://www.lawofone.info/s/19#17.

4. Law of One, Session 41, Question 26, https://www.lawofone.info/results.php?s=41#26.

5. Law of One, Session 57, Question 17, https://www.lawofone.info/results.php?s=57#17.

6. Law of One, Session 60, Question 16, https://www.lawofone.info/results.php?s=60#16.

7. Law of One, Session 22, Question 26, https://www.lawofone.info/results.php?s=22#26.

8. Law of One, Session 71, Questions 19–20, https://www.lawofone.info/results.php?s=71#19.

9. Law of One, Session 14, Question 18, https://www.lawofone.info/results.php?s=14#18.

10. Law of One, Session 3, Question 11, https://www.lawofone.info/results.php?s=3#11.

11. Law of One, Session 3, Question 12, https://www.lawofone.info/s/3#12.

12. English Standard Bible, Isaiah 26:4, https://biblehub.com/esv/isaiah/26.htm.

13. Crossway Bibles, "43 Bible Verses about the Rock of Ages" (December 29, 2019), https://www.openbible.info/topics/rock_of_ages.

14. King James Bible, Psalms 118:22, https://biblehub.com/nkjv/psalms/118.htm.

15. English Standard Bible, Isaiah 28:16, https://biblehub.com/esv/isaiah/28.htm.

16. King James Bible, Matthew 16:18, https://biblehub.com/kjv/matthew/16.htm.

17. Law of One, Session 3, Question 13, https://www.lawofone.info/s/3#13.

18. Law of One, Session 3, Question 14, https://www.lawofone.info/s/3#14.

19. Martin Gray, "Giza Pyramids," World-Mysteries.com, 2003, https://web.archive.org /web/20160528121838/https://old.world-mysteries.com/gw_mgray5.htm.

20. Ibid.

21. Peter Lemesurier, *The Great Pyramid Decoded* (Rockport, MA: Element Books, 1977), 8.

22. John Zajac, "The Great Pyramid: A Dreamland Report," *After Dark Newsletter* 1, no. 2 (February 1995), http://www.europa.com/~edge/pyramid.html.

23. Gray, "Giza Pyramids."

24. Zajac, "Great Pyramid."

25. Gray, "Giza Pyramids."

26. Ibid.

27. Lemesurier, *The Great Pyramid Decoded,* 3–4.

28. Peter Tompkins, *Secrets of the Great Pyramid* (New York: Harper & Row, 1971, 1978).

29. Ibid.

30. Ibid., 1.

31. Ibid., 2.

32. Ibid.

33. Gray, "Giza Pyramids."

34. Tompkins, *Secrets of the Great Pyramid,* 3.

35. Ibid.

36. Bernard Pietsch, "The Well Tempered Solar System: Anatomy of the King's Chamber," 2000, http://sonic.net/bernard/kings-chamber.html.

37. Christopher Dunn, *The Giza Power Plant: Technologies of Ancient Egypt* (Rochester, VT: Bear & Company, 1998), http://www.gizapower.com.

38. Ibid.

39. Gray, "Giza Pyramids."

40. Peter Lemesurier, *Gods of the Dawn* (London: Thorsons/HarperCollins, 1999), 84.

41. Ibid., 85.

42. Joseph Jochmans, "The Great Pyramid: How Old Is It Really?," Forgotten Ages Research, 2009 (Accessed May 2010), https://web.archive.org/web/20110530161019/http://www .forgottenagesresearch.com/mystery-monuments-series/The-Great-PyramidHow -Old-is-It-Really.htm [Broken link, original not archived].

43. Edgar Cayce, *The Edgar Cayce Readings* (Virginia Beach, VA: Association for Research and Enlightenment, June 30, 1932), Reading 5748-5, http://arescott.tripod.com /EConWB.html.

44. Tompkins, *Secrets of the Great Pyramid,* 17.

45. Gray, "Giza Pyramids."

46. Tompkins, *Secrets of the Great Pyramid,* 18.

47. Ibid., 17.

48. Ibid., 67.

49. Ibid., 68.

50. Ibid., 69.

51. Ibid., 72.

52. Ibid., 73.

53. Ibid., 74.

NOTES

538

54. Lemesurier, *The Great Pyramid Decoded*, 309.
55. Ibid.
56. Mario Latendresse, "The 153 Big Fishes," University of Montreal, http://www.iro.umon treal.ca/~latendre/poissonsA.html.
57. Toy, C. H., and L. Blau, Jewish Encyclopedia: "TETRAGRAMMATON, 1906," Wikipedia.
58. Lemesurier, *The Great Pyramid Decoded*, 27–28.

CHAPTER NINETEEN

1. Edgar Cayce, *The Edgar Cayce Readings* (Virginia Beach, VA: Association for Research and Enlightenment, June 30, 1932), Reading Number 294-151.
2. Peter Lemesurier, *Gods of the Dawn* (London: Thorsons/HarperCollins, 1999), 71.
3. Ibid., 93.
4. Ibid., 86.
5. Peter Tompkins, *Secrets of the Great Pyramid* (New York: Harper and Row, 1971, 1978), 87.
6. Ibid., 94.
7. Ibid., 6.
8. Jo Marchant, "Cosmic-Ray Particles Reveal Secret Chamber in Egypt's Great Pyramid," *Nature*, November 2, 2017, corrected November 6, 2017, https://www.nature.com/news /cosmic-ray-particles-reveal-secret-chamber-in-egypt-s-great-pyramid-1.22939.
9. Ibid., 6.
10. David Pratt, "The Great Pyramid," November 1997, http://web.archive.org/web /20080216115839/http://ourworld.compuserve.com/homepages/dp5/pyramid.htm.
11. Tompkins, *Secrets of the Great Pyramid*, 9.
12. Ibid., 10.
13. Library of Congress American Memory, "Today in History: May 24," accessed May 2010, http://rs6.loc.gov/ammem/today/may24.html.
14. AllSands, "The History of the Telegraph," accessed May 2010, http://www.allsands.com /history/objects/historyofthet_ahg_gn.htm.
15. Din Timelines, "1845 to 1849," accessed May 2010, http://www.din-timelines.com/1845 -1849_timeline.shtml.
16. Ken Polsson, "Chronology of World History: 1845," accessed May 2010, http://kpolsson .com/worldhis/worl845.htm.
17. Ibid.
18. Ibid.
19. Otavalo Ecuador, "The Galapagos Islands," accessed May 2010, http://www.otavalo.com /galapgs/eglpgs.html.
20. Nivea Ferreira-Schut, "Darwin's Chilean Earthquake: The Connection Between the Events in 1835 and 2010," March 1, 2010, accessed May 2010, http://geologyecology .suite101.com/article.cfm/darwins-chilean-earthquake.
21. The History Place, "The Potato Famine," accessed May 2010, http://www.historyplace .com/worldhistory/famine/begins.htm.
22. The History Place, "Irish Potato Famine: Gone to America," accessed May 2010, http:// www.historyplace.com/worldhistory/famine/america.htm.
23. BBC H2G2, "The Potato: Its Unexpected Historical Impact," March 8, 2008, accessed May 2010, http://www.bbc.co.uk/dna/h2g2/alabaster/A18740522.
24. Eyewitness to History, "Riding the Overland Stage, 1861," accessed May 2010, http:// www.eyewitnesstohistory.com/stage.htm.

25. Polsson, *Chronology of World History*.

26. Ibid.

27. Gray, "Giza Pyramids," https://old.world-mysteries.com/gw_mgray5.htm.

28. Glenn Greenwald, "NSA Collecting Phone Records of Millions of Verizon Customers Daily," *Guardian*, June 6, 2013, https://www.theguardian.com/world/2013/jun/06/nsa-phone-records-verizon-court-order.

29. Peter Lemesurier, *The Great Pyramid Decoded* (Rockport, MA: Element Books, 1977, 1993), 109.

30. King James Bible, John 6:35, https://biblehub.com/kjv/john/6.htm.

31. King James Bible, John 6:51, https://biblehub.com/kjv/john/6.htm.

32. Law of One, Session 73, Question 13, https://www.lawofone.info/s/73#13.

33. M. Short and E. B. Joel, "How to Use a Breadboard," Sparkfun, https://learn.sparkfun.com/tutorials/how-to-use-a-breadboard/history.

34. Law of One, Session 6, Questions 16–18, https://www.lawofone.info/s/6#16.

35. Law of One, Session 6, Question 18, https://www.lawofone.info/s/6#18.

36. Law of One, Session 17, Question 29, https://www.lawofone.info/s/17#29.

37. Matila Ghyka, *The Geometry of Art and Life* (New York: Dover, 1946, 1977), 62–66.

38. Ibid., 21.

39. Ibid., 28.

40. Ibid., 25.

41. Ibid., 27.

42. Ibid., 28.

43. Ibid., 35.

44. Ibid., 36.

45. Zecharia Sitchin, *The Stairway to Heaven*, Book 1 of Earth Chronicles series (New York: Avon Books, 1983), 253–82.

46. Pratt, "The Great Pyramid."

47. Ibid., 30.

48. Ibid., 31.

49. Ibid., 32.

CHAPTER TWENTY

1. David Pratt, "The Great Pyramid," November 1997, 284, http://web.archive.org/web/20080216115839; http://ourworld.compuserve.com/homepages/dp5/pyramid.htm.

2. Ibid.

3. Ibid., 320.

4. Ibid., 287.

5. Peter Tompkins, *Secrets of the Great Pyramid* (New York: Harper & Row, 1971, 1978), 100.

6. Wikipedia, "Pyramid Inch" (Accessed May 2010), http://en.wikipedia.org/wiki/Pyramid_inch.

7. Peter Lemesurier, *The Great Pyramid Decoded* (Rockport, MA: Element Books, 1977, 1993), 24.

8. Ibid., 106.

9. Law of One, Session 17, Question 22, https://www.lawofone.info/s/17#22.

10. Lemesurier, *Great Pyramid Decoded*, 51.

11. Law of One, Session 16, Question 19, https://www.lawofone.info/s/16#19.

12. *New Advent Catholic Encyclopedia*, "St. Francis of Assisi" (Accessed May 2010), http://www.newadvent.org/cathen/06221a.htm.

13. E. L. Cutts, *Scenes and Characters of the Middle Ages* (2003; Prior editions beginning in 1911) (Accessed by Google Books, May 2010), 43.

14. History Orb, "Today in History for Year 1223" (Accessed May 2010), http://www.history orb.com/date/1223.

15. *New Advent Catholic Encyclopedia*, "St. Francis of Assisi."

16. Smithsonian Institution, *Report of the Board of Regents,* Vol. 1909 (Board of Regents, United States National Museum, Smithsonian Institution, July 1896) (Accessed via Google Books, May 2010), 627.

17. Ed Dubrowsky, *Salamanca: The Heart of Spain's Golden Age,* documentary, June 1, 1998, http://www.amazon.com/Salamanca-Heart-Spains-Golden-Age/dp/1563881055.

18. Gabriel Gottfried Bredow, *A Compendium of Universal History* (London: Longman, Green, Longman and Roberts, 1860) (Accessed May 2010 via Google Books), 162–63.

19. Antoon Vollemaere and Pieter De Keyser, "Myth and Location of Aztlan: Motecuhzoma's Expedition to Colhuacan" (Accessed May 2010), http://users.skynet.be/fa039055/duran mot.htm.

20. John Louis Nuelsen, *Luther the Leader* (Jennings and Graham, 1906) (Accessed via Google Books, May 2010), 117.

21. Johan Huizinga, *Erasmus and the Age of Reformation* (London: Harper & Row, 1957), 148 (Accessed via Google Books, May 2010).

22. *Scientific American,* New Series 17, no. 25 (December 21, 1867): 390 (Accessed via Google Books, May 2010).

23. Dilshad Hasan, *Islam Philosophy and Ideology* (New Delhi: Anmol Publications Pvt. Ltd., 2005) (Accessed via Google Books, May 2010), 62–63.

24. *Encyclopedia of Irish and World Art*, "Renaissance Art in Rome" (Accessed May 2010), http://www.visual-arts-cork.com/history-of-art/renaissance-in-rome.htm.

25. Guy Bedouelle, *The History of the Church* (London: Lit Verlag, 2002) (Accessed via Google Books, May 2010), 88.

26. Ibid.

27. Ibid.

28. Bredow, *A Compendium of Universal History*, 169.

29. Lemesurier, *The Great Pyramid Decoded,* 129.

30. Wikipedia, "Revolutions of 1848" (Accessed May 2010), http://en.wikipedia.org/wiki /Revolutions_of_1848,

31. Lindsey Williams, "Do Mystery Patterns Shape Our Lives?," July 29, 1970 (Accessed May 2010), http://www.lindseywilliams.org/index.htm?LAL_Archives/Do_Mystery _Patterns_Shape_Our_Lives.htm-mainFrame.

32. Ibid.

33. G. Edward Griffin, *The Creature from Jekyll Island: A Second Look at the Federal Reserve*, 5th ed. (New York: American Media, Inc., 1994).

34. The Nobel Prize, "The Nobel Prize in Physics 1921: Albert Einstein" (Accessed May 2010), http://nobelprize.org/nobel_prizes/physics/laureates/1921/einstein-bio.html.

35. Wikipedia, "Revolutions of 1848."

36. History Central, "World History 1910–1911" (Accessed May 2010), http://www.history central.com/dates/1910.html.

37. Ibid.

38. Ibid.

39. Brainy History, "1914 in History" (Accessed May 2010), http://www.brainyhistory.com /years/1914.html.

40. Lemesurier, *The Great Pyramid Decoded,* 133.

41. Kimberley Amadeo, "The Great Recession of 2008 Explained with Dates," *The Balance* (December 14, 2019), https://www.thebalance.com/the-great-recession-of-2008-explanation-with-dates-4056832.

42. Kimberley Amadeo, "2007 Financial Crisis Explanation, Causes, and Timeline," *The Balance* (November 20, 2019), https://www.thebalance.com/2007-financial-crisis-overview-3306138.

43. Ibid.

44. Lemesurier, *Great Pyramid Decoded*, 157.

45. Law of One, Session 17, Question 24, https://www.lawofone.info/s/17#24.

46. Law of One, Session 65, Question 12, https://www.lawofone.info/s/65#12.

47. Brainy History, "2004 in History" (Accessed May 2010), http://www.brainyhistory.com/years/2004.html.

48. Ibid.

49. Jin Wook Choi, "The 2007–2010 U.S. Financial Crisis: Its Origins, Progressions and Solutions," *Journal of Economic Asymmetries* 10, no. 2 (November 2013), 65–77, https://www.sciencedirect.com/science/article/pii/S1703494913000121.

50. Ibid.

51. "Dodd-Frank Act," History.com, August 21, 2018, Original January 26, 2018, https://www.history.com/topics/21st-century/dodd-frank-act.

52. Wikipedia, "The Battle of Los Angeles" (Accessed May 2010), http://en.wikipedia.org/wiki/Battle_of_Los_Angeles.

53. C. Scott Littleton, "Eyewitness to History: The Battle of Los Angeles," Sign of the Times, May 24, 2007 (Accessed May 2010), http://www.sott.net/articles/show/132795-Eyewitness+to+History:+The+Battle+of+of+Los+Angeles.

54. Billy Booth, "1942—The Battle of Los Angeles Summary," liveaboutdotcom (Accessed May 2010), http://ufos.about.com/od/bestufocasefiles/p/losangeles1942.htm.

55. Littleton, "Eyewitness to History: The Battle of Los Angeles."

56. Wikipedia, "The Battle of Los Angeles."

57. Ibid.

58. Littleton, "Eyewitness to History: The Battle of Los Angeles."

59. Booth, "1942—The Battle of Los Angeles Summary."

60. Littleton, "Eyewitness to History: The Battle of Los Angeles."

61. Booth, "1942—The Battle of Los Angeles Summary."

62. Ibid.

63. Richard Pallardy, "Deepwater Horizon Oil Spill," *Encyclopaedia Britannica*, https://www.britannica.com/event/Deepwater-Horizon-oil-spill/Cleanup-efforts.

64. "Explaining Greece's Debt Crisis," *New York Times* (June 17, 2016), https://www.nytimes.com/interactive/2016/business/international/greece-debt-crisis-euro.html.

65. Ker Than, "Haiti Earthquake 'Strange,' Strongest in 200 Years," *National Geographic News*, January 14, 2010, https://www.nationalgeographic.com/news/2010/1/100113-haiti-earthquake-red-cross/.

66. Richard Pallardy and John P. Rafferty, "Chile Earthquake of 2010," *Encyclopedia Britannica*, https://www.britannica.com/event/Chile-earthquake-of-2010.

67. Ker Than, "Chile Earthquake Altered Earth Axis, Shortened Day," *National Geographic News*, March 3, 2010, https://www.nationalgeographic.com/news/2010/3/100302-chile-earthquake-earth-axis-shortened-day/.

68. Ibid.

69. "Two killed, 100 Injured in Mexican Earthquake," CNN, April 5, 2010, http://www.cnn.com/2010/WORLD/americas/04/04/mexico.earthquake/index.html.

70. Baerbel Langmann et al., "Volcanic Ash Over Europe During the Eruption of Eyjafjal-lajokull on Iceland, April–May 2010," *Atmospheric Environment* 48 (March 2012), 1–8, https://www.sciencedirect.com/science/article/abs/pii/S1352231011003256.

71. Cain Nunns, "Life on the Mentawai Islands: Dsplaced, Robbed and Washed Away," *Guardian*, November 16, 2010, https://www.theguardian.com/world/2010/nov/16/mentawai-islands-indonesia-tsunami.

72. Erin Blakemore, "New Analysis about 2010 Deadly Indonesia Tsunami Earthquake May Help Save Lives," *Washington Post*, January 11, 2020, https://www.washingtonpost.com/science/new-analysis-about-2010-deadly-indonesia-tsunami-earthquake-may-help-save-lives/2020/01/10/04a2a3c0-3263-11ea-a053-dc6d944ba776_story.html.

73. "Iran: Earthquakes—Dec 2010," Reliefweb, https://reliefweb.int/disaster/eq-2010-000254-irn.

74. Law of One, Session 40, Questions 10 and 11, https://www.lawofone.info/s/40#10.

75. Dictionary.com, "Discrete," https://www.dictionary.com/browse/discrete?s=t.

76. Law of One, Session 59, Question 24, https://www.lawofone.info/s/59#24.

77. Law of One, Session 17, Question 1, https://www.lawofone.info/s/17#1.

78. Law of One, Session 11, Question 16, https://www.lawofone.info/s/11#16.

79. Law of One, Session 11, Question 17, https://www.lawofone.info/s/11#17.

80. William T. Still, *New World Order: The Ancient Plan of Secret Societies* (Lafayette, LA: Huntington House Publishers, 1990).

CHAPTER TWENTY-ONE

1. Law of One, Session 46, Question 12, https://www.lawofone.info/s/46#12.

2. Fritz Springmeier, *Bloodlines of the Illuminati*, 3rd ed. (Pentracks Publications/TGS Printing Distributing, 2005), http://www.whale.to/b/sp/bloodlines.html.

3. Law of One, chronological search on the term *Orion*, https://www.lawofone.info/results.php?q=orion&o=s.

4. Law of One, Session 7, Questions 14 and 15, https://www.lawofone.info/s/7#14.

5. Ernest Scott, *The People of the Secret* (London: Octagon Press, 1983), 120.

6. Ibid., 121.

7. Ibid., 60.

8. Ibid., 179.

9. Ibid., 196–97.

10. *Encylopaedia Britannica*, "Saracen," Britannica.com, https://www.britannica.com/topic/Saracen.

11. Law of One, Session 2, Question 2, https://www.lawofone.info/s/2#2.

12. Scott, *The People of the Secret*, 198.

13. Ibid., 199.

14. Ibid., 200.

15. Dictionary.com, "Demiurge," https://www.dictionary.com/browse/demiurge?s=t.

16. Ibid.

17. Stephan A. Hoeller, "The Gnostic World View: A Brief Summary of Gnosticism," The Gnosis Archive, http://gnosis.org/gnintro.htm.

18. Scott, *The People of the Secret*, 251–53.

19. Tom Head, "New Documentary Says SA Group Tried Spreading AIDS to 'Cement White Rule,'" *South African*, January 28, 2019, https://www.thesouthafrican.com/news/cold-case-hammarskjold-keith-maxwell-aids-south-africa/.

20. David Wilcock, "DECLAS: Social Media Nukes an Entire Generation . . . But Why?, Section Two: Tech Doofus Mass Censorship," June 25, 2019, https://divinecosmos.com/davids-blog/22962-social-media-nukes/2/.

21. Law of One, Session 16, Question 45, https://www.lawofone.info/s/16#45.
22. Law of One, Session 16, Question 46, https://www.lawofone.info/s/16#46.
23. Law of One, Session 11, Question 18, https://www.lawofone.info/s/11#18.

CHAPTER TWENTY-TWO

1. Law of One, Session 53, Question 3, https://www.lawofone.info/s/53#3.
2. Raymond E. Fowler, *The Watchers II* (Leland, NC: Wild Flower Press, 1995), xiv.
3. Budd Hopkins, David M. Jacobs, John E. Mack, and Ron Westrum, *Unusual Personal Experiences: An Analysis of the Data from Three National Surveys Conducted by the Roper Organization* (Las Vegas, NV: Bigelow Holding Corporation, 1992), 7.
4. Fowler, *The Watchers II*, xxi.
5. Thomas E. Bullard, *UFO Abductions: The Measure of a Mystery* (Mount Rainier, MD: Fund for UFO Research, 1987).
6. Ibid., 52.
7. Raymond E. Fowler, *The Watchers* (New York: Bantam, 1990), xii.
8. King James Bible, Book of Daniel, https://biblehub.com/kjv/daniel/4.htm.
9. Fowler, *The Watchers*, 173.
10. *Companion Bible,* Notes: Daniel 4:13 (London: Lamp Press), 1186.
11. Boyd Rice, "Chaldean Genesis: The Secret Legacy of the Architect-Priests," from Dragon KeyPress website, October 21, 2004, https://www.bibliotecapleyades.net/merovingians /merovingios_08.htm.
12. Law of One, search for the term *guardians*, https://www.lawofone.info/results.php?q =guardians.
13. Law of One, Session 7, Question 9, https://www.lawofone.info/s/7#9.
14. Law of One, Session 10, Question 9, https://www.lawofone.info/s/10#9.
15. Law of One, Session 50, Question 5, https://www.lawofone.info/s/50#5.
16. Law of One, Session 51, Question 1, https://www.lawofone.info/s/51#1.
17. Fowler, *The Watchers II*, 109.
18. Ibid., 167.
19. Ibid., 134.
20. Ibid., 105.
21. Ibid., 155.
22. Jacques Vallée, *Passport to Magonia* (Chicago, Henry Regnery, 1969).
23. Fowler, *The Watchers II*, 207.
24. Ibid., 211.
25. Vallée, *Passport to Magonia*, 100.
26. Ibid., 87.
27. Fowler, *The Watchers II*, 208.
28. Vallée, *Passport to Magonia*, 101.
29. Fowler, *The Watchers II*, 208.
30. John A. Keel, *UFOs: Operation Trojan Horse* (New York: G. P. Putnam's Sons, 1970), 230–31.
31. Fowler, *The Watchers II*, 209.
32. Vallée, *Passport to Magonia*, 107.
33. Fowler, *The Watchers II*, 210.
34. Ibid.
35. Ibid., 35.
36. Ibid., 45.
37. Ibid., 55.
38. Ibid., 56.

39. Ibid., 63.
40. Ibid., 77.
41. Ibid., 79–80.
42. Ibid., 82.
43. Ibid., 128.
44. Ibid., 130.
45. Ibid., 146.
46. Ibid., 220.

CHAPTER TWENTY-THREE

1. Michael Hesemann, *The Cosmic Connection: Worldwide Crop Formations and ET Contacts,* 1st ed. (Nevada City, CA: Gateway Books, 1995).
2. Philip J. Corso and William Birnes, *The Day After Roswell: The Truth Exposed After Fifty Years!* (New York: Pocket Books, 1994).
3. Dan Sherman, *Above Black: Project Preserve Destiny. Insider Account of Alien Contact & Government Cover-Up,* 6th ed., Order Dept., LLC, 1998.
4. David Wilcock, "11/30/96: The Advent of the Wilcock Readings," Divine Cosmos, November 30, 1996, https://divinecosmos.com/read-free-books-here/readings-in-text-form/159-113096-the-advent-of-the-wilcock-readings/.
5. *Encyclopedia Britannica,* "Al-Tamim," Britannica.com, https://www.britannica.com/place/Al-Tamim.
6. Wilcock, "11/30/96: The Advent of the Wilcock Readings."
7. Chris Kirkman, "The Life of Mother Teresa," *Sun Sentinel,* September 6, 1997, https://www.sun-sentinel.com/news/fl-xpm-1997-09-06-9709170186-story.html.
8. Wilcock, "11/30/96: The Advent of the Wilcock Readings."
9. Ibid.
10. Ibid.
11. Ibid.
12. Ibid.
13. Ibid.
14. Ibid.
15. Ibid.

CHAPTER TWENTY-FOUR

1. Patricia Pereira, *Songs of the Arcturians: The Arcturian Star Chronicles,* Volume 1 (New York: Atria Books/Beyond Words Publishing, 1996).
2. Wilcock, "11/30/96: The Advent of the Wilcock Readings," Divine Cosmos, November 30, 1996, https://divinecosmos.com/read-free-books-here/readings-in-text-form/159-113096-the-advent-of-the-wilcock-readings/.
3. Ganesha Speaks, "Virgo Traits," https://www.ganeshaspeaks.com/zodiac-signs/virgo/traits/.
4. Wilcock, "11/30/96: The Advent of the Wilcock Readings."
5. Ibid.
6. Wilcock, "The Advent of the Wilcock Readings," original Archive.org snapshot of Ascension2000.com, April 9, 2001 (Included to establish time reference, well before author's Gaiam TV job started in 2013), https://web.archive.org/web/20010409202343/http://ascension2000.com/Readings/readings01.html.
7. Wilcock, "11/30/96: The Advent of the Wilcock Readings."

8. David Wilcock, "12/14/96: Readings: First Half of December 1996," Divine Cosmos, December 14, 1996, updated March 14, 2009, https://divinecosmos.com/read-free -books-here/readings-in-text-form/160-121496-readings-first-half-of-december -1996/.

9. Ibid.

10. Ibid.

11. Dictionary.com, "Parlance," https://www.dictionary.com/browse/parlance?s=t.

12. Wilcock, "12/14/96: Readings: First Half of December 1996."

13. Ibid.

14. Ibid.

15. Ibid.

16. Ibid.

17. Ibid.

18. Ibid.

19. Sherman H. Skolnick, "The Overthrow of the American Republic—Part 32: US /Iraq Plots and Secret Weapons," Skolnick's Report, April 4, 2003, https://rense.com /general36/skolov32.htm.

20. Wilcock, "12/14/96: Readings: First Half of December 1996."

21. Ibid.

22. David Wilcock, "12/31/96: Readings: Second Half of December 1996," Divine Cosmos, December 31, 1996, https://divinecosmos.com/read-free-books-here/readings-in-text -form/161-123196-readings-second-half-of-december-1996/.

23. David Wilcock, "7/3/98: Prophecy: NYC Terrorist Attack?," Divine Cosmos, July 3, 1998, https://divinecosmos.com/read-free-books-here/readings-in-text-form/438-7398 -prophecy-nyc-terrorist-attack/.

CHAPTER TWENTY-FIVE

1. Wilcock, "12/31/96: Readings: Second Half of December 1996," Divine Cosmos, December 31, 1996, https://divinecosmos.com/read-free-books-here/readings-in-text -form/161-123196-readings-second-half-of-december-1996/.

2. The Association for Research and Enlightenment, Edgar Cayce Reading 262-57, January 7, 1934, http://www.huttoncommentaries.com/article.php?a_id=48.

3. Law of One, Session 12, Question 15, https://www.lawofone.info/s/12#15.

4. Dictionary.com, "Intransigent," https://www.dictionary.com/browse/intransigent?s=t.

5. David Wilcock, "Wilcock Readings Section 21: Dream Voice Gives the Word: You Have to Move," September 18–30, 1997. Archive.org copy from March 3, 2001, https://web .archive.org/web/20010303151344/http://ascension2000.com/Readings/r21.htm.

6. Ibid.

7. Jesse Bering, "Ian Stevenson's Case for the Afterlife: Are We 'Skeptics' Really Just Cyn-ics?," Scientific American, November 2, 2013, https://blogs.scientificamerican.com /bering-in-mind/ian-stevensone28099s-case-for-the-afterlife-are-we-e28098skepticse 28099-really-just-cynics/.

8. David Wilcock, "November Section Two: The Shocking Announcement Is Made," Divine Cosmos, transcripts from November 15–30, 1997. Archive.org snapshot from February 9, 2002, https://web.archive.org/web/20020209022912/http://ascension2000 .com/Readings/r25.htm.

9. Edgar Cayce Reading #294-151, July 29, 1932, https://file1.hpage.com/002608/96/html /reading_294-151.htm.

10. Church, W. H., *Many Happy Returns: The Lives of Edgar Cacye* (New York: Harper & Row, 1984), 226.

11. David Wilcock and Richard C. Hoagland, "Interplanetary Day After Tomorrow," Part 1, May 14, 2004, https://web.archive.org/web/20040521121710/http://www.enterprise mission.com/_articles/05-14-2004/Interplanetary_1.htm.

12. David Wilcock and Richard C. Hoagland, "Interplanetary Day After Tomorrow," Part 2, June 3, 2004, https://web.archive.org/web/20040703021145/http://www.enter prisemission.com/_articles/05-27-2004_Interplanetary_Part_2/InterplanetaryDayAfter -Part2.htm.

13. David Wilcock and Richard C. Hoagland, "Interplanetary Day After Tomorrow," Part 3, June 4, 2004, https://web.archive.org/web/20040723032515/http://www.enter prisemission.com:80/_articles/06-03-2004_Interplanetary_Part_3/InterplanetaryDay After-Part3-amended2.htm.

14. David Wilcock, "The Revealing: Endgame of the New World Order," Divine Cosmos, February 26, 2007, https://divinecosmos.com/davids-blog/296-the-revealing/; https:// divinecosmos.com/davids-blog/297-endgame-of-the-new-world-order-part-ii-the -proof-in-the-plunge/ [Part II].

15. Law of One, "Calling," https://www.lawofoneinfo/results.pho?1=calling.

16. Law of One, Session 7, https://www.lawofoneinfo/s/7.

17. Law of One, Session 24, Question 8, https://www.lawofoneinfo/s/24#8.

18. Free, Wynn, and David Wilcock, *The Reincarnation of Edgar Cayce Draft of Part 1 Chapter 5: Prophecy Fulfilled*, http://divinecosmos.com/books-free-online-the-reincar nation-of-edgar-cayce-draft-of-pt-1/116-chapter-05-prophecy-fulfilled/.

19. David Wilcock, "ET Update on Global Politics, Immediate Future Earth Changes and Ascension Events," Divine Cosmos, June 23, 1999. Archived on November 28, 1999, https://web.archive.org/web/19991128144250/http://ascension2000.com/6.23Update .html.

20. David Margolick, "The Path to Florida," *Vanity Fair*, March 19, 2014, https://www .vanityfair.com/news/2004/10/florida-election-2000.

21. Wilcock, "ET Update on Global Politics, Immediate Future Earth Changes and Ascen- sion Events."

22. David Wilcock, "11/3/99: Prophecy: Stock Market Crash!," *Divine Cosmos*, November 3, 1999, https://divinecosmos.com/read-free-books-here/readings-in-text-form/221-11399 -prophecy-stock-market-crash/.

23. "Stock Market Crash!," web.archive.org, October 4, 1999, https://web.archive.org/web /20000311065417/http://www.ascension2000.com:80/10.04.99.htm.

24. "The Great Awakening: 2012, Ascension and NWO Defeat," Divine Cosmos, April 15, 2009, https://divinecosmos.com/davids-blog/467-the-great-awakening-2012 -ascension-and-nwo-defeat/.

25. Ascension2000.com, https://web.archive.org/web/19991128124257/http://ascension2000 .com:80/.

26. Ibid.

27. Law of One, Session 14, Question 14, https://www.lawofone.info/s/14#14.

28. Law of One, Session 15, Question 14, https://www.lawofone.info/s/15#14.

29. Law of One, Session 1, Question 0, https://www.lawofone.info/results.php?s=1#0.

30. Law of One, Session 26, Question 36, https://www.lawofone.info/results.php?s=26#36.

Index

Note: Page numbers in *italics* refer to illustrations.

AUTHOR'S NOTE

About the Coronavirus

This manuscript was completed and locked on January 21, 2020. On April 6, I was permitted to add this final page on the last day before printing began. In Chapter 24, page 479, under "The Coming Car Crash," I quoted from a reading on December 3, 1996. After "[These] discussions [are] reminiscent of our talk so long ago. The memories come quickly, like fleeting ghosts," the original reading then said, "By 2010, germs will have rid the earth of many problems. Overpopulation is nothing to scoff at." You can go back to Archive.org captures of the site in the Notes section and see this passage from as far back as 2000.

This passage always disturbed me and I thought it was bad data, so I did not include it in this book. However, at the time of this writing I have done five YouTube videos on the pandemic, with a total of 3.5 million views and nearly sixteen hours of content. I argued that this may be a man-made virus—released to slow or prevent the unsealing of thousands of indictments against top Deep State criminals.

The prophecy gives us the year 2010, which is only one digit away from 2020: 20 minus 1 is 19. The Deep State's apparent agenda for potentially releasing "germs" like this is to combat overpopulation, but the reading actually implies that the Deep State will be defeated, not the people. Hence it says that "germs will have rid the earth of many problems," meaning the problems caused by the Deep State. "Nothing to scoff at" sounds like "nothing to cough at," and the COVID-19 virus creates a dry cough that produces "nothing," as in no mucus.

Furthermore, "scoff at" sounds roughly like "covid." When we add *have rid* from the previous sentence after the word *germs*, SCOFF HAVE RID contains the letters CO V ID in them, and 20 minus one is 19. What deeper problems will COVID-19 end up ridding us of on Earth? At the time I write this, I do believe I know the answer. Also notice that after the deleted portion on page 479, the reading said, "It is about to be centralized again. I am sorry." This appears to be the beings apologizing for how this crisis would temporarily centralize power and control by forcing everyone to stay home, greatly disrupting the economy.

DAVID
WILCOCK

"David Wilcock is a leading thinker who makes a magnificent case . . . that a Golden Age is indeed within our grasp and can be brought into manifestation if only we choose to make it so."

–Graham Hancock,
author of *Fingerprints of the Gods*